Cannabis, Sacred and Profane

Also Available from Bloomsbury

Mortality and Music: Popular Music and the Awareness of Death,
Christopher Partridge

Acute Religious Experiences: Madness, Psychosis and Religious Studies,
Richard Saville-Smith

The Bloomsbury Handbook of Religion and Popular Music,
Edited by Christopher Partridge and Marcus Moberg

Cannabis, Sacred and Profane

Christopher Partridge

BLOOMSBURY ACADEMIC
LONDON • NEW YORK • OXFORD • NEW DELHI • SYDNEY

BLOOMSBURY ACADEMIC

Bloomsbury Publishing Plc

50 Bedford Square, London, WC1B 3DP, UK
1385 Broadway, New York, NY 10018, USA
29 Earlsfort Terrace, Dublin 2, Ireland

BLOOMSBURY, BLOOMSBURY ACADEMIC and the Diana logo are trademarks of Bloomsbury Publishing Plc

First published in Great Britain 2024

Copyright © Christopher Partridge, 2024

Christopher Partridge has asserted his right under the Copyright, Designs and Patents Act, 1988, to be identified as Author of this work.

For legal purposes the Acknowledgements on p. ix constitute an extension of this copyright page.

Cover images: Leaf of marijuana © dickcraft / istock; vintage movie poster © SilverScreen / Alamy

All rights reserved. No part of this publication may be reproduced or transmitted in any form or by any means, electronic or mechanical, including photocopying, recording, or any information storage or retrieval system, without prior permission in writing from the publishers.

Bloomsbury Publishing Plc does not have any control over, or responsibility for, any third-party websites referred to or in this book. All internet addresses given in this book were correct at the time of going to press. The author and publisher regret any inconvenience caused if addresses have changed or sites have ceased to exist, but can accept no responsibility for any such changes.

A catalogue record for this book is available from the British Library.

Library of Congress Cataloging-in-Publication Data

Names: Partridge, Christopher H. (Christopher Hugh), 1961- author.
Title: Cannabis, sacred and profane / Christopher Partridge.
Description: London; New York : Bloomsbury Academic, 2024. | Includes bibliographical references and index.
Identifiers: LCCN 2023059778 (print) | LCCN 2023059779 (ebook) | ISBN 9781350115880 (pb) | ISBN 9781350115897 (hb) | ISBN 9781350115903 (epdf) | ISBN 9781350115910 (ebook)
Subjects: LCSH: Cannabis—History. | Cannabis—Social aspects.
Classification: LCC HV5822.C3 P38 2024 (print) | LCC HV5822.C3 (ebook) | DDC 394.1/4—dc23/eng/20240226
LC record available at https://lccn.loc.gov/2023059778
LC ebook record available at https://lccn.loc.gov/2023059779

ISBN:	HB:	978-1-3501-1589-7
	PB:	978-1-3501-1588-0
	ePDF:	978-1-3501-1590-3
	eBook:	978-1-3501-1591-0

Typeset by RefineCatch Limited, Bungay, Suffolk
Printed and bound in Great Britain

To find out more about our authors and books visit www.bloomsbury.com and sign up for our newsletters

Dum spiro spero

Ted Henry Partridge
(3 September, 2023)

Contents

Acknowledgements   ix

Introduction   1
Sacred and profane   3
Mundane   7

1   Cannabis   13
Background notes on the plant and its cultivation   13
A note on terminology   20
Ganja, charas, and *bhāṅg*   23
Smoking   26
Edibles and drinkables   35
Concluding comments   38

2   Profane Cannabis   43
Notes on profanation   43
The *ḥashīshīyyīn*   47
Racism, violence, criminality, and insanity   53
Harry Anslinger and the moral crusade   61
Jazz, blues, race, and cannabis   66
Pot pulp fiction, true crime, and moralizing tracts   69
Psychiatry, racism, and cannabis psychosis   73
Conservative Christian responses to legal cannabis consumption   75
Concluding comments   79

3   Medicinal Cannabis   83
Romantic radicalism, the turn to the self, and medicinal cannabis   84
Background notes on the early history of medicinal marijuana   88
Nineteenth-century medical research   100
Intoxication and insanity   108
Epidemiology, pharmacology, and the demonization of cannabis in the nineteenth century   119
Medicinal cannabis since the 1960s   124

	Listening to the voices of the suffering	131
	Concluding comments	135
4	**Sacred Cannabis**	139
	The Orient, mysticism, and hashish in the nineteenth century	141
	The hashish eater	147
	Mesmerism and spiritualism in the nineteenth century	158
	Early theosophy	171
	Victorian occultism	174
	Temperance and ambivalence	186
	Rastafari and cannabis	190
	Imagining cannabis and religion in premodern societies	196
	Contemporary cannabis spirituality	209
	420	219
	Concluding comments	220
Notes		225
Bibliography		293
Index		339

Acknowledgements

The time needed to write this book was made available by a period of research leave granted by the Faculty of Arts and Social Sciences at Lancaster University.

I am indebted to Lalle Pursglove at Bloomsbury for her enthusiasm and support for the project. Also, for her patience and help, I am indebted to Emily Wootton at Bloomsbury. My thanks also go to the anonymous reviewer of the final manuscript both for carefully reading it and also for offering helpful suggestions. The cannabis leaf image used in the book is courtesy of widodo/Alamy Stock Vector.

Writing books inevitably takes time and attention away from loved ones. I want to thank my partner, Marcia, for her love and patience.

Finally, this book is dedicated to our first grandchild, Ted, who has brought so much happiness into our lives.

Introduction

At seven o'clock in the evening, after long hesitation, I took hashish ... I lie on the bed ... I think three-quarters of an hour have already passed. But it is only twenty minutes ... At last I left the hotel, the effects seeming non-existent or so weak that the precaution of staying at home was unnecessary ... My walking stick begins to give me special pleasure. One becomes so tender, fears that a shadow falling on the paper might hurt it ... One reads the notices on the urinals. It would not surprise me if this or that person came up to me. But when no one does I am not disappointed, either ... Now the hashish eater's demands on time and space come into force. As is known, these are absolutely regal. Versailles, for one who has taken hashish, is not too large, or eternity too long. Against the background of these immense dimensions of inner experience, of absolute duration, and immeasurable space, a wonderful, beatific humour dwells all the more fondly on the contingencies of the world of space and time.[1]

Walter Benjamin (1928)

The cannabis experience is typically gentle, pleasurable, and immersive. As the drug takes effect, the user becomes aware of heightened perception. Users frequently report feelings of being awed by the beauty of nature, or of being absorbed in a work of art, or of getting lost in music, or of experiencing a type of mystical transcendence. An everyday object can become the locus of an epiphany. Space and time seem to become fluid. As such the cannabis experience has a countercultural quality, in that it can lead to new and subversive ideas about the world.[2]

This potential of the cannabis experience was discussed by the German philosopher Walter Benjamin, who, between the years 1927 and 1934, embarked on a series of experiments with hashish in Berlin, Marseilles, and Ibiza. He had initially been encouraged to consume what he considered to be a toxic substance by his friend, the physician Ernst Joël who, along with the neurologist Fritz Fränkel, was carrying out research into the effects of psychoactive drugs. Benjamin recorded his thoughts in a loose collection of 'protocols', which, although fascinating, are preliminary and unsystematic. Indeed, he fully intended writing a 'truly exceptional book about hashish', and the fact that it remained unrealized was a source of regret for him.[3] Moreover, like many users, while he enjoyed taking hashish alone, it is clear that he benefitted from getting high with friends and acquaintances, including, most notably, the Marxist philosopher Ernst Bloch – who would go on to discuss the significance of cannabis intoxication in *The Principle of Hope*.[4]

Benjamin was particularly intrigued by the potential of hashish to enhance the imagination by inducing what Bloch referred to as a 'freewheeling, rapturous daydream'.[5] More specifically, he was fascinated by the ability of hashish to subvert or reconfigure the subject–object relationship. To some extent, this can be understood with reference to his well-known conception of the 'aura' which, interestingly, he initially mentioned in an unpublished report about his experiment with hashish in March, 1930.[6] The term was then used rather differently in his 1931 essay, 'A Small History of Photography',[7] in that it became an aesthetic category. Later, in 'The Work of Art in the Age of Mechanical Reproduction', he further developed this aesthetic distinction between 'auratic' and 'nonauratic' art forms.[8] The point here, however, is that, for Benjamin, while 'aura' refers to the authenticity or unique aesthetic authority of an original work of art, there is – possibly because it originally occurred to him while under the influence of hashish – something almost psychedelic about his understanding of it. 'What is aura, actually? A strange weave of space and time: the unique appearance or semblance of distance, no matter how close it may be.'[9] Again, in referring to the aura, in his later work, he was primarily thinking about the here-and-nowness of an original work of art, and its presence before the viewer, which cannot be fully replicated in reproductions. But there is something more about it that makes it special, something that draws one into it, that constitutes, to use a phrase of the theologian Emil Brunner, 'truth as encounter' (*Warheit als begegnung*).[10] Something important is communicated in the very encounter itself. Again, he references the perception of space and time, both of which seem strange and non-ordinary. This, of course, is characteristic of the cannabis experience. It's as if the states of waking and sleeping have merged. One becomes lost in the encounter, in the aura, in the meaning emanating from the object. With cannabis, of course, one need not stand before an original work of art; the experience can happen with everyday objects, like notices on urinals. As such, they become sites of illumination; something shines through; insights are gained; there is an *apokálypsis* – a revelation. As such, Benjamin suggested that his reflections on the cannabis experience may 'turn out to be a very worthwhile supplement to [his] philosophical observations ...'[11]

While such induced experiences are often interpreted as 'sacred' – as in Aldous Huxley's discussion of induced mysticism in *The Doors of Perception*[12] – Benjamin preferred to interpret them as moments of 'profane illumination' – serendipitous encounters that modify our perception of reality. Indeed, instead of viewing them through a religious lens, he found the lens of surrealism more helpful. Having been introduced to the surrealists just prior to his experiences with hashish, not only was he sympathetic to their 'bitter, passionate revolt against Catholicism',[13] but, drawing on their ideas, he 'sought to infuse thinking with the energies of a dream – but in the interests of a *waking* dream'[14] (similar to Bloch's 'freewheeling, rapturous daydream'). 'In a state of intoxication, the thread of ratiocination is loosened, unravelled, not dissolved; with the emptying out of personality, there is a diffusion of perspective. Thinking is sensualized ...'[15] Again, everyday objects become transformed into conduits of meaning: 'My walking stick begins to give me special pleasure. One becomes so tender, fears that a shadow falling on the paper might hurt it ...' Unlike

Huxley, for Benjamin these experiences represented a suspension of the opposition between the sacred and the secular. Although a profane illumination is, to some extent, a survival of a premodern religious impulse, it is 'a materialist and anthropological inspiration'. Indeed, like the surrealists, for Benjamin, any traces of mysticism were channelled into the realization of revolutionary social, political, and aesthetic goals.[16]

The central term in Benjamin's discussions of the cannabis experience is *Rausch*, which, of course, Nietzsche had used, very influentially, of Dionysian knowledge. It is a state of immersive intoxication, trance, and ecstasy, during which the boundary between the self and observed everyday objects breaks down. Christina Halperin expresses this point nicely: 'Scholars have tended to either ignore the ordinary or consider it as highly subjective, particular, unnoticed, self-evident, and mundane. The ordinary contrasts with the reflexive, critical, objectifying, and supernatural. For Benjamin, ordinary objects have the potential to dialectically dance between these binaries.'[17] This became conspicuously apparent when he was stoned.

Overall, Benjamin's analysis of the cannabis experience, although unsystematic and idiosyncratic, raises a number of questions that subsequent thinkers and everyday users have sought to address. Are induced altered states of consciousness able to generate moments of illumination? Does the experience have any philosophical, cultural, social or spiritual value? For some users, the experiences can be so personally significant that they can only be understood as 'sacred' in some sense. For others, they are set apart as profane states that require regulation. For yet others they are simply moments of mundane, everyday intoxication.

Sacred and profane

This brings us to the understanding of the 'sacred' and the 'profane' in this book. The terms are not used in the same sense as they are typically understood in the study of religion. Studies such as, for example, Mircea Eliade's *The Sacred and the Profane* (1957) and R.C. Zaehner's *Mysticism, Sacred and Profane* (1961)[18] interpret 'the sacred' in a narrow, explicitly religious sense. The sacred is synonymous with 'religion'. Eliade, for example, argued that 'the history of religions – from the most primitive to the most highly developed – is constituted ... by manifestations of sacred realities'.[19] These may be special stones, special places, special texts, special people, or special times, all of which are set apart as things of 'a wholly different order, a reality that does not belong to our world ...'[20] A crucifix may be fashioned out of rusty metal, but its association with a messianic individual invests it with a sacred significance that separates from other pieces of rusty metal. It is set apart as 'sacred'. The profane is the other aspect of the binary, in that it identifies that which is not sacred and, more particularly, that which constitutes a challenge to the sacred: good and evil; God and the Devil; the Church and the world; sin and salvation.

While these categories are relevant and important, the following analysis will draw primarily on understandings of the sacred and the profane developed within cultural sociology. While there are continuities between the above ontological notions and those developed within cultural sociology, the latter frees the sacred and the profane from religion and theology, by demonstrating that these categories are central to all human cultural, social, and political life. This is *not* to say that we are all religious 'deep down', but rather that the categories are better used to describe what humans consider to be absolute realities. That is to say, the sacred-profane binary identifies that which exerts an overpowering moral claim on a person or a community. Let's unpack these ideas a little more, beginning with profanation.

After an introduction to the plant and its uses in Chapter 1, the second chapter examines the construction of cannabis as profane. The discussion focuses on the demonization of cannabis and the social construction of its users as deviant. It analyses the ways in which power has been used in society to encourage Othering discourses. As Michel Foucault commented, 'power is everywhere ... power is not an institution, and not a structure; neither is it a certain strength we are endowed with; it is the name that one attributes to a complex strategical situation in a particular society.'[21] Through a complex arrangement of cultural and social forces we come to believe certain things. While there are a number of ways in which these can be exposed, the work of the French sociologist Émile Durkheim is particularly helpful in this respect. Especially useful is his notion of *faits sociaux* ('social facts').

For Durkheim, the discipline of sociology is concerned with the analysis of social facts, by which he meant social phenomena and forces. Describing such 'facts' as 'things',[22] he argued that they are realities external to the individual, existing independently of an individual's thought about them and predating the individual. Hence, one is born into a world of social facts, just as much as one is born into a world of physical facts. In this sense, he insisted, sociology is no less a science than psychology or biology. It is the scientific study of 'a category of facts with very distinctive characteristics: it consists of ways of acting, thinking, and feeling external to the individual, and endowed with a power of coercion, by reason of which they control him.'[23] Hence, while, on the one hand, such facts should not be confused with biological phenomena, on the other hand, neither are they the concern of psychology, in that they are external to the individual consciousness. In summary, 'a social fact is every way of acting, fixed or not, capable of exercising on the individual an external constraint; or, again, every way of acting which is general throughout a given society, while at the same time existing in its own right independent of its individual manifestations.'[24]

Produced throughout human history, social facts are effectively representations of moral consensus arising from a society's 'collective consciousness'. They are those givens that provide the conditions for thought and action within a community. They form the 'mainstream' of normative values. Indeed, in many cases we may not understand or even be aware of these social forces acting upon us. The laws of a society, the conventions that govern behaviour, the systems of signs used to convey ideas, the notions that shape a person's relationships with family and friends, the monetary systems with which people are involved when they purchase a cup of coffee, attitudes to cannabis consumption, all function independently of any particular member of society. In this sense, whether we are aware of it or not, social facts exert considerable coercive power over our beliefs and behaviour.[25] In freely conforming to these forces we barely feel their power. Like a boat floating down a river, the power of the current is hidden. Effortlessly, we go with the flow, with little resistance or sense of the forces that determine the direction of travel. However, our experience of the river is reversed once we decide to stop the boat midstream or attempt to row upstream. Immediately, we are faced with the full force of the current. The energy that was all but invisible immediately becomes powerfully evident as it works against us. Likewise, to act against an accepted norm is to push against a social current. Social activists know that this can be very uncomfortable, if not dangerous. As Zygmunt Bauman puts it, 'bitter and painful awakening awaits all those who by ignorance or ill will behave as if "social facts" were but figments of imagination. We cannot go unpunished through the space they fill, just like we cannot try to pass through a locked door without bruising our heads or knees'.[26] Hence, certain drugs, such as alcohol, can be consumed without feeling any sense of opprobrium or social resistance. This, however, is often not the case with cannabis.

There is a relationship between the sacred and this understanding of social facts.[27] As indicated above, Durkheim has helped us to view the sacred in terms of what people perceive to be absolute and normative – taken-for-granted norms. These normative realities can be understood in terms of 'sacred forms', which exert a profound moral and affective claim over our lives. The profane, on the other hand, is that which poses a threat to those sacred forms. Again, while constructions of the sacred-profane binary can often be traced back to a society's religious past, they are better understood as operating independently from religion. As Gordon Lynch has commented, 'gender, human rights, the care of children, nature, and the neo-liberal marketplace, all have sacralized significance in modern social life, but our understanding of the nature and operation of these sacred forms is not helped by framing them as "religious" phenomena'.[28]

Having said that, the influence of religion (as moral gatekeeper) is often still evident in the identification of the sacred and the profane. Hence, it is often implicated in discourses of demonization and stigmatization (concepts which are themselves shaped by our religious past). As we will see regarding cannabis consumption, religious groups or religiously inspired individuals have often been at the forefront of campaigns to ban recreational drug use as a profane influence on society. Unsurprisingly, therefore – as we will see in Chapter 2 – during the twentieth century much anti-cannabis propaganda referenced religious ideas to add gravity to its often ill-informed claims. Indeed, if demonization is 'a speech act used to create an image of the enemy as evil or in league with the Devil',[29] then cannabis has, quite literally, been demonized, in that much of the early propaganda drew explicitly on Christian demonological themes to construct an understanding of it as Satanic.[30] It is 'the Devil's weed', the 'weed with roots in Hell', and 'the weed that bewitches'.[31] Such anti-cannabis propaganda also frequently used images of users surrounded by key signifiers of the profane. The poster for the 1942 film *The Devil's Harvest* is a good example. Alongside an illustration of Satan embracing a languid young woman inhaling 'the smoke of hell' is the claim that cannabis is 'a vicious racket with its arms around your children'.[32]

This, again, is a good example of the construction of the profane. While, nowadays, relatively few people accept a traditional religious understanding of the world, modern culture is, nevertheless, organized around a sacred-profane binary code. This, as Jeffrey Alexander has argued, 'serves the mythological function of dividing the known world into the sacred and the profane, thereby providing a clear and compelling picture of how contemporaries must act to manoeuvre the space in between. In this sense, the discourse of modernity bears a striking resemblance to metaphysical and religious salvation discourse of various kinds.'[33] In other words, following Durkheim, from a cultural sociological perspective, we can view areas of value-conflict in modern societies as sites of struggle between, on the one hand, purity and goodness (the sacred) and, on the other hand, pollution and evil (the profane). Concerning demonization and the construction of the profane, Alexander provides an evocative description of the consequences of profanation in his discussion of the civil narratives of good and evil, which complements the above discussion of social facts. The profane represents the worst in a national community and is considered by many to be the embodiment of evil:

> The objects it identifies threaten the core community from somewhere outside it. From this marginal position, they present a powerful source of pollution. To be close to these polluted objects – the actors, structures, and processes that are constituted by repressive discourse – is dangerous. Not only can one's reputation be sullied and one's status endangered, but one's very security can be threatened. To have one's self or movement identified in terms of these objects causes anguish, disgust, and alarm. Collective representations of this polluting code are perceived as a threat to the very center of civil society itself.[34]

Because the profane accrues a transgressive charge relative to the strength of the sacred, the more powerful the sacred form (such as the protection of vulnerable young people), the greater the sense of revulsion generated by that which threatens to breach it. Indeed, the revulsion occasioned by the transgression of a sacred form, such as the abuse of children or the violation of a human right, can be so powerful that it can, as Alexander indicates, sanction extreme acts of retribution – even violence and death. As one grandfather once commented to me in a discussion about his grandson's occasional cannabis use, 'if I could find the guy who sold it to him, I'd beat him so hard he wouldn't get up.' This would have been very unlikely, but it does indicate the emotional charge occasioned by the profane. Individuals feel morally constrained to act. The threat of profanation must be expunged at all costs in order to limit its pollution within society and to restore the authority and integrity of the sacred. This helps to explain the draconian punishments meted out to some cannabis users. For example, in July 2011, Lee Carroll Brooker, a 75-year-old disabled war veteran suffering chronic pain, was given a life sentence with no possibility of release for growing thirty-four marijuana plants for personal medicinal use. He had no intention of selling or buying cannabis. He simply grew it and consumed it to relieve pain. Even the judge, Larry Anderson, stated that, 'If the court could sentence you to a term that is less than life without parole, I would. However, the law is very specific ... there is no discretion.'[35]

It's worth stressing, however, that the sacred-profane binary is not ontologically fixed. That is to say, there is no sense that this or that object, space, idea, time or practice is always sacred or profane. Being the products of culture and social forces, constructions of the sacred and the profane are protean.[36] Again, this is different from the ontological understandings of the sacred and the profane in the work of Eliade and Zaehner. In cultural sociology, identifying the sacred and the profane is a process of continual negotiation. What is sacred in one culture, may be profane in another culture, and what is sacred during one historical period, may be profane during another. This is certainly true of drug use, which, during the modern period, has, not only been demonized by religious and civil authorities,[37] but has also, at other times, been sanctioned, not only for medical and religious purposes, but also for recreational use.[38] Hence, not only has the medical use of cannabis been legalized in a number of countries, but following Uruguay's creation of a regulated cannabis market,[39] recreational use has been legalized in Canada, South Africa, Georgia, and Germany, along with several American states. Indeed, in 2020, a number of Democratic presidential candidates in the United States not only supported the legalization of marijuana, but they also proposed major changes to the country's criminal justice system. For example, several of the candidates wanted to address past criminal convictions. 'We will,' insisted Bernie Sanders, 'legalize marijuana and vacate and expunge past marijuana convictions.'[40]

This has led to a reaction from self-appointed moral gatekeepers, particularly conservative Christians who feel constrained to view cannabis consumption as profane. While most people understand that consuming any intoxicant is risky, particularly alcohol, the problem for cannabis users is that, because of the history of their chosen psychoactive substance (as discussed in Chapter 2), it is vulnerable to exaggeration and misinformation in conservative cultures. Hence, although we now have a better understanding of the psychoactive effects of cannabis (see Chapter 1), nevertheless, for a still large, but diminishing section of society, it continues to be freighted with much of the profane baggage it acquired during early twentieth-century campaigns against it.

Interestingly, while discourses of profanation are gradually being subverted, cannabis has maintained a liminal space in the West that distinguishes it from other intoxicants. Again, this is largely because of its history in Western societies. While cultures of resistance from the Beats onwards, have, in their own way, contributed to the normalization of cannabis, they have also fetishized it as a transgressive, subversive substance – a direct challenge to conservative values. Although this means that it can still (just about) be employed in popular culture as a signifier of bohemianism, it also means that, within traditionally conservative cultures, particularly religious cultures, there is nervousness and dissonance – especially in societies in which it has been legalized. In Chapter 2 we will discuss some Christian responses to cannabis in societies in which it is increasingly 'normalized'. (The normalization thesis, which was developed by drug researchers in the UK during the 1990s, refers to the process whereby increased socio-cultural familiarity leads to growing tolerance for, and eventually acceptance of an illicit substance.[41])

This brings us to another development. For an increasing number of consumers, cannabis use is neither sacred nor profane. It is mundane.

Mundane

The notion of the mundane is a little fuzzy. For example, Chapter 3 could have been neatly entitled 'Mundane Cannabis', rather than 'Medicinal Cannabis', but often the fact that it is considered medicinal links it to core sacred forms in the West: health;

healing; wellbeing; happiness. Hence, unsurprisingly, in cultures in which health and wellbeing are sacred forms, the growing popularity of medicinal cannabis has, not only been central to its normalization, but has also had a sacralizing impact. Having said that, for many of those I have spoken to while researching this book, cannabis is simply mundane.

Apart from its illegality, cannabis consumption is viewed in much the same way as opening a bottle of beer or pouring a glass of wine. Consequently, some users, such as the British singer Shaun Ryder, become angry when it is referred to as a drug: 'I don't class weed as a drug. We should get that out of the window, calling marijuana a fucking drug.'[42] This is often the response of drinkers who become annoyed when their favourite recreational psychoactive substance is referred to as 'a drug'. In other words, they don't want alcohol embroiled in discourses of profanation. Culturally, drinking and drug-taking are two distinct activities. Pharmacologically, of course, they are not. Alcohol/ethanol is a strong psychoactive drug, which, while embedded in Western culture, is arguably more socially and psychologically problematic than cannabis.[43]

Despite attempts to stoke the fires of profanation or, indeed, efforts to sacralize cannabis, again, for many people it is not 'special' or 'set apart' in any significant positive or negative sense.[44] It is simply an ordinary intoxicant, relaxant, and soporific; it is a food supplement and a natural aid to health and wellbeing. This understanding of the mundanity of cannabis is, of course, supported by frequent references to everyday use in popular culture and the media. Numerous stoner films from *The Big Lebowski* (1998) and *Saving Grace* (2000) to *Pineapple Express* (2007), *Ted* (2012) and *Green is Gold* (2016), as well as TV series such as *Ideal* (2005–2011), *Weeds* (2005–2012), *High Maintenance* (2012–2020) and *Brassic* (2019–), all contribute to the normalization of cannabis.[45] Again, to take an admittedly random example, just this morning, before I started work, I read a review of *The Wicker Man: 50th Anniversary Release* in the British political and cultural magazine *The New Statesman*. It was described as 'a film to watch together, shriek through, toke through, eat crisps through'.[46] Cannabis and crisps! While recreational use is still illegal in the UK, many readers will have understood the reference to 'toking' and few will have been concerned by it. This is because, regardless of any residual concern about negative side effects, cannabis is an increasingly unremarkable and ubiquitous drug. Many non-users are able to identify the aroma of cannabis because, not only are most outdoor popular music events accompanied by its distinctive fragrance, but also one doesn't have to spend much time on the streets of Western towns and cities to smell it in the air. Again, who does not know what a cannabis leaf looks like? While many people would have trouble identifying the leaf of a beech tree, or a cedar, or a eucalyptus, this is not the case with cannabis. While it used to be an immediately recognizable countercultural signifier, images of the leaf now adorn the packaging of everyday CBD and hemp products, many of which are sold in superstores, pharmacists, health food outlets, and retailers. Consequently, over the past couple of decades it has become light on 'subcultural capital'.[47] Cannabis is certainly no longer demonized as the deviant drug of Rastas, rappers, hippies, and beatniks. It is going through a process of rapid normalization.

A good example of the normalization of cannabis in a society in which it is still illegal is the changing attitude of the police in the UK. Although we will see that the classification has shifted over the years, arguably for political reasons, it is currently a Class B controlled drug under the UK's Misuse of Drugs Act, 1971. As such, it is illegal to possess, supply or produce. Possession for personal use carries a maximum sentence of five years' imprisonment and an unlimited fine. However, as cannabis becomes increasingly mundane, so penalties such as imprisonment for personal use are becoming rare, with users much more likely to be issued with a police caution. There is a growing concern that the prosecution of otherwise law-abiding citizens 'creates criminal records that damage future education and employment opportunities, visa applications, and potentially, access to housing and parental rights/access'.[48] But, again, bearing in mind its increased normalization, anti-cannabis legislation is beginning to look odd and out of step with public opinion. For example, a 2020 survey of 16,017 UK university students found that 43.9 per cent described cannabis as their drug of choice.[49] Consequently, the authorities are turning a blind eye to its use in order to focus police resources elsewhere. Indeed, there are now a growing number of 'consumption rooms' throughout the country.[50]

Perhaps the most famous of these consumption rooms is the Teesside Cannabis Club and Exhale Harm Reduction Centre, which was established in 2014 by Michael Fisher in the English market town of Stockton-on-Tees. Supported by Ron Hogg, a local Labour politician, who, at the time, was also the Durham Police and Crime Commissioner, the idea was inspired by similar projects in Denmark. The aim is simply to provide safe, educational, community spaces for cannabis users. For a £120 annual membership fee, users of all ages can smoke their own cannabis in peace, listen to music, enjoy the company of others and receive advice about drug use. 'The walls are plastered with flyers and educational resources, and on the back of the toilet door is a list of mental health helplines, refuges, charities, and local alcohol and drug support services.'[51] Moreover, it is significant that, according to Fisher, 'over the years members have been referred through authorities such as the NHS, social services and the Department of Work and Pensions.'[52] The comments of members are revealing: 'This place has helped me in so many ways, it has been a lifesaver.' Again, 'I joined in 2016 to help me get away from the stigma, it gets me out and about and helps with my mobility and I don't have to deal with backstreet dealers anymore.' Similarly a woman suffering chronic pain states the following: 'This is exactly what's needed. It's not nice being a female and having to go to a drug dealer and buy off the street. You're putting yourself in an unsafe environment.' She continues, 'I came across the club on Instagram and there's a huge community here. When you're not in a working environment everyday you do feel isolated. It's nice to be able to come here and relax with like-minded people. You can socialise without alcohol having to be involved. I don't mind people drinking but going out and getting bashed about when you're living with chronic pain is not a nice environment to be in.'[53] Moreover, bearing in mind that it used to be considered a drug of transgressive youth cultures, it is significant that many of the members are older people, with up to 40 per cent being pensioners. Furthermore, one of the benefits of the club has been its success in promoting cannabis as an 'exit drug', rather than a 'gateway drug'. Discourses of profanation tend to be weakened by education. Many of the members consume cannabis as a way of leaving lives of addiction to more problematic drugs, such as alcohol and opiates. Of course, because the drug is still illegal and perceived as profane by some non-users, changes in the management of the local police force have led to periodic raids and arrests. Overall, however, because regional law enforcement authorities have the power to use their own discretion about how they police their local areas, some police forces are beginning to consider ceasing the active pursuance of individual users and small-scale growers.[54] There have even been recent discussions about whether to provide it free to inmates of British prisons in order to assess the extent to which it is able to reduce violence, overdose deaths, and addiction to stronger drugs.[55]

Since the late 1950s a number of progressive thinkers have contributed to this gradual normalization of cannabis in Britain. For example, on 1 June 1964, the psychiatrist R.D. Laing wrote a letter to a medical journal following the conviction of a colleague for cannabis possession. He argued that there was 'a strong case to point out to doctors that it is possible for them to prescribe this drug with discrimination and, moreover, to think seriously about making it as available to the public as nicotine or alcohol.' Indeed, he cautiously continued, 'I would be far happier if my own teenage children would, *without breaking the law*, smoke marihuana when they wished, rather than start on the road of so many of their elders to nicotine and ethyl alcohol addiction.'[56] Such views about cannabis were, in the 1960s, so controversial that the editors of the journal refused to print the article. Over the 60 years since Laing sought to challenge the profanation of cannabis, a lot has changed. While more research is still required, it is now, as we will see in the following pages, not difficult to find published research supporting much the same view as Laing's. For example, David Nutt, who is currently the Professor of Neuropsychopharmacology and the Director of the Neuropsychopharmacology Unit in the Division of Brain Sciences at Imperial College London, has argued that not only is cannabis a more benign drug than alcohol,[57] but, actually, much of what we've been told about it being a dangerous drug is 'lies and myths and fearmongering.'[58] Not only was Laing correct, but now that robust research is being disseminated,[59] so cannabis is becoming increasingly mundane and, slowly but surely, newly enacted legislation is making room for medical cannabis.

The key point, however, is that, although cannabis still retains a countercultural veneer, and although it is still, therefore, viewed as 'special' in some sense, whether as sacred or profane, it is no longer as special as it once was. Again, as discussed in Chapter 3, one of the principal catalysts for the gradual normalization of cannabis has been the promotion of CBD (a non-psychoactive cannabinoid – see Chapter 1) as an everyday, natural cure-all. As a result, the profane signification linking cannabis to the counterculture and, subsequently, to a number of transgressive youth subcultures, is being incrementally eroded as the new focus on health and wellbeing is promoted. Stories about, for example, Kim Kardashian using it when 'freaking out' over the birth of her fourth baby or why we should give it to anxious dogs are having a normalizing effect.[60] Overall, the twenty-first century has witnessed a significant challenge to the once stable relationship between cannabis and transgression. As we will see in Chapter 3, there has been a significant growth in demand for medical cannabis and CBD products in high- and middle-income countries. Indeed, by 2019, one in seven Americans claimed to have used CBD,[61] and, by 2022, 64 per cent of US adults believed CBD to be safer than alcohol.[62] As one user in the UK related to me, purchasing cannabis is 'a monthly bill, just like rent, milk, or electricity'.[63] Again, another user simply stated, 'it's one of my five-a-day'.[64] The signification is shifting. It is less exotic than it used to be, less profane, and less identified with youth subcultures.

None of this is surprising, of course, bearing in mind the statistics for recreational cannabis use. For example, researchers in London found that residents support decriminalizing cannabis by 50 per cent to 33 per cent, with younger Londoners being significantly more likely to support a change in the law. Overall, 52 per cent of 18–24 year olds, 56 per cent of 25–49 year olds, 45 per cent of 50–64 year olds and 34 per cent of those aged over 65 support decriminalization.[65] As to usage, across England and Wales almost 8 per cent of adults aged between 16 and 59 years old reported that they had used cannabis in 2020 – with this figure increasing to almost 19 per cent among 16 to 24-year-olds.[66] This trend is also reflected in studies of global drug use. There are now around 209 million recreational users globally.[67] Indeed, according to the United Nations Office on Drugs and Crime, between 2010 and 2020, there was an increase of 23 per cent in the number of cannabis users.[68] In Europe, cannabis remains the most widely used illicit drug, with 22.2 million adults (7 per cent of the population) reporting consuming it in some form during 2022.[69] Familiarity with cannabis consumption or some use of it during a person's life – whether they currently consume it or not – is now very high. Nearly 48 million European males and around 31 million females reported some use of cannabis. In France 44.8 per cent of the population reported that they had used cannabis.[70] Again, this trend has been evident in a number of reports over the past decade. In the US, 49 per cent of the adult population have tried it, which is significant when one considers that, 'more than 50 years ago, just 4% said they had tried the drug.' That percentage, moreover, 'surpassed 20% in 1977, 30% in 1985, and 40% in 2015'.[71] Furthermore, it has become 'socially and culturally accepted by many members of the non-drug using population and ... increasingly culturally embedded in wider society'.[72] While, in 2016, 57 per cent of Americans supported the legalization of cannabis,[73] by 2020 this had increased to 68 per cent. Moreover, as one might expect, the younger the cohort, the higher the percentage of those supporting legalization. So, for example, 79 per cent of people aged 18–29 and 75 per cent of those aged 30 to 49 believe that cannabis should be legalized. Indeed, in 2021, the Pew Research Center published a study showing that 'among adults overall, 91% say marijuana should be legal in some form.'[74] Even those socially conservative sections of society within which normalization is typically resisted as a profane threat to core social values are seeing a shift. Hence, in the US, while just under half of Republicans and conservatives support legalization – compared to over 80 per cent of Democrats and liberals, and more than 70 per cent of independents and moderates – this is still a significant shift compared to attitudes during most of the twentieth century.[75] Again, while it is to be expected that 'US adults who are affiliated with a religion are less likely than religiously unaffiliated adults to support broadly legal marijuana',[76] even amongst these people – who, in the past, enthusiastically embraced Ronald Reagan's 'war on drugs'[77] – there is clear evidence of a softening of attitudes.[78] For example, 'among people who identify with any religious group, just over half (54 per cent) believe marijuana should be legal for medical *and* recreational use, while roughly a third (35 per cent) say it should only be legal for medical use.' Of course, the more religiously conservative people are, the more likely they are resist the normalization of cannabis. So, while 62 per cent of non-Evangelical, Protestant Christians believe marijuana should be legal for medical *and* recreational use, this percentage falls to 44 per cent for those identifying as Evangelicals.[79] Even this, however, demonstrates a significant socio-cultural shift, in that 50 years ago there was only a tiny percentage of left-leaning Evangelicals who would have supported the recreational use of cannabis. Nowadays, an increasing number of Christians challenge the view that cannabis use *per se* is 'a sin' and many support its medicinal use. Moreover, as discussed in Chapter 4, a small, but growing number of Christians are also willing to consider its use as a spiritual aid.[80] Again, the point is simply that cannabis is becoming an unremarkable feature of late-modern life.[81]

What follows is not a comprehensive history of cannabis and nor is it an apologia for its consumption. Rather it is simply an attempt to understand the social and cultural significance of cannabis use in the modern West. What are the cultural processes that have led to it being considered either sacred or profane? How has the growth of our understanding of its pharmacological actions and their effects informed attitudes to the plant? However, before turning to address these issues, we begin with an introduction to the plant and its uses. While I hope that all readers will benefit from this initial discussion, it has been written for those unfamiliar with cannabis culture.

1

Cannabis

As one of the oldest cultivated, multipurpose plants, cannabis has a complex and meandering ethnohistory. Whether we think of its use in rope and cloth, in building materials, in medicinal preparations, in food and drink, as a magico-religious aid, or as a recreational intoxicant, throughout history, somewhere on the planet, humans have been weaving, twisting, compressing, rolling, baking, eating, drinking and smoking cannabis.[1] This has led to a bewildering breadth of practices, beliefs and terminology. Moreover, since the 1960s, a voluminous literature on cannabis has been published across a range of disciplines, from pharmacology to anthropology, from history to politics, from food studies to geography, and from criminology to philosophy.[2] In this sense, we can agree with Brian Preston that we are living on 'pot planet'.[3] Having said that, not all readers will be familiar with cannabis, its cultivation and its uses. Hence, the aim of this chapter is to provide a basic introduction for those readers unfamiliar with the plant, as well as, perhaps, providing some useful information for aficionados.

Background notes on the plant and its cultivation

Cannabis is an annual, dioecious (male and female plants), anemophilous (wind-pollinated) flowering herb. As such, it relies on air currents to carry the grains of pollen from male to female plants. Of course, modern cultivation techniques rarely rely on wind-pollination, in that, typically, growers gather pollen and, over a period of several days, using a brush or even their fingers, simply sprinkle it on the female plant.

Cannabis is prototypical of the relatively small botanical family, Cannabaceae. That said, nineteenth-century botanists tended to identify *Cannabis* as a member of the nettle family (Urticaceae) and then the mulberry family (Moraceae). Although the Cannabaceae family of plants had initially been proposed by the Russian botanist Ivan Martinov in 1820, it would be another century until the English botanist, Alfred Barton Rendle, formally established the relationship with *Cannabis*. 'Cannabinaceae'[4] is, he noted, 'a very small family containing only two genera, *Humulus*, with two species, one of which, *H. Lupulus*, is the Hop, and *Cannabis sativa* (Hemp).'[5] Indeed, although some botanists have continued to debate this relationship, as Robert Clarke and Mark Merlin have commented, 'recent research on the structural organization of nuclear ribosomal (rDNA) has shown a high degree of sequence similarity in the rDNA coding regions of *Cannabis sativa* and *Humulus lupulus*, thus supporting the lumping together of

Cannabis and *Humulus* into one family, Cannabaceae.'[6] (Much has been made of this close family relationship, not least by those interested in brewing beer.[7])

There has also been some debate concerning the number of species, of which popular introductions will typically mention three. *Cannabis sativa* was initially classified by the Swedish botanist Carolus Linnaeus (Carl von Linné) in 1753. Essentially, he argued that *Cannabis* was the genus, consisting of a single species, *sativa*. Following Linnaeus, in 1785, *Cannabis indica* was classified by the French biologist Jean Baptiste Lamarck. He noted that, while *Cannabis sativa* was tall and fibrous, *Cannabis indica* was shorter and more psychoactive. Hence, he concluded that it must be a distinct species. This polytypic (i.e. more than one species) understanding dominated as other supposedly new 'species' were added.[8] For example, in 1924, *Cannabis ruderalis* was identified by the Russian botanist Dmitri Erastovich Janischevsky. Unlike *sativa* and *indica* this is a small, stalky, hardy plant with a low psychoactive impact that is native to Central and Eastern Europe and Russia.

During the twentieth century, however, the tide began to turn as botanists again concluded that all *Cannabis* plants do in fact belong to the single species of *Cannabis sativa*. This monotypic approach lasted for a few decades up until the 1970s when it was again re-examined. Some botanists, such as Richard Evans Schultes and William Emboden, reasserted the view that the genus *Cannabis* is, indeed, polytypic, consisting of the three species noted above. This led to further taxonomical challenges in favour of a monotypic classification. According to Ernest Small and Arthur Cronquist, '*Cannabis* consists of a single highly variable species' – *Cannabis sativa*.[9] More recently and influentially, the geneticist Karl Hillig has identified 'a fundamental split within the *Cannabis* gene pool'.[10] Basically, he has proposed a polytypic understanding of *Cannabis*, which, again, recognizes the above three species, *Cannabis sativa*, *Cannabis indica*, and *Cannabis ruderalis*. However, as far as this book is concerned, there is little to be gained from unpacking the details of these debates.[11] That said, for clarity, following Hillig, Clarke and Merlin, a polytypic interpretation will be adopted, focusing particularly on *sativa* and *indica*. This is the position that is now more or less assumed within everyday cannabis cultures.

As an interesting historical aside, it's worth noting that the taxonomic classification of *Cannabis* has not simply been the arcane pursuit of a few botanists. It has found its way into the courts. In the 1970s, drug legislation in the United States and Canada specifically identified products of *Cannabis sativa* as prohibited materials. This inevitably led creative defence lawyers to argue that their clients' plants, which had been seized by the police, were actually not *Cannabis sativa*. Rather, they were far more likely to have been its close relative, *Cannabis indica*. Hence, although the seized material was more psychoactive, it was, strictly speaking, not prohibited by a law that addressed only *sativa* possession. In a number of cases, Small testified for the prosecution, while Richard Evans Schultes testified for the defence. However, while some of these cases were dismissed, generally speaking, the prosecution succeeded in arguing that, despite the debate within botanical circles, the intent of the law was clear: *Cannabis* – *sativa* or otherwise – was illegal.[12]

As for the various parts of the plant, let's begin with the seeds. These are typically a shade of brown and about the size of a peppercorn or a matchhead. They are ovular and pointed at each end, with a ridge that transverses longitudinally along one side from tip to tip. This ridge splits as the taproot appears during germination.

Interestingly, even in countries where cannabis cultivation is illegal, it is not difficult to acquire seeds. For example, in the UK, it is legal to purchase seeds from seed banks, to feed them to birds, to use them for fishing, and to store them, but *not* to germinate them.

Growers who do use seed banks will be familiar with a number of types of seed, namely 'regular'/'photoperiod', 'feminized', and 'auto-flowering'.[13] The term 'photoperiod' simply refers to the hours of light required in a twenty-four hour period in order to initiate and to maintain the flowering phase. So, for example, while indoor *Cannabis* strains tend to grow according to 12/12 photoperiod, most outdoor plants will require longer exposure to light (e.g. 17/7). However, those indoor growers who want an easier life can purchase auto-flowering seeds. These produce plants that are relatively quick and easy to grow, in that the shift to the flowering stage is 'automatic'. Such seeds are typically the product of hybridizing the plant genetics with the highly resilient *Cannabis ruderalis*, which tends to grow irrespective of the photoperiod. As such, they are often ready to harvest in under ten weeks, more or less regardless of the environmental conditions. Again, for reasons which will become apparent, growers also tend to choose feminized seeds that have been genetically engineered to ensure that the adult plant will be a flowering female, rather than a male.

After the seeds have germinated, usually within a week, they produce two cotyledons (small seed leaves). Shortly after this, the first identifiable serrated *Cannabis* leaves appear as a pair above and at right angles to the cotyledons. Given an open, sunlit environment, light, well-drained soil, sufficient nutrients, and an adequate water supply, depending on the species, *Cannabis sativa* plants are capable of growing to a height of six metres (twenty feet)[14] in a growing season of four to six months. *Indica* plants tend to be smaller – unless they are hybridized with *sativa*.

During the flowering phase, the male and female plants become easier to identify: 'the density of leaves on the upper parts of the plants begins to differ, with the male plant having fewer leaves than the female plant. The male plant forms flowers in long loose clusters (six to twelve inches long) from buds with claw shaped bracts on branches at the top of the plant, while the female plant forms flowers in tight crowded clusters from buds with tubular-shaped bracts.'[15] This is important for growers interested in the medicinal and psychoactive properties of the plant, because it is the upper leaves of the female plant, the unfertilized flower heads, and the flower bracts that are the primary source of the phytochemicals known as 'cannabinoids'.

While the non-psychoactive compound cannabinol (CBN) was initially identified in 1896,[16] it wasn't until 1940 that its chemical structure was correctly determined by the American chemist Roger Adams.[17] Indeed, it wasn't until the 1940s and 1950s that pharmacological experiments with single cannabinoids were first performed. The majority of this research and the principal focus of socio-cultural interest has been the plant's primary psychoactive constituent, 'delta 9-tetrahydrocannabinol' (Δ^9 THC or simply THC).[18] More recently, another phytocannabinoid, 'cannabidiol' (CBD) has become the focus of attention for those interested in the non-psychoactive therapeutic uses of the plant. The structures and stereochemistry of CBD and Δ^9-THC were initially elucidated in the laboratory of Raphael Mechoulam in 1963 (CBD) and in 1964

(Δ^9-THC), when they were first isolated from cannabis.[19] However, as will be discussed in Chapter 3, cannabis research has not been straightforward. Mechoulam, for example, notes the following:

> As cannabis was an illicit substance, it was not readily available to most scientists. Even if obtained legally, research with it was a laboratory nightmare. In many countries special security precautions had to be undertaken. In most universities, researchers could not follow the security regulations effectively, and pharmaceutical companies did not want the presumed notoriety of 'trying to make money out of marijuana.' From a scientific point of view, cannabis research had effectively been suppressed.[20]

However, because Mechoulam was blissfully unaware of these legal problems, he asked the police where he could secure some hashish. Fortunately for the future of cannabis research, they too were ignorant of the details of the legislation and happily supplied the kindly scientist with some hashish to take back to his laboratory. As he later commented: 'I obtained hashish from the police ... [who] were also unaware that they were not supposed to give it to me for research ...' Hence, he 'went happily ahead isolating the cannabis constituents'. It wasn't long before his friend, Yechiel, joined him: 'we collaborated for six or seven years. We isolated the major typical constituents of the plant, which we named "cannabinoids."'[21]

The production of cannabinoids in the plant varies according to, for example, genetic differences between plant lineages and environmental factors. Of course, like any organism, *Cannabis* plants are a product of both their genetic constitution ('genotype') and their environment. This combination leads to a particular constellation of observable characteristics, such as size, colour, smell, taste, and so on. Together, these are known as the plant's 'phenotype'. Both the genotype and the phenotype have become important in contemporary *Cannabis* genetics.

Having said that, as indicated above, it's not just the appearance, smell, and taste that are important to growers and users. In particular, cultivars are being produced to maximize the levels of certain cannabinoids. While some of these, such as CBD, are popular because they are known to have a number of non-psychoactive, medicinal properties, the aim of much genetic manipulation has been to modify the plant's psychoactive potency.

It's worth noting here that this is significant when thinking about the history of the plant's use as a psychoactive technology. 'Humans have,' noted Small, 'domesticated *Cannabis*, causing it to evolve in divergent ways to supply different products. Virtually all major crops have undergone domestication, although the degree of divergence among the different kinds of cannabis plant is more extreme than in most plants.'[22] So, was wild, ancient cannabis much the same as the little bag of weed that can be purchased today? No, it wasn't, not least because THC levels in ancient wild cannabis plant populations are likely to have been much lower than they are today. Again, as Robert Clarke and Mark Merlin have noted, while there are a number of variables to be accounted for, generally speaking, 'all cultivated drug varieties are higher in THC than fibre varieties or wild or feral spontaneous populations'.[23] Although some campaigners might disagree, actually, most researchers would concur with Clarke and Merlin that 'it is readily apparent that domestication of *Cannabis* from drug use, especially during the latter half of the twentieth century, significantly raised THC levels in dried floral clusters'.[24] For example, a recent analysis of the available data demonstrated that, while the situation is complex, 'the cannabis products available on the illicit market and in coffee shops in the Netherlands are more potent today than before the turn of the millennium.'[25]

Not only has domestication led to an increase in THC levels, but it has led to an expanding range of strains/cultivars. One of the most well-known of these is 'skunk', an influential, frequently demonized, highly potent strain that was first developed by the American Sacred Seed Company in the late 1970s. It was initially a blend of several varieties from around the world, notably, 'Afghani Indica', 'Acapulco Gold', 'Mexican Sativa', and 'Columbian Gold Sativa', which, together, as the name suggests, gave it a distinctive, pungent aroma. Having said that, while 'Skunk #1' is a specific strain, 'skunk' is now a popular generic term among non-afficionados for all high-potency strains. However, largely because of a link between highly potent strains and instances of psychosis in some users – although recent research has questioned this[26] – the term 'skunk' is now freighted with negative baggage. Indeed, because skunk is now central to discourses of profanation about cannabis, as we will see in Chapter 3, those who seek to promote medical cannabis frequently distance their products from association with, not just skunk, but also with THC *per se*. That is to say, popular ideas about skunk have tainted cannabis and created problems for those wanting to promote its use as a non-psychoactive medicine.

One can, of course, understand why this has happened. Strains grown primarily for recreational purposes can contain from 2 per cent to over 30 per cent THC. For example, 'The Toad' developed on Tyson Ranch (owned by the former boxer Mike Tyson) and 'Brownie Scout' cultivated by Green Thumb Industries have both been tested at around 37 per cent THC. Both of these, which can induce a psychedelic-like experience, are derived from a very popular strain called 'Girl Scout Cookies' (GSC) – which has around 19 per cent THC and a flavour profile slightly reminiscent of the cookies sold by Girls Scouts in the United States to raise funds. A highly potent, *indica*-dominant strain, GSC was made by combining two other well-known and potent strains of cannabis, 'OG Kush' and 'Durban Poison' – and, it is rumoured, 'Granddaddy Purple'. It was developed by the well-known San Francisco collective, 'Cookies Fam', and is particularly linked to one of its members, the rapper and cannabis entrepreneur 'Berner' (Gilbert Antony Milam, Jr). Although the link to Berner is questioned by some, it is certainly true that, along with his business partner, 'Jigga' (Jai Chang) – with whom he founded 'Cookies', one of the leading global cannabis brands – he has produced some of the most popular GSC-derived strains.

To return to the earlier point, however, cannabis cultivation is not just about potency. As a craft, which is now taught at specialist educational institutions, such as particularly Oaksterdam University,[27] cannabis cultivation is an academic discipline and strains are treated to much the same sensory examination and evaluation as sommeliers interrogate fine wines. The appearance, the aroma, the taste, the type of psychoactive effect produced and so on are all judged and described in evocative detail.

Indeed, because cannabis cultivation is a craft, not only are there educational courses serving the cannabis industry, but there are now a number of competitions to assess the quality of the produce. For example, in Amsterdam, in 1988, Steven Hager, who was, at the time, the editor of the leading cannabis magazine, *High Times*, established the 'Cannabis Cup'. Similarly, in California, the 'Emerald Cup' is becoming an increasingly important industry event.

Central to the quality of the phenotypes judged at these competitions are the terpenes. These give the various strains their distinctive colours, aromas, and flavours. That is to say, the overall effect of cannabis is produced by a range of compounds functioning synergistically. Put simply, just as drinking pure alcohol is not the same experience as drinking a fine wine or whisky, so consuming pure THC will not produce the same overall aesthetic and psychoactive experience as when it is consumed with the rest of the plant. This is because numerous different compounds work together with the cannabinoids to achieve an effect that they would be unable to achieve alone. Indeed, in 1998, this process was given a name by Mechoulam and Shimon Ben-Shabat: 'the entourage effect'.[28] This effect, of course, is not surprising, bearing in mind that *Cannabis* has more than four hundred chemicals, over a hundred of which are cannabinoids, accompanied by a range of terpenes, flavonoids, and other phenolic compounds.[29]

As we have already briefly noted, as a result of crossbreeding, the number of evocatively named strains is growing all the time.[30] For example, 'Skunk #1' is a *sativa*-based hybrid strain. Another very popular strain is 'Kush', which is either wholly *Cannabis indica* or mixed with a strain of *sativa*. So, for example, 'Afghan Kush', 'Hindu Kush', 'Green Kush', and 'Purple Kush' are all pure *indica* strains, whereas 'Blueberry Kush' and 'Golden Jamaican Kush' are hybrids. Others, such as 'Haze', are either wholly *sativa* or again a hybrid. Each strain is carefully described to customers, sometimes with reference to the pedigree or even the original growers, particularly if they are well-known for their craft, such as the veteran American grower, Daniel John Short.[31] So, for example, 'Blueberry', we are told, 'is oozing with fruity flavours – as one would expect from a strain that features Juicy Fruit Thai in its pedigree. Bred by the distinguished horticulturalist D.J. Short, he also used Afghani *indica* and Purple Thai to get the balance just right. A Cannabis Cup winner in 2000, this one is guaranteed to keep you on your toes.'[32] Again, 'Stella Blue' is 'one of those rare Dutch *sativas* that live up to their reputation. Stella Blue is strong on fruit flavours with just a hint of aniseed. A Cannabis Cup prize winner in 1995, Stella Blue has since gone the distance and established itself as a firm favourite in many of Amsterdam's most discerning coffee shops. One for the connoisseur.'[33] Likewise, 'Rock Bud' was a Cannabis Cup winner in 1998. It is 'a reliable Dutch *indica* delivering a fresh sweet smoke. It blends subtle fruit flavours of strawberry, banana, and lemon. Don't be fooled though. It's got a kick like a mule and chances are that you'll be lying flat on your back ten minutes later. Best reserved for those quiet nights in.'[34] Similarly, the popular, award-winning *sativa*-dominant strain 'Super Lemon Haze', originally cultivated by Franco Loja from a combination of 'Lemon Skunk' and 'Silver Haze', produces buds that are green and yellow with amber hairs on the trichomes that can appear as if they are tinted yellow. Largely because of its dominant terpene, 'limonene', it smells and tastes like freshly peeled lemons.

It's also worth noting that, nowadays, while users are treated to an enormous variety of strains, the cannabis smoked during the 1960s was rather different. Indeed, much of the cannabis produced in the 1960s was 'landrace'. That is to say, it was a pure *indica* or *sativa* strain, often grown in its natural environment. As with vinification, the 'terroir' is enormously important for landrace strains, in that the soil, the climate, the topography, and the growing practices developed in particular locations all impart unique characteristics to the finished product. While most cannabis is now hybrid, it is still possible to acquire popular landrace strains, the names of which sometimes betray the geographical area where they originated, such as 'Durban Poison', 'Kilimanjaro', 'Acapulco Gold', 'Panama Red', 'Columbian Gold', 'Thai', 'Afghan Black', and 'Hindu Kush'.

As indicated above, not all cannabis is cultivated for recreational or medicinal usage. It is also produced for the bast fibre taken from the main stalk. This is 'hemp'. As with the breeding of psychoactive strains, hemp farmers have carefully cultivated *Cannabis sativa* to maximize the length and quality of the fibre. (Indeed, hemp typically has less than 0.3 per cent THC.) As Clarke and Merlin comment, those hemp varieties that are 'selected for fibre production have longer and more flexible fibres, while seed and drug varieties have shorter and more brittle fibres. Unbranched, slender stalks with long internodes are preferred for fibre production ... Fibre cultivars have also been selected for total fibre yield, and exceptional plants of Hungarian fibre cultivars can produce over 40 percent dry weight of bast fibre.'[35]

Finally, as indicated above, the primary source of cannabinoids are the upper leaves, the unfertilized flower heads, and the flower bracts of the female plant. Of particular value are the tiny 'trichomes' (glandular hairs) found on the flowers. These trichomes produce resin rich in cannabinoids.[36] In terms of the evolution of the plant, this resinous substance was possibly 'a defense against herbivory (attack by plant-eating organisms), although glands may also prevent desiccation by lowering airflow and reflecting sunlight'.[37] Whatever the reason for the plant's evolution of trichomes, they have been enormously important in the history of cannabis cultivation. Along with fragments of flowers (which contain the most trichomes) and leaves, the resin is separated from the plant using various methods and then compressed into blocks. This is 'hashish', which is often more potent than the unprocessed cannabis flower. As one popular user's guide comments regarding 'the relative merits of grass versus hash', 'if one were to judge it purely by strength of the smoke, then hash is the clear winner. This is because, in its purest state, hash contains significantly more THC ... than grass.'[38] As to its production, this was probably a by-product of harvesting for other uses. As Chris Duvall notes, '*Cannabis* is a sticky, resinous plant, and the most basic technique of hashish production is to collect resin accumulated on the skin. A more developed technique is to dry harvested plants, sift the resinous hairs from the other material and press the sifted dust into lumps of hashish.'[39] Again, 'from North Africa to central Asia, labourers used simple sieves to produce mountains of hashish. Less efficient methods were used locally. In Pakistan, workers in confined spaces beat dried plants with sticks, collecting the copious resinous dust on hanging sheets while wearing respiratory masks. Current hashish production in Afghanistan uses a similar technique.'[40]

A note on terminology

Observant readers will no doubt have noticed that, for much of this chapter, the word '*Cannabis*' has been capitalized and italicized. This is because much of the discussion has focused on the scientific literature. '*Cannabis*' is used in plant taxonomy, while 'cannabis' is generally used outside botanical discussions. Hence, throughout the rest of the book, unless specifically discussing the botanical details of the plant and its scientific classification, reference will simply be made to 'cannabis'.

Joseph Berke and Calvin Hernton note that 'cannabis, in the form of a leafy mixture (marijuana) or resinous exudate (hashish) is used throughout the world by tens of millions of people. In Western countries marijuana and hashish are generally smoked rather than eaten and both are commonly known as "pot."'[41] Berke was an American psychotherapist who had moved to London in 1965 to work with the pioneering Scottish psychiatrist R.D. Laing. Hernton was an American sociologist who had also travelled to Britain in 1965 to work with Laing. The above quotation, which is taken from their 1974 study of British cannabis users, reflects the Euro-American context of the late 1960s and early 1970s. 'Pot', for example, was a ubiquitous Western, countercultural term for recreational cannabis during this period. Likewise, 'pothead' was frequently used as a largely derogatory term for regular users. It even found its way into academic literature, such as Michael Schofield's engaging 1971 psycho-sociological study, *The Strange Case of Pot*.[42] Again, while in Britain 'grass' and 'weed' tended to be the terms used for the leaves and flowers prepared for recreational use,[43] in the United States the word 'marijuana' was much more common. It still is.

Berke and Hernton, also mention 'hashish'. Etymologically, while the term has multiple origins, and is taken primarily from the Arabic, '*ḥašīš*', it is also traceable to the Latin, '*lhasis*' and the Dutch term '*assis*'. In Arabic, the term simply refers to 'dry grass' or 'herb' and first appeared as a reference to a psychoactive hemp-based product in the mid-thirteenth century. The influential botanist Ibn al-Bayṭār (1197–1248), in his most widely read text, *Kitāb al-Jāmiʿ li-Mufradāt al-Adwiya wa-l-Aghdhiya* (*Compendium on Simple Medicaments and Foods*), noted that '*ḥashīsh* is an Egyptian nickname for a third variety of hemp called "the Indian hemp" (*al-qinnab al-hindī*), the consumption of which was believed to trigger intoxicating and euphoric effects.'[44] By the eighteenth century the term was widely used, particularly amongst the poor in Islamic societies, which prohibited alcohol consumption. For example, in 1774, the German cartographer Carsten Niebuhr, reporting on his travels through Arabia, noted that 'the lower people are fond of raising their spirits to a state of intoxication. As they have no strong drink, they, for this purpose, smoke *Haschisch*, which is the dried leaves of a sort of hemp.'[45]

Nowadays, however, 'hash'/'hashish' tends to refer to cannabis resin – a light to dark brown substance visually resembling a stock/bouillon cube. While trends have changed, between the 1960s and 1980s resin was typically heated over a flame, crumbled into tobacco and rolled into a cigarette. There are other ways of smoking hash, such as the use of a pipe or chillum, but this was the dominant method of smoking it in Europe.[46] Moreover, it was the most popular form of cannabis available in Britain. As Gary Potter comments, as late as 1997, two-thirds of the cannabis consumed in the UK was resin, 'with 42% of the total cannabis consumed being hashish of Moroccan origin.'[47] Again, Mel Thomas notes that 'all that was readily available was hashish, predominantly something called Moroccan "soap bar" ... There was also a soft and pliable black hash of dubious Afghan origin, as well as a nasty, thinly pressed Lebanese variety known as "flat pack."'[48] The dominance of hashish, particularly in the UK, was, as Howard Marks has discussed in his autobiography, largely because it was easier to smuggle into the country. For example, 'a hundred pounds of hashish' could be 'stuffed under the back seat and in the door panels' of a car.[49]

It should also be noted that, whereas it is fairly obvious why some terms, such as 'grass', 'weed' and 'bud'[50] are used for cannabis, the origins of other terms, such as 'pot', are, etymologically, more difficult to determine. Indeed, the term 'pot' seems to have appeared in America in the 1930s and has, not unreasonably, been linked to the Mexican Spanish etymons '*potaguaya*' or '*potiguaya*'. Furthermore, some believe that these terms are a corruption of '*potación de guaya*' ('drink of grief'), which appears to have been a beverage produced by soaking cannabis in alcohol. However, while all this would make good sense, actually this derivation lacks significant corroborating evidence.[51]

Having said that, in the final analysis, whether one refers to 'pot', 'grass', 'weed', 'herb', 'bud', 'hash', 'gear', 'chronic', 'tea', 'jive', 'kaya', 'zamal', or any of the other numerous terms in the argot of global cannabis culture, it is difficult to be dogmatic about etymology. Words for drugs travel underground and change over time and from place to place. Indeed, while the term 'pot' is frequently used in the study by Berke and Hernton, one of the most common terms for cannabis during this period was 'dope'[52] – a term which has been used for a number of recreational, illegal drugs. Indeed, in the late nineteenth and early twentieth centuries, as part of a process of othering and profanation, certain 'drugs' were referred to as 'dope' and their users were demonized as 'dope-fiends'.[53] However, by the late 1960s, the signification of 'dope' had changed. Within liminal, transgressive youth culture it had become a largely positive term for cannabis and, indeed, nowadays, 'dope' has been almost entirely sanitized and invested with subcultural capital. Central to this process has been its use within popular culture. For example, Gilbert Shelton's popular comic strip character, Freewheelin' Franklin, issued the following humorous nugget of weed wisdom: 'dope will get you through times of no money better than money will get you through times of no dope.'[54]

Shelton's *Fabulous Furry Freak Brothers*, which first saw the light of day in 1968, was a significant influence on hippie cannabis culture. Many countercultural users during the 1970s were familiar with the characters, wore the badges, and shared the comics. This is worth mentioning here, because, just as Al Aronowitz and Bob Dylan introduced The Beatles to cannabis on 28 August 1964,[55] so, more widely, the influence of American cannabis culture on European youth culture became ubiquitous during the 1960s and 1970s. This led to the dissemination of popular American terminology. Indeed, The Beatles were not the first to be introduced to cannabis by Americans. Even before the 1960s, the impact of American drug culture was being felt. For example, Graham Keen, one of the voices from the English underground interviewed by Jonathon Green, recalled that, in 1959, he hitchhiked to London to see a friend. 'I got up to town, we got on the Northern Line to go up to Highgate in the rush hour and he said, "Read this," and gave me a copy of [Allen Ginsberg's] *Howl*. Then I read [Jack Kerouac's] *On the Road* and it was those two books for ever after. That brought in the Beats and from then on we were looking for dope.'⁵⁶ The globalization of American literature, music, and film contributed significantly to the construction of European cannabis cultures.

Of particular note is the fact that the drug became a staple within the jazz and blues music scenes. A fascinating window on American jazz culture during the 1930s and 1940s can be found in *Really the Blues* by the clarinettist Mezz Mezzrow (Milton Mesirow). In it, he introduces the reader to the contemporary argot for cannabis – e.g. 'guage', 'grass', 'grefa', 'gunga', 'muggles', 'muta', 'reefer', 'tea', and 'weed'. Indeed, his own name even entered the cannabis lexicon. As he recalled, 'new words came into being to meet the situation: *the mezz* and *the mighty mezz*, referring, I blush to say, to tea and to me both; *mezzroll*, to describe the kind of fat, well-packed, and clean cigarette I used to roll (this word later got corrupted to *meserole* and it's still used to mean a certain size and shape of reefer ...).'⁵⁷ As we will see in the next chapter, in repressive and racist societies, musicians began to use such codified terms for the drug to avoid detection. This transgressive, non-mainstream discourse was then quickly adopted within the counterculture of the 1960s as the use and knowledge of cannabis became increasingly invested with subcultural capital.

Another term for cannabis, '*ganja*', which became common during the 1970s, can also be linked to a particular genre of popular music. The term, which is the most popular word for cannabis in Jamaica, began to be used within Western musical subcultures influenced by reggae. That said, while, in Chapter 3, we will discuss *ganja*'s association with Rastafarianism in 1970s popular culture, like 'hashish', it was already a well-travelled term. Indeed, it is actually a Hindi word and, as a result of the British presence in India, it had already been introduced into Europe several centuries previously.⁵⁸

Finally, some, such as Duvall, have questioned whether the term 'marijuana' originated in Mexico, as is commonly believed. This, of course, is debateable. Although its usage can be traced to Mexico in the mid-nineteenth century, as Alan Piper has discussed, the origins of the term remain stubbornly obscure.⁵⁹ A number of theories have been posited over the years. For example, Weston La Barre has suggested that the term 'may derive from a Chinese word for hemp, brought by Chinese coolie labourers in western Mexico'.⁶⁰ Again, Piper also notes a theory suggested by Victor Mair that 'the root of the word *marijuana* might be a Semitic loan word in Spanish, having an Arabic origin, later being imported to Mexico from Moorish Spain'.⁶¹ More recently, Duvall has sought to link it to Africa. Noting its similarity to the Central African Bantu term '*mariamba*', which means 'some cannabis to smoke',⁶² he criticizes those writers who have 'portrayed *marihuana* as either a "Mexican" term lacking any linguistic identity or a word whose roots lay only in Mexican indigenous languages'. He continues, 'in recent decades, a few etymologists have looked beyond Mexico for possible roots, but have rarely considered Africa.' However, 'an African etymology for *marihuana*', he insists, 'is a hypothesis that is supported by historical context and can be tested through formal linguistic analysis. All other proposed etymologies are untenable. Some rest on made-up words that are absolutely undocumented, like the alleged Portuguese *maraguango*.'⁶³ Again, while this etymological link is still a little tenuous, overall, Duvall does make a cogent case for the idea that 'African knowledge underlies practices of psychoactive cannabis use around the Atlantic'.[64]

It's worth noting here that, until recently, the significance of the role Africa played in the global diffusion of cannabis has been neglected. Brian du Toit and others began to realize this back in the 1970s.[65] That is to say, studies in the history of cannabis use have highlighted a larger problem regarding the accuracy of scholarship informed by colonial bias. In short, there seems to have been a marginalization of African contributions to world culture. In fact, in terms of cannabis culture, 'African knowledge is fundamental to now dominant global practices of cannabis use, particularly the act of smoking the herb and the technology of the water pipe. In the Atlantic World, African knowledge of psychoactive cannabis spread widely with slave trading. In many societies that received slaves from Central African ports between 1730 and 1900, African vocabulary and technology are historically documented.'[66] Hence, African knowledge, practice, and terminology are important for our understanding of contemporary global cannabis cultures. Most importantly, whereas in Asia the plant was typically consumed in food and drink, in Africa it was introduced into ethnobotanies that included pipe smoking. Duvall, for example, has discussed the history of cannabis use in sub-Saharan Africa, notably its use by pre-existing indigenous smoking cultures in the Zambezi River valley. Subsequently cannabis smoking spread throughout the continent and later throughout the Atlantic world as a result of the transportation of exploited Africans. That said, we will see that there is some debate as to whether African slaves were primarily responsible for spreading its recreational use in the Caribbean. Indeed, it's rather more likely that its use was linked to indentured labourers from India.

Ganja, *charas*, and *bhāṅg*

This brings us to the three terms used for cannabis preparations in India, which have, at times, served as a folk standard of potency in the West,[67] namely '*bhang*', '*ganja*' and '*charas*'.[68] The Sanskrit term *bhāṅg* – which, as we will see in Chapter 3, is mentioned in the *Atharvaveda* (1000–900 BCE) – while simply used to refer to the plant, also popularly refers to the least potent and the cheapest of cannabis preparations consumed on the Indian subcontinent. As well as being used as a remedy for a number of ailments in Ayurvedic medicine, *bhang* is also consumed during religious festivals, notably Mahashivaratri and Holi.

It did not, however, remain in India. It travelled. Maritime trade transported cannabis from India to the Arabian Peninsula and, eventually, by the mid-twelfth century to Egypt and East Africa.[69] During the first millennium CE, the seasonal monsoon winds assisted intrepid travellers across the Arabian Sea, from western India towards the Red Sea and East Africa. Evidence for this growing trade can be found in, for example, the *bhang* cognates that occur around the Red Sea. As Duvall comments, 'Arabic *bango*, which means "psychoactive cannabis herbal material," is spoken in Sudan, Yemen, and Egypt.'[70] Moreover, whereas, in India, *bhang* had traditionally been prepared as a paste from the dried leaves, seeds, and stems of cannabis, which was then introduced into foods and drinks – e.g. *bhaṅgā* and *bhang lassi* – in sub-Saharan Africa it became part of a pipe-smoking culture. Indeed, there is, as Nikolaas van der Merwe has discussed, archaeological evidence of cannabis being smoked in pipes in Ethiopia from the thirteenth century CE.[71]

Although, during the 1300s and 1400s CE, '*gañjā*' and *bhang* were synonymous in some texts from around the Ganges valley,[72] generally speaking they refer to distinct preparations in the history of cannabis. Unlike *bhang*, the Hindi term *gāṇjhā* typically refers to the flowering tops of cultivated female plants. Consequently, because cannabinoids are concentrated in the pistillate inflorescences, *ganja* tends to be stronger than *bhang*. While both were occasionally smoked prior to 1500 CE, they were primarily consumed in food or drink.

Because, as indicated above, many readers will associate the term '*ganja*' with Jamaica and particularly Rastafarianism (as will be discussed in Chapter 4),[73] it's worth saying a little more about its introduction to the Caribbean. Essentially, while it has been argued by Kenneth Bilby that cannabis culture arrived with African slaves,[74] it's difficult to ignore the evidence suggesting that its use as a recreational drug was introduced to Antillean culture by workers from the Indian subcontinent. As a result of a decline in socioeconomic conditions in British India, the end of slavery early in the nineteenth century, and an inability to attract European workers to the plantations, between 1838 and 1917, more than 500,000 Indians were transported to the Caribbean under 'the Indian indenture system'.[75] Around 36,000 Indian labourers arrived in Jamaica between 1845 and 1917. They farmed cattle, grew vegetables, cultivated rice, and, in some cases, propagated that '"pernicious plant" – *ganja*'.[76] As Gurbakhsh Singh Chopra notes, the recreational smoking of *ganja* was particular popular among poor Indians.[77]

Having made that point, we should note that cannabis was known in Jamaica prior to the arrival of workers from India. Hemp, of course, was already used by the British for cloth and cordage. Indeed, although it has been assumed that studies of plant life in Jamaica 'failed to note cannabis in the local flora' until later in the nineteenth century,[78] actually, one of the first botanical references to '*Cannabis sativa*' appeared in 1794 in Arthur Broughton's 'Appendix' to the first volume of Bryan Edwards' *The History, Civil and Commercial, of the British West Indies*.[79] This Appendix is simply 'a catalogue of exotic plants in the garden of Hinton East'[80] at Spring Garden, Gordon Town. As Hinton East was a prominent Jamaican slave owner of English parentage who established a private botanic garden, *Cannabis* may have been transported there as an interesting botanical specimen.

As to its cultivation and usage in Jamaica beyond the confines of East's botanical garden, while we have noted Bilby's argument that the recreational use of *Cannabis* travelled there with slaves, we have also indicated that this is very difficult to substantiate. Even he has acknowledged that 'documentation of cannabis use among Africans during the slavery period is lacking'.[81] Again, as Vera Rubin and Lambros Comitas have discussed, although 'it is generally believed that the psychoactive use of cannabis was introduced to the West Indies by African slaves', there is a conspicuous lack of evidence for its use therapeutically or recreationally by 'African slaves, or by freedmen in the Antilles during the pre-emancipation era'.[82] Hence, they too conclude that 'strong circumstantial evidence suggests that the multipurpose use of cannabis was introduced to the British West Indies by indentured labourers from India, the first of whom arrived in ... Jamaica in 1845'.[83] However, the key point as far as this discussion is concerned is that, not only does the term *ganja* become popular following the arrival of Indian labourers, but also other cannabis-related Indian terms, such as '*kali*' and '*chillum*' (a pipe used for smoking cannabis) are also introduced to Jamaican cannabis cultures. African terms, on the other hand, such as '*kif*' and '*dagga*' seem not to have been used during this early period. Later, of course, during the twentieth century, the influence of Central African cannabis cultures are evident in the use of terms such as '*diamba*' and '*makoni*'.

It is also worth noting that the complex of beliefs and cultural attitudes allied to cannabis use among working-class Jamaicans parallels that of India. This includes, for example, as Rubin and Comitas discuss, 'the methods of preparation and use, the role of *ganja* in folk medicine, in divine origin mythology, in pragmatic ritual uses, and the social class framework of use and attitudes towards *ganja*.'[84] In the final analysis, the anthropological evidence from Jamaica and also the testimonies in reports, such as that of the Indian Hemp Drugs Commission, established by the British government in 1893,[85] clearly suggest that 'the *ganja* complex is a cultural innovation from the period of East Indian indenture, diffused to the black cane cutters through association with indentured workers on the sugar plantations and incorporated into working-class lifestyles.'[86]

Moreover, whether it was initially used by Africans or Indians, the colonial opposition to *ganja*, while rooted in racism, was also fundamentally related to social class. Hence, witnesses who testified before the Indian Hemp Drugs Commission,

> stated that its 'use is confined to lower-class people,' who are treated by the educated 'higher-class' people with disrespect and referred to as *ganjari*, a term of contempt, like 'drunkard.' One witness stated that 'good cultivating farmer caste' never used *ganja* or *bhang* as a stimulant to hard work, but increased the consumption of ghee and milk for increased energy ... Adverse witnesses correlated the use of cannabis with dissipation, debauchery, crime, violence, disease, and insanity.[87]

This correlation of cannabis with dissipation, debauchery, crime, violence, disease and insanity is, we will see in the next chapter, a recurring theme.

Hence, demonized by the colonial authorities as a largely working-class vice suspected of inducing violence and insanity, the Hindi term eventually entered the legal vocabulary of Jamaica.[88] Indeed, the first official mention of *ganja* appeared in an 1883–1884 report from an institution for the mentally unwell, in which it was identified as a probable cause for 'lunacy'.[89] A few years later, a 1893 report produced by the 'Protector of Immigrants' noted that the recreational use of the plant 'rendered men incapable of working and while under its influence they might commit a crime almost without their knowledge ... The Colonial Secretary said that honourable members thought ganjah most dangerous as compared with other drugs; but an analysis of it had been made in India and it was found to be one of the least dangerous.' Nevertheless, the report continued, while 'it might be the least of the evils they had in India ... taken by itself it might still be a most terrible evil. It was certainly something which the Government should take up.'[90] This they did in 1913, when the Legislative Council of Jamaica ratified the International Opium Convention (1912). A clause relating to '*ganja*' was inserted into the legislation that prohibited its cultivation and importation.[91]

Having considered *bhang* and *ganja*, we come to '*charas*', which is basically another term for 'hashish' or compressed cannabis resin concentrate. Consequently, as we have seen, visually, it is quite different to either *bhang* or *ganja*, being a hard, brown block, ball, or finger of resin, rather than leaves and flowers. It is also known for its potency. Indeed, not only have the terms *bhang*, *ganja*, and *charas* been used as a folk standard of potency, but, relatedly, 'indica' and 'sativa' have also served as references for the psychoactive effects of the plant, rather than botanical references (which would be typed in italics), indica being the more potent. This is relevant to the current discussion, because, as Duvall notes, 'the ideal images of the folk species are that indica plants were originally *charas* cultivars, bred to be short so that people could collect resin by rubbing their bodies against standing plants. Sativa plants, on the other hand, are tall-growing *ganja* cultivars.'[92] Hence, regardless of how it was grown and what strains were used, *charas* is almost synonymous with psychoactive potency.

Before we continue, it's perhaps worth noting that very little is known regarding when, where, and how the plant was first cultivated for increased THC production. Indeed, 'little is known about the prehistoric use of cannabis outside eastern China, where it was domesticated as an oil-seed crop.'[93] Nevertheless, as we will see in the third and fourth chapters, we do know that, as time progressed, humans began using the plant, not only for food and fibre, but also medicinally and ritually. Indeed, whether we think of its use in the making of cordage or cloth, or its utility as a cooking oil and a food supplement, or its medicinal value, or its employment within religious contexts, or simply its widespread popularity as a recreational drug, the number of cannabis-related technologies has expanded over the years. Again, while there is little value in providing an inventory of these technologies, it will be helpful to mention a few of the more prominent.

Smoking

In their study of the ethnobotany of cannabis, Clarke and Merlin imagine our ancestors' initial encounter with the plant and make some suggestions regarding how and why their relationship with the plant might have developed.

> It was in the springtime many thousands of years ago. A long ice age had recently ended, and a small group of nomadic people was on the move, venturing far from their ancestral territory. Finding a suitable clearing near the bend of a meandering river, they stopped to camp ... As time passed, they increasingly disturbed the clearing surrounding their settlement and in the process, inadvertently created a nitrogen-rich soil environment by depositing organic waste materials in dump heaps ... One plant that often colonizes dump heaps or waste areas in open environments is *Cannabis* ... Toward the end of the short, warm summer, women gathering seasonal fruits and nuts discovered stands of wild hemp full of ripe seeds

along the river near their settlement ... Women experimented with these plants, letting them dry and flailing them against cleared ground ... The group's store of knowledge developed slowly ... They knew initially that edible *Cannabis* seeds borne in clusters on the female plants contained a nutritious oily substance. Soon they discovered that they could also be used as a source of oil for cooking, fuel, or even a base material for crude soap ... These early settlers eventually learned they could peel bark from the hollow *cannabis* stalk and extract long fibers that were easily utilized. They also learned that hemp fibers were very strong, long lasting, and water resistant ... But was the need for fiber or food the only reason for their interest in *Cannabis*? Perhaps it was first used for its spiritual or euphoric value and thus initially employed for entertainment or ceremonial purposes. In their ceaseless quest for food, they could have firs realized *Cannabis*'s psychoactive potential ... Psychoactive *Cannabis* resin ... can induce rapturous and joyous sensations, ranging from mild reverie and a general sense of wellbeing to ecstasy and hallucination. In our ancient past, these experiences probably generated a deeper interest in the plant than they do for some today.[94]

While this account would be very difficult, if not impossible to substantiate, what evidence we do have suggests that it's probably not too far from the truth.

Historically, while it's likely that cannabis was first consumed orally in food or drink, we have seen that from a fairly early period it was probably also smoked. Indeed, our ancestors seem to have quickly realized that if any significant psychoactive experience was to be enjoyed, 'decarboxylation' is a necessary first step. Decarboxylation is the process by which the cannabinoid 'tetrahydrocannabinolic acid' (THCA), which is not psychoactive, is converted into THC, which is.[95] While, to some extent, decarboxylation can occur naturally over time as the harvested plant dries, the most effective method of speeding up the process is by applying heat. Indeed, nowadays, even those who cook with cannabis will usually decarboxylate their key ingredient in the oven prior to incorporating it in their recipe of choice. However, by far the quickest and easiest method for a user to decarboxylate the harvested flower is by igniting it and inhaling the smoke.

Unsurprisingly, therefore, although 'edibles' (the term used for cannabis-infused food products) are becoming increasingly popular in health-conscious societies, recreationally, the plant is still primarily smoked rather than eaten. While this can be done using a number of methods, from 'vaporizers' to 'bongs' and from 'hot knives' to 'chillums', by far the most popular way to deliver THC to the brain is by means of a cannabis cigarette. Gradually, over the course the twentieth century, this has become the preferred method. Having said that, linked to the development of the medicinal cigarettes, which became popular in France,[96] cannabis cigarettes began to be produced commercially around the mid-nineteenth century. Between the 1850s and 1930s, the Parisian pharmaceutical manufacturer Grimault & Co. produced *Cigarettes Indiennes* ('Indian cigarettes'), which were made from a mixture of dried plants, including tobacco, belladonna, datura, and *Cannabis indica*.[97] Between 1860 and 1820, the company placed over 4,000 advertisements in French newspapers, magazines, and journals for their *Cigarettes Indiennes*. It also advertised its psychoactive cigarettes in publications in the UK, the US, Australia, New Zealand, Canada, Germany, Mexico, and Spain. The product was even promoted in leading medical publications, such as *The Lancet* in the UK and *The Boston Medical and Surgical Journal* in the US. The company's dubious, but largely uncontested claim was that they were a 'sovereign remedy' for a number of respiratory ailments, including asthma.[98] As such, not only did intoxicating cigarettes become relatively popular, but, arguably, they helped to promote this particular method of consuming medicinal plants.

By the 1920s, while still considered by some to be an effective treatment for asthma, we have seen that the recreational use of cannabis was becoming popular within the jazz scene. Consequently, they were increasingly referred to as 'jazz cigarettes'. Indeed, Mezz Mezzrow became a supplier of cannabis in Harlem. That said, as he noted in his autobiography, *Really the Blues*, 'I want to make one thing clear: I never advocated that anybody should use marihuana, and I sure don't mean to start now . . . I never "pushed" it like a salesman . . . I had it for anybody who came asking, if he was a friend of mine.'[99] He quickly gained a lot of 'friends' and they came asking: 'overnight I was the most popular man in Harlem.'[100] As we have seen, even his own name was used to refer to a particular type of cannabis cigarette. Nowadays, while few people will be aware of the term 'meserole', there's no shortage of words for cannabis cigarettes, many of which similarly emerge out of the argot of particular subcultures or scenes. That said, there a few common, transnational terms, of which, perhaps the most ubiquitous are currently 'spliff', 'joint', and 'blunt'. Concerning the first of these, although the etymology of 'spliff' is uncertain, one of its earliest recorded uses appeared in 1929 in the Jamaican newspaper *Kingston Daily Gleaner*, where we learn that 'the deceased was smoking a ganja spliff'.[101] Nowadays, generally speaking, a 'spliff' refers to a cigarette that is made up of a mixture of tobacco and cannabis. A 'joint', on the other hand, typically uses no tobacco. It is simply cannabis rolled in a cigarette paper. That said, the meanings are of course not fixed. They shift over time and from culture to culture. Hence, although older smokers I have spoken to in the UK often don't recognize the distinction between a 'joint' and a 'spliff', it is increasingly common amongst younger users.

Again, in Europe, the term 'blunt', rather than 'joint', is sometimes used of cannabis-only cigarettes. That said, strictly speaking, blunts are constructed by rolling cannabis in a hollowed-out cigar or a tobacco leaf wrap – originally the US cigar brand Philly Blunt. As one popular cannabis website notes,

> selecting the right tobacco wrap is at the heart of rolling blunts, as blunt aficionados tend to be very loyal to one particular brand of tobacco wrapping paper, using their brand of choice almost exclusively. There are two main ways to procure your tobacco wrapping paper. Traditionally, you purchase a pre-rolled cigar or cigarillo, empty out the contents, and then repurpose the tobacco wrapping paper by filling it with weed before re-rolling it into a blunt . . . The other type of blunt wrap is a tobacco leaf paper that comes as-is and is not a pre-filled cigar or cigarillo.[102]

The article concludes by noting that 'blunts are excellent choices for cannabis connoisseurs who favor strong aromas and flavors accompanied by a slow burn and intense high'.[103]

It's also worth noting that, while the blunt has grown in popularity in recent years, it was initially closely linked to another US popular music scene, namely, New York hip-hop during the 1990s. Indeed, it became an important subcultural signifier. As David Foster has commented, 'blunts meant hip-hop. They meant urban culture, New York culture, and, frankly, black culture.'[104] As such, the blunt distinguished cannabis consumption from earlier subcultural associations, which tended to be linked to the largely white, middleclass counterculture of the 1960s and 1970s. Hence, as Foster comments, 'Biggie and Nas rapped about blunts ... Redman came out with a song entitled, "How To Roll A Blunt"',[105] and one of the most well-known early albums from the period is Diamond D's *Stunts, Blunts, and Hip Hop* (1992). It is unsurprising, therefore, that the skilled rolling of blunts became a marker of subcultural capital. That is to say, there emerged 'a direct correlation between your blunt-rolling ability and coolness status ... Everyone had his own individual style and technique ... As we became more skilled and elitist, we learned we could ... maximize the weed flavour and minimize the actual Phillies Blunt flavour.'[106] From hip hop it spread into other urban music scenes, such as drum 'n' bass (e.g. Big Bud's 'Blunt' from the 1999 album *Infinity + Infinity*). Indeed, there's even a record label named after the original product, Philly Blunt Records, which is affiliated to the British drum 'n' bass label V Recordings. Hence, from its origins in hip hop culture, smoking blunts quickly became popular in cannabis culture more widely.

A traditional component of a cannabis cigarette, which all smokers are familiar with, is the 'roach'. This term, which originally referred to the stub of a cigarette, became popular in the jazz scene in North America.[107] As the journalist Meyer Berger noted in his 1938 article for *The New Yorker*, 'Tea for a Viper' – 'tea' being jazz argot for cannabis and 'viper' being argot for a cannabis smoker – 'a pinched-off smoke, or stub, is a roach.'[108] While some smokers will dispose of these, other users will save them and then re-roll the 'roach weed' into another cigarette. As to the smoking of roaches, because these stubs can burn the fingers, small metal clips – 'roach clips' (tweezers etc.) – are used to hold them. Having said that, in the UK, Europe and the Commonwealth, the term 'roach' typically refers to a small strip of rolled card inserted into the end of the spliff/joint. It effectively replaces the filter in a normal tobacco cigarette – although some smokers roll a roach around a filter. As such, there is often no need for a roach clip. Indeed, while some users still rip pieces of card from the rolling paper packaging, nowadays, specifically designed cardboard roaches can be purchased separately. Indeed, it is interesting to note that, as cannabis normalization progresses, some large manufacturers, such as Rizla, now produce cardboard roaches ('paper tips') and even include them with their rolling papers. That said, more health-conscious smokers tend to use cigarette filters. Although some users have told me that they don't get *quite as high* using cigarette filters, others disagree, arguing that they haven't noticed any change at all in the psychoactive impact. This latter assessment is likely to be more accurate, since filters have been shown to be largely ineffective at their primary task. In other words, there is little evidence to support the widely accepted claim that filters significantly reduce smoking-related health risks. Even the cigarette manufacturer Philip Morris conceded that this was the case, but nevertheless insisted that, when it comes to marketing cigarettes, 'the illusion of filtration is as important as the fact of filtration'.[109] Filters were even designed to turn brown to foster this illusion.[110] Hence, for the cannabis smoker, it is unsurprising that filters do little more than rolled cardboard roaches. Having said that, even if filters are not as effective as cigarette manufacturers claim or smokers assume, they are arguably preferable to unfiltered cigarettes.

So much of the ritual around cannabis smoking involves anticipation of the actual event. The scrutiny of the raw cannabis (particularly its aroma), the construction of the joint, the communal sharing, and the gradual shift of perspective as one settles into being high are all part of the experience. Indeed, this is so important that, for many users nowadays, something is lost when one replaces smoking with edibles. Even back in 1953, when recreational cannabis use was not nearly as popular as it is nowadays, Howard Becker's sociological study of users argued that, essentially, smokers need to 'learn to be high'.[111] He was, of course, wrong. Although the cannabis will not have been as potent as it is nowadays, nevertheless, people who smoke cannabis get high. No education necessary! Hence, his naive claim that 'the novice does not ordinarily get high the first time he smokes marihuana, and several attempts are usually necessary to induce this state',[112] is, generally speaking, nonsense. However, Becker's thesis has more to offer than that, in that he also claimed that, once intoxicated, users learn how *to be* high. They learn to smoke in a particular way and, more importantly, they learn to interpret the effects of being high. They also learn to manage the time around smoking. For example, smokers generally make sure they're not going to be interrupted and, bearing in mind the brain fog that some users experience, as Nicholas Lezard reminds us regarding the use of intoxicants generally, 'plan it so the next day is a day off you can use to recharge your batteries.'[113]

Particularly since its association with the counterculture of the 1960s, which invested cannabis with significant subcultural capital, the rituals around its consumption have been just as important for the user's experience as they have for the interpretation of the experience itself.[114] As Tim Pilcher has commented, 'every true stoner knows that smoking a joint isn't just a case of throwing grass into a rolling paper and lighting it. There's the ritual.'[115] This ritual is clearly articulated by Nick Jones: 'First there is the exquisite ritual and anticipation of building it: the delicate origami of pasting the papers together; the cooking and crumbling of the hash or the grinding of the grass; the leisurely rub to achieve the consistency of the mix; the coiling of the cardboard roach; the firm, yet gentle rolling action; the gentle licking of the adhesive strip and the final flamboyant flourish of twisting the touchpaper.'[116] Again, what Jones eloquently communicates is the emotional significance of the ritual journey to the joint. It's a process quite different from simply taking a cigarette from a packet, lighting it and smoking it. While, arguably, there are similarities with the ritual of self-rolling a tobacco cigarette, the process of rolling a joint, a spliff, or a blunt tends to be invested with far more meaning. It is so, not simply because the user is preparing to relax into a more profound altered state of consciousness than that produced by nicotine, but also because of the cultural significance of cannabis and the subcultural capital invested in performing the ritual well. The user is preparing to leave everyday reality and enter a very particular heterotopia. It's interesting to watch a group of users visibly relax as they all prepare to roll their first joints of the evening. One can almost feel the mood in the room lighten. Everyone is on the same page, bound together by a desire to get high, listen to music, and enjoy each other's company. As Jones puts it, 'after the first few drags, your mood mellows, your body relaxes, and you are enveloped in a comfortable glow of wellbeing.'[117] Much of this understanding of the experience is, as Becker argued, learned. Whether users listen to a particular genre of music, or create a particular space with incense, or sit in a particular chair, or roll the joint on a particular album cover, or engage in any number of ritualized activities, they perform certain learned behaviours.[118] Indeed, as Patrick Matthews has commented, there is 'connoisseurship, a set of expectations, a way of talking about the experience, the rituals of sharing joints, and an idea of how stoned to get and how to behave when stoned, all of which matter'.[119]

While cannabis is smoked in numerous settings, alone or with friends, for most users the antecedent period of anticipation is part of the pleasure and central to the construction of what drug researchers sometimes call 'set and setting'. Informed by memories of relaxation and pleasure, along with a knowledge of cannabis cultures, anticipation is an important part of the preparation of 'the set' (i.e. mindset). 'The setting' (i.e. context) is also important. Of course, for many users, because cannabis is a social drug, the ideal setting includes like-minded friends with whom to share conversation, food, music, and so on. However, regardless of whether it is smoked alone or with others, the manipulation of the set and the construction of the setting are learned activities. Some older users, for example, who remember smoking in Easternized, countercultural settings, may burn incense.

Unsurprisingly, in contexts where cannabis is understood to be a sacrament, these rituals are sacralised. For example, one well-known cannabis guru, connoisseur, and grower, Swami Chaitanya, describes the process as a form of mindfulness:

> All of the senses are engaged in the evaluation and preparation of the joint. The look of the bud and the fragrance of the terpenes engage the visual and olfactory centers. Then the tactile awareness comes in as you feel the flower when you break it apart, releasing even greater aromas. You sense the dampness, oiliness, waxiness, and texture of the material. Grinding the buds even stimulates the auditory faculty, particularly when one knocks the grinder pieces together to dislodge plant material. Most likely you are also considering the provenance of the flower during the process. Rolling the joint is tactile and somewhat dexterity challenging, yet there is a subtle satisfaction in having produced a well-turned cylinder ... The penultimate step of the ritual is to puff on the unlit joint prior to lighting, which should give you a taste of the terpene profile of the raw plant. We call it 'taking a dry hit.' To fully employ cannabis as a sacrament, the precursor to lighting the joint, taking a bong rip, using the dab rig, or eating the edible, would be to acknowledge the source of the divinity empowering the plant with a mantra, a prayer or a simple statement of affirmation. Another ritual use would be to enlist its aid in a healing or in a creative endeavour with a specific request to the spirit in the plant.[120]

As touched upon in this quotation, of particular significance for many smokers is the attendant paraphernalia. Perhaps the most conspicuous item that many smokers will cherish is their 'stash box'. This is often an old box with sentimental value. While users can purchase boxes specifically designed for storing cannabis, along with the necessary equipment and materials – rolling papers, roaches, grinders, and so on – often, particularly in the case of seasoned users, they are boxes that have been used for many years. Again, while in the Easternized counterculture of the 1960s and 1970s, they were principally carved, wooden, Oriental boxes, nowadays they tend to be custom-made 'rolling boxes' that include everything required for building the perfect cannabis cigarette, including a V-shaped tray into which the rolling paper is placed while filling it. Indeed, there are even odour-absorbing stash boxes designed (for obvious reasons) to inhibit the smell of the cannabis when closed.

As indicated above, for most smokers, once the contents of the stash box have been unpacked, a bud of cannabis is chosen, broken up, and placed in the grinder. These are plastic, wood, or, preferably, metal cylinders used for grinding large portions of cannabis flower into small particles suitable for rolling a cigarette or packing into a pipe bowl. The top is opened, the cannabis is placed inside between the grinder's teeth. After replacing the top, it is twisted until the contents are ground up and fall through small holes into a second chamber below the teeth. Indeed, some grinders include a third chamber to catch the 'kief'/'keef' (i.e. very small particles of dust-like ground cannabis, including loose, potent cannabis trichomes). Then, having anticipated the moment for some time, the smoker fills the cigarette paper and begins rolling. This is a skill distinct from that of rolling tobacco cigarette. Not only is cannabis not quite as easy to roll – although combining it with tobacco helps – but often the cigarette is given a slight cone shape. Indeed, typically, in countries where it's legal, users can purchase pre-rolled cigarettes, which are almost always conical. While they have become common in cannabis culture as the classic, if slightly more difficult method of rolling a cannabis cigarette, the reason for them is simply because they are more capacious than the usual cylindrical cigarettes. As such, they have become invested with subcultural capital within the cannabis community. Some even argue that the conical shape inhibits 'canoeing' (i.e. burning unevenly), produces smoother smoke, and is actually more potent. Whatever the truth about the benefits of conical spliffs/joints, they have, to some extent, been fetishized within cannabis culture. Hence, photographs and drawings of joints nearly always portray them as conical. (If you want to view one, simply type 'cannabis joints' into your search engine and click 'images'.) Again, rolling cone-shaped joints is part of the user's subcultural cannabis education.

In other cultures, of course, different methods are used. For example, in some Asian cultures, smokers empty cigarettes, mix the tobacco with cannabis, and refill the hollowed out cigarette with the mixture. Preston, for example, recalls observing this method in Nepal. The smoker

> squeezes and kneads the tobacco out of a filter cigarette. No damage to the paper. He keeps half of the tobacco and uses his fingers to make it more powdery in the palm of his hand. Now he adds the pot ... He keeps mixing it for a bit, then puts the hollow cigarette between his lips, brings his palm within range, and scoops up the pot using subtle lip action to control the cigarette like a shovel ... They possess amazing lip dexterity. They scoop it all up, stopping at intervals to tap the

joint on the wrist or a tabletop to make sure it's packing nice and tight. Top it off with a pinch or two placed by the fingertips, fold up the end, and *voila*, you are ready to smoke, and you've kept that industrial-strength filter in place to take care of the tar.[121]

Regardless of how people prefer to roll their spliffs, joints, and blunts – and there are numerous creative interpretations[122] – the anticipation builds as the process moves towards taking the first 'toke'. (Initially used in America in the 1950s to refer to cigarette smoking, the verb 'toke' is now specifically used to refer to smoking cannabis.[123]) The very act of taking a toke – breathing in the fragrant smoke – is important. It's not just that users relax, but, more significantly, that they pass into a gentler reality in which the sharp edges of life are smoothed and everyday life seems just a bit more interesting and profound. 'After the initial inhalation I experience an overall upward movement, both mental and physical. I reach a place after a while, where everyday sensations and experiences become magnified, slowed down, and capable of a fuller, richer appreciation.'[124] Again, Preston recalls that, 'at the first toke that strange bodily sense of eagerness and impatience takes hold, a longing for the remembered indolent happiness of being high. The mere taste of it in the mouth and lungs brings on the longing. Then comes the payoff – that great *whoooooooooosh* of feeling uplifted, like some unseen force is tucking its hands into your armpits and whispering, "Come fly with me." I feel light, giddy, high.'[125] Indeed, as part of this experience, the arts become more engaging and the world seems increasingly beautiful. 'Everything I look at and touch has a certain beauty that I could never see before. Life appears to have extra meaning which is difficult to grasp in everyday life, but pot smoking makes it come easily and makes it all clear.'[126] Again, as is well-known, the appreciation of music in particular is noticeably enhanced during cannabis intoxication.[127] 'Music is beautiful when you're high. Every note is separate, perfect, and complete ... Beauty and love are epitomized in each note.'[128]

Of course, as indicated above, the cigarette isn't the only way to smoke cannabis. There are more ancient technologies. For example, archaeologists in Africa have discovered cannabis residue in Ethiopian clay or stone pipe bowls from 1325 CE.[129] It's likely that cannabis pipes were used earlier than this, but difficult to substantiate as the materials used disintegrate over time. As Duvall has discussed, early 'water-pipe containers were mostly biodegradable, made of bamboo, calabash, coconut, horn, or wood. Some pipes were entirely biodegradable, such as dry pipes made from banana leaves.'[130] However, what does seem to be clear is that 'African knowledge is fundamental to now dominant global practices of cannabis use, particularly the act of smoking the herb and the technology of the water pipe.'[131]

Again, while this isn't intended to be a comprehensive guide to cannabis smoking paraphernalia, it is worth noting a few of the more popular contemporary smoking devices. Let's begin with the 'chillum'. Taken from the Hindi word '*chilam*', this is the part of a 'hookah pipe' designed to hold the smoking material. The hookah itself – also referred to as a 'narghile', an 'argileh', a 'shisha', a 'hubble-bubble', and a 'goza' – is a water pipe sometimes depicted in Orientalist paintings, such as Rudolf Ernst's 'Arab Smoking a Nargilah'. It's usually quite large and consists of a water chamber, which is connected to a small tobacco bowl by a solid pipe. Attached to the water chamber (but located above the liquid) is the hose, a long flexible tube from which the user inhales smoke that has passed from the bowl, down the solid pipe, and bubbled through the water. Think, for example, of John Tenniel's evocative drawing of the caterpillar, comfortably perched on a mushroom, smoking a hookah in Lewis Carroll's *Alice's Adventures in Wonderland*.[132] Although the hookah itself is sometimes referred to as a chillum, again, strictly speaking the chillum is the straight, conical pipe that serves as the tobacco bowl.[133] Nowadays, the term refers to any hand-held, straight, conical pipe used for smoking cannabis. That is to say, few smokers think of a chillum as part of a hookah, but rather understand it to be an entirely separate pipe. Such chillums are made in a range of sizes from a number of materials, including wood, stone, metal, and glass. Again, Preston helpfully describes his own usage: 'We're using a chillum, cupped upright in the hands, with a little square of torn cloth – red, yellow, and green – as a filter over the bottom end. A chillum has to be loaded, held, and smoked upright.'[134] Typically, chillums will also include a 'filter stone', which is dropped into the top of the pipe before the cannabis is added. This stone, which usually has grooved sides in order to allow the smoke to pass through the pipe, prevents the rather unpleasant experience of inhaling burning particles. Also, a '*safi/saafe*' (i.e. damp cloth) is wrapped around the mouthpiece as another residue filter, as well as a method of cooling the smoke a little.

Situated somewhere between a chillum and a blunt are glass blunts. The most popular, 'twisty glass blunts', which come in a range of sizes, obviate the need for rolling papers and roaches. It simply consists of a glass tube and a mouthpiece, attached to which is a screw the length of the tube. The cannabis is loaded into the glass tube, the mouthpiece is screwed through the cannabis, and the blunt is lit. The smoke, which is forced around the raised helical thread gradually cools down, thereby giving the user a more pleasurable experience.

However, far more popular nowadays are vaporisers and vape pens. Vaporisers are designed to be used with dried cannabis, but most can also be used with hash. Typically, they are sleek, discrete, beautifully designed electrical devices which can be recharged with a USB cable. Using either convection (hot air) or conduction (direct contact) methods, they quickly heat the cannabis without burning or combusting it, thereby enabling the user to inhale a smokeless vapour. As such it is generally considered to be far less injurious to the user's health. Even sleeker and more discrete are vape pens, some of which are fashioned in the form of actual cigarettes or cigars. These use cartridges of cannabis concentrate, which, although usually very strong, is generally more healthy, and, as the vapour doesn't smell of cannabis, they allow discrete consumption in public. (Having said that, because the active ingredient cannot be inspected by the user, some unscrupulous, illegal producers have added cheaper, synthetic cannabis, such as 'Spice',[135] to concentrates. This is a far more dangerous drug and, indeed, bears little relation to cannabis.[136])

Perhaps the most common pipe used in Western cannabis cultures – a pipe which isn't technically very different from the hookah and water pipes found in Africa – is the 'bong'. Originally a Thai word for the tubular section of bamboo, the bong is an immediately recognisable water pipe. Indeed, it has become a popular signifier of cannabis culture. For example, if a film director wants to indicate that the protagonist is countercultural or bohemian in some general sense, a bong on the table usually does the trick. The smoke is drawn through water contained in a chamber usually made of glass, ceramic, or plastic. While bongs can be constructed out of almost any watertight receptacle, including plastic bottles, over the years there have been a broad range of designs, some of which reference contemporary politics. For example, in the early 1970s a bong was designed in the image of President Nixon, who had 'vowed that marijuana use would not become legal during his tenure'.[137] Likewise, there's now a number of Donald Trump bong designs.

Finally, there are several other creative methods that smokers employ to increase intoxication. For example, 'moon rocks' – closely associated with the rapper and record producer Korupt (Ricardo Emmanuel Brown) – are a combination of the buds of a strong strain of cannabis, traditionally 'Girl Scout Cookies', dipped in 'hash oil' (a cannabis concentrate), and then rolled in kief. The result is an expensive, but highly desirable cannabis bud, which has had its THC potency more than doubled. In the words of one user,

> Each hit is damn near its own experience. And the high? … Starting in the head and eventually spreading throughout the entire body, down to your toes, a moon rock high is a slow burn that will make you realize you've reached a mountaintop that you may not be ready to climb. I once smoked a gram of moon rocks at 5.00 pm, and when I woke up the next morning at 7.00 am, I was still on Mars waiting for the train back to Earth.[138]

Again, another method of increasing intoxication is simply to light up in a small, poorly ventilated space. This is known as 'hotboxing'. Perhaps the most popular space in which to do this – following the example of Cheech and Chong in their 1978 stoner film *Up in Smoke* – is a parked car with the windows closed. The aim, of course, is to immerse oneself in smoke.

Most users will be aware that, when it comes to getting high, the most efficient and effective method is to use the digestive system rather than the lungs.

Edibles and drinkables

Increasingly, those conscious of the negative health implications of inhaled smoke are turning to 'edibles' (cannabis-infused food) and 'drinkables' (cannabis-infused drinks). That said, cannabis-infused food has a long history.[139] For example, we have already seen that *bhang* was widely used on the Indian subcontinent in drinks and edible pastes. Similarly, *majoun* is an old Islamic confection made of, amongst other ingredients, honey, nuts, figs, ghee, poppy seeds, nux vomica, and cannabis. Indeed, its use was fairly common as an ingredient in premodern Islamic societies. For example, in 1250, shortly after his accession to the throne as the second Mamlūk sultan of Egypt, al-Malik 'Izz al-Dīn al-Aybak, introduced a tax on hashish. Hence, as Danilo Marino has commented, 'the eating of hashish for non-mystical purposes must have been widespread in society as a recreational habit; if that were not the case, political authorities would not have introduced a tax on hashish consumption.'[140] Again, *dawamesc*, a variation of *majoun*, which is a North African green paste made from ground cannabis flowers, mixed with sugar, orange juice, cinnamon, cloves, cardamon, nutmeg, musk, pistachios, and pine nuts. As we will see in Chapter 3, in the mid-nineteenth century, it was used in Paris by the pioneering psychiatrist Jacques-Joseph Moreau, who, as we will see in Chapter 4, introduced it, in varying dosages, to fellow luminaries at the *Club des Hashischins*. These included Théophile Gautier, Victor Hugo, Alexandre Dumas, Gerard de Nerval, Honore de Balzac, and Charles Baudelaire. Again, during the 1860s in the United States, the Gunjah Wallah Company in New York distributed 'hasheesh candy, the Eastern Gunjah of Enchantment, or Oriental exhilarant and nervine compound'. According to the widely published advertisements, it was 'a pleasurable and harmless stimulant confectionized for Nervousness, Debility, Confusion of Thoughts, Loss of Appetite, Depression of Spirits, Nervous Headache, Chills and Fever, Impotence, Nervous Debility, Want of vitality, &c.' The advertisement continued: 'Afflicted Sufferers, try it. Seekers after pleasure and the marvellous, try it. It will do you good.'[141] While it is doubtful that it was the panacea the Gunjah Wallah Company claimed it to be, again, these advertisements do indicate that its use was widespread.

Interestingly, it has even been argued that a mediocre 1968 film about the counterculture, *I Love You, Alice B. Toklas*, transformed *majoun* into one of the most widely used edibles, the hash brownie. The film's title references a 74-year-old American-born member of the Parisian avant-garde, who, in 1954, published a recipe for 'haschich fudge' in a memoir-cum-cookbook. Alice Babette Toklas, the life partner of the American author Gertrude Stein (who had recently died), was struggling with hepatitis and desperately in need of money – but was also keen to avoid selling Stein's enviable collection of early twentieth-century European avant-garde art. Feeling the pressure of an imminent publishing deadline,[142] in order to complete her manuscript for *The Alice B. Toklas Cookbook* she contacted friends and acquaintances to ask for interesting recipes. Ernest Hemmingway, for example, promised her a recipe for cooking a lion. Although the recipe never arrived, she did receive an equally unusual one from her friend, the avant-garde author, sound artist and painter Brion Gysin.[143] Trusting Gysin's recommendation and under pressure, she simply added his recipe to the manuscript without actually attempting to make the 'fudge' – which was a type of *majoun*. Indeed, she seems to have had little or no knowledge of the active ingredient. Nevertheless, although one of the least helpful recipes for *majoun* one is likely to read, Gysin persuaded her that it 'is the food of Paradise', which 'might provide an entertaining refreshment for a Ladies' Bridge Club or a chapter meeting of the DAR [Daughters of the American Revolution].' It would certainly do that! As he pointed out, 'euphoria and brilliant storms of laughter, ecstatic reveries and extensions of one's personality on several simultaneous planes are to be complacently expected. Almost anything Saint Teresa did, you can do better if you can bear to be ravished by *un évanouissement réveillé*.'[144] While the recipe was removed by her disapproving American editor, the British first edition and the second American edition included it, making it an instant sensation in the burgeoning countercultural environment of the 1960s.

This brings us to the film. In 1968, a romantic comedy about the counterculture, *I Love You, Alice B. Toklas*, used her recipe as a plot device. The prudish protagonist, Harold Fine (played by Peter Sellers), is transformed into a hippie by the free-spirited, countercultural Nancy (played by Leigh Taylor-Young), who seduces him with her 'groovy' confectionary. Prior to that point, the principal method of using cannabis was to smoke it. It was this film, Robyn Griggs Lawrence has argued, that 'morphed *majoun* into the pot brownie, and turned the pot brownie into a Western icon forevermore'.[145] Having said that, although others have credited *The Alice B. Toklas Cookbook* as the catalyst for 'modern marijuana edibles era',[146] bearing in mind that those who had travelled to North Africa and Asia had encountered *bhang*, *majoun*, and *dawamesc*, and also that, as we will see, nineteenth-century users in the United States and Europe, such as the esteemed members of the *Club des Hashischins*, had also preferred edibles, this assessment is a little blinkered. Nevertheless, Toklas can almost certainly be credited with publishing the first recipe in a modern Western cookbook.

It should also be noted that the method suggested in *The Alice B. Toklas Cookbook* is rarely used today: 'a bunch of *canibus* [sic] *sativa* can be pulverized. This, along with the spices, should be dusted over the mixed fruit and nuts, kneaded together.'[147] While this may induce a mild effect, it is unlikely to produce visions to rival those of Teresa of Ávila. Nowadays, most cooks will begin by making 'cannabutter' (cannabis-infused butter) or a cannabis-infused oil. Because CBD and THC are not water-soluble, but rather need to bind to fat molecules, butter, and vegetable oils are ideal. That said, it does require time and patience, in that the infusion/extraction process typically takes a few hours. Ground cannabis, which, ideally, has first been decarboxylated in the oven, is mixed with butter or vegetable oil in a pan and left to simmer for a few hours in order to extract as much of the THC and CBD as possible. It is then strained into a bowl to be stored and used in any of the many ways in which one normally utilizes butter and oils. Indeed, there are now numerous user-friendly books and online guides to cooking with cannabis.[148]

Moreover, as indicated above and as users will testify, there is plenty of evidence to suggest that the psychoactive impact of THC is increased when absorbed through the digestive tract, rather than the lungs. This is because it is primarily processed by the liver, which produces 11-hydroxy-THC, which is more – possibly, significantly more[149] – psychoactive than THC.[150] Basically, THCA, which, we have seen, is converted into THC during the decarboxylation process, is, following oral consumption, converted into 11-hydroxy-THC by the liver – this is the 'first-pass effect' or 'first-pass metabolism'. From the liver, the more potent 11-hydroxy-THC passes into the blood. This is different from smoking, of course, which doesn't trouble the liver with much metabolizing work. The THC simply passes from the lungs into the blood.

It's also important to note that using the liver to metabolize THC takes time. Consequently, the effects of intoxication only begin to be felt after about an hour or so. Full intoxication is experienced after about 90 minutes and lasts far longer than when the cannabis is smoked – up to eight hours. Hence, if too much is consumed and the experience is unpleasant, there isn't a lot one can do. Indeed, consuming high doses of THC is not unusual because, firstly, cannabis-infused foods, such as 'space cakes' – not to mention the growing variety of manufactured products, including chocolate, mints, gummies, dried fruit, and ice cream – are very enjoyable. Moreover, because one needs to wait around ninety minutes to gauge the level psychoactive impact, it's not unusual for users to assume that they have consumed too little and proceed, impatiently, to eat more. This has, understandably, led to some concern amongst health professionals about the growing popularity of edibles.[151]

As well as foods, in those parts of the world where cannabis is legal, adults can purchase a range of drinks infused with THC: coffee, soft drinks, energy drinks, and, of course, beers. While there are a number of hemp beers on the market, which are flavoured using cannabis products, such as seeds, there are a growing number of non-alcoholic beers that are infused with either THC or CBD.[152] For example, Coastal Haze by the San Diego-based High Style Brewing Company is a non-alcoholic beer infused with THC. Moreover, helpfully, the company developed the product so that the effects could be felt in under half an hour. As Lyden Henderson of High Style commented, 'it was very important for us to develop a "self-regulating" product, meaning that by the time a consumer is finished with their first High Style, they should know whether their individual tolerance will allow them to have another. This is ideal for social settings or an evening of relaxation, as once you start feeling the effects of the cannabis, you should stay at that level for about 4-5 hours.'[153]

While cannabis-infused beers are typically required to be non-alcoholic, there is a growing market for cannabis tinctures. Traditionally, tinctures, such as laudanum (ethanol and opium) – which was widely used during the Victorian period – are concentrates made by dissolving organic products in high-proof alcohol. There are two methods of doing this with cannabis: the 'hot method' (or 'green dragon' method) and the 'cold method'. The latter is the traditional method. Essentially, cannabis flowers are sealed in a jar filled with high-proof alcohol and shaken daily for a few weeks. This promotes the absorption of the cannabinoids by the alcohol. The contents are then filtered and bottled. The hot method, as the name implies, simply introduces heat in order to speed up the process to just over a couple of hours. However, while, for obvious reasons, the 'green dragon' method is popular, for equally obvious reasons it is also dangerous, in that the combination of inflammable liquid, heat, and stoners seeking a short cut to paradise is not a good one. Whatever method is used, once the liquid has been decanted into small bottles, it is typically administered sublingually with a pipette or added to food and drink.

Concluding comments

Many readers familiar with cannabis culture will be aware of much of what has been discussed in this chapter. Users tend to be well-informed about their drug of choice. Indeed, I have spoken to a number of smokers who clearly consider themselves to be cannabis connoisseurs. In my conversations, they have been keen to reveal their knowledge of different strains, provenance, paraphernalia, and so on, as well as, probably quite rightly, occasionally correcting my own apparently limited understanding of their changing culture. Being 'in the know' and set apart from the ignorant mainstream is important. We can think of this in terms of 'subcultural capital', an idea developed by Sarah Thornton with reference to Pierre Bourdieu's notion of 'cultural capital' – i.e. knowledge that has accumulated over time and that confers social status. For Bourdieu, this leads to a system of distinction in which cultural hierarchies are established that correspond to social hierarchies.[154] For example, one's knowledge about certain art forms, such as opera, one's accent, the educational institutions one attended, one's social connections ('name-dropping') are all indicators of cultural capital. *Subcultural* capital, on the other hand, while ostensibly distinct, actually functions in much the same way. Having observed the cultural knowledge, styles, and artifacts valued by those involved in the dance scene/club culture of the 1990s, Thornton came to 'conceive of "hipness" as a form of *subcultural capital*'. A person is 'hip' or 'cool' because of what they know, how they dress, their ability to dance in a particular way, their understanding of music, and so on: 'subcultural capital confers status on its owner in the eyes of the relevant beholder.'[155] Again, just as books or artworks in a family home display cultural capital to visitors, so subcultural capital is objectified in hairstyles and fashion, and articulated in the form musical taste, correct use of argot, and so on. The point is that this type of capital raises the status of individuals amongst their peers, differentiating them from members of other groups and creating a hierarchy within the subculture. Indeed, to be rejected by mainstream society as transgressive or profane in some sense, is also a valued marker of distinction.

It's also important to understand that, following Bourdieu's analysis, cultural capital can be transformed into economic capital. Indeed, the cannabis industry is a good example of the ways in which subcultural capital can be converted into cultural capital and, eventually, into economic capital. That is to say, the gradual acceptance and legalisation of cannabis (particularly CBD) has led to this transformation. In other words, cannabis culture has generated what Bourdieu referred to as 'advantageous attributions' that lubricate social and economic advantage.[156] Hence, on the one hand, subcultural capital attracts attributions of authenticity, coolness, and distinction. This, as we have seen, is evident in the hip hop scene, in that it is socially advantageous to know, for example, how to roll a blunt. Indeed, blunts emerged as a way of distinguishing the hip hop subculture from other subcultures that smoked cannabis, such as those of white rockers and hippies. As Thornton has commented, 'the social logic of subcultural capital reveals itself most clearly in what it dislikes and by what it emphatically is not.'[157] However, on the other hand, because subcultural users trust the judgement of those who have accrued subcultural capital, the latter are in a very good position to turn their knowledge to their economic advantage, as well as to influence the subculture and campaign on related issues. Good examples of this are Nikki Lastreto and Swami Chaitanya, who established Swami Select, a craft cannabis growing business in California. The following extract from their website clearly describes part of the journey from subcultural capital to economic capital.

> Called 'the Swami of Pot' by *Rolling Stone* ... Swami Chaitanya is a radical human being. Having started life as an East Coast academic and now an Emerald Triangle homesteader in his seventies, Swami has helped shape both cannabis culture and policy over the years, making the transition himself from a rebellious outlaw to a respected thought leader in a multibillion dollar industry. A self-described 'original

hippie,' Swami moved to San Francisco in 1967. From there, he travelled the world, living in South America, Europe, and India for many years before settling in Northern California's Mendocino County in the heart of the Emerald Triangle. Also a well-known figure in the music festival scene, Swami speaks and teaches publicly on meditation, spirituality, and more.[158]

It should be noted that, although they have been able to convert subcultural capital into economic capital, because they have not sought to build a large-scale commercial activity, but have rather remained 'craft producers' still closely connected to their subcultural roots, they are still 'cool' and 'authentic', rather than cannabis capitalists in an increasingly profitable, mainstream business. Nevertheless, the point is that, as a result of legalisation in California, they are a good example of how subcultural capital can be transformed into economic capital.

It's also worth briefly noting that there are a number of motivations for growing and selling cannabis, from those driven by ideology to those driven by purely commercial concerns.[159] Indeed, it is often those growers, such as Lastreto and Swami Chaitanya, who are motivated by politics, or spirituality, or environmental activism, or social/medical issues, or, a mixture of all of these, that accrue subcultural capital. Rather than motivated primarily by profit, they are committed firstly, to the cultivation of a quality product, secondly, to cannabis as a social good, and, thirdly, to defending the rights of those who want to use it.

> Swami Select mindfully cultivates craft cannabis in native Mendocino soil under the full sun, moon, and stars in the heart of Northern California's famed Emerald Triangle. Through our commitment to regenerative, responsible farming methods, we provide conscious connoisseurs with premium cannabis flowers for inspirational use.[160]

As Potter has commented, 'growers are often politically and ecologically minded (with a heavy link between the two, and with cannabis seen by many to be a political or ecological issue as much as simply a "drugs" issue).'[161] Again, for such users and producers, cannabis production is never merely about drugs and profit. It is linked to a number of 'sacred forms' (as discussed in the Introduction) relating, most notably, to health, wellbeing, and the environment.

Finally, we will see that, typically, those unfamiliar with the plant and its uses tend to base what knowledge they have on a range of popular discourses of profanation, including reports about its psychoactive effects and potential harms. While, of course, cannabis use isn't risk free and can lead to adverse effects on the mental health of some users,[162] including dependency, generally speaking the risk of addiction is lower than that of other drugs, including alcohol and nicotine.[163] As David Nutt has noted, 'there are a whole range of scare stories about cannabis that have been made up and/or exaggerated to justify political decisions and to try to put people off using it.'[164] (We will explore these discourses of profanation in the next chapter.) However, while there are risks with any drug use, both prescribed and recreational, overall users report experiences of geniality, a feeling of wellbeing, and a sense of euphoria. As Adolph

Steeze, the Court Apothecary at Bucharest, observed in 1846, the person under its influence feels with perfect consciousness in the best of humours; all impressions from without produce the most grateful sensations: pleasant illusions pass before his eyes, and he feels comfortably happy; he thinks himself the happiest man on earth, and the world appears to him paradise.' Furthermore, 'from this imaginative state he passes into the everyday state, with a perfect recollection of all sensations, and of everything he has done and of every word he has spoken.'[165] It's unusual for users to experience the Goyaesque 'bad trip' sometimes associated with psychedelics, such as LSD.

Having said that, just as most drinkers will be familiar with the sensation of 'the spins', nausea and vomiting, so most cannabis users will experience a 'whitey' (also known as a 'white-out', a 'green-out', and 'greening'). This is usually the result of strong cannabis or a large quantity being consumed over a short period of time. A whitey can also occur when the user mixes cannabis with alcohol or fails to consume enough fluids and/or food. Essentially, there is an increase in blood pressure and heart rate, the user's complexion becomes pallid and sweaty, and they feel faint and nauseous. However, this is typically temporary and, after an hour or so, users begin to feel better.[166] Unless the user is vulnerable to poor mental health (depression, anxiety, and psychosis),[167] generally speaking, this is as bad it gets for the casual cannabis consumer. However, as we will see in the following chapter, regardless of its long history, it's ubiquitous use, and recent research in a number of areas from sociology to neuropharmacology, for much of the twentieth century it has struggled with, to use Erving Goffman's phrase, a 'spoiled identity'.[168] In the following chapter, we explore the roots and consequences of this spoiled identity.

2

Profane Cannabis

Throughout much of the modern period, cannabis has been portrayed as the demonized Other. This was, in part, the result of popular constructions of African, Asian, and South American societies as uncivilized cultural and economic backwaters populated by the drug-addled, the immoral, the criminal, and the mad, all of which tended to be conflated in the Occidental imagination. Hence, as people were introduced to the word 'hashish' in the West, so they were being taught to associate it with mental illness, immorality, and criminality.[1] Drug users were portrayed as unwitting dupes consuming a substance that was as dangerous to themselves as it was to civilized, Christian societies. Hence, in discussing cultural constructions of cannabis use, we are examining both complex social attitudes to the Other and also the mechanisms of biopower.[2]

Notes on profanation

As discussed in the Introduction, the understanding of the sacred-profane binary discussed in this book is indebted to the work of Émile Durkheim and subsequent cultural sociology. We have seen that the sacred can be thought of in terms of what people perceive to be absolute and normative. It concerns those taken-for-granted norms that we value as 'good' in society. These normative realities can be understood in terms of 'sacred forms', which exert a profound moral claim over our lives. The profane, on the other hand, is that which poses a threat to those sacred forms. These understandings are not, we have seen, ontologically fixed. There is no sense that this or that object, space, idea or practice is always sacred or profane. Being the products of cultural contexts and social forces, notions of the sacred/profane are historically contingent structures of meaning that are constantly being negotiated. As such, what is sacred in one culture, may be profane or mundane in another culture, and what is sacred during one historical period, may be profane or mundane at another time.

This is important because it helps us to understand why attitudes to cannabis change from place to place and from time to time. Indeed, attitudes towards or away from profanation can often occur relatively rapidly. This typically happens when the discourse about cannabis is managed through the media, which is able to subjugate one sacred form for another. Take the recent change of approach to cannabis in the UK. On 1 November 2018, the Conservative Home Secretary, Sajid Javid, introduced legislation that made it possible for people to legally access cannabis for medical reasons. The following year, in their manifesto for the 2019 general election, the Liberal Democrats felt confident enough to propose a framework for a regulated cannabis market in the UK. Likewise, in 2019 even the Church of England relaxed its previously held policy of excluding investment in all ventures that profit from cannabis, arguing that it would now consider working with companies that carry out research into medicinal uses of the drug. In other words, there was a change in the cultural perception of cannabis, which enabled the Church to view it as an opportunity for investment. Not only was cannabis now no longer irredeemably profane, but it may even serve a sacred function. In the words of Edward Mason, Head of Responsible Investment at the Church Commissioners for England, 'we are content with it being used for proper medicinal purposes.'[3] Rather predictably this led to headlines such as 'Church of England Blesses Medicinal Use of Marijuana'[4] and 'Higher Power: Church of England Backs Medicinal Cannabis'.[5] The point is that, this revision of the Church of England's policy and the British government's position is indicative of a subjugation of sacred forms. That is to say, there are hierarchies of sacred forms that tend to be reordered according to social pressure and cultural change. The change in cannabis legislation followed a public outcry related to another, more compelling sacred form, namely the care and protection of children. The media had championed the case of two young epileptics, Alfie Dingley and Billy Caldwell. Their parents had effectively used the media to call the government to account for having denied their children access to cannabis oil. This was significant because the oil had a dramatic positive impact on their children's seizures. The sacrality of the care of children effectively trumped any concerns that society had about the availability of cannabis.[6] Consequently, the prohibition of cannabis became a subjugated sacred form. The government was forced to act because certain discourses about the threat posed by cannabis lost some of their power as people focused on the health and wellbeing of children.

Previously, cannabis was considered to be too profane for a government to have even considered legalization. Politicians, of course, tended to avoid such discussions in order to avoid the perception of being 'soft' on drugs. Hence, when statements were made, they were frequently peppered with terms such as 'menace', 'threat', and 'scourge'. To some extent, this is understandable, in that, as indicated above, identification with a perceived source of profanation is no small matter. Not only can it be socially disadvantageous to be the object of demonization, but it can be dangerous. Consequently, regardless of any scientific evidence supporting the legalization of cannabis, pollution by association is not something political parties are willing to risk. Cannabis is too culturally profane. Take, for example, the case of the neuropsychopharmacologist Professor David Nutt, Chair of the British government's Advisory Council on the Misuse of Drugs (ACMD).[7] He was fired by the British Home Secretary, Alan Johnson, for questioning the government's re-grading of cannabis from a 'Class C' drug to 'Class B'. In July 2009, in a lecture delivered at the Centre for Crime and Justice Studies at King's College London, Nutt had argued that, based on peer-reviewed scientific research, drugs should be classified according to the harm they cause. He was particularly concerned that the government, led by Prime Minister Gordon Brown, had bypassed the ACMD, ignored inconvenient scientific evidence, and promoted the profanation of cannabis by focusing on skunk and peddling the erroneous claim that it was 'lethal'. As Nutt has since commented, while the AMCD 'never knew for sure why Brown took this line',[8] they suspected that, facing a general election, the Labour Party sought the support of the British right-wing press, particularly *The Daily Mail* and the *Daily Telegraph*, both of which, informed by the conservative anti-drugs organization EURAD (Europe Against Drugs), demonized cannabis.[9] Nutt responded by pointing out that any change in the law required the government to provide 'more accurate and credible information':

> If you think that scaring kids will stop them using, you're probably wrong. They are often quite knowledgeable about drugs and the internet has made access to information extremely simple. We have to tell them the truth, so that they use us as their preferred source of information. A fully scientifically-based Misuse of Drugs Act where drug classification accurately reflects harms would be a powerful educational tool. Using the Act in a political way to give messages other than those relating to relative harms undermines the Act and does great damage to the educational message.[10]

Johnson was clearly panicked by the political implications of this statement. He could not risk the taint of being associated with anyone who did not demonize drugs. So, he asked for Nutt's resignation. As Nutt recalls, 'I replied that I wasn't going to resign because I had been telling the truth about comparative drug harms, a truth that needed to be openly discussed because it had implications for policing and punishments.'[11] Johnson responded by firing him on the grounds that he opposed government policy. In a public defence of this decision, he claimed that, not only had Nutt strayed away from science and into politics, but he and the other experts on the AMCD were wrong. However, perhaps unsurprisingly, many noted that, rather than the findings of the AMCD being wrong, it was actually Johnson who was sacrificing evidenced-based science on the altar of party politics. This was significantly problematic for a number of reasons. For example, as *Chemistry World* commented in 2009, 'the decision to ask Nutt to resign has ... caused the scientific community and a number of politicians to round on Johnson, saying his actions throw the role of scientific advisers into question and punish Nutt for voicing his scientific opinion.'[12] Again, as Nutt pointed out in his response, 'I gave a lecture on the assessment of drug harms and how these relate to the legislation controlling drugs. According to Alan Johnson, the Home Secretary, some contents of this lecture meant I had crossed the line from science to policy and so he sacked me. I do not know which comments were beyond the line or, indeed, where the line was.'[13] The government's rejection of the science and Nutt's dismissal led to the resignations of a number of members of the AMCD, including Les King, the senior chemist on the ACMD, and Marion Walker, the Clinical Director of Berkshire Healthcare NHS Foundation Trust's substance misuse service and the Royal Pharmaceutical Society's representative on the ACMD. As King later commented, Nutt's sacking 'was disgraceful'. He continued, 'I've provided chemical advice over many years, and the thing that has really irked me is the way that the government has come to the advisory council with a predetermined expectation of what the conclusion of various reviews would be ...'[14] That he in particular felt constrained to resign highlighted the fact that, according to *Chemistry World*, the ACMD was unable to function effectively.[15] Indeed, a week after Nutt's dismissal, the Liberal Democrat politician and science spokesperson, Evan Harris, attacked Johnson for misleading Parliament in his original statement. Moreover, John Beddington, the Chief Scientific Advisor to the government, stated that he agreed with Nutt's position on cannabis, it being an accurate reflection of the scientific evidence. Consequently, when Beddington was asked if he agreed with Nutt that cannabis was less harmful than cigarettes and alcohol, he was unequivocal: 'I think the scientific evidence is absolutely clear-cut. I would agree with it.'[16] Again, thinking from the perspective of cultural sociology, we can understand Johnson's knee-jerk response. Nutt's assessment of cannabis was too culturally toxic. As a report of the Home Affairs Committee candidly declared, 'it is seen as particularly controversial to suggest that drug laws should be amended.'[17] The situation had changed nine years later for Javid, not only because of the global cultural de-toxification of cannabis, but, more directly, because it had been sacralised by media reports of its ability to help sick children.

Again, increasingly robust research is challenging popular perceptions of the drug. Take, for example, the widespread perception that cannabis transforms active, intelligent people into lethargic, demotivated, anhedonic dullards. A good example of this is Mark Fisher's irritable anti-cannabis rant about the 'chronic demotivation' of stoners. 'What,' he writes, 'is supposed to be good about dope? The problem with it is not just the resultant psychosis, but the *actual state* it puts people into in the first place – chronically demotivated, lethargic, filled with the kind of idiot porcine self-satisfaction that is the dialectical obverse of feeling paranoid.' He continues, '"Better to be Socrates dissatisfied than a pig satisfied . . .": not for stoners, whose only commitment is to the pleasure principle, to the shortest route to total relaxation.' While there's nothing wrong with seeking a shortcut to relaxation, his overall point is that this particular shortcut transforms people into satisfied pigs. As a left-wing cultural theorist, his concern was that cannabis undermines creativity and disables critical thinking. 'Stoner stupefaction seeks only to remove tension, to become a zombified consumer . . .'[18] He continues, 'young people voluntarily subordinating themselves to this pacification program is not exactly politically positive.' Indeed, he even suggests the broadly conspiratorial notion that governments are only considering relaxing restrictions around cannabis use because it is politically expedient. With reference to Mark E. Smith's comment in the song 'Backdrop' (The Fall, *Backdrop*, 2001) regarding a young person's 'state-subsidized cannabis haze', he argues that users become politically disengaged. To some extent, of course, this is similar to Karl Marx's reference to opium and religion: 'Religion is the sigh of the oppressed creature, the heart of a heartless world, and the soul of soulless conditions. It is the *opium* of the people. The abolition of religion as the illusory happiness of the people is a demand for their true happiness.'[19] Cannabis is like opium, in that it is a drug that dulls the senses, anaesthetizes the user against the suffering of the present, distorts reality, inhibits critical thinking and undermines political activism.

In response to Fisher's stigmatization of cannabis users, three general points can be made. Firstly, few would deny that drug dependency is less than ideal for thoughtful analysis. Secondly, few people think a person is ideally placed to offer astute social commentary while intoxicated. Finally, Fisher's rather crude caricature flies in the face of the facts. For example, recent research published in the *International Journal of Neuropsychopharmacology* fundamentally challenges his claims. The project involved 274 adolescent and adult users who consume cannabis on average four days a week and a group of non-users (matched for age and gender). The results show that the former group is no more likely to lack motivation and critical thinking than the latter.

> Cannabis use has historically been linked with amotivation, which is reflected in prevalent, pejorative 'lazy stoner' stereotypes. In this study, we counter this cliché by showing that a relatively large group of adolescent and adult cannabis users and controls did not differ on several measures of reward and motivation. Specifically, people who used cannabis on average [four days a week] did not report greater apathy or anhedonia, reduced willingness to expend effort for reward, or reduced reward wanting or liking compared with people who did not use cannabis. Additionally, while adolescents had greater apathy and anhedonia than adults, cannabis use did not augment this difference; thus, adolescents were not more sensitive to the putatively damaging effect of cannabis.[20]

Hence, again, the frequently cited notion that cannabis use induces everyday lethargy – a notion which has been central to depictions of stoners in popular culture (e.g. the Dude in *The Big Lebowski*) and, indeed, to anti-drug campaigns, such as the ill-advised 'stoner sloth' campaign in Australia[21] – is now difficult to support. Of course, some users do report a hangover or 'brain fog' the morning after, but, as with all hangovers, this usually clears and they get on with their day like everyone else.

This brings us to discourses of demonization of cannabis in the West. In order to understand the cultural context within which cannabis was constructed as profane, we need to go back to what might, at first sight, appear to be a rather unusual time and location, namely, the mountains of Persia and Syria between 1090 CE and 1275 CE.

The *ḥashīshīyyīn*

In modern Western culture cannabis has always been something of an agathokakological drug, in that it has been perceived as both a technology of sublime pleasure, even a sacrament, and also a profane threat both to an individual's sanity and also to civilized society. While it was understood to have the ability to induce 'the freewheeling, rapturous daydream',[22] it also became linked in the Western imagination – despite its well-known soporific effects and its tendency to induce lethargy – to those who 'are thirsty for human blood, kill the innocent for a price, and care nothing either for life or salvation'.[23] While we will see that there are a number of reasons for the development of these twin perspectives, one of the key supporting narratives was rooted in popular Orientalist discourses surrounding an obscure late-eleventh-century Nezārī Ismaʿili sect known as 'the Assassins'. These discourses can be traced back to Muslim propaganda,[24] which was subsequently elaborated by Europeans to validate their own prejudices about the Orient. This is conspicuous in both Marco Polo's formative account and also the subsequent influential research and speculation of the nineteenth-century French scholar Antoine Isaac Sylvestre de Sacy.

Who were the Assassins? They were *fidaʾi*s (self-sacrificing devotees) who were loyal to the Iranian Ismaʿili convert and theologian Ḥasan-e Ṣabbāḥ. Ismaʿilism is a branch of Shia Islam that emerged in the eighth and ninth centuries, following a succession dispute in which their choice – Ismail – lost. Covertly organized, they established an extensive web of learned missionaries who sought to find and educate new students. In the second half of the eleventh century, the seventeen-year-old Ḥasan began training in the Persian city of Rayy to become an Ismaʿili missionary (*daʾi*). He was then sent to Cairo, where he remained for three years, after which he pursued missionary work in Persia. Over time he gathered Ismaʿili converts and began to organize them against the oppressive Turko-Persian Seljuq empire. His new faction, the Persian Nezāri Ismaʿilis, mounted a decentralized revolutionary effort against the Seljuqs. Greatly outnumbered, Ḥasan's principal tactics were guerrilla warfare, espionage and carefully orchestrated assassinations. Such covert tactics were designed to create a culture of fear.[25] Eventually, in 1090, as a result of a well-executed plan of infiltration, he secured for his headquarters the fortress of Alamut, located in the central Elburz mountains of the Rudbār region (northwest of modern Tehran). As Farhad Daftary, comments, 'this signaled the commencement of the Persian Ismaʿilis' open revolt against the Seljuqs and also effectively marked the foundation of what was to become the Nezāri Ismaʿili state of Persia.'[26] Ḥasan quickly set about making the fortress impregnable, as well as developing irrigation systems in the Alamut valley to create a society self-sufficient in food production. He also established an impressive library at Alamut, which amassed a large collection of manuscripts and scientific instruments. These significant achievements fuelled stories of well-educated, highly skilled, secretive, and ruthless Assassins living amongst majestic gardens modelled on Qur'anic descriptions of Paradise.

As stories of the Assassins spread and as something of a moral panic took hold, so they became what John Hutnyk has called 'pantomime demons': 'whatever the actuality of threat or ideological purchase, a repetition compulsion operates a monstrous theatre. Grotesque characters are created and maintained by political opportunity, convenient stereotype and ... an uncritical celebrity scholarship.'[27] This is a good description of the emergent Western discourses that demonized Ḥasan and the Assassins. They became ruthless pantomime characters embedded in Orientalist exaggeration and myth. As Bernard Lewis comments, the word 'assassin' first appeared in 'the chronicles of the Crusades, as the name of a strange group of Muslim sectaries in the Levant, led by a mysterious figure known as the Old Man of the Mountain, and abhorrent, by their beliefs and practices, to good Christians and Muslims alike.'[28]

It should be noted that there is often some confusion in popular stories about Ḥasan-e Sabbah. He actually died in 1124 and his sect continued under the leadership of Kiyā Buzurg-Ummid (who died in 1138). He, in turn, was followed by Muhammad Buzurg-Ummid and then by Ḥasan II – Ḥasan ʿAlā Zikrihi's Salām. The point is that, it was almost certainly Ḥasan II's period of rule that influenced the stories that were later collected by Marco Polo and other Europeans. Indeed, it was Ḥasan II's chief subordinate in Syria, Rashid ad-Din Sinān, who was known as the Old Man of the Mountain and accorded, by some, semi-divine status. That is to say, it was almost certainly Sinān who was the original 'Old Man of the Mountain' described by the Crusaders and it was he who would make the Nezāri Isma'ilis notorious in medieval Europe as the Assassins. Ruling from his fortress in Maṣyāf, he was feared for his practice of sending assassins to murder his enemies and, indeed, tried several times to kill the Ayyūbid leader Saladin, who opposed the Isma'ilis. Nevertheless, regardless of the historical details, a popular account designed to demonize Ḥasan and the Assassins emerged in the West.

One of the earliest descriptions of these Syrian Assassins can be found in the report of an envoy sent to Egypt and Syria in 1175 by Emperor Frederick Barbarossa, in which it was noted that 'on the confines of Damascus, Antioch, and Aleppo there is a certain race of Saracens in the mountains, who in their own vernacular are called *Heyssessini*, and in Roman *segnors de Montana*. This breed of men live without law; they eat swine's flesh against the law of the Saracens; and make use of all women without distinction, including their mothers and sisters.'[29] Again, even though some medieval poems use the loyalty of the Assassins to speak of courtly love,[30] generally they were constructed as devilish pantomime characters. Their very existence was a profane threat to all that the Christian West held sacred. 'They have among them a Master, who strikes the greatest fear into all Saracen princes both far and near, as well as the neighbouring Christian lords. For he has the habit of killing them in an astonishing way.'[31] According to some accounts, he selected some of the sons of his subjects, removed them from their families, and educated them to a high standard, including teaching them several languages, which enabled them to insinuate themselves into other societies undetected. Central to this training was an unquestioning commitment 'to obey the lord of their land in all his words and commands; and that if they do so, he, who has the power over all living gods, will give them the joys of paradise. They are also taught that they cannot be saved if they resist his will in anything.'[32] Hence, when summoned into their leader's presence, they prostrated themselves before him and fervently declared unconditional obedience. 'Thereupon the Prince gives each one of them a golden dagger and sends them out to kill whichever prince he has marked down.'[33]

While some stories about the Assassins had circulated amongst the Crusaders for a number of years, in 1192 attitudes hardened against the sect when two of their number assassinated Conrad of Montferrat, a north Italian nobleman who was preparing for his coronation as the King of Jerusalem. That said, because of the covert nature of the killings, there has been some debate about who actually ordered the killing of Conrad, some sources blaming Richard I, others claiming it was Saladin, while still others were convinced that it was the Old Man of the Mountain, Sinān.[34] Nevertheless, this first Crusader victim led to a proliferation of Orientalist propaganda. Most of the chroniclers of the Third Crusade made reference to the Assassins, to their strange beliefs, to their macabre methods, and to their redoubtable leader.[35]

It is within this Orientalist field of discourse that cannabis emerged as a profane agent for altering states of consciousness. It is here that we find the cultural origins of 'reefer madness'. Arnold of Lübeck (d. *c*.1212), a Benedictine Abbot and chronicler, is particularly significant in this respect. The author of the earliest Western source to refer to a mysterious psychoactive substance states that the Old Man of the Mountain, 'by his witchcraft, so bemused the men of his country that they neither worship nor believe in any God but himself. Likewise, he entices them in a strange manner with such hopes and with promises of such pleasures with eternal enjoyment, that they prefer rather to die than to live'. This was achieved by intoxicating them with 'such a potion that they are plunged into ecstasy and oblivion', during which they experience 'certain fantastic dreams, full of pleasures and delights'.[36] It was this potion, which was able to induce visions of Paradise, that became identified with cannabis in subsequent versions of the legend.

As indicated above, the Syrian Nezārī Ismaʿīlīs were at their strongest under the leadership of Rashid al-Dinan Sinān until his death in 1193. It was during this period that chroniclers of the Crusades, European travellers, and diplomatic emissaries began to write about them as 'the Assassins'. The term itself seems to have been based on variants of the Arabic word *hashish* (plural, *ḥashīshīyya*) that was applied by other Muslims to the Syrian Nezārī Ismaʿīlīs. From the outset it seems to have been a term of profanation, which identified them as 'irreligious social outcasts' – like those reprobates in society who use hashish. Although a smear, it was adopted by the Crusaders and their European observers in the Levant (who had very little understanding of Islam). Within this context, as Daftary says, 'the Frankish circles themselves began to fabricate and put into circulation both in the Latin Orient and in Europe a number of tales', none of which can be found in contemporary Muslim sources, 'including the most hostile ones written during the 12th-13th centuries'.[37] Consequently, unlike the indigenous pejorative use of the term *ḥashīshīyya*, which was not a description of actual practice, the Crusaders understood the slur literally. Indeed, as with some twentieth-century conservative reactions to youth culture, the assumed relationship explained the unusual behaviour of the Nezārī Ismaʿīlīs – they were under the influence of a demonic weed.

While interest in the legend of the Assassins continued in the West, stimulated by the work of writers such as Denis Labey de Batilly in 1603, Henricus Bangertus in 1659, and Étienne Maurice Falconet in 1751,[38] it was Napoleon Bonaparte's expedition to Egypt in 1798 that proved particularly significant for its reception history. Inspiring a groundswell of interest in the Orient, the expedition began a cultural process that finally fixed the occidental understanding of the Assassins' relationship with hashish and firmly established ideas about 'reefer madness'.[39] It also needs to be understood that the plant itself was believed to be a product of where and how it was grown. As David Guba Jr has noted in his discussion of attitudes to cannabis in nineteenth-century France, when cultivated cannabis (*Cannabis sativa*) was harvested from European soil it was understood to be 'good'. It was highly 'productive' hemp that, as rope and cloth, served the nation. Oriental cannabis (*Cannabis indica*), on the other hand, was understood in terms of a profane intoxicant that 'disturbs the brain'. That is to say, the difference between *Cannabis sativa* and *Cannabis indica* was not based on 'fixed biological distinctions' intrinsic to the plant, but rather it was 'the direct result of contrasting climates, soil, and processes of cultivation'.[40] This is why, as we will see, Orientalist travel writing from the sixteenth century to the eighteenth century associated cannabis grown outside Europe with the uncivilized beliefs and practices of non-European peoples. This served, as Guba puts it, to embed 'hashish and its psychoactive effects within a growing discourse about the non-Western world that highlighted barbarism, violence, and cultural otherness'.[41]

Of particular note in this respect was the work of Silvestre de Sacy – 'the first modern and institutional European Orientalist'[42] – who, on 19 May 1809, read a paper to the Institut de France on the Assassins.[43] In addition to a number of sources used by earlier scholars, he was 'able to draw on a rich collection of Arabic manuscripts in the Bibliothèque Nationale in Paris, including several of the major Arabic chronicles of the Crusades hitherto unknown to Western scholarship'. As such, notes Lewis, 'his analysis of the sources wholly superseded the efforts of earlier European writers'.[44] He is particularly significant in that it was he who argued that 'the word *assassin* is a corruption of the word *Hachishin*, and was given to the Ismaelians because they made use of an intoxicating liquor called hashish'.[45] The earliest recorded use of the designation *hashīshīyya* as a derogatory term appears in a reference to the Syrian Nezāri Isma'ilis in a polemical text produced around 1123.[46] It was such evidence that led de Sacy to his etymological link between the term *hashīshīyyīn* and the Western rendering of that term, '*assassin*'. His subsequent erroneous claim that the terminology was indicative of a particular practice was widely accepted. For example, the English Victorian Orientalist, Edward William Lane – who translated *One Thousand and One Nights*, lived in Cairo, wore Arabian dress, and spent time sequestered in hashish dens – concluded that 'De Sacy has ... rightly pronounced [assassin] to be a corruption of "Hhash'shásheém."'[47]

As to the etymology of the widely used term *hashīsh*, initially, in Arabic, it was simply used to refer to grass, dried herbs or cattle fodder. However, eventually, as Lewis has commented, 'it was specialized to denote Indian hemp, *Cannabis sativa*, the narcotic effects of which were already known to Muslims in the Middle Ages.'[48] Indeed, Franz Rosenthal makes the point that hashish became 'the most widely used of the hallucinatory drugs employed by medieval Muslims'.[49] That is to say, over time it acquired a more restricted meaning and was, particularly in the West, used to refer to cannabis resin.

Regardless of its popular currency, de Sacy's argument that the assassins weaponized hashish suffers from a paucity of evidence. Firstly, we have seen that *hashīshīyyīn* was a pejorative term originally used of the Nezāri Isma'ilis. Despite the fact that it was 'the most widely used of the hallucinatory drugs employed by medieval Muslims', as Rosenthal discusses, 'it is clear that Muslim authorities often considered it necessary to try to curb the use of drugs.'[50] Indeed, Daftary makes the point that, 'in the entire mediaeval discussion of hashish by Muslim writers ... users were plainly regarded as social outcasts and criminals, and the *hashīshīyya* were branded as dangerous to Islam and society, and condemned as such by majority opinion at least from the latter part of the eleventh century.'[51] Hence, again, it is now generally agreed that, 'it was in the abusive senses of "low-class rabble" and "irreligious social outcasts" that the term *hashīshīyya* seems to have been used' during the twelfth and thirteenth centuries, rather than because they 'secretly used hashish in a regular manner.'[52] That said, as Rosenthal comments, 'its use cut through all layers of the population' and was 'common to Zayd and 'Amr, meaning everybody'. Nevertheless, he continues, 'a certain class distinction was made between confirmed addicts and the rest of the people. This distinction was no doubt largely fictitious, yet, it enjoyed the reputation of being true and definite. Hashish eaters were believed to be low-class people either by nature or by being reduced to that state through their habit...'[53] This brings us to my second point. Because the use of cannabis as a psychoactive substance was well known at the time, it is unlikely to have been considered a mysterious 'potion'. Thirdly, unlike some hallucinogenic substances, hashish is a mild psychoactive, which is very unlikely to have induced stable visions of Paradise with the levels of clarity and cogency claimed in the early stories.[54] Finally, the quantities required for a powerful hallucinogenic experience would have been unhelpful to a militia that sought to execute people covertly and with great sophistication, agility, and precision.

Nevertheless, Orientalist stereotypes of exotic, cannabis-intoxicated Muslims continued to fascinate Westerners. Of particular note is the work of the Viennese Orientalist Joseph von Hammer-Purgstall. While his *Geschichte der Assassinen aus morgenländischen Quellen* (1818) – which was translated into French in 1833 and into English in 1835 – simply repeated Marco Polo's account of Islamic murderers inspired by hashish-induced visions of Paradise, it proved to be enormously popular and influential.[55] Regarding 'the origin of the name in question', he makes the point that, 'although I have not gleaned it from any of the Oriental historians that I have consulted, I have no doubt whatever that denomination was given to the Ismailites, on account of their using an intoxicating liquid, or preparation, still known in the east by the name *Hashish*.' He continues:

> the intoxication produced by the *hashish*, causes ecstasy similar to that which the Orientals produce by the use of opium; and from the testimony of a great number of travellers, we may affirm, that those who fell into this state of delirium, imagine they enjoy the ordinary objects of their desires, and taste felicity at a cheap rate; but the too frequent enjoyment changes the animal economy, and produces, first, marasmus, and then, death. Some, even in this state of temporary insanity, losing all knowledge of their debility, commit the most brutal actions, so as to disturb the public peace.[56]

Of course, Hammer-Purgstall was aware of the principal flaw evident in the original accounts. Why would an elite militia use cannabis?

> If the use of intoxicating substances . . . is able to disturb the reason . . . how could it be proper for people who had need of all their *sangfroid* and mental calmness, in order to execute the murders with which they were charged . . . and skillfully seize the instant which fortune offered for their purpose? This is certainly not the conduct of delirious beings, not of madmen, carried away by a fury which they are no longer able to control.[57]

His less than convincing response made full use of Marco Polo's account.

> The whole object of their education went to convince them, that, by blindly obeying the orders of their chief, they insured to themselves, after death, the

enjoyment of every pleasure that can flatter the senses. For this purpose, the prince had delightful gardens laid out near his palace; there, in pavilions, decorated with everything rich and brilliant that Asiatic luxury can devise, dwelt young beauties, dedicated solely to the pleasures of those for whom these enchanting regions were destined. Thither, from time to time, the princes of the Ismailites caused the young people, whom they wished to make the blind instruments of their will, to be transported. After administering to them a beverage which threw them into a deep sleep, and deprived them, for some time, of the use of their faculties, they were carried into those pavilions, which were fully worthy of the gardens of Armida; on their awaking, everything which met their eyes, or struck their ears, threw them into *a rapture which deprived reason of all control over their minds*; and uncertain whether they were still on earth, or whether they had already entered upon the enjoyment of that felicity, the picture of which had so often been presented to their imagination, they yielded in transport to all the kinds of seduction, by which they were surrounded. After they had passed some days in these gardens, the same means which had been adopted to introduce them, without their being conscious of it, were again made use of to remove them. Advantage was carefully taken of the first moments of an awakening, which had broken the charm of so much enjoyment, to make them relate to their young companions, the wonders of which they had been the witnesses; and *they remained themselves convinced, that the happiness which they had experienced in the few days which had so soon elapsed, was but the prelude, and, as it were a foretaste of that which they might secure the eternal possession, by submission to the orders of their prince.*[58]

It was these cannabis-induced periods of blissful transcendence and the hope that these inspired that led them to obey the Old Man of the Mountain with such devotion. That is to say, hashish was utilized as a technology of psychological manipulation during training, rather than as an intoxicant during their murderous missions. Nevertheless, the basic narrative was a powerful one, which excited the Orientalist imagination and, we will see, informed the reception of cannabis in the West.

Racism, violence, criminality, and insanity

During the nineteenth century, the idea of cannabis as an Oriental psychoactive with the power to disturb the mind and inspire malevolence became fixed in the Western imagination. As early as 1779, Henry Draper Steel's widely consulted *Portable Instructions for Purchasing the Drugs and Spices of Asia and the East Indies* describes 'bangue' (i.e. cannabis) intoxication in terms of insanity and uncontrolled violence. 'The effects of this drug are to confound the understanding, set the imagination loose and induce a kind of folly or forgetfulness.' He continues with a quotation from John Henry Grose, whose Orientalist observations were popular in Britain in the mid-eighteenth century and whose views about the relationship between cannabis, violence, and criminality had a lasting influence.

Bangue is an intoxicating herb, in the use of which it is hard to say what pleasure can be found, it being very disagreeable to the taste and violent in its operation which produces temporary madness, that, in some, when designedly taken for this purpose, ends in running, what they call a muck, furiously killing every one they meet without distinction till themselves are knocked on the head like mad dogs.⁵⁹

Although the drug isn't explicitly linked to the legend of the Assassins, it is difficult to avoid making the connection. Certainly, as the nineteenth century progressed and particularly following the publication of Hammer-Purgstall's *Geschichte der Assassinen aus morgenländischen Quellen* (1818), while this more general relationship between cannabis, insanity, and violence became fixed, increasingly references were made to the Assassins. For example, in Britain, in 1860, the English Botanist, Mordecai Cubitt Cooke published his famous survey of narcotic plants, *The Seven Sisters of Sleep*, in which he made explicit reference to the Assassins, 'a famous heretical sect among the Mahometans', which, 'while in a state of intoxication from the use of the drug', kill Christians 'without themselves having any fear of death'.⁶⁰ While 'a small dose seems only to influence the moral faculties giving to the intellectual powers greater vivacity and momentary vigour', a larger dose, he observed, 'seems to awaken a new sensibility and calls into action dormant capabilities of enjoyment. Not only is the imagination excited, but an intensity of energy pervades all the passions and affections of the mind.'⁶¹ Of course, he was also keen to warn his readers that 'the incautious use of hemp is also noticed as leading to, or ending in, insanity, especially among young persons who try it for the first time'. Indeed, 'this state may be recognized by the strange balancing gait of the victim, a constant rubbing of the hands, perpetual giggling, and a propensity to caress and chafe the feet of bystanders, of whatever rank.' Moreover, 'the eye wears an expression of cunning and merriment which can scarcely be mistaken. In a few cases, the patients are violent – in all, voraciously hungry.'⁶² While some of these characteristics will, no doubt, be recognizable to users (especially giggling and an increased appetite/'munchies'), viewed from a Victorian Orientalist and conspicuously racist perspective, they were matters of concern. Asian users, 'who are naturally and nationally superstitious and credulous',⁶³ exhibited 'strange freaks and antics'.⁶⁴

> The ready and active brain of the Oriental – always associating places and people, actions and accidents, men and manners, with the unseen agency of ghosts and genii – under the influence of haschisch, gave full scope to their imaginations, letting loose upon the traveller a torrent of romance, and peopling every corner of his route with legions of spirits, set him wondering to himself whether he had really escaped from the common-place world of his nativity into another sphere specially devoted to the occupation of ethereal beings.⁶⁵

Indeed, while he conceded that the hallucinations of Asian users 'may be only symptoms of a previously disordered intellect', he noted that cannabis use may also 'be the starting point from which insanity is developed'.⁶⁶ There are people whose minds are 'diseased through the use of haschisch'.⁶⁷

Hence, while we will see in the next chapter that cannabis medical preparations enjoyed some popularity during the nineteenth century, it was used with some apprehension because of a growing body of evidence linking it to insanity in Asia. For example, as James Mills discusses, 'British officers gathered evidence that convinced the Government of India that there was a direct link between cannabis use and mental illness.'[68] And, of course, the discursive formation of madness during this period tended to frame it as a profane mental state.[69] Indeed, the perceived relationship between insanity and cannabis was directly linked to the perceived relationship between madness and violence. More specifically, as discussed by Foucault, insanity was interpreted as a sort of regression to bestiality. 'Madness ... took its face from the mask of the beast. The men chained to the walls of the cells were not seen as people who had lost their reason, but as beasts filled with snarling, natural rage, as though madness at its furthest point was liberated from the moral unreason where its milder forms languished, and was revealed in all its immediate, animal violence.'[70] The cannabis of Orientalist discourse supported this construction of madness. That is to say, cannabis appeared to induce a temporary madness, which, in turn, led to extreme violence. This, in turn, paved the way for a link between cannabis and crime. Unsurprisingly, therefore, the British in India expressed grave reservations about cannabis use, with some even exploring ways to prohibit its use as a recreational drug.[71]

By the middle of the nineteenth century, even in popular scientific literature, discussions of cannabis often revealed explicit concerns about its threat to Western civilization. For example, in 1858, in an ostensibly objective article published in the *Scientific American*, cannabis was analysed with reference to the legend of the Assassins, which was, again, embedded in virulent racist discourse: 'The drowsy appearance and indolent character of Eastern nations is not only due to the climate of the countries,' but also to the widespread 'use of powerful narcotic drugs'. Whereas 'the Chinese have their opium which they chew and smoke to great excess ... the Ottomans ... prefer the intoxication produced by hasheesh ... the first smokers and eaters of [which] were called hasheeshins, from which our word "assassin" is derived.' Again, the article notes that their custom of hashish eating 'was first practised in the days of the Crusaders by a powerful enemy of theirs, "The Old Man of the Mountain," as he was called, and who obtained the most implicit obedience from many followers by supplying them with this drug.'[72] Unfortunately, to consume cannabis is also to enter into a Faustian pact. Magnificent visions and great moments of elation are exchanged for a person's sanity. Those 'who are in the habit of using this drug usually terminate their existence as lunatics'. As some evidence for this claim, the article notes that 'since the French have had Algeria their insane hospitals have been filled with the victims of hasheesh'.[73] We will see in the next chapter that this claim was based on the accounts of a number of French psychiatrists. Indeed, hashish and the legend of the Assassins became tropes for violence and insanity. For example, this is evident in Guba's discussion of the analysis of political violence in the conservative newspaper *Gazette de France*:

> The article in the *Gazette* connected the republican backlash against Napoleon III's usurpation of power to the Hungarian nationalist János Libényi's recent assassination attempt on Austria's emperor Franz Joseph that February, blaming

both attacks on 'universal republicanism, that hashish of modern regicides.' To drive the point home, the article gave a short history of the 'Muslim fanatics who assassinated kings in the 11th century,' describing them as 'regicides pushed to criminality by an intoxicating drink called hashish, whence came the name Hachichins, of which we made the word assassin.'[74]

This type of thinking continued into the twentieth century. In the United States, it was particularly stimulated by a wave of immigration following the 1910 Mexican Revolution. The decade-long armed struggle, which transformed Mexican culture and government, drove many poor people into the American southwest. Unhappily, but unsurprisingly, this led to an increase in tension, fear, and prejudice, which eventually led to a 'moral panic'. A few words from Stanley Cohen's seminal analysis of moral panics are worth quoting here:

> A crucial dimension for understanding the reaction to deviance both by the public as a whole and by agents of social control, is the nature of the information that is received about the behaviour in question. Each society possesses a set of ideas about what causes deviation – is it due, say, to sickness or willful perversity? – and a set of images of who constitutes the typical deviant – is he an innocent lad being led astray, or is he a psychopathic thug? – and these conceptions shape what is done about the behaviour.[75]

While the objections raised against the classic moral panic thesis are cogent and need to be acknowledged,[76] nevertheless, we should not throw the baby out with the bathwater. While Cohen's work may be flawed and not entirely applicable in all cases, it is clear that sensational newspaper articles were central to the identification of Mexican immigrants as deviant and to the construction of cannabis as a profane threat to societal values. These 'folk devils' were accused of numerous crimes and acts of indecency, which, over time, became linked to the 'killer weed'. On 2 January 1913, the *El Paso Times* reported that the region of El Paso–Juárez 'was thrown into a panic … when an unidentified Mexican ran amuck, killing one policeman, wounding another, and cutting two horses before he was knocked unconscious and arrested'.[77] While, in 1913, very few people had heard of cannabis, and, indeed, even the police typically dismissed it as 'not warranting major attempts at enforcement',[78] there were crusading 'moral entrepreneurs'[79] who argued that its use had a corrosive influence on American's Christian society. Such crusaders were spurred into action by events that appeared to establish a link between immigrants, extreme violence, and cannabis use. Like the Assassins, foreign killers were possessed by a dark, unpredictable energy. Hence, continues the above report, 'according to the police, the man was a victim of "marihuana," the "Mexican opium."' Because he 'had been smoking the drug all day',[80] certain dark, primal forces within the human nature had been unleashed. Two years later, on 14 June 1915, El Paso became the first city in the US to outlaw cannabis use. A report published in the *El Paso Times* proudly stated that 'El Paso is the first city in the country to take a stand against the traffic in marihuana, known to be the deadliest drug on the market'.[81] It then repeated the insanity-violence-criminality rationale for the decision: 'Marihuana is known to create a lust for human blood in the users and some of the most atrocious crimes committed in the city and elsewhere have been attributed to these fiends'.[82]

Informed by the Orientalist construction of the Assassins, the racist demonization of cannabis gained ground in the 1920s. Even the 1929 *Preliminary Report on Indian Hemp and Peyote* by US Surgeon General Hugh Cummings mixed basic pharmacology with Orientalist myths circulated by the media.

> Those who are habitually accustomed to use the drug are said to develop a delirious rage after its administration during which they are temporarily, at least, irresponsible and liable to commit violent crimes ... It is sometimes alleged that the murderous frenzy of the Malay, characterized as running 'amok,' is the result of the habitual use of hashish. It is also said that the Mohammadan leaders, opposing the Crusades, utilized the services of individuals addicted to the use of hashish for secret murders. The frenzy produced by the drug led to these persons being called 'haschischin,' 'hashshash,' or hashish from which the modern word 'assassin' is derived.[83]

Significantly, this deeply flawed report was the first official statement by the scientific establishment of the United States government on the effects of cannabis.

The relationship between 'blood lust', criminality, insanity, and race, which was, again, largely constructed and disseminated by the mass media, became an increasingly popular theme in anti-cannabis propaganda during the 1920s. For example, in Canada, the first female magistrate in the country, prominent women's rights activist Emily Murphy, published *The Black Candle*, which explicitly linked drug use to immigration, race, insanity, and violence. The first part of the book, which brought together a number of articles she had already published in *Maclean's*, a popular Canadian current affairs and news magazine, had been written as a direct result of her experiences of 'an illicit traffic in narcotic drugs', while serving as 'a Police Magistrate and Judge of the Juvenile Court at Edmonton'.[84] In her discussion of 'this weed of madness',[85] she makes a point of noting that 'it is ... a peculiarity of hasheesh that its fantasia almost invariably takes Oriental form'.[86] Moreover, noting the connection between the words 'hasheesh' and 'assassin', she comments that 'addicts to this drug, while under its influence, are immune to pain, and could be severely injured without having any realization of their condition. While in this condition they become raving maniacs and are liable to kill or indulge in any form of violence to other persons, using the most savage methods of cruelty without ... any sense of moral responsibility'.[87] She also noted that users experience 'hallucinations which are commonly sexual in character among Eastern races'.[88]

Similarly, in 1927, the *Chicago Daily Tribune*, which had begun to lobby heavily for anti-cannabis legislation, reported that hashish was a drug that led to 'expressions of wild extravagance' and claimed numerous young American 'victims'. We know this because it has 'been one of the curses of India and other Oriental countries for generations'.[89] Likewise, even *The New York Times* – known for its sober, careful, and conservative reportage – contributed to the growing moral panic. In a 1927 article entitled 'Mexican Family Go Insane', readers were informed that a widow and her four children had accidentally eaten some cannabis that was growing amongst vegetables in their garden. The result was immediate and irreversible. Neighbours, hearing 'outbursts of crazed laughter', rushed to the house and witnessed the disturbing effects of the demonic intoxicant. The report confirmed that 'there is no hope of saving the children's lives and ... the mother will be insane for the rest of her life'.[90] Again, in 1923 the *San Francisco Examiner* published an article under the title 'Marihuana Makes Fiends of Boys in 30 Days: Hashish Goads Users to Blood Lust'. The article claimed to present evidence that 'hasheesh makes a murderer who kills for the love of killing out of the mildest mannered man who ever laughed at the idea that any "habit" could ever get him.'[91] The violence, of course, was unnatural and irrational. Cannabis begins by attacking the mental health of users; this leads them to attack their families; eventually they become a threat to wider society. When a person smokes cannabis nobody is safe. In 1928, the popular campaigning journalist Winifred Black – who had been recruited by William Randolph Hearst to write for the *San Francisco Examiner* – published a book on 'the murder drug' entitled *Dope: The Story of the Living Dead*.[92] While she was, no doubt, genuinely worried about the effects of the drug on society, one doesn't have to read much of the book to realise that its aim was to generate a moral panic. Throughout, her argument is based on extravagant nonsense. Not only did she insist that enough cannabis can be grown 'in a window-box to drive the whole population of the United States stark, staring, raving mad', but also that, once consumed, the user has 'selected murder and torture and hideous cruelty ...'[93]

Regardless of the conspicuous lack of evidence marshalled by journalists such as Black, their work was of central strategic importance to the creation of a moral panic.[94] The media encouraged people to view cannabis simplistically as a 'deadly, dreadful poison that racks and tears not only the body, but the very heart and soul of every human being who once becomes a slave to it in any of its cruel and devastating forms'. The public increasingly came to believe that cannabis was 'a short cut to the insane asylum'. Many accepted newspaper reports which claimed that the mind of a person who smokes 'marihuana cigarettes for a month' is turned into 'a storehouse of horrid spectres'.[95]

The set of ideas that framed cannabis as a dangerous, foreign influence, reflected concerns, not only about cannabis being transported across the Mexican border, but also about the activities of sailors and West Indian migrants arriving at port cities along the Gulf of Mexico. That is to say, there was a concern that US borders were too porous to protect the population against alien pollution. The sacrality of the nation, understood as Christian and Caucasian, was being threatened. As early as 1912, Henry Finger, an American delegate to the First International Opium Conference, noted that the people of San Francisco were frightened by 'the "large influx of Hindoos ... demanding *Cannabis indica*," who were initiating "the whites into their habit"'.[96] Consequently, vulnerable young Americans were growing up without the protection they needed. This concern was made explicit in a number of short films and newspaper articles. For example, the 1924 film *Notch Number One* (also known as *High on the Range*) explicitly linked cannabis to Mexican immigration. Viewers were informed that it's 'a devilish narcotic' that leads smokers to 'go bughouse, loco, and want to raise hell ...'[97] Again, in

1926, the *New Orleans Tribune* published a series of articles on cannabis that highlighted both its corrosive effect on the health and the morality of young people:

> We saw children, some of them not more than twelve years old, under the influence of the drug; we overheard two marijuana-smokers planning crime; we saw large cars loaded with the sons and daughters of wealthy and prominent New Orleans families parked in dark streets in the Vieux Carre ... We saw these young men and women smoking marijuana and some of them were already stupefied by the drug ... Marijuana cigarettes can be bought in New Orleans with almost the same ease that one can buy a sandwich. The number of addicts is impossible to estimate.

By 1930, cannabis was becoming known, not only as a Mexican problem, but also as 'a dangerous Oriental drug' and understood to be 'very common in the negro settlements'. It was the profane drug of the racial Other. This racial perspective was also directly linked to the belief that it was 'smoked by the scarlet women downtown' and the 'men who live off fallen women'. Profane races were linked to profane spaces. From here it was being cynically distributed to 'children [who] can and do buy marijuana freely'.[98] (The corruption of children, as we have seen, constitutes a commonly perceived threat to the sacred.)

Interestingly, such was the nature of this campaigning reportage and the growing panic that the government became uneasy about the extravagant language used. Although we have seen that the 1929 *Preliminary Report on Indian Hemp and Peyote* by the US Surgeon General was hardly a model of restrained analysis, nevertheless, the Treasury Department, in its 1931 report, while not denying the profanity of cannabis, sought to provide a more sober assessment of the problem:

> A great deal of public interest has been aroused by newspaper articles appearing from time to time on the evils of the abuse of marihuana, or Indian hemp, and more attention has been focussed on specific cases reported of the abuse of the drug than would otherwise have been the case. This publicity tends to magnify the extent of the evil and lends color to an inference that there is an alarming spread of the improper use of the drug, whereas the actual increase in such use may not have been inordinately large.[99]

Nevertheless, the magnification continued.

The links between race, violence, crime, insanity, and cannabis, around which the nascent moral campaign of the 1920s had been organised, were further encouraged by the rise of anti-immigrant sentiment during the Great Depression (1929–1939). It was during this period that the effort to demonize the drug reached its peak. The 1930s witnessed a steep increase in the publication of articles, not only in newspapers, but also in reputable magazines, such as, again, *Scientific American*, claiming that 'marihuana produces a wide variety of symptoms in the user', including 'a desire to fight and kill'.[100] As indicted above, often such claims were supported by references to the legend of the assassins. For example, a physician, Albert Emile Fossier, published an influential article in 1931 in *New Orleans Medical and Surgical Journal* entitled 'The Marihuana Menace', which began with the following words:

> History tells us that about the year 1090 AD, the military and religious order or sect of the Assassins was founded in Persia by Hassan ben Sabbat. This diabolical, fanatical, cruel, and murderous tribe, although isolated in the mountains of Lebanon, and in the valleys and glens of Persia and Syria became remarkable for its secret murders committed in blind obedience to the will of their chief, and the heinousness of its crimes was bruited the world over. Their numerous acts of cruelty cast dire panic and consternation in the stoutest hearts not only in Asia, but in Europe as well. This branch of the Shi'ite sect, known as Ismalites, was called Hashishan, derived from hashish, a confection of hemp leaves, *Cannabis indica*. From the Arabic 'hashishan' we have the English word 'Assassin'.[101]

Fosser continues:

> under its addiction the most brutal and bestial crimes have been perpetrated, armies were transformed into fanatical hordes, dervishes have performed apparently impossible feats of human endurance, and intellectuals have soared to the heights of imagination; withal, nations and races in the grasp of its nefarious influence have degraded to the lowest planes of civilization.[102]

Of particular note during this period were a number of influential films, the most famous of which was *Reefer Madness* (1936). Originally entitled *Teach Your Children*, the film leaned heavily on earlier journalistic accounts and reports such as Fosser's. Posters for the film declared that it is 'the sweet pill that makes life bitter' and those who smoke it risk 'drug-crazed abandon' – 'women cry for it, men die for it'. Indeed, the film opened with a warning that set out the principal ideas disseminated in newspapers:

> The motion picture you are about to witness may startle you. It would not have been possible otherwise to sufficiently emphasize the frightful toll of the new drug menace which is destroying the youth of America in alarmingly-increasing numbers. *Marihuana* is that drug – a violent narcotic – and unspeakable scourge – *the Real Public Enemy Number One!* It's first effect is sudden, violent, uncontrollable laughter; then comes dangerous hallucinations – space expands – time slows down, almost stands still … fixed ideas come next, conjuring up monstrous extravagances – followed by emotional disturbances, the total inability to direct thoughts, the loss of all power to resist physical emotions … leading finally to acts of shocking violence … ending often in incurable insanity. In picturing its soul-destroying effects no attempt was made to equivocate. The scenes and incidents, while fictionalized for the purposes of this story, are based upon actual research into the results of Marihuana addiction.

Perhaps needless to say, the film was peppered with inaccuracies, such as the novel and rather odd claim that users smoke dried cannabis 'berries' that are even 'more vicious and more deadly' than 'opium, morphine, and heroin'. Nevertheless, nonsense though much of it was, it was an important contributor to anti-cannabis propaganda and, indeed, to the overall profanation of drugs during the mid-twentieth century.

Harry Anslinger and the moral crusade

Howard Becker almost certainly had Harry Anslinger in mind when he wrote the following words:

> The existing rules do not satisfy the [moral crusader] because there is some evil which profoundly disturbs him. He feels that nothing can be right in the world until rules are made to correct it. He operates with an absolute ethic; what he sees is truly and totally evil with no qualification. Any means is justified to do away with it. The crusader is fervent and righteous, often self-righteous.[103]

Anslinger was the most influential anti-cannabis propagandist in the United States.[104] For thirty-two years, from 1930, when the Federal Bureau of Narcotics (FBN) was founded, until his retirement in 1962, he had the last word in debates about the control of narcotics.

He was born on 20 May 1892 in Altoona, Pennsylvania. He attended Pennsylvania State College (1913–1915) and received his Bachelor of Laws from the American University in 1930. He served in the US Government (1918–1963) and held consular posts in the Netherlands, Germany, Venezuela, and the Bahamas (1918–1926). In the Treasury Department, he was Chief of Division of Foreign Control (1926–1929), Assistant Commissioner of Prohibition (1929–1930), and the first commissioner of the FBN (1930–1963). He was the US representative at League of Nations conferences on narcotics and served on the United Nations Narcotic Drugs Commission.

While there are a number of personal, social, and cultural reasons for his virulent opposition to drugs and drug users, it is difficult to avoid the impact of a particular childhood experience:

> As a youngster of twelve, visiting the house of the neighboring farmer, I heard the screaming of a woman on the second floor. I had never heard such cries of pain before. The woman, I learned later, was addicted ... to morphine ... All I remember was that I heard a woman in pain, whose cries seemed to fill my whole twelve-year-old being ... I never forgot those screams.[105]

That said, although this traumatic event was clearly a contributory factor, we will see that his particular opposition to cannabis has roots in other areas of his life and personality, not least his deeply held racism.

On 11 August 1930, Anslinger became the first commissioner of the FBN, which largely replaced the Bureau of Prohibition – formerly the Prohibition Unit, which had been established in 1920 to enforce the National Prohibition Act of 1919 (the Volstead Act). While the regulation of narcotics had occurred at state level, much of the control of drug trafficking happened at federal level and was largely cooperative, in that it relied on the Customs Service, Border Patrol, Coast Guard, the Justice Department, the Treasury, and a number of special agents. However, when the FBN was established, it was small, had little power, and bleak prospects. Indeed, there was only ever a relatively small number of federal agents involved in the control of narcotics – about 175 in 1920, rising to around 270 during the 1930s – and many of those who had worked for the Bureau of Prohibition were demoralized. Not only had their war on alcohol been unsuccessful, but they were also widely (and rightly) suspected of corruption. Anslinger wanted change. Determined to win the war on drugs, he sought to instil in FBN agents the steely conviction of moral crusaders.

Having said that, he was initially sceptical that a campaign against cannabis would be successful. Because it grew 'like dandelions',[106] there was too much of it to control. However, following the failure to prohibit alcohol consumption, there was a need for another moral focus. Hence, he was persuaded that opposition to cannabis could be useful in a wider campaign against narcotics. Like many prohibitionists, he was convinced that the moral and economic progress of the nation depended on controlling the deviant tendencies of the masses. This, of course, was not a novel idea in the US. As Mark Thornton discusses, 'there is little doubt about the importance of prohibition in American history and its role in social problems ... Temperance (along with slavery) was a primary reform movement in antebellum America, and prohibition was a determining political issue at the state and local level.' Moreover, he notes, 'the Progressive Era (1900–1920) marks the pinnacle of American prohibitionism. As America "progressed" to become an imperial power, it did so in part on the international prohibition of narcotics and the Harrison Narcotics Act.'[107] It's worth noting here that, following the 1906 Pure Food and Drug Act – which sought to control the traffic and labeling of food and medicine, which frequently contained opiates and cocaine[108] – the Harrison Narcotics Act of 1914 was the first federal regulation to restrict the sale of drugs. That said, while there was evidence of an increase in the numbers of addicts, because drug manufacturers used opium and cocaine in preparations that doctors then sold to the public, they sought to use their political and financial muscle to make sure that any legislation did not negatively affect their profit margins. Certainly, during the nineteenth century, manufacturers had been, as David Musto[109] has commented, 'remarkably effective ... in preventing any congressional action to require even the disclosure of dangerous drugs in commercial preparations.'[110] Moreover, those who had benefitted from the lack of legislation prior to the Harrison Act were in competition. For example, the American Medical Association lobbied for laws that did not impinge on the rights of doctors to sell drugs, while pharmacists wanted a monopoly on dispensing drugs. As such, the Harrison Act ended up being the result of a series of compromises between pharmaceutical companies, the medical profession, anti-drug campaigners, and bureaucrats. Moreover, as far as cannabis was concerned, while it was mentioned in early drafts of the legislation, it was edited out of the final draft. Essentially, this was because, having being entered into the *United States Pharmacopia* in 1850, it was still used in some medicines. Consequently, simply on business grounds, it was opposed by the American Pharmaceutical Association and the American Medical Association.

For Anslinger, however, it was an ideal vehicle to exploit the relationship, as he understood it, between politics, drugs, and deviance. We have seen that, by the late 1920s there was an increasing concern that it was a dangerous narcotic, fuelling violent crime among the Mexican community in the south-western states. While there was little evidence for this, nevertheless, by 1933, several of these states had legislated against cannabis and there was growing support for national prohibition. Hence, bearing in mind that Anslinger only had relatively few agents at that time, he reasoned that, if propaganda was carefully managed, cannabis could be an effective way of securing more support for his campaign against narcotics. Hence, a number of accounts, such as the following, were introduced into public discourse.

> From time to time, instances are brought to light of acts committed by persons under the influence of, or addicted to marihuana, which illustrate the viciousness of this drug. In Colorado, a man under the influence of marihuana attempted to shoot his wife, but killed his grandmother instead and then committed suicide. A Florida youth, while under the influence of the drug, murdered five members of his family with an ax. On November 23, 1935, in Baltimore, Maryland, a twenty-five-year-old Puerto Rican charged with criminally assaulting a ten-year-old girl entered a plea on the grounds of temporary insanity caused by smoking marihuana cigarettes...[111]

Anslinger acted swiftly and brutally. In an effort to cauterize the moral wound in American society, he quickly adopted a policy of high fines and severe mandatory prison sentences for initial convictions. However, policing forty-eight states on a slim budget during the Great Depression proved beyond even his abilities. His solution was to require each state to finance a local war on drugs. In order to enforce this, he campaigned for the passing of a Uniform Narcotic Drug Act. This had been proposed initially in 1924 by the National Conference of Commissioners on Uniform State Laws. The 1925 meeting of commissioners received the first draft, which included cannabis in its list of 'habit-forming drugs'. However, it was not discussed and a second tentative draft was presented in 1928. Again, this was not discussed. Indeed, this was indicative of the commissioners' lack of concern between 1924 and 1928. As the President of the National Conference of Commissioners commented, 'in some states we do not recognize the importance because it has not been called to our attention'.[112] Finally, a third draft, which was submitted in 1930, removed cannabis altogether from its list of habit-forming drugs, mentioning it only in a supplemental provision.

Needless to say, Anslinger was furious at the lack of progress and particularly frustrated with the general disinterest in cannabis prohibition. Following his appointment as commissioner of the FBN, he insisted on being centrally involved in the drafting process. As Richard Bonnie and Charles H. Whitebread II comment, 'the Bureau's involvement converted the cannabis provision from an appendage of little importance to a major bone of contention. Anslinger, having chosen the Uniform Act as the Bureau's first priority on the marihuana issue, seems to have decided soon after his ascendancy to seek the total prohibition of domestic marihuana cultivation, sale, possession, and even use for medical purposes.'[113] He was directly opposed by

Dr. William Woodward, the Head of the American Medical Association's Bureau of Legal Medicine and Legislation. The pharmaceutical industry were keen to retain the optional inclusion of cannabis in any legislation. Hence, again, the fourth draft presented to the conference of commissioners included the optional cannabis provision. Again, Anslinger insisted on total prohibition, but was rebuffed and the conference requested a final draft. Determined to influence it, Anslinger decided to involve the media who were happy to collude in his campaign of demonization. The general approach taken was to disseminate the tried and tested narratives linking cannabis to Mexicans, insanity, violence, and immorality. The aim was to generate a moral panic that would force the commissioners to include the total prohibition of cannabis in the Act. However, in the end, largely because of the pressure from the pharmaceutical industry, the Uniform State Narcotic Drug Act of 1934 did not require absolute prohibition.

Having said that, although the FBN was forced to concede defeat, the Act did include an important shift that would have significant consequences in the decades to come. Although the cannabis provision remained supplemental to the main body of the Act, any state wishing to regulate the sale and possession of cannabis was instructed simply to add it to the definition of 'narcotic drugs'. 'All the other provisions of the Act would then apply to marihuana as well as to opiates and cocaine.'[114] Moreover, because cannabis was mentioned in the Act, it effectively became defined as a 'narcotic' along with cocaine and opiates. This was an important step forward for Anslinger. Indeed, the very debate preceding the 1934 Uniform State Narcotic Drug Act moved cannabis into the American consciousness. At the beginning of the campaign many Americans were not even aware of it. By the time the Act was passed, things had changed. As Anslinger himself observed in 1937, 'ten years ago we had only heard about [cannabis] throughout the Southwest ... [It] has only become a national menace in the last three years.'[115]

Not only was there an increased awareness, but Anslinger and the FBN also attracted attention to their campaign. Indeed, they had begun to divide opinion in American society. Some viewed Anslinger as a force for good, while others questioned his draconian approach. As Wayne Morgan has noted, on the one hand, 'supporters saw him as a stalwart opponent of the insidious drug traffic that threatened the nation's vitality. His belief in strong law enforcement won their approval, as did his opposition to what they saw as soft-minded theorists and humanitarians.' On the other hand, his critics viewed him as 'a persecutor of hapless addicts, foe of enlightened medical and psychological reforms, and builder of a tyrannical bureaucratic empire'.[116] For the most part, however, as the 1930s wore on, legislators became increasingly convinced by his crusading rhetoric and the moral panic he began to generate. Cannabis was a social evil that threatened the very foundations of American society.

In particular, as noted above, Anslinger successfully related cannabis to other drugs already considered social evils, such as cocaine and opiates. Moreover, he also began to develop the notion of cannabis as a 'gateway drug'. Towards the end of his career, in 1955, he was invited before a special judiciary subcommittee headed by Senator Price Daniel, a conservative Democrat from Texas. 'Now,' asked Daniel, 'do I understand it from you that, while we are discussing marihuana, the real danger is that the use of marihuana leads many people eventually to the use of heroin, and the drugs that do cause them complete addiction? Is that true?' Anslinger agreed that 'if used over a long period, it does lead to heroin addiction'. Daniel then pushed him a little further: 'As I understand it from having read your book [*The Traffic in Narcotics*], an habitual user of marihuana or even a user to a small extent presents a problem to the community ... Marihuana can cause a person to commit crimes and do many heinous things. Is that correct?' Anslinger was unequivocal: 'That is correct. It is a dangerous drug, and is so regarded all over the world.'[117]

While Anslinger was hard-working and committed to his cause, much of his success in promoting opposition to cannabis can be attributed to the people he gathered around him. As well as politicians who supported him, such as Senator Daniel, there were a number of key people that he relied upon. For example, Malachi Harney, a technical assistant to the Secretary of the Treasury, became an important strategist whose ideas influenced the FBN's enforcement policies. Another influential supporter was Richmond Pearson Hobson, a Representative of Alabama who had been a rear admiral in the United States Navy and a veteran of the Spanish–American War. An eloquent and enthusiastic supporter of alcohol prohibition, he broadened the scope of his activities to include narcotics. He helped to found the International Narcotic Education Association in 1923, the World Conference on Narcotic Education in 1926, and the World Narcotic Defense Association in 1927. Like Anslinger, he promoted his views about the relationship between narcotics and crime in any way he could. In particular, he proposed changes in school textbooks to alert young people to the dangers of drugs.[118] That said, many considered Hobson's propaganda to be extreme and lacking any foundation in credible evidence. In 1932, a member of the American Medical Association even referred to the World Narcotic Defense Association as 'a rather pernicious group working under the direction of Mr. Hobson ...'[119] Anslinger disagreed. Hobson's networks, lobbying, and anti-drug rhetoric were just what the country needed in a time of moral crisis. Indeed, largely as a result of the earlier campaigns of Hobson and others, by the time the FBN was established in 1930, many of the core themes articulated by Anslinger were fairly standard.[120]

Nevertheless, Anslinger was key. According to Becker's 'Anslinger hypothesis', the FBN's demonization of cannabis played a key role in bringing it to the attention of the general public. Despite the work of Hobson, Black and others, prior to Anslinger there was still little interest in cannabis across much of North America. There were pockets of moral concern, but, overall, it was largely unknown and certainly not considered to be a social problem. It was the FBN's moral crusade that was primarily responsible for the widespread conceptualization of cannabis as 'the killer weed'. Indeed, during the 1930s, the FBN's publications became the principal resource for journalists writing sensational 'dope' stories. 'The articles designed to arouse the public to the dangers of marihuana identified use of the drug as a violation of the value of self-control and the prohibition on search for "illicit pleasure," thus legitimizing the drive against marihuana in the eyes of the public ...The Federal Bureau of Narcotics, then, provided most of the enterprise which produced public awareness of the problem ...'[121]

Anslinger's understanding of cannabis use as 'a violation of the value of self-control' was supported by another sacred form in 1930s America, namely, the disapproval of the pursuit of states of ecstasy that are not the by-product or reward of actions considered 'proper in their own right, such as hard work or religious fervor'. It is, continues Becker, 'only when people pursue ecstasy for its own sake that we condemn their action as a search for "illicit pleasure"'.[122] This was, in turn, linked to another sacred form rooted in the Protestant ethic: 'the individual should exercise complete responsibility for what he does and what happens to him; he should never do anything that might cause loss of self-control'.[123] Cannabis was profane, in part, because it was perceived to be a substance that threatens these core values or sacred forms by inducing altered states that lead to a loss of control.

Jazz, blues, race, and cannabis

The above sacred forms were, we have seen, woven into yet another, more pernicious discourse shared, not only by prohibitionist leaders, but also by many Americans during the 1930s, namely racism. Venomous racist attitudes were endemic within Western societies. In fact, such was its significance in America during the first half of the twentieth century that, not only was it condoned within churches, but it was often considered 'Christian'. As the prominent moral and political theologian Reinhold Niebuhr bemoaned in 1923, 'if there were a drunken orgy somewhere, I would bet ten to one a church member was not in it . . . But if there were a lynching, I would be ten to one a church member was in it.'[124] Indeed, as Jon Michael Spencer has shown, 'verse upon verse of the blues easily could be cited to illustrate the prevalent theme of ecclesial hypocrisy'.[125] For example, in his 1941 song 'The Good Lawd's Children,' the blues musician Peetie Wheatstraw reflected on the deeply unchristian attitudes and behaviour of churchgoers: 'why do they treat me like they do?' Although they 'kneel and pray', they 'serve the devil in the night', and 'serve the Lord in the day'.[126] It is unsurprising, therefore, that within Christian racist discourse, non-white cultures were linked to other sources of profanation in society, particularly intoxicants. Hobson, for example, even argued that, whereas 'alcohol will actually make a brute out of a negro, causing him to commit unnatural crimes', and while the overall effect 'on the white man' is similar, because the latter is 'further evolved, it takes longer time to reduce him to the same level'.[127]

In a 1970 article in the *Virginia Law Review*, Bonnie and Whitebread make an important point regarding the impact of racism on discussions about cannabis. 'Since marijuana was an intoxicant consumed only by immigrant Mexicans in the South and West and by ghetto Blacks in the East, the legislators might have accurately reflected a public hostility to the drug wholly without regard to its pharmacological effects.' They continue: 'to the extent that alcohol prohibition was motivated, or at least quickened, by ethnic prejudice against the Irish, marijuana prohibition, once proposed, was an inevitable by-product of anti-Mexican penalties'.[128] Put simply, racism drove the agenda. Indeed, in 1971, Musto drew on a broader range of evidence to show that 'the fear of marihuana was more intense' in areas of the United States 'with a concentration of Mexican immigrants who tended to use marihuana as a drug of entertainment or relaxation'.[129] This thesis was further developed in Musto's influential 1973 book, *The American Disease: Origins of Narcotic Control*, which cogently argued that, while the FBN was responsible for much of the anti-cannabis propaganda that led to the Marihuana

Tax Act of 1937,[130] there had also been significant political pressure from enforcement agencies and other groups who opposed Mexican immigration.[131] According to the propaganda, the combination of Mexicans and cannabis led to violence and criminality.

As we have seen, however, anti-drug propaganda didn't just focus on Mexicans. Anslinger systematically demonized African Americans and their cultures, particularly jazz and blues music, which appeared unrestrained, ecstatic and, therefore, profane. Again, the music, influenced by the effects of the drug, unleashed illegitimate ecstasy. Of course, this need not be viewed as profane. As we will see in the next chapter, the effects of cannabis on the composition, performance, and the reception of music might just as easily be sacralized as demonized. Certainly, musicians spoke about the creative influence of the drug.[132] As Paul Garon discusses in *Blues and the Poetic Spirit*, just as the Romantics 'utilized their drug experiences as points of departure for elaborate philosophical investigations',[133] several jazz and blues artists used drugs, not only to escape the experience of grinding poverty and oppression, but also as a technology of inspiration. When, in the song 'If You're a Viper', Rosetta Howard and Harlam Hamfats 'dreamed about a reefer five foot long ... but not too strong', they articulated not simply an experience of being lifted above their material conditions, but also a vision of a better life: 'I'm the queen of everything ... Light a tea and let it be ... When your throat gets dry, you know you're high, everything is dandy.' It is unsurprising, therefore, that musicians celebrated cannabis in their music.[134] For example, in 1928 Louis Armstrong recorded 'Muggles' (a popular slang term for cannabis), in 1932 Cab Calloway recorded J. Russel Robinson's composition 'The Reefer Man', and in 1937 Chick Webb and his Orchestra released the upbeat 'When I Get Low, I Get High' (sung by Ella Fitzgerald). While such songs often used whimsy and hyperbole to glamorize the inspirational effects of cannabis, the FBN seized upon them as objective accounts of its profane influence.[135]

In an interesting discussion of jazz and cannabis, Johann Hari explains how it transgressed everything Anslinger believed in:

> It is improvised, relaxed, free-form. It follows its own rhythm. Worst of all, it is a mongrel music made up of European, Caribbean, and African echoes, all mating on American shores. To Anslinger, this was musical anarchy and evidence of a recurrence of the primitive impulses that lurk in black people, waiting to emerge. 'It sounded,' his internal memos said, 'like the jungles in the dead of night.' Another memo warned that 'unbelievably ancient indecent rites of the East Indies are resurrected' in this black man's music. The lives of the jazzmen, he said, 'reek of filth.'[136]

Moreover, such music was only possible because those who created it did so under the influence of cannabis. Indeed, Anslinger suggested that 'musicians appear to be among the principal users of marijuana'.[137] 'Music hath charms, but not [jazz] music. It hails the drug,'[138] which, he claimed,

> makes a rubber band out of time, stretching it to unbelievable lengths. The musician who uses 'reefers' finds that the musical beat seemingly comes to him

quite slowly, thus allowing him to interpolate any number of improvised notes with comparative ease. Under the influence of marijuana, he does not realize that he is tapping the keys with a furious speed impossible for one in a normal state of mind; marijuana has stretched out the time of the music until a dozen notes may be crowded into the space normally occupied by one.[139]

Having made the link between race, music, and cannabis, the FBN sought to increase social concern about the drug by establishing continuities with other profane areas of social life. For example, aware that 'roughly 1 man in 10,000 selective service registrants examined for military duty was rejected primarily because of drug addiction',[140] Anslinger argued that, due to their cannabis use, jazz and blues musicians should be considered 'draft dodgers'. Indeed, he asked the Selective Service System to provide a list of musicians whose alleged cannabis use had led to their rejection for military service. The list contained the names of many prominent musicians. These were then identified as prime sources of immorality that threatened to pollute society. The idea of pollution is important here, in that anyone who came into contact with their music became suspect. The moral purity of society was at stake. Consequently, the FBN compiled another list that included members of the orchestras and bands with which they were associated. The likelihood was that they too had been infected by 'reefer madness'.

The FBN's wartime efforts to lay siege to the jazz world failed. Jazz musicians were careful not to inform on their fellow musicians and they immediately recognized those agents that sought to infiltrate their world. Hence, on the whole, the big names of jazz avoided prosecution.[141] That said, some were arrested. A famous early conviction was that of Louis Armstrong, who was arrested for smoking outside the Cotton Club in November 1930. He was imprisoned for ten days and received a six-month suspended sentence.

Despite the overall failure of the campaign against the jazz community, during the 1940s and 1950s, spurred on by the passing of the Marijuana Tax Act of 1937, Anslinger redoubled FBN's efforts. In particular, he was keen to exploit growing moral concern about popular music culture. There was evidence to suggest that young people were being influenced by their musical idols. In 1948, Anslinger sent a letter to Edward Foley, the Under Secretary of the Treasury, which he wanted him to forward to James Petrillo, the Head of the American Federation of Musicians of the United States and Canada (AFM). In it, he argued that 'there is a real juvenile delinquency threat in the marihuana antics of these persons'. He continued, 'I am bringing this situation to your attention because I feel that you might suggest ways in which your organization could assist in eliminating the anti-social activities of this segment of the musician profession.'[142] Foley dismissed the letter, believing, correctly, that the AFM would not respond positively. Nevertheless, he did propagate the idea that there was a fundamental connection between popular music, cannabis, and the corruption of the young. As such, the relationship was increasingly widely reported as fact. As the *Minneapolis Tribune* put it, 'the use of marihuana is on the increase. Not only is it being used by dance band musicians, but by boys and girls who listen and dance to these bands.'[143] This music–cannabis–youth connection would become central to discourses of demonization over the next couple of decades – and, we will see, also to the countercultural reception of cannabis, in that it became a subcultural mark of transgression in a way that alcohol never did.

Whereas cannabis would be embraced by much of the popular music industry in the 1960s and 1970s, initially – largely because of Anslinger's influential campaign – there was significant unease about the relationship between jazz, blues, and cannabis. After all, few profit-driven organizations want to be the focus of opprobrium and social censure. As Mike Levin, a reporter for the influential jazz magazine *Down Beat*, put it, 'the business neither deserves nor can stand a national campaign of this sort.'[144] Hence, in 1941, an editorial entitled 'Marijuana – A Scourge' in *The Keynote* (the publication of the Detroit Federation of Musicians) issued the following statement: 'the comparatively few musicians who are addicted to its use have gained for the entire music profession a reputation among law enforcement officers, and to some extent the general public, that is most unsavory, and every day bring disgrace and worse to the good reputation of the great majority who do not use it.' Much of the editorial articulated ideas that had been propagated by Anslinger and the FBN: 'Marijuana causes far more than mere moral degradation – it breaks down the mentality of its slaves' who become 'wrecked human beings ... jabbering idiots ... [who] can't think at all'. Consequently, 'any member found guilty of the use of marijuana ... shall be immediately expelled from membership.'[145] Likewise, in 1943, Levin went on the offensive against users in the music industry. 'This is one of the sorriest messes that we've seen ... "Musician" is going to be synonymous with "weed hound" ... The whole situation is an ugly one, but it must be faced now and wiped out now ... The Narcotic Bureau has the names and facts concerning many of the musicians ... We can only suggest to anyone who uses the stuff: STOP IT NOW, BEFORE YOU GET YOURSELF AND YOUR FRIENDS IN A POTFULL OF TROUBLE!'[146] Anslinger was delighted with this support from the jazz world and even included Levin's article in the US Treasury Department's report for 1941.

Pot pulp fiction, true crime, and moralizing tracts

Another contributing factor to the growing moral panic about cannabis was the link between race and sex, which was, of course, directly related to the growing concerns about popular music culture. Interracial socializing was already actively suppressed as a profane threat to American values, so the idea that young people, particularly women, might be disinhibited by the combined effects of cannabis and music concerned many at the time. There were numerous reports of African American men raping young white girls, which, during the 1930s, began to include cannabis use: 'Two negros took a girl of fourteen years old and kept her for two days in a hut under the influence of marihuana. Upon recovery she was found to be suffering from syphilis.'[147]

Unsurprisingly, much was made of this relationship between sex and drugs by popular pulp fiction writers such as Cornell Woolrich (under the pseudonym William Irish), Robert Campbell Bragg (under the pseudonym of N.R. de Mexico), and Jody Scott and George Thurston Leite (who together wrote under the pseudonym of

Thurston Scott). Like much pulp literature of the period, such as the magazine *Snappy Stories* and even the popular science fiction publication *Amazing Stories*, the cover illustrations of 'pot pulp' books were frequently salacious. For example, the cover of Mexico's *Marijuana Girl* promises its readers a story about a teenager who 'traded her body for drugs and kicks'.[148] Drawing on FBN's propaganda, the book is about a young girl, Joyce Taylor, attracted to the New York jazz clubs. Lured into smoking cannabis, she quickly becomes immersed in profane culture of sex, music, and drugs. These stories and the artwork used to market them increased both the circulation of pot pulp literature and the perception of profanity regarding the subject matter. Cannabis belonged in the shadowy corners of society.

As well as cannabis's alleged relationship to race, music, and sex, Anslinger, of course, made much of earlier reports linking it to extreme violence. In July 1937, he co-authored the most famous anti-cannabis article of the period with Courtney Ryley Cooper (a popular writer, anti-drug propagandist, and circus performer) for *The American Magazine*: 'Marijuana: Assassin of Youth'.[149] Their argument, which was central to the case for the Marijuana Tax Act, was that young people 'on the weed' were responsible for a number of serious crimes, including extreme violence and murder. In particular, much was made of the case of Victor Licata, a 21-year-old Mexican who slaughtered his family with an axe on 16 October 1933 in Ybor City, Tampa, Florida.[150] Because Licata was a cannabis user, the local newspaper reported the macabre killings as the work of an 'axe-murdering marijuana addict'. Indeed, according to the *Tampa Daily Times*, he 'had a dream, a horrible nightmare that snapped the last bit of sensibility out of his dope-tortured brain and made him a butcher'. It was 'the kind of nightmare that lifts its ugly head out of a deadly combination of raw moonshine and dope'.[151] This mention of 'dope' attracted Anslinger's attention and quickly became central to his campaign. Furthermore, popular publications, such as the 'true crime' magazine *Inside Detective*, supported Anslinger's crusade. In 1938, shortly after the publication of 'Marijuana: Assassin of Youth', *Inside Detective* reported the case in gory detail, linking Licata's savagery to his consumption of cannabis. Again, the principal argument is clear, namely, that cannabis and young people – who tend, by nature, to be 'thrill-seekers' – cannot be allowed to mix.

> In its issue of last November, *Inside Detective* revealed the degenerative effect of marihuana on the human mind, and began a campaign against this ever-spreading menace of thrill-seeking youth.
>
> Herewith is presented a true story of the appalling horror the sinister weed brought to a respected Florida family. Read it carefully – then consult your municipal government to find out what steps are being taken to smash the marihuana traffic in your community. Are your children safe from the 'reefer' evil?[152]

Of course, Licata's crime was not quite as straightforward as Anslinger had claimed. He was known to have had poor mental health and, indeed, eleven days after the murder, a psychiatric examination found him to be unfit to stand trial. He was subsequently committed to the Florida State Hospital for the Insane, where he remained until 1950, when he took his own life. While the link between cannabis and mental health is a complex one, and while, no doubt, Licata was unwise to smoke it at a time when he was experiencing hallucinations and homicidal impulses,[153] Anslinger simply used the case to support his 'reefer madness' rhetoric. He implied that Licata's mental health was a direct result of cannabis use. His argument was, quite simply, cannabis infects young minds, corrodes the conscience, undermines Christian morality, and, as such, threatens society.

As well as recounting Licata's murderous rampage and several other selected tales of the macabre, unsurprisingly – as indicated by the title of his article, 'Marijuana: Assassin of Youth' – Anslinger supported his case by appealing to the legend of the Assassins. On 27 April 1937, in his testimony to Congress in support of the 'Marijuana Act', he made the relationship explicit.

> This drug is as old as civilization itself. Homer wrote about, as a drug that made men forget their homes, and that turned them into swine.[154] In Persia, a thousand years before Christ, there was a religious and military order founded which was called the Assassins, and they derived their name from the drug called hashish, which is now known in this country as marihuana. They were noted for their acts of cruelty, and the word 'assassin' very aptly describes the drug.[155]

While much of this is nonsense, nevertheless, his argument had a formative impact on anti-cannabis discourses within American society. Indeed, as some indication of his influence, his article was republished in February 1938 in *Reader's Digest*, a widely read general interest family magazine. Despite the fact that there was actually no credible evidence to support his interpretation of the Assassins, widespread public ignorance, the American culture of deference, an appetite for conspiracies, and a penchant for the scandalous ensured an easy passage into public discourse for stories about unchristian, un-American substances corrupting the minds of young people and threatening society. As the sociologist Jerry Mandel commented in 1966, since Anslinger's testimony, 'no US case seemed so convincing as the story of the Assassins'.[156] Indeed, in the same year, another propaganda film was released, not only with the same title as Anslinger's article, but which also repeated some of his extravagant claims: *Assassin of Youth* (1937). Again, also in 1937, an article in *Hygeia Magazine* published by the American Medical Association declared that 'Oriental thugs long ago learned that hashish produced the proper mental stated to prepare one for a heinous crime. In fact, the English word "assassin" is derived from the Arabic "hashishin," or "hemp-eaters"'.[157]

Hence, on the one hand, not only could money be made from publishing salacious stories about 'reefer madness' and sex-obsessed young 'thrill-seekers', but, on the other hand, moral crusaders were quick to board Anslinger's cannabis-Assassin bandwagon. For example, Rev. Robert James Devine republished his booklet, *The Moloch of Marihuana* (c. 1934), under the title *Assassin of Youth: Marihuana*. Published by Fundamental Truth Publishers, an evangelical publishing house, the aim of the booklet was to demonize the drug by linking it to Moloch, an Ancient Near Eastern deity associated in Leviticus with child sacrifice.[158] Many of Devine's churchgoing readers would have understood the link he was making between cannabis, profane religion and the death of children. A new Moloch was threatening America's young people and subverting Christian values. He makes this case by marshalling a range of dubious evidence, including selections from newspaper reports about cannabis-related crime. 'If it has the power to drive cattle "loco" or crazy' – which it doesn't – 'or to make an elephant "run amok"' – which, again, it doesn't – what, he asks, 'will it not do to adolescent youths?'[159] The arresting cover for both booklets, drawn by J.N. Curry, depicts drug 'peddlers' sacrificing America's youth to 'the Moloch of marihuana' and, thereby, effectively throwing them into the flames of hell, while complacent clergy, policemen, and other officials fail to grasp the awful significance of the threat to American society.

As indicated above, the line between moralizing and salaciousness was frequently blurred and often transgressed. This is particularly evident in the comic books of the period. By the 1940s cannabis had become a useful plot device. In the struggle between good and evil – between a carefully regulated Christian society, on the one hand, and a chaotic 'dope' industry, on the other – young people were being corrupted and drawn into lives and sex, violence, and insanity. Stories often included a young person making a naïve claim such as 'one puff never hurt anybody', only to discover the opposite. From the moment a hapless young person breathes in the demon smoke, she is effectively, if not actually, possessed. Cannabis is, as the comic hero Kerry Drake (created by Alfred Andriola) described it, 'a poison that causes *insanity, crime, and wrecked lives!* An innocent looking weed that can turn a nice kid ... into a *homicidal maniac!*'[160]

'Exactly one year after Superman debuted in *Action Comics* #1 (June 1938),' notes Craig Yoe, 'the Man of Steel's creators, Jerry Siegel and Joe Shuster, had their crime fighters ... battling marijuana pushers in *Adventure Comics* #39 (June 1939).'[161] The title of the story, 'Reefer Madness', was lifted from the film and supported its central theme. Indeed, over the next couple of decades, several comic book genres, from crime to romance, explored the profane effects of cannabis in ways that betrayed the influence of FBN propaganda – all of which, of course, supports Becker's 'Anslinger hypothesis'. Cannabis was often explicitly linked to other narcotics, sometimes as a gateway drug to cocaine and opiates, and sometimes as simply one of a number of drugs covered by the umbrella term 'dope'. For example, '"International Public Enemy #1," a crime story found in *Wanted Comics* #13 (May 1948), reads: "Statistics show that the use of dope (such as heroin, opium, marijuana, etc.) is, and always has been, the cruellest and most ruthless murderer of mankind in the history of the world."' The story, which includes images of 'Satan, drug addicts strangling women in their negligees, prostitutes by the waterfront, and machine gun murders between mobsters', was explicitly aimed at young people.[162] While this type of content would normally have been considered too corrupting for general consumption, such were the dangers of cannabis that it was judged acceptable. Again, we can think of this in terms of a subjugation of sacred forms. The protection of society, and particularly adolescents, from stories of 'weird orgies, wild parties', and 'unleashed passions'[163] had been trumped by the threat posed to society by cannabis.

Perhaps needless to say, cultural globalization meant that these ideas were not confined to the United States. They quickly crossed the Atlantic. For example, in the

UK, on 25 July 1939, *The Daily Mirror*, a popular tabloid newspaper, published an article that, while claiming to be objective reportage of events in Soho, was actually a repetition of Anslinger's rhetoric. It was entitled 'Terror! Just a Cigarette, You'd Think, but it was Made from a Sinister Weed and an Innocent Girl Falls Victim to This'. Accompanied by a posed photograph of a young woman smoking, it focused on the corruption of innocent young females, because 'for women the menace of the [marihuana] cigarette is greater than for men'.

> One girl, just over twenty, known among her friends for her quietness and modesty, suddenly threw all caution to the winds. She began staying out late at nights. Her parents became anxious when she began to walk about the house without clothes. They stopped her when she attempted to go into the street like that. At times she became violent and showed abnormal strength. Then she would flop down in a corner weeping and crouching like an animal. Soon she left home.[164]

Again,

> A young and lovely woman, her clothes in shreds, stood perilously perched on a window ledge. Behind her was a man. He, too, was wild-looking and dishevelled ... They were both marihuana addicts. As she disappeared, she could be heard screaming: 'I can fly. Well, I don't care if I die.'[165]

This is less reportage and more a case of the repetition of reefer madness rhetoric, including references to sex, violence, 'reefer clubs', 'coloured' men, 'addicts', 'criminals', drug lunatics, and dope peddlers'. It even repeated the claim that 'marihuana drives its victims into society, forcing them to violence, often murder'. Indeed, this is supported by a report, conspicuously based on the Licata story, that a young man 'killed his mother, father, brother, and two sisters with an axe'.[166]

Psychiatry, racism, and cannabis psychosis

During the 1980s and 1990s, particularly in the UK, concerns were expressed about diagnoses of 'cannabis psychosis'. Part of the problem was that the disorder was ill-defined. While it was clear that cannabis induced psychosis in some users, there was disagreement regarding its distinctive features. Consequently, room was left for interpretation.[167] More worryingly, there was evidence to suggest that interpretations were racially biased. In particular, evidence emerged during the 1980s of disproportionate diagnoses of cannabis psychosis amongst young Black men. For example, in 1987, Dermot McGovern and Rosemarie Cope published research that demonstrated that Black patients in Birmingham and the neighbouring borough of Sandwell were ninety-five times more likely to receive a diagnosis of cannabis psychosis than white patients.[168] While McGovern and Cope were careful to reject the idea that psychiatry was deliberately being used as an agent of social control, or indeed that the profession was institutionally racist, they did conclude that 'racial ... and cultural differences between psychiatrists and patients leads to a less competent diagnosis'. Consequently, they insisted, there was 'an urgent need for research on the accuracy of diagnoses in Afro Caribbeans'.[169]

While the study of McGovern and Cope was worrying enough, others have been more strident in their critique of psychiatric interpretations of cannabis induced psychosis. Indeed, some have gone so far as to trace the roots of racism back to imperial psychiatry. Certainly, there is little doubt that, as Andrew Scull has commented, 'Western physicians looked with condescension on indigenous beliefs and practices.'[170] Again, Jamie Banks has made the point that psychiatry, as 'a medical discipline born from the mores of European colonialism', is guilty of 'encouraging practitioners to think of their patients and their maladies in particular ways. This includes an implicit emphasis on the *differences* between practitioner and patient, be they in terms of gender, class, race, or state of mind.'[171] This context is significant when considering psychoactive substances such as cannabis, which is, as we have seen, heavily freighted with negative cultural baggage linked to Orientalism, race, and deviance. This point is brought into focus if we employ social constructionism to understand psychiatry's relationship to race. That is to say, the problem becomes clear if we view medical knowledge as *a product of*, rather than existing independently of social forces. In 1989, for example, Chris Ranger argued, that his reading of the emerging literature on cannabis psychosis, along with interviews with psychiatrists and mental health support workers, convinced him that 'the development of "cannabis psychosis" as a disease category has been strongly influenced by factors of race and culture.'[172] For example, one of his interviewees commented that it frequently appeared to be the case that 'psychiatrists see "locks," think "Rasta," and conclude "abusing ganja."'[173] In other words, 'the main factor ... to influence psychiatrists in making their diagnosis of "cannabis psychosis" was the appearance of the patient. If a young, Black (i.e. Afro-Caribbean) man presented with "locks" (the plaited hair associated with Rastafarianism) it was considered probable that any disturbed behaviour would be attributed to this psychosis.'[174] Essentially, there seems to be evidence of a lazy, cultural segue from race to drug abuse. This was exacerbated if patients presented with cultural cues that indicated deviance, such as long hair or the use of particular argot. Cannabis, it was assumed, is not only part of a deviant lifestyle, which could be assumed if one had a particular hairstyle, such as dreadlocks, but it is particularly prevalent within some communities, such as the Afro-Caribbean community in the UK during the 1980s and the Mexican community in the US during the 1920s. This racial stereotyping in psychiatry was confirmed a year later, in 1990, when another study found that 'cannabis psychosis and acute reactive psychosis tended to be diagnosed more often...'[175]

Similarly, in the United States, although studies, including the 'National Survey on Drug Use and Health', have found that white people have higher prevalence rates of substance abuse disorders than do other racial and ethnic groups, nevertheless, 'Blacks are overrepresented in the health and criminal justice systems.'[176] Again, there seems to be an easy segue from a Black person presenting with poor mental health to the assumption that the condition is induced by cannabis.

Conservative Christian responses to legal cannabis consumption

As cannabis gradually becomes normalized and legal, and as the evidence supporting its medicinal use becomes increasingly difficult to ignore, so the arguments in support of profanation look less convincing.[177] Consequently, conservative religious leaders and theologians whose thinking has been shaped by the twentieth century's discourses of profanation struggle to provide cogent arguments against its use. While in the past, theologians, priests, and pastors could simply cite its illegality and repeat versions of refer madness rhetoric, such responses are no longer tenable. This is now widely recognised. As the website Catholic Answers points out, 'American Christians in general, and American Catholics in particular, have based their moral condemnation of marijuana largely on the legal prohibition against it. But those prohibitions are going up in smoke, and the change in legislation might not seem to leave our moral intuitions against pot smoking or marijuana brownies much rational basis.'[178]

Moreover, although there are a spectrum of approaches to cannabis consumption, even attitudes within conservative religious communities are beginning to shift. A good example of this type of thinking is the well-known Evangelical teacher and pastor John Piper, who makes it clear that he would 'not oppose a kind of medical use of marijuana that is controlled by appropriate physician oversight and prescriptions.' He continues:

> We have lots of drugs that are sold by prescription that, if they were abused, would be as destructive or even more destructive than marijuana. I had a friend who shared with me, very soberly one time, that he had a son who had a long-standing old ankle injury. He said, 'I know from his experience that the only relief he can get is with a slight use of marijuana.' So, if there were a way to use marijuana the way we use aspirin or the way we use an antibiotic – with careful oversight – in principle, I wouldn't oppose that.[179]

Having said that, he still counsels against recreational cannabis use because 'it leads away from the kind of sober, self-controlled use of the mind for the glory of God.'[180] This is a common concern within conservative religious cultures for which it is still a profane signifier.

So, in the face of the scientific evidence and its gradual legalization across the Western world,[181] how do conservative cultures maintain their opposition to it as a profane psychoactive? Essentially, as Piper indicates, the argument is now carefully framed in a way that focuses on intoxication and the religious life. The plant itself may have some therapeutic benefits, but the experience of intoxication is *distinctively* profane. That is to say, it is profane in a way that other socially acceptable intoxicants and medicines are not. It is important to defend this distinction, of course, because many Christians drink or take medicines which have a mild psychoactive effect. Again, as the Catholic Answers website comments: 'we don't as a rule ban moderate consumption of alcohol, even though it's a psychoactive substance. And we all likely know someone on an antidepressant or antianxiety medication – we may even be taking one ourselves. So, if we're okay with synthetic psychopharmaceuticals, why would we draw the line at ingesting something plant-based to alter our mood?'[182] Moreover, this problem is exacerbated by evidence demonstrating that, overall, cannabis is less harmful than alcohol.[183] All drugs are risky and can have a detrimental impact on the mental and physical health of some people who are vulnerable to them (addiction, psychosis, etc.). However, as Leslie Iverson, Professor of Pharmacology at Oxford University, comments, to a large extent their effects on the brain 'are quite similar. A number of studies performed under laboratory conditions have reported that users actually find it difficult to distinguish between the immediate subjective effects of acute intoxication with the two drugs.' There are some differences, of course, in that 'whereas marijuana tends to make users relaxed and tranquil, alcohol may release aggressive and violent behaviour. In terms of the long-term effects of chronic use', he continues, 'alcohol has none of the subtlety of marijuana. Heavy long-term use can lead to organic brain damage and psychosis or dementia (a condition known as Korsakoff syndrome), while even moderately heavy use can lead to quite severe persistent intellectual impairment.'[184]

With these points in mind, why is it claimed by conservative religious commentators that cannabis is distinctively profane? Of course, they may not be aware of the scientific evidence or, because of the fear of pollution and the cultural power of taboo,[185] choose to ignore it. Ostensibly, however, their principal argument is based on the Bible's prohibition of drunkenness. All intoxication is profane. Todd Miles, for example, has argued that, although 'the marijuana high is different from alcohol drunkenness, the effects of drunkenness – namely, impairment of physical ability, cognitive ability, and judgment – also occur with the marijuana high, so the biblical prohibition on drunkenness applies to marijuana intoxication'.[186] Hence, cannabis is no different to wine in being, as Kevin Vanhoozer insists, inconsistent with 'gospel citizenship'.[187] Again, arguments based on 1 Corinthians 6.19 regarding the body as a 'temple of the Holy Spirit', also apply to all intoxicants. However, we need not discuss the basic argument in favour of abstinence, in that a number of religions place restrictions on intoxicating substances. Whether we agree with total abstinence or not, there is a basic internal logic to the position. However, as far as this discussion is concerned, problems emerge for religious communities when one intoxicant is accepted and another is not.

How does one distinguish between an intoxicant that many Christians feel comfortable with and another that they are suspicious of? Take, for example, the claim of John Paul II that 'there exists, certainly, a definite difference between the use of drugs [including cannabis] and the use of alcohol: while the moderate use of the latter as a drink does not violate moral norms, and hence only its abuse is to be condemned, the use of drugs, on the contrary, is always illicit'.[188] Indeed, the Catholic Answers website claims that alcohol is 'a digestible substance and is still believed to have health benefits. That's why the *Catechism* classifies alcohol as food and not as a drug.'[189] This, of course, is just as true, if not more true of cannabis – particularly CBD. However, again, the point of this discussion is not to challenge theological responses to cannabis consumption. Those decisions are for religious institutions and their members. The aim here is simply to show how conservative communities with particular constructions of the sacred manage changing attitudes to a once profane substance that is currently going through a process of normalization. Put bluntly, how does one demonize a mild psychoactive substance, while protecting the right of Christians to use another? The easiest response is to reference earlier tropes and prejudices. For example, Vanhoozer poses the following question: 'What has Christ to do with stoner culture – the practices and products that result from being laid back, in mind and body?'[190] This sentence links cannabis with a particular culture that Christians immediately identify as a profane threat to core sacred forms. Cannabis users are 'stoners'. They are lazy dropouts who are disengaged from society. Cannabis is central to, if not the principal cause of a morally and spiritually bankrupt culture antithetical to the Christian life. 'Can disciples be simultaneously saints and slackers? Could recreational marijuana be the latest opportunity of sloth: not mere laziness, but the deadlier sin of not caring enough to stay awake?'[191] Hence, Christians who choose to relax with cannabis are on a slippery slope to acedia.

Wine, on the other hand, does not do this. Indeed, it has a long history within Christianity. In her book *The Spirituality of Wine*, Gisela Kreglinger discusses its theological significance: 'From Genesis to the book of Revelation, the theme of wine features rather prominently in Scripture ... Wine has an important role in the life of the church.' Indeed, she argues that the history of wine in Christianity 'is a history that is often forgotten and needs to be rediscovered, remembered, and celebrated. From the early church in the Ancient Near East to its growth in medieval western Europe and its expansion in Central and North America, the history of wine in the church is long and rich.'[192] It is also, of course, one of the eucharistic elements. In other words, unlike cannabis, it is couched in sacred discourse. More broadly, in Western culture it has a role as a repository and marker of social, cultural, and symbolic capital. Sophisticated wine drinkers are certainly not laid-back stoners. 'Note the difference,' Vanhoozer says, 'between drinking alcohol and smoking pot: a glass of wine complements food, but doesn't result in intoxication, whereas the whole point of consuming cannabis for recreational purposes is to get "high."'[193] Again, Miles is clear that 'while both intoxicate, alcohol impacts the brain in a different manner to marijuana. A little wine does not intoxicate; it is not clear that marijuana can be smoked in moderation without effects.'[194] The point is, of course, naïve, if not disingenuous. Yes, cannabis users like to get intoxicated, as do wine drinkers. This is unsurprising, since intoxication is pleasurable. As Kreglinger notes in her discussion of the spirituality of wine, 'intoxication can have very positive effects, and critics often overlook these benefits'. She continues, 'in places where wine-drinking is part of the culture, distinctions between mild intoxication and drunkenness are more naturally in place.'[195] Indeed, she argues that 'gentle intoxication can enhance our festive play before God, and wine can play an important role in that ... The psalmist reminds us that wine's primary purpose is to bring joy to our lives here on earth (Ps 104: 15).'[196] The point here is that all this is true of cannabis. Indeed, a number of older users I have spoken to simply use it to 'take the edge off' at the end of a long day. Sometimes they have a glass of wine and sometimes they have a weak brownie. But they are clear that they don't want to get stoned. They are not 'stoners'; they just want to wind down. As Kreglinger discusses, even in small quantities wine does have a psychoactive effect and most occasional drinkers appreciate this. Yes, they enjoy it with a meal, but, honestly, they also use it to feel mildly intoxicated and relax.

Having enjoyed wine most of their adult lives, they are aware that small doses are very unlikely to lead to a loss of inhibitions and drunkenness. Again, the same is true of cannabis. Not every user is a stoner, just as not every drinker is a drunkard.

If Vanhoozer and Miles are claiming that even the mildest psychoactive effect is sinful, then total abstinence would be the wisest course of action. Otherwise, to engage in consumption without intoxication, there would be a need to attend to the Christian's blood alcohol concentration (the per cent of alcohol in a person's blood stream). The higher the percentage, the more likely one is to experience profane levels of intoxication. Theoretically, I suppose, one could use a breathalyser or blood test kit to measure levels of transgression by intoxication, but this would, of course, be ridiculous. However, the point here is simply that, as the scientific evidence confirms, both substances are intoxicating, but neither need lead to high levels of inebriation. It is quite possible for a person to have a glass of wine, a weak brownie, or a small joint without becoming incoherent. The sensible advice should simply be: don't drink too much wine and don't consume too much cannabis. To claim that one substance is profane because it produces a particular level and type of intoxication makes little sense.

Why do Christians feel constrained to produce these rather arcane arguments? While, in the case of cannabis, they are largely the result of the profane discourses discussed above, more generally, the nervousness around intoxication is rooted in Jesus's command to keep watch and stay alert (Mark 13.32–37). Intoxication is a threat to this state of mind. Cannabis, Vanhoozer insists, 'clouds our ability to perceive the world clearly and dulls our sense of urgency about what disciples should be doing.'[197] Leaving on one side the fact that alcohol does this more effectively, such arguments ignore the fact that, for occasional or mild users, the effect is only ever temporary. While a lot depends on a number of variables – e.g. the dosage, the presence of food in the body, age, sex, and weight – both alcohol and cannabis leave the body. Indeed, a key factor would be the drug's 'half-life' – how long it takes for the concentration in the body to drop by 50 per cent. For most people, the effects of cannabis or alcohol intoxication diminish overnight, leaving them able to carry on with their lives as normal the next day. So, again, the argument seems to be determined by a certain cultural bias against cannabis.

In summary, the process of normalization presents significant problems for some conservative religious communities, particularly those that accept the use of other intoxicants such as alcohol. On the one hand, there is an effort, pastorally, to provide guidance regarding a mild intoxicant that increasing numbers of people use therapeutically, if not recreationally. On the other hand, conservative social thinking has been informed by a history of profanation. This thinking has been bolstered in Christianity by, for example, conversion narratives that include testimonies about deliverance from intoxicants and the profane cultures in which they are used. For example, such concerns are evident in bestselling Christian books, such as David Wilkerson's *The Cross and the Switchblade*[198] and Nicky Cruz's *Run Baby Run* in which cannabis draws young people into lives of crime and addiction: '"Johnny always seemed to have a supply of reefers and I thought it was a lot of fun." Maria paused as if remembering those first days as she began her descent into hell . . .'[199] Again, informed by early twentieth-century anti-cannabis rhetoric, these texts, perhaps unwittingly, repeat the links between cannabis and violence. So, for example, Cruz tells us that 'Jesus ... gave me new purpose in life. No longer am I smoking pot and fighting and killing.'[200] This link between cannabis and profane culture has meant that, as Miles admits, until very recently, churches ignored the issue of whether Christians should use cannabis or not: 'it was just self-evident that marijuana use was sinful, and the question was not even worth considering.' Indeed, as some indication of how polluting the whole subject was, he notes that, 'if people did have questions, they were too ashamed or embarrassed to ask.'[201] Normalization and increased education about cannabis are gradually enabling such conversations to take place. Indeed, as we will see in Chapter 4, there are now growing numbers of progressive Christians who are beginning to use cannabis as part of their spiritual practice.

Concluding comments

It has *not* been the aim of this chapter to provide a comprehensive overview of the history of cannabis legislation or, indeed, anti-cannabis propaganda. That would be a little too ambitious for a single chapter. Rather it has examined how a relatively unknown plant became known and, in the process, became constructed as a profane threat to certain sacred forms. The discussion has, in other words, interrogated the cultural politics of cannabis. It is concerned with what Foucault has discussed in terms of 'biopower' and 'biopolitics', those forms of power directed towards us as human beings that seek to manage our lives according to certain conceptions of what is normal and acceptable.[202] A dominant culture, for example, say, white, Western Christian culture, 'holds power and is entitled to define the norm, and against those who deviate from that norm, against those who pose a threat to the biological heritage.'[203] Cannabis, the cultures, and the communities in which it is used are perceived as presenting just such a threat.

Of course, while much of the discussion has focused on the significance of race, the history of the profanation of cannabis is a bit more complex than that. Indeed, the chapter has touched upon a number of important questions linked to biopower and biopolitics. Which voices are heard and which are silenced? Why is wine panegyrized and cannabis demonized? Which images of social life have been projected as normal and which have been marginalized? We have seen that the published information about cannabis was not the result of careful analysis, but rather the product of underlying prejudices and moral emotion rooted in attitudes to race, sex, violence, young people, and religion.

Often, these discourses were shaped by the media and popular culture. In other words, we have seen that the demonization of cannabis and the marginalization of its users were rooted, less in science and empirical evidence, and more in myth and prejudice.[204] For example, at the time of the Marihuana Tax Act of 1937, very few people knew much about cannabis. As Thornton discusses, 'marijuana prohibition is ... a curiosity because it was enacted before the use of marijuana as a recreational drug became widespread.'[205] Moreover, even the scientific community had limited knowledge of the plant's effects.[206] As Herbert Wollner, the consulting chemist at the Treasury

Department admitted in a 1938 memorandum to Anslinger, 'virtually nothing is known concerning the nature of the narcotic principle, its physiological behavior, and the ultimate effect upon the social group.'[207] Nevertheless, although Anslinger was eventually persuaded to hold a conference to discuss the science on 5 December 1938, it is clear that actual evidence was of little interest to him. Rather, his concern was to manage the population, to demonize particular cultures, and to control what people were putting into their bodies.

We have also seen that, central to the shaping of these discourses of profanation has been the power of media and popular culture. Aware of this power, Anslinger and the FBN made full use of them in order to deliberately create a moral panic. As Cohen has noted, moral panics about drug use have 'been remarkably consistent for something like a hundred years: the evil pusher and the vulnerable user; the slippery slope from "soft" to "hard" drugs; the transition from safe to dangerous; the logic of prohibition.'[208] Central to this process has been 'labelling'. (This, we have seen, is evident within conservative religious discourse against cannabis.) As Becker argued, profane culture 'is created by society', in that *social groups create deviance by making the rules whose infraction constitutes deviance,* and by applying those rules to particular people and labelling them as outsiders. From this point of view, deviance is *not* a quality of the act the person commits, but rather a consequence of the application by others of rules and sanctions to an "offender." The deviant is the one to whom that label has successfully been applied; deviant behavior is behavior that people so label.'[209] Again, access to the media is key to the labelling process.

It's worth noting here a model of the process through which social problems rise and fall provided by Stephen Hilgartner and Charles Bosk: a 'social problem exists primarily in terms of how it is defined and conceived in society.'[210] If moral entrepreneurs, such as Anslinger, are able to gain access to public arenas, including popular culture, the media, the judicial system, and political institutions, they are able to shape public discourse. They are able to secure ideologically charged labels in social discourse. However, because public arenas have limited capacity to carry issues, in that they are constantly competing for attention, there is an ongoing need to increase salience. The central activity of moral campaigners (such as particularly those within conservative religious cultures), therefore, is rhetorical. They have to persuade people to adhere to a particular symbolic-moral universe and to use particular labels.[211] As Joel Best has argued, 'rhetoric plays a central role in claims-making about social problems.'[212] This rhetoric, moreover, draws much of its power from examples of atrocities with which the public can empathise. 'Claims-makers routinely use examples or case histories to typify social problems.' Indeed, although Best's book focuses on child abuse, he makes the point that a good example of this is how 'the Federal Bureau of Narcotics ... personified marijuana smokers as homicidal drug fiends. . .'[213] He is right. Anslinger was able to persuade people, not only that there was a problem, but that it was a problem of a particularly deviant sort – as is evident from the profane acts committed by medieval Muslims, corrupt Mexicans, depraved African Americans, and sleazy jazz musicians.

Graphic accounts of the peculiarly acute dangers cannabis presented both to young people and, more broadly, to Western civilization ensured that Anslinger's accounts of cannabis and its users went viral. As we have seen, central to this process was the use of memorable labels and images that drew heavily on Christian culture and established cannabis as a threat to society. This innocent looking plant was actually 'the assassin of youth'. It was 'a weed with roots in hell' and joints were 'Satan's cigarettes', which, if smoked, would lead quickly to mental illness, degradation, unbridled lust, prostitution, crime, and even murder. Again, the dramatic and deeply profane nature of the stories influenced by Anslinger's rhetoric ensured that they migrated from one public arena to another, accumulating support from the media, the political establishment, the judiciary, and the Church. The anti-cannabis rhetoric of the FBN became hegemonic in American society. It wasn't wholly uncontested, but it was increasingly accepted as common sense. The FBN created a language to talk about cannabis.

Part of the reason that Anslinger needed to expend enormous energy on his campaign to shape the discourse about cannabis was, again, because his cause was not supported by evidence from either pharmacology or the social sciences. This left some key agents of change of unconvinced. As Best comments, 'those with the power to act may choose to do so once they adopt the claimants' interpretation, or in more sensitive cases, policy-makers may delay action until there is evidence that the claims-makers have successfully shifted public opinion on the issue, making it safe to change policy.'[214] This, of course, is what the British Home Secretary, Sajid Javid, was able to do in 2018 when he made it possible for people to legally access cannabis for medical reasons. Again, we have seen that this was not the case in 2009. Because the claims-makers had not successfully shifted public opinion about cannabis, Johnson panicked and fired Nutt. However, because campaigners, such as Anslinger, are not patient and sometimes work with ideas that lack scientific credibility, they need to find other methods of influencing policy. As such, they 'learn ways to mobilize and maintain public support; they learn how to get press coverage by constructing claims that are newsworthy; and they learn to identify key policymakers and recognise the levers that can move policy'. While, as Best continues, 'these lessons may come through personal experience, or through watching the successes and failures of other claims-makers promoting other issues', typically, the result is 'increasingly polished claims'.[215] Anslinger learned his trade during Prohibition (1920–1933). He became a moral entrepreneur who promoted his cause by projecting his own prejudices and exploiting cultural biases. He was generally aware of what would and what would not work; he knew who he needed on his side; he was acutely aware of the importance of the media; and he was aware that he could exploit American cultural politics, whether it was rooted in fears about Mexican immigration, concerns about African American popular culture (particularly jazz and blues), moral anxiety about illicit sex, religious worries about demonic influence, or general nervousness about the perils of a 'thrill-seeking' youths. Within a couple of decades, cannabis became the drug of the outsider, the marginalized, and the profane. This wasn't wholly Anslinger's work, of course. As we have seen, there were a number of key figures, factors, and forces responsible for the demonization of cannabis. Of particular significance were the popular comics and pulp fiction that discussed the corrupting effects of cannabis and the newspapers that carried articles about its alleged relationship to violence, mental illness, and immigration.[216] Anslinger was, however, the driving force.

Once the FBN had begun its rhetorical work, which led to something approaching a 'reefer madness' industry, it was difficult for those interested in communicating the science of cannabis to be heard. Indeed, individuals who sought a sober assessment of its effects risked the danger of pollution by association. Their unwillingness to support sensational stories and their careful reliance on empirical evidence opened them up to the suspicion of complacency about a major social problem. As far as the anti-cannabis campaigners were concerned, they were part of the problem. For Christian campaigners, they were on the side of the Devil, unwitting servants of Satan. In short, anti-cannabis propaganda demonized any assessment of the drug that did not fully support its rhetoric of profanation.

By the 1960s, cannabis culture emerged as an explicitly deviant culture. That it did so, of course, eventually led to its sacralization. That is to say, because cannabis was associated with the marginalized, with jazz and blues, and with discourses of transgression, it was identified as special in a way that alcohol was not. It was invested with significant subcultural capital. As such, it became the intoxicant of choice within beat culture and, subsequently, within the counterculture of the 1960s.[217] This, in turn, increased its perception as a profane threat within conservative cultures.

3

Medicinal Cannabis

Advocates of medicinal cannabis frequently point out that, 'for thousands of years, societies around the world' have used the plant for health and healing.[1] Epilepsy, arthritis, Alzheimer's disease, Parkinson's disease, multiple sclerosis, depression, nausea, poor appetite, strokes, inflammation, cancer-related symptoms, and a range of other maladies are all believed to respond positively to cannabis.[2] Indeed, many users would agree with Dee Dussault that the plant should not 'be seen as a form of "complementary" or "alternative" medicine'. Rather, it is, she claims, 'a nutritional supplement that millions of people all over the world already use to cope with the stresses of modern living. More and more sensible people are turning to it for this reason, as well as for its anticarcinogenic, antioxidant, anti-inflammatory, anti-anxiety and antidepressive, neuroprotectant, and pain-killing properties.'[3] The increasingly popular argument is that, within this complex plant, there are hundreds of different cannabinoids, terpenoids, and flavonoids that work together to ease the troubled mind and heal the ailing body. Hence, insists Christian Rätsch, 'if hemp preparations were freed from the morass of illegality, then they could make an enormous contribution to health around the globe.'[4] While there is no shortage of popular assessments of the medicinal value of cannabis, it is true that recent research into two cannabinoids in particular, cannabidiol (CBD) and tetrahydrocannabinol (THC), has led to a conspicuous and growing optimism about the medicinal potential of the plant.[5] Moreover, CBD in particular has become a trendy wellness ingredient. Lacking the psychoactive effects of THC, it can now be found in juice, moisturizer, ice cream, bath salts, dog treats, textiles, sports bras, and even stress medication for elephants.[6] There are few things, it would seem, that cannot be improved by the addition of CBD. It is the new alchemical elixir for the twenty-first century. It transforms base products into health and wellbeing gold.

While the CBD craze has contributed significantly to the rebranding of cannabis as an *elixir vitae*, of particular importance has been the socio-cultural impact of the growing body of medical and pharmacological research. Medical science, which is now beginning to demonstrate the health benefits of cannabis for the care of the most vulnerable members of society, is rapidly changing the discourse. For example, a recent study of epilepsy in children concluded that 'CBD-enriched cannabis extract is shaping up to be a very promising anti-seizure option.'[7] Hence, as with many other such studies into a range of conditions, the authors of the report concluded that 'we strongly support the need for controlled studies of cannabis products using consistent formulations and strict methodology to assess the effectiveness of various compounds in the plant, to analyze pharmacodynamics as well as pharmacokinetic aspects, and to test the long-term efficacy of cannabis...'[8] Again, not only does this type of rigorous scientific work serve to promote pharmacological interest in the plant, including the funding of research, but it also has an enormous impact on the popular perception of cannabis. Positive reportage about the results of cannabis research, which typically includes sympathetic interviews with patients whose suffering has been alleviated, is rapidly transforming its profane image as a drug that ensnares unwitting users into a life of addiction and violence.

Having said that, as discussed below, there are still some concerns within the medical community about risks associated with THC. Much of this concern relates to evidence that regular cannabis use increases the risk of developing psychotic illnesses such as schizophrenia.[9] This concern, moreover, tends to support previous popular discourses of demonization that link cannabis consumption to madness and violence.

These competing discourses of profanation and sacralization are evident throughout the history of medical cannabis in the modern West. The aim of this chapter is to provide an analytical introduction to some of the salient moments in this complicated history.

Romantic radicalism, the turn to the self, and medicinal cannabis

'For thousands of years,' Dussault tells her readers, 'yogis, mystics, and shamans have been using cannabis and other plant medicines to leave behind ordinary states of consciousness and explore portals to other dimensions of experience like relaxation, embodiment, pleasure, and creativity.'[10] Similarly, Jack Herer, in his bestselling overview of cannabis culture, argues that the world is 'facing many problems these days, and we feel that the key to these problems is locked away in the traditions of the past, not in the gilded cage of man's greed'. Rather, 'we must embrace the ways of our ancestors', including the use of cannabis. This will enable us to 'achieve a balance that has been lost in our world'.[11]

Romantic constructions of history and indigenous cultures are frequently referenced as part of a popular apologia for medicinal cannabis. Indeed, this is interesting in itself, in that it is an example of the growing romanticization of cannabis. We need to learn from our ancestors that 'the entire plant is a treasure trove of life-giving richness'.[12] It is frequently claimed that, before paracetamol, benzodiazepines, and other modern pain killers and anxiolytics, which are known to be toxic and inimical to human wellbeing, cannabis was used as a safe, natural, effective, herbal remedy. There is, as we will see in the next chapter, a romanticizing of the premodern.[13]

Moreover, this turn to premodernity is part of a broader contemporary discourse that relates the use of natural, organic products directly to health and wellbeing.[14] Ashley Koshie, for example, insists that 'we need ... to be devoid of chemical toxins, and for this we should change completely to natural medicine ... The reign of pharmaceutical companies has to end; we need a revival of soul. A change of progress toward natural elements.'[15] This type of thinking was central to the rationale for cannabis use within the counterculture of the 1960s and 1970s, in that it was part of a broader ideological suspicion of technocracy and orientation toward nature.[16] Hence, terms such as 'mother's milk' – a soy and cannabis beverage used for pain relief – helped to promote this perception of a harmless, natural remedy.[17]

Concerning the countercultural resistance to technocracy, which is traditionally conspicuous within cannabis culture, this is still evident in popular discourses about the growth and power of the pharmaceutical industry. While recent medical literature increasingly advocates a blended approach, in which cannabis is used alongside other drugs and therapies, there is, nevertheless, a suspicion of 'big pharma'.[18] Indeed, 'big pharma' is demonized as a profane threat to wellbeing driven by the desire for profit.[19] From articles in popular magazines to T-shirts declaring 'Beware of the Legal Pusher', pharmaceutical companies are frequently challenged within cannabis culture. Mark Miller, for example, in a broad discussion of the 'reasons why pot is better than prescription drugs', notes that, on the one hand, medical marijuana 'shines over and above pharmaceutical drugs in treating many ailments when the two are pitted one-on-one', while, on the other hand, pharmaceutical companies are 'fuelling a dangerous dynamic in which too many irresponsible physicians are handing out prescription drugs like candy'. He continues, 'unlike virtually every prescription medication that carries a risk of overdose, this is not the case with cannabis, in which the result of consuming too much is an early night's (or day's) sleep'.[20] Again, in a discussion of the history of medical cannabis, another popular writer makes the following comment:

> Unfortunately, these days humanity is governed by its need to acquire money and wealth rather than striving for a society free of illness and filled with happiness ... The fact that drug companies today have so much power is a terrible thing it puts too many important decisions in the hands of people who are only concerned with the bottom line. The fact that we live in such a technologically advanced society yet have such a backwards thinking when it comes to how we allow people to govern us, especially when it concerns our health. It's amazing that in some way our ancestors were wiser than us.[21]

Indeed, in order to establish the potential of medicinal cannabis, it's not unusual for even broadly scientific discussions to reference its historical usage. For example, in an article discussing the treatment of cancer, we are told that 'the cannabis plant has been used in nearly every culture for centuries ... It has been used as a medicine for nearly 3,000 years and cited in ancient texts as having healing properties in over 100 ailments'.[22] Again, in another article, we are informed that 'it has always been used as medicine' and that 'we have co-evolved with this plant for thousands and thousands of years'.[23]

This romanticization of the indigenous and the premodern overlaps significantly with occultural discourses in the holistic milieu. In other words, the arguments for medical cannabis are continuous with a range of esoteric, spiritual, and countercultural discourses. For example, in a recent article in *Dispense Magazine*, which serves the medical cannabis industry, it was noted that 'since the 1960s, there has been a growing movement towards more natural, holistic, and integrative ways of health and healing.

The focus has been on nutrition, exercise, and other lifestyle changes with lots of Eastern philosophies included.' Indeed, Richard Greer, the Director of Solevo Wellness (a medical marijuana dispensary based in Pittsburgh), makes the point that the evidence suggests that 'cannabis patients are more open, in general, to other alternative or holistic modalities and practices.'[24]

As indicated above, there is an underlying feeling that the modern period has seen a regression, rather than a progression of our understanding of human wellbeing. This is rooted in a concern about our gradual alienation from the natural world, which was accelerated during the industrial revolution of the eighteenth century. Not only was there a shift away from economies based on agriculture to economies based on mechanization and the factory system, but this had an enormous impact on our understanding of the causes and treatments of disease. While much of this has been undeniably beneficial, some worry that modern medicine has thrown the baby out with the bath water. Particularly since the emergence of the counterculture of the 1960s, the progress of environmental activism, peace protest, and the growth of various back-to-the-land movements, increasing numbers of people have questioned the benefits of technological progress. There have been frequent attempts to create what, in a 1971 *Rolling Stone* article, Thomas Albright and Charles Perry referred to as 'a future age which often harks back to a past one'.[25] During the 1960s and 1970s the ideas informing such projects were sympathetically and influentially explored in magazines such as *The Whole Earth Catalog*[26] and analysed by theorists such as Theodore Roszak and Charles Reich.[27] For most of us, Roszak observes,

> the jargon and mathematical elaborations of the experts are so much mumbo jumbo. But, we feel certain, it is all mumbo jumbo that *works* – or at least seems to work, after some fashion that the same experts tell us should be satisfactory. If those who know best tell us that progress consists in computerizing the making of political and military decisions, who are we to say this is not the best way to run our politics? If enough experts told us that strontium 90 and smog were good for us, doubtless most of us would take their word for it.[28]

Indeed, Roszak, who became well-known for popularizing the term 'counterculture', was particularly interested in the significance of the broadly Romantic opposition to 'industrial culture' and 'the myth of progress'. He developed a form of what I have referred to as 'Romantic radicalism'.[29] For example, he made the following general point in an interesting interview at the close of the 1970s:

> I've developed a kind of genealogy for the counterculture which reaches back at least to the early Romantic poets with their suspicion of science and technology, and their suspicion of the state, which also came up in the 1960s. But it seems to me that what happened within the last generation was that the set of sensibilities which had been restricted to poets and philosophers and were a rather rarefied and marginal aspect of the culture had gotten very widespread in the society and had taken on the dimension of a politically significant force, mainly in a kind of generation of dissent. So, what you have is a kind of popularization, maybe in

some cases a vulgarization, of sensibilities which had been born many generations before among poets and philosophers.[30]

A good example of this neo-romantic suspicion of technocracy and the turn to nature can be found in the philosophy of Chellis Glendinning. She begins her book *When Technology Wounds* with a strident statement: 'I am a technology survivor.' Having taken oral contraceptives she contracted systemic candidiasis and, eventually, pelvic inflammatory disease. 'The antibiotics used to treat it worsened the candida problem until I suffered a total collapse'. This led to a twenty-year struggle with ill-health until she eventually visited 'a holistic doctor who specialized in diseases of immune dysfunction. Seeing him led me away, once and for all, from the Western medical technologies that had caused the illness and toward alternative approaches that catalyze the body's ability to heal.' She 'became sick from an encounter with a health-threatening technology, and ... survived'.[31]

The reason for mentioning this turn to nature and away from 'big pharma' is to highlight the intellectual and cultural context within which many of the attitudes to medicinal cannabis have been shaped. This, of course, is not to deny that there are medical researchers and users who are simply interested in the science of cannabinoids with very little interest in the countercultural field of discourse. However, while the results of scientific research are beginning to come to the fore in discussions around drug development and policy, cannabis still carries a lot of broadly neo-romantic political and cultural baggage.

Furthermore, this type of thinking is, in part, the product of the subjectivized culture of the late-modern West. As Charles Taylor has observed, we have witnessed a 'massive subjective turn of modern culture, a new form of inwardness, in which we come to think of ourselves as creatures with inner depths'.[32] As such, many of our contemporaries treat these inner depths, these feelings and thoughts, as an ultimate source of authority. Unsurprisingly, therefore, strategies for healing, health and wellbeing have been democratized. Increasingly, they are no longer the preserve of the medical establishment. They are a core part of a 'responsible person's' self-care. As Robert Wuthnow put it, 'care, in the sense of attending to the self in its daily journey, becomes the key word, rather than the various cures suggested by medicine.'[33] Again, as Wade Clark Roof has commented, 'the body is central to healing experiences ... Whatever the type of healing, all such experiences are grounded in an embodied self that is in a continuous process of development and idealization'[34] – hence, the very common use of 'journey' and 'growth' metaphors within the holistic milieu. '"Health" is an idealization of a kind of self, and "healing" is part of the process by which growth towards the ideal is achieved.'[35] For those resistant to technocracy, suspicious of the motives of pharmaceutical companies, concerned about the exploitation of the natural world, committed to countercultural consciousness raising, and at home within the holistic milieu, cannabis has a lot to offer. Moreover, that medical science seems, increasingly, to support certain countercultural ideas about health, healing, and wellbeing is significant, in that it serves to validate, not only cannabis consumption, but also the broader neo-romantic turn in the late-modern world.

Background notes on the early history of medicinal marijuana

The history of the therapeutic use of cannabis is long and complex.[36] From the fragmentary evidence available, it seems likely that, from a very early period, humans recognized hemp to be a remarkable multicomponent natural resource that could be used to aid healing. Certainly, there is a range of ancient *materia medica* from Assyria, Egypt, India, China, Greece, and Rome that provides good evidence of a belief in its medicinal properties.

In 1934, it was argued by the Egyptologist and antiquarian Warren Dawson that the hieroglyphic word *šmšmt* (*shemshemet*) referred to cannabis. 'The word occurs in the Pyramid texts with an elaborate determinative and is spoken of as a plant from which ropes are made, which makes the equivalence with hemp, *Cannabis sativa* ... likely.'[37] Not only have a number of scholars found this tentative conclusion persuasive, but it has led to much speculation about the role of cannabis in ancient Egypt. For example, John Nunn, Paula Veiga, Ethan Russo and Christian Rätsch all broadly accept Dawson's translation of *shemshemet* and, on that basis, cite a range of ancient *materia medica* which suggest a number of cannabis nostrums and medicaments. Russo has even suggested that, not only are there references to the plant in medical papyri, but it is likely that 'the oldest written description of cannabis' can be found in ancient Egypt.[38] Again, Nunn, who insisted that 'there is general agreement with the view of Dawson that *shemshemet* means cannabis', argued that it was 'administered by mouth, rectum, vagina, bandaged to the skin, applied to the eyes, and by fumigation.'[39] More recently, Veiga has noted that, in the Ebers Papyrus (c. 1550 BCE) – the oldest extant complete medical papyrus – reference is made to a preparation of *shemshemet* for the treatment of gonorrhoea. Women who suffered from the condition were advised to mix it with honey and to insert it into the vagina in order to reduce pain and inflammation (Ebers Papyrus, Formula No. 821).[40] Similarly, Rätsch claims that, not only do 'inscriptions on the pyramids and papyruses bear witness to diverse uses of marijuana as medicine', but 'high concentrations of cannabinoids have been measured in nine Egyptian mummies.'[41]

While this evidence seems fairly conclusive, it should be noted that much of it rests on Dawson's translation of *shemshemet*, which has been challenged. William Benson Harer Jr, for example, has noted that Dawson's reasoning was flawed. Not only did he base his translation on a single reference to its use as rope, but it is far more likely that cannabis was introduced as a medicine in Egypt following the Arab invasion (639–642 CE).

> He decided that the Egyptian word *shemshemet* must be *Cannabis sativa*, or marijuana, because he found a single Old Kingdom statement that rope was made from *shemshemet*, 'which makes the equivalence with hemp.' Since the rope he knew was made from hemp, he reasoned that this meant they used cannabis fibers, too. While this seems logical, no sample of ancient Egyptian rope has been found to be made of cannabis hemp. They used flax, raffia, palm, camel hair, and other

fibers, but no actual cannabis hemp ... The topic is further confused by the word 'hemp' being applied generically to rope made from any plant fibers as well as those specifically from cannabis sativa ... Dawson also found four prescriptions in the Ebers papyrus which used *shemshemet*. Almost anything could have been considered for the meaning, but he chose cannabis without any further corroboration even though the word *shemshemet* was not in a context that could suggest any pharmacologic effect on the central nervous system. Furthermore, there is no evidence that the actual plant was introduced to Egypt prior to the Arab conquest in the seventh century AD ... Dawson's designation became enshrined when his interpretation was entered into the *Grundriss der Medizin der alten Ägypten*. With that imprimatur, it has become ubiquitous in popular literature about ancient Egypt. Nevertheless, the facts only confirm that marijuana use in ancient Egypt is a myth.[42]

Although we might not want to go so far as to insist that 'marijuana use in ancient Egypt is a myth', nevertheless, it is clear that the matter is not quite as straightforward as it is often claimed. After all, as Russo has discussed, while a number of scholars 'remain unconvinced ... that *shemshemet* denotes cannabis ... recent physical evidence of its presence has been excavated. Hemp fibers were found in the tomb of Amenophis IV (Akhenaten) at El-'Amarna, *circa* 1350 BC and confirmed in two separate scientific analyses.' Furthermore, he notes that '*Cannabis* pollen has also been identified from mid-third-millennium BCE soil samples from Nagada and in geological strata of similar vintage in the eastern Nile Delta.'[43] Again, several pollen grains have been discovered 'inside the mummy of Rameses II, who died *circa* 1213 BCE ... Samples containing cannabis pollen from another mummy have also been documented, *circa*. 100 BC, during the Ptolemaic era.'[44] Similar evidence has also recently been cited by a number of other scholars.[45]

If the archaeological evidence for medicinal cannabis use in ancient Egypt has been controversial, this is certainly not the case in other areas of the ancient world. For example, between 1947 and 1951, and again in 1954, the Ukrainian archaeologist and anthropologist, Sergei Ivanovich Rudenko, supervised an excavation of five Scythian *kurgans* (burial mounds/barrows) at Pazyryk in Siberia. As well as finding a spectacular tattooed mummy, the excavation discovered a number of carefully crafted artifacts in an almost perfect state of preservation, including equipment for inhaling cannabis smoke. As will be discussed in the next chapter, Rudenko later concluded that 'smoking hemp, like smoking hashish, took place without a doubt, not just as a ceremony of purification after burial, but in ordinary life; hashish was used as a narcotic ...'[46]

We have seen that cannabis is generally believed to be an Asiatic plant.[47] Central China in particular is important for our understanding of the early uses of cannabis. Not only has this region provided some of the earliest evidence of cannabis that we have – 11,000-year-old pollen – but it has also provided some of the earliest evidence of humans using it.[48] It was one of the ancient crop plants of China. As Mark Merlin comments, 'over hundreds, perhaps thousands of years, early inhabitants of Central and/or East Asia domesticated *Cannabis* varieties from wild plants into artificially selected, cultivated crops. Chinese historical records and archaeological data suggest that the history of hemp cultivation and use in Eastern Asia is approximately 5,000 to 6,000 years old. China, therefore, may have been the first region to cultivate, and even use hemp.'[49] For example, a notable archaeological discovery which provides good physical evidence of its ethnobotanical significance is the remains of cannabis found at the 2,500-year-old Yanghai Tombs in Xinjiang. As one recent study of the burial site has noted, 'all the cannabis remains could be used for psychoactive purposes, which would suggest that the deceased man knew of the narcotic value of cannabis. Moreover, based on the analysis of all the funerary objects in Room 90, Tomb No.1, the owner was considered to be a shaman.'[50]

This link with shamanism is important. While, as we will discuss in the next chapter, the modern construction of 'shamanism' by both scholars and practitioners is problematic,[51] nevertheless, for our purposes, we can think of 'the shaman' as a social and religious functionary whose repertoire includes healing and a knowledge of how certain natural elements can be utilized medicinally.[52] Concerning cannabis, while there is still a great deal of uncertainty about its role in ancient cultures, nevertheless, archaeological evidence does indicate that it was sometimes employed by shamans ritually and medicinally.[53]

> Together with the musical instrument and the cannabis, which are unique among the Yanghai Tombs, the shamanistic status of the deceased becomes all the more apparent. Due to its apparently prolonged use as a pestle, the inner surface of the wooden bowl containing cannabis had become smooth, and one side became perforated. The cannabis was presumably pulverized with a mortar before being consumed for psychoactive purposes. Thus, we assume that the deceased was more concerned with the intoxicant and/or medicinal value of the cannabis remains.[54]

Again, the point here is simply that, what is known of 'Chinese shamanism' (*wū jiào*) in the region during this early period suggests that cannabis was used ritually (possibly to induce trance states) and medicinally[55] – although, of course, religion and healing are frequently difficult to separate in ancient and indigenous societies, not least because physical maladies were frequently thought to have spiritual causes.

Furthermore, evidence for ancient Chinese cannabis cultivation can be found in the oldest extant book of poetry, the *Book of Odes* (*Shijing* or *Shih-ching*), which comprises 305 works dating from the eleventh to seventh centuries BCE: 'When we plant hemp, how do we do it? Across and along we put in rows.' Again, 'In the ninth month we take the seeding hemp.'[56] Furthermore, some of the earliest discussions about the medicinal use of cannabis are found in *bencao*, Chinese *materia medica*, 800 of which were gathered together by Li Shizhen (1518–1593) in a collection known as the *Bencao Gangmu* (本草纲目, *Compendium of Materia Medica*). However, because some of the terminology is problematic, clarity regarding the detail is still lacking. As Joseph Brand and Zhongzhen Zhao have commented, 'few reliable translations of Chinese monographs on cannabis from traditional *bencao* texts exist, which has led to significant gaps in the Western understanding about how cannabis was used in Chinese medicine.' Furthermore, 'a number of modern and historical Chinese sources contradict each other in terms of which plant parts correspond to certain traditional drug names ... complicating the interpretation of their medical actions.'[57] Nevertheless, again, while some of the details are unclear, what is clear is that cannabis was used in traditional Chinese medicine.

The Chinese character for hemp, 'ma' (麻) is around 3,000 years old and was, in the ancient *chuan* script, 'derived from ideographic components representing fibers hanging on a rack and placed under a roofed shack. Having evolved from the ancient to the later styles, it remains the character for hemp.'[58] Interestingly, at a very early period, 'separate characters were assigned to male and female hemp plants, its seeds, fruits, etc.'[59] This indicates, not only the antiquity of its cultivation, but also a relatively sophisticated knowledge of the plant and an understanding of the distinct ways in which it might be employed. Moreover, notes Hui-Lin Li, 'the original character *ma* in later usage assumed two additional connotations. One connotation meant "numerous" or "chaotic," derived from the nature of the plant's fibers. The second connotation was one of "numbness" or "senselessness," apparently derived from the stupefying effects of the fruits and leaves.'[60]

Within the *bencao* texts, three terms are used for cannabis – all of which include the root word *ma* (麻) – *mafen* (麻蕡), *mahua* (麻花), and *mabo* (麻勃). The most frequently used term, *mafen*, refers to 'the immature inflorescence of the female flower or the mature infructescence of the seeded female flower' – the 'rising spike on the cannabis flower' – which, readers are informed, 'should be harvested on the 7th day of the 7th month (based on the lunar calendar)'.[61] *Mafen* was first listed in the *Shennong Bencaojing* (*Divine Farmer's Classic of Materia Medica*), the extant text of which dates back to the Eastern Han Dynasty, between 100 CE and 220 CE.[62] Although produced and compiled by a number of authors and editors, it is attributed to the frequently cited Shennong/Shen-nung ('divine peasant/farmer'), a mythological divine ruler who, it was believed, taught the Chinese both agriculture and herbalism.[63] In one tradition Shennong is credited with introducing the five key grains or cereals in ancient Chinese agriculture: rice, barley, millet, soybeans, and cannabis. That said, he experimented with numerous herbs in order to compile his pharmacopeia, which was completed in, it is claimed, 2737 BCE. However, as JulieAnn Nugent-Head comments, 'the book is not simply a compendium of all the herbs that were in use during the Eastern Han Dynasty, but rather constitutes a careful selection of only 365 herbs ... correlating with the number of days in a year.'[64] She continues, 'the choice of a number correlating with a natural cycle was clearly more important than simply listing every medicinal herb known at the time.'[65] Furthermore, these medicinal plants are ordered into three categories: 'upper' (*shang*) herbs, which are non-poisonous and revitalizing; 'middle' (*zhong*) herbs, which, while toxic in larger dosages, are nevertheless useful; and 'inferior' (*xia*) herbs, which, while poisonous, are efficacious for the rapid reduction of fever and an aid for digestion.[66] This categorization became the basis of the *Shennong Bencaojing*, which, along with a commentary – the *Additional Records of Famous Physicians* (*Ming Yi Bie Lu*) – contains some of the key statements about the medicinal use of cannabis that were repeated in later texts.[67]

As to the uses of *mafen*, while only cannabis seeds are used in contemporary Chinese medicine,[68] the *bencao* texts indicate that, in the past, all the plant was used, including 'the female inflorescence, leaf, and root, as well as the cortex of the stalk and the water used to process the stalk into fibre'.[69] That said, even in ancient usage there was clearly a preference for the female plant, almost certainly because of its psychoactive properties. Hence, although there is little detail, it is noted that, while 'prolonged consumption frees the spirit and lightens the body',[70] users should be aware that 'excessive consumption causes one to see ghosts and run about frenetically'. More generally, cannabis was used for 'gout, female disorders, rheumatism, malaria, beriberi, constipation, and absent mindedness'.[71] While one would not normally think of cannabis as a cure for absent mindedness, there is little doubt that it was valued for its perceived analgesic properties. Hence, again, in the *Additional Records of Famous Physicians*, *mafen* is noted for its ability to relieve an 'impediment', which, in Chinese medicine, typically refers to a painful obstruction.[72] Indeed, the renowned Chinese Physician Hua Tuo developed a cannabis-based anaesthetic in order to perform surgery. This was noted by nineteenth-century Western practitioners who were themselves seeking to develop anaesthesia. For example, Alexander Christison, President of the Medical Society of Edinburgh, is pleased to record that, 'in a communication to the *Académie des Sciences* in 1849, extracts are produced from a Chinese work showing that so far back as AD 220, a Chinese physician named Hao-Tho [*sic*] produced insensibility in his patients by means of a preparation of hemp, and that operations in his patients were then performed without pain to the patient'.[73] As to the precise nature of Hua Tuo's concoction, although the details are not clear, a number of scholars have speculated that he mixed the resin with wine – a preparation called *ma-yo*. It was, says Solomon Snyder, 'employed as an anaesthetic for controlling pain during surgical operations. Besides alleviating pain, it seems to have had the ability to cause amnesia for the operation, much like the "twilight sleep" produced during scopolamine, a drug used to prevent secretions during operations and as a sedative.'[74] Similarly, Emboden and Rätsch have argued that it was probably a mixture of hemp, wine, and possibly monkshood.[75] Whatever the ingredients, as Emboden says, Hao Tuo recorded 'testimonials by his patients praising their pain-free operations'.[76] While it is very unlikely that surgery will have been pain-free, the mild analgesic properties of cannabis are relatively well-known.

Beyond China, some of the earliest references to medicinal cannabis can be found in India.[77] In an 1892 survey of references to cannabis in Sanskrit and Hindi texts, George Abraham Grierson noted that the principal terms used for the plant are *bhanga*, *Indravana*, and (possibly) *Vijaya* or *Jaya*, references to which date back to 'about the year 1300 AD'.[78] While this indicates some of the terms by which medicinal cannabis was known in nineteenth-century India, actually, in the earliest Sanskrit texts, two primary terms are used: *bhaṅgā* (which seems to be synonymous with *Vijayā*) and *śaṇa*. The latter essentially refers to what we now call 'hemp', namely a plant that is useful for making rope and weaving textiles. *Bhaṅgā*, on the other hand, identifies a plant with medicinal and psychoactive properties – possibly *any plant* that fitted that description (such as datura, belladonna, and henbane). As Duvall comments, 'the original meaning of *bhaṅgā* was probably something like "psychoactive drug plant."'[79] That is to say, initially the term *bhaṅgā* seems primarily to have indicated use, rather than identifying a particular botanical specimen. Nevertheless, as we have seen in

Chapter 1, *bhaṅgā/bhang* eventually came to refer to cannabis as a psychoactive, medicinal plant.

The distinction between *bhaṅgā* and *śaṇa* probably emerged in the southwestern Himalayas. Neolithic farmers first entered the mid-elevation Hindu Kush around 5,000 years ago and *śaṇa* was most likely the word already used for *Cannabis sativa*. 'When Proto-Indo-European speakers moved into the southwestern Himalayas, the people recognized *indica* and found that it could be used in the same ways as *sativa* – hempseeds collected for food and stems for fibre. The name *śaṇa* was transferred to *indica*.'[80]

Perhaps the earliest (pre-Vedic) Sanskrit reference to cannabis appears in the *Atharvaveda*: 'to the five kingdoms of the plants which Soma rules as Lord we speak: Darbha, hemp [*bhaṅgā*], mighty power: may these deliver us from woe' (11.6.15);[81] 'May hemp [*bhaṅgā*] and *Jaṅgiḍa* [which may have been a synonym for *ganja*[82]] preserve me from *vishkanda*' (2.4.5).[83] While it's not entirely clear what is being referred to – which has led to speculation in popular histories of cannabis – what is evident is that, as Clarke and Merlin suggest, the plant 'was believed by the ancient Aryan settlers of India to possess sedative, cooling, and febrifuge properties'.[84] As Harold Kalant has commented, from an early period it 'formed part of the therapeutic armamentarium of traditional Indian medicine ...'[85] For example, the ancient Indian *Ayurveda* holistic health system – derived from the Sanskrit words *ayur* (life) and *veda* (knowledge) – includes purified *bhanga* as an aid to digestion and a cure for constipation.[86] Again, Shri Dwarakanath has noted that references to cannabis

> appear in veterinary and medical works belonging to the twelfth to thirteenth centuries A.D. onwards ... *Sharangadhara Samhita*, a compendium of therapeutics (thirteenth century A.D.), has included medicaments titrated with the fresh extract of *bhang*. Authoritative *Ayurvedic* works on *materia medica* such as *Dhanwantari nighantu* (eighth century A.D.), *Madanapala nighantu* (1374 A.D.), and *Rajanighantu* (1450 A.D.) have described the properties, actions, and indications of both cannabis and opium. Bhavamishra (fifteenth century A.D.), a contemporary of Paracelsus, has in his compendium on medicine and therapeutics, *Bhavaprakasha*, described the properties, actions, indications, and formulations of both cannabis and opium. Much later, *Ayurvedic* medical works have given increasing importance to [cannabis] and included [it] in a large number of formulations ... It would appear that cannabis ... [has] also been employed by traditional folk medicine in the treatment of diseases even as early as the fourth to third century B.C. During the last two centuries, traditional folk medicine and the classical Indian medicine have become almost synonymous. Many drugs, including those containing cannabis ... have entered into the practice of classical *Ayurveda*.[87]

This is unsurprising in that, as Kalant says, 'many of the uses were similar to those for which it is currently advocated in our own society. Among its claimed benefits were sedative, relaxant, anxiolytic, and anticonvulsant actions – all of which also made it useful in the treatment of alcohol and opiate withdrawal – analgesia, appetite stimulation, antipyretic and antibacterial effects, and relief of diarrhoea.'[88] Indeed, contemporary Ayurvedic practitioners use it for the treatment of cancer patients: 'administration of *Shodhita Bhanga* (water-wash processed *Cannabis*) leaves powder in dose of 250mg thrice a day with 50ml of cow's milk and 4g sugar as an adjuvant, for a period of 1 month; significantly relieves pain, anxiety, and depression of cancer patients without creating any major side effects, dependency, and withdrawal symptoms.'[89]

Of particular note is the fact that, throughout history, it seems that cannabis played a particular role in gynaecology and obstetrics. We have seen, for example, that there is an early reference to its gynaecological use in the Ebers Papyrus. Again, in the plateau region of Iran and further west it seems clear that, as Duvall has noted, 'midwifery was possibly where the plant found greatest use. The Zoroastrian *Zend Avesta* (perhaps 700 BCE) ... listed *bhangem* among the four abortifacients ...'[90] Indeed, some of the earliest gynaecological references can be found in the library of the seventh-century BCE Neo-Assyrian King Ashurbanipal. This collection included Sumerian and Akkadian medical stone tablets dating to 2000 BCE. Of particular note is the word '*azallû*', which the Assyriologist and cuneiformist Reginald Campbell Thompson has argued refers to *Cannabis indica*, which was used 'in a prescription for difficult childbirth.'[91] Again, in the *Venidad* – a collection of texts within the *Avesta*, some of which are particularly ancient and probably reflect earlier oral traditions – it is clear that *bhaṅgā* was considered an effective abortifacient. The following passage (Fargard 15.IIb.13–14) discusses the case of a young woman seeking an abortion:

> If a man come near unto a damsel ... and she conceives by him, and she says, 'I have conceived by thee'; and he replies, 'Go then to the old woman' [i.e. midwife] and apply to her for one of her drugs, that she may procure the miscarriage'; And the damsel goes to the old woman and applies to her for one of her drugs, that she may procure her miscarriage; and the old woman brings her some *bhaṅgā*, or *Shaeta*, a drug that kills in the womb or one that expels out of the womb, or some other of the drugs that produce miscarriage and [the man says] 'Cause thy fruit to perish!' and she causes her fruit to perish; the sin is on the head of all three, the man, the damsel, and the old woman.[92]

Further west, near Jerusalem, at an archaeological site in the town of Beit Shemesh, the body of a young teenage girl who had apparently died during childbirth was discovered in a tomb from the late Roman period. In the abdominal area of her skeleton, '6.97g of a grey, carbonized material was recovered and analysed'. This turned out to be *Cannabis sativa* that had been 'burned in a vessel and administered to the young girl as an inhalant to facilitate the birth process'.[93] It appears to have been believed that cannabis increased 'the force of uterine contractions, concomitant with a significant reduction of labour pain.'[94] While a recent study of the use of plant-induced abortions in Morocco concluded that there is little evidence that cannabis does 'increase the force of uterine contractions',[95] nevertheless, as well as being frequently commended in pre- and early modern discussions of gynaecology, it is still used for that reason within traditional and folk medicine.[96]

The idea that certain plants and compounds are able to remove bodily obstructions brings us to humoral theory in Western medicine, evidence of which, with reference to cannabis, can be found in a number of pre-and early modern medical books.[97] For example, Thomas Short's *Medicina Britannica* (1751) offers the following advice:

> Take Heads of great Hemp, Number five; Tops of Feverfew and Penny-royal, of each half a Handful; boil in New-wort a Pint to a half, strain and drink it off going to Bed, repeat it for two or three Nights; it is a Remedy to bring down the *Menses minime fallax*. I once ordered only the Hemp alone, where they had been obstructed not only Months, but some years, with success; and, when it could not break the Uterine or Vaginal Vessels, the Woman threw up Blood from the Lungs, but had them naturally the next Time.[98]

The theory of humours can be traced back to the fifth century BCE and to the Greek physician Hippocrates, whose ideas were developed by Galen in the second century CE. From that point on it became medical orthodoxy in Western medicine until the seventeenth century when the circulation of blood began to be understood. However, even then, in practice, it continued into the nineteenth century.[99] Essentially, it focused on the balance of certain fluids (i.e. 'humours') within the body, which were believed to be central to its functioning: blood, phlegm, black bile, and yellow bile. Correctly assessing the levels of a body's humours was important for understanding disease, health, and wellbeing. Indeed, it explained almost anything from happiness to sadness and from the effects of recreational intoxication to sexual desire. For example, individuals with a predominance of blood were identified by their ruddy complexion and 'sanguine' disposition. Similarly, people were said to be 'phlegmatic' if they had a predominance of phlegm. Again, an increase in black bile generally led to 'melancholia', while too much 'choler' (yellow bile) produced a choleric temperament and biliousness. That said, regardless of one's dominant temperament, the balance of humours could be altered by diet, geographical location, climate, time of the year, and astrological phenomena. This was because, along with much else, each of the humours was directly related to the four elements – earth, air, fire, and water – as well as the four cardinal directions – north, south, east, and west. Hence, early modern medical practice required complex analysis. It also required a good understanding of the pharmacological properties of local flora and fauna. The point here is that, as the knowledge of herbalism grew in the West, it became increasingly aware of the value of hemp. Arguably the earliest reference to cannabis in English appears in 1621, in Burton's celebrated text *The Anatomy of Melancholy*. He recommends its use, for example, as an effective sedative. 'Waking by reason of their continual cares, fears, sorrows, dry brains, is a symptom that much crucifies melancholy men, and must therefore be speedily helped, and sleep by all means procured, which sometimes is a sufficient remedy of itself without any other physic.' Having recommended a number of compounds and 'simples' (i.e. herbs), he reminds his readers that 'country folks commonly make use of a posset of hemp-seed'. While he concedes that the influential German scholar, Leonhart Fuchs (Leonhartus Fuchsius), in his 1542 Latin work *De historia stirpium commentarii insignes*, 'so much discommends' the use of cannabis, nevertheless, he insisted, because 'I have seen the good effect', the plant 'may be used where better medicines are not to be had'.[100]

Similarly, like Burton, Nicholas Culpeper in *The English Physician* (1652) notes that cannabis 'consumeth wind' and 'openeth obstructions of the gall, and causeth digestion of choler'. It also 'stayeth lasks and continual fluxes, easeth the colic, allayeth the troublesome humours of the bowels, and stayeth bleeding at the mouth, nose, or any other place'. Furthermore, 'it will destroy the worms either in man or beast; and, by dropping the juice into the ears, it will kill the worms, and bring forth earwigs and other insects gotten therein.'[101] Likewise, a century later, Thomas Short's *Medicina Britannica* (1751), which shows the influence of Culpeper's work, notes the following of cannabis:

> Its Emulsion is ... good, if there is no Fever, and given at first. Its Juice is the Bane of Infects, in Wounds or Ulcers. A Decoction of the Seed, poured on the Ground, brings Earth-worms out of their Holes ... Hens, fed with the Seed, lay Eggs plentifully all Winter, and are very fat. An Oil express'd from it quicky cures all Burns, and draws out the Heat and Pain. The Juice drop'd into the Ears eases their Pain. An Emulsion of the Seed takes out fresh Marks of the Small Pox. A Decoction of the Seed eases the Pain of the Cholic. It kills Worms in the Bowels or Ears of Man or Bead.[102]

Apart from much else, it is clear that cannabis was widely available in premodern Europe as a mundane medicinal herb. It was certainly not considered profane. As Culpeper remarks in 1652, hemp 'is so common a plant, and so well known by almost every inhabitant of this kingdom, that a description of it would be altogether superfluous'.[103] By 1855, in a volume entitled *Papers Regarding the Cultivation of Hemp in India*, it is recorded that 'Hemp is cultivated in almost every part of Europe for Home consumption, but only in large quantities for export in Russia and Poland, though the finest quality of Hemp comes from Italy. French Hemp is also much esteemed, as well as that grown in both England and Ireland. Hemp is cultivated in almost every province of Russia ...'[104]

The mundanity of cannabis is evident in that, from the sixteenth century onwards, its supply became an increasingly pressing concern for the British government, which was seeking to establish Britain as a maritime and imperial power. The expanding empire needed hemp to make ropes, rigging, sails, sacks, and so on. As noted by Malachy Postlethwayt in his *Universal Dictionary of Trade and Commerce* (1766), Britain's 'whole mercantile, as well as royal maritime power, depends on supplying ourselves with [hemp] cordage'.[105] Indeed, as early as 1563, Queen Elizabeth I required landowners with 60 acres of land to cultivate hemp or pay a £5 fine. Unfortunately, such was the increasing demand for hemp that even this plan did not produce the requisite quantities. Indeed, by the beginning of the nineteenth century its supply had become a significant problem for the government. For example, Robert Wissett, Clerk to the Committee of Warehouses of the East India Company, made the following comment in his 1808 volume *A Treatise on Hemp*:

> With regard to the *native* growth of Hemp, although the recent vast importations of corn sufficiently indicate the inadequacy of our harvests to feed our growing

population, and consequently may seem to imply that no soil should be diverted to any other crop, which may be advantageously appropriated to the culture of grain; – yet there are circumstances and soils, the nature of which, when impartially considered, will more than counterbalance the apparent objection.[106]

In other words, politically, hemp was becoming more important than corn.

By the turn of the nineteenth century, notes Mills, 'India was established as the main source of information for the British about the hemp plant and about medicinal and intoxicating preparations made from it.'[107] Furthermore, it was identified as the most promising in terms of resourcing hemp. Initially, however, there was some bemusement about its cultivation in India. While it was grown in large quantities, it was used less for cordage and more for medicine and intoxication. Although popular eighteenth-century books such as John Henry Grose's *A Voyage to the East Indies with Observations on Various Parts There* (1757)[108] had amused its readers with tales of cannabis intoxication and the exotic lives of a stoned Eastern elite, as well as positing an influential link between cannabis, criminality, and death, the British government's interest in India's cannabis production was driven by the need for hemp fibre. However, it soon became apparent that the indigenous penchant for getting high – about which the government and traders had little interest or knowledge – was a significant problem. As Wissett noted in 1804, 'the Hemp plant has been cultivated in Bengal from time immemorial for the purpose of intoxication; but it is never used by the natives for cordage or cloth as in Europe. The plant is called by them *ganja* and the intoxicating preparation made from it *Bang*.'[109] This was problematic because they found it difficult to persuade Indian growers to change their cultivation methods. Indians wanted *bhang* not rope. On the face of it, of course, this doesn't appear be a particularly difficult problem to solve. Why not just make rope out of the hemp produced for *bhang*? Unfortunately, the problem was not quite as straightforward as that. This is evident in the following extract taken from the *Transactions of the Agricultural and Horticultural Society of India*, Vol. 8 (1840) – reprinted in 1855 as an appendix in *Papers Regarding the Cultivation of Hemp in India*:

> it is well known that no plant is so commonly cultivated in many parts of India as the true Hemp plant which is there called *ganja*, but which differs in no respect from the European plant, though the natives employ it only for the purposes of yielding *bhang*. But, cultivated for this purpose, instead of being sown thick as it ought to be when intended for cordages, it is sown thin by the natives, who afterwards transplant the young plants and place them at distances of 9 or 10 feet from each other. The effect of this is to expose them more freely to light, heat, and air, by the agency of which the plant is enabled to perfect its secretions in a more complete manner, and the *bhang* consequently will be more intoxicating in nature ... *This mode of cultivation has, however, the disadvantage of being more expensive, from taking up more space than desirable when the plants are required to yield the best quality of fibre for cordage.*[110]

Hemp that is carefully cultivated for psychoactive purposes is not particularly useful or profitable for making cordage. The whole approach to cannabis cultivation in India needed to change. However, the British, who had managed to get their own way so often, failed to persuade Indian growers to revise their cultivation methods in order to produce cheaper and stronger hemp. The Indians wanted a product that would be attractive to the drug markets of Asia. However, while this was of little use to the British government and traders, it was of increasing interest to medical researchers attached to the East India Company. Indeed, it should be noted that, as Mills has commented, 'medical publications from the 1700s show that there was an awareness of the properties of the hemp plant that meant that it could be used both as a medicine and as an intoxicant. However,' he continues, 'the nature of the entries in these books points to the fact that there was little direct experience of the medicinal preparations of the plant.'[111] This situation changed significantly as the nineteenth century progressed.

Finally, as we have indicated, the reception of cannabis as an intoxicant in Europe was significantly aided by the failure of Napoleon's Egyptian campaign. In order to understand why, a few salient contextual details need to be noted, central to which is the fact that, at the end of the eighteenth century, France was at war with Britain.[112] As such, the French were keen to disrupt British dominance of the seas, as well as its trade routes with India. To this end, the ruling Directory of the Republic of France authorised a military expedition to 'the Orient' (a contemporary term for what would now be referred to as 'the Middle East') to establish a base from which it could then expand its influence. Napoleon Bonaparte, a Corsican general famous for his campaigns in Italy – but not yet Napoleon I – was given command of the expedition. In 1798, he led his Armée d'Orient to Egypt. It's also worth noting that, while the expedition's primary aim was political, it had a historically significant secondary purpose, namely to collect scientific, historical, and cultural information about Egypt. Hence, along with 35,000 soldiers, Napoleon enlisted more than 160 scholars and artists, officially known as the 'Commission of the Sciences and Arts of Egypt'. These scholars and artists were far more successful in their efforts than the soldiers. Their research, which was carried out over many years, gave birth to modern Egyptology and, indeed, Egyptosophy – the Romantic Orientalist occult fascination with what was imagined to be the religion and culture of the ancient Egyptians.[113] The Armée d'Orient, on the other hand, after initial successes at Alexandria and Cairo, began to struggle. Most notably, in what came to be known as the Battle of the Nile (1–3 August 1798), Horatio Nelson and the British Navy, which had discovered the French fleet anchored off the Egyptian coast at Abukir/Abu Qir, destroyed it. This meant that Napoleon's forces were now effectively stranded. While the land campaigns continued with some success, they struggled to suppress local revolts. Also, many of the soldiers who had managed to avoid dying in battle, succumbed to disease.[114] Eventually, in 1799, facing failure, Napoleon returned to Europe to pursue his own ambition, leaving his soldiers under the command of the celebrated French military strategist General Jean-Baptiste Kléber. Unfortunately for the French, he was assassinated in June 1800 by Suliman El-Halebi, a Kurdish student from Aleppo. Kléber's successor, General Jacques-François de Menou, was faced with a dire and deteriorating situation. Furthermore, Menou was not the military strategist that Kléber had been and nor did he enjoy the same degree of loyalty from his officers. As one of his colleagues put it, 'he was without any sort of military talent, but he was not lacking in bravery.'[115] This was a dangerous combination, which led to a number of bold, but ultimately ill-fated decisions. Eventually, having stumbled from one calamity to the next, and following a number of insurrections in Cairo and an unnecessarily lengthy siege at Alexandria, he was forced to capitulate to the British in August 1801.[116] In October 1801, the remaining soldiers of the Armée d'Orient were allowed to return to Europe.

While fascinating in many important respects, Napoleon's Egyptian campaign is relevant to the current discussion because it was these returning French soldiers that carried hashish back to a Europe that had become increasingly fascinated with all things Oriental. Although recreational cannabis use in Egypt was contentious, it was also widely employed medicinally, recreationally, and religiously. Alcohol, on the other hand, was not freely available in an Islamic country. Consequently, having been marooned following the Battle of the Nile, with their supply lines cut by the British Navy, French soldiers began looking for a substitute intoxicant. Keen to relax, they began smoking the local recreational drug, consuming cannabis delicacies, and drinking hashish-laced beverages. Although it is sometimes argued that Napoleon banned the use of cannabis, actually, both he and Kléber seemed unconcerned by its growing popularity among the troops. At least it kept them in good spirits. Menou, on the other hand, had married into an upper-class Sunni family after taking command of Egypt following the assassination of Kléber. As a Sunni convert, like many well-to-do Sunnis, he viewed intoxication as an offence against Islamic law and a profane threat to the social order. Moreover, from his own particular perspective, he was concerned that cannabis would present an obstacle to Franco-Egyptian co-operation. He was particularly bothered by correspondence from his generals in Rosetta and Alexandria who were worried about the behaviour of intoxicated soldiers, some of whom were (whether as a result of the cannabis or not) mistreating local people. This shocked Menou and, in early September 1800, he issued a warning to the Armée d'Orient: 'I am unhappy with many of you ... I have received serious complaints about soldiers mistreating native inhabitants. What! You are republicans and you are not generous! You are French and you would be barbarians! Ah! I want to believe these insults and excesses delivered by many of you are the result of intoxication.' He then drives home his point by making the familiar profanatory connection between cannabis and crime. 'The intoxicated man is nothing but a frantic, who succumbs to all impulses, and who can commit the most horrible crimes.'[117] Indeed, 'those who are accustomed to drinking this liquor and smoking this seed lose reason and fall into a violent delirium, which often leads them to commit excesses of all kinds.'[118] For this conservative Muslim convert, cannabis became understood as a profane threat to the social order. Be that as it may, his admonition went unheeded. Consequently, it appears that he felt that his hand had been forced and that some form of legislation was required. On 8 October, he issued an *ordre du jour* banning the consumption, production, and distribution of hashish throughout Egypt. Furthermore, businesses that traded in hashish were shut down, their proprietors were imprisoned for three months and smugglers were subject to draconian fines. Still, hashish retained its popularity and its supply continued.

Whereas few in France had reliable access to hashish, as David Guba comments, 'this dearth of supply did little to stymie the rise in popularity of the intoxicant as a discursive marker of the Oriental world in the developing French imperial imaginary.'[119]

While attitudes to hashish in nineteenth-century France were mixed, generally speaking, as we will see below, increased familiarity within medical circles led to an interest its pharmacological potential. Even if it was dangerous and profane, there was a belief that it could be sanitized and redeemed by occidental science.

Nineteenth-century medical research

Western medicine during the early years of the nineteenth century was practised by a broad range of surgeons, apothecaries, and quacks, some of whom had studied at university, while others had very little formal education. Indeed, humoral theory and folk remedies were still being referenced in medical texts.[120] However, as the nineteenth century progressed, so did medicine, not least because many of the diseases erroneously accounted for by earlier theories were shown to be caused by germs.[121] Indeed, by the 1850s, germ theory had effectively condemned folk medicine to medical history. It was during this revolutionary period in the emergence of modern medical research, that cannabis came to the attention of scientists in Europe and America.[122] While Antoine Isaac Silvestre de Sacy had mentioned the possibility of its use in 1809,[123] it would be another three decades before Western physicians would begin to experiment with it. Initially, much of this experimentation was conducted in India. As Mills has discussed, 'of all the places in the world that British administrators and merchants were trading in and travelling to, it was India that their awareness of hemp narcotics was being formed.'[124]

While we have seen that cannabis had been used both recreationally and medicinally in Asia for centuries, it was not until William Brooke O'Shaughnessy read a paper to a gathering of students and scholars at the Medical and Physical Society of Calcutta in 1839 that its star began to rise in modern Western medicine. It's not the case, of course, that O'Shaughnessy was the first Western scholar to recognize the therapeutic potential of cannabis, but rather it was his careful research and influence that significantly promoted its use among the medical establishment. When his findings were published in India in 1839,[125] they stimulated great interest in pharmaceutical circles and, as such, were subsequently republished in a number of scholarly medical publications.[126] It is largely as a result of this research that he is now popularly viewed as the father of modern medical cannabis research; the one who 'introduced cannabis to modern Western medicine';[127] 'the first western medical practitioner to publish articles promoting the use of a medicine he derived from the hemp plant.'[128] As the *New Scientist* commented in 2018, 'thanks to one man's researches, cannabis [became] the drug of choice for ailments from migraine to epilepsy.'[129]

Born in Limerick, Ireland, in October 1809, O'Shaughnessy's intelligence was conspicuous from a very young age. By the age of 18, he had secured admission to the University of Edinburgh to study medicine, chemistry, and forensic toxicology, graduating in 1829 with a thesis entitled *De Metastasi Rheumatismi Acuti*. That year he also began working as a clinical assistant to the social reformer and philanthropist, William Allison. Two years later, in September 1831, England experienced a devastating cholera pandemic. As the death rate rapidly increased, 'the medical profession grasped at an array of empirical remedies ranging from cayenne pepper given by mouth to turpentine enemas.'[130] O'Shaughnessy, however, studied the chemical pathology of the blood in cholera, which eventually led to the first successful use of intravenous replacement therapy.

> On January 7, 1832, he presented his data to the Central Board of Health in London and published them immediately thereafter in a brilliant monograph. This delightful book deserves a small place among medicine's classics as a demonstration of O'Shaughnessy's command of the literature, his clear and incisive logic, and astonishing grasp of acid-base physiology. He related the functions of carbon dioxide, oxygen, and the 'colouring matter of the blood,' and finally he showed the essential elements of the chemical pathology of cholera.[131]

It's perhaps also worth noting that, along with much else, O'Shaughnessy was involved in the design and construction of the first telegraph system in India. At 3,500 miles in length, this was a significant achievement,[132] for which, in 1856, he was knighted by Queen Victoria. He was also subsequently appointed as Director General of Telegraphs.

O'Shaughnessy spent two periods in India, between 1833 and 1841 and between 1852 and 1860. It was during his first trip that he researched the medicinal properties of cannabis (and other indigenous plants, including opium) and during his second trip that he conducted the engineering work for which he was knighted. Concerning his initial journey to India, having recently got married and disappointed by his failure to secure the Chair in Medical Jurisprudence in the University of London, on 8 August 1833, he joined the service of the British East India Company as an assistant surgeon in the Bengal service. Such was O'Shaughnessy's ability that, within two years, he had been promoted to the rank of surgeon and also appointed as the first Professor of Chemistry at the newly established Calcutta Medical College. Although, initially, he had little grasp of indigenous languages, he arrived in India at a time of increasing Anglicization. Consequently, whereas basic medical training had not previously been conducted in English, this changed in 1835 when the Medical College was opened.

It was at this time that O'Shaughnessy turned his mind to the pharmacological potential of cannabis, which, he observed, was being used in Ayurvedic and Islamic medicine. Fascinated by what he had learned from local practitioners, he travelled widely and read all he could. Several times, he noted his surprise that, to his knowledge, the plant was not used medicinally, or indeed, recreationally in Europe.[133]

It is worth taking a moment here to note that, although his view of cannabis is generally positive, nevertheless, he betrays the Orientalist influence of earlier Western discussions. For example, in the above quotation, not only does he refer to indigenous recreational users as 'dissipated and depraved', but he rehearses a number of typically Orientalist notions, such as those that link the drug to criminals, to the poor, and, indeed, to the Assassins. Cannabis, he says, is a 'drug which is still greedily consumed by *the* dregs *of the* populace, and from the consumption of which sprung the excesses which led to the name of "Assassin" being given to Saracens in the Holy Wars.'[134] This is unsurprising, but it does indicate the insidious nature of demonization, which even influences minds that are otherwise enlightened and progressive. Having said that, guided by his rigorous application of the scientific method, O'Shaughnessy's work also demonstrates an embryonic shift in attitudes. While acknowledging that he had been 'guided' by the large amount of 'preliminary information before [him]' in order 'to gain more accurate knowledge of the action, powers, and possible medicinal applications of this extraordinary agent',[135] it is clear that he is bothered by discourses of profanation. His own research had indicated that such notions were misleading. Indeed, he seems to have become increasingly convinced that, when compared to other popular intoxicants, such as alcohol, there are minimal negative effects. 'As to the evil sequelae so unanimously dwelt on by all writers, these did not appear to me so numerous, so immediate, or so formidable, as many which may be clearly traced to over-indulgence in other powerful stimulants or narcotics – *viz*, alcohol, opium, or tobacco.'[136] By 1844, he was able to describe cannabis simply as 'a powerful, but safe narcotic.'[137] This is an important point, even at this early stage, medical science, driven by empirical evidence and objectivity, is able to undermine discourses of profanation. Consequently, while he accepted that cannabis could become a social problem, actually, he insisted, it has the potential to be of great benefit to society. Cannabis has the potential to be a social good. Hence, rather than focusing on 'evil sequelae' rooted in prejudice and rumour, O'Shaughnessy is 'led ... to the belief that, in Hemp, the [medical] profession has gained an anti-convulsive remedy of the greatest value. Entertaining this conviction, be it true or false, I deem it my duty to publish it without any avoidable delay in order that the most extensive and the speediest trial may be given to the proposed remedy.'[138] Likewise, a review of his work in *The Lancet* – a prestigious British medical journal founded in 1823 – noted that 'the labours of Dr O'Shaughnessy, as a scientific chemist, are already known in the most favourable manner to our readers; but unlike the greater number of chemists, he combines practice with theory and directs his scientific discoveries to the advancement of medicine as a healing art.'[139] The review concluded by expressing the hope that 'some of our hospital physicians will, without delay, procure the remedy which Dr O'Shaughnessy has thus favourably introduced, and determine how far it may sustain its reputation as a "powerful anti-convulsive" in this country.'[140]

O'Shaughnessy published a number of influential works in the early 1940s that increased interest in medical cannabis, including *The Bengal Dispensatory and Pharmacopœia* in 1841.[141] Indeed, his work is fascinating for a number of reasons. Not only is it an interesting early analysis of cannabis, it is also ground-breaking in its use of ethnography, self-dosing, and animal experimentation. Concerning the last of these, he was led, he declared, 'to one remarkable result – that while carnivorous animals, such as fish, dogs, cats, swine, vultures, crows, and adjutants, invariably and speedily exhibited the intoxicating influence of the drug, the graminivorous, such as the horse, deer, monkey, goat, sheep, and cow, experienced but trivial effects from any dose we administered.'[142] He was particularly taken with, not to say amused by, its effects on dogs.

> Ten grains of Nipalese *churrus*, dissolved in spirit, were given to a middling-sized dog. In half an hour he became stupid and sleepy, dozing at intervals, starting up, wagging his tail, as if extremely contented; he ate some food greedily; on being called to, he staggered to and fro, and his face assumed a look of utter helpless

drunkenness. These symptoms lasted about two hours, and then gradually passed away; in six hours he was perfectly well and lively.

One drachm of *majoon* was given to a small-sized dog; he ate it with great delight, and in twenty minutes was ridiculously drunk; in four hours his symptoms passed away, also without harm.[143]

The fact that, 'in none of these, or several other experiments, was there the least indication of pain, or any degree of convulsive movement observed',[144] gave him confidence to experiment on himself and his patients. 'Encouraged by these results, no hesitation could be felt as to the perfect safety of giving the resin of Hemp an extensive trial in the cases in which its apparent powers promised the greatest degree of utility.'[145] Hence, convinced of its pharmacological efficacy, in 1842, O'Shaughnessy encouraged Peter Squire, 'the well-known pharmacist of Oxford Street',[146] London, to develop a cannabis tincture. 'Squire's Extract' was quickly followed by a number of other preparations, such as, perhaps most famously, Dr. John Collis Brown's 'Chlorodyne', the principal ingredients for which were cannabis tincture, laudanum, and chloroform. This was clearly a potent mixture that, no doubt, secured its unrivalled popularity as an effective remover of almost any symptom one could experience.[147] While cannabis never rivalled opium in the nineteenth century, for a number of years it did become a relatively widely used ingredient in pharmaceutical preparations.

A good example of a prominent Victorian physician who became convinced of the therapeutic benefits of cannabis is Sir John Russell Reynolds, 'Physician-in-Ordinary to Her Majesty's Household.' In an interesting 1890 article, 'On the Therapeutic Uses and Toxic Effects of *Cannabis Indica*', he insists that 'Indian hemp, when pure and administered carefully, is one of the most valuable medicines we possess.'[148] Unsurprisingly, therefore, he recommended the drug as an effective remedy for a broad range of conditions, including sleeplessness, neuralgia, and 'spasmodic dysmenorrhea'.[149] A century later, in the 1990s, this connection led to speculation about Queen Victoria's cannabis use. Did Reynolds prescribe cannabis to the Queen to ease her discomfort during times of painful dysmenorrhea? Certainly, there are many campaigners and scholars who, it would seem, have simply assumed that this was the case.[150] Philip Leveque, for example, boldly declares that 'Queen Victoria was the first woman to use marijuana for PMS.' He continues:

> This occurred a few months after Dr. O'Shaughnessy brought cannabis to England about 1840 ... It was prescribed by a Dr. Sir Russel Reynolds physician to Queen Victoria ... The Queen obviously found that cannabis/marijuana worked well. She used it also for morning sickness and obstetrical anaesthesia with no harm to foetuses ... The new most promising therapy for PMS was discovered by Queen Victoria about 1850.[151]

Again, Russo has commented that 'Sir John Russell Reynolds was personal physician to Queen Victoria, and it has been widely acknowledged that she received monthly doses of *Cannabis indica* for menstrual discomfort throughout her adult life.'[152] And, according to Raphael Mechoulam, the Israeli chemist who isolated THC, Reynolds acquired cannabis for the Queen, not to ease menstrual discomfort, but to reduce the severity of her migraines.[153] Moreover, in Britain, in 1998, when the legalization of medical cannabis was being debated, the relationship between Queen Victoria and cannabis was officially referenced in a report by the Science and Technology Committee of the House of Lords.[154] The same year, another member of the British royal family, Prince Charles, was drawn into the narrative and linked to Victoria. In an article in *The Guardian* by Amelia Gentleman, we are told that 'anti-establishment forces campaigning to legalise cannabis could be joined by an altogether more orthodox figure – the Prince of Wales has hinted that he approves of its use as an alternative method of pain relief. During a visit to a day care centre this week he suggested to a multiple sclerosis sufferer that cannabis might ease her crippling pain.' Gentleman concludes her article by noting that 'Prince Charles is not the first member of the royal family to support use of cannabis as medicine. Queen Victoria is said to have used it to ease period pains.'[155] This claim was quickly recycled, appearing three times in *The Guardian* in 1999 and nine times in 2000.[156]

Attractive though this 'widely acknowledged' theory may be to many, actually, it is highly speculative. Firstly, there is no evidence that Reynolds administered cannabis to the Queen. Indeed, the report of the House of Lords, Science and Technology Committee, while referencing the claim, also notes that 'there is no actual proof of this at all'.[157] Secondly, while it is frequently assumed that Reynolds was the Queen's personal physician, actually he was only one of a number of physicians and surgeons that constituted the Queen's 'medical household'.[158] Thirdly, even if he had wanted to reveal the details of Victoria's menstrual cramps, which is unlikely, he could not have done so, since he was only appointed in 1878, by which time she would have been approaching her sixtieth birthday. As such, menstruation was almost certainly a distant memory. Finally, while, of course, it could be argued that Reynolds might have been consulted prior to his appointment, or, indeed, that one of his predecessors might have administered cannabis to the Queen, or that it was prescribed to her later in life for an entirely different condition (such as migraine), again, there is a conspicuous absence of evidence.[159]

We should, of course, not be surprised that such stories quickly gain traction, particularly within campaigning circles. If anything is going to promote medical cannabis and challenge discourses of profanation, it is its commendation by an eminent Victorian physician and its use by a famously morally conservative monarch. The very claim that 'respectable' members of the royal family use cannabis is, in itself, sacralizing.

Despite the impressive research by O'Shaughnessy and others, and although a number of tinctures were prepared by apothecaries, most physicians did not prescribe it, preferring opiates instead. Nevertheless, as the second half of the century progressed, myths about the pharmacological efficacy of cannabis were increasingly disseminated. This was conspicuously the case in advertisements for cannabis-based products. For example, one advertisement declared that the 'cheapest, best, and most agreeable medicine in the world is hasheesh'. Readers were informed that it is 'the great Eastern remedy, used for thousands of years by ancient Hindoos, Persians, Jews, Greeks, Chinese, Japanese, Arabians, Egyptians, Chaldeans, and the Assyrians. Sacred and profane history alike inform us, says Rev. John Wesley, that these were the most

Beautiful, Happy, Healthy, Cheerful, and Long-lived people that ever existed.'[160] While, of course, Wesley, the founder of Methodist movement in the Church of England, was hardly an authority on the health and wellbeing of ancient peoples or, indeed, cannabis consumption, by simply linking a prominent Christian with the drug, no matter how loosely, performed much the same role as linking it to Queen Victoria. The overall impact was sacralizing. Not only does cannabis heal, promote beauty, cultivate happiness, and ensure a long life, but it is mentioned in the same sentence as a well-known religious figure who represents core Christian values. Indeed, one advertisement went so far as to claim that 'no clergyman, actor, singer, lawyer or in fact anyone should be without it'.[161] It's a cure-all substance that deserves to be at the heart of society.

It should also be noted that, as we will see below, one of the reasons for it falling out of favour in medical circles in the late nineteenth century was the fact that it suffered from poor quality control and, as such, lacked the stability of other preparations. Not only was it not the secret of youth and beauty, but also it often failed to relieve symptoms that much smaller doses of opium could. Moreover, in the large quantities taken in the nineteenth century, it often produced unwanted psychoactive effects that disturbed the more sober-minded members of society. Hence, by the turn of the twentieth century, it struggled to rival newer drugs such as aspirin, chloral hydrate,[162] and barbiturates, all of which were chemically more stable than cannabis, less psychoactive, and able to produce more predictable results. Moreover, the invention and subsequent popularity of the hypodermic syringe contributed significantly to the decline of medicinal cannabis use, in that, unlike opiates, it was not water-soluble and, therefore, couldn't be injected.

Prior to the invention of the hypodermic syringe in 1853 and the development of more effective drugs, there was a short period when cannabis was viewed as the new wonder drug. Indeed, we should also note that, despite the claim that O'Shaughnessy 'introduced cannabis to modern Western medicine',[163] in fact, at the same time, it was becoming increasingly popular elsewhere in Europe. As we will see, there were, for example, a number of French physicians convinced of its pharmacological value for a broad range of ailments. Although they were still fundamentally influenced by earlier Romantic Orientalist constructions of Muslim otherness, which were, in turn, informed by an uncritical reading of de Sacy's account of hashish and the Assassins, many French pharmacists and physicians viewed hashish as both exotic and, in its raw form, dangerous.[164] They shared Théophile Gautier's view of cannabis as 'a strange food which had been used centuries ago by an imposter sheik as a means of exciting his illuminati to murder'.[165] Nevertheless, we will also see that some were convinced that occidental science could subdue it and control it. Indeed, during the nineteenth century, Paris became an important centre for cannabis experimentation. As Guba notes, 'throughout the 1840s and 1850s dozens of French pharmacists staked their careers on hashish, publishing dissertations, monographs, and peer-review articles on its medicinal and scientific benefits.'[166]

Of particular note in this regard is the French epidemiologist Louis-Rémy Aubert-Roche, a Chief Physician in Egypt, who was, as *Médecin en chef de la Compagnie*, responsible for the oversight of medical care during the construction of the Suez Canal.[167] Alongside him was the talented and influential physician, Antoine Barthélémy

Clot (known in Egypt as 'Clot-Bey'[168]). Their medical work became particularly important during a prolonged and devastating plague epidemic in Egypt that broke out in July 1834. Apart from much else, the disease highlighted a heated debate between those who believed that it was contracted by direct human contact (contagionists) and those who thought it was the result of environmental factors (anticontagionists). Moreover, the contagionists supported the ruthless quarantine procedures sanctioned by the Viceroy of Egypt, Muhammad Ali. For obvious strategic reasons, the Viceroy was keen to protect his armed forces and those at work in Egypt's dockyards and factories producing military equipment. To this end, he bestowed unrestricted powers on the Quarantine Board, which had organized a large lazaretto in Alexandria.[169] Because it was believed that disease was transmitted from unhealthy people to healthy people, any symptoms led to immediate imprisonment. However, the anticontagionists argued that the policy was misconceived and rooted in medieval superstition. It was, therefore, counterproductive. In this pre-germ theory period, Aubert-Roche was, like Clot-Bey and many of his medical contemporaries, a committed anticontagionist.[170] He believed the plague to be a disease of the central nervous system that was contracted as a result of 'bad air' or 'miasma' in unsanitary conditions, poorly ventilated areas, and geographical locations that incubated disease, such as the lazaretto that was built in Alexandria near the stagnant, infested waters of Lake Mariout. Poverty, poor living conditions, and neglected hygiene cultivated disease. Indeed, these were environmental factors that Auber-Roche particularly associated with Arabs and Black Africans.[171] Hence, throughout his book *De la peste ou le typhus d'Orient*,[172] he lampooned the contagionists for being superstitious, in that they effectively believed in an evil influence that could be passed from person to person and that required exorcism by quarantining. It was more akin to witchcraft than medical science. As Guba notes, 'Auber-Roche railed against the members of the health commissions in Alexandria and Cairo, who, in his mind, fell victim to the superstitions of contagionism during the plague outbreak of 1834–35 and thus took ineffective measures to arrest its spread and treat its victims.'[173] Of course, as the nineteenth century progressed, so germ theory challenged many of the basic assumptions of anticontagionism. That said, its emphasis on the importance of environmental factors for pathogenesis was an important contribution in the history of medicine.

It is within this Egyptian context, that Aubert-Roche discovered that his patients responded to cannabis: 'from all that I have seen and observed, the plague is by no means an inflammatory disease, but rather a disease caused by damage to the nervous system ...' Consequently, since hashish is 'a substance that acts upon the nervous system', it is unsurprising that it 'has given me the best results'.[174] Indeed, following a number of case studies demonstrating the ability of cannabis to arrest the effects of the plague and even cure some patients, he became convinced that stimulation by hashish intoxication was the key. 'It was ... my duty as a doctor to look for a drug that acted on the nervous system since the plague was a disease of this system ... Hashish presented itself quite naturally.'[175] In 1840, he published his *magnum opus*, *De la peste ou typhus d'Orient*, in which he provided a forty-page discussion of the efficacy of hashish. Clot-Bey too was convinced and, indeed, published 'some thoughts on the effects of hashish',[176] as did Clot-Bey's colleague Alexandre Willemin, who, in 1848, delivered a paper about the treatment of cholera in Egypt to the Académie de Médecine in Paris, in which emphasized 'the salutary effects of the active ingredient of *Cannabis indica* in the treatment of this disease'.[177] Indeed, as a committed and influential anticontagionist, Willemin had been evangelistic about the medicinal benefits of cannabis for some years. As Guba notes, 'during the first half of the nineteenth century, dozens of French pharmacists and physicians embraced Willemin's theories and believed that hashish, though a dangerous and exotic intoxicant of the Orient, could be tamed by Western pharmaceutical sciences and, once refined, used by physicians to treat a variety of deadly and much-feared diseases'.[178] One such pharmacist was Joseph-Bernard Gastinel who had established a large business in Cairo. He too was convinced that hashish stimulated the central nervous system and, indeed, was able to 'successfully reverse' any damage done to the brain by cholera.

Again, it's worth noting that, while this discussion has focused on a few key figures, actually there were many French physicians and pharmacists who were bewitched by pharmacological promise of hashish. Certainly, during the 1840s and 1850s numerous articles were published about the benefits of cannabis. Indeed, as Guba has noted, 'the first mention of hashish in nineteenth-century medical literature appeared in *Histoire médicale de l'Armée d'Orient* (1802), a collection of first-hand accounts of the medical challenges faced by the French Army of the Orient during their Egyptian campaign between the summers of 1789 and 1801.'[179]

While it would be unhelpful to trawl through all these discussions, it is worth making a few comments about Aubert-Roche's discussion of cannabis in *De la peste ou typhus d'Orient*. Firstly, as we have seen, it clearly betrays the influence of de Sacy's work.[180] 'I had learned from M. de Sacy and other authors that there existed in the East a hemp-like plant ... M. de Sacy gave it the name of hashish.'[181] Essentially, de Sacy's narrative, as well as other Orientalist notions about the instability of the Arab mind, effectively linked hashish with the violence of the Assassins. This, in turn, suggested to Aubert-Roche that cannabis was 'a substance that had a significant impact on the central nervous system'.[182] Again, from the outset, cannabis in nineteenth-century French medicine was rooted in an Orientalist discourse of profanation. Guba makes this point very persuasively.

> In the early 1800s, French doctors wrote about hashish as an Oriental intoxicant and routinely emplotted the drug within a fictionalized narrative of Muslim and Arab savagery. These pharmacists and physicians almost always pulled from Silvestre de Sacy's Assassin's myth as a key thread in this tapestry. And with each citation they further concretized de Sacy's argument concerning the etymological and physical connection between assassination and hashish as a baseline for understanding the medicinal potential of the 'Oriental' drug.[183]

Having said that, like O'Shaughnessy, Aubert-Roche became convinced that, regardless of its danger, cannabis 'may well become very useful in medicine'. Hence, he insisted, 'it is a drug not to be neglected.'[184] Indeed, to alleviate any fears that his patients might have about the profane effects of cannabis, he stated that, should he find himself in the unfortunate position of being a plague victim, he would not hesitate to reach for hashish. Moreover, he had himself witnessed the recovery of eleven patients in the hospitals of Alexandria and Cairo to whom cannabis had been administered as a confection called *dawamesc* taken with a good cup of coffee.[185] His hope was that, like him, 'those who experience it will recognize its therapeutic value against the plague and other diseases.'[186] Indeed, in commending cannabis, Aubert-Roche believed that he was providing a valuable service to 'humanity and science'. Of course, there is no question that, on the one hand, the legend of Ḥasan-e Ṣabbāḥ, particularly as told by de Sacy,[187] tainted the perception of hashish in the nineteenth century. However, the key argument here is that Aubert-Roche, Clot-Bey, O'Shaughnessy, Willemin and others began a process that had the effect of subverting discourses of profanation and encouraging a reassessment of cannabis as a social good.

Intoxication and insanity

Arguably the most important figure in the history of medicinal cannabis during the nineteenth century was Aubert-Roche's friend, the psychiatrist Jacques-Joseph Moreau de Tours.[188] In his ground-breaking 1845 book, *Du Hachisch et de l'Aliénation mentale. Études psychologiques*[189] – translated as *Hashish and Mental Illness*[190] – he argued that cannabis offered enormous potential for the study and treatment of mental illness. Hence, unlike Auber-Roche's *De la peste ou typhus d'Orient*, which was published several years before, it is a book about mental health, rather than epidemiology. It is also distinguished by its emphasis on subjective experience and self-dosing: 'personal experience is the criterion of truth here. I challenge the right of anyone to discuss the effects of hashish if he is not speaking for himself and if he has not been in a position to evaluate them in the light of sufficient repeated use.'[191] Indeed, Moreau insisted that, 'to understand an ordinary depression, it is necessary to have experienced one; to comprehend the ravings of a madman, it is necessary to have raved oneself, but without having lost the awareness of one's madness, without having lost the power to evaluate one's psychic changes occurring in the mind.'[192]

It is this methodological focus on personal experience that drew him to experiment with cannabis. Not only does it induce altered states of consciousness that are of a similar character to insanity, but it does so in a way that leaves the consciousness intact, thereby enabling observation from within. There is also a certain clarity to the experience, which is not always the case during intoxication with other psychoactives. He knew this because he had also explored the therapeutic potential of a number of other drugs, including, in 1841, the dissociative hallucinogen *Datura stramonium*.[193] Hence, he soon settled on *Cannabis indica* as his drug of choice. Indeed, not only can he be considered the first 'alienist'[194] to record clinical experiments with hashish,[195] but he is sometimes considered to be the first researcher in the history of psychiatry with a general, experimental interest in psychopharmacology.[196] Having said that, this is not entirely true, for we know from comments in, for example, Alphonse Karr's *Le Livre De Bord*,[197] that some psychiatrists, such as Alexandre Brière de Boismont and Jean Etienne Dominique Esquirol (both of whom will be discussed below), attended sessions organized by Stéphane Ajasson de Grandsagne, who, although not a psychiatrist, promoted the experimental study of hashish.[198] In a very similar way to what Moreau would later do at *Le Club des Hachichins* (discussed in the next chapter), Ajasson observed the behaviour of friends and colleagues under the influence of hashish. Nevertheless, Moreau's theory and approach to psychopharmacological research can be considered pioneering. However, before looking a more closely at this research, it will be helpful to provide a few details about the psychiatric context which helped to shape Moreau's thinking.

Moreau was born on 2 June (or possibly 3 June[199]) 1804, in the small village of Montrésor about thirty miles from Tours. Although the forename written on his birth certificate is 'Jacques', he preferred 'Joseph'. But, because he was required to use his birth name on official documents, he either added a second 'J' or simply wrote both names in full. As to the toponym 'de Tours', this was possibly adopted as a tribute to the institution where he began his career under the guidance of his esteemed mentor, Pierre-Fidèle Bretonneau, from whom he learned the importance of close observation and personal experience in psychiatric research. That said, although he dedicated his doctoral thesis to Bretonneau,[200] it is conspicuously influenced by Esquirol – to whom he would later dedicate his book on cannabis.[201] On 6 July 1826, thanks to a recommendation from Bretonneau, he began an internship at the Charenton asylum in Paris under the watchful eye of Esquirol, who had become the asylum's director.

Esquirol had been the favourite student of the pioneering physician Philippe Pinel at Salpêtrière Hospital. This is significant because Pinel was an important figure in shifting the focus of modern psychiatry from understanding insanity as a social problem to treating it as a medical problem. Central to this shift was the development of what became known as *traitement morale*. 'I ... discovered,' declared Pinel, 'that insanity was curable in many instances, by mildness of treatment and attention to the state of the mind exclusively, and when coercion was indispensable, that it might be very effectually applied without corporal indignity.'[202] Again, concerning medication, Pinel insisted on the careful and judicious use of drugs, 'for, in diseases of the mind, as well as in all other ailments, it is an art of no little importance to administer medicines properly; but, it is an art of much greater and more difficult acquisition to know when to suspend or altogether omit them.'[203] This patient-centred approach had a formative impact on the work of Esquirol, as is evident at Charenton, in that he implemented a more enlightened, humane, case-study informed method of treating the mentally unwell. His aim was to increase self-control and enable a slow adjustment to the demands of everyday life.

Pinel and Esquirol were not alone in their concern to develop a humane approach to the care of the mentally ill. In 1792, towards the end of the period that Michel Foucault refers to as 'the great confinement' (mid-seventeenth century to around 1800),[204] the Quaker tea merchant William Tuke began building the York Retreat in Britain. When it finally opened its doors in 1796, it was evident that life for the insane was going to be very different. Apart from much else, corporal punishment was prohibited and chains were not, as a rule, used to restrain patients. It was an altogether more comfortable and compassionate environment for the mentally vulnerable. Treatment was based on personalised attention and therapeutic care, the aim being to restore the self-esteem and self-control of patients. Indeed, it was Tuke's son Samuel who popularized the term 'moral treatment'. That said, as Foucault has argued, while life for the insane was certainly improved, these were still institutions within which individuals were sequestered away from friends, family, and the rest of society.[205] Moreover, separation was not just physical, but categorical, in that patients became a different class of people. While Foucault's argument is provocative, sweeping and the details are a little inaccurate in some respects, it is, nevertheless, an important observation. Indeed, as the nineteenth century progressed and as asylums became bigger and patients more numerous, so therapy gave way, all too easily, to custody. Patients became problems to be contained and medicated. Nevertheless, overall, care of the insane was improved and the implementation of *traitement morale* provided the ideal medical context for the type of research that Moreau would become interested in.

On Pinel's death in 1826, Esquirol became the most influential alienist in France and Charenton became known as *l'Hôpital Esquirol*. As Rafael Huertas has noted, he became 'an outstanding reformer of asylum institutions in post-revolutionary France. His effort in introducing the Law on Alienated Persons of 1838 is, unquestionably, one of his major contributions to the history of psychiatric care.'[206] Also in 1838, he published *Des maladies mentales*, 'the first *modern* textbook on psychiatry',[207] which is significant in a number of respects, not least because it introduces the term 'hallucination'[208] into psychiatric literature, describing it as 'a thorough conviction of the perception of a sensation, when no external object, suited to excite this sensation, has impressed the senses'.[209] Again, with reference to certain practices in ancient Greece and, more recently, in Britain, he argued for the importance of therapeutic travel:

> the ancients prescribed travelling ... The English now send their melancholics into the southern provinces of France, into Italy, and even into the colonies. I have always observed that the insane are relieved by a long voyage ... Travelling acts ... by exciting all the assimilative functions. It promotes sleep, the appetite and secretions ... Such are the agents which exercise a direct influence over the brain, and consequently over the intellectual and moral disorders of the insane.[210]

Hence, as well as prescribing regimens that would distract his less affluent patients (such as knitting and gardening), for those who could afford it, he prescribed therapeutic tourism around Europe, Asia and North Africa.[211] All of this had a profound influence on a Moreau's development as a psychiatrist with an interest in psychoactive substances. Indeed, it was while he was a travelling companion of one of Esquirol's wealthy patients that Moreau became interested in the potential offered by hashish. Keen to experience all he could, not only did he relish travel, but he immersed himself in the cultures of the countries he visited. As Bo Holmstedt has commented, 'travel ... became a necessity for Moreau. He ... was young and had no desire to settle down, he longed to see foreign countries ... The young Moreau wished to learn and profit as much as possible from what he saw and heard, and for this reason he adopted the dress and the customs of the countries he passed though.'[212] This, we will see, included hashish intoxication.

While Moreau was greatly indebted to Esquirol, he was not an uncritical mentee.[213] He questioned his approach to *traitement morale* and particularly disagreed with the ideas of another member of Esquirol's circle, namely Brière de Boismont.[214] Indeed, eventually he and Moreau came to represent two opposing camps in the early understanding of mental illness: the 'physiologists' and the 'psychologists' (or, as they were sometimes termed, the 'spiritualists'[215]). While they shared a number of presuppositions, including contemporary Orientalist constructions of cannabis intoxication, they disagreed over the root cause of insanity. For Brière de Boismont, as Guba has commented, 'mental illness was not solely a physiological phenomenon but also and more often a disorder of one's moral and spiritual constitution.' This understanding directly contradicted that of Moreau 'who understood mental illness as a physiological phenomenon rooted in the organic process of the brain understood as an organ and not as a scientifically repackaged soul …'[216] While they 'shared an Orientalist perception of hashish that equated its psychotropic effects with the irrational violence supposedly at the core of the Arabo-Muslim soul, their opposing medical philosophies assigned contrasting medicinal properties to the drug.'[217] Indeed, their distinct interpretations of hashish fell on each side of the sacred-profane divide. For Moreau, like Auber-Roche, it offered enormous potential for him to serve humanity and science. For Brière de Boismont, it offered nothing good to humanity and science, leading only to insanity and violence. As such, it should be legislated against as a dangerous substance.

Central to Brière de Boismont's conception of mental illness was an older belief in its metaphysical origin. While, of course, madness had already, as Foucault has discussed, taken root in the world of morality,[218] Brière de Boismont, a rationalist Christian, was keen to incorporate this explanatory relationship into modern medicine. As such, his work is a good example of, following Foucault, the transition from the 'classical age' (seventeenth and eighteenth centuries, when madness was perceived as 'unreason' and when the insane were locked up with criminals and other moral deviants) to the 'modern era'.[219] Like the blasphemers, prostitutes, thieves, and murderers with whom the insane frequently shared their cells, in the classical age they were considered responsible agents who had chosen the path against truth and reason. Again, the argument was moral, even theological, but not medical. It is this transitional psychiatric context which is so clearly demonstrated in the work of Brière de Boismont.[220] He was motivated by the belief that he needed to safeguard the relationship between medical science and traditional Christian dogma regarding the spirituality of the soul and moral freedom.[221] This is clear from the outset in his influential 1845 study of hallucinations, *Des hallucinations ou histoire raisonnée des apparitions, des visions, des songes, de l'extase, du magnétisme et du somnambulisme*.[222] While one may be able to trace hallucinations back to physical causes, actually, he argued, these are 'secondary', in that 'the first causes of hallucinations must be sought for in the violation of some great principle, in the erroneous direction of ideas, and by consequence in the abnormal production of their perceptible signs'.[223] Indeed, he asks, 'does not the analysis of the different kinds of delirium present a solid and experimental foundation to metaphysics? Is not the study of mysticism an indispensable preparation to the study of derangement …?'[224] For Brière de Boismont, psychiatry is an examination of 'the most profound mysteries of the soul'. It is 'a ceaseless examination of those high spiritual questions which are declared useless in medicine'. Consequently, 'religious dogmas, history, philosophy, morality, are intimately connected with its study.'[225] So, while he did not consider his work to be theological *per se*, he did assure his readers that it is 'full of respect for the creeds which have thrown so bright a refulgence on the world, to which humanity owes its greatest conquests, and which can alone save it from the abyss...'[226]

Furthermore, Brière de Boismont's work fed into an important nineteenth-century debate regarding the problematic link between madness and civilization.[227] Essentially, his argument was that insanity occurs more frequently and its manifestations are more diverse in civilized societies.'[228] Driven by theologically informed prejudice, he insisted that the development of Western civilization had generated 'a climate of individualism, scepticism, opulence, and idleness favouring the emergence of all kinds of moral and mental disorders.'[229] This is important because it informed his understanding of hashish. Bearing in mind that his thinking was shaped by Orientalism,[230] it is unsurprising that he questioned its medicinal value.[231] For Brière de Boismont there was a clear link between cannabis intoxication and 'a psychological "error of reason" rooted in the religious fanaticism of Islam and the inherent barbarism of the Arab world.'[232] Hence, in opposition to those physiologists, such as Moreau, who sought to develop cannabis-based therapies, he argued that it was a profane influence that exacerbated mental illness. For example, he noted that 'several lunatics in the hospital at Cairo ... had lost their reason simply from the use of haschisch.'[233] He concluded his argument by stating that 'a prolonged indulgence in this drug must necessarily have a fatal effect on the health'. Even 'the momentary loss of reason', which recreational users experience during intoxication, 'although it be intentional, presents but a melancholy spectacle.'[234] Hence, he effectively demonized the drug, linking it to a range of social evils, especially violence. For example, he tells us that 'a frightful scene occurred on the 30th May, on board the Empress, a packet-ship ... on the run from Trebizond to Constantinople.' Amongst the passengers, there were

> two Afghan dervishes of Candahar. At three in the afternoon, their prayers being concluded, the dervishes were seized with a paroxysm of frenzy, the consequences of which were terrible. In an instant, they had shot a young Greek, stabbed an Armenian and Lloyd's agent from Trebizond. Six other passengers were more or less dangerously wounded. Finally, by order of the captain, the sailors killed the dervishes with the bayonet.[235]

His point is that 'they commenced their carnage without provocation' and 'from the report of several passengers, it appears certain that they had become intoxicated with haschisch.'[236] Hence, again, in a respectful, but direct challenge to Moreau, Brière de Boismont concluded that the use of cannabis and other psychoactive drugs in psychiatry exacerbated mental instability and, as such, prevented the insane from fully adjusting to everyday life in civilized societies.[237] Psychiatry should 'focus on restoring one's moral and social constitution via a *"traitment morale,"* rather than on pharmaceuticals aimed at homoeopathically stimulating the central nervous system into normal function.'[238] Moreau, of course, fundamentally disagreed.

Following the successful defence of his thesis on 9 June 1830, Esquirol invited Moreau to accompany one of his patients to Switzerland and Italy for around twelve months during 1831 and 1832. A second trip of eleven months, from late 1836 until the end of 1837, took him to Malta, Smyrna, Cairo, Constantinople and Beirut.[239] Incorporating research into his trip,[240] as well as visiting a number of asylums, he began his study of hashish. 'Since my travels in the Orient, I have steadfastly pursued a serious study of the effects of hashish.'[241]

On Moreau's return to France, Esquirol supported his application for a position as an attending physician at the Hospitals of Bicêtre and La Salpêtrière in Paris. Moreover, it's worth noting that, in 1842, he travelled to the small Belgium town of Geel, which had become associated with the veneration of Dymphna, the patron saint of mental illness and anxiety. Since the Middle Ages, pilgrims suffering with poor mental health made their way to Geel in search of help.[242] Although the clergy and their assistants did what they could for the pilgrims, and even extended their premises to accommodate them, eventually they found themselves unable to cope with the numbers arriving. Consequently, here, in this small town, psychiatric care was gradually de-institutionalized as, incredibly, Geel's inhabitants began inviting the mentally unwell into their own homes and caring for them. Over time they became part of the community, contributing when and where they could. This began a pioneering tradition of psychiatric care. Moreau, of course, was fascinated by this approach, as Esquirol had been before him. Furthermore, we have seen that he had become convinced that it was important for the alienist to live among the mentally ill in order to understand them more intimately.[243] Indeed, this humane approach galvanized his opposition to a popular interpretation of moral treatment defended by his fellow physician at Bicêtre, François Leuret. While the chains had been removed, as noted above, they were still imprisoned, institutionalized, and subjected to disciplinary measures as part of their treatment. This was very different from what Moreau had seen at Geel. He was particularly concerned that, in Paris, some of the treatment was coercive, such as the threat of cold showers to encourage patients to renounce their delusions. According to this approach, once patients acquiesced and acknowledged that their experiences were delusional, they were declared sane. For Moreau, such treatment was blunt, cruel, and often ineffective. Hence, influenced by his experiences at Geel and intrigued by what he had witnessed in the Orient, he began to explore new treatment regimens and new ways to research mental illness. It was arguably this rethinking that galvanized his commitment to the study of hashish as a method of understanding mental illness.

While it's not entirely clear when Moreau first came across hashish, as indicated above, it was probably in 1836, during his second trip accompanying patients from Charenton.[244] Certainly, he experienced its widespread use in Egypt. As he reported, not only do 'almost all Moslems eat hashish', but 'a very great number of them are addicted to it'.[245] Moreover, as Holmstedt notes, there is clear evidence that he tried hashish himself on his second trip, since his 'in his travel reports he writes rather lyrically about "pleasures impossible to interpret" which this "marvellous substance" brings about and which "would be impossible to describe to anybody who has not experienced it."'[246] Having said that, in *Du Hachisch et de l'Aliénation mentale*, he seems to suggest that he himself had not experienced it until December 1841.

> In 1841 ... [on] Thursday, December 5, I had taken hashish, and I knew the effects, *not from experience* but because a person who had visited the Orient had told me

about them, and I quietly awaited the happy delirium that was supposed to seize me. I sat at the table, and I cannot add, as some people do, 'after having relished this delicious paste,' because to me it tasted horrible. I swallowed it with great effort.[247]

The account continues in this vein, becoming increasingly fantastical. Indeed, it is difficult to avoid the conclusion that, not only was Moreau inexperienced, but that he employed a degree of dramatic license in order both to engage his readers and also to establish a link with the experience of mania. Having said that, it also needs to be borne in mind that he almost certainly consumed larger quantities than would be normal today. Again, as noted in the first chapter, edibles deliver a higher dose of THC than smoked cannabis and the body processes it differently. As he noted, 'a dosage the size of a walnut, about 30g of *dawamesc*, is necessary to attain some results. With half or even a quarter of that amount, one feels more or less elated and may be inclined to laughter. It is only with a much larger dose that the results known in the Middle East by the Italian term *fantasia* can be obtained.'[248] Whether or not he exaggerated its effects, it is clear that he opted for the 'much larger dose'.

> Bursting into laughter, I left the dining room. Soon I felt the need to hear and make music; I sat down at the piano, and I began to play an air from *Black Domino*. I interrupted myself after several measures because a truly diabolic spectacle greeted my eyes: I thought I saw the image of my brother standing atop the piano. He stirred and presented a forked tail, all black and ending with three lanters, one red, one green, and one white. This apparition presented itself to me several times in the course of the evening. 'Why,' I suddenly cried, 'do you nail down my limbs? I feel as if I am turning into lead. Oh, I am so heavy!' They took my hands to raise me, and I fell heavily to the ground. I kneeled in the manner of Moslems, saying, 'My father, I accuse myself, etc.,' as though I were starting confession. They picked me up and I underwent a sudden change. I picked up a little stove with which to dance the polka ... Then a frightening thing happened to me: I choked, I suffocated, I fell into an immense, bottomless shaft, the well of Bicêtre.[249] Like a drowning man who seeks his salvation in a feeble reed that eludes him, so I wanted to clutch the stones that encircled the well. But they fell with me into that bottomless abyss. This sensation was painful, but it did not last long, before I cried, 'I am falling down a shaft,' and my friends brought me back to the room I had just left.[250]

Again, it's important to understand that these records were a central part of his research. Indeed, the very fact that he was able to record his experiences, which could then be studied when he was in a more sober frame of mind was important. As Holmstedt has commented, hashish was a valuable research tool because of its ability 'to keep intact "consciousness and the innermost feeling" of the user.' As such 'he could analyze all his impressions and still be aware of the disorganization of his mental faculties.'[251] Furthermore, he also invited colleagues and friends to record his words, acts, gestures, and facial expressions during intoxication. Everything about the hashish experience was documented. Furthermore, as well as self-dosing, Moreau also used his students as guinea pigs, most of whom, no doubt, did not complain.

What did Moreau learn from his states of intoxication? A key conclusion concerned the origin and pathogenesis of insanity.

> We shall see ... that when the effects of hashish are revealed in organic troubles ... it transpires that these effects are completely analogous to those reported by mental patients who have been able to study and follow the development of their illness from its inception. Mental patients and users of hashish express themselves similarly when they want to convey what they have experienced. It seems as if they had all been under the same morbid influence.[252]

Because he was convinced that hashish had given him access to an under researched region of the psyche, which other 'so-called scientists' had avoided by relegating it to 'the ill-defined area of metaphysics',[253] he was in a position to investigate the development of insanity. In other words, he was convinced that cannabis was psychotomimetic. Indeed, he went so far as to insist that 'there is not a single, elementary manifestation of mental illness that cannot be found in the mental changes caused by hashish, from simple manic excitement to frenzied delirium, from the feeblest impulse, the simplest fixation, to the merest injury to the senses, to the most irresistible drive, the wildest delirium, the most varied disorders of feelings'.[254] Hence, again, in hashish, Moreau had discovered an invaluable psychiatric research tool, in that it enabled him to induce, control, and observe the early stages of insanity: 'I saw in hashish, or rather in its effect upon the mental faculties, a significant means of exploring the genesis of mental illness. I was convinced that it could solve the enigma of mental illness and lead to the hidden source of the mysterious disorder we call "*madness*."'[255] Up until this point in the history of medicine, what he calls the '*fait primordial*' (the 'primary fact')[256] of insanity had been inaccessible: 'this primitive, necessary source of the fundamental components of delirium has completely eluded the observation of our predecessors.'[257] Hashish changed all that. 'I had only to transfer the main characteristics of delirium to those of hashish intoxication and to apply to my study the insights gathered from self-observation.'[258]

As to what he discovered by means of this novel method of investigation, firstly, he claimed that cannabis intoxication had confirmed to him that 'the dispositions of the mind which make a man different from others by the originality of his thoughts and conceptions and by superior intelligence stem from the same organic conditions that may give rise to insanity'.[259] Secondly, he was, therefore, 'able to go back to the origin of the phenomenon of delirium'.[260] Thirdly, this led him to the conclusion that 'all forms, all occurrences of delirium or of actual madness, all fixations, hallucinations, irresistible impulses, and so forth, owe their origin to a primary mental change, identical in all cases, that is evidently the essential condition of their existence'.[261] But, what was this 'primary change', this 'initial intellectual modification' that could be stimulated by hashish and that also seemed to be evident in the early stages of mental illness? '*C'est l'excitation maniaque.*'[262] That is to say, insanity has its roots in a basic 'manic excitement', which can be understood as a type of 'disaggregation' of ideas, a 'disintegration, a veritable dissolution of that mental structure known as the mental faculties'.[263] As a result of the self-administration of hashish, he was now in a position to describe this experience as 'similar to what happens when a substance undergoes the solvent action of another substance: the separation, the isolation of ideas and molecules that formed a harmonious and complete whole when they were united'.[264] Although he recognized that being high is not precisely the same as being insane, not least because the experience passes after a short period of time, nevertheless, during intoxication he was immersed in a disorienting psychosis: 'every kind of dream-creature passed through my fantasies: goatsuckers, fiddle-faddle beasts, buddled goslings, unicorns, griffons, incubi, an entire menagerie of monstrous nightmares fluttered, hopped, skipped, and squeaked through the room'.[265] As he gradually adjusted to this hashish heterotopia, he clearly felt that he had entered a world that would have been familiar to his patients. Hence, whereas he had once tried to understand their accounts of delusions from an etic perspective, as a detached observer, he could now understand them from an emic perspective. He was, for a short period of time, an insider. He had experienced madness.

This brings us to the fourth conclusion that Moreau reached as a result of hashish intoxication, namely that delirium and dreaming are actually the same states of consciousness. His experiences led him 'to postulate, for delirium in general, a psychological nature, not only analogous, but *absolutely identical* to a dream-state'. This identity, 'which eludes casual observation, since it cannot be seen in others, is definitely confirmed, and even *perceived*, by introspection'.[266] Indeed, on the basis of his research, he argued that 'it appears that hallucinations, like all the phenomena of delirium without exception, are derived essentially from excitement, a cerebral change which, from a psychological point of view, is identical to an ordinary dream state'.[267] What was this cerebral change? Again, *c'est l'excitation maniaque*. This is important, because he sought to provide psychiatry with 'a new vantage point from which [to] study the phenomenon of hallucinations in its totality'.[268] That said, Moreau was not the first to draw the analogy between dreams and delirium. Indeed, their *similarity* may have even been suggested to him by Esquirol, who had made the connection years before. However, the latter did not research the connection using hashish and, as such, failed to observe that delirium and the dream state are identical states. Moreover, in Moreau's hashish-induced experience of insanity, sleep, and wakefulness become confused: 'the fusion or, if you wish, the attraction established between the dream state and the waking state is so complete that one who experiences it is hardly aware of it, and when recounting his visions, he explains them as he would ordinary sensations'.[269] Essentially, his conclusion was that intoxication and delirium can be understood as types of a waking or lucid dream.

While *Du Hachisch et de l'Aliénation mentale* was popular and did much to elevate the reputation of Moreau and, indeed, hashish, it was also controversial. Some queried the existence of a *fait primordial*, some questioned his claim that the dream state and delirium were identical, and yet others were concerned about the physical and moral consequences of cannabis use. Brière de Boismont was, of course particularly critical:

> we do not coincide more now than we formerly did in the opinion of our honourable brother on the primordial fact of the delirium which he calls maniacal

excitement, and on the absolute identity of the physiological nature of delirium with the dream state. Without confounding all our ideas of the value of words, it is difficult to give the name of maniacal excitement to the condition of a man who, having a false idea or sensation, appreciates them at their just value, and yet is unable to escape their influence, any more than it is possible to conceive a dream to be physiologically and psychologically identical with delirium.[270]

However, of those who were more sympathetic to Moreau's views, perhaps the most common criticism levelled at the book concerned the limited amount of case studies on which he based his conclusions. Take, for example, the editor of the *American Journal of Insanity*, Amariah Brigham, who, whilst acknowledging that the effects of cannabis seemed to be 'very remarkable', nevertheless, regretted that Moreau 'had not waited until a further trial of this remedy had enabled him to speak from that large experience which would be far more convincing than a dozen books of conjectures, and predictions of future results to be obtained from its use.' His concern was that, Moreau had focused on a small number of interesting cases along with conclusions drawn from the analysis of his own experiences: 'a small part of his work [was] occupied with the details of its effects on patients, and, in fact, he had not administered it to many.' Indeed, 'on the stupid and demented it had no effect; on others, none that were permanent.' Hence, Brigham continued, 'in those cases in which he supposes it proved highly useful, contributing to their recovery, we do not feel at all certain that the cannabis had much to do with their restoration, as such cases, we should expect, would recover with equal rapidity without it.'[271] Having said that, Brigham was impressed enough with Moreau's work to do a little research himself:

> Desirous of testing the efficacy of this remedy in cases of insanity, we procured ... about two ounces of the pure extract direct from Calcutta. Most of this we have used in the Lunatic Asylum at Utica, in doses varying from one to six grains. From our limited experience we regard it as a very energetic remedy, and well worthy of further trial with the insane, and thank M. Moreau for having called attention to its use.[272]

While Moreau's impact on medical science may have been negligible,[273] and while the overall inconclusiveness of his findings almost certainly denied him the prestigious Montyon Prize for medicine in 1846,[274] his influence on nineteenth-century cannabis culture was significant. As we will see in the next chapter, beginning in 1842, he organised a series of monthly sessions at the Hôtel de Pimodan on the Île Saint Louis in Paris, during which he and a number of eminent thinkers would enjoy a little *dawamesc* and discuss the significance of their experiences.

It should also be noted that, although Moreau was principally concerned with research into mental illness, he was also interested in the use of hashish for the treatment of certain diseases, notably rabies and cholera. Indeed, Edmond DeCourtive, one of his most promising interns at Bicêtre, even noted, rather presciently, its potential for the alleviation of symptoms and the improvement of the quality of life during the terminal stages of cancer.[275]

Finally, while Moreau's influence in the area of psychopharmacology was truncated, for several decades following the publication of his 1845 book *Du Hachisch et de l'Aliénation*, it was unrivalled.[276] During this period, almost a hundred articles were published in French medical and scientific journals, many of which referenced his work. Moreover, several French doctoral theses betraying the influence of his ideas were submitted for examination.[277] The first such thesis was *Haschish: Étude historique, chimique et physiologique* by DeCourtive,[278] who had been encouraged to explore the properties of hashish by Moreau.[279] Having read *Du Hachisch et de l'Aliénation mentale* – which, he notes, 'caused a great sensation in the medical and literary world'[280] – he became fascinated with the therapeutic potential of cannabis. This is not to say that its profane reputation didn't worry him. It did. Nevertheless, supported by Moreau, he became convinced that its mysterious endogenous Oriental energy could be harnessed by the superior exogenous power of occidental medicine. This is evident in an account of an experience he had under the influence of the drug in which he revealed his understanding of its potential, as well as betraying his estimation of his own pharmacological brilliance in harnessing its power. As Guba notes, he recalls:

> having a 'waking dream' in which he attended his *soutenance*, or thesis defence, intoxicated on hashish as a means, of course, of demonstrating the drug's 'marvels.' Before morphing into lizards (and one into a glass orb), his committee members expressed outraged at his assertions, but were soon bowled over by the rush of students and international scholars who entered the hall to express their congratulations on his findings and his 'great contribution to humanity.' After the European admirers rushed the hall, a group of Chinese entered to 'acknowledge that opium had produced nothing so marvellous as hashish ...'[281]

In this hallucinated doctoral examination, the profane is transformed into the sacred; the demonized, exotic intoxicant becomes the wonder drug; the student is lauded and the drug is celebrated.

In DeCourtive's actual thesis, which he successfully defended at the École Spéciale de Pharmacie de Paris on 11 April 1848, Orientalist discourse is conspicuous. He even included a short history of the 'Haschaschins', which, leaning heavily on the work of Marco Polo and de Sacy, describes them as 'frenzied absolutists and servile executioners'.[282] Unsurprisingly, therefore, throughout the thesis cannabis is treated as 'a dangerous and exotic intoxicant whose provenance is the darkest elements of the Muslim world'.[283] Consequently, DeCourtive understood his work in terms of a civilizing/sacalizing project. He wanted to draw out the active ingredient, 'pure hashish', in order to sanitize it, control it and introduce it into Western medicine. On the one hand, he argued, 'it is easy to conceive how important it is not to introduce into therapeutics suspicious preparations ... which are not well known'; on the other hand, 'medicine must willingly accept with passion pure hashish. I thus seek to naturalize *Cannabis indica* among us, without prejudice to the less psychoactive, but still precious *Cannabis sativa*, as these substances can render great services to humanity.'[284] This last point is an important one. *Cannabis sativa*, which is grown in the West, is related to *Cannabis indica*, which is grown in the East. The latter is more psychoactive than the former, but they are both the same species. This, as Guba has noted, 'went against the grain of established botany', which tended to divide them into two distinct species.[285] As Antoine Lieutaud reminded his readers in 1850, *Cannabis indica*, had, until recently been 'mistakenly viewed as a distinct species from our ordinary hemp'.[286] This is significant because it was a mistake rooted more in culture than in botany. It was a binary that, as Guba has commented, 'firmly posited cannabis as medicine on the wrong side of the occidental/Orient civilizational divide'.[287] That is to say, it was commonly accepted that the strong psychoactive plant used to make potent hashish was distinct from the utilitarian plant used to make rope. By demonstrating that both plants can be used to alter consciousness, DeCourtive believed that he could neutralize much of the Western prejudice against the cannabis. As we have seen, he didn't object to the Orientalist demonization of *Cannabis indica*. He simply argued that its relationship to *Cannabis sativa* required a revision of its status in Western societies. It wasn't irredeemably profane. It was simply a more potent variety of *Cannabis sativa* that had adapted to a warmer climate. As such, it could be subdued and controlled by Western medical science. Moreover, he argued that, while the Orient is undoubtedly savage and unchristian, it is not all bad. In fact, it is well known as 'the cradle of humanity'.[288] Hence, we should not be surprised if we discover Oriental substances with significant medicinal value – even if they do need to be civilized and regulated.

In the final analysis, however, such arguments gradually lost their cogency. As the nineteenth century drew to a close, the conclusions of Brière de Boismont and other naysayers gained ascendency over those of Auber-Roche, Moreau and DeCourtive. The culture changed and as it did the healing herb became, again, the 'Devil's weed'.

Epidemiology, pharmacology, and the demonization of cannabis in the nineteenth century

Even during the decades of the mid-nineteenth century, when the scientific gaze led to a gradual acceptance of cannabis within and beyond the medical community, it was never entirely culturally disinfected. As we have seen, it continued to be freighted with centuries of negative Orientalist baggage. There was always a suspicion that it contained the seeds of moral turpitude. It was only the civilizing influence of Western science that protected its users from profanation. Of course, everyday recreational users had no such protection. They risked exposing themselves to a mysterious and dark Oriental energy. Hence, when cannabis was eventually discredited by the medical profession, it became detached from the civilizing discourses of Western science.

An initial problem that faced nineteenth-century pharmacologists was the elusiveness of the standardized dose.[289] Of course, this wasn't the only problem that cannabis faced, and hashish wasn't the only drug that faced the problem,[290] but it was an important issue. '*Cannabis indica*', observed the American psychiatrist George Beard, 'has the reputation of untrustworthiness and unreliability, both of preparation and of action.'[291] While it wasn't too demanding for a medical professional to weigh a gobbet of *dawamesc*, the problem was that the strength of the gobbet could not be regulated. Both Moreau and Aubert-Roche frequently expressed frustration over their inability to control the potency of the drug, which seemed to fluctuate from one consignment to the next. One dose of hashish gently lifted the user's mood, while the next induced vivid hallucinations and paranoia. This problem was significantly exacerbated by the fact that imported hashish was not always pure. Indeed, it was not uncommon for it to be infused with opium, *Datura*, or even Spanish fly/*Cantharides* (*Lytta vesicatoria*), which, needless to say, could modify the psychoactive impact considerably. Consequently, much effort was put into refining hashish and isolating its psychoactive ingredient.[292] Indeed, this was one of the tasks with which DeCourtive was charged by Moreau at Bicêtre. However, as we now know, in the final analysis, it was a task that would remain uncompleted for another century. As noted in the first chapter, it was not until the early 1940s that the American chemist Roger Adams first identified and synthesized CBD and demonstrated its relationship to cannabinol (CBN) and THC.[293] Moreover, it would be another two decades before delta-9-THC, the chemical principally responsible for its psychoactive effects, was isolated by the Israeli chemists Raphael Mechoulam and Yechiel Gaoni.[294]

While cannabis research was hampered by its entanglement in Orientalist prejudice during the nineteenth century, nevertheless, small but significant steps were made by DeCourtive in Paris, by O'Shaughnessy in Calcutta, and by the brothers Thomas and Henry Smith in their laboratory at 21 Duke Street, Edinburgh. Of particular note was the Smiths' isolation of an enriched material they called 'cannabine'.[295] The process of production is described by them in some detail and concludes as follows:

> The resin is brown in mass, but of a fawn colour, in thin layers. Heated on a platinum foil ... melts into a liquid, takes fire, burns with a bright white flame, and disappears entirely. Two-thirds of a grain acts upon ourselves as a powerful narcotic, and one grain [i.e. *c.* 65 mg] produces complete intoxication. In this character it is quite analogous to alcohol, but in its hypnotic and soothing effects on the nervous system, its resemblance to morphia is very great ... One experiment of ours shows that the peculiar action of hemp resin on the human system is not easily destroyed, and is retained with great tenacity. We heated in the open air a dose of the resin, spread out so as to cover nearly two square inches of the bottom of an evaporating basin, at a temperature of 180° Fahr., for eight hours continuously, notwithstanding which treatment it appeared to us on trial not to have suffered the least diminution of its energy. The resin contains the whole power of the plant, which we have proved by taking a quantity of the plant equivalent to a dose of the resin. We could observe no difference in the strength of the action.[296]

Unfortunately, the consistent duplication of these results proved somewhat elusive. Nevertheless, their research in the 1830s and 1840s contributed to the increase of interest in medicinal cannabis and their formula for 'cannabine', which was translated into French in 1846,[297] is cited in DeCourtive's thesis.[298]

So invested were a growing number of researchers in the pharmacological potential of cannabis during this period that, inevitably, there was competition. This is particularly evident in French literature. For example, in the 1850 edition of the popular pharmaceutical directory *L'Officine, ou Répertoire générale de pharmacie pratique*, the Parisian pharmacist François Dorvault[299] argued that, 'while a Scot and Irishman broke new ground, it was truly the French pharmacists who perfected and simplified the process.'[300] Although, with the benefit of hindsight, this is debateable, at the time the competition to produce standardized doses was fierce. This competitiveness reached its apotheosis in what became known as 'L'affaire Gastinel'. In 1847, the *Bulletin de l'Académie nationale de médicine* reported a claim made by the French pharmacist Gastinel, who, we have seen, was working in Cairo with Clot-Bey. His claim was made in a letter to the French consulate in Cairo, which was subsequently forwarded to the Académie Nationale de Médicine in Paris. He argued that he had finally done what others could not do, namely isolate the active alkaloid in hashish. This had, he believed, enabled him to make a powerful hashish tincture – which he called 'haschischine' – that could be administered in standardized doses. Unfortunately for Gastinel, the Académie Nationale de Médicine disagreed. It concluded that his claims suffered from a conspicuous lack of evidence and, indeed, did not seem to be particularly original. More tellingly, he was unable to produce a sample of his tincture for examination. The judgment of the Académie Nationale de Médicine was unequivocal. Not only had he 'confined himself to only words ... giving no evidence', but, it was pointed out that 'in England, churrus, hashish, alcohol extracts, pure resin, volatile oil, all have already undergone numerous experiments. Has M. Gastinel advanced the state of research? We do not see it.'[301] Not only was Gastinel displeased by this decision, but he was incensed by the largely positive reviews DeCourtive's thesis had received in France. It was he, not DeCourtive, who had broken new ground in cannabis research: 'I think it necessary to demand from the Academy a priority which I think was sufficiently established, for it has been about a year since my discovery was registered here at the Consulate of France and transmitted to the Ministry of Foreign Affairs, where it could be found if necessary.' He continued, 'knowing for a long time the powerful action which hashish exercises over the nervous system, I foresaw the whole course which medicine might derive from it in the treatment of severe neuroses.'[302]

Without unpacking the details of the Gastinel Affair, the point here is simply that, although for a short period during the nineteenth century, cannabis was believed to offer modern medicine enormous potential, much of this belief was based on conspicuously slight evidence. Consequently, not only did the quest to produce a standardized version of this new 'heroic remedy' become highly competitive, but it failed.

Furthermore, it's interesting to note that, as part of the process to produce a Western medicine from Oriental raw material, there was a shift away from using *dawamesc* and towards using tincture in the mid-1840s. That is to say, while not wanting to labour the point, cannabis was subjected to a process of cultural cleansing in an effort to reclassify it as a safe medicine. *Dawamesc* was a conspicuous marker of Oriental otherness, while tincture was clearly located with the fold of Western medicine. As Guba discusses, 'interconnected medical, colonial, and cultural discourses concerning hashish in 1840s France arguably produced an opportunity for the drug to establish itself among the accepted narcotics in French medicine. *The shift away from dawamesc reflects this attempt by French pharmacists and physicians in the mid- to late 1840s to legitimize hashish as an accepted narcotic in the modern pharmacist's tool kit.*'[303] The preference for tincture, while having a scientific rationale, was, more importantly, symbolic of a shift from the profane to the sacred, from Oriental chaos to occidental order. Unfortunately, as we have seen, hashish was too embedded in Orientalist discourse for this to be ultimately successful. Again, the attempt to civilize it failed.

Over time, both the struggle to standardize cannabis, to control its effects, and its Oriental otherness began to erode confidence in its value as an ingredient in medicine. Increasingly, it came to be seen as less of a wonder drug and more of a problem. However, the decisive blow to the future of cannabis in nineteenth-century medicine came during the second outbreak of cholera in Paris in 1849.[304] Prior to the outbreak, many believed that they had in their possession a medical solution. Indeed, Gastinel, in his attempt to promote his claim to be the primary cannabis researcher, reported the following:

> I have a new fact to report. You know, no doubt, that cholera is wreaking havoc here in Cairo and in many other cities of Egypt. Knowing, according to certain journals, that in India hashish was sometimes given successfully against cholera, I have communicated it, from the invasion of the epidemic, to several physicians who hastened to make use of the active principle of hashish. I can report several cases of healing ascertained through this new agent. But the remarkable case I know of is that of Dr. Willemin, a medical physician, who was nearly lost to cholera. He was torn from death by the beneficent reaction of the active principle of hashish, a reaction which probably would not have occurred without this precious excitant.[305]

Willemin, who was convalescing in Paris, personally testified that he had indeed been cured of cholera by cannabis. 'I thus believe,' declared Willemin, 'that of all the remedies proposed against cholera there are none more effective than the active principle of *Cannabis indica*.'[306] To support his case, he provided numerous lozenges and tinctures prepared by Gastinel for the Académie to test. Of course, these preparations, Gastinel believed, would also serve to force a revision of the judgment against him. He was wrong. The Académie de Médicine reasserted DeCourtive's primacy regarding the 'perfecting of cannabine in France'. Having said that, members of the Académie were so impressed by Willemin's moving testimony that they recommended cannabis to the Commission du choléra. Bearing in mind that other suggested remedies included 'the common truffle',[307] which the Académie summarily dismissed, it is also reasonable to assume that its members were desperate for a cure. In such circumstances, hashish seemed far more promising. The result was, as Guba comments, 'numerous public health practitioners and policy-makers in Paris [adopted] hashish tincture as a treatment against cholera in metropolitan France'.[308] By April 1849, almost 13,000 Parisians who had contracted the disease had been treated with cannabis tincture. However, by March, as men, women, and children died in their thousands,[309] it was becoming clear to many physicians that they might as well have administered truffles to their patients. Cannabis tincture was not the 'médicament précieux' (precious medicine), the 'remède héroïque' (heroic remedy)[310] that they had hoped it would be. As Dorvault wrote, 'during the invasion of this terrible scourge in Paris, four months ago, some doctors of the hospitals tried to use this substance according to the indications of Willemin. As the results obtained were inconclusive, *haschischine* was almost entirely put aside.'[311] While Gastinel objected, claiming that the strength of the cannabis used in Paris was insufficient, and while Willemin continued to repeat his assertion that hashish had been effective in restoring him back to rude health, it became clear that, regardless of its strength, the tincture had failed. The symptoms may have been relieved a little by cannabis, but the progress of the disease had not been halted at all. Hence, while some pharmacists continued to insist that it had potential as a medicine, most abandoned it. Indeed, in the following decades it was increasingly profaned by the medical profession as a substance that was not only ineffective against disease, but was actually toxic and, again following de Sacy, capable of inducing insanity and bouts of extreme violence.

This brings us back to the work of Brière de Boismont.[312] Even during the heyday of nineteenth-century cannabis research, there were those who expressed concern about its negative efficacy as a medicine and its positive efficacy as an agent of profanation and madness. Hence, as France emerged from the cholera epidemic with a revised understanding of the value of hashish, so Brière de Boismont's claim that 'madness is often a consequence of prolonged use of this substance'[313] began to gain support. As we have seen, he was convinced that de Sacy's account of the Assassins[314] had established a link between cannabis intoxication, Islamic violence, and insanity: 'haschisch ... occasioned ... similar phenomena to those which had been noticed in the adepts of the Old Man of the Mountain.'[315] Again, 'the individuals under the influence of haschisch felt a maniacal exaltation; ideas succeeded each other with rapidity and incoherence; it might be said, with an ebullition which raised them above the influence of the will. The mind was under the empire of hallucinations and illusions.'[316] This type of demonizing discourse eventually gained traction in both medical and political circles and continued into the twentieth century. For example, in Britain, on 16 July 1891, the Member of Parliament, Mark Stewart stood up in the House of Commons and declared that 'the lunatic asylums of India are filled with ganja smokers'.[317] Again, in 1924, the influential German pharmacologist Louis Lewin commented that, 'in the lunatic asylum in Cairo ... 60 men and 4 or 5 women owed their mental state to hashish,' some of which exhibited 'a state of violent fury' that was 'not always curable'.[318]

These culturally inscribed notions were supported by epidemiological advances during the late nineteenth century. Not the least of these was the verification of contagionism and the discovery of the bacillus *Vibrio cholerae* as the cause of cholera. Not only did it become evident that hashish was impotent against epidemics, but it was also clear that the anticontagionist thesis – which was a core part of the rationale for using the drug – was fundamentally flawed. Again, this all served to construct cannabis as a problematic substance.

To develop this point a little, it's also worth noting that, as Stephen Snelders, Charles Kaplan and Toine Pieters have argued, 'interest in cannabis was not high because the drug did not belong to the new "scientific" era of modern psychopharmacology starting in 1869. Cannabis did not look forward to the hopes of the final conquest of physiological and mental diseases by modern medicine; on the contrary, it looked backward to an ancient, obsolete medical tradition, which became regarded as the "unscientific" era of mesmerist and romantic speculations.'[319] Hence, the combination of the inability to produce standardized doses, the ineffectiveness of cannabis in the face of epidemics, the falsification of the claims made by prominent pharmacists and physicians, the Orientalist demonization of hashish, and its relationship to premodern medicine, all served to undermine interest in it as a modern drug. Furthermore, as noted above, unlike opiates, because cannabis is a not a water-soluble drug it could not be given by injection. When the hypodermic syringe was developed in 1853 by the Scottish physician Alexander Wood and, simultaneously, in France by the surgeon Charles Pravaz, it was immediately popular with doctors. Hence, because cannabis had to be administered orally and also took some time to take effect, it was dismissed by the medical profession. As Iversen comments, 'the doctor might have to remain with the patient for more than an hour after giving the drug, in order to make sure not only that it was having the desired effect, but also that the dosage had not been too high.'[320] Again, as such, for many years, it lost its protection by the medical establishment against profanation in Western societies.

Of course, we have already indicated that there were exceptions. Even into the twentieth century, cannabis could be bought as a popular tincture in apothecaries. Indeed, pharmaceutical companies, such as E. Merck in Germany, Burroughs, Wellcome & Co in the UK, and, in the US, Bristol Myers Squibb, Parke-Davis and Co., and Eli Lilly all produced cannabis-based preparations. Hence, it didn't simply disappear from the cabinets of doctors or medical researchers. For example, in Germany, Bernhard Fronmüller, a physician at the hospital in Fürth, conducted a large study of patients with sleep disorders, the results of which were published in his 1869 book, *Klinische Studien über die Schlafmachende Wirkung der Narkotischen Arzneimittel*. He introduced his patients to a range of narcotics, including cannabis. He found that the plant was an effective treatment for insomnia in 53 per cent of his patients, partially effective in 21.5 per cent, and minimally or not at all effective in 25.5 per cent. He also noted the impressive analgesic and anti-inflammatory properties of cannabis, as well as its apparent ability to stimulate the appetite.[321] A couple of decades later, in his widely used 1892 volume, *The Principles and Practice of Medicine*, the eminent Canadian physician, Sir William Osler, considered *Cannabis indica* to be 'probably the most satisfactory remedy' for the alleviation of pain in patients suffering from migraines, gout, and rheumatism.[322] Moreover, we will see in the next chapter that, while the latter half of the nineteenth century witnessed a general decline of interest in cannabis as a medicine, other areas of Western culture embraced it.

Medicinal cannabis since the 1960s

Interest in medical cannabis declined during the final decades of the nineteenth century and the first half of the twentieth century. This, however, was not the case in the latter half of the twentieth century. Advances in understanding the chemistry of the plant, particularly since the 1940s, laid the foundations for its cultural reconstruction as a healing herb.[323] As noted earlier in this chapter, this understanding was assisted by a sociocultural milieu shaped by a postmaterialist turn to the self, a neo-romantic focus on nature, an interest in ancient remedies, and a growing suspicion of technocracy and 'big pharma'. Certainly, anybody familiar with cannabis literature will be aware of the suspicion many users have regarding the claims of politicians and the motives of large multinational drug companies. That is to say, there is often a perception that those responsible for drug policies are guided by agendas that do not always seek to promote the wellbeing of individual members of society. For example, the British 'Seed Our Future Campaign' has argued that 'we are experiencing an economic, environmental, health, and food emergency here in the UK. It is clear that our government has failed in protecting us, our security, and our environment. The government protect corporations whose sole interest is making profit for shareholders, opposed to acting in the interests of people and the environment.'[324]

Cannabis campaigners have not been alone in arguing that the legislative process often has an irrational relationship to drugs. While, of course, it cannot be denied that recreational drug use is one of the major social, legal, and public health challenges facing societies,[325] a number of pharmacologists have noted that, while some highly toxic chemicals with distressing side effects are sanctioned, other more benign substances are prohibited. That is to say, it is clear to some that the classification of drugs has more to do with culture than chemistry.[326] For example, it is often pointed out that evidence-based assessments of the harms of recreational drugs conclude that cannabis is less harmful than both alcohol and tobacco.[327] This argument was cogently articulated as far back as the 1960s. For example, the psychiatrist and psychoanalyst Anthony Storr had noted in 1967 that 'marijuana is not a drug of addiction and is, medically speaking, far less harmful than alcohol and tobacco'.[328] Again, in 1971, with reference to a 1942 psychiatric report, the prominent Harvard University Professor of Psychiatry, Lester Grinspoon, made the same point in his influential study, *Marihuana Reconsidered*.[329] He also suggested that concerns about the dangers of cannabis were rooted more in ignorance and culturally constructed fear, than science. Indeed, he bemoaned the fact that, up until the 1960s, compared to studies of alcohol, there had been relatively little scientific research undertaken into the effects of cannabis consumption. While, of course, a number of articles had discussed its various uses, he noted that 'only a fraction of these are reasonably sound medical or scientific articles'.[330] This seemed odd to Grinspoon, for, while the heyday of medical exploration in the nineteenth century 'did not establish it as the hoped for panacea ... one might have expected that such an attempt, with the promising leads that were generated, would not have been so soon almost abandoned.' He continued, 'one would certainly have expected that, after the early 1940s, when tetrahydrocannabinols had been identified as pure substances having cannabis-like action, the search for marihuana's therapeutic utility would have been pressed with considerable vigour.' Furthermore, this is particularly surprising bearing in mind that cannabis 'has through the ages served as an indigenous medicine in vast areas of the world and for which many undocumented anecdotal claims for therapeutic utility in various ailments have been made.'[331] Of course, from the perspective of cultural sociology this is not surprising. The paucity of pharmacological research prior to the 1970s was largely the result of, as discussed in the previous chapter, the profanation of the drug in Western societies. That's not to say that such research was completely prohibited, only that it was not made easy. For example, the pharmacologist, Roger Pertwee, a co-founder of the International Cannabinoid Research Society, began his work in this area at Oxford University in the late 1960s. He then moved to the University of Aberdeen in 1974 where, in the early

1990s, he became a co-discoverer of endocannabinoids. However, reflecting on his early work, he noted that cannabis research was not straightforward. For example, he and other researchers were not able to work on actual cannabis plants: 'I actually never worked directly with herbal cannabis. But back at that time it was possible to extract cannabinoids from tincture of cannabis, which was then a legal cannabis-based medicine in the UK.' However, this didn't last long, for there were 'concerns raised about the recreational use of cannabis...' Consequently, even cannabis-based medicines were 'unfortunately eventually banned in the UK'.[332] This helps to explain why research into medical cannabis was hindered in the twentieth century, becoming increasingly difficult throughout the 1960s when concerns were being raised about its recreational consumption in white youth cultures. Indeed, it's worth spending a little time looking at the background to the changes that took place in the 1960s.

Cannabis had been outlawed in Britain since the passing of the 1928 Dangerous Drugs Act, which had classified it as a narcotic similar to heroin and cocaine. Hence, although, earlier in the century, it was not a major cause of concern for the police – largely because it was not common and they knew little about it – because the Act made no distinction between possession and supply, the small number of convicted offenders tended to be imprisoned. By the 1950s, however, it was becoming a cause for concern. Moreover, this concern was informed by a conspicuous racist bias, in that, prior to the mid-1960s, enforcement primarily focused on immigrants from the Caribbean. Furthermore, the popular press encouraged these attitudes. For example, in 1950, the police raided two jazz clubs in London, Club Eleven in Soho and the Paramount Dance Hall on Tottenham Court Road. Because cannabis was discovered and the audiences were racially mixed, the narrative was immediately framed in terms of Black pushers and white victims. Moreover, this was embedded within a vicious miscegenation narrative. Hence, regardless of who was smoking cannabis, reports of the arrests suggested that Black men were forcing white British girls to smoke the drug in order to seduce them. As one article put it, 'teen-aged girls are falling victim to marijuana cigarettes, given them by coloured seamen'.[333] Again, readers were told that, 'sometimes the dealer tantalises his victims, refusing to sell until one of the girls has danced with him. Eyes rolling, body twitching, a sixteen-year-old girl then slides into the motions of bebop in the arms of the black peddler.'[334] Such ideas were unfortunately encouraged by the authorities. For example, Henry Bryan Spear, who joined the Home Office Drugs Inspectorate in February 1952, argued that the upsurge in drug use in the United Kingdom was 'first seen in connection with the use of cannabis, a drug which first began to appear in the United Kingdom in appreciable quantities in the immediate post-war years, when its use was almost entirely confined to the newly established immigrant communities of certain large cities.'[335] However, this focus began to shift in 1964, when it became evident that cannabis was becoming popular within a burgeoning largely white youth culture. Indeed, 1964 was the first year in which white offenders outnumbered Black offenders. Hence, as it became clear that cannabis was being used much more widely, it quickly became a growing area of social concern. The number of white youths arrested rose year on year, including a number of high-profile arrests, such as the musicians Donovan in mid-1966 and Mick Jagger and Keith Richards in February 1967.[336] This led to responses from prominent public figures and medical professionals. For example, the well-known Scottish psychiatrist R.D. Laing wrote a letter to the editor of a medical journal after one of his colleagues was imprisoned for possession. He pleaded for physicians, psychiatrists, and researchers to do more to present the facts about cannabis and resist the growing moral panic: 'Does not this case point urgently to the need for the medical profession to do what we can to dispel the mounting panic in the country, reflected in the police and the judiciary, at the effects of this drug that is not known to have an deleterious effects whatever?'[337] More widely, articles in prominent magazines, such as the American magazine *LIFE*, explained that 'fears concerning marijuana have proved to be exaggerated. Pot is not physically addicting, nor need it lead to crime, immorality, or stronger drugs.'[338] Hence, during the 1960s, cannabis became a contested issue in the Western world. It was prohibited by governments and demonized in the popular press, but promoted in popular culture and enjoyed by growing numbers of young (and not so young) people.

Of some significance in the UK was the campaigning work of the Soma Research Association, led by Chicago-born Steven Adams who was studying parapsychology at Oxford University. On Monday 24 July 1967, Soma, financially supported by the musician Paul McCartney, took out a full-page advertisement in *The Times* entitled 'The Law Against Marijuana is Immoral in Principle and Unworkable in Practice.'[339] It was, noted Adams, 'signed by 65 people, including the Nobel Laureate Francis Crick, novelist Graham Greene, 15 doctors of medicine, one member of the Wootton Committee, members of Parliament and The Beatles.'[340] Signatories also included a number of prominent public figures and intellectuals, including David Dimbleby, David Hockney, Francis Huxley, R.D. Laing, Jonathon Miller, Patrick Nowell-Smith, Anthony Storr and Kenneth Tynan. As Adams commented, 'Soma was looking for a way to put the topic of cannabis law reform on the political agenda, and also to influence the terms of the deliberations of the Wootton Committee. In particular, the aim was to persuade the subcommittee to report on cannabis alone, rather than in conjunction with LSD.'[341] Although the *News of the World* tabloid newspaper insisted that 'this dangerous man must be stopped',[342] the advertisement was successful. With such a list of well-respected voices expressing their disapproval of contemporary cannabis legislation, the advertisement was hard to ignore. Not only did it lead to debates in the media and in Parliament, but it was cited on the first page of the 1968[343] 'Wootton Report' on cannabis, which was compiled by the Home Office Advisory Committee on Drug Dependence, chaired by Baroness Barbara Wootton:

> An advertisement in *The Times* on the 24th July, 1967, represented that the long-asserted dangers of cannabis were exaggerated and that the law was socially damaging, if not unworkable. This was followed by a wave of debate about these issues in Parliament, the Press, and elsewhere, and reports of enquiries e.g. by the National Council for Civil Liberties. This publicity made more explicit the nature of some current 'protest' about official policy on drugs; defined more clearly some of the main issues in our study; and letters to give greater attention to the legal aspects of the problem. Government spokesmen made it clear that any future development of policy on cannabis would have to take account of the Advisory Committee's report.[344]

Moreover, while the initial aim of the report was to examine both cannabis and LSD, in accordance with a recommendation of Soma, the panel 'decided to give first priority to presenting [their] views on cannabis.'[345] Furthermore, it also agreed with Soma that most of the popular fears about cannabis were baseless. Not only is it less dangerous than the other recreational drugs, but most users can give it up without significant withdrawal symptoms. Moreover, as in the United States, so in Britain, there was no substantive evidence to suggest that it encouraged users to experiment with addictive drugs, such as opiates, or that it led them into a life of crime – other than, of course, the crime of possessing cannabis. Hence, while the report did not recommend legalization, it did recommend leniency. It also suggested that more research into the effects of the cannabis needed to be done, not least the therapeutic benefits of cannabis because, so far, 'trustworthy reports have been few and vague.'[346]

While the Wootten Report made a number of important recommendations, as is so often the case, the government rejected them. The Home Secretary, James Callaghan, made the following statement: 'I think that it came as a surprise, if not a shock, to most people, when that notorious advertisement appeared in *The Times* in 1967, to find that there is a lobby in favour of legalising cannabis. The House should recognise that this lobby exists, and my reading of the Report is that the Wootton Sub-Committee was over-influenced by this lobby.' Hence, he argued that the report 'was compromised at the end,' because 'those who were in favour of legalising "pot" were all the time pushing the other members of the Committee back, so that eventually these remarkable conclusions emerged that it would be wrong to legalise it, but that the penalties should be reduced.'[347] That said, a year later, Callaghan relented and decided to implement the main proposals of the report. Moreover, while he suggested increasing the penalties for most drugs offences, including trafficking in cannabis, he introduced a distinction not drawn in the Wootton Report between penalties for possession and supply, which enabled him to significantly reduce the penalties for possession. Although, because the Labour Party lost the General Election, Callaghan was unable to see his Misuse of Drugs Bill become law, it was reintroduced by the incoming Conservative government. When the Misuse of Drugs Act received the Royal Assent in 1973, the Lord Chancellor, Quintin Hogg, instructed magistrates on sentencing: 'Set aside your prejudice, if you have one, and reserve the sentence of imprisonment for suitably flagrant cases of large-scale trafficking.'[348]

Despite these shifts towards greater tolerance of cannabis, and despite the fact the Wootton Report had noted that 'pharmacological developments gave our study new and much increased significance,'[349] as Pertwee commented, scientific research was made very difficult because the change in law had made the supply of cannabis a particularly serious offence. Hence, the supply of the necessary raw material was now too difficult. This, of course, need not have been the case, since the subcommittee's comments on medical cannabis are fairly positive and also testify to a growing medical interest in the drug. For example, it was noted that in the Wootton Report that:

> cannabis can be prescribed by doctors in the form of extract of cannabis and alcoholic tincture of cannabis. Until very recently, the demand for these preparations has been virtually negligible. In recent months, however, there has been a striking increase in the amounts prescribed. Our enquiries, supported by

what we were told by our witnesses, indicate there are a number of doctors who are beginning to experiment with the use of cannabis in the treatment of disturbed adolescents, heroin, and amphetamine dependence, and even alcoholism. While we do not expect cannabis prescription will ever become standard medication in the treatment of these conditions, it is quite likely that the amount dispensed on medical prescriptions will continue to increase and that this process may be accelerated when synthetic cannabis derivatives, properly standardised, become available. We see no objection to this and believe that any new legislation should be such as to permit its continuance. We think, however, that when cannabis or its derivatives are prescribed, records of this of the kind that can be inspected by H.M. Inspectors of Drugs should be available. This will enable the prescribing trend over the next few years to be kept under methodological review.[350]

Indeed, one of the recommendations of the Wootton Report was that 'preparations of cannabis and its derivatives should continue to be available on prescription for purposes of medical treatment and research'.[351] Hence, while certain provisions could have been inserted into the legislation in order to protect research into the use of medical cannabis, in effect, it continued to be demonized as a social scourge.

In North America, following the passing of the Marijuana Tax Act in 1937, cannabis-based preparations were removed from the *United States Pharmacopoeia*. Since then, as Martin Lee has commented, 'federal drug warriors ... erected a labyrinth of legal and institutional obstacles to inhibit research and prevent the therapeutic use of the herb.'[352] Again, this profanation of medical cannabis was based less on robust scientific research and more on cultural bias. Indeed, many medical professionals who actually took the time to review the available research, even during the 1960s, tended to adopt a more tolerant approach to its therapeutic benefits.[353] Grinspoon is a good example of one such researcher: 'Upset by the growing use of this dangerous drug by young people who were ignoring the government's warnings about its toxicity, I decided to review the science on which the warnings were based. Much to my surprise, I discovered that I had been brainwashed, as had most other people, by an almost ubiquitous cannabis catechism which was based primarily on fear, not science.'[354] Furthermore, after his son was 'stricken with a grave illness in 1967' and began using cannabis, he realised how 'miraculously useful it was to him'. This led him 'to explore the clinical and scientific evidence of its usefulness as a medicine'.[355]

Some federal funding into medical cannabis research did begin in 1970 and, in 1976, small steps were taken to distribute it through a 'compassionate use' programme. Essentially, in the United States, 'compassionate use' or 'expanded access' is the utilization of an investigational new drug (IND) outside of clinical trials to treat patients with serious or immediately life-threatening diseases or conditions when there are no comparable or satisfactory alternative treatment options. However, the application process was complex and only six patients were admitted onto the medical marijuana programme between 1976 and 1988.[356] Nevertheless, demand rose considerably when it became evident that it was helpful in treating the symptoms of AIDS. In 1991, Kenneth Jenks, a haemophiliac who had contracted AIDS through a blood transfusion, and his wife, Barbara, became the first patients to receive medical cannabis under the auspices of the compassionate IND programme. However, as the number of applications from AIDS patients grew, the Bush administration responded with a conspicuous lack of compassion. It shut down the entire programme in March 1992. As Lee has commented, 'no new candidates would be accepted. The eight patients who were already getting ganja from Uncle Sam would continue to receive their medication thanks to a grandfather clause. Everyone else, in effect, were told to drop dead.'[357] While some medical cannabis campaigners were hopeful that Bill Clinton would reintroduce the Compassionate IND programme following his election in November 1992, they were disappointed. Indeed, the President who famously stated that, when he was in England, he experimented with cannabis but 'didn't inhale it',[358] escalated the war on drugs. However, this had 'the unintended effect of fuelling the rise of the medical marijuana movement'.[359] Indeed, in 1993, partly in response this new draconian environment, Grinspoon and his colleague James Bakalar published *Marihuana, the Forbidden Medicine*, which included numerous testimonies of the sick and the dying who had benefitted from cannabis. Marijuana, they argued, is 'a wonder drug because of its virtual lack of toxicity, its medical versatility, and its potential ... to be much less expensive than the conventional drugs it will replace.'[360] Since then, increasing numbers of medical professionals have familiarized themselves with the published research and accepted a version of this view. For example, the American psychiatrist Julie Holland has argued that 'the study of cannabis and cannabinoids could be enormously beneficial to the field of psychiatry. Cannabis has been used for the treatment of depression, anxiety, inattention, malaise, and insomnia for thousands of years. Millions of people around the world are using marijuana to "self-medicate" these symptoms and others. For these two reasons alone, it would behove us to have a better understanding of the medicinal properties of this plant.'[361]

While many physicians and psychiatrists would, of course, be more cautious about promoting the benefits of cannabis, nevertheless, contemporary research is now furnishing us with the evidence needed for an informed understanding of the plant's therapeutic potential. This work is regularly published in dedicated journals, such as *Cannabis and Cannabinoid Research, Journal of Cannabis Research, Journal of Cannabis Therapeutics* and *Medical Cannabis and Cannabinoids*, as well as in the principal journals of psychiatry, oncology, pain management, and so on. Indeed, over the past few decades, this research has led to, amongst other advances, the development of cannabinoid pharmaceuticals such as Epidyolex for children and adults with epilepsy and other seizures, and nabiximols (Sativex) for those suffering with multiple sclerosis. Furthermore, synthetic cannabinoid products have also been developed, such as dronabinol (Marinol, Syndros, and Adversa) and nabilone (Cesamet) for chemotherapy patients.[362] These advances seem to have had a subtle, but positive impact on public attitudes towards cannabis. Indeed, as we have seen was the case in the nineteenth century with the use of tinctures, rather than preparations such as *dawamesc*, the very act of turning cannabis into a pill or bottled liquid preparation is a normalizing, if not sacralizing process for many in mainstream society. While some users, of course, champion homegrown 'natural medicine' over the products manufactured by 'big pharma', generally speaking, the transformation of 'weed', a profane, countercultural plant, into 'medicine', something that *looks like* everyday medication, has changed the perception of it. Indeed, it's not difficult to identify the basic semantic changes of key signifiers. There has been a shift from 'dope' to 'medicine', from 'getting high' to 'getting healthy', and from 'intoxication' to 'improved wellbeing'. The meanings of cannabis have shifted from the profane side of the equation to the sacred side.

Listening to the voices of the suffering

Of particular importance for the popular rebranding of cannabis within mainstream society have been the voices of the suffering, particularly the parents of sick children and those struggling with the pain caused by terminal illnesses such as cancer. While chronic pain and life-threatening conditions are always fundamentally profane, when children are involved the sense of the seriousness of the situation is significantly intensified. As we have seen, if we think of 'the sacred' in terms of the ways people relate to and experience certain things that are considered to be 'set apart' from everyday life in some absolute sense, the wellbeing of children is one of the most important. As such, we can think of the care of children in terms of a 'sacred form'. That is to say, it is one of those moral assumptions that are believed to be so fundamentally self-evident, so essential to civilized social life, that they are beyond question. As such, its violation, as in the case of child abuse, elicits a sense of revulsion and a demand for some form of restitution. Indeed, as we have seen, such sacred forms need to be understood in a relational or oppositional sense, in that, to quote Mary Douglas's influential study *Purity and Danger*, 'sacred things and places are to be protected from defilement. Holiness and impurity are at opposite poles.'[363] Hence, as discussed in the Introduction, social and cultural constructions of the sacred are tied to constructions of the profane, in that the latter is constituted as a threat to the former, a threat that needs to be removed. Moreover, not only is the profane constructed as a threat to the sacred, but it accrues a transgressive charge relative to the strength of the sacred: the stronger the sense of the sacred, the greater the revulsion evoked by that which threatens to profane it. In the case of children who are sick and dying, the sense of needing to heal can be so powerful that something must be done at all costs. Hence, if cannabis can help a severely sick child, then any sense of it being profane is effectively subjugated by the needs of that child. It was this, I suggest, that led the British Home Secretary, Sajid Javid, to make a step in the direction of legalizing cannabis for medicinal use. In 2018, he intervened to permit the use of cannabis oil to treat severely epileptic twelve-year-old Billy Caldwell, who had been admitted to hospital with seizures after supplies his mother had purchased in Canada were confiscated at Heathrow. The very idea of the law condemning a child to suffering was not only unconscionable, but it was also fundamentally profane. Something needed to be done. Likewise, in June 2018, a seven-year-old boy, Alfie Dingley, was granted a special licence to use medicinal cannabis oil. The fact that he suffered from PCDH19, an extremely rare form of clustering epilepsy, which caused him to have up to 150 seizures a month, could not be tolerated when there was medication available. As his mother has commented in a moving article in the *British Medical Journal*, 'I have watched my son struggle to breathe when he is having a seizure, seen my daughter cry when I leave her, and noticed my partner anxious and worried about the future.' She continues, 'we became campaigners because we had no choice. We are our child's only advocates, and we must do all we can to be heard. I have watched my child develop and enjoy life, and every child with intractable epilepsy should have the right to try cannabis medicines that could save them from a life of suffering.'[364] She now works for End Our Pain, a charity that seeks improved availability of medical cannabis: 'Medical cannabis was legalised in 2018. But patients still can't get access. Their terrible suffering continues. Help us to help them.'[365] Driven by the needs of suffering children, End Our Pain is now supported by numerus celebrities and politicians who have been persuaded that cannabis is, again, a 'healing herb', rather than the 'Devil's weed'.

Likewise, the very fact that cannabis has been shown to alleviate the symptoms of a painful, life-threatening disease such as cancer effectively sacralizes it. 'How bad can marijuana be?' asked one patient struggling with the brutal effects of chemotherapy and depression. 'I'm putting nothing but poisons into my body right now, and this is natural. Marijuana has helped with more than the chemo and getting me to feel better and eat again. It's helped me to cope with everything that's happened to me over a short period of time.'[366] More sensationally, scientists have found that 'THC and other cannabinoids such as CBD slow the growth of, and/or cause death in certain types of cancer cells growing in lab dishes.' Similarly, 'some animal studies also suggest certain cannabinoids may slow the growth and reduce the spread of some forms of cancer.'[367] That said, while research has demonstrated that cannabis can be an effective treatment for some of the symptoms of cancer and chemotherapy,[368] despite some extravagant claims to the contrary,[369] it has not, as yet, been shown that it can cure the disease.[370] Nevertheless, narratives which portray it as a friend to the suffering and an enemy of a profane disease such as cancer serve to sacralize it.

Similarly, one side effect of cannabis intoxication that has been found to be particularly helpful is well-known to recreational users as 'the munchies'. Because cannabis stimulates the appetite and enhances the appreciation of food, it has frequently (if not always legally) been used to help those suffering from a poor appetite, such as those struggling with cancer and HIV.[371] Likewise, while there is still debate about its efficacy to manage pain,[372] there is evidence to suggest that patients who are administered cannabis in clinical trials require less pain medication.[373] Indeed, there is even some evidence to suggest that, while smoking cannabis undoubtedly delivers a number of harmful substances into users' bodies, nevertheless, 'inhaled (smoked or vaporized) marijuana can be a helpful treatment of neuropathic pain'.[374] There is also some evidence to suggest that 'smoked marijuana . . . can be helpful in treating nausea and vomiting from cancer chemotherapy.'[375] This is interesting because there is a sense in which smoking, which is increasingly demonized in Western societies, is sanitized as an acceptable delivery method for medical cannabis. The key sacred form here is the health of the body and the alleviation of its suffering. Smoking, which obviously threatens health, becomes acceptable – less profane – as a delivery method for a substance that alleviates the suffering of the vulnerable and dying.

Not only are medical professionals beginning to advocate its use as the results of reliable research become more widely available, but an increasing number of specialist websites and magazines, such as *Treating Yourself*, *Cannabis Health*, *Dispense Magazine* and *CBD Health and Wellness*, are reshaping the discourse. Again, they are doing this, not only by providing accessible introductions to the latest research, but also by sharing stories of people with chronic health conditions whose lives have been changed by the drug. However, interestingly, these testimonies, perhaps unwittingly, tend to distance the medical use of cannabis from recreational use. That is to say, it is frequently pointed out that, before taking cannabis as a medicine, such users had very little knowledge of the drug. In this way, their stories serve to distance medicinal use from earlier demonizing narratives about cannabis users as pitiable and profane countercultural dropouts. They are 'normal' members of society who, having read the science and experienced the effects of cannabis, have become advocates for its legalization. For example, in the magazine *Cannabis Health*, Lorna Bland comments that 'there is a perception of the type of person who consumes cannabis, and I'm everything that kind of person is not'. She continues, 'I discovered cannabis in my 50s. I was of the generation where it was perceived to be a bad thing. I've never been drunk, so I certainly had no interest in getting high – which is what I associated with consuming cannabis.' Hence, she concluded, 'I've had to adjust my mindset to the idea that this isn't a dangerous thing, it is therapeutic medication ... It has absolutely transformed my life.'[376] Indeed, in 2018, she became one of the first recipients of a medical cannabis prescription in the UK. Since then, this 'normal' citizen has become an enthusiastic advocate of medical cannabis. Indeed, it is surprising how many people are overcoming culturally inscribed prejudice and embracing cannabis as a natural cure. As one veteran cannabis dealer told me, an increasing number of his customers are now older people with health conditions, rather than younger people who are using it primarily for recreational reasons. These are everyday folk who simply want to feel well and, for the first time in their lives, are having to break the law to do so.

Some of these users belong to what have, in the UK, been called 'cannabis compassion clubs' – the use of the word 'compassion' is, of course, culturally significant – or, in the United States, 'medical marijuana cooperatives'. Typically, these collectives grow cannabis and distribute it to small numbers of patients.[377] In the United States many of these are now legal and regulated. For example, cooperatives that register with the Washington State Liquor and Cannabis Board are allowed to grow up to sixty plants for the personal use of up to four patients. In the UK, largely because cannabis is illegal and, consequently, grown and distributed in an unregulated environment, some providers cannot be trusted. Hence covert 'compassion clubs' have emerged. These are local community groups that dispense cannabis to people in need. They rarely advertise their presence, becoming known primarily by word of mouth. For example, at Humshaugh, near Hexham in North East England, a 66-year-old grandmother, Pat Tabram, was arrested for 'compassionately' cooking cannabis-infused casseroles for her neighbours. Initially, she raised the money to buy cannabis with other pensioners after starting to use it medicinally to treat pain, firstly following a car accident and then as a result of cancer (from which she died in 2014). Eventually, she began growing it herself. As she put it, 'I used to be on NHS medications, but I found the side-effects were so bad that I stopped taking them.'[378] There was enormous sympathy for her, and the issue became something of a *cause célèbre*, making her an unwitting and unlikely poster girl for the legalization of cannabis.[379] However, as she stated after her second conviction, 'I am old and I am tired and I am disappointed ... in the attitude of the court regarding someone my age with my health problems and the way

I deal with it. I just want to go home and get some rest.'[380] Consequently, many who might formerly have profaned cannabis, began to wonder why an old woman couldn't simply be allowed to take the medication she needed to make her life more bearable. Hence, again, stories such as this, which portray brave, vulnerable, otherwise law-abiding people struggling to control their pain with a remedy proven to be effective have served to undermine fears generated by years of socio-cultural demonization.

This cultural shift in attitudes towards medical cannabis is conspicuously evident in Canada and the United States. For example, in 1996, Terrance Parker, who had, since the age of four, suffered from frequent epileptic seizures which had led to over a hundred hospitalizations, was arrested for growing cannabis.[381] Whereas prescription drugs and a right temporal lobotomy had proved ineffective, he discovered that cannabis alleviated his symptoms. On the advice of his doctor, he documented its impact on his health and wellbeing in a diary. This convinced his doctor to write a letter in support of his continued use of cannabis as a way of controlling his debilitating seizures. Parker appealed to the Canadian Charter of Rights and Freedoms for the right to smoke the drug legally. In 2000, the Ontario Court of Appeal agreed that denying him medical cannabis was an infringement of his Charter right to life, liberty, and security. Furthermore, the Court of Appeal indicated that the federal government needed to revise its cannabis legislation. Consequently, in 2001, the 'Marihuana Medical Access Regulations' allowed medical patients to grow four plants and licensed producers to cultivate larger crops for sale online to those with valid prescriptions. Following more legislation for medical cannabis, eventually, on 19 June 2018, the 'Cannabis Act' was passed, which has served to create 'a strict legal framework for controlling the production, distribution, sale, and possession of cannabis across Canada'.[382] While medical issues were not alone in paving the way for the 'Cannabis Act', in that it also sought to address drug-related crime and secure significant revenue, as far as the public perception of cannabis was concerned, pharmacological research and testimonies such as that of Parker were central to undermining discourses of demonization.

Likewise, in the United States, at the time of writing, thirty-six states and four territories allow for the medical use of cannabis products, and eighteen states, two territories, and the District of Columbia have enacted legislation to regulate cannabis for nonmedical use. While there are still negative media reports about its side effects, including a number of disturbing psychiatric conditions,[383] there is a growing body of evidence to support its pharmacological value. For example, Mary Bridgeman and Daniel Abazia, both professors of pharmacy, have commented that,

> despite lingering controversy, the use of botanical cannabis for medicinal purposes represents the revival of a plant with historical significance re-emerging in present day health care. Legislation governing the use of medicinal cannabis continues to evolve rapidly, necessitating that pharmacists and other clinicians keep abreast of new or changing state regulations and institutional implications. Ultimately, as the medicinal cannabis landscape continues to evolve, hospitals, acute care facilities, clinics, hospices, and long-term care centers need to consider the implications, address logistical concerns, and explore the feasibility of permitting patient access to this treatment.[384]

Assessments such as this contribute significantly to the growing number of positive reports in the media, which increasingly frame cannabis use in ways that undermine previous constructions of it as profane.[385] Again, studies of the therapeutic value of cannabis and the testimonies of those who have benefitted from its use have, more than almost anything else, shifted the narrative away from profanation and towards sacralization. That this is so, is evident from reports of the growing acceptance of the recreational/non-medical use of cannabis. For example, in a recent UK poll, 52 per cent either 'strongly supported' or 'tended to support' legalization, 15 per cent didn't know what they thought, and 32 per cent still opposed any changes to the law.[386] Likewise, in the United States, 'an overwhelming share of U.S. adults (88%) say either that marijuana should be legal for medical and recreational use (59%) or that it should be legal for medical use only (30%). Just one-in-ten (10%) say marijuana should not be legal.'[387] Although there is still some way to go, generally speaking, cannabis can be considered an increasingly mundane psychoactive.

Concluding comments

While there are a number of lacunae in this chapter, it's aim has not been to provide a comprehensive history of medicinal cannabis or, indeed, to provide a pharmacological analysis of the plant. That would have been rather too ambitious. The aim has simply been to excavate alternative histories of systems of medical knowledge in order to make sense of discourses that have influenced the fluctuating fortunes of cannabis, including its increased normalization/mundanity.[388] Hence, as well as providing an introduction to the role it has played in modern medicine, the chapter has also sought to demonstrate the socio-cultural significance of health and healing. As such, indirectly, it has been a discussion of the sacralization of medicine. As we have seen, social and cultural constructions of the sacred are tied to constructions of the profane, in that the latter is constituted as a threat to the former. If that threat can be mitigated or even neutralized, the active agent tends to be sacralized. This is particularly the case when there is a threat to the health of the body and society. Hence, the threat of suffering and/or death highlights the sacred–profane binary. (Significantly, of course, religious discourses utilize the language of healing and health in their soteriologies.) Medicine is, in some fundamentally important sense, sacred because it restores the body to health and resists the progress of death. Indeed, as we have seen, so powerful is this discourse around medicine that it can reverse earlier constructions of profanity. For example, in the case of cannabis, while in previous centuries, as Gabriel Nahas has commented, there was 'a cultural cleavage that kept the Europeans from adopting this Oriental habit'[389] – largely because of the prevalence of a demonizing Orientalism – this changed when prominent nineteenth-century Western physicians became convinced of the pharmacological value of hashish. Likewise, during the twentieth century, the simple addition of the word 'medical' to 'cannabis'/'marijuana' has fundamentally altered its signification. Of course, as we have seen, the fact that the term 'medical cannabis' is based on an impressive volume of reliable research, along with an increased understanding of the brain cannabinoid system, has been central to the transformation of the popular understanding of the drug.[390]

More specifically, central to this transformation of signification have been testimonies about its efficacy in alleviating the suffering of the most vulnerable members of society. As we have seen, this is evident in recent campaigns that seek changes to the law in order to allow suffering children to access cannabis-based medication. In the previous chapter we discussed the dynamics of profanation regarding the corrupting influence of the 'demon weed' on young people. Medical science has begun to invert this narrative.[391] The fact that suffering and dying children are being helped by cannabis is changing social attitudes towards it. Death and disease, which are fundamentally profane, have brought their opposing sacred forms, health and wellbeing, into focus. As absolute, normative realities, sacred forms, such as the protection and health of children, are obvious. As Gordon Lynch comments, they 'operate as more fundamental assumptions than what we might describe as "good"'. As he says, 'children simply are precious'. Hence, it is precisely when such a sacred form is threatened, whether by child abuse or a painful and terminal disease, that 'such assumed realities come to figure in the foreground of consciousness as vulnerable to the harmful and polluting effects of the profane ...'.[392] Hence, regardless of the fact that many once considered cannabis to be the 'demon weed', because it has been shown to alleviate the suffering of children, it is sacralized. Cannabis inhibits a profane threat to a child's health. Again, we have seen how, regardless of its relationship to the Orient, the signification of cannabis was transformed in the nineteenth century during a time of plague because it was understood (erroneously, as it turned out) to be a miracle cure. For a short time, some physicians were convinced that it had stayed the Grim Reaper's scythe.

Having said that, as one might expect, bearing in mind the history of cannabis in Western societies, the current situation is a complex mix of competing discourses. For example, partly as a result of its multifarious properties, it has often been treated as both sacred and profane. Just as we have seen Western colonialism value hemp for cordage and cloth, while also demonizing the use of Oriental hashish as an intoxicant capable of inducing madness and violence, so, more recently, advertising and discussions promoting the health benefits of CBD often unwittingly make a point of distancing it from its darker, wilder sister, THC. The concern about cannabis intoxication – which, again, is often informed by discourses that relate it to madness, savagery, violence, and crime – has been supported in recent years by the 'skunk-psychosis' narrative. As discussed in the first chapter, 'skunk' is a family of cannabis strains noted for their distinctive pungent aroma, as well as high yields of THC-rich flowers. Although popular amongst growers and users, skunk has been linked to an increased risk of psychosis in some people.[393] Hence, it's not difficult to find media headlines such as 'superskunk schizophrenia timebomb' and 'skunk blamed for ... psychosis epidemic'.[394] While the public concern is understandable, this profanation of THC, not only supports demonizing discourses, but it also informs the cultural reception of the whole plant.

Hence, those seeking to promote CBD as a medicine feel obliged to distance it from THC and the desire to get 'high'. This, in turn, tends to undermine the efforts of those seeking to promote medical cannabis *per se*, rather than just CBD. For example, the CBD supplier, Essentia Pura, proudly promote their product as free of compounds that are 'potentially dangerous, like THC'.[395] THC has been exorcised and the plant is now free of its profane agent. Again, Rachna Patel, a physician who has made much of the use of CBD in her practice, points out that it is unlike THC, that 'notorious and notable compound found in cannabis ... CBD doesn't get you high, but it does effectively relieve a wide range of medical conditions ...'.[396] Like many other CBD advocates, she draws a clear distinction between getting high and getting healthy. It's not that she doesn't recognise the therapeutic value of THC. She does. As she says, 'the general perception out there is that the totality of the medical benefits is derived solely from CBD, but, in fact, that's not the case. While it's true that some medical conditions do benefit more from CBD, there are other conditions that benefit more from THC. And then there are medical conditions that benefit from both THC and CBD'.[397] The point is that much advertising and popular discussion foregrounds the benefits of CBD as a cannabis product that will heal, not harm. This, as Patel acknowledges, is 'the general perception out there'. In other words, the discourse around CBD is typically shaped by anti-intoxication rhetoric: 'get healthy, not high'.[398] As such, even if inadvertently, the popular promotion CBD as a medicine tends to construct a sacred-profane binary.

This, of course, is not to say that the focus on medical CBD has not had a positive impact on the overall perception of cannabis. Again, the picture is complex, changing and different from one society to the next. Generally speaking, however, not only is the therapeutic value of CBD being recognized, but this recognition is leading to a wider acceptance of cannabis *per se*, both as a medicine and as a recreational intoxicant. Despite the continued profanation of THC, the increased recognition of CBD's medicinal properties seems to be having an overall sanitizing effect.[399] As indicated above, attitudes across the Western world are changing. For example, a recent Gallup poll found that 49 per cent of Americans have used cannabis. This is an increase from 45 per cent in 2019. Indeed, the significance of this increase becomes evident when one considers that, in 1969, when Americans were first surveyed about cannabis use, only 4 per cent of adults said that they had tried it. This was a period, of course, when cannabis was the demonized, countercultural, drop-out drug of youth culture. Since then, following the progress of medical cannabis research, the number of those supporting legalization has increased steadily, rising to around a third of the population in 1985, and to above 40 per cent in 2015.[400] Indeed, in a recent poll, 68 per cent of American adults wanted cannabis legalized.[401]

As well as the underlying, if increasingly diluted, sacred/profane distinction between CBD and THC, it's also worth noting a distinction between the natural and the manufactured. On the one hand, we have seen that many users in a broadly neo-romantic culture embrace cannabis as an ancient and natural healing herb distinct from the modern, manufactured toxins of 'big pharma'. As noted in a recent article on cannabis healthcare, while 'parents are often wary about giving their kids pharmaceutical drugs if it's not absolutely necessary ... CBD is prized because it's natural.'[402] Because 'nature' and 'the natural' are increasingly important sacred forms in Western societies, the idea of a 'healing plant', rather than a manufactured chemical in the form of a pill, is enormously attractive.

On the other hand, however, many in mainstream society are comforted by the notion of mass-produced pharmaceuticals. Indeed, there is still a suspicion that 'medicinal cannabis' is a contradiction in terms. As Wendy Chapkis and Richard Webb point out,

> Medicine is standardized, synthetic, and pure; marijuana involved the unrefined and promiscuous coupling of more than four hundred components rooted in the dirt... Medicine presents itself as an objective science safeguarded by the ritual of the double-blind, randomized clinical trial. The therapeutic value of marijuana relies largely on the 'soft science' of subjective experience and anecdotal evidence. From the perspective of its critics, then, cannabis is an effeminate interloper in the masculine world of real medicine, a dangerous drug pushed on a credulous public by illegitimate quacks.[403]

However, again, this is changing. Part of the process of the cultural sanitization or 'de-profanation' of cannabis in mainstream society has been the growing education about pharmacological research into its medicinal properties and, also, the production of pills and bottled medicines. For example, we have seen that, in the mid-1840s, the development of Western medicine from Oriental raw material included a shift away from using *dawamesc* and towards using tincture. This was effectively a process of cultural cleansing in an effort to reclassify cannabis as a safe, Western medicine. *Dawamesc* was a conspicuous marker of Oriental otherness, while tincture was clearly located with the fold of Western medicine. Similarly, for many today, the production of pills, bottled medicines, and substances with names that sound like other products behind the pharmacist's counter, such as Epidyolex, tend to sanitize cannabis by normalizing it. In other words, the process strips cannabis of its countercultural, drop-out, drug culture associations and transforms into something that can be administered with a pipette or stored in a blister pack. That's 'proper' medicine.

Finally, related to the above, it's worth noting that some campaigners for medical cannabis have been concerned about what we might call 'tainted terminology'. We have noted that the addition of the word 'medical' to 'marijuana' has fundamentally altered its signification. However, particularly in the United States, the word 'marijuana' is so closely linked to recreational drug use and to earlier discourses of profanation, that even the addition of the word 'medical' doesn't help very much. For example, in 2005, Julie Falco, a multiple sclerosis sufferer who campaigned for the legalization of medical cannabis in Illinois, stopped using what she referred to as 'the M word'. It became clear to her that 'it prevented legislators from taking the plant's medicinal uses seriously'.[404] The political opponents to legalizing medical cannabis, she insisted, simply rehearse 'old thinking and old stigma. You know, smoking pot and reefer madness, all the old stereotypes. That's where they are, and that's where they're stuck.'[405] Hence, in the US, campaigners are beginning to replace 'marijuana' with words such as 'cannabis' or 'cannabinoid', which aligns it with the terminology most widely used in medical science. This is an astute observation, which, apart from much else, takes account of the political importance of discourses of the sacred and the profane.

4

Sacred Cannabis

Cannabis, like all psychoactive substances, is a 'technology of transcendence'.[1] It typically alters perspective and, as well as relaxing the user, it induces a feeling of being gently lifted above the quotidian details of life. The user experiences a lightness of spirit (which often leads to an appreciation of the absurd and to laughter), an openness to others, and heightened perception. Indeed, although cannabis is not a psychedelic, nevertheless, as we have seen, some potent strains and preparations can induce a surrealistic, dreamlike state, which can be interpreted as, in some sense, 'mystical'. As Allen Ginsberg put it, 'marijuana is a metaphysical herb . . .'[2] Similarly, Ram Dass found it to be a useful technology of transcendence: 'I see it as an elevator to shift my planes of consciousness.'[3] Moreover, even when intoxication is not understood in such explicitly spiritual terms, because it generates novel ideas and connects ostensibly disparate thoughts, it is often, following Walter Benjamin, interpreted as a moment of 'profane illumination'.[4] In other words, for many users, cannabis is something of a secular philosopher's stone, in that it is able to transform the mundane into the special and the meaningful. It becomes a lens through which to look at the world differently. Again, as Benjamin put it in a letter to his friend Gershom Scholem, the influential scholar of Jewish mysticism, by inducing 'a wonderful, beatific humour' and a blurring of the usual distinctions and limits that constrain the embodied self, the insights gained 'may well turn out to be a very worthwhile supplement to . . . philosophical observations . . .'[5]

Many, of course, would disagree with this assessment. Even the philosopher Dale Jacquette, who edited a collection of essays on philosophy and cannabis,[6] concluded that the drug offered 'not very much'[7] to philosophical analysis.

> It is a well-worn cliché that the halo of brilliance surrounding our thinking when we are high does not generally stand the test of critical evaluation in the sober aftermath. I do not personally believe that using cannabis can enhance philosophical creativity or produce insights or ideas, let alone good philosophical solutions to important philosophical problems that would not otherwise occur to a philosopher straight. Progress in philosophy requires clear memory, astute critical faculties, and the ability to draw fine-grained distinctions, together with the patience and discipline to work these things out with the necessary circumspection and care.[8]

However, as discussed in Chapter 2 in relation to Mark Fisher's comments regarding 'stoner stupefaction' and 'zombified' users,[9] such assessments miss the point somewhat. Indeed, few informed users and researchers would claim that intoxication aids rigorous analysis. It doesn't! Having said that, many do feel that, as Benjamin noted, being high can be a catalyst for a moment of 'profane illumination'. As with all peak experiences, these moments can then be reflected upon in the cold light of day. Just as one might reflect philosophically, sociologically, psychologically, or theologically on experiences of sickness, bereavement, fear, happiness, love, awe, or the sublime, so the unfamiliar ideas and feelings evoked during intoxication can provide the raw material for meaning-making. Again, as Benjamin argued, experiences alone, whether induced by drugs or not, are insufficient to stimulate cultural analysis. Rather, as Dave Boothroyd has pointed out, 'it's not the experience alone, but the specific critical appropriation of the experience; it is about the relationship between thinking about the experience and the experience itself and about critical practice ...'.[10] Psychoactive substances are merely technologies that provide opportunities for critical reflection.

Hence, while it would be difficult to develop a convincing argument that all the ideas that bubble to the surface while under the influence of cannabis are pregnant with meaning, it is unsurprising that there is a long history of users committed to the view that valuable insights can be gleaned from critical reflection on the experience. To be high is to be intellectually and emotionally relocated. As such, again, the user is enabled to perceive the world from a novel vantage point. 'The gates to a world of grotesquerie seem to be opening,' observed Benjamin in his notes about his first cannabis experience. He continued, 'You are fixated on the intellectual sphere as a man possessed may be fixated on the sexual: under its spell, sucked into it.'[11] That is to say, the user's focus can settle on an object, an image, a sound, or a piece of music in a way that generates a meaning-making affective space. Again, this can then lead to the emergence of new insights and ideas. Some of these may be idiosyncratic and humorous, but others may feel like moments of revelation.

Even when the cannabis high is understood in terms of a secular, fundamentally mundane experience of enjoyable intoxication, it frequently engenders moments of profane illumination, which can, in turn, lead the user to question the nature of consensus reality. That is to say, during the experience, the spheres of the secular and the non-secular overlap as the user's perspective shifts, perception heightens, and relaxation is induced. Along with an enhanced appreciation of art, music, food, and, some would argue, sex,[12] the quotidian is illuminated and questioned. Things are not quite as they initially appeared to be.

Focusing on accounts from the nineteenth century onwards, this final chapter will examine the ways in which cannabis and the experience it induces are sacralized. To some extent, of course, we have already touched on this in the previous chapter, in that we have seen how medicinal usage has shifted the perception of cannabis away from its profanation and towards an understanding of it as mundane and, in some cases, sacred. In this chapter we will be looking specifically at its construction as a substance capable of inducing spiritual experiences of transcendence.[13]

The Orient, mysticism, and hashish in the nineteenth century

'This is the time of the Assassins,' declared Arthur Rimbaud.[14] On a number of levels this was an astute observation. As we have seen, the widely circulated Orientalist legend of Ḥasan-e Ṣabbāḥ is woven into the reception of hashish in the West. In nineteenth-century France, not only did it inform the thinking of Jacques-Joseph Moreau de Tours and Alexandre Dumas, but Charles Baudelaire took the title of his book from the mythic 'artificial paradise' created by Ḥasan. Indeed, the name of his sect was also adopted by a loosely organized Parisian *séance* of literati with which Baudelaire was involved. *Le Club des Hachichins* met monthly between 1845 and 1849 at the Hôtel Pimodan on the Île Saint-Louis. It may have gone unnoticed had it not been for the fact that one of their number, Théophile Gautier, published a semi-fictional essay, 'Le Club des Hachichins',[15] in *Revue des Deux Mondes* on 1 February 1846, which recounts the story of the relationship between Ḥasan, the Assassins, hashish, and visions of Paradise. This Orientalist reading of the cannabis experience has, in the modern West, been central to its construction as sacred. There is something special about this 'Eastern' herb.

As well as Moreau, Baudelaire, Gautier and Dumas, other French luminaries who could be found in various states of euphoria and reflection at the Hôtel Pimodan, included Louis Aubert-Roche, Victor Hugo, Eugène Delacroix, Honoré Daumier, Alphonse Karr, Gérard de Nerval and Honoré de Balzac. Inspired by the medical work of Moreau (see Chapter 3), members of *Le Club des Hachichins* met to discuss ideas, to experiment with dream states and to observe each other in varying degrees of intoxication. Indeed, the central significance of Moreau for the Parisian *hachichins* is indicated in Gautier's references to 'the doctor'.[16] The following passage describes an initial visit to one of their meetings:

> I recognized the apartment by its revolving door whose crushed and shiny Utrecht velvet, yellowing braid, and battered studs witnessed to long service. I rang and was admitted with the customary precautions and found myself in a great room illuminated at one end by a few lamps ... 'There he is!' voices cried in unison, 'let him have his portion!' The doctor was standing by a sideboard on which was placed a tray laden with little Japanese saucers. He was extracting morsels of paste or greenish conserve ... The doctor's face radiated enthusiasm: his eyes were sparkling, his cheeks flushed with crimson, the veins at his temples were swollen, and his dilated nostrils snuffed the air. 'This will be deducted from you portion of Paradise,' he said as he handed me my due ration ... Now, the green paste which the doctor had just distributed to us was the very same with which the Old man of the Mountain had secretly dosed his fanatics, leading them to believe that it was within his power to bestow on them the paradise of Mahomet ... Assuredly, those who had seen me leave my home at the hour at which ordinary mortals take their dinner had no inkling that I was going to the Ile Saint-Louis, a virtuous and patriarchal neighbourhood if ever there was one, to consume a strange food which had been used centuries ago by an imposter of a sheik as a means of exciting his

illuminati to murder. Nothing in my perfectly bourgeois rig could have made me suspect of such an excess of Orientalism; I had rather the appearance of a nephews going to dine with his elderly aunt than of a believer on the point of tasting the joys of Mahomet's heaven in the company of a dozen French 'Arabs.'[17]

It was this sense of transcendence and the Orientalist construction of induced Paradise, for which 'reality merely served as a jumping off ground for the splendors of the hallucination',[18] that became central to the French ḥashīshīyya and that contributed so significantly to the sacralization of hashish in the West. 'I was in the happy stage of hashish that Orientals call *kief*,' declared Gautier. 'I could no longer feel my body; the bonds of matter and spirit had been untied: I moved by sheer willpower in a medium which offered no resistance at all.'[19] This, he reasoned, must be what we experience in the afterlife: 'I understood the pleasures tasted by spirits and angels according to their degree of perfection, as they traverse the ether and the heavens, and what might be the pastime of Eternity in paradise. No trace of materiality mingled with this ecstasy; no earthly desire impaired its purity.'[20] (Such hyperbole is, we will see, not unusual in drug literature. Users seem drawn to exaggerate the colourful otherness and deep profundity of their experiences.)

Arguably the most important drug writing to emerge out of these *séances* was Baudelaire's 'Du vin et du hachish' (1851) and *Les Paradis Artificiels* (1860).[21] That said, while he frequently enjoyed wine and became addicted to opium, there is little evidence to suggest that he was a regular consumer of cannabis. 'That he once or twice tried hashish, as a psychological experience, is possible and even probable,' says Gautier, 'but he did not make continuous use of it.' Indeed, what Gautier refers to as 'this happiness, bought at the chemist's and carried in the pocket' was, he says, 'repugnant' to Baudelaire. 'He compared the ecstasy that it produced to that of a maniac, for whom painted cloth and coarse decorations replaced real furniture and the garden enriched with living flowers.'[22] Gautier's point is an important one and needs to be borne in mind when considering Baudelaire's assessment of cannabis. Indeed, to claim, as Catherine Osborn has done, that Baudelaire was 'an understanding loving brother' to the hippies of the 1960s,[23] misunderstands him. In fact, he writes in the love–hate style of an addict caught somewhere between the ethereal Romanticism of Thomas De Quincey[24] and the brutal realism of William Burroughs.[25] On the one hand, Baudelaire lauds the cannabis experience as liberating and inspiring, unlocking inner worlds and lifting the user above the tedium and darkness of everyday life. He even employs conspicuous hyperbole when describing the high. On the other hand, however, he is highly critical of drug use and sought to distance himself from the perception of being immersed in an intoxicated life. Hence, regardless of the many hours he spent under the influence of one substance or another, he frequently warned against intoxication and famously described induced altered states as 'artificial paradises'. Cannabis, in particular, harboured a 'stupefying spirit' that quickly takes possession of the user's mind, inducing a profoundly antisocial attitude, which 'renders the individual useless to his fellow man'.[26] This, of course, is reminiscent of the discourses of profanation discussed in Chapter 2. He bemoans cannabis consumption as both 'useless and dangerous', in that it is so effective in eroding morality, undermining creativity, and causing 'intellectual death', that, 'if there existed a government in whose interest it were to corrupt its citizens, it would have to encourage the use of hashish'.[27] Moreover, it leads a person 'to admire himself and precipitates him day by day toward the very brink of the luminous abyss in which he admires his Narcissan face'.[28] Hence, while he admits that the effects of hashish are 'not without charm', which is why users 'set such great store' by them, in fact, the paradises to which they are transported 'are not really as beautiful as they appear beneath their temporary disguises and magical tinsel trappings. Such thoughts belong to the earth rather than to heaven and owe a great part of their beauty to nervous irritation, to the eagerness with which the mind embraces them.'[29]

A few points need to be borne in mind when considering Baudelaire's comments on cannabis use. Firstly, he was taking high doses of hashish. Secondly, as an opium addict, he learned to fear the effects of drug use on a person's everyday life. Thirdly, it seems clear that he conflated the experiences of opium and hashish in his writing. Finally, like DeQuicey, whom he admired, he makes liberal use of poetic licence to embroider his accounts of cannabis intoxication. Combined, these points make it difficult to take his descriptions of the cannabis experience at face value. Nevertheless, as his work has been so influential, it's worth outlining his understanding of its principal characteristics.

(1) The perception of time is so altered that, within just a few minutes, an 'eternity' can be experienced and (2) within that experience of timelessness, the angst of mortal life dissolves.[30] While most users will experience a distorted perception of time, few, if any, would describe being high as an experience of eternity: 'One lives several lives in the space of an hour.'[31] He even describes a feeling that 'soon the very idea of time will disappear'.[32] Hence, 'when on the morrow you observe the light of day in your room, your first sensation is astonishment. Time had completely disappeared. It had been night just before and now it is day. "Have I slept or not? Did my state of intoxication last all night and, the concept of time having been suppressed, did the entire night signify for me less than the space of a second? Or have I perhaps lain enveloped in the veils of a vision-filled slumber?" There is no possibility of knowing.'[33]

(3) Because one is lifted 'so much above material things',[34] there is also an erosion of the sense of space. Again, generally speaking, this is a relatively common experience. Relatedly, but more controversially, he also argues that (4) there is an erosion of the perception of the distinct identity of the self over against other objects in the world. While some users might recognize this experience, few will agree with Baudelaire that the 'personality vanishes'. He continues, 'the sense of objectivity that creates certain pantheistical poets and great actors becomes so powerful that you are confounded with external objects. Now you are a tree moaning in the wind and murmuring vegetable melodies to nature. Now you hover in the azure of an immensely extended sky.'[35] Again, 'you are seated, smoking a pipe; you think you are sitting inside the pipe, but the pipe, rather, is smoking you; you exhale yourself in spirals of blue clouds.'[36] Furthermore, 'a final, crowning thought springs from the dreamer's brain: '*I have become God!* ... Which French philosopher is it who said, in mockery of modern German doctrines, "I am a god who has not dined well"? That irony would fail to make an impression on a man under the sway of hashish; he would calmly reply: "I may not have dined well, yet I am a God!"'[37] (Again, these are by no means common experiences for the cannabis user.)

(5) Related to the perception of unity with the external world are Baudelaire's comments on the relationship between music and hashish intoxication – a relationship that is now well documented.[38] In particular, he notes that music 'will associate itself with the objects around you', enchanting them, and drawing the intoxicated observer into a unity with them. At one with the music, indistinguishable from it, the listener is no longer an isolated self, but rather merges with and becomes part of the sonic environment.

(6) Hashish intoxication can be an evocative experience, within which users discover their muse. Hence, it can, says Baudelaire, 'give you infinite poems'.[39] Having said that, he was suspicious of easy shortcuts that erode creativity, bypass serious reflection, and undermine morality. 'In the very infallibility of the means lies its immorality, just as the supposed infallibility of magic lies in the diabolical stigma with which it is attached.'[40] There is something morally and creatively constructive about the time, effort, and privations endured by the ascetic, the mystic, and the artist; there is something important to be gained from the dark night of the soul that is denied to the person who seeks to arrive at the same destination by a chemical shortcut.

(7) Moreover, large doses of hashish can engender a conviction that 'every philosophical [and religious] problem has been solved. All the knotty questions with which theologians have battled and which are the despair of thinking humanity have become pellucid, limpid.'[41] While there is little that troubles the emotional and intellectual pond in which the intoxicated mind floats, this is not because anything has been solved, but only because, being intoxicated, the user is satisfied with an unconvincing, ill-thought through solution. Most users I have spoken to recognize this experience. The troubles of the world are solved during an evening spent with friends smoking cannabis.

(8) Finally, central to the artificial paradise induced by cannabis is the user's immersion in a sense of pleasure. Although users may experience several initial, transitory, negative effects, it isn't long before they realize that 'every sorrow has disappeared' or at least been significantly depleted. 'It is what the Orientals call *kief* – it is the absolute of happiness ... It is a calm and frozen beatitude.'[42] Again, with some hyperbole, he says, 'you have ceased to struggle, you are transported, you are no longer your own master, and little do you care.'[43] This is the central issue for Baudelaire. While drugs are undoubtedly pleasurable and, in many respects, inspirational, in the final analysis, they create artificial paradises in which all problems temporarily evaporate in a cloud of unknowing.

The human yearning for the eternal, for the ideal, for infinite paradise explains, argues Baudelaire, the human appetite for intoxicated states. 'Alas! the vices of man, however frightful they seem, contain the proof (if only in their infinite applications!) of his taste for the infinite; and yet it is a taste that quite frequently goes astray.'[44]

Not everyone at the close of the nineteenth century agreed with Baudelaire's negative assessment of the cannabis experience. Gustave Flaubert, for example, was particularly critical of his work on drugs: 'One senses something like a leaven of Catholicism here and there. I would have preferred you not to condemn hashish, opium, overindulgence. How do you know what may ultimately come of all that?'[45] Flaubert, unsurprisingly, was far more positive about the value of altered states. Could not these experiences be genuinely mystical? In his series of religious tableaux, *La Tentation de Saint Antoine* (1874),[46] he discusses a night in the life of the fourth-century Christian anchorite mystic Saint Anthony, during which he is tormented. Weakened, as many Desert Fathers were, from the rigors of asceticism and haunted by sinful thoughts and remorse, he slipped into hallucinatory altered states during which he experienced sensual excess and philosophical doubt. Rooted in, as Foucault puts it, 'the ancient imagination of the Orient',[47] the account locates Anthony on the borderlands of madness and mysticism. In many ways, it is an examination and, indeed, a celebration of the potential of the mind during altered states of consciousness. Whether the visionary states are induced by the privations of asceticism or by drugs is beside the point, in that both alter brain chemistry and produce hallucinations that can have profound personal, social, and religious implications. In an evocative passage deeply resonant of Romantic Idealism, Flaubert has Anthony declaring the following:

> O joy! O bliss! I have beheld the birth of life. I have seen the beginning of motion! My pulses throb even to the point of bursting. I long to fly, to swim, to bark, to bellow, to howl. Would that I had wings, a carapace, a shell – that I could breathe out smoke, wield a trunk – make my body writhe – divide myself everywhere – be in everything – emanate with all the odours – develop myself like the plants – flow like water – vibrate like sound – shine like light – assume all forms – penetrate each atom – descend to the very bottom of matter – be matter itself![48]

Again, these are important experiences that, Flaubert feels, Baudelaire dismisses too lightly in his assessment of cannabis intoxication: 'how do you know what may come of all that?'

As will be evident from the previous discussion, and as discussed in Chapter 2, nineteenth-century Orientalism informed the reception of hashish in the West. In particular, we have noted the significance of Marco Polo's rendering of the legend of the Assassins. For example, the Marxist philosopher Ernst Bloch references Ḥasan in *The Principle of Hope* when discussing hashish-induced daydreaming.[49] Later in the twentieth century, Ḥasan was effectively transformed from, as Marcus Boon puts it, an 'Oriental despot' into a 'medieval dandy'. He became a revolutionary icon for 'the dope-smoking radicals of the 1960s, decked out in caftans while plotting to overthrow the state'.[50] This is evident in subsequent popular music, from obscure experimental projects such as Vagina Dentata Organ's *Music For The Hashishins: In Memoriam Of Hasan Sabbah* (1983) to 'Hassan I Sahba', a popular rock song written by Robert Calvert and Paul Rudolph for Hawkwind's *Quark, Strangeness and Charm* (1977).[51]

The legend of the Assassins was not, of course, the only influence on the Orientalist construction of hashish. Of particular note in this respect was *Les Mille et une nuits*, translated by Antoine Galland, which appeared in twelve volumes between 1704 and 1717.[52] Widely known in English as the *Arabian Nights*, it had a significant impact on Western conceptions of the Orient as an exotic, enchanted heterotopia. This is evident throughout Western drug culture, from Samuel Taylor Coleridge's 'Kubla Khan' to twentieth-century anti-cannabis propaganda. By the 1880s, it had, as Sadie Plant notes, 'inspired all of the nineteenth century's writers on drugs'.[53] Even the experience of the American physician Harry Hubbell Kane, when he 'indulged in a few pipefuls of the narcotic hemp' in a New York 'hashish-house', immediately 'brought to mind the scenes of the *Arabian Nights*'.[54] Likewise, Silas Burroughs, who, in 1880, with Henry Wellcome, founded the pharmaceutical company Burroughs, Wellcome & Co, is described by an anonymous correspondent in 1892 as taking 'a few whiffs of the hashish-pipe' and being 'instantly carried off to the seventh heaven of imaginary delight'.[55] Burroughs himself described the experience as one of being 'transported, like Aladdin, to the moonlit Alhambra ... or down to the Red Sea and beyond the pinnacles of Sinai to gaze at distant Mecca ...'[56] It is, of course, of particular significance that the members of *Le Club des Hachichins* were 'in love with the Eastern flavour of hashish and the stories with which it seemed to come equipped'.[57] For example, in *The Count of Monte Cristo*, Dumas embeds his enthusiasm for hashish in a narrative explicitly influenced by the *Arabian Nights*.[58] Again, the point is that discourses developed around cannabis use in the nineteenth century, which were influenced by exotic tales from the Orient, particularly the *Arabian Nights* and the legend of the Assassins, have continued to inform the reception of hashish and discourses of sacralization and transgression up to the present day.

One of the earliest Orientalist references to cannabis in America can be found in 'The Haschish', a poem published in 1854 by the Quaker poet and abolitionist John Greenleaf Whittier:

> Of all that Orient lands can vaunt
> Of marvels with our own competing,
> The strangest is the Haschisch plant,
> And what will follow on its eating.[59]

This is one of Whittier's anti-slavery poems in which he compares the muddled thinking of hashish intoxication with the arguments of the apologists for slavery. As with Baudelaire, he argues that hashish may make 'fools or knaves of all who use it'. However, he continues, while cannabis may have the power to enslave an individual, it is relatively benign when compared to cotton, which has enslaved a numberless multitude: 'The hempen Haschish of the East / Is powerless to our Western Cotton!'[60] However, what interests us here is Whittier's articulation of the relationship between hashish and visions of the Orient. In other words, while it is unlikely that he partook of hashish himself, he betrays an assumption that narcotic plants have an organic connection to the cultures of the lands in which they were germinated. Hence, as soon as the 'genie' of hashish is released into the brain, it possesses the user's mind, evoking (to quote Calvert again) 'a thousand and one nights / In the perfumed garden of delights'.[61] That is to say, by virtue of its geographical origins, hashish tends to induce visions of an Oriental nature: 'such scenes that Eastern plant awakes.' As we will see, this Romantic association between the origins of a drug and the nature of the altered state induced is not limited to Whittier.

An anonymous article, rather different in tone, which eulogized hashish intoxication, also published in 1854, appeared in *Putnam's Monthly Magazine*. Entitled 'The Vision of Hasheesh', the anonymous author was actually Bayard Taylor, the illustrious poet, travel writer and United States Envoy to Prussia.[62] Unlike Whittier's poem and much closer to the writing of Gautier and Flaubert, Taylor's article was a sensational account of his own experiences of transcendence: 'the spirit ... of Hasheesh had entire possession of me. I was cast upon the flood of his illusions, and drifted helplessly whithersoever he might choose to bear me.'[63] However, like Whittier and *Le Club des Hachichins*, the relationship between the Orient and cannabis was key to the latter's sacralization: 'I suddenly found myself at the foot of the great Pyramid of Cheops ... I wished to ascend it and the wish alone placed me above its apex, lifted thousands of feet above the wheat-fields and palm-groves of Egypt.' He continues, 'I was moving over the desert, not upon the rocking dromedary, but seated in a barque made of mother-of-pearl, and studded with jewels of surpassing lustre. The sand was made of grains of gold, and my keel slid through them without jar or sound.'[64] Indeed, travelling further East in his vision, he too reveals the influence of the *Arabian Nights*: 'Mahomet's Paradise, with its palaces of ruby and emerald, its airs of musk and cassia, and its rivers colder than snow and sweeter than honey, would have been a poor and mean terminus for my arcade of rainbows. Yet in the character of this paradise, in the gorgeous fancies of the *Arabian Nights*, in the glow and luxury of all Oriental poetry, I now recognize more or less of the agency of hasheesh.'[65]

The hashish eater

Taylor's writing was particularly significant as the catalyst for one of the most influential hashish texts of the nineteenth century, Fitz Hugh Ludlow's *The Hasheesh Eater: Being Passages from the Life of a Pythagorean* (1857).[66] Ludlow recalls that he had been 'moved ... powerfully to curiosity and admiration' by a 'most graphic' discussion of hashish 'from the pen of Bayard Taylor'.[67] Hence, while some, such as Boon, have argued that *The Hasheesh Eater* 'inaugurated writing about drugs in America',[68] this is erroneous. Indeed, because Taylor's article was published anonymously, some early commentators mistakenly thought that it had been written by Ludlow himself.[69] (Moreover, even earlier, in 1842, William Blair had already published 'An Opium Eater in America' in *The Knickerbocker*.[70])

Like many young people today, Ludlow was a teenager when he began experimenting with hashish in 1854. He had been introduced to 'a preparation of the East Indian hemp, a powerful agent in cases of lock-jaw', by a local apothecary in his hometown of Poughkeepsie.[71] However, after several years of committed and increasing cannabis use, including his time as a student at Union College, he became convinced that he had succumbed to addiction. Having chanced upon Taylor's article in a local bookshop, he believed that he had found a kindred spirit who might be able to help him: 'As none other could counsel me, he might counsel. For the first time in all the tremendous stretch of my spell-bound eternity heard I the voice of sympathy or saw I an exemplar of escape.'[72] He immediately wrote to the editor of *Putnam's Monthly Magazine*, who put him in touch with Taylor. In his response, Taylor suggested that, as a form of catharsis, he should reflect upon and record the details of his experiences. However, this self-therapy, not only failed to terminate his cannabis habit, but, following Taylor's example, it led him to write an anonymous article on hashish for *Putnam's Monthly Magazine*: 'The Apocalypse of Hashish.'[73] Impressed, Taylor encouraged him to continue writing. By early 1857 he had a 365-page manuscript, which was quickly accepted for publication by Harper and Brothers in New York on 1 July of that year. Having received a number of prominent reviews, including one in the fashionable *Harper's Monthly Magazine*, the book sold well and three further editions followed. It finally went out of print during the Civil War (1861–1865) and was not published again until 1903, when it was reprinted by S.G. Rains & Co. Including illustrations by Aubrey Beardlesy (who was himself familiar with hashish),[74] it quickly acquired a certain countercultural gravitas, which attracted the attention of, among others, the occultist Aleister Crowley and the broadcaster and novelist Algernon Blackwood. Later in the century, the horror and fantasy author Howard Phillips Lovecraft would also express his indebtedness to *The Hasheesh Eater*, as would the Beat generation and key figures of the 1960s psychedelic counterculture and beyond, such as Timothy Leary and Terence McKenna.[75] As Donald Dulchinos discusses, the Beats reprinted the book 'in a broadside in 1960 alongside works of Kerouac, Ginsberg and Jean-Paul Sartre, and passed on the knowledge to the hippie generation, through the publication of the book by ... City Lights Books'. Moreover, 'excerpts and analyses of *The Hasheesh Eater* appeared in half a dozen books on the Sixties' drug scene, as well as in the *Berkeley Barb* ...'[76] Indeed, Mckenna even recorded readings from the book for a set of tapes he produced with his wife, Katherine Harrison McKenna, entitled *Victorian Tales of Cannabis*.[77]

Like Baudelaire, Ludlow was deeply influenced by De Quincey, and, like De Quincey, his favourite childhood book was the *Arabian Nights*. Indeed, it is difficult to overestimate the significance of both De Quincey's *Confessions of an English Opium Eater* and the *Arabian Nights* for Ludlow. De Quincey was, he says, 'the most wondrous, most inspired Dreamer ...'[78] Indeed, he is admirably candid regarding the importance of *Confessions* for the development of *The Hasheesh Eater*: 'Frankly do I say that I admire De Quincey to such a degree that, were not imitation base and he inimitable, I know no master of style in whose footsteps I should more earnestly seek to tread.'[79] Nevertheless, base or not, *The Hasheesh Eater* can, without much effort, be read as a somewhat inferior and rather sensational imitation of De Quincey's *Confessions*. While he notes that 'the state of insight which [De Quincey] attained through opium, I reached by the way of hasheesh',[80] and while he claims that his account is one of 'unexaggerated fact, its occurrences being recorded precisely as they impressed themselves upon me',[81] one can be forgiven for assuming that De Quincey's influence was far more potent than that of the hashish. Although he obviously consumed prodigious amounts of hashish, nevertheless, the accounts of his remarkable and vivid experiences – including his addiction – seem, like Baudelaire's descriptions, closer to those of an opium-eater.[82] Moreover, from the first page, which opens with a quotation from Coleridge's 'Kubla Khan', to its appendix, which commends the 'lively hasheesh vision' described in *The Count of Monte Cristo*, Ludlow's book is infused with Romantic Orientalism: 'we try to imitate Eastern narrative, but in vain.'[83] As well as numerous references to Oriental culture, he sometimes chose to use Islamic rather than Christian theological terms: 'genie' (*jinn*, supernatural beings) – 'I was seized by the hand of the hasheesh genie'; and 'Eblis' (*Iblīs*, the Arabic term for 'Devil'; the leader of the *jinn* who refused to prostrate himself before Adam) – 'the hell of Eblis and its inextinguishable pangs'.[84] Again, his understanding of the Orient was informed by his reading of the *Arabian Nights*: 'The singular energy and scope of imagination which characterize all Oriental tales, and especially that great typical representative of the species, the *Arabian Nights*, were my ceaseless marvel from earliest childhood.' He continues:

> The book of Arabian and Turkish story has very few thoughtful readers among the nations of the West, who can rest contented with admiring its bold flights into unknown regions of imagery, and close the mystic pages that have enchanted them without an inquiry as to the influences which have turned the human mind into such rare channels of thought. Sooner or later comes the question of the producing causes, and it is in the power of few – very few of us – to answer that question right.[85]

The reason 'very few' were capable of revealing the mystery of the *Arabian Nights*, was because, at that time, very few had experienced the esoteric delights of cannabis: 'I believe, and now with all due modesty assert, I unlocked the secret, not by hypothesis, not by processes of reasoning, but by journeying through those self-same fields of weird experience which are dinted by the sandals of the glorious old dreamers of the East.' In other words, 'the secret lies in the use of hasheesh'.[86] That is to say, he suggested that, firstly, as with all drug-induced mysticism, the path to wisdom was to be found in a direct experience induced by the appropriate psychoactive substance and, secondly, that hashish had, as Plant put it, 'a privileged connection, a sympathetic link to all the cultures in which the drug had ever been used'.[87] Concerning this latter point, Ludlow noticed that, for example, several of his friends who had taken hashish had also experienced visions of Oriental scenes. This was not uncommon within Romanticism, and, of course, might simply be a case of users associating the drug with stories they were already familiar with. Ludlow, however, disputed this explanation. Rather, he insisted, during hashish intoxication, the mind becomes so detached from everyday life that it is difficult even to process such ideas. Hence, the only explanation must be that the mind is subjected to the force of an alien influence, which has over millennia shaped the Oriental mind and, therefore, been formative in the development of some of the key characteristics of its culture.[88] This being so, he claimed that users can experience that culture simply by consuming the same drug. This is, of course, nonsense, but it is central to Ludlow's understanding of the importance of hashish – and, indeed, evident in much subsequent drug literature.

> It is not one of the least singular facts of hashish that its fantasia almost invariably takes an Oriental form. This cannot be explained upon the hypothesis that the experimenter remembers it as the indulgence in use among people of the East, for at the acme of the delirium there is no consciousness remaining in the mind of its being an unnatural state. The very idea of the drug is utterly forgotten, and present reality shuts out all inquiry into grounds for belief. The only

supposition which at all accounts for the fact to my own mind is that the *hasheesh is the antecedent instead of the result of the peculiar characteristics of Oriental mind and manners.*[89]

Oriental art, literature, music, and 'the sum total of Eastern manners', are all, he says, 'the embodiment and symbol of the Eastern mind', and that mind 'is very much the product of those stimulants which are in use throughout that portion of the world, and among these hasheesh holds the regency, as swaying the broadest domain of mind, and most authoritatively ruling all faculties within it'. Hence, 'wherever this drug comes into contact with a sensitive organization, the same fruit of supernatural beauty or horror will characterize the visions produced'. He concludes, therefore, that 'it is hasheesh which makes both the Syrian and the Saxon Oriental'.[90] Indeed, Ludlow is nothing if not consistent. The English too, he insists, can trace their own peculiar culture back to cigarettes and alcohol: 'beer, mildly toned by the moderate use of tobacco' accounts for the 'reticence, solidity, reflectiveness' of the English.[91]

To summarize, drugs induce states of mind, which are formative of cultural characteristics. Hence, hashish can be understood as a technology which enables the transcendence of the user's own culture, establishing a 'sympathetic link' with the same Oriental mind that produced the *Arabian Nights*. Intoxicated, a person is able, says Ludlow, to stand on 'the same mounts of vision where they stood, listening to the same gurgling melody that broke from their enchanted fountains ...' He continues, 'plunging into their rayless caverns of sorcery, and imprisoned with their genie in the unutterable silence of the fathomless sea, have I dearly bought the right to come to men with the chart of my wanderings in my hands, and unfold to them the foundations of the fabric of Oriental story.'[92]

As indicated above, it is hardly surprising that the *Arabian Nights* was so central to reflection on the 'hashish state' during the nineteenth century, in that it was such a significant component of Orientalist occulture. Indeed, its importance for writers such as Ludlow, Taylor and Dumas had less to do with the fact that hashish use is mentioned in the *Arabian Nights* and more to do with the exotic, spiritual world it presented to them. It's worth noting that, not only is hashish not dwelt upon in the *Arabian Nights*, but when it is mentioned, as Robert Irwin comments, it is often within 'simple, crudely constructed tales, aimed at an audience which had a taste for bawdy or even lavatorial humour',[93] which would have been of little interest to Ludlow and Taylor, if not Dumas. For example, in 'The Tale of the Hashish Eater', a beggar, having being given a large lump to eat, believes himself to be reclining in a palace, while being washed by servants in preparation for a promised liaison with a beautiful young woman. However, while still excited at the prospect of his encounter, his head began to clear, the vision faded, and he found himself surrounded by a group of people 'laughing at him with all their hearts at his naked zabb, which stood up in the air as far as humanly possible ...'[94] Again, such stories detract from the spiritual significance with which nineteenth-century writers such as Ludlow sought to invest hashish. Hence, rather than turning to the portrayal of hashish intoxication in the *Arabian Nights*, those seeking access to paradise focused on earlier drug writing, such as that of De Quincey and the Romantics. Nevertheless, the key point is that, as noted above, Westerners, who had been enchanted by stories of the Orient, believed that they had found in hashish a psychoactive substance capable of spiritually transporting them in an easterly direction.

Informing all this, of course, was an enthusiasm for Romantic ideas, the essence of which, as Bernard Reardon comments, 'lies in the inexpungable feeling that the finite is not self-explanatory and self-justifying, but that behind it and within it – shining, as it were, through it – there is always an infinite "beyond," and that he who has once glimpsed the infinity that permeates as well as transcends all finitude can never again rest content with the paltry this-and-that, the rationalized simplicities, of everyday life'.[95] Hashish intoxication meshed neatly with these concerns. Terrible though some of the visions could be – Ludlow often describes, with the hyperbole of Baudelaire, the experience as 'a daring venture into the realms of insanity and death'[96] – the altered states it induced confirmed that behind and within the material world there is indeed an infinite beyond, that, once glimpsed, leaves the user frustrated with 'the paltry this-and-that' of everyday life and with a greater appreciation of the depth and breadth of reality. Hence, again, like Baudelaire, even when denouncing hashish as 'the witch-plant of hell' or 'the weed of madness' or 'the drug of sorcery', he is keen to stress 'its revelation of interior mysteries'.[97]

Ludlow's own Romantic tendencies were the result of, not only the experience of hashish intoxication, along with his reading of De Quincey and the English Romantics, but also, arguably, the influence of Laurens Perseus Hickok, his Professor of Mental and Moral Philosophy at Union College, Schenectady, New York. An ordained minister, Hickok had also been a Professor of Theology at both Western Reserve College (1836) and Auburn Theological Seminary (1844).[98] According to Ludlow, he was 'almost the only real metaphysician of America, perhaps the greatest now living anywhere, and worthy to be classed with the strongest and deepest thinkers of any age or land ...'[99] Certainly, his magnum opus, *Rational Psychology; or, The Subjective Idea and the Objective Law of All Intelligence* (1849),[100] is regarded by some as one of the most important studies in psychology produced during the nineteenth century[101] – although it should be noted that his thought is highly idiosyncratic and, regardless of the plaudits it received at the time, by the close of the nineteenth century it was rarely mentioned in key works of psychology.[102] Nevertheless, Hickok can be considered an important early American interpreter of German Idealism. A large and complex work, *Rational Psychology* is essentially an attempt to provide a way for the study of the mind to progress beyond a description of the facts of conscious experience (he is critical of both John Locke and David Hume). Influenced by Kant's *Critique of Pure Reason*, he wanted to excavate the universal *a priori* principles that determine what we experience empirically. 'In this science [rational psychology], we pass from the facts of experience wholly out beyond it, and seek for the *rationale* of experience itself in the necessary and universal principles which must be conditional for all facts of a possible experience. We seek to determine how it is possible for an experience to be, from those *à priori* conditions which render all the functions of an intellectual agency themselves intelligible.'[103] In passing from 'the facts of experience wholly out beyond it', he embraced Kant's distinction between noumena and phenomena[104] – the noumenon is *the thing in itself* (*Ding an sich*) unknowable through the senses; the phenomenon is *the thing as it appears* to an observer as an object of the senses. This is not to say that the noumenal world of transcendental objects is entirely obscured from reason, so that we can know nothing about it. Hickok agreed with Kant that 'practical reason' – for example, the capacity to function as a moral agent – makes little sense unless one postulates the reality of a noumenal world in which God exists, a Platonic world of the highest knowledge, truths, and values, of which the objects in the phenomenal world are merely representations. The problem with Kantian epistemology, as far as Hickok was concerned, was that 'ontology, in reference to the Soul, Nature, and God, must be left to opinion and faith, and can never become science'.[105] In other words, Kant was unable to account for our knowledge of the noumenal world, which then led his Idealist successors to 'Absolute Idealism, and ultimately to Ideal Pantheism'.[106] Hickok sought to correct this in his rational psychology.

Ludlow follows Hickok, in that his thought betrays the influences of both Kant and German Idealism – which, of course, he also found in De Quincey and the English Romantics. Again, like Hickok, with a philosophy rooted in Reformed theology, while indebted to Idealism, he was also suspicious of pantheistic tendencies. Nevertheless, he commended the Idealists for being 'climbers over … that ring-fence of knowledge brought in through mere physical passages, with which a tyrannous oligarchy of reasoners would circumscribe all our wanderings in search of facts and laws.'[107] Kant, he argued, 'awakened … by the very perplexity which set boundaries to the mind of Hume, stands forth as the resurrectionist of the long-buried idea, and is followed, with more or less non-essential departure from his main track, by Fichte, Hegel and Schelling; for, although the first of the trio may be styled a pure Idealist, he follows Kant pre-eminently in the assertion of far higher grounds of knowledge than the sense.'[108] This was key for Hickok and it is key for Ludlow: there are 'far higher grounds of knowledge than the sense'. Hence, building on Hickok's interpretation of Kant and Idealism – which he sometimes referred to as 'Transcendentalism'[109] – he posited the existence of a 'Notional'[110] (i.e. noumenal) world unavailable to sense experience, but which can be accessed by practical reason and intuited while hallucinating: 'Great reason have I to be thankful … that I was suckled at the breast of Transcendentalism,' for, he says, 'the first moment when it flashed upon me … that we were not confined for our knowledge to the mere ungrouped and unsettled appearances of the Sense, was like a revelation; it expanded and dignified the soul with a sudden access of glories such as no earthly kingship could give. At that moment spirit appeared to me for the first time something more than a hopeless bond-slave of matter.'[111]

Central to his thesis, therefore, is the argument that hallucinations are intimations of a level of reality distinct from that available to the senses – i.e. a transcendent, noumenal reality. Therefore, a person in the 'hasheesh state'[112] can be understood to inhabit a different 'world' than that inhabited by a person in the 'natural', or 'unexalted state'.[113] Hashish induces an experience during which the phenomenal world 'is utterly violated'. Hence, 'in the hasheesh-eater a virtual change of worlds has taken place, through the preternatural scope and activity of all his faculties. Truth has not become expanded, but his vision has grown telescopic; that in which others see only as a dim nebula, or do not see at all' – the noumenal – 'he looks into with a penetrating scrutiny'. Indeed, 'where the luminous mist or the perfect void had been, he finds wondrous constellations of spiritual being, determines their bearings, and reads the law of their sublime harmony.'[114] Such preternatural insights into the noumenal world, into the world of necessary *a priori* truths, are difficult to communicate with any accuracy to one who has only experienced the phenomenal world and knowledge acquired through sense experience (what Kant referred to as *a posteriori* knowledge). 'To his neighbor in the natural state he turns to give expression to his visions, but finds that to him the symbols which convey the apocalypse [unveiling/revelation] to his own mind are meaningless, because, in our ordinary life, the thoughts which they convey have no existence; their two planes are utterly different.'[115] Although he moves towards a more mystical conception of direct experience, nevertheless, his ideas can be traced back through Hickok and De Quincey to Idealism and Kant. Hashish visionaries have 'spoken forth the symbols presented to their minds; yet from these symbols men around them, in the unexalted state, drew an entirely different significance from the true one, or, perceiving none at all, laughed as what was said as an absurdity.'[116]

Having discussed the philosophical ideas informing Ludlow's notion of 'separate worlds'[117] – the 'Ideal' and the 'Non-Ideal', the 'Visionary' and the 'Practical'[118] – we should also note that he was the son of a Presbyterian clergyman, the student of a Reformed philosophical theologian, and, in many respects, a deeply Christian thinker himself. As his friend, the painter Frank Carpenter recorded in an article for the *New York Evening Mail* following his death, 'I never knew him under any circumstances, to shrink from bearing his testimony to the central truth of Christianity.'[119] Again, as Dulchinos puts it, he was 'thoroughly grounded in "the old time religion"'.[120] Consequently, while indebted to 'Transcendentalism', it was Christian theology – albeit an idiosyncratic, esoterically nuanced theology – that informed his interpretation of 'the hasheesh state'.[121] For example, he relates his own experiences to those mentioned in 2 Corinthians 12.3–4: 'And I knew such a man (whether in the body, or out of the body, I cannot tell: God knoweth). How that he was caught up into paradise, and heard unspeakable words, which it is not lawful for a man to utter.' This passage fascinated him: 'I often thought of St. Paul's God-given trance.' However, he says, 'never was I more convinced of anything in my life than that our translation, "which it is not lawful for a man to utter," is wholly inadequate. It should be, "which it is impossible to utter to man;" for this alone harmonizes with that state of intuition in which the words are "speechless words," and the truths beheld have no symbol on earth which will embody them.'[122] Again, his understanding of the ineffability of the 'hasheesh state' is informed, not only by the Kantian distinction between *a priori* knowledge and *a posteriori* knowledge, but also by a theological distinction between revealed knowledge and natural knowledge. Those limited to the latter, find the former absurd. Again, although 1 Corinthians 1.18–20 is not mentioned, it is difficult to resist the thought that it was at least at the back of his mind during the writing of *The Hasheesh Easter*: 'For the message of the cross is foolishness to those who are perishing, but to us who are being saved it is the power of God. For it is written: "I will destroy the wisdom of the wise; the intelligence of the intelligent I will frustrate." Where is the wise person? Where is the teacher of the law? Where is the philosopher of this age? Has not God made foolish the wisdom of the world?' Likewise, according to Ludlow, hashish destroys the wisdom of the wise and confounds the philosopher with insights unavailable and unintelligible to those whose understanding is restricted to empirical knowledge and human logic.

'Blind philosophers! Nature refuses to cramp herself within your impossible law; she rejects your generalization; she throws off the shackles of your theory!'[123]

The hashish experience, however, in a particularly profound and intimate way, did reveal 'the message of the cross' to Ludlow. Throughout both *The Hasheesh Eater* and 'The Apocalypse of Hasheesh' he records – again, no doubt with some hyperbole – vivid and terrifying hallucinations, during which he witnessed the torments of hell and multitudes who have 'stamped upon their foreheads ... the dreadful sign of all hope of better things forever lost.'[124] Believing these to be accurate visions of the afterlife, he became consumed with a deep unease as to the security of his own salvation. There is, he insists, 'such a thing as damnation, for I have seen it. Shall I be saved?' The only way he could be sure of his redemption was to see his name inscribed in the 'Book of Life' (Revelation 3.5, 20.15, 21.27): 'Oh thou Angel of Destiny, in whose book all the names of the saved are written, I call on thee to open unto me the leaves!' As his hashish vision unfolds, 'the dread registrar' descends and stands before him:

> Silently he stretched out to me the great volume of record, and with devouring eyes I scanned the pages, turning them over in wild haste that did not preclude the most rigid scrutiny. Leaf after leaf flew back; from top to bottom I consumed them in my gaze of agony. Here and there I recognized a familiar name, but even my joy at such revelations took nothing from the cruelty of the suspense in which I looked to find my own. With a face cold as marble I came to the last page, and had not found it yet. Drops of torture beaded my brow as with eye and finger I ran down the final column. One, two, three – I came to the bottom – the last. I was not there!'[125]

Emerging traumatized from the hallucination, he became aware of a crucifix on the wall in front of him on which 'Christ, the Merciful was nailed.' He clearly interpreted this as divine intervention: 'I sprang from my seat; I rushed toward him; I embraced his knees; I looked intensely into his face in voiceless entreaty. That sad face sweetly smiled upon me, and I saw that my unspoken prayer was granted. Through my soul, as through a porous film, swept a wind of balm, and left it clean.'[126] Such expressions of Christian devotion, rooted in visions of hell and the experience of abandonment by God (*resignation ad infernum*) are, of course, not unprecedented within the history of mysticism; references are made to the Harrowing of Hell (*Descensus Christi ad Inferos*; 1 Peter 3.19–20) and particularly to Christ's own experience of abandonment during the crucifixion: 'My God, my God, why hast thou forsaken me?' (Matthew 27.46; citing Psalm 21.2). As Bernard McGinn says, 'the delights of rapture and contemplative vision by no means exhaust the variety of ways in which mystics have described their consciousness of God ... Some mystics taught that a willingness to be consigned to hell, if that be God's will, was a necessary aspect of the mystical path.'[127] Although Ludlow never refers directly to any Christian mystics, nevertheless, he says that he 'thirsted ... for mystical discoveries'[128] and, referring to his experiences as 'visions', clearly understood them as mystical revelations. Indeed, *The Hasheesh Eater* can be understood as a work of Christian mysticism.

Another of Ludlow's experiences during the 'hasheesh state', which needs to be interpreted carefully – particularly bearing in mind that he may be exaggerating the experience – also has something of a precedent in the history of Christian mysticism, namely, the moment of immediacy and directness when the self becomes indistinct from the divine. As McGinn discusses, there are a number of mystics 'who claim that God and soul become identically one'. At that point, they 'explicitly insist on the absence of all mediation'.[129] This type of union, which is particularly associated with the German mystic Meister Eckhart, Ludlow claims to have experienced on a number of occasions in relation to Christ.

That said, almost certainly because he is conscious of how his statements will be received within Christian circles, not least by his Presbyterian father, his accounts betray a certain ambivalence. On the one hand, he links them to the pride of Eblis/Satan[130] – a central theme in Christian demonology[131] – which, he says, 'is so often characteristic of the fantasia'.[132] For example, he describes how 'he grew colossal in a delirium of pride. I felt myself at the centre of all the world's immortal glory'.[133] On the other hand, while we have seen that he understood himself to be ontologically distinct from Christ, nevertheless he recalls a vision in which he merges with the crucified Christ:

> It was now with Christ the crucified that I identified myself. In dim horror I perceived the nails piercing my hands and my feet, but it was not this that seemed the burden of my suffering. Upon my head, in a tremendous, ever-thickening cloud, came slowly down the guilt of all the ages past and all the world to come. By a dreadful quickening, I beheld every atrocity and nameless crime coming up from all time on lines that centred in myself. The thorns clung to my brow, and bloody drops stood like dew upon my hair, yet these were not the instruments of my agony. I was withered like a leaf in the breath of a righteous vengeance. The curtain of a lurid blackness hung between me and heaven; mercy was dumb, and I bore the anger of Omnipotence alone. Out of the fiery distance demon chants of triumphant blasphemy came surging on my ear, and whispers of ferocious wickedness ruffled the leaden air about my cross.[134]

Elsewhere, he records a similar experience, but with an eschatological focus on the millennial rule of Christ and the establishment of a new heaven and new earth (cf. Isaiah 65.17–25; Revelation 21.1–4):

> My powers became superhuman; my knowledge covered the universe; my scope of sight was infinite. I was invested with a grand mission to humanity, and slowly it dawned upon me that I was the Christ, come in the power and the radiance of his millennial descent, and bearing to the world the restoration of perfect peace. I spoke, and it was done: with a single sentence I regenerated the Creation. A smile of exultation beamed from the awakened earth. I could hear her low music of rejoicing as she perceived that the fullness of the times with which, for centuries, she had travailed in woe, had at length been brought forth. All men once more lived in love to God and their neighbor, and, secure in an eternal compact, began marching on harmoniously to the sublime end of spiritual greatness. The nature of all beasts grew mild; the satyr walked down from his mountain fastness, and led his young fearlessly into the presence of his old foe, the leopard; the kite and the

dove imped their wings upon the same branch; out of the depths of the jungle the tiger stepped forth and gently drew near to fawn upon his king. The terrible lustre of his eyes was dissolved into the serene light of love, and as I caressed his spotted hide, he returned the kindness with a thankful purr.[135]

Again, such visions are perhaps what one should expect of a Christian on drugs, in that both the set (the pharmacology of a drug and the personality of the user) and the setting (the physical and social context in which a drug is taken) have a formative impact on the experience.[136] Having said that, regardless of the nature of these experiences – and indeed whether they were as vivid as he claims – they had an important and lasting impact. He understood them to be spiritual lessons, revelations of truth, which instilled in him 'the conviction that, encumbered with a mortal body, [he] was suffering that which the untrammeled immortal soul could alone endure. The spirit seemed to be learning its franchise and, whether in joy or pain, shook the bars of the flesh mightily, as if determined to escape from its cage.'[137] In other words, his disembodied soul was permitted to experience both the majesty and suffering of Christ.

Finally, this brings us to another key theme. In his discussion of 2 Corinthians 12.3–4, in which, as noted above, he compared his experience of transcendence to that of Paul, he makes the following point: 'Though far from believing that my own ecstasy, or that of any hasheesh-eater, has claim to such inspiration as an apostle's, the states are still analogous in this respect, that they both share the nature of disembodiment, and the soul, in both, beholds realities of greater or less significance, such as may never be apprehended again out of the light of eternity.'[138] That is to say, he interprets his experiences in terms of a dualist anthropology (i.e. the human is comprised of a soul within a body): 'the conception of our human duality was presented to me in a manner more striking than before.'[139] Indeed, he makes specific use of the Greek term ἔκστασις (ecstasy) to describe the intoxicate state, for hashish is able to liberate the soul from its embodied incarceration.

> In the course of my delirium, the soul, I plainly discovered, had indeed departed from the body. I was that soul utterly divorced from corporeal nature, disjoined, clarified, purified. From the air in which I hovered, I looked down upon my former receptacle. Animal life, with all its processes, still continued to go on; the chest heaved with the regular rise and fall of breathing, the temples throbbed, and the cheek flushed. I scrutinized the body with wonderment; it seemed no more to concern me than that of another being.[140]

This experience confirmed to him the Platonic notion that the body is little more than a container for the soul. That is to say, the discarnate soul is still 'possessed of all the human capacities, intellect, susceptibility, and will … complete in every respect; yet, like a grand motor, it had abandoned the machine which it once energized, and in perfect independence stood apart.'[141]

Once released by hashish, the soul ceases to be subject to the laws of the material world. Firstly, 'I was restrained by no objects of a denser class. To myself I was visible and tangible, yet I knew that no material eyes could see me. Through the walls of the room I was able to pass and repass, and through the ceiling to behold the stars unobscured.'[142] Secondly, not only was he freed from material constraints, but also, as such, he was freed from spatial constraints: 'Hasheesh I called "the drug of travel," and I had only to direct my thoughts strongly toward a particular part of the world ... to make my whole fantasia in the strongest possible degree topographical.' Should anyone, he says, 'suggest to me, however faintly, mountain, wilderness, or market-place, and straightaway I was in it.'[143] Finally, hashish also liberated him from temporal constraints:

> I remember that ... I had looked at my watch to measure the cycles through which I had passed. The impulse seized me to look again. The minute hand stood half way between fifteen and sixteen minutes past eleven. The watch must have stopped; I held it to my ear; no, it was still going. I had travelled through all that immeasurable chain of dreams in thirty seconds. 'My God!' I cried, 'I am in eternity.' In the presence of that first fist sublime revelation of the soul's own time, and her capacity for an infinite life, I stood trembling with breathless awe. Till I die that moment of unveiling will stand in clear relief from all the rest of my existence. I hold it still in unimpaired remembrance as one of the unutterable sanctities of my being. The years of all my earthly life to come can never be as long as those thirty seconds.[144]

As such, released from the moorings of space and time, he 'swam up against the current of all time; I walked through Luxor and Palmyra as they were of old; on Babylon the bittern had not built her nest, and I gazed on the unbroken columns of the Parthenon.'[145]

While, again, it could be argued that, regardless of any hyperbole, this is no more than one should expect of a person who had recently consumed large quantities of hashish, Ludlow is keen to establish that the experience had a greater significance than that: 'this was neither hallucination nor dream. The sight of my reason was preternaturally intense, and I remembered that this was one of the states which frequently occur to men immediately before their death has become apparent to lookers-on.'[146] Indeed, central to his argument throughout *The Hasheesh Eater* is that the drug 'is no thing to be played with as a bauble',[147] for it induces an experience normally limited to the postmortem soul. Hashish does what death will eventually do; it separates body and soul. As such, perilous though the experience is, it provides an apology for both 'human duality' and also the widely held Platonic doctrine of incorporeal immortality – at death the body is evacuated and dies, while all that is essential to the identity and nature of the self (the soul) survives.[148] There are even times during 'the hasheesh state ... at the moment of the most rapturous exultation', when 'the soul hears the outcry of the physical nature pouring up to the height of its vision out of the walls of flesh ... The cords which bind the two mysterious portions of our duality together have been stretched to their ultimate tensity, and the body, for the sake of its own existence, calls the soul back into the husk which it cannot carry with it.'[149] Indeed, he recalls an experience during which 'a voice of command called on me to return into my body, saying in the midst of my exultation over what I thought was my final disenfranchisement from the corporeal, "The time is not yet." I returned, and again felt the animal nature joined to me by its mysterious threads of conduction. Once more soul and body were one.'[150] Again, he says, there have been times of transcendent rapture that have been interrupted by a feeling of restraint, as if 'the cords' connecting body to soul 'were real sinews' inhibiting progress to the celestial sphere.

Mesmerism and spiritualism in the nineteenth century

As well as members of *Le Club des Hachichins*, there were a number of occultists in France experimenting with hashish, the most significant of which was undoubtedly Louis-Alphonse Cahagnet,[151] a mesmerist and follower of the Swedish thinker Emanuel Swedenborg, who described himself as a simple '*ouvrier*' – much of whose working life was spent as a cabinetmaker and furniture restorer. While his work within Spiritualism can be considered innovative and influential, it should be noted that, as Frank Podmore commented in 1902, 'in the Paris of his day Cahagnet seems to have stood almost alone. He belonged to no school; he persuaded few of his contemporaries to share his views of the somnambulist revelations which he recorded; and, but for the advent of Modern Spiritualism from America, he would, it may be hazarded, have found few readers.'[152] Indeed, much of the content of these revelations was, as he put it, 'of the usual post-Swedenborgian kind', in that they relate 'the constitution of the spirit spheres, the occupations of the deceased, the bliss of the after-life, and visions of angelic beings clothed in white, walking on beautiful lawns, in the light of a fairer day than ours'.[153] However, while Podmore is cautious regarding the validity of the early revelations, as Cahagnet's work progressed, so it became more rigorous and cogent. Finally, he says, 'in the whole literature of Spiritualism, I know of no records of the kind which reach a higher evidential standard, nor any in which the writer's good faith and intelligence are alike so conspicuous.'[154]

One of key early figures in the American reception of Cahagnet who was clearly persuaded by the veracity of his experiments was Paschal Beverly Randolph, who first met him during a visit to Paris in 1855. Indeed, while, as John Patrick Deveney notes, Randolph's encounter with Cahagnet 'must have been an eye-opener'[155] – certainly regarding the use of hashish – it is clear that he was already familiar with many of his ideas, as well as those of other French mesmerists, such as Baron Jules du Potet. He would almost certainly have been well acquainted with Cahagnet's three-volume work *Arcanes de la Vie Future Devoilés* (1848, 1849, 1854) and *Sanctuaire du Spiritualisme* (1850).[156] Both the first volume of *Arcanes de la Vie Future Devoilés* and *Sanctuaire du Spiritualisme* had been translated in America in 1851 – although Randolph's French was good enough for him to have read the originals.[157] Hence, while we will see that he sought to legitimize his use of hashish with reference to Oriental usage – the turn East being, as we have seen, increasingly common in the late nineteenth century, not least in occult circles[158] – more important for the development of his ideas was the work of Cahagnet and the drug culture of the burgeoning French *fin de siècle*. That is to say, not only was Cahagnet's work increasingly widely disseminated during this period,[159] but there is some comparative evidence to suggest that Randolph owed a particular debt to his cardinal work on hashish and mesmerism, *Sanctuaire du Spiritualisme*.[160] Indeed, it is perhaps not insignificant that, in 1859, under the title 'Hashish Visions', an account of one of Cahagnet's hashish experiments taken from the book was published as an article in the *Spiritual Telegraph and Fireside Preacher* – a popular occult publication with which Randolph had a close association.[161] Moreover, if there was any doubt about Cahagnet's influence on Randolph, this is removed by his published comments regarding his time in Paris. For example, he records that, using hashish, 'Alphonse Cahagnet, myself, and others, have been enabled to pass through eternal doors, forever closed to the embodied man save by this celestial key, and passing through them, in holy calm to explore the ineffable and serene mysteries of the human soul, and attain unto conviction of immortality...'.[162]

Before continuing to look a little more closely at Cahagnet's work, some clarification regarding Spiritualist mesmerism is required in order to understand the rationale for using hashish. It should not be a surprise to discover that, although cannabis use was not universally condemned within Spiritualism and Theosophy during this period, it was not well understood and, therefore, treated with varying degrees of suspicion. That said, many were increasingly intrigued by the possibility that states of intoxication might be spiritually significant. For example, in a report of a letter sent by Wilkie Collins to the co-founder of the Theosophical Society, Henry Steel Olcott, in *Supplement to The Theosophist* concerning the imagination and 'flashes of divine knowledge from the divine consciousness', the point is made that 'sometimes these inspirations come when the physical brain is stupefied by liquor or drugs, *a fact* but little known'.[163] Others, however, while acknowledging that 'opium, hashish, Indian hemp, and such things are resorted to with the vague and ill-defined idea of transferring the consciousness to astral realms, which is the well-known, intoxicating effect such drugs have', were nevertheless concerned that, 'like all other abnormal processes, the ultimate result is destructful to the one who indulges himself in this manner'.[164] Yet others, such as Adolph d'Assier, argued that those who use 'the hashish of the Orientals' have 'obtained no other effects than simple hallucinations'.[165] Hence, Spiritualists who had been persuaded that drugs were indeed useful needed to make their case carefully and cogently. This tended to be done with reference to already established practices. For example, we will see that Randolph included effusive accounts of his own experience that typically dovetailed with the concerns of Spiritualists: 'I gained more light... than from all the "spiritual" experiences of my entire life – real, positive, genuine, unmistakable light – nor has my soul ever parted with one jot of that light to this day'.[166] Hence, if more conservative Spiritualists had reservations, they also had to concede that, even if potentially dangerous, cannabis had some value within the occult world.

Of particular interest to Spiritualists was the fact that, as an article in the British occult journal *Light* indicated in 1893, 'hashish-smokers frequently get into a state much resembling hypnotism'.[167] This, of course, suggested a direct connection with the techniques of mesmerism/magnetism (the antecedent of hypnotism).[168] This is key to understanding the significance of hashish within Spiritualism during this period.

To unpack this last point a little, while the history of 'animal magnetism' and hypnotism is relatively convoluted,[169] essentially it is a theory based on a system of physical healing developed in the latter half of the eighteenth century by the German physician Franz Anton Mesmer. He used the term 'animal magnetism' because his theory was based on the premise that there exists throughout the universe 'something that he called "magnetic fluid" which permeates every living thing ("animal" here meaning anything that is animate, especially human beings)'.[170] Because he believed that illness was the result of blocks in the natural flow of magnetic fluid within an organism, he concluded that healing could be promoted by their removal. While, initially, he used iron magnets, which were beginning to come into general use, he eventually became convinced that 'the most powerful "magnet" was the physician's own body and that he could heal his patients by directing magnetic fluid in a concentrated form (through what he called "magnetic passes" or sweeping movements of the hands over the body) into the patient'.[171] Building on this work, Mesmer's student, Marquis de Puységur, noted that some of his patients fell into states of trance as he worked with them. Moreover, 'although appearing to be asleep, magnetized subjects were still conscious and could reply to questions and convey information. In this state of "magnetic sleep," as Puységur called it, the patient was very suggestible. Upon awakening from magnetic sleep, the patient would remember nothing that had taken place while asleep'.[172] Having said that, it was apparent from their communications during the trance state that they retained a continuous memory from one sleep state to the next. Hence, 'noting these two separate chains of memory that accompanied the two distinct states of consciousness, he came to view magnetic sleep and the waking states as "two different existences." From this beginning, the notion that we all possess a mind seemingly separate from ordinary awareness operating covertly within the human psyche began to take root'.[173] He also made much of the similarity between magnetic sleep and the natural phenomenon of somnambulism (sleepwalking), 'the only difference between the two states being that in magnetic sleep the subject is in a special connection or "rapport" with the magnetizer, whereas in sleepwalking the sleeper is in rapport with no one'.[174] Moreover, Puységur also noticed a change in the personality of subjects during 'magnetic somnambulism', in that they seemed to exhibit an unusual vitality. In addition, notes Adam Crabtree, they would 'sometimes exhibit certain metanormal abilities, such as the capacity to read the magnetizer's thoughts and a certain degree of clairvoyance, taking the forms of diagnosing the subject's own illness and those of others, along with the ability to prescribe effective remedies'.[175] Although Puységur resisted any mystical or occult interpretations of magnetism, they quickly became central to its reception in the West – which is largely why the term 'hypnotism' was adopted in the late nineteenth century, in an attempt to return the practice back to the world of medical science.

Cahagnet was firmly rooted within the tradition of mesmerism, in that he used the technique to induce trance states in his '*somnambules extatiques*', the most famous of which was Adèle Maginot. Typically, a session would proceed as follows: he would induce magnetic sleep in the medium, which he understood in terms of a distinct spiritual state; he would then name the spirit he wanted to communicate with; the somnambule would contact the spirit and provide a description, which served as a form of identification; thus verified, he would proceed to ask a series of questions of the entity, the answers to which were provided by the medium while in the somnambulic state. Again, this information often concerned the nature of the spiritual world, including heaven and the afterlife, current events in distant locations, prognoses of medical conditions, and even predictions of death – Adèle is even said to have predicted Cahagnet's own death following a period of six years, which, claimed William Gregory in 1851, 'on good authority' happened just as she had indicated.[176] However, while such claims were certainly sensational, his approach was not unusual within Spiritualism. Far more unusual was his claim to have used hashish to induce somnambulic ecstasy.[177]

In his earlier work, Cahagnet only infrequently mentions 'narcotics'. Of course, it would have been remarkable if he hadn't mentioned them at all, for, as we have seen, they were being used increasingly by French literati and, as such, cannabis-induced altered states had a growing presence within the emerging occulture of the *fin de siècle*. Nevertheless, he seemed initially suspicious of these developments, fearing that they might compromise the practice of magnetism. For example, in one recorded communication through Adèle, he is informed that 'there are narcotics which produce hallucinations more or less agreeable, and display to us pictures, scenes, somewhat similar to ecstasy', but that they also 'convey trouble into the nervous system' and 'disturb the soul in its vital functions…'.[178] Indeed, while the intoxicated mind can 'perceive the most burlesque scenes tacked on to rational ones… it knows not how to separate them, knows not where it is, knows not what they are; the reservoir of its imagination overflows, and hurries into the absurd.'[179] (Interestingly, the influential occultist Éliphas Lévi expressed very similar concerns and, as such, warned against the use of hashish.[180]) Consequently, he insisted that magnetism is 'the only means of attaining the ends I have proposed to myself; any other state, effected by the ordinary means of narcotics, leaves the individual too much dependent on the resources of his belief, the influence of his desires, and naught but very suspicious results are obtained.'[181] Again, through Adèle, he asked the spirit of Swedenborg the following question: 'Could you inform me of a means whereby I could enter into a state necessary to communicate directly with you, by the aid of certain narcotic combinations?' Swedenborg's answer is clear: 'The only practicable means is magnetism; any other state, provoked by narcotics, irritates the nerves, influences the ideas by disorganizing them, and cannot, consequently, be so good as the magnetic state.'[182] It's also worth noting here, that, betraying the influence of Cahagnet, Randolph expresses similar reservations: 'In attempting to gain lucidity,' rather than using 'narcotic agents… I strongly advise purely magnetical means…'.[183]

Having said that, before his own hashish revelation, Cahagnet does commend narcotics for occult purposes, but 'for external use only'. For example, he seems to have engaged in some early experiments with a range of rather bizarre preparations, such as narcotic pomade, the principal ingredients of which were 'flowers of hemp, flowers of red poppy or the wild poppy, then five *grammes* of hashish in a *hecto* of lard'. This should then be applied in 'the evening, before going to bed'. For the maximum clairvoyant effect, a person should – partly following his magnetic technique – 'rub it behind the ears, descend along the neck to the carotid arteries, then use it under the armpits, and in the region of the grand sympathetic, which passes under the left breast. Then rub in the same manner the loins, the soles of the feet, the thick part of the arms, and the chest'. Then sleep 'well penetrated with the subject which you desire to understand'.[184] Again, he suggests that profit might be gained from the use of a 'narcotic mirror', which was a method of scrying using the reflective surface of 'water distilled from Narcotic plants', instead of, for example, a crystal ball. He recommended, 'Belladonna, Henbane, Mandragora, and flowers of hemp, then a head of a bruised poppy, and three grammes of opium, macerated for forty-eight hours in a glass retort, of the capacity of two *litres* circumference, a full moiety of good red wine, after which put all to heat upon a sand-bath to distill.'[185] He concluded with some advice to his readers (not that many would have needed it): 'care should be taken that this water is not swallowed ...'[186]

Following his hashish revelation, his approach shifted significantly. By 1850, swallowing was strongly advised! In *Sanctuaire du Spiritualisme*, he discusses, with some enthusiasm, his experiments with hashish as a magnetic technology.[187] The book begins with forty-five '*propositions métaphysiques*',[188] which provide the reader with a basic outline of his Spiritualist presuppositions: 'life is only one thought which *observes* another thought'; 'that which exists *in general* is only a manifestation of Divine thought'; 'the spiritual world is a *state* of thought'; 'the material world is a *state* of thought'; 'we cannot glance at the smallest object which surrounds us, either as emanating from God, or fashioned by the hands of men, without seeing it as a Divine thought ...'[189] Moreover, based on the broadly Neoplatonic notion that 'each germ is the whole of its species', he concludes that 'the human soul is the whole of these species, and God is the sum of these wholes'.[190] Consequently, his articulation of what he calls 'this Platonic proposition'[191] is indicative of a shift in Spiritualism away from a concern with external disembodied spirits and towards a focus on the nature of humanity: all that can be known about the macrocosm can be discovered by exploring the microcosm. Hence the importance of the somnambulic state, the significance of which his own experiences with cannabis had confirmed to him: 'I was a universe in miniature.'[192]

As to his preference for hashish over other drugs, initially, he had tried opium, as well as a broad range of natural herbs and chemicals. However, he says, 'I obtained nothing.'[193] Nevertheless, he continued, for 'with perseverance, as they say, one conquers everything'.[194] Finally, a friend of his recalled that he had seen a card carrying an advertisement for '*Haschish d'Orient*' at an apothecary on the rue de l'Ancienne-Comédie. 'I ran forthwith to procure myself some of this precious drug.'[195] Within a few hours everything had changed. What he experienced was, far from being a disorganization of the mind (as he had previously suspected), actually an insight into the organization of reality: 'it would be an error to imagine it only as an hallucination.'[196] Indeed, with specific reference to 'the most curious' work of Moreau,[197] he believed hashish to have provided him with a direct experience of mesmerism's teaching regarding two distinct orders of reality: an exterior world, experienced during normal waking consciousness, and an ideal interior world, experienced during altered states. Of course, Cahagnet was not entirely happy with Moreau's psychiatric terminology (see Chapter 3), but this was a small matter that could be dealt with easily: 'let us hope that in a short time the words *madness, hallucination*, and *imagination* will be erased from our scientific language to be replaced by those of internal life and external life.'[198] Again, to those who might be tempted to consider that the visions produced 'by artificial means' (i.e. cannabis) are merely dream states (e.g. Baudelaire's 'artificial paradises'), he says, quite categorically, 'I regard it as a reality, not as a dream. Dreaming belongs solely to this world ...' Hashish enables us 'to penetrate thither momentarily ...'[199]

Furthermore, he believed that his intoxication had confirmed to him that '*birth* and *death* are the entrance of man into two different states'.[200] Take, for example, the following account recorded in *The Sanctuary of Spiritualism* and reprinted in the *Spiritual Telegraph and Fireside Preacher*: 'I could perceive what it was to die, and in this manner: I saw myself die; my body was stretched out on the bed, and my soul escaped from all parts of it like a thick black smoke, but instead of being dissipated in the atmosphere, this smoke was condensed two feet above my body, and formed a body in every respect like that which I had quitted.'[201] He then passed 'into a state of which I preserved no recollection. I think I did not speak, and know not how long a time I continued in it.'[202] Finally, he returned to consciousness, but was aware that he was still 'disengaged from matter'. Nevertheless, Adèle and his wife were able to communicate with him, which, he concluded, proved the independent existence of an incorporeal spiritual self within a 'miserable material envelope'.[203]

> I make use, indeed, of my material mouth to speak. That is true; without that you would not understand me; but it is not my body that speaks, it is my Spirit; it ascends to my mouth and issues from it, as by a door or a window, under the form of a small flame, to communicate with you. At this moment, I seem as though I were at my window, and that I am speaking to someone in the street; it is no longer my material envelope that thinks and acts, it is myself. In our psychological conversations, we call our bodies pitchers. Oh, they are in truth really pitchers, or rather not even pitchers, for pitchers still imply stone – they are miserable matter![204]

Moreover, the hashish-induced state, he concluded, is much the same as the ecstasy experienced by 'Swedenborg, whom we so much venerate'. He did not, he insisted, experience 'a different state from mine. I see what he has seen and comprehend what he has comprehended. Oh, I am as great as Swedenborg myself! I am his equal.'[205] Indeed, not only did he subsequently edit a digest of Swedenborg's *Heaven and Hell*,[206] but it is significant that he used Antoine-Joseph Pernety's translation, which represents him as a mystic and an admirer of Jacob Böhme.[207] This enabled Cahagnet to portray Swedenborg as 'an ecstatic' whose teaching was akin to his own.[208] Indeed, postmortem messages from the spirit of Swedenborg in support of Cahagnet's teaching, not only dominate the first volume of his *Arcanes de la Vie Future Devoilés*, but continue under the influence of hashish in *Sanctuaire du Spiritualisme* – which is dedicated to him.

From his idiosyncratic Swedenborgian perspective, Cahagnet's *Sanctuaire du Spiritualisme* discusses one of the core doctrines of drug-induced mysticism,[209] namely, the ability of psychoactives to penetrate everyday perception, to subvert hegemonic ideas learned in the material world, and to reveal the spiritual dimension of reality. Indeed, one of the most common drug-induced experiences provided further confirmation for Cahagnet, as it would do for Randolph, of the independent existence of the soul, which, when released from the body, is not subject to the usual spatial and temporal constraints: 'this second, I will that I shall last ten thousand years,' he states under the influence of hashish. 'Well, it has lasted ten thousand years; at this moment ten thousand years are only a second; I comprehend all that, and also that it can be so. Good God! I comprehend eternity.'[210] Hence, the state induced by hashish is, he says, so different from the material state that it is wholly impossible, while subjected to its influence, to appreciate the time that slips away, and the space that exists between the succession and continuance of these images. I felt a conviction that I hovered over the centre and above this microscopic universe, which nevertheless presented to me the semblances of form and space, producing the same effect and impression as materiel forms and spaces. Being swayed by the idea of observation and comparison between this state and the material state, I could not but pronounce in favour of the former. The materiel state appeared in all respects inferior...[211]

However, it's important to understand that Cahagnet is not here imagining an induced out-of-body experience in the sense in which that was typically understood.[212] In other words, the experience was not, strictly speaking, one of leaving his body, but rather one of going within, of experiencing the self as microcosm: 'Swedenborg is right in saying that we have in us a universe, since I can clasp the universe in one embrace.'[213] Consequently, because 'the spiritual world' can be understood as 'a state of thought'[214] – which, again, he understands in terms of a larger experience of reality – the common cannabis experience of transcending space and time is effectively achieved by going within. 'I found myself in the spots I desired to visit, without ceasing to observe that I perceived them in myself – that they were my domain. I had got the solution I had been in search of; I understood what man was – I was a universe in miniature; and I appreciated how it was a clairvoyant could be in Egypt or China without journeying thither.'[215]

Finally, for Cahagnet, all this can be interpreted in terms of divine providence: '*c'est par la volonté de Dieu que j'ai cette dernière extase.*'[216] It has been, he says, 'demonstrated to me that these hallucinations, so called by all those who have taken this beverage, and on whom similar effects have been produced, were intended to establish sacred truths...'[217] Indeed, Randolph reached a similar conclusion. 'I ... most sacredly believe that, properly used, it is an agent especially ordained by God himself to aid man in his search for light on the nature of the human soul.'[218] Moreover, he insists that, throughout history, numerous esoteric thinkers have received inspiration under the influence of hashish: 'thousands of people in all ages have used it to procure insight into the mysteries that surrounded them on all sides. There is no doubt that Confucius, Pythagoras, and his disciples, the Alchemists, Hermetists, Illuminati, and mystic brethren of all ages used it to exalt them while making their researches for the Philosopher's Stone, Secret of Perpetual Youth, and the Elixir of Life.'[219] He even goes so far as to argue that 'Mahomet derived all his knowledge and power from its use in the cave of Mecca.'[220]

Turning now to Randolph and American Spiritualism, his discussions of hashish were a significant, but relatively small part of a much larger body of work. As well as being 'an eloquent advocate of social reform', he was perhaps most well-known as 'arguably the founding father of modern sexual magic'.[221] Born in 1825 to a wealthy Virginian father and a Madagascan slave mother, he was a 'free Black' (i.e. not a slave) who referred to himself as 'the man with two souls'.[222] He was orphaned at the age of seven and raised in the squalid urban slums of New York. Brought up in the almshouse in which his mother had died, he was largely self-educated. Nevertheless, although, until very recently, he is rarely mentioned in surveys of Spiritualism,[223] it is clear that he rose to prominence as a popular and prolific thinker in the burgeoning American Spiritualist movement during the 1850s and 1860s. Even in Britain, his works were advertised in popular publications[224] and he was received at conferences as the 'famous' and 'celebrated American medium'.[225] Indeed, at the height of his powers, wherever he went he seemed incapable of disappointing his audience. He demonstrated an acute awareness of contemporary interests and what might entertain particular audiences. For example, at one meeting of the Charing Cross Spirit Circle in London, he caused some excitement when he delivered a trance address 'inspired by Sir Humphry Davy'[226] (the British chemist, inventor, and President of the Royal Society).[227]

Unfortunately, influential though he was within nineteenth-century Spiritualism, his life was, in many respects, a tragic one. While he can be considered, as Lana Finley comments, '*the* foundational figure of African American esotericism',[228] perhaps unsurprisingly, the African American community rejected him on account of his explicit experimentation with sex, drugs, and the occult. Furthermore, towards the end of his life, his fortunes shifted swiftly and significantly. In May 1873, he 'suffered a serious injury that left his left arm and side partially paralyzed. Apparently, while walking over a railroad trestle in Toledo – one has to suspect that he was intoxicated – he found himself between "two converging locomotives, one behind and one before," and fell twenty-five feet to the ground'.[229] Although he was still able to continue his work within Spiritualism, he became increasingly dependent on alcohol. Eventually, consumed by jealously, believing his young wife, Kate Corson, to have been unfaithful, he shot himself.[230]

Baudelaire was once unfairly attacked for being 'at once a mystic ... an erotomaniac, [and] an eater of hashish ...'[231] To describe Randolph in these terms would not be unfair. Moreover, unlike Baudelaire, there is little that is novel in his writing, much of which lacks systematic thought and suggests exaggeration, even fabrication. In particular, although often unacknowledged, it is clear that he drew heavily on the works of Bayard Taylor, Ludlow, Dumas, Gautier, and, of course, Cahagnet. Indeed, his discussion of his own hashish use contains basic contradictions. For example, in 1867 he makes the following point: 'people often ask me if I use hashish, and I reply, I took it twice on purpose, and twice accidentally, many years ago. I have not used it since, not that I fear its power, but because I need it not.'[232] Two years later, in 1869, in an article for the *Religio-Philosophical Journal*, responding to a person envious of his achievements, who, he claimed, 'thought to build himself up by tearing me down ... telling people I was a hashish eater', he insisted that 'I never took an eighth of an ounce in my life'.[233] Another year on, and we find him claiming that, while he had only experimented with the drug twice, he deeply regretted the experiences: 'may God forgive me for so doing. Nothing on earth could induce me to repeat [the experiments], or suffer others to do so, for I know no possible good, but much of unmitigated evil, can result therefore.'[234] While these contradictions might be overlooked, his story begins to unravel when one discovers that ten years previously, in December, 1860, he had already declared that 'five times – perhaps six – in my life, and that within a period of twelve years, I have experimented with hashish upon myself, in order to reach through the gloom toward the light,' commenting that 'I shall do it again, when I get ready', for 'I gained more light in any two of these experiments than from all the "spiritual" experiences of my entire life – real, positive, genuine, unmistakable light – nor has my soul ever parted with one jot of that light to this day. Under its influence, I became developed to what I am – intellectually reaching by it a certain point from which my soul has never ebbed again.'[235] Indeed, two months earlier, in October, he had already indicated that his use was far more frequent than a mere five or six times and that, within Spiritualist circles, he was viewed as an authority on the subject. For example, in an address on hashish to the Boston Spiritual Conference of 1860, he began by remarking that 'this Conference has, during its recent sessions, repeatedly called for my views on the question [of the spiritual value of intoxication].'[236] Moreover, in an advertisement published in the *Banner of Light* on 6 October 1860, he revealed that he had brought a large quantity of hashish from Europe, which he had been selling to persons with an interest in induced transcendence:

> In reply to numerous correspondents, let me say that nearly all the hashish I brought with me from Europe (and none other is fit to use) is exhausted. The balance I will sell at four dollars a bottle, with full directions how to secure the celestial, and avoid the ill fantasia. I have only twenty-five cases left out of three hundred and fifty, so that those who want the genuine Oriental article must send at once to Dr. D.P. Randolph, 17 Bromfield Street, Boston, Mass.[237]

It is rather difficult, therefore, to take much of what he has to say at face value. Of course, having said that, it needs to be borne in mind that, as an African American in the nineteenth century, he was continually treading on thin ice and conscious of the need to manage his public image carefully. This is evident throughout his work. Hence, in discussing his use of hashish, he will have been very conscious of the prevailing cultural currents, the sensibilities of the audience he was addressing, the need to make a living from a community that was often suspicious of drug use, and, of course, any rumours that may have been circulating about him.

As indicated above, Randolph had spent time in Europe, his first, and most important trips being in 1855 and 1857, and the final journey being at some point in 1873 or 1874. During his travels he became acquainted with 'the *haut ton* of European Spiritualism'.[238] It's also clear that he had familiarized himself with the bourgeoning intellectual and esoteric currents of *fin de siècle* Paris, where drugs and occultism had a relatively easy relationship – certainly several members of Le Club des Hachichins expressed an interest in esotericism. Moreover, in accordance with the Romantic penchant for the Orient, Randolph also spent time in Asia Minor and the Middle East, where he claims to have garnered occult knowledge, particularly from the Nusa'iri[239] (Ansaireh/Ansayree): 'I became affiliated with some dervishes and fakirs,' through whom 'I found the road to other knowledges'.[240] These 'devout practitioners of a simple, but sublime and holy magic', guided his 'soul into labyrinths of knowledge', which they 'themselves did not even suspect the existence of'.[241] Such claims are, of course, common within occultism, betraying again the significance of Orientalism in the nineteenth century. As I have argued elsewhere, occult travellers during this period simply assumed the superiority of the Western intellect in the discernment of esoteric knowledge.[242] Their innate intellectual insight enabled them to sift out the core mystical ideas of Oriental religion. Indeed, as Edward Said has commented, in Western systems of knowledge about the Orient, 'the Orient is less a place than a *topos*, a set of references, a congeries of characteristics, that seems to have its origin in a quotation, or a fragment of text, or a citation from someone's work on the Orient, or some bit of previous imagining, or an amalgam of all of these.'[243] This was certainly true of Randolph, for whom the Orient was an idea that became a space to be plundered. Exotic theories, symbols, and practices, which could be presented as ancient and authentic, untainted by the institutions and theologies of the West, enchanted his Romantic mind. As Ludlow put it, 'we are all of us taught to say, "The children of the East live under a sunnier sky than their Western brethren; they are the repositors of centuries of tradition; their semi-civilized imagination is unbound by the fetters of logic and the schools."'[244]

The principal critic of *fin de siècle* culture, Max Nordau, is scathing of occultism in this respect – and it has to be said, he was not entirely wide of the mark: 'the greater number of "occultists," as they call themselves, in their treatises on occult arts and magic sciences,' claim to have, 'without any pretext of "modernity," without any concession to honest investigation of nature ... direct recourse to the most ancient traditions.'[245] Indeed, Randolph was convinced that, not only could he accurately interpret ancient Oriental religion, but that, unhindered by the underdeveloped cultures within which it was embedded, he could attain a level of proficiency beyond that available to indigenous practitioners. His work in this respect was, he believed, necessary because the world was 'approaching the termination of the Christian civilization ... bidding farewell to many of its modes, moods, sentiments, thoughts, and procedures, and ... entering upon a new epoch of human history', which would witness the emergence of humanity's currently latent occult powers.[246] Hope for the future, he argued, was to be found in the 'semi-civilized' Orient, unbound by the fetters of Western logic, for here there was a repository of occult knowledge that would 'revolutionize the globe'.[247] Such knowledge was prized and Randolph confidently declared that, after only a short period of time, he had learned immeasurably more than teachers in the East had been able to discover for themselves: 'I became practically, what I was naturally – a mystic, and in time chief of the lofty brethren; taking clues left by the masters, and pursuing them farther than they had ever been before; actually discovering the Elixir of Life; the universal Solvent or celestial Alkahest; the water of beauty and perpetual youth, and the philosopher's stone.'[248] Indeed, while Randolph claimed that his own teaching amounted to 'a résumé' of what he had 'acquired in the Orient', and that it differed '*in toto* from all Occidental knowledge and the practice of spiritism',[249] it was, in fact, little more than a development of the latter. This is conspicuously the case concerning hashish, which was almost certainly the principal ingredient in the 'celestial Alkahest' – what he elsewhere refers to as 'Alla-chichi' and 'Dowam meskh'.[250]

His influences are conspicuous. As well as references to *The Count of Monte Cristo* and the *Arabian Nights*,[251] he tells us that, 'lured by what Cahagnet wrote about the use of narcotic agents and strengthened by the hope of what Théophile Gautier, Bayard Taylor, Fitz Hugh Ludlow and various other travellers wrote regarding the use of [hashish], early in the year 1855, I was led to make two experiments...'[252] Indeed, their

Orientalism, including their references to the legend of the Assassins, had a formative influence on Randolph's interpretation of the hashish experience. For example, his comments on 'the Hashish and Dowameskh extasia and fantasia', which he links to 'dreams and their meanings',[253] betray the influence of *Le Club des Hachichins* and particularly Dumas, who he claimed to know as a friend – which is certainly possible, bearing in mind Dumas' penchant for Spiritualism and his presence in Paris during Randolph's visit.[254] Again, his use of the term '*fantasia*' for the hashish experience, which he will also have read in Ludlow and popular articles on the subject,[255] was commonly used by Gautier, Moreau and, no doubt, Dumas.[256] More significantly, however, he fetishizes the Parisians' preferred way of consuming the drug. That is to say, as indicated above, he makes much of the significance of 'Dowam meskh'/'Dowameskh'. Described by Gautier as 'a greenish conserve',[257] it is described by Baudelaire as follows:

> In Arab countries, the rich extract of hashish is usually obtained by cooking the plant's freshly culled crowns in butter with a little water. The preparation thus arising, after evaporation has rid it of moisture, resembles a greenish-yellow pomade and retains the unpleasant odor of hashish and rancid butter. In this form, it is taken in small pellets of two to four grams. Because of its repugnant odor, which intensifies over time, the Arabs mix the rich extract into a sweet jam. The most commonly employed of these preparations is *dawamesk*, a blend of rich extract, sugar, and diverse flavorings, such as vanilla, cinnamon, pistachio, almond, and nutmeg.[258]

Dowameskh was important for Randolph – as it was for Moreau, Gautier, and Dumas – largely because it was an authentic Oriental preparation. Indeed, writing during his brief period as a purveyor of hashish, he stresses the importance of using the highest-grade Oriental hashish – such as that which he himself had in stock! His comments, while idiosyncratic and misleading, are nevertheless worth quoting:

> a deal of misapprehension exists in this country as to what this substance really is. Most people think that it is the ordinary extract of *Cannabis indica*. A greater mistake was never made. 'Hashish' is a slang term, used in the Orient, just as we use the term 'rum' in a generic sense. We use 'rum' when we mean alcoholic stimulants of whatever shape or form; and just so does the term 'hashish' stand for a whole class of exhilarants, although in European lands and here, it is mainly given to the inspissated juice of India hemp, which juice, as well as the common 'extracts,' are better calculated to make those who use them, under the delusive hope of making half-hour trips to heaven by the 'Hashish Express,' repent their folly, than even our modern tangle foot whiskey, which we well know will kill at forty rods. All these mongrel extracts of hemp are on a par with that staple article extract of American commerce.[259]

However, he says, there are 'higher preparations, which, while coming under the general term "hashish," or exhilarants, are as superior to all the "extracts" as is pure grape juice to New England "R.G."'[260] In particular, there are three Oriental varieties of which hemp is the basis: 'First, *affiyooni*, the common "drunk" [*sic*],' by which he is almost certainly referring to *bhang*, which, we have seen, was used recreationally as a mild intoxicant. Second (probably drawing on 'The Tale of the Hashish Eater' in the *Arabian Nights*), he identifies '*dabreeb*', which, he claims, is used 'in Oriental lands' as 'the grand sexual invigorator of the harems. It is one of the perpetuators of polygamy, inasmuch as it keeps up the vigor to a greater length of time; and, without it, one wife would suffice one husband ... Its effect is to increase the vital energies, make a beggar feel himself a Lord'.²⁶¹ The third preparation is 'dowam meskh', which has been used 'for ages by the Orientals' as a technology of transcendence, for 'beyond all question', it is 'one of the most remarkable things on earth'. Claiming to 'speak from experience', he assured his readers that it

> leads the soul to glory ineffable and imparts a rapture and bliss not to be measured by mortal standards. It is the 'royal road' to a kind of mediumship, whose magnificent revealments are as superior to those of the so-called 'state', as is the blazing sun to a common candle; and I have no doubt that the clairvoyance it induces is as far superior to the ordinary sort, as gold is better than block tin for jewelry. True, it will not produce this holy state in all, but will in a majority of cases. It not only affects the body, but the very soul itself, and produces an ecstasy, and mental and spiritual illumination, whose unutterable glory, superlative grandeur, and awful sublimity, transcend my powers of description.²⁶²

Indeed, in order to establish a link with the Orient, in a similar way to Ludlow, he argued that the *Arabian Nights* is not simply a collection of imaginative stories, but is rather the result of 'so many doses of hashish, penned as the visions occurred'.²⁶³ That is to say, there is that which is of esoteric import in the very stories themselves, because 'whoever wrote the *Arabian Nights*, did so under hashish, and thousands of people in all ages have used it to procure an insight into the mysteries that surrounded them on all sides'.²⁶⁴ The overall point is that, at some level, *the* Oriental provenance of hashish legitimizes its significance as an occult technology of transcendence. This is why, of course, he informs his readers that the knowledge imparted in his work originated in the teachings of 'dervishes and fakirs'.²⁶⁵

In order to further understand his interpretation of the hashish experience, more needs to be said about the basic contours of his esoteric thought. While his teaching is rather convoluted and evolved over a number of years, nevertheless, by 1862, his core ideas had begun to take shape. In *Dealings with the Dead*²⁶⁶ (which doesn't discuss hashish) he sets out his broadly Neoplatonic cosmology, consisting of a 'Central Sun', the origin of the 'All', within which God is immanently present.²⁶⁷ 'Coruscating out eternally from this sun are three forms of fire or light. One of these becomes matter, another is the highest form of the all-pervading and sustaining fluid of the magnetists, and the last is the stream of soul monads – thoughts of God ... "Individual monads – all men and women – are scintillas or parts of this great thought of the Mighty Thinker, God; they are coruscations from the Over-Soul, while matter is constituted of ethereal from God's Infinite Body."'²⁶⁸ This is not far from Cahagnet's 'Platonic proposition'. However, while Randolph also argued that 'man is a microcosm – a universe in miniature'[269] – his vision, depicting a celestial hierarchy, is grander and more Neoplatonic than that of Cahagnet. Not only is 'man a world within himself', but, 'he is an entire system of worlds'; 'the Soul, I soon discovered, was a Vastitude in and of itself'.[270] He refers to this interior microcosm as the 'Soul-world' (distinct from the mundane 'Spirit-world'), within which the soul progresses back towards its source, God. That is to say, the origin of the 'monad', which becomes a soul, is in 'the Over-soul himself'.[271] Indeed, he provided the reader with an autobiographical account of the development of the monad, beginning with its genesis in the 'heart of God'. Although its progress is one of transmigration, it can also be likened to Hegel's triumphalist Idealist narrative of the self-comprehension of *Geist*, in that he described a gradual unfolding, over long periods of time and through various forms of matter and animal life (including racial and cultural hierarchies[272]), into a self-conscious, immortal soul: 'I awoke to a consciousness of self, and man, the immortal, stood revealed!'[273] As a self-conscious soul, Randolph could now reflect on that Neoplatonic process: 'with me there were myriads of others, for in every molecule of spiritual and material substance, was imbedded one of my brethren, all longing to escape and return to the heart of God, whence we had been sent forth to perfect his great design.'[274]

Randolph also defended a tripartite theological anthropology, which distinguished the soul from both the spirit and the body: 'The spirit of a human being is the product of the physical body; the human being is a triplicate, composed of soul, or the thinking principle, the body, and an intermediate link, called spirit; *possessing all the organs of and shaped like the body*, and which serves to connect this last with the soul, while on earth, and being its eternal casket after death.'[275] Elsewhere, he referred to the spirit as 'a phantasmal projection' and a 'out-attachment of the supreme self'.[276] Having said that, this theological anthropology seemed to have been ignored when it came to explaining the spiritual significance of hashish intoxication, in that the role of the spirit seemed to have been ignored. On the one hand, the drug-induced states that enabled one to explore inner space – the 'vastness of the soul' and the 'universe within'. On the other hand, cannabis was effectively able to detach the soul from 'its material envelope'.[277]

Writing in 1860, slightly before the publication of *Dealings with the Dead*, he suggested that hashish was able visibly to manifest his 'soul' outside his body: 'I rolled up a pill of Hashish and Taraxacum about as large as a small pea, took it, and retired to rest . . . I slept in the upper part of the house, with door locked.'[278] At breakfast the next day, an occupant of the house

> stated that, notwithstanding the room where he slept was, as usual, securely fastened, and a light burning, yet that I was seen in that room, not as a shadow or spirit, but as an apparently opake [*sic*] form, which reflected the light from the lamp. The figure was unmistakably mine, but its features were bland, and wore none of the lines of care, sorrow-plowed, which mark my unfortunate body. The figure had life, for it mutely expressed solicitude for my host, a man for whom I had great regard, who is well-known as a gentleman and thinker . . . Now, the body of that soul lay alive upstairs, proving, he says, that the body 'is only second cousin to the soul – a relationship which it can toss off at will.'[279]

It could be argued, of course, that the reason this account makes no reference to 'the spirit' – which is odd in the light of his claim that it is 'shaped like the body' – is because he was still in the process of working out his theological anthropology in 1860. Likewise, in another article published the same year, he recalled a similar cannabis experience to that described by Cahagnet:

> On 29th of March, 1858, just after my return from Europe – I think it was on Sunday – being desirous of entering the clairvoyant state, and no magnetizer at hand, I took a jar of Dowam meskh from my trunk, rolled up a pill, took it, and waited quite four hours without feeling the least effect. I then returned the jar to the trunk, and walked out, thinking I had had my labor for my pains. Presently I returned to my lodgings ... I became seized with an irresistible impulse to open the window and the blinds. I did so, and ... lay down upon the bed. And now a tremendous experience followed; and *on this* experience I predicate *my* immortal nature, and of course that of all other human beings; for to me it passes belief – it is KNOWLEDGE ... I became conscious of being entirely free from the body, and with folded arms stood looking calmly at the body on the bed. I saw it distinctly! I watched the pulses through its heart; I saw it gently breathing ...[280]

Nevertheless, in the final analysis, he concluded that, while 'it is by no means an easy task to define where the objective begins and the subjective terminates, hashish will, in the hands of judicious persons, be the means of solving many a knotty problem connected with the soul, its nature, and destiny'.[281]

Early theosophy

At this point, it's worth considering some comments of Theosophy's principal thinker, Helena Petrovna Blavatsky. While her work can be used selectively to support abstinence, there is also a clear appreciation of the use of drugs as spiritual aids. On the one hand, she insists that 'a Sadhu who uses *ganja* and *sooka* – intoxicant drugs – is but a sham ascetic. Instead of leading his followers to *Moksha*, he does but drag them along with himself into the ditch ... A pretty business that, for a religious teacher!'[282] On the other hand, she also indicated that she was herself not a stranger to this 'pretty business'. To begin with, as Hannah Wolff observed in 1891, she was a heavy smoker who 'rolled and smoked cigarettes with marvellous rapidity'.[283] She even claimed that the effects of smoking tobacco were spiritually beneficial: 'my most precious thoughts come to me in my smoking hours. My mind is then tranquil, and I feel lifted from the earth, and I close my eyes and float on an on, anywhere or wherever I wish.'[284] More significantly, however, there is good evidence to suggest that she used cannabis – and may even have been referring to its effects in that last comment. For example, after a meeting with her, Wolff recorded in a letter originally sent to the editor of *The Better Way* that, not only was it 'evident from the first that she smoked tobacco to great excess', but also that she 'was addicted to the use of hashish'. Indeed, Wolff described how 'she, several times, endeavoured to persuade me to try the effect upon myself'. She also reported that

Blavatsky related to her that 'she had smoked opium, seen its visions, and dreamed its dreams, but that the beatitudes enjoyed in the use of haschish were as heaven to its hell. She said she found nothing to compare with its effects in arousing and stimulating the imagination.'[285] This account is supported by the comments of Blavatsky's friend Albert Rawson. Not only does he confirm that 'she had tried hasheesh in Cairo with success', as had Taylor and Randolph,[286] but he also confirmed that 'she again indulged in it in [New York] under the care of myself and Dr. Edward Sutton Smith, who had had a large experience with the drug among his patients'.[287] Indeed, according to Rawson, she once declared to him that 'hasheesh multiplies one's life a thousand fold. My experiences are as real as if they were ordinary events of actual life. Ah! I have the explanation. It is a recollection of my former existences, my previous incarnations. It is a wonderful drug, and it clears up a profound mystery.'[288]

It is not surprising, therefore, that, regardless of her Orientalist comments concerning the sham sadhus who use *ganja* in India,[289] elsewhere in her work she was more approving of the cannabis experience. For example, in *Isis Unveiled*, she argued that some plants have 'mystical properties in a most wonderful degree'. Unfortunately, 'the secrets of the herbs of dreams and enchantments are ... lost to European science'. They are, she claimed, 'unknown to it, except in a few marked instances, such as opium and hashish'.[290] Again, while in the modern Western world 'the psychical effects of even these few upon the human system are regarded as evidences of a temporary mental disorder', there are other interpretations of altered states available to the occultist: 'the women of Thessaly and Epirus, the female hierophants of the rites of Sabazius, did not carry their secrets away with the downfall of their sanctuaries. They are still preserved, and those who are aware of the nature of *Soma*, know the properties of other plants as well.'[291] This last point is important for Blavatsky, in that, as well as the undeniable effects of hashish and opium, her interest in psychoactive substances was primarily informed by references to *soma* in Vedic literature. Moreover, although she identified *soma* as *asclepias acida*,[292] rather than cannabis, it is arguable that her understanding of *soma* was informed by her personal knowledge of hashish intoxication. And, for Blavatsky, references to *soma* in these ancient religious texts validated the use of a range of psychoactive substances within esotericism: 'in the *Rig Veda*, Indra is the highest and greatest of the Gods, and his *Soma*-drinking is allegorical of his highly spiritual nature.'[293] Furthermore, she pointed out that, not only is *soma* associated with the gods, but, 'in mystical phraseology' it is 'the name of the sacred beverage drunk by the Brahmins and the Initiates during their mysteries and sacrificial rites'.[294] This ancient ritual usage further validated the use of drugs within occult practice. Indeed, not only did she claim that, as well as being a substance capable of inducing 'mystic visions and trance revelations',[295] it could also be identified with 'the Elixir of Life'.[296] As such, 'the real property of the true *Soma* was (and *is*) to make a new *man* of the Initiate, after he is *reborn*, namely once that he begins to live in his *astral* body'.[297] A person under the influence of 'the occult force in the *Soma*',[298]

> finds himself both linked to his external body, and yet away from it in his spiritual form. The latter, freed from the former, soars for the time being in the ethereal higher regions, becoming virtually 'as one of the gods', and yet preserving in his

physical brain the memory of what he sees and learns. Plainly speaking, *Soma* is the fruit of the Tree of Knowledge forbidden by the jealous Elohim to Adam and Eve or *Yahve*, 'lest Man should become as one of us.'[299]

In other words, the altered states produced suggest its potency as an elixir of immortality and an imparter of *gnosis*. This is why, 'the initiated received "*Soma*," sacred drink, which helped liberate his soul from the body' and why 'in the Eleusinian mysteries it was the sacred drink offered at Epopteia'.[300]

As far as this discussion is concerned, her comments are interesting because, not only do they tell us something about the significance of her experiences of cannabis intoxication, but also they resemble those recorded by Cahagnet and Randolph. These were clearly ideas circulating within nineteenth-century Spiritualism. As she commented, 'even in that early period and before the "Rochester" wave of Spiritualism [i.e. the modern Spiritualist Movement inspired by the Fox sisters] had swept over any considerable portion of civilized society in Europe, it was shown that the same phenomenon could be produced by means of various narcotics and drugs.'[301] Moreover, to repeat the point, for Blavatsky, whether she was referencing *soma* or nitrous oxide, her understanding of the altered states produced seems to have been informed by her consumption of hashish and by her familiarity with cannabis literature. For example, recognizing that some of her readers, fearing social censure, might be timid about sharing experiences of intoxication, she refers them to the Parisian cannabis culture, where there are 'bolder people', who fear 'neither a charge of lunacy nor the unpleasant prospect of being regarded as wards in "Old Nick's Chancery".' While she was familiar with the work of 'our Brother Cahagnet'[302] – who, indeed, would become an Honorary Fellow of the Theosophical Society[303] – she particularly mentions 'Théophile Gautier, the famous French author',[304] who, she opines, used hashish to understand the experience of the opium-eater. Again, this, of course, is significant in that, as argued above, Blavatsky seemed to believe that cannabis intoxication was able to provide insights into the experiences induced by other psychoactive substances (even *soma*). 'Few are those acquainted with the French literature of that day, who have not read the charming story told by that author, in which he describes the dreams of an opium-eater. To analyse the impressions at first hand, he took a large dose of hashish.'[305]

This general experimental approach to cannabis, however, clearly worried some members of the Theosophical Society. As we will see below, several prominent occultists of the period betrayed an ambivalence to the spiritual use of hashish. Theosophists were no different. While, on the one hand, from a relatively early period in its history, the Theosophical Society advised against the use of drugs as detrimental to spiritual progress,[306] on the other hand, there is good evidence to suggest a more inquisitive attitude amongst early Theosophists. For example, as well as Blavatsky's penchant for hashish, Wilhelm Hübbe-Schleiden travelled to India to pursue *ganga*-induced 'God-intoxicatedness'.[307] That said, the bias within the movement was always towards abstinence and the development of natural occult abilities. Indeed, Hübbe-Schleiden's enthusiasm eventually turned to ambivalence. He became increasingly disillusioned with the results and worried that his experiments were at odds with the growing focus on temperance within the Society, particularly encouraged by both

Charles Webster Leadbeater, Annie Besant and Angarika Dharmapala.[308] Leadbeater, for example, insisted that, 'if we administer drugs of any sort, at the best we can act only upon the physical nerve, and through it to some limited extent upon the fluids surrounding it; whereas mesmerism acts directly upon the fluids themselves, and so goes straight to the root of the evil.'[309] It is unsurprising, therefore, that he warned against attempting to 'throw open the doors which nature has kept closed' by the 'use of alcohol or narcotic drugs'. This is because they interfere with the 'etheric web' – a layer around the human aura that separates the physical and the astral bodies. It is important that this web remains intact because it prevents the 'thought forms' and entities of the astral plane from intruding, uninvited, into the field of waking consciousness. The problem, says Leadbeater, is that

> certain drugs and drinks – notably alcohol and all the narcotics, including tobacco – contain matter which on breaking up volatilizes, and some of it passes from the physical plane to the astral ... When this takes place in the body of man these constituents rush out through the chakras in the opposite direction to that for which they are intended, and in doing this repeatedly they seriously injure and finally destroy the delicate web.[310]

As we will see below, these concerns were shared by a number of occultists during the nineteenth and early twentieth centuries.

Victorian occultism

Romantic Idealist notions of dream states and theories of the imagination helped to shape the interpretation of drug-induced altered states within late nineteenth-century occultism. Indeed, as Michael Saylor has noted, 'numerous *fin de siècle* writers ... promoted the Romantics' valorisation of the imagination as a faculty that was equal to, rather than subordinate to reason.'[311] Many occultists understood that, as Alex Owen comments – quoting the occultist Edmund William Berridge's *Some Thoughts on the Imagination* (1892) – '"imagination is a reality," and that "when the Imagination creates an image – and the Will directs and uses that image, marvellous magical effects might be obtained."' Hence, she continues, 'magicians of the Golden Dawn were taught that "Imagination is the Creative Faculty of the human mind, the plastic energy – the Formative Power," but that it must be harnessed to the magician's will in an intense display if controlled creativity of powerful and desired magical effects are to be achieved.'[312] Likewise, the self-experimentation with hashish of scientific thinkers such as Moreau, the exotic cannabis experiences described by Ludlow and members of *Le Club des Hachichins*, the metaphysical speculation emerging within Spiritualism and Theosophy, and the Orientalist lens through which hashish was typically viewed, all contributed to the understanding of altered states during this period.

One of the first occult orders of the *fin de siècle* to experiment with drugs was the Hermetic Brotherhood of Luxor, a short-lived secretive order established to teach practical occultism. Known to have been operating in the mid-1880s, it was indebted to the ideas of Randolph – although the relationship with him is not explicitly spelled out in their extant materials[313] – and drew several of its small membership from the Theosophical Society. Central to their work was clairvoyance and the ability to transcend the body in the form of an 'astral double' – as Cahagnet and Randolph claimed to have done under the influence of hashish. Indeed, the practice of clairvoyance included inducing 'the Sleep of Sialam', which was, apparently, an 'exalted conscious trance state in which the initiate communed with the Powers, Potencies, and Intelligences of the celestial hierarchies'.[314] It would be surprising therefore, bearing in mind the availability and popularity of hashish within European mesmerism and the influence of Randolph, if it had not been used. Although, the official materials of the H.B. of L. (as it was known) make no mention of cannabis, there is a direct reference to the ritual use of psychoactive substances in a letter from Rev. William Alexander Ayton to an American neophyte.

> An Altar had to be extemporised, lamps burning, flowers on it, incense burning, and invocation of the elements, what purported to be the real *Soma* juice drunk at a certain stage. The Adepts were supposed to be present in Astral form. I hesitated very much to drink this drug sent to me by a perfect stranger, & I thought of omitting it. However, I opened the bottle & smelt of it. All my life I have been used to drugs, & I at once recognized this. I knew its effects were most powerful, but I decided to take it. Whether it was hallucination produced by this drug I know not, but I was conscious of another presence, tho' I cannot say I absolutely saw any form. I was fully 3 hours at it from midnight.[315]

While the H.B. of L. was not particularly prominent, its interest in drugs can also be found among members of a far more significant occult organization, the Hermetic Order of the Golden Dawn – although, unlike the H.B. of L., it did not sanction the use drugs in initiation rituals or, indeed, encourage drug use at all.[316] Founded by three members of the Societas Rosicruciana in Anglia, Samuel Liddell MacGregor Mathers, William Wynn Westcott and William Robert Woodman, drawing on the rituals and teaching within Freemasonry and Rosicrucianism, the Golden Dawn focused on disciplined ritual practice in the service of an 'ancient wisdom'. It was established, as Robert Gilbert comments, 'in response to a demand among occultists for a society in which the occult arts and sciences could be practiced rather than simply studied'.[317] It did this by resurrecting a Rosicrucian magical tradition that united practical occultism with metaphysical speculation in a way that addressed late-Victorian concerns regarding progress and future regeneration. While it was, as Owen comments, 'a child of its moment', it also did 'more than any other Order to influence the development of modern magic in Britain, Europe, and the United States during the course of the twentieth century. It was without doubt the hidden jewel in the crown of the *fin de siècle* "mystical revival."'[318]

Part of this influence, of course, lay in its ability to attract some of the most creative artists and thinkers of the *fin de siècle*. The 'Hermetic science' taught by the Golden Dawn – which was, as Waite put it, 'a method of transcending the phenomenal world, and attaining to a reality which is behind the phenomena'[319] – could be, some believed, augmented by the use of psychoactive substances. In particular, Allan Bennett, Aleister Crowley, W.B. Yeats and Maud Gonne all experimented with psychoactives as occult technologies, as did a number of their acquaintances, including the Victorian sexual psychologist Havelock Ellis and the British writers John Addington Symonds, Ernest Dowson, and particularly Arthur Symons.[320]

As Symons tells us, the fact that he 'took hashish fairly frequently in Fountain Court and in Paris' because 'the sensations' it induced 'were wonderful',[321] stimulated much speculation about the significance of intoxication. Again, with reference to Dowson, he comments on 'that slow intoxication, that elaborate experiment in visionary sensations'.[322] Also interested in exploring the potential that cannabis might be able to offer to the occult life, was Yeats. Although, for many years, his occultism, rather predictably, bemused scholars of his work who tended to treat it as an idiosyncratic and irrational digression, it is now generally acknowledged to be 'vital to and inseparable from his aesthetic concerns'.[323] As he himself reflected, 'some were looking for spiritual happiness or some form of unknown power, but I had a practical object. I wished for a system of thought that would leave my imagination free to create as it chose and yet make all that it created, or could create, part of the one history, and that the soul's.'[324] He eventually found this system in the ceremonial magic of the Golden Dawn and acknowledged Mathers as an important influence on his development as a poet: 'It was through him mainly that I began certain studies and experiences, that were to convince me that images well up before the mind's eye from a deeper source than conscious or subconscious memory.'[325]

Having said that, he had begun to tread the occult path during his childhood in Sligo. Not only did the stories of Irish folklore he heard as a small boy serve as a resource for enchantment throughout his life, but, George Pollexfen, his uncle, was an astrologer who would also become a member of the Golden Dawn. Moreover, as Denis Donoghue comments, 'his friend, the artist and poet George Russell was a seer. Aunt Isabella Pollexfen gave Yeats a copy of A.P. Sinnett's *Esoteric Buddhism* (1884).'[326] Indeed, Alfred Percy Sinnett's Theosophical work was particularly significant in that it seemed to sharpen his focus. Certainly, as George Mills Harper has argued, 'his renditions of the kinds of stories that had long fascinated him' demonstrate the influence of Theosophy, the formal study of which can be dated to 16 June 1885, when he, with Russell and a number of friends, including Charles Johnson, founded the Dublin Hermetic Society. Two years later, during the Christmas of 1887, having been greatly impressed by a meeting with Blavatsky, he joined the Esoteric Section of the Theosophical Society. Over the next couple of years, however, his interests began to shift towardS ceremonial occultism and, on 7 March 1890, at the invitation of Mathers, he became a member of the Golden Dawn, a move which had the effect of alienating him from the Theosophical Society.[327] Later in life, following the demise of the Golden Dawn, he continued his interests as a member of the Order of the Stella Matutina and also as an Associate Member of the Society for Psychical Research (1913–1928).

As a Romantic occultist during the *fin de siècle*, it is unsurprising that he became interested in drug-induced transcendence. Because, as Margaret Mills Harper has commented, 'from start to finish' his work 'suggests the pre-eminence of what can be envisioned over what can be rationally explained',[328] the psychoactive properties of certain drugs were, at some level, always going to appeal to him. There is, we have seen, something about cannabis-induced altered states that coheres with the romantic imagination, particularly when that imagination views the world through an occult lens. There is an overlap. This is evident in statements by Yeats such as the following: 'much as a hashish eater will discover in the folds of a curtain a figure beautifully drawn and full of delicate detail all built up out of shadows that show to other eyes, or later to his own, a different form or none, Swedenborg discovered in the Bible the personal symbolism of his vision.'[329] Having said that, not only is relatively little known of Yeats's occultism,[330] but even less is known about his experiments with cannabis, beyond a few isolated comments that weave esotericism and intoxication together.[331]

Having been introduced to hashish by Symons in 1890,[332] he began experimenting within the occult milieu of *fin de siècle* Paris.

> I took the Indian hemp with certain followers of Saint-Martin on the ground floor of a house in the Latin Quarter. I had never taken it before, and was instructed by a boisterous young poet, whose English was no better than my French. He gave me a little pellet, if I am not forgetting, an hour before dinner, and another after we had dined together at some restaurant. As we were going through the streets to the meeting-place of the Martinists, I felt suddenly that a cloud I was looking at floated in an immense space, and for an instant my being rushed out, as it seemed, into that space with ecstasy.[333]

This led to a concern regarding the possibility of becoming detached from oneself while under the influence of cannabis and losing agency. While he tells us that he became himself again following this experience, he notes that 'the poet' who had provided him with hashish 'was wholly above himself, and presently he pointed to one of the streetlamps now brightening in the fading twilight, and cried at the top of his voice, "Why do you look at me with your great eye?"'[334] While this might be dismissed as the result of inexperience, for Yeats it was an indication of the dangers of cannabis. Again, he recalls an incident when 'a Martinist ran towards me with a piece of paper on which he had drawn a circle with a dot in it, and pointing at it with his finger he cried out, "God, God!" Some immeasurable mystery had been revealed, and his eyes shone.' Yeats was, of course, impressed by such intimations of revelation from the beyond, but, again, was also concerned by the outburst. 'The boisterous poet, who was an old eater of the Indian hemp, had told me that it took one three months growing used to it, three months more enjoying it, and three months being cured of it.' His point was that, 'these men were in their second period', which accounted for their enthusiasm, but, he insists, 'I never forgot myself, never really rose above myself for more than a moment, and was even able to feel the absurdity of that gaiety.'[335] It would be disastrous for his work, he reasoned, should his mind and spirit be impaired by hashish. As he put it, 'the hangman's rope' (made of hemp) is 'brother to that Indian happiness . . .'[336] Cannabis consumption came at a price he was not willing to pay. As Mary Catherine Flannery has commented, 'drugs, like any other excess, are for Yeats the same as death; hashish and peyote are escapes not available to him. He will never enjoy "immemorial impartiality," as he was never fully part of the tragic generation.'[337] In other words, he tended to observe *fin de siècle* decadence at a distance. Hence, although he did use drugs again, in 'The Stirring of the Bones', at the end of the second section of *Autobiographies*, we find him 'affirming consciousness and magic as the sources of inspiration', rather than psychoactives. 'Yeats knew what would not only save him from absorption [in the tragic culture of *fin de siècle* decadence], but also make him a great poet: the conscious use of rituals which would induce visions and help him to incarnate ideas from the *Anima Mundi*' (i.e. the Neoplatonic 'world soul').[338]

Regardless of Yeats's cautious approach to cannabis, there is little doubt that he valued the few experiences of induced transcendence that he had shared with his muse and the object of his unrequited love, Maud Gonne. Both were bewitched by the occult potential of dream states and intrigued by the prospect that these might be induced by psychoactive substances. Indeed, as Donoghue comments, the most erotic moments in her letters to him 'are those in which the theme is a shared vision, a dream of spiritual union. Maud was keen on such intimacies with Yeats, it was only physical conjunction with him she avoided'.[339] Hence, that drugs might foster such spiritual intimacy was appealing to both. They first took hashish together while in Paris in 1894.[340] Then, in a letter to Yeats in 1897, Gonne notes that she had received a 'dream drug'[341] from him, which was almost certainly some mescaline he had acquired from Havelock Ellis. Again, in 1898, they attempted spiritual union while geographically separated first with 'mescalin on 16 September', and then with 'hashish four days later'.[342]

Gonne also indicated that she very occasionally took hashish alone and, on one such occasion, managed to induce an out-of-body experience. In a chapter in her autobiography entitled 'Occult Experiments', she notes that, 'once, when I had got hold of some haschish, that strange Indian drug, I took the prescribed dose and nothing happened'. So, not unreasonably, she 'took a much larger dose'. This time, following a period of sleep and slight paralysis in her legs, she 'saw a tall shadow standing at the foot of [her] bed'. She continues, 'it said, or more exactly, the thought drifted through my mind: "You can now go out of your body and go anywhere you like but you must always keep the thought of your body as a thread by which to return. If you lose that you may not be able to return."' Immediately, she tells us, 'I wished to see my sister, Kathleen, and at once I was standing by her bed. She was asleep and her little son, Toby, was asleep beside her. I tried to make her know I was there by putting my hand upon her, but she slept on.' Gonne then began to notice that the house she had travelled to appeared unfamiliar. It was certainly not her sister's home in Dublin. She explored further and discovered her brother-in-law sleeping in what should have been the children's room. She then recalled the injunction that she should not 'lose the thought' of her own body if she wished to be reunited with it. 'I thought of it. I had a vague, fleeting impression of sea and clouds and wind and was back in my room in Paris and saw my body asleep on the bed; then, with the sensation of falling from a height, I was really lying in my bed, conscious of my heart pounding queerly.' The next day she wrote to her sister. 'My letter, sent to her Dublin house in Ely Place, had been forwarded to her at Howth.' Her sister replied, confirming her experience, for 'Toby had been ill; she had taken him to convalesce at Howth in the little house in which we had lived as children ... He slept in her bed. Her husband slept in the room opposite. It was all exactly as I had seen.' This hashish-induced experience thus led her to the conviction – as it had done for Cahagnet and Randolph – 'of the possibility of being able to leave the body and see people and things at a distance and to travel as quick as thought.' Hence, she noted, if the practice 'could be developed', then 'how interesting and how useful!'[343] But – and this, we have seen, was a common refrain within much Victorian occultism, as well as being a conviction shared by Yeats – drugs could only ever be a step along the way to the development of one's innate psychic abilities. While powerful aids to transcendence, hashish was invariably detrimental to one's innate abilities. Hence, while noting that her cannabis experiments were 'interesting' and 'useful', in the final analysis, she says, 'I wanted to do it by the power of will and not with haschish.'[344]

Finally, there was another prominent member of the Golden Dawn who adopted a rather more enthusiastic and less cautious approach to drugs, not least cannabis. Aleister Crowley was the epitome of the *fin de siècle* occultist.[345] He gloried in accusations of Satanism, delighted in tabloid vilifications of him as 'A Wizard of Wickedness', 'the Wickedest Man in the World', and the 'King of Depravity',[346] and, with reference to 'the Beast' (Θηρίον, *Therion*) in the biblical Book of Revelation, he occasionally referred to himself as 'the Great Beast' or the 'Master Therion'. Indeed, in several respects, he was also a good example of 'the tragic generation' eulogized by Yeats. While Yeats did not, of course, have him in mind – considering him to be an 'unspeakable mad person' who had produced, 'amid much foul rhetoric', 'about six lines ... of real poetry'[347] – the significant personal wealth Crowley had inherited[348] afforded him the luxury of being able to pursue almost any whim that occurred to him, and to embrace decadence, in much the same way that Joris-Karl Huysmans recounts the perverse pleasures of the wealthy and reclusive aesthete Des Esseintes.[349] Likewise, just as Yeats's tragic generation was haunted by disillusionment, *ennui*, and despair, often as a result of the persistent quest for intense experiences, so too there was a shadow across Crowley's life. His exhaustive search for moments of ecstasy did not always end happily and, in the case of drugs, led to the debilitating pain and ignominy of heroin addiction.

While there are references to drugs and short discussions of their effects scattered throughout his work, like Randolph, only a small percentage of his corpus specifically addresses the subject. Even fewer discuss the use of cannabis in occult practice. The principal studies of cannabis published by Crowley were gathered together under the title 'The Herb Dangerous' in successive issues of his journal *The Equinox*:[350] 'A Pharmaceutical Study of Cannabis Sativa' (March 1909) by E.P. Whineray – a London pharmacist who often supplied Crowley with drugs; his own essay 'The Psychology of Hashish' (September 1909); his own translation of Baudelaire's 'The Poem of Hashish' (March 1910); and finally, extracts from Ludlow's *The Hasheesh Eater* (September 1910).[351]

Reading through this material it quickly becomes apparent that Crowley was impressed by the ability of cannabis to produce what the psychologist Abraham Maslow would later call 'peak experiences' – 'an illumination, a revelation, an insight'.[352] 'Hashish ... gives proof of a new order of consciousness, and (it seems to me) it is this *prima facie* case that the mystics have always needed to make out, and never have made out.'[353] Consequently, as Martin Booth discusses, he came to believe that 'the taking of drugs – at least, the right "magical" drugs – should precede all magical ceremonies because they made access to mystical experiences all the easier.' Moreover, 'he believed that they were genuinely magical and he made use of the way in which they enabled him to re-examine his basic beliefs and values from a new point of view, reassessing the world from a magical and mystical perspective. One of the primary aims of his life was the extension of his consciousness by whatever means . . .'[354] More specifically, hashish was treated as a powerful occult technology in the service of 'scientific illuminism', the core idea behind which was distilled into the motto, 'the method of science; the aim of religion'.[355] Essentially, he argued that, individually, the approaches of both science and religion had failed in their attempts to access the true nature of reality. Crowley, therefore, sought to develop a *via media* in the form of an esoteric system that combined the methodologies of both. Cannabis was useful in such a system because, under the right conditions, it was able to induce *reproducible* (i.e. 'scientific') moments of revelation. That is to say, apart from being peculiarly effective in the production of altered states of consciousness, it equipped the user with a certain level of control. One could, with reasonable accuracy, determine, not only the time and place of a mystical experience, but also its intensity and nature. As such, it was an appealing substance for a mystic wanting to apply the scientific method to occult practice. Indeed, he was particularly impressed and influenced by the research of William James into nitrous oxide intoxication and induced mysticism. 'Since 1898,' he tells us, 'I have been principally occupied in studying the effects of various drugs upon the human organism, with special reference to the parallelisms between psychical phenomena of drug-neuroses, insanities, and mystical illuminations. The main object has been to see whether it is possible to produce the indubitably useful (see William James, *Varieties of Religious Experience*) results of "ecstasy" in the laboratory.'[356] While Crowley was no James, this does indicate something of the direction of his thought regarding the use of drugs in occult practice.

This brings us to his Thelemic philosophy. Keenly focused on the importance of 'the will' (θέλημα, *thelema*), he famously insisted that '"Do what thou wilt shall be the whole of the law." "Love is the law, love under will." "There is no law beyond Do what thou wilt."'[357] Central to this broadly egoistic philosophy was the notion of the 'True Will', which expressed his conviction that all beings have their own purpose to which, at the expense of all else, they must devote themselves. This is not to say that Crowley's egoism advocated simply doing only what one wants, but rather it insisted on the importance of discovering one's purpose in life – in accordance with the cosmic laws of the universe – followed by the fulfilling of that purpose. In short, one's True Will must be identified and realized. 'Magick' – the term he used for his system, which he defined as 'the Science and Art of causing Change to occur in conformity with the Will'[358] – enabled the identification and realization of the True Will.[359] Flowing from this, his declaration that 'every man and woman is a star'[360] suggested the potentiality within all of us for glorification. As long as we follow our proper course, the struggles of life that inhibit progress towards glorification will dissolve. Although, again, Crowley would discover that drugs can lead to a dulled and diminished will, he was also convinced that, in the right hands (and head), they could be incorporated into the Thelemic system.

If hashish is able to create a hunger for glorification and mystical experience, then, as far as Crowley was concerned, it is an effective means to an important end. This is essentially Israel Regardie's thesis concerning Crowley's understanding of the esoteric significance of cannabis. (Not only was Regardie an influential ceremonial magician, scholar of the Golden Dawn, and interpreter of Crowleyan magic, but it's worth noting that he too was no stranger to cannabis.) Having worked as Crowley's secretary for four years,[361] he argued that he was primarily interested in the ability of hashish to induce 'a foretaste or some adumbration of the mystical experience towards which he was focusing all his energies'.[362] That is to say, Crowley believed that, 'if the Neophyte could taste the glory and the ineffability of his goals by means of an introductory dose of hashish, he would then be willing to embark upon a lifelong program of self-discipline to make the divine an intrinsic part of his being.'[363] However, having said that, he was also very keen to avoid accusations of attempting 'a short cut by the means of such drugs as opium and hasheesh'.[364] It was, insisted Regardie, '*never* the intention of Crowley at any time, to use drugs as a substitute for the body-mind-discipline, which he insisted upon beyond all other things. This was the furthest notion from his mind.'[365] While the evidence suggests that it was not always the furthest notion from his mind,[366] nevertheless, it is true that he at least claimed that he had 'no use for hashish save as a preliminary demonstration that there exists another world attainable – somehow'.[367] His argument was that, 'since human nature is human nature after all, and since people tend to become discouraged and, from there, give up the struggle for enlightenment', then, as Regardie noted, 'if they could be given some inkling of what the ineffable experience could be like, perhaps ... they would be willing to overcome their own inertia and despondency – and work. It was the carrot to be waved in front of the donkey's nose. But waved *only long enough* to get the donkey started.'[368] As Gonne had intimated, while hashish is a useful occult technology, the aim should always be to move beyond it and to develop one's innate spiritual potential and magical skill. Unfortunately, while Gonne managed to do this, Crowley did not and eventually succumbed to heroin addiction.

The 'drug-life' began for Crowley when he was introduced to psychoactives by his friend, mentor, and fellow member of the Golden Dawn, Allan Bennett. While Bennett could have led a materially comfortable life, his commitment to occultism and then to Buddhism, as well as his chronic asthma, led to frequent periods of poverty. Indeed, as with many in the nineteenth century, it was the medication prescribed to alleviate his suffering that revealed to him the spiritual potential of drugs.[369] As Crowley commented, 'his cycle of life was to take opium for about a month,' then 'when the effect wore off ... he had to inject morphine. After a month of this he switched to cocaine, which he took until he began to see "things" and was then reduced to chloroform.'[370] As Bennett's life became increasingly organized around periods of intoxication, so he became convinced that 'there exists a drug whose use will open the gates of the World behind the Veil of Matter'.[371] Crowley was so impressed by his arguments, that once Bennett had 'imparted to him the rudiments of his pharmacological knowledge',[372] he began in earnest experimenting with opium, cocaine, ether, and hashish in an attempt to gain access 'behind the veil of the universe' where 'live the mystic and the true artist'.[373] (Such substances were, of course, all legally available in Britain until the passing of the Dangerous Drugs Act in 1920.) Together, says Crowley, he and Bennett, 'for many months ... studied and practiced Ceremonial Magic, and ransacked the ancient books and MSS of the reputed sages for a key to the great mysteries of life and death'. He continues:

Through the ages we found this one constant story. Stripped of its local and chronological accidents, it usually came to this – the writer would tell of a young man, a seeker after Hidden Wisdom, who, in one circumstance or another, meets an adept; who, after sundry ordeals, obtains from the said adept, for good or ill, a certain mysterious drug or potion, with the result (at least) of opening the gate of the Other-world. This potion was identified with the Elixir Vitae of the physical Alchemists, or one of their 'Tinctures', most likely the 'White Tincture' which transforms the base metal (normal perception of life) to silver (poetic conception)...[374]

Crowley would later bemoan the project as a series of 'fruitless attempts to poison ourselves with every drug in (and out of) the Pharmacopœia', because, 'like Huckleberry Finn's prayer, nuffin' come of it'.[375] This, however, is disingenuous, in that it is clear that his experiments with Bennett, who he referred to as 'a flawless genius',[376] were important to him and informed his thinking about drugs. Indeed, far from nuffin' coming of it, as we will see, a great deal came of it.

An ardent admirer of Richard Burton, the Victorian Orientalist, travel writer and translator of the *Arabian Nights*, in 1903, Crowley, with his new wife Rose Kelly, began his own journey to the Orient. During these and subsequent travels, not only did he betray the influence of Burton's interests and idiosyncrasies,[377] but, he claims that, in at least one respect, he went beyond the great man 'who solved nigh every other riddle of the Eastern Sphinx'.[378] Whereas Burton used hashish and regarded it as 'no more than a vice',[379] Crowley discovered its true significance. In India, for example, he related how he was taught 'systems of meditation' in which 'lesser Yogis employed hashish ... to obtain Samadhi, that oneness with the Universe...'[380] Moreover, while this was no doubt true, arguably more significant was what he was reading during this period: 'I also had the advantage of falling across Ludlow's book, and was struck by the circumstance that he, obviously ignorant of Vendantist and Yogic doctrines, yet approximately expressed them, though in a degraded and distorted form.'[381] In other words, not only does he claim that hashish was used to attain states of transcendence that were normally the result of disciplined meditation, but he also argued that accounts of cannabis intoxication in the West come very close to describing the experiences of mystics in the East. Nevertheless, he was careful to insist that cannabis should be used as a tool *along with* 'discipline and training in the meditative arts'.[382] That said, although we have noted Regardie's argument that he understood hashish primarily as an initial introduction to mystical experience, he does concede that Crowley taught users to 'expect far better results with its use than if the tool of meditation alone was used, and vice versa'.[383] Indeed, 'there might be occasions, even when one had acquired supreme skill in mediation, when an additional fillip or stimulus provided by judicious and temperate use of hashish would enable one to surmount the sterility and grimness of the long-protracted discipline, to soar exaltedly above the armored restriction of the ego-functions into the ineffable.'[384] As such, cannabis, 'the grass of the Arabs', can be considered a 'Holy herb ... which might be appointed for ... Enlightenment'.[385] Hence, again, he insisted that, while some might accuse him of 'pure sloth or weariness',[386] of laziness in occult practice, in fact he used hashish as a technology to 'loosen the girders of the soul'.[387] Indeed, in 1907, in an analysis of Crowley's philosophy (which is actually more of an erudite exercise in ingratiation), John F.C. Fuller claimed that this was precisely the case: 'hasheesh may in some way be the loosener of the girders of the soul, but this is all.'[388] However, that this was all it was for Crowley is doubtful. Again, it is difficult to avoid the conclusion that he found in hashish a shortcut to transcendence, which, regardless of his emphasis on the importance of skill, knowledge, and sober ritual, he was never quite able to leave behind. Hence, it is unsurprising to discover that, not only did he struggle to meditate, but also that he found hashish to be a significant help in realizing his spiritual goals.

> I was aware of the prime agony of meditation, the 'dryness' ... which hardens and sterilizes the soul. The very practice which should flood it with light leads only to darkness more terrible than death ... Meditation therefore annoyed me, as tightening and constricting the soul. I began to ask myself if the 'dryness' was an essential part of the process. If by some means I could shake its catafalque of Mind, might not the Infinite Divine Spirit leap unfettered to the Light? Who shall roll away the stone?[389]

The answer, of course, was the 'burning daughter of the Jinn' – hashish.[390]

Its perhaps worth noting that of some significance in his experience of hashish was the perception of transcending of space and time. We have seen that this sense of spatiotemporal transcendence/distortion, which is a common feature of the cannabis experience, invests it with an otherworldly significance. In a way reminiscent of Ludlow, he notes in his magnum opus, *Magick: Liber ABA*, Book 4, that hashish enables us to understand that 'Time and Space are forms by which we obtain (distorted) images of Ideas. Our measures of Time and Space are crude conventions, and differ widely for different Beings.'[391] The point is that hashish intoxication 'involveth the Mystery of the Transcending of Time, so that in One Hour of our Terrestrial Measure did I gather the Harvest of an Aeon, and in Ten Lives I could not declare it.'[392]

Although Crowley used a number of drugs within ritual contexts, particularly peyote, hashish, certainly early in his occult career, was never far from his mind. This was evident in, for example, his 'Augoeides invocations'. The relatively obscure Neoplatonic term, αυγοειδης (*augoeides*) – which refers to luminosity – appears infrequently in modern occultism. Crowley almost certainly lifted it from Edward Bulwer Lytton's Rosicrucian novel *Zanoni*, in which it is discussed in a technical footnote on the 'mystical Platonists'.[393] Lytton's novel, which relates the story of Zanoni and Mejnour, the two last survivors of an ancient sect, describes them as seers who have managed to transcend time, freeing themselves from earthly passions, and being unaffected by the ravages of death and decay. They were able to do this because they had found a way of living continually in the realm of the spirit, an advanced state that only the most accomplished mystics can hope to achieve. While the path to this state is extraordinarily difficult, requiring absolute devotion in order to survive the daunting trials of mind and body, Lytton also suggested that assistance might be found in a 'golden elixir' that 'some of the alchemists enjoyed.'[394] The suggestion of an 'immortal elixir', an 'elixir that baffles death'[395] which, moreover, enables a person to invoke spiritual entities (as

Bennett had claimed),[396] was certainly of interest to Crowley (as it had been to Blavatsky). Also of interest to him was the notion of Augoeides as the individual 'sphere of the soul', which says Lytton, 'is luminous when nothing external has contact with the soul itself; but when lit by its own light, it sees the truth of all things and the truth centred in itself'.[397] Although, at times, Crowley understood the Augoeides invocation in terms of communion with a distinct spiritual entity, his Holy Guardian Angel, at other times he used it to refer to his 'Higher Self'/'Genius' (concepts which were, again, common in Theosophy). Furthermore, as Marco Pasi comments, 'the ritual of the Augoeides is interesting because it took place almost exclusively in an imagined ritual space'[398] – which, of course, he understood hashish to be peculiarly effective in evoking.

The Augoeides invocation, moreover, formed part of the 'Abramelin Operation' as set out in *The Book of the Sacred Magic of Abramelin the Mage* – a translation by Mathers of an esoteric German grimoire, which had been translated into French, and which he had discovered in the *Bibliothèque de l'Arsenal* in Paris. The text, which became influential within the Order of the Golden Dawn, was, according to Mathers, known to Bulwer Lytton and the French occultist Éliphas Lévi. It included its own founding myth, which identified it as the magical system of Abramelin/Abra-Melin, an Egyptian mage, who passed on his knowledge to Abraham von Worms, a medieval Jewish scholar. Essentially, the ritual consists of a series of laborious and elaborate preparations, undertaken over a long period of time, the aim of which is to obtain the 'knowledge and conversation' of one's 'Holy Guardian Angel'. Having performed the ritual in his imagination, Crowley claimed that he had managed to achieve the same result as if he had performed it physically, namely 'Knowledge and Conversation of the Holy Guardian Angel'. It was, as Pasi says, subsequently 'perceived by him as one of the most important magical achievements of his entire life'.[399] The point here is that, in his discussion of the significance of hashish, he mentions an experience of 'what Abramelin the Mage calls the Knowledge and Conversation of the Holy Guardian Angel, another (and less metaphysically pretentious) way of speaking of the "Higher Self" or "Genius."'[400] Again, speaking of 'that supreme state in which the man has built himself up into God',[401] 'the final and perfect identity of the Self with the Holy Guardian Angel', he notes that, while 'one may doubt whether the drug alone ever does this', there are those for whom hashish can be an important instrument in the ritual: 'it is perhaps only the destined adept who, momentarily freed by the dissolving action of the drug from the chain of the four lower *Skandhas*, obtains this knowledge which is his by right, totally inept as he may be to do so by any ordinary methods.'[402] While there is necessarily some speculation in the above discussion, what is clear is that, influenced by Bennett, *Zanoni* and *The Book of the Sacred Magic of Abramelin the Mage*, as well as by his reading of Ludlow and Baudelaire, he used hashish-induced altered states to 'loosen the girders of the soul' within ritual contexts.

As to Regardie's discussion of Crowley's use of hashish, this needs to be understood as part of a broader Crowleyan apology.[403] More specifically, while he betrays a conspicuously more restrained attitude to drug use than that of his mentor and a preference for ceremonial work far closer to the teaching of the Golden Dawn, it is worth noting that his essay was written in 1968. Regardie got to know Timothy Leary and developed a relationship that, as Gerald Suster notes, 'stimulated his productivity'.[404] While deploring the undisciplined use of psychoactives and indeed Crowley's own addiction to heroin and cocaine, he began to appreciate 'the use of mind-expanding drugs for willed magical and mystical purposes'.[405] He argued that 'drugs are just tools for the exploration and enhancement of consciousness'. Each drug, he insisted, 'should be employed for a specific purpose and used with intelligence and will'.[406] Hence, although he rejected the idea of 'Crowley as a Victorian hippie',[407] nevertheless, in an effort to reintroduce his work to a new generation of seekers, he sought to demonstrate its relevance to the counterculture of the 1960s and 1970s by explicitly drawing parallels between 'The Psychology of Hashish' and the ideas articulated by Abraham Maslow, Aldous Huxley, Robert de Ropp, David Solomon, Alan Watts and, particularly, Leary.[408] Indeed, he commended 'wholeheartedly' *The Psychedelic Experience* by Leary, Ralph Metzner and Richard Alpert, as 'the only single text which approximates, albeit distantly, the hashish essays of Crowley'. He continues: 'were Crowley alive today and familiar with this work, I am altogether confident that he would have immediately written a "rave" review of it in one of his *Equinox* publications.'[409] Again, he claimed that, not only would Crowley have greeted LSD as 'the drug of choice, the ideal chemical instrument he had yearned for as the experimental aid to the magico-mystical system he had developed',[410] but also that Huxley, Watts and Leary in their own discussions of the drug were essentially following a trajectory initiated by him in the early years of the twentieth century when he experimented with cannabis. Indeed, possibly influenced by Regardie, the British occultist Kenneth Grant even argued that Leary 'identified himself so entirely with the current initiated by Crowley ... that he considers one of his aims to be the completion of the work of preparing the world for cosmic consciousness, which Crowley had begun'.[411] Regardie, however, went further, insisting that Huxley's argument that psychedelics can be used 'to potentiate the non-verbal education of adolescents and to remind adults that the real world is very different from the misshapen universe they have created for themselves by means of their culture conditioned prejudices', reflects the principal tenets of Crowley's philosophy; Watts' conviction that there is 'no essential difference between the experiences induced, under favorable conditions, by ... chemicals and the states of "cosmic consciousness" recorded by R.M. Bucke, William James, Evelyn Underhill, Raynor Johnson and other investigators of mysticism ...' concurs with the findings of Crowley's own research; Leary's assertion that 'the most effective way to cut through the game structure of Western life is the use of ... consciousness-expanding drugs ...' goes some way towards Crowley's own conclusions.[412] However, as far as Regardie is concerned, while there are significant lines of continuity between their attempts to dislocate a person's sense of reality, Crowley 'had the edge over most of our present-day researchers'[413] because he incorporated drug-induced transcendence into an occult system. This, he believed, was Crowley's genius from which the new generation of hippie explorers needed to learn.[414] That said, Regardie was open-minded enough to learn from the counterculture. As Suster notes, 'he enjoyed the effects of cannabis'. Despite his earlier resistance to recreational drug use, 'at the age of 76 he would serve coffee, cognac, and powerful hash cookies for those diners at his home who wanted them, including himself.'[415]

Temperance and ambivalence

Whereas some people embraced the spiritual potential of cannabis, others, partly motivated by accounts of notable drug casualties, became enthusiastic supporters of temperance.[416] Stories of addicted occultists were problematic because both esotericism and intoxication were often understood in terms of a profane influence within a Christian society. That is to say, cannabis use and the occult shared a space on the rejected margins of late-nineteenth-century Victorian society. They both tended to be linked to irrationality, profanity, immorality, insanity, and even the 'Satanic'.[417] This meant that those occultists wanting to maintain a certain level of respectability and, indeed, to attract new members had to do what they could to distance themselves from everything else commonly associated with that profane space. As Marlene Tromp discusses, 'one of the most distressing indignities for Spiritualists and damning for non-Spiritualists was the abuse of alcohol and drugs in the movement.'[418]

Addiction in occult circles was often simply because drugs provided an escape from the enormous stress that many mediums (particularly females) were undoubtedly subjected to, not only by fellow Spiritualists desiring confirmation of their beliefs and contact with dead loved ones, but also by rival mediums competing for clients and, of course, detractors seeking to prove their work to be fraudulent.[419] As Owen comments, as well as providing 'temporary escape from the problem of declining powers and popularity ... it was also one way of dealing with the pressure of constant séances and the unremitting demand for exciting phenomena. The pressures on mediums were enormous.'[420] For example, it was well-known that Kate Fox – whose experiences with her sister on 31 March 1848, are usually identified as the inauguration of the modern Spiritualist movement – succumbed to alcoholism.[421] 'It was rumoured as early as 1867,' notes Owen, that she 'had begun to drink heavily, and after her husband's death in 1881, she deteriorated rapidly. In England her reputation was discredited, and in New York she was arrested for drunkenness and idleness and her children were taken away.'[422]

Along with these moral concerns, there were also some related theological issues. For example, James Burns claimed that alcohol 'perverts all the magnetic sphere, turning the wholesome emanations of the system into poison, and laying the drinker open to evil spirits, besides degrading his own spirit in its operation through the body'.[423] Likewise, the English industrialist and Spiritualist Alfred Smedley admonished believers to 'banish the drink from your midst', and 'do what you can to prevent its victims from being sent prematurely, or at all, into "the land of souls"; then will your hours of spirit-communion be secure against unwelcome visitation.'[424] The link made by Burns and Smedley between intoxicants and 'evil spirits' and 'unwelcome visitation' is an interesting one, in that the argument would seem to draw on common discourses in religion around purity and pollution,[425] focusing particularly on the identification of healthy food with healthy spiritual communion. In other words, just as the consumption of sacred substances at the Eucharist leads to 'holy communion', so the consumption of unclean substances, taints the spirit, and leads to 'profane communion'. Hence, the rejection of cannabis within Spiritualism needs to be understood in relation to an emerging discourse on purity, particularly the power of food to enhance, not only a healthy body, but also a healthy spiritual life. For example, Tromp notes that the medium Elizabeth d'Espérance 'insisted that her sitters avoid alcohol and tobacco for up to six months prior to a séance because their ingestion might damage the spiritual energy and thus the phenomenon of the séance'.[426]

Nevertheless, just as there were those in the occult world who eschewed cannabis as a curse, and others who welcomed it as a blessing, many more were ambivalent. On the one hand, they could not deny the esoteric use of narcotics in the spiritually rich Orient and nor could they deny their conspicuous ability to induce states of transcendence. On the other hand, they felt the force of the arguments supporting abstinence. Indeed, as we have seen, many occultists promoted the development of innate human abilities and spiritual techniques. While cannabis might be useful, it should not be relied upon and might even serve to undermine those abilities. For example, the influential Spiritualist, Emma Hardinge Britten argued that, because 'Hasheesh, Napellus, Opium, the juice of the Indian *Soma*, or Egyptian Lotus plant, besides many other narcotics of special virtues, constitute a large portion of the preparatory exercises by which Oriental Ecstatics produce their abnormal conditions', they might be considered for use within Western occultism. Nevertheless, she rarely discussed drugs and, in the final analysis, was far more concerned to identify 'the all-omnipotent and restless power' of the human will in occult practice; 'the power of faith, is the power of will, the essence of Soul, and Soul's action in producing forms, and emulation of the creative functions of Divine Will.'[427] Hence, Britten commended 'temperance, chastity, and purity'.[428] Again, throughout the history of occultism 'the more utterly ascetic' priests and prophets were able to be, 'the more exalted their spiritual powers'. She concluded that, 'without a certain amount of fasting and asceticism, let none expect to succeed in magical practices ...'[429] Again, with Cahagnet and Randolph in mind, she argued that, while some had discovered that 'somnambulism ... could be induced sometimes by drugs, vapours, and aromal essences ... the best and most efficacious method of exalting the spirit into the superior world and putting the body to sleep was ... through animal magnetism'. She therefore advised her readers that, although 'the use of certain drugs ... might produce temporary excitement in the person upon whom they are exercised, nevertheless ... the effect is temporary'.[430]

Crowley, we have seen, was much more positive about the potential of cannabis, as well as several other more powerful psychoactives. Nevertheless, there are still the traces of ambivalence towards them in his work. Firstly, it is clear from his discussions of drug legislation, as well as a number of other comments scattered throughout his work, that he was conscious of the growing social concern about increasing drug use. For example, he observed that 'every other Chinese laundry is a distributing centre for cocaine, morphia, and heroin. Negroes and street peddlers also do a roaring trade. Some people figure that one in every five persons in Manhattan is addicted to one or other of these drugs.'[431] While he disputes the figures, nevertheless, he says, 'the craving for amusement is maniacal among this people who care so little for art, literature, or music, who have, in short, none of the resources that the folk of other nations, in their own cultivated minds, possess.'[432] He was a snob and this clearly bothered him. He did not want to be associated with this sphere of society.

Furthermore, like Britten, there was a concern that the power of the will might be undermined. For Crowley's particular understanding of the significance of the will, the problem was acute. For example, he was highly critical of those whose pursuit of the 'True Will' had been compromised. He was adamant that 'only weaklings fell victim to a drug'.[433] This, of course, meant that his own experience of 'the restless wretchedness of a morphineuse deprived of the drug'[434] was a deeply humiliating one. Therefore, again, there were times when, like most addicts, he simply denied that he had a problem and insisted to his followers that drugs had no power over him. Indeed, he seemed to believe this and, because he did, he struggled with the brutal reality of addiction. Unlike his hashish use, which he could control, he was disturbed that he could not resist using heroin and cocaine: 'it is for these and these only that I hanker.'[435] 'Heroin was,' as Symonds recalls, 'essential to his existence. He needed, too, rather a lot of heroin owing to his body's toleration: seven or eight or more grains a day, a phenomenal amount really if one considers that the usual dose is one-sixteenth or one-eighth of a grain. More than once I had steadied him while he injected himself in the armpit.'[436] Indeed, for much of the latter half of his life, drugs haunted and enslaved him.

A particularly interesting example of ambivalence towards hashish is the idiosyncratic and doughty social activist, scientist, and Baptist missionary, Adele Marion Fielde. Indeed, ambivalence seemed central to her thought, rooted in an irrepressible inquisitiveness. Although she was born into a warm, liberal Baptist family and was always serious about her faith, as a young woman she chose, with her parents' blessing, to join the more liberal and tolerant Universalist tradition. However, in her late twenties she became engaged to a Baptist missionary working in Siam and agreed to return to the Baptist fold. She travelled to Siam to get married, but on her arrival in 1865 was told that her husband-to-be had died several months previously. Although she agreed to continue his work, she was not well-received within the conservative Baptist missionary community. Apart from her critical theological mind, she liked to dance and play cards with the diplomatic community. Eventually, this led to her dismissal. However, she was later reinstated and reassigned to China, where she began training Chinese women to work as Bible teachers. She also established schools, wrote a curriculum, and engaged in humanitarian work. On her retirement from the mission field, she returned to America to pursue both a career in science (providing important research into the behaviour of ants) and also social activism (particularly in the area of women's suffrage), becoming one of the founders of New York's League for Political Education.

While she subscribed to Baptist Christian theology for most of her life, and while she naturally tended towards a rationalist scientific understanding of the world, it's clear that, following an early 'psychic experience' – an account of which she sent to the Society for Psychical Research in 1907[437] – her restless intellect was always ready to look beyond the doctrines of her tradition to the burgeoning occulture of *fin de siècle* America.[438] This led, later in life, to an interest in Spiritualism and psychical research. Moreover, in 1868, while still working as a missionary in Siam, she began secretly experimenting with hashish.[439] In 1888, following her retirement from the missionary society, she produced an account of her experiences as part of what she understood to be a scientific investigation into 'the problem of consciousness'.[440] This is significant for a number of reasons, not least because a summary of the article was republished by Britten in her Spiritualist journal *Two Worlds* under the title 'The Psychic Effects of

Hashish' – although she masculinizes her as 'Mr. A.M. Fielde ... the well-known chemist'.[441] While she was concerned about problems related to drug use, nevertheless, she suggested both that hashish can contribute to the scientific verification of psychic phenomena and also believed, like Moreau, that there is a 'close relationship between states of real insanity and transitory affections induced by psychic poisons'.[442]

The record of her initial experience of hashish intoxication, which seems to have increased her interest in the occult, repeats many of those discussed above, focusing particularly on the manifestation of a 'second self': 'about ten minutes after laying down the pipe, I suddenly became conscious of dual being. My usual self was awake, was aware of all my actual circumstances, was perceiving with clearness and recalling with precision the facts of my commonplace existence. I knew that I was lying on my back in a chamber of a native house, at ten o'clock at night, and was observing with open eyes the details in my familiar surroundings.'[443] Furthermore, she recalls that her 'double was standing in an arched and pillared hall, whose walls, furniture, and drapery were all encrusted with tinted gems, that shone with soft and exceeding brilliancy ... In the midst of this radiance and beauty I was infinitely joyous. Every atom in me quivered in unspeakable spiritual bliss, and,' she notes, 'I said, "This is the house not made with hands, and I am now in heaven."'[444] In other words, she seems to have interpreted the experience in terms of either astral travel or a foretaste of celestial rapture. Whatever the case, she understood it in terms of a profound mystical experience.

Moreover, the liberation of her 'second self' also seemed to evoke an experience of pantheism, which she describes in a way that suggests the influence of Transcendentalism. For example, she records her 'double' morphing into 'an automatic musical instrument, a complex arrangement of strings and keys, trembling in rapture while sending forth an enchanting melody'.[445] Again, 'my duplicate became a boundless sea, ravishingly cool, utterly free, rising in vast billows under an illimitable sky, and feeling in every drop of every wave the transport of my own pulsations. Then I became a continent, with wide meadows and verdant forests. A breeze swept over me and ruffled all my leaves. I felt my vital forces working in every blade of grass and every spreading tree, sending them gently upward. The thrill of growth was in them all, and growth was ecstasy.'[446] Again, the influence of Spiritualism is evident in that she recalls that, during intoxication, she understood clairvoyance and hypnotism. Moreover, the article betrays the confluence of Christian theology and Idealism evident in the work of 'Professor Ludlow, the hasheesh-eater of Albany',[447] which she was clearly familiar with and which informed her interpretation. The point is that, while she was aware of the problems drugs caused,[448] and certainly did not commend their use, she did not deny that, under certain conditions, they induced experiences that could not be ignored.

As well as the moral issues surrounding drug use, perhaps the most frequently cited concern relates to spiritual shortcuts.[449] On the one hand, as Gonne had remarked, if hashish could be used to release the self from its corporeal ties and, therefore, from the tyranny of the physical laws governing material existence, then 'how interesting and how useful!'[450] On the other hand, does this lead to spiritual apathy? That is to say, there seems to be some evidence within nineteenth- and early twentieth-century occultism of what Max Weber referred to as the Protestant ethic. He was referring to the value attached to disciplined hard work, which, especially in Calvinism, is directly related to salvation, in that duty, employment, and prosperity are signs of one's election.[451] Religion, likewise, requires commitment and effort. Cannabis is a problematic technology, therefore, because it suggests a quick route to mystical states that bypasses effort. This type of thinking is, for example, evident in Baudelaire's writing.

> If the Church condemns sorcery and magic, it is because they are contrary to the intentions of God, because they abolish the accomplishments of time, and would render the conditions of purity and morality superfluous – and because the Church will accept as legitimate and true only those riches earned by assiduous good intention. The gambler who has found a sure means of winning is called a swindler; what then should we call the man who wishes to purchase happiness and genius for the price of a few coins? In the very infallibility of the means lies its immorality, just as the supposed infallibility of magic lies in the diabolical stigma with which it is attached.[452]

There is something fundamentally worthwhile to be gained from the effort given to religious and cultural work that is denied to the person who seeks to arrive at the same destination by a psychoactive shortcut. Even Crowley worried that visions induced 'artificially' do not carry the same authority as experiences induced by magical skill and spiritual forces. As Symonds recalls of Crowley, although he had been taking psychoactive substances for some years, 'he did not want to reveal this in case anyone should think that his ... visions and conversations with the gods were only mescaline dreams'.[453]

Little sleep will be lost on account of such concerns by followers of some of the more recent religions and spiritualities that use cannabis. Rather, it is far more likely to be celebrated as an important, divinely ordained sacrament. The most well-known such religious tradition is Rastafari.

Rastafari and cannabis

Jamaica, the third largest island in the West Indies, is known, not only as a popular tourist destination, but also for reggae and Rastafari, both of which are the product of colonialism. Throughout the island there are place names and large plantation mansions that serve to remind Jamaicans that their land was, until 1962, a British colony and, until 1 August 1838, an important sugar producer as a result of the labour of enslaved West Africans. This is important for the present discussion because Rastafari is a religio-cultural response to the colonial and postcolonial experiences associated with plantation society.

As time passed and as new generations of Jamaicans reflected on their history, their longing for a better life had a sacralising effect on their perception of Africa, in that it gradually came to be understood as the biblical Promised Land. This, in turn, led to the emergence of Ethiopianism, in that there was a conflation of 'Ethiopia' and 'Africa', so that the former was used as a synonym for the latter. As Ennis Edmonds comments, 'this identification is supported by a 1542 map taken from the *Geographia* of Claudius and edited by Sebastian Muenster. On the map, the word *AETHIOPIA* is inscribed across the land mass we now know as Africa.'[454] Hence, over time, 'Ethiopia, with its long history and religious tradition, came to represent the pride of Africa and Africans everywhere.' That is to say, 'behind the back-to-Africa movements of the nineteenth century ... was this tradition of extolling the greatness of Ethiopia/Africa.'[455] This, we will see, provided fertile soil for the emergence of Rastafari.

Furthermore, as indicated above, some of the terms used to describe experiences of oppression and to articulate the hope for liberation were taken from the Hebrew Bible/Old Testament and invested with new meaning. On the one hand, Africa was now viewed in terms of the biblical Promised Land and an imagined historic African Golden Age became the blueprint for future millennial Zion.[456] On the other hand, the oppressive societies in which the African diaspora were now living were understood in terms of 'Babylon'. Moreover, reinterpreting the story of the Israelites' journey out of Egypt, not only did Jamaicans think of Africa in terms of the divinely ordained Promised Land, but they understood the Atlantic Ocean in terms of the River Jordan which needed to be crossed. The point is that, as Dick Hebdige has commented, the Bible became the 'central determining force in both reggae music and popular West Indian consciousness in general ... It is the supremely ambiguous means through which the Black community can most readily make sense of its subordinate position within an alien society.'[457]

As to the emergence of an identifiable back-to-Africa movement, a key early influence was Edward Wilmot Blyden (1832–1912) – now considered the pioneer of Pan-Africanism.[458] While we needn't unpack Blyden's thought here,[459] it is significant that, drawing again on imagery from the Hebrew Bible, he expressed the following hope: 'The Negro leader of the Exodus who will succeed will be a Negro of Negroes, like Moses was a Hebrew of the Hebrews – even if brought up in Pharaoh's palace [i.e. at the heart of the land of oppression] he will be found. No half Hebrew and half Egyptian will do the work ... for this work heart, soul, and faith are needed.'[460] That political saviour, many came to believe, was Marcus Garvey. He would be the 'Negro of the Negroes'. As Leonard Barrett noted, 'the movement that was to embody the Ethiopian ideology par excellence was the back-to-Africa Movement of Marcus Garvey. It was in Garvey – the prophet of African redemption – that the spirit of Ethiopianism came into full blossom.'[461]

Born in 1887 at St Ann's Bay, Jamaica, Garvey was the leader of the first genuine, modern large-scale Black liberation movement and, with reference to Blyden's 'prophecy', was popularly referred to during his lifetime as 'Black Moses'. In a 1913 article, which he wrote during his first visit to London, he predicted that West Indians would become instrumental in founding an empire equivalent to the 'Empire of the North'.[462] In 1914, he returned to Jamaica and, on 20 July that year, founded the Universal Negro Improvement Association (UNIA) in Kingston. Very quickly the UNIA, and Garveyism in general, became influential and international, being the movement for African repatriation and self-government that many oppressed Africans had, since Blyden, been longing for. As Peter Clarke pointed out, 'the Garvey movement, like the Rastafarian movement, was born perhaps as much from despair of ending injustice and discrimination in America as it was from a vision of Africa as a "Land without Evil".[463] Not only did Garvey encourage Africans to consider returning to their homeland, but he insisted that they should be proud of their blackness, lay the foundations for a new superior African civilization, correct the prejudiced white histories of Africa, recognize African civilization as the world's first and greatest, and worship a Black God 'through the spectacles of Ethiopia'.[464]

While Garvey's dream of physical repatriation was not realized during his lifetime, he did succeed in increasing the self-confidence of Africans and, more particularly, preparing the way for the emergence of Rastafari. Indeed, for many Rastas, this focusing of the mind on Africa can be understood in terms of a 'return to Africa'. Hence, there is a sense in which Garvey did fulfil his Mosaic calling. Psychologically, emotionally, culturally, and spiritually, Garvey led his people back to the Promised Land. Of particular importance for Rastafari, however, were Garvey's comments concerning an African redeemer. For example, he interpreted Psalm 68.31 as follows: 'We go from the white man to the yellow man and see the same unenviable characteristics in the Japanese. Therefore, we must believe that the Psalmist had great hopes of the race of ours when he prophesied "Princes shall come out of Egypt and Ethiopia shall stretch forth his hands to God"'.[465] Indeed, while there is little evidence for the claim, many Rastas also believe him to have prophesied the following: 'Look to Africa for the crowning of a Black King; he shall be the Redeemer'[466] or 'Look to Africa when a black king shall be crowned for the day of deliverance is near'.[467] Who would this royal redeemer be? The answer, for Garvey and for many Garveyites, came in 1930 with the enthronement of Haile Selassie I.

On 2 November 1930, Ras (meaning 'Prince') Tafari Makonnen, the great grandson of King Saheka Selassie of Shoa, was crowned Negus of Ethiopia. Declaring himself to be in the line of King Solomon and taking the name Haile Selassie I, as well as 'King of Kings' and 'Lion of the Tribe of Judah' – which are important biblical references – it is not surprising that, when he was crowned in St George's Cathedral in Addis Ababa in front of representatives from many nations, those who had been inspired by Ethiopianism and Garvey's teaching saw more than the accession of another Ethiopian ruler. In Haile Selassie I/Ras Tafari many saw the Messiah, the fulfilment of biblical prophesy, even God incarnate. While not all Rastas accept a theology of Selassie's divinity, it is a popular belief and was almost certainly first taught by Leonard Howell, who – with Joseph Hibbert, Archibald Dunkley, and Robert Hinds – was one of the principal architects of Rastafari. However, as far as this discussion is concerned, Howell is particularly significant because he purchased the Pinnacle plantation in the hills outside Kingston, where he founded the Ethiopian Salvation Society and began cultivating cannabis. Moreover, it was during this period that the spiritual practice of smoking *ganja* was introduced.[468]

As noted in the first chapter, while *ganja* is now widely associated with Rastafari, by the time Howell began using it, the word itself was already well-travelled. Indeed, we have seen that *ganja* is actually a Hindi word and its use was introduced to Jamaica by East Indian indentured labourers.[469] That said, by the 1970s, as Lambros Comitas has discussed, the majority of *ganja* users in Jamaica were not East Indians (who formed only a small minority of the population), but rather 'Black labouring people, both rural and urban ...'.[470] With the emergence of Rastafari, however, its use became invested with new meanings. It was both an act of resistance and a sacrament. It was, as Barrett has discussed, 'a reactionary device to the society and an index of an authentic form of freedom from the establishment'.[471] Indeed, not only did *ganja* smoking become part of a culture of resistance, but, as Barrett suggests, it was probably 'the first instrument of protest engaged in by the movement to show its freedom from the laws of "Babylon"'.[472] That said, there was only a minority of Jamaicans that used *ganja*. Most rejected its use, including Garvey, who considered it 'a dangerous weed'. He understood why it was used, in that 'most people who smoke *ganja* do so' in order to forget 'troubles and worries brought upon them by the bad conditions that exist in the country'.[473] However, as far as Garvey was concerned, *ganja* use brought its own problems, not the least of which were that, firstly, it undermined the desire to engage acts of resistance, secondly, it was un-Christian, and, thirdly, it degraded 'the true African personality'.[474]

Nevertheless, although condemned by Garvey and profaned by many Jamaicans as an illegal drug associated with the working class, *ganja* use became a key feature of much Rastafarian spirituality. That said, not all Rastas smoke cannabis. For example, some years ago, in 2004, the Rastafarian poet Benjamin Zephaniah made the following comment to me about a photograph accompanying an encyclopaedia article I had written on Rastafari:

> As soon as I looked at the piece ... the photo stood out. I was having a conversation recently with some brothers and we were talking about the experiences we've had trying to tell police officers that we didn't smoke – they wouldn't have it. An officer once told me that in training they are told that it is a fact that all Rastafarians smoke, which makes life hard for people like me. And I remember that, somehow, it was worked out that there were more non-smoking Rastas than smoking ones.

Whether or not it's true that the majority of Rastas abstain, it's certainly the case that many do enjoy *ganja* and revere it as, not only a sacrament, but as a key component of 'livity' (natural living). God/Jah has provided, in nature, all that is required for a healthy, happy life. Hence, most Rastas avoid processed foods, some become vegetarian or vegan, and, while others eat meat or fish, they subscribe to the dietary laws set out in Leviticus 11 – for example, they avoid fish without scales, pork, and crustaceans. Of particular significance for Rastas are herbs, the healing powers of which can be used for the maintenance of optimal health and for a range of ailments. 'The herb' is the prime example of 'ital' (natural/vital) produce. As Afari has commented, 'for the Rastafarians, *ganja* is a sacred herb which is blessed with extensive medicinal, nutritional, pharmaceutical, industrial, biological, cosmetological, cosmological, spiritual, intellectual, and therapeutic properties for the benefit and upliftment of all humanity'.[475] That *ganja* is able to promote health is, for Rastas, a cogent verification of its sacred status. Consequently, the current pharmacological interest in the plant is often cited as empirical evidence of its unique value.[476] *Ganja* is, quite simply, good for humans. As Peter Tosh famously insisted in his song 'Legalize It', it's good for a whole range of maladies from the flu to umara composis.[477]

Despite Garvey's concerns, *ganja* was also understood to be politically, psychologically, and spiritually significant, in that it liberates minds disturbed and muddled by the 'Babylon system' (i.e. colonial oppression). Its effects subvert the forces of Babylon by enabling users to think clearly and critically. 'The proper use of herbs has a central role to play in freeing the mind from the fuckery of colonialism. It provides the inspiration necessary to transcend alienating structures of thought.'[478] Again, as Vera Rubin and Comitas found in their survey of Jamaican users, 'most respondents associated the use of *ganja* with clear thinking, meditation, and concentration ...'[479] More importantly, spiritually, it makes the user more receptive to the divine within.[480] Herbs ... are the key to the lock of understanding; God chooses to reveal himself through herbs.'[481]

Partly because Haile Selassie I, as a member of the Ethiopian Orthodox Tewahedo Church, advocated Bible reading, it is, as we have seen, revered within Rastafari.[482] Having said that, because the Bible is so closely linked to Christian mission, colonialism, and cultures of oppression, it is also subjected to a hermeneutics of suspicion. It needs to be 'read with a clear and open conscience and mind'[483] and, to aid this, *ganja* is used. Indeed, Rastafari teaches that *ganja* consumption is, not only helpful for understanding the Bible, but it is itself biblical. To this end, Rastas will cite passages such as Genesis 1.29 – 'And God said, Behold, I have given you every herb bearing seed, which is upon the face of the earth' – and especially Revelation 22.2 – 'And the leaves of the tree of life are for the healing of the nations'. References to the 'tree of life' are also understood to be direct references to *ganja*. Rastas will even claim that it grew on the grave of Solomon, the famously wise King of Israel (1 Kings 3.9–12). As such, it is claimed that cannabis engenders 'wisdom'.[484] For example, the following words, which link the above biblical passages, are printed on the record cover of Jah Power Band vs. Sly and the Revolutionaries, *Sensi Dub*, Vol. 7/1: 'The Herb of Wisdom which was found in the Tomb of Solomon is for the Healing of the Nations.'

Furthermore, *ganja* is central to the development of 'I 'n' I consciousness'. What does this mean? Firstly, it's important to understand that the distinctive use of the personal pronoun is a key characteristic of 'dread talk' (Rastafarian argot) and frequently used to modify a range of English words.[485] Dread talk ('I-ance') is, as Velma Pollard has noted, 'a comparatively recent adjustment of the lexicon of Jamaican Creole to reflect the religious, political, and philosophical positions of the believers in Rastafari.'[486] As such, at one level, it is a linguistic attempt at separation from the dominant culture of Babylon, an expression of resistance that asserts the dignity of the Rasta in an oppressive context. Hence, whereas, in Jamaican creole, the first-person singular is often expressed by the pronoun 'me', as Joseph Owens comments, Rastas perceive this 'as expressive of sub-service, as representative of the self-degradation that was expected of the slaves by their masters. It makes persons into objects, not subjects. As a consequence, the pronoun "I" has a special importance to Rastas and is expressly opposed to the servile "me".'[487] However, at another level, it is also fundamentally theological. 'In the first instance,' says Jack Johnson-Hill, 'it connotes a sense in which the self is believed to be inextricably linked with symbols of divine agency such as Selassie-I, Rastafar-I, God or "Jah". For example, the "I" of the self is fundamentally related to the "I" in Selassie-I. That is, in the Rastafarian imagination the Roman numeral in the title "Hailie Selassie I" does not connote "the first" as much as it evokes the "I" of the I-n-I relation.'[488] More specifically, 'by referring to oneself in the first person singular as I-n-I, there is a virtual equation between oneself and God.'[489] While this highlights the significance of the individual within Rastafari, it also emphasizes the importance of community, in that it identifies Jah's presence within all persons. I 'n' I declares that we share a common divine essence. Properly understood, therefore, I 'n' I is a theologically sophisticated way of emphasizing divine immanence and the threefold relationship between the self, other selves, and the divine Self. It also modifes a range of terms in order to highlight this relationship in all aspects of life: 'Ivine' (divine); 'Iration' (creation); 'Ises' (praises); 'Iman' (Rastaman); 'Ites' (heights – meaning spiritual highs); 'Ital' (vital – indicating a concern to live authentically in relation to nature); 'Itals' (pure food, usually vegetarian); 'Ifrica' (Africa); 'Irie' (meaning both spiritually high and feeling good – a common Rasta greeting); 'Isus' (Jesus).

With the above in mind, cannabis is used regularly, if not daily, because it aids meditation on the significance of the I 'n' I relationship. As Afari puts it, 'constant reasoning and meditation serves to maintain the focus, sustain and energize the links ... that connects the Rastafarians, one to the other, and to the Most High, Jah Rastafari. In this connection, Rastafari perpetuates an itinuous (continuous) meditation, prayer, reasoning, vigilance, brainstorm, and focus within the movement, and on the Most High.'[490] Furthermore, while cannabis is important for individual meditation and Bible study, it is particularly important for 'reasoning' at 'grounding' sessions. Grounding 'takes place when a few Rastas gather to smoke *ganja* spliffs or to "draw the chalice" and to reflect on their faith or on a current or historical event that impinges on their lives'.[491] Reasoning, which typically begins with smoking *ganja*, is an essential part of grounding. Basically, it's an open-ended discussion in the service of 'overstanding'[492] some point of belief or how a particular teaching might be used to interpret history, or politics, or culture. As respondents to the survey by Rubin and Comitas commented: 'This is a time for discussing God, creation, the ruling of man, the signs of the time, such as war and depression.' 'It helps you to think about the future.' 'You plan your life.' 'If you have something to consider, you smoke *ganja* to help you.' '*Ganja* makes you more conscious. You meditate about life's problems and don't talk about silly things.'[493]

While many Rastas smoke spliffs, they are understood to be 'a convenient, less elaborate and less potent application of the principles employed in the usage of the chalice'.[494] That is to say, central to Rastafarian rituals and reasoning sessions is the communal sharing of the 'chalice'. The chalice is essentially a chillum pipe (as discussed in Chapter 1), but, for many Rastas, 'the chillum pipe ... should not be called a "pipe" ... but a cup or chalice ...'.[495] This preference for the word 'chalice' is significant, of course, because it is invested with Christian eucharistic signification. As Afari explains, 'the chalice ... which can be likened to the Christian churches' communion cup, is an instrument of worship and is, therefore, a sacred object for the Rastafarians. The chalice is used to offer up herbal incense as a sacrament unto the Most High.'[496] Moreover, just as the chalice in the Eucharist is a shared cup, so the chalice in Rastafari is shared: 'pass the chalice in a circle.'[497] Indeed, Afari provides an interesting comparative discussion of the chalice in Rastafari and Christianity:

While the Christian communion is administered as liquid (wine or grape juice) and solid (bread), the Rastafarian chalice encompasses solid (the herbs), liquid (the water, used as a coolant and a filter), and gas (the fumes and smoke). With the Christian churches' communion, the bread (solid) represents the body (of Christ) and the wine or grape juice (liquid) represents the blood (of Christ). While, with the Rastafarian chalice, the herbs as well as the chalice itself (solid) represent the earth, the water (liquid) represents the seas, and the smoke fumes (gas) represents the heavens or spirit.[498]

However, regardless of how it's interpreted, cannabis is 'overstood' as a dynamic agent that enters a worshipper's body, purifies the spirit, challenges the mind and guides the self towards union with the divine. The mindful breathing in of the smoke, holding it, and exhaling, followed by the gentle psychoactive lift, 'induces a state of mind that is conducive to meditation and introspection'.[499] Again, it also creates 'church', in that both the ritual and the psychoactive effect of THC increases sociality, draws the worshipping community together, and, as such, actively promotes love and peace.

Some of the general ideas developed within Rastafari, not least the use of the Bible, are evident in other cannabis-based religions. However, before we turn to look at some of these cannabis theologies, we need to briefly comment on a recurrent theme, namely the romantic reconstruction of the past.

Imagining cannabis and religion in premodern societies

'Who the fuck do you think wrote the Book of Revelation? A bunch of stone-sober clerics?'[500] Although Hunter S. Thompson's comment regarding the authorship of Revelation would be considered unusual in biblical scholarship, this is not the case in popular drug literature. Indeed, when presented with the weird, awful, and disorienting apocalyptic visions in the final book of the Bible, one can understand the assumption that it is the work of a mind altered by drugs. Certainly, as Will Self discusses, it is such a singular text filled with dramatic and frightening language that those whose consciousness has been altered by psychosis or drugs, or, indeed, those who are drawn to secret meanings, symbols, and conspiracies, find it difficult to resist.[501] It's not surprising, therefore, that the mystical writings, apocalyptic discourses, and visionary texts that populate the history of religions are frequently assumed to be linked to drug use. Similarly, although there is now a large (and growing) corpus of historical and ethnographic research about humanity's relationship with cannabis in its various forms,[502] there are also a number of significant lacunae which are quickly filled with conjecture about its use in religion. From gaps in the archaeological record to ambiguous references to plants and deities in ancient literature, much thought has been devoted to establishing a long history of ritual cannabis use. Of course, while much of this is conjecture, it should be noted that using the imagination is not simply the preserve of popular theorists and Internet speculation. As the influential archaeologist Andrew Sherratt once commented, for the prehistorian, a gap in the evidence 'is a challenge to the imagination, to extrapolate a plausible reconstruction from the nearest kind of evidence available, and by the application of general principles ... The evidence will catch up in its own time ... Life is too short for faint-heartedness.'[503] While Sherratt had his critics, nevertheless, his point is an important one. Indeed, in his own academic work, on the basis of hemp cord impressions on pots and ostraca, as well as the discovery of charred seeds, he cautiously speculated about the ritual use of cannabis in ancient cultures.[504] That said, he was also clear that 'evidence for the employment of substances such as opium and cannabis at various times in the past should not immediately be interpreted as an indication either of profound ritual significance or of widespread employment for largely hedonistic purposes – they may simply belong to the *materia medica*'.[505] Unfortunately, when it comes to popular speculation, the imagination is less restrained and the arguments more dogmatic. Indeed, claims about ancient cannabis use in religious contexts tend to be ideologically driven, rather than evidence based. For example, Philip Farber insists that 'we can say *with certitude* that human spirituality coevolved with entheogens, psychoactive plants that activate the mystical parts of our brains, and that cannabis was one of the more frequently used ones'.[506] It would seem that the principal aim of cannabis apologists is to sacralise the plant they fetishize. As such, their use of scholarship and the available evidence is typically selective and uncritical.

Perhaps the most influential popular writer to use scholarship in this way is Chris Bennett – who Steven Hager (formerly the editor of *High Times*) considers to be 'the most important religious scholar of our time'.[507] Take, for example, Bennett's use of Sherratt's work, about which he is far more dogmatic than Sherratt was himself. 'Oxford archaeologist Andrew Sherratt points to the earliest evidence of cannabis as a sacrament ... Sherratt also points to even older ceramic tripod bowls ... as further indications of humanity's primordial relationship with cannabis.'[508] Then, on the basis of what Bennett refers to as the 'profound history' of cannabis and religion, he claims that he has been able to trace its ritual use 'from the Stone Age to the present'. That's a bold claim! And it needs to be, because it is used to support the following conclusion: 'cannabis has had an evolutionary partnership with humanity that stretches back more than ten thousand years ... and any law that stands in the way of that relationship is an abomination to both God and nature.'[509] This is a good example of an observation by Carol Sherman and Andrew Smith: 'cannabis advocates point to the plant's long history as a kind of grandfather clause justification for its modern-day acceptance.'[510] They have a cause and they select any quotations and available evidence they need to advance it – an approach, which is, of course, not dissimilar to those who seek to demonize cannabis. In other words, cannabis apologists, such as Bennett, betray conspicuous confirmation bias – the tendency to look for evidence and to interpret information according to a set of prior beliefs. While confirmation bias is largely unintentional, again, it does mean that both apologists and detractors tend to seize on quotations and scraps of evidence with little regard for the context or the overall debate to which the original research was contributing. Again, this problem has been exacerbated in the Internet age, in that there is now such a wide range of information and disinformation available.[511] However, the principal argument here is that, despite any accuracy in their accounts, their reconstructions of the past are typically detraditionalized conjecture informed by a modern romantic turn to the self.[512]

What do I mean by this? Essentially, with the demise of the authority of tradition in late-modern societies, many of our contemporaries select information about the past or, indeed, contemporary indigenous cultures in accordance with a particular romantic, social imaginary. This notion of a 'social imaginary', as developed by Charles Taylor, is also useful here.

> By social imaginary, I mean something much broader and deeper than the intellectual schemes people may entertain when they think about social reality in a disengaged mode. I am thinking, rather, of the ways people imagine their social existence, how they fit together with others, how things go on between them and their fellows, the expectations that are normally met, and the deeper normative notions and images that underlie these expectations.

He continues:

> There are important differences between social imaginary and social theory. I adopt the term imaginary (i) because my focus is on the way ordinary people 'imagine' their social surroundings, and this is often not expressed in theoretical terms, but is carried in images, stories, and legends. It is also the case that (ii) theory is often the possession of a small minority, whereas what is interesting in the social imaginary is that it is shared by large groups of people, if not the whole society. Which leads to a third difference: (iii) the social imaginary is that common understanding that makes possible common practices and a widely shared sense of legitimacy.[513]

The overall point as far as this discussion is concerned is that a social imaginary – carried in neo-romantic images, stories, and legends – legitimizes certain reconstructions of the past and informs confirmation bias. Indeed, because of the widespread neo-romantic turn to the self and to the natural world in Western societies, even if people are persuaded by discourses of profanation about cannabis, they tend to be, as we have seen in the previous chapter, sympathetic to arguments regarding ancient, plant-based remedies and aids. The ubiquitous references to the archaic and the natural in texts ranging from popular songs to advertising, and from contemporary literature to discussions about climate change are indicative of the power of this social imaginary. Again, the point here is that this has significantly contributed to a shift in the public perception of cannabis.

More specifically concerning the nature of the neo-romantic social imaginary, it is informed by a number of core overlapping themes: caring for the self; the promotion of wellbeing; the epistemic authority of personal experience; the questioning of external authority in matters of religion and politics; protecting the planet in an age of climate change; utilising natural products; resisting the destructive power of technology in industrialized societies (such as 'big pharma').[514] Once the preserve of the counterculture,[515] there is a growing sense that these ideas, which have been neglected in the modern period, can now be retrieved from both indigenous and premodern cultures: 'peoples long ago, or now on the brink of extinction' had 'a richer, subtler knowledge of consciousness than we modern Western-style societies possess today.'[516] Indeed, there is a feeling that modernity has witnessed a regression, rather than a progression in our understanding of the self and its relationship to the natural world.

Conspicuous examples of this neo-romantic bias are evident in discussions of 'shamanism', which is not, of course, limited to cannabis culture. As Ronald Hutton has pointed out, 'since the 1970s, the word "shamanism" has become one of the most heavily worked among scholars of anthropology and religious studies, as well as having a major presence in countercultural groups in the western world.'[517] Indeed, while most scholars are aware that what we now refer to as 'shamanism' originally derived from Siberia, nowadays, the term is used indiscriminately. As Graham Harvey put it, 'absolutely anything and everything can be (indeed, probably has been) labelled "shamanic" or "shamanism."'[518] Hence, most researchers in the area accept that this slippery term is 'a scholarly construct, used to group together beliefs and activities across the world which appear to have a relationship with those observed in Siberia. It is also generally admitted that no commonly agreed definition has ever been ascribed to the term, and that the recent boom in studies associated with it has only worsened the confusion and diversity in its use.'[519] Moreover, popular neo-romantic constructions of the premodern have led to shamanism becoming 'one of the phenomena against which modern western civilization has defined itself'. As such, Hutton continues, 'it takes place within a set of complex adversarial relationships: between the developed world and indigenous peoples; between science and magic; between established and charismatic religion; and between institutional and "alternative" medicine.'[520] It is unsurprising, therefore, that, in cannabis literature the term 'shaman' is often (not always) little more than shorthand for a stoned religious functionary who reflects the desires and concerns of the late-modern neo-romantic social imaginary: 'to induce the necessary trance, *most* shamans use various psychoactive drugs ... [and] since ancient times, hemp has been a shamanic drug.'[521]

Arguably the most influential text in discussions of modern shamanism, which has been widely cited in popular drug literature, is Mircea Eliade's *Shamanism: Archaic Techniques of Ecstasy*, originally published in French in 1951.[522] It is difficult to overestimate the occultural significance of this book. However, what is often not noted in popular discussions is that Eliade's work has not gone unchallenged and, in some respects, is highly speculative. For example, although Eliade described shamanism in terms of 'archaic techniques of ecstasy' and the earliest form of religion, as Andrei Znamenski has commented, 'many scholars now believe that "ecstasy" (altered state) is not a necessary attribute of shamanism', even though 'for many Western seekers, this is one of the basic pillars of this spiritual practice'.[523] This is certainly the case when it comes to cannabis apologists who cite Eliade's speculation about the hemp-induced experiences of ecstasy.[524] There are, however, a couple of things to note regarding Eliade's speculation about the use of narcotics within early shamanism. Firstly, he considered drug-induced trance to be 'a vulgar substitute for "pure" trance' that 'points to a decadence in shamanic technique'.[525] Eliade exalted the shaman as a master technician of ecstatic states who, originally, didn't need to use psychoactive substances. Drug use only appeared as an occasional late 'vulgarization of the mystical technique' within the shamanic repertoire. There are, he insisted, '"difficult ways" and "easy ways" of realizing mystical ecstasy…' and hemp was one of the easy ways employed by lesser shamans.[526]

Secondly, because he lacked expertise in (or, indeed, interest in) drug-induced experiences, he seems to have misunderstood the relatively mild nature of the cannabis experience, which he simply conflated with other experiences induced by psychedelic substances such as 'the pre-eminently shamanic mushroom *Agaricus muscarius*' (fly agaric).[527] He was unaware that hemp – which is not a psychedelic and, at this early period, will not have had have had the THC content of modern skunk – could not have produced the experiences of shamanic ecstasy he described. (Hence, his research seems to have included embroidered accounts of the cannabis experience, such as those of Ludlow!) The point here is simply that, Eliade's work needs to be treated cautiously, particularly by those who seek to support theories of cannabis-induced shamanic ecstasy.

The comments about shamanism in popular cannabis literature are part of the general argument that hemp was used in ancient rituals to induce altered states of consciousness. That said, such claims are even made in the more restrained work of widely cited scholars such as the botanist Richard Evans Schultes:

> Hemp's value in folk medicine was obviously associated closely with the discovery of its euphoric and hallucinogenic properties, and knowledge of the narcotic effects of *Cannabis* may date almost as far back as a fibre. Beset by hunger, early man experimented with all plant materials that he could chew. He could not have avoided discovering the intoxicating properties of *Cannabis*, for in his quest for nutritious seeds and oil, he certainly ate the sticky tops of the plant, the most narcotic part. The euphoric, ecstatic, and hallucinatory aspects of the intoxication may have introduced him to an other-worldly plane from which emerged religious beliefs, perhaps even the concept of deity. The plant became accepted as a special gift of the gods, a sacred medium for communion with the spiritual world.[528]

Again, although this claim is highly speculative, because it was made by a well-known scholar, it tends to be accepted uncritically and widely cited as authoritative.[529]

Unfortunately, it cannot be adequately substantiated. While, of course, it would be unwise to insist that psychoactive substances – particularly hallucinogens – made no contribution to the initial manifestation of religious interest in early *Homo sapiens* and, more specifically, to their perception of what Gerardus van der Leeuw referred to as 'Something Other',[530] the notion that the consumption of raw hemp was the catalyst for 'the concept of deity' lacks credibility. Apart from anything else, although 'it remains a largely unanswered question as to when, where, and how the plant was first cultivated for higher psychoactive tetrahydrocannabinol (THC) production',[531] again, it is unlikely to have had the necessary psychoactive potency.

This, of course, is not to say that it wasn't used in ancient rituals. It was. For example, recent chemical analyses of archaeological artifacts recovered at the Jirzankal Cemetary (*c*. 500 BCE) in the Pamir Mountains and the Jiayi Cemetery in Turpan have revealed the remains of charred cannabis, which appear to have been heated under hot stones in wooden braziers during mortuary ceremonies. The team analysing the cannabis reported the following:

We extracted organic material from 10 wooden brazier fragments and 4 burnt stones and analyzed them using gas chromatography–mass spectrometry ... In our first test, biomarkers of cannabis were found on the internal charred layer of one wooden vessel ... Subsequently, we analyzed ancient cannabis (dating to 790-520 BCE) from the Jiayi Cemetery, Turpan, to obtain a chemical reference signal. This analysis demonstrated that CBN, cannabidiol (CBD), and cannabicyclol (CBL) are all preserved in ancient cannabis. A secondary round of testing, based on the reference signal, identified CBN, which is the oxidative metabolite of THC, on the remaining wooden vessels from the Jirzankal Cemetery. We detected the chemical signature of CBN on all of the burnt residues, except for one, from the inside of the wooden braziers and on two of the stones. As a control, no cannabinoids were found on the samples that we collected from the exteriors of the vessels. The experimental results ... suggest that cannabis plants were intentionally burned by laying hot stones in the braziers.[532]

Although THC *per se* wasn't found, this is to be expected because it decomposes and oxidizes into CBN if exposed to air, light or heat. However, the fact that evidence of CBN was found and, on examination, suggested 'higher THC levels than typically found in wild plants',[533] indicates that, at an early stage, plants *may* have been purposely selected for potency. Hence, although our knowledge of the domestication of cannabis and its cultural history is increasing, firstly, any knowledge we do have about ancient usage is still limited, and, secondly, the cannabis used, even if cultivated for potency, is unlikely to have had the THC content of many of the strains that users are familiar with today. Hence, again, many of the popular claims made about ancient usage and induced ecstasy tend to suffer from confirmation bias and fail to account for all the available evidence.

This brings us to another issue. We have seen that writers, such as Bennett, claim that there is a 'profound history' of the ritual use of cannabis 'from the Stone Age to the present ... that stretches back more than ten thousand years ...'[534] Again, according to Roger Christie, 'cannabis has been a constant overseer of human welfare throughout humanity's long journey'.[535] The problem is that, as John Oman pointed out many years ago, 'no facts known to us carry us back anywhere near even the beginnings of religion'.[536]

At this point, it's worth noting a useful distinction that Oman makes between 'beginning' and 'origin'. He used the term 'beginning' to refer to the earliest recognizable forms of religion and reserved the term 'origin' for the earliest subjective stirrings of religious interest in the human mind. His point is that, whereas archaeology can furnish scholars with evidence of the beginning of religious behaviour, when it comes to the initial formation of something approaching 'the idea of deity', this 'is not even within the range of history at all ...' It can only ever be the result of speculation.[537] Hence, 'all that history can possibly deal with is the beginning: and even to an absolute beginning no research brings us anywhere near.'[538] Since Oman wrote those words in 1931, the situation has not improved enough to warrant extravagant claims about cannabis use at the *beginnings* of religion, let alone at the *origin* of religion. This, of course, is *not* to say that historians and archaeologists cannot help us toward a greater understanding of the role of psychoactives in ancient religion, but only that their work needs to be treated with due caution.[539] Again, unfortunately, this tends not to be the case in cannabis culture.

One of the most widely cited books on cannabis in religious history is *Green Gold and the Tree of Life: Marijuana in Magic and Religion* by Chris Bennett, Lynn Osburn, and Judy Osburn. Although it is an enjoyable book with many thought-provoking insights, it is also a good example of neo-romantic revisionism. The book argues that, not only did hemp play 'a prominent role in the development of the religions and civilizations of Asia, the Middle East, Europe, and Africa', but that 'the insights gained from the marijuana high by the ancient worshippers were considered to be of divine origin and the plant itself an "angel" or messenger of the gods.'[540] Again, the problem is that much of this is speculative. While we know that hemp was first domesticated in early Neolithic times in East Asia, becoming one of the earliest known textile fibres, and that 'all current hemp and drug cultivars diverged from an ancestral gene pool currently represented by feral plants and landraces in China,'[541] as Chris Duvall discusses, 'psychoactive use in the region has always been limited. Chinese documents suggest psychoactivity as early as 1500 BCE, but clear and consistent evidence dates from the Han Dynasty (200 BCE–200CE).'[542] This is a long way from the *beginning* of religion, let alone the *origin* of religion.

As well as discussion of its use in ancient China, there are, as one might expect, numerous references to its use in India, where, according to William Emboden, it is 'inseparable from most of the religious philosophies'. This, he says, accounts for the fact that 'the greatest vocabulary for *Cannabis* and its derivatives emerged from India.'[543] Of particular note are the attempts made to link it to *soma* in the Ṛgveda (c.1200–900 BCE). (We have already noted the references to *soma* in early Theosophical literature.) This is important, not only because of the antiquity of the Ṛgveda, but also because 120 of the 1,028 Sanskrit hymns are devoted to *soma* – which seems to be a psychoactive plant that is also worshipped as a deity. In terms of ritual consumption, the Ṛgveda describes a process, whereby *soma* was pressed in wooden bowls and its juice filtered through woollen gauze, after which it was mixed with water and milk, and drunk. The result was, apparently, hallucinations.[544] As one of the hymns declares, 'we have drunk the Soma; we have become immortal; we have gone to the light; we have found the gods ... The glorious drops I have drunk set me free in wide space' (8.48.). Unsurprisingly, therefore, since their translation, western writers with an interest in altered states of consciousness have been fascinated with what *soma* might be and, over the years, numerous suggestions have been made. Indeed, in *Brave New World* (1932), Aldous Huxley even chose it as the name for his powerful hallucinogen with a 'euphoric, narcotic' effect and 'all the advantages of Christianity and alcohol', but 'none of their defects': '*soma*, delicious *soma*, half a gramme for a half-holiday, a gramme for a weekend, two grammes for a trip to the gorgeous East, three for a dark eternity on the moon.'[545]

Perhaps the most widely discussed argument about the identification of *soma* was that of the mycologist Gordon Wasson.[546] He became convinced that he had identified the 'plant-god of the Aryans' as the fly agaric mushroom.[547] Although many were persuaded by Wasson's thesis, including Robert Graves, Roger Heim,

Richard Schultes, Weston La Barre, Albert Hofmann, Claude Lévi-Strauss, and Joseph Needham, others, including a number of Vedic scholars, such as John Brough, were not.[548] One of the principal problems with Wasson's thesis is that it rested on his speculation about the existence of a widespread primitive fly agaric cult throughout Eurasia.[549] Indeed, a large part of his book on *soma* is devoted to the study of fly agaric consumption in Siberia, which, he suggested, had continuities with the rituals described in the Ṛgveda. Brough denied this.[550] Separated by thousands of miles and without any evidence to the contrary, it is very unlikely that there was much cross-cultural communication between Siberian shamanism and the religion of the Ṛgveda.[551]

In more recent years, a similar type of speculation has focussed on cannabis. Indeed, Bennett has made a particular point of replacing Wasson's mushroom thesis with his own argument about cannabis.[552] Drawing on scholarly discussions of *haoma* in the Avesta – the earliest sacred texts belonging to Zoroastrianism – which is a cognate of *soma*, he argues that both refer to cannabis, thereby demonstrating that it was used sacramentally from early in Indo-European history. Indeed, he insists that the process of making *soma* and consuming it prior to fermentation, as indicated in the Ṛgveda, describes precisely the way *bhang* is made and consumed in India today. Hence, he claims that cannabis is one of the most ancient and widespread psychoactive substances to be used in religion. While we need not debate the identification of *soma* – which is highly problematic – the point here is simply to note that, despite the lack of concrete evidence, significant effort is put into weaving a narrative of cannabis use into accounts of the early history of religions. Again, it seems to be a case of authors sacralizing a plant they fetishize.

As one might expect in cultures shaped by Christianity, this desire to weave cannabis into religious history has also led to a significant interest in what the Bible has to offer.[553] As in Rastafari, Genesis 1.29 is frequently cited: 'And God said, "Behold, I have given you every plant yielding seed which is upon the face of all the earth, and every tree with seed in its fruit; you shall have them for food."'[554] According to Lydia Decker – who named her cannabis pressure group after the verse, 'Genesis 1:29' – it means that cannabis is 'meant to be eaten, whether in oil, whether in an edible.'[555] The problem is, of course, that, just as basil, coriander, and mint are not mentioned, so there is nothing here to suggest that cannabis was in the author's mind when referring to 'every plant yielding seed'. Admittedly, the use of the determiner 'every' logically includes *all* angiosperms and gymnosperms. However, this would also include hemlock, white snakeroot, oleander, and a number of other poisonous plants. Indeed, rather than referring to specific plants, the passage appears to be simply a reminder that God has provided everything required for sustenance – for both humans and animals.[556] This is also the case with other biblical references to God's provision of food, such as Ezekiel 34.29.[557] In the final analysis, the Bible contains no references to cannabis, positive or negative.[558] While many people still do cite the Bible as support for their cannabis use, there is a growing recognition that it's not particularly helpful. For example, Craig Gross, the founder of Christian Cannabis, concedes that, while 'scripture does not forbid responsible cannabis consumption … neither does it condone it. In fact, scripture says nothing about it at all.'[559]

At this point, it's worth briefly discussing the work of the scholar to provide the most cogent argument for cannabis use in the Bible, the anthropologist Sula Benet. The following thesis is frequently cited in popular cannabis literature.

> Both in the original Hebrew text of the Old Testament and in the Aramaic translation, the word *kaneh* or *keneh* is used either alone or linked to the adjective *bosm* in Hebrew and *busma* in Aramaic, meaning aromatic. It is *cana* in Sanskrit, *qunnabu* in Assyrian, *kenab* in Persian, *kannab* in Arabic, and *kanbun* in Chaldean. In Exodus 30:23, God directed Moses to make a holy oil composed of 'myrrh, sweet cinnamon, *kaneh bosm*, and *kassia*.' In many ancient languages, including Hebrew, the root *kan* has a double meaning – both hemp and reed. In many translations of the Bible's original Hebrew, we find *kaneh bosm* variously and erroneously translated as 'calamus' and 'aromatic reed,' a vague term. Calamus (*Calamus aromaticus*) is a fragrant marsh plant. The error occurred in the oldest Greek translation of the Hebrew Bible, the Septuagint, in the third century BC, where the terms *kaneh, kaneh bosm* were incorrectly translated as 'calamus.' And in the many translations that followed ... the same error was repeated ... In the course of time, the two words *kaneh* and *bosm* were fused into one, *kanabos* or *kannabus*, known to us from the Mishna, the body of traditional Hebrew law. The word bears an unmistakable similarity to the Scythian 'cannabis.' Is it too far-fetched to assume that the Semitic word *kanbosm* and the Scythian word *cannabis* mean the same thing?[560]

Unfortunately for this theory, it is a little too far-fetched. Certainly, *kaneh* can be translated as 'stalk' or 'branch', and is applied to 'plants or plant parts that have a stalklike or spearlike appearance', such as a reed.[561] Indeed, as Lytton John Musselman comments, the word was simply used for 'unrelated plants that have a similar appearance.'[562] That said, the Israeli botanist Michael Zohary has argued that 'the Hebrew *kaneh* is a reed that grows in swamps and marshes.'[563] It appears in passages, such as 1 Kings 14.15: 'the Lord will smite Israel as a *reed* is shaken in the water.' Zohary continues:

> The identity of *kaneh* (English, 'cane') with 'reed' has linguistic and contextual attestation and is further supported by the use of the term for fencing, the shaft of a lamp stand (Exodus 25:31), measures of length (Ezekiel 40:5), and reed pens ... The history of the word helps to explain its usage. Of Sumerian origin, it entered into Semitic languages with the meaning of 'reed' or 'cane', and later 'measuring rod', both of which senses passed into Greek.[564]

Exodus 30.23 is also cited because it refers to the recipe for anointing oil: 'the finest spices: of liquid myrrh five hundred shekels, and of sweet-smelling cinnamon half as much, that is, two hundred and fifty, and of aromatic cane two hundred and fifty.' However, again, the problem is that there were several other plants that could be described as 'aromatic canes/reeds.'[565] As Zohary has pointed out, 'the Hebrew words *kaneh hatov, knei-bosem*, and sometimes *kaneh* by itself are believed to designate herbaceous perennial aromatic grasses.' Consequently, 'it is hopeless to speculate about which of the three or four possible species was intended. It is even doubtful whether the biblical authors had in mind any particular species of the genus *Cymbopogon*, although one of them does grow wild in Israel.'[566]

Consequently, logically, the cannabis argument cannot be ruled out. Not only did hemp grow in the ancient Near East, but *k'neh/qâneh* is simply a descriptive term for similar looking plants. Hence, because it can be translated 'reed' or 'stalk' and because *bosem* can be translated 'spice' and 'sweet odour',[567] with a bit of imagination, *k'neh bosm* can be said to describe cannabis – unless, of course, you agree with the first-century Greek physician Pedanius Dioscorides, who considered it to have 'a foul odour'.[568] The point here, however, is that cannabis apologists are not too concerned that Benet's thesis is problematic and that it is rarely positively mentioned nowadays in scholarly literature. They have faith in their interpretation of the Bible and her theory does the important work of providing some academic support for that interpretation. They can simply declare that 'modern scholarship shows that cannabis was used sacramentally by Moses and the ancient Israelites'.[569]

As well as the effort to find references to cannabis in the Bible, apologists and spiritual seekers are also keen to associate the plant with belief in a range of deities: 'cannabis is a gift from Shiva',[570] 'the original pothead';[571] '*bhang* was consecrated to the dark goddess Kali';[572] 'incense is made from the leaf tops of cannabis by priests under the guidance of Thoth and Osiris and in concert with the apothecary skill of Isis';[573] 'among the German peoples, hemp was sacred to Freya, the goddess of love.'[574] However, perhaps the deity most frequently cited in connection with cannabis is Ma Ku (Magu), a Chinese goddess generally associated with health and longevity.[575] 'Ma' (麻) is the Chinese term for 'hemp' and 'Ku' (姑) means, variously, 'aunt', 'maiden', 'priestess', 'damsel', or 'goddess.' Hence, Magu is commonly translated 'hemp maiden.'[576] Joseph Needham, for example, notes that 'the Hemp Damsel, Ma Ku, was goddess of the slopes of Thai Shan, where [cannabis] was supposed to be gathered on the seventh day or the seventh month, a day of séance banquets in the Taoist communities.'[577] While this may be true, in recent cannabis literature she is detraditionalized – detached from her traditional context within ancient Daoism – becoming more of a signifier for healing, health, and wellbeing. For example, the spiritual teacher Kathleen Harrison informs us that Ma Ku is 'the name of the deity resident in hemp ... the spirit of she who grows, she who clothes us, she who binds us, she who ties it all together.'[578] Again, Jamie Della informs her readers that Ma Ku is 'honoured as the protectress of health and healing as well as the vitality of the earth itself ... Like a guardian at the gate, cannabis invites her human partners into her dance of creativity.'[579]

Finally, while there is good archaeological evidence for its use in ancient China, when it comes to documentary evidence, one of the earliest references to the ritual use of cannabis was provided by Herodotus in the fifth century BCE in a discussion of the Scythians. Needless to say, this ancient account is widely referenced in cannabis literature, both popular and academic.[580]

Originally of Iranian stock, the Scythians migrated westward from Central Asia to southern Russia and Ukraine in the eighth and seventh centuries BCE, where they established a powerful empire in the area we now know as Crimea.⁵⁸¹ In *The Histories* (Book 4.73ff), Herodotus recorded the use of cannabis (κάνναβις) during Scythian funerary ceremonies.

> After burying their dead, the Scythians purify themselves. First, they anoint and rinse their hair, then, for their bodies, they lean three poles against one another, cover the poles with felted woollen blankets, making sure they fit together as tightly as possible, and then put red-hot stones from the fire on a dish which has been placed in the middle of the pole-and-blanket structure.
>
> Now, there is a plant growing in their country called cannabis, which closely resembles flax, except that cannabis is thicker-stemmed and taller. In Scythia, in fact, it is far taller. It grows wild, but is also cultivated, and the Thracians use it, as well as flax, for making clothes ... Anyway, the Scythians take cannabis seeds, crawl in under the felt blankets, and throw the seeds on the glowing stones. The seeds emit a dense smoke and fumes, much more than any vapour-bath in Greece. The Scythians shriek with delight at the fumes. This is their equivalent of a bath, since they never wash their bodies with water. Their women, however, pound cypress, cedar, and frankincense wood on a rough piece of stone, and add water until they have a thick paste which they then smear all over their bodies and faces. This not only makes them smell nice, but when they remove the paste the day after, they turn out to be all clean and shining.⁵⁸²

Interestingly, Sergei Rudenko's discovery of tent poles and braziers, along with hemp and melilot seeds in Scythian *kurgans* at Pazyryk in Siberia, provides important support for Herodotus's account.⁵⁸³ While Rudenko was convinced that he was able to demonstrate that the Scythians used cannabis for intoxication and that this was what Herodotus was referring to, there are a few issues that need to be borne in mind. Firstly, Herodotus suggested that the Scythians used the smoke for ritual cleansing purposes, 'since they never wash their bodies with water.'⁵⁸⁴ While this may betray some misunderstanding about what the Scythians were doing, actually, fumigation for the purposes of ritual cleansing (such as 'smudging') is not unknown in the history of religions.⁵⁸⁵ Hence, cannabis may simply have been one of the herbs used during something like a smudging ritual, rather than for intoxication.

Secondly, the primary indication that Herodotus was describing Scythian intoxication is the reference to shrieking with delight at the fumes. However, this is problematic because Herodotus mentions only 'seeds'. Although some scholars simply assume that burning cannabis seeds would be enough to intoxicate a group of heavy-drinking⁵⁸⁶ Scythians, and even refer to them as 'psychoactive cannabis seeds',⁵⁸⁷ induced euphoria is highly unlikely. Nowadays, of course, seeds and hemp oil are generally consumed, without intoxication, as part of an everyday healthy diet because they are rich in unsaturated fats and protein, while containing little to no cholesterol. Although, of course, the outer shells of the seeds may become contaminated as a result of their proximity to the flowers and trichomes, generally speaking, 'they produce negligible, if any, quantities of THC endogenously'.⁵⁸⁸ Hence, while it is possible that the Scythians felt some mild psychoactive effect, the fumes of hemp seeds are unlikely to have been powerful enough to elicit shrieks of delight. Of course, we might speculate that Herodotus was actually referring to the more potent and pungent seed-bearing flowers, rather than just the seeds. This is a possibility that has recently been argued by Alan Sumler. His argument is based on the claim that 'the ancient Greeks and Romans referred to cannabis efflorescence as seed or flower, without any preference for one term or the other', and that 'when their medical recipes instruct us to use cannabis seed or flower, they are referring to the efflorescence with the seed inside'.[589] This goes some way to supporting his theory that Herodotus is describing a 'hotboxing' session and that, as a point of reference, he likens it to a Greek vapor bath.[590] Hence, his overall argument is that the Scythians burned flowers for intoxication, rather than seeds for incense and ritual cleansing. Indeed, although Sumler fails to provide evidence for his claim that Herodotus didn't distinguish between flowers and seeds, it's worth noting that Galen reported that 'there are some who fry and consume [the seed] together with other desserts. I call "desserts" those foods which are consumed after dinner in order to stimulate an appetite for drinking. The seed creates a feeling of warmth, and – if consumed in large amounts – affects the head by sending to it a warm and toxic vapour.'[591] The point is that, if Galen's observation is accurate, it would appear that more than the seeds are being fried. However, while Sumler's explanation is promising, it needs to be noted that, despite Galen's comment, actually, the Greeks did understand the distinction between a seed (σπέρμα, *sperma*) and a flower (ἄνθος, *anthos*), which is why they had distinct terminology.[592] Dioscorides even refers to the 'spherical-shaped seeds' of cannabis.[593] Moreover, it's also worth bearing in mind that, even if the whole flower was used, under normal conditions, by the time a plant has produced seeds, its potency has begun to decrease.

This brings us to the slight problem of the reported impact of cannabis on the Scythians. Whereas one might expect the Scythians to 'shriek with delight' after consuming alcohol – of which they were widely known to be heavy drinkers – this seems unlikely after smoking weak cannabis. Although it's a complex drug that affects people in different ways according to set and setting, as Leslie Iverson notes, current research indicates that 'the user feels relaxed and calm, in a dreamlike state disconnected from the real world. The intoxicated subject often has difficulty carrying on a coherent conversation and may drift into daydreams and fantasies. Drowsiness and sleep may eventually ensue.'[594] Likewise, Mitch Earleywine discusses research that demonstrates that it typically induces feelings of relaxation. Data from a sample of '100 people who used the drug at least 50 times revealed consistent reports of peaceful and relaxed feelings when smoking ... More than 90% said that the drug made them feel mellow or relaxed.' That said, he also noted that 'more than 60% reported that the drug made them euphoric'.[595] Usually, along with the other effects, this presents as laughter and giddiness. This research suggests that, even if they were exposed to enough THC to experience intoxication, most Scythians would probably have been too relaxed to shriek – but a few may have become giddy. Having said that, even nowadays with the significantly more potent strains available, there are surely very few users who get high and shriek. Certainly, this is unlikely from just breathing in airborne fumes. Even 'hotboxing', Cheech and Chong style, requires actually smoking cannabis. Perhaps Herodotus simply observed drunk Scythians amidst the incense fumes of burning seeds. Indeed, the Greek grammarian, Hesychius of Alexandria, gave 'the word "hemp" a synonym which translates as "Scythian incense".[596]

The fact that Herodotus doesn't seem to know too much about the effects of cannabis is to be expected. While there has been much speculation about ancient Greek and Roman usage in recent years,[597] actually, relatively little was known about the plant in classical antiquity.[598] As Theodore Brunner has commented, 'ancient writers show a considerable degree of ignorance on the subject'.[599] For example, although Pliny the Elder discussed a number of domestic and medical applications, he appears unaware of its potential as an intoxicant.[600] Even when cannabis was discussed by medical writers, such as Dioscorides, Galen, and Oribasius, they disregard its 'tops and leaves altogether, claiming that many of the symptoms ... are the result of seed consumption'.[601] For example, according to Dioscorides, it is 'a useful plant for weaving very strong ropes. Its leaves are like those of the ash tree... The juice [oil] of the fresh seed, dropped into the ear, is beneficial for earaches'.[602] Likewise, Theodoras Priscianus repeats the popular view that 'warm juice pressed from cannabis seeds is useful in treating ear-aches... and comments on the dehydrating, anti-flatulent, and impotency-producing properties of the seeds ...'.[603] Galen thought cannabis was 'hard to digest, bad for the stomach, unwholesome, and a cause of headaches',[604] while Pseudo-Apuleius believed that it was helpful for 'treating cold-sores',[605] and Marcellus Empiricus suggested tying 'hemp-root' to the right arm in order to stem blood flow.[606] Consequently, while we cannot be sure why the Scythians shrieked with delight, Brunner is surely correct to urge caution: 'the evidence available from Greek and Latin literary sources – while establishing the fact that certain properties inherent in cannabis were known and used for medicinal purposes – does not permit us to postulate use of the plant as an intoxicant in Greece and Rome.'[607]

The aim of this section has not been to recount and debate the various interpretations of the available historical evidence or to dismiss popular discussions of the relationship between cannabis and religion. Although there has been some analysis of methodology and the arguments employed, the overall purpose of the discussion has been to highlight some of the ways in which cannabis apologists seek to portray the role of the plant in ancient religion. It has been suggested that the reason for the largely neo-romantic reconstructions of the past, as well as the effort to weave it into religious history, is not merely to rehabilitate the plant after a period of profanation in the West, but, more specifically, to sacralize it. In other words, much effort is made to identify cannabis as special, or sacred, by demonstrating its significance as a technology of transcendence at a very early period in religious history. Hence, popular research is not disinterested, but rather it is informed by a late modern neo-romantic social imaginary. Was it sanctioned by God in the Bible? Was it the ancient plant-god *soma*? Was it sacred to the Scythians? Was it associated with deities from around the world, including Shiva, Kali, Thoth, Osiris, Isis, Freya, and Ma Ku? Was it part of the shamanic toolkit from an early period? Did it have a role in the evolution of religion? More often than not, the answer that popular cannabis apologists give to all such questions is, categorically, 'yes'. This supports their arguments that THC is woven into human religious and cultural history and that, therefore, its profanation in the late-modern period is anomalous.

Contemporary cannabis spirituality

It is not unusual within religiously oriented cannabis culture for the plant to be personified. For example, it is variously described as a 'spiritual ally',[608] a 'very advanced teacher plant' with 'subtle energies' and a 'consciousness' that can be communicated with.[609] 'Cannabis is always teaching, challenging one to think outside the box... She is one of my gurus and I am her devotee.'[610] Indeed, Douglas Rushkoff tells us that cannabis deserves 'a level of respect, trepidation, and devotion that most people aren't prepared or expecting to give her.'[611] Again, with reference to 'Amazonian shamanism', Kathleen Harrison has indicated that we can foster a personal relationship with the plant: 'think of your liaison with cannabis as a relationship with an old friend... or a familiar lover... [Cannabis] encourages us to see our own folly... She suggests ways we might mend the small rifts in our human relations by forgiving someone... She helps us see the humour in our own daily dramas...'[612] Once this relationship has been established, the user can then seek to become an apprentice to cannabis in a way that is mutually beneficial:

> The principle and the aim is that the apprentice and the plant spirit learn to recognise each other as allies... Just as we can learn to grow cannabis well, we can also learn to listen to it, to share her song. The apprentice usually partakes of the herb with ritual... The plant is your honoured guest... You may be pleasing yourself or your close friends, but you are also pleasing the spirit of cannabis when you slip into a more conscious attentive frame of mind in order invite her into your body and your consciousness, into your ceremony of awareness... It takes a long time to really get to know a person, and the same is true of a plant... especially of plants that we put into our bodies and that alter us... As a way to meet... or get to know a plant... I suggest beginning with the personal approach by asking questions such as: Who are you? Why are you here? May I kneel down by you? Can we possibly get to know each other?[613]

Moreover, whether we think of cannabis use in yoga, meditation, or Bible study, as it becomes increasingly normalised, so it is being used in a wide range of religious settings. For example, Dee Dussault makes the point that 'sharing some nice bud with friends, shaking off the day, and connecting over a few laughs is the perfect way to start yoga practice... Ganja yoga with friends is an awesome way to bring conscious relaxation into socializing.'[614] This is supported by a survey of Buddhists, which discovered that a number of them 'specifically mentioned the benefits of smoking cannabis within Buddhist practice.'[615] As one respondent wrote, 'I think marijuana is extremely in line with Buddhist ideas of equilibrium, experiencing the highs and lows of life, yet never letting anything become extreme one way or the other.'[616] Again, another found that cannabis 'helps concentration, focusing, and mindfulness, and reduces the ego's influence over the individual personality. Enhances one's current mood and/or mindset, slows perception of time, leading one to believe time is a mental construction.'[617] Likewise, Jennifer, another use, insisted that smoking cannabis as part of her religious practice enabled her to 'quiet the mind' and 'practice mindfulness more readily than I am able to when I am not using anything. The combination of meditation and cannabis use frees me from the racing thoughts that anxiety brings.'[618] Similarly, Ashley claimed that 'marijuana calms the monkey mind and enables me to reach a state of deep relaxation much faster. It also helps me to become more self-reflective.'[619]

While the use of cannabis might be expected in contemplative religious practice and countercultural mystical trajectories, perhaps a little more surprising is the fact that it's becoming increasingly common in Christian spiritual practice. Although we have seen that it is not mentioned in the Bible, this hasn't stopped it being used as a legitimate Christian spiritual aid. Typically, Christians begin using it for a medical condition, then theologically rationalize it as a plant created by God for the benefit of worshippers. Take, again, Craig Gross, who, having grown up in an Evangelical family, eschewed cigarettes, drink, and drugs for much of his life. Then, at the age of 36, he tried cannabis to ease a chronic and debilitating medical condition. He discovered that not only did it alleviate his pain, but also that it helped his devotional life: 'after having used cannabis frequently throughout the past five years of my life, my wellness – be it mental, physical, and/or emotional – has improved exponentially. I would even go so far as to say that these benefits have led to spiritual growth, enlightenment, the dissolving of my pride, and pragmatic life change. My wife would attest to this truth.'[620] This led him to found Christian Cannabis, which now markets a range of products, including pre-rolled joints, tea, gummies, mints, and CBD oils. Gross is not alone in holding these views. Indeed, there are now a growing number of Christians, some of them Evangelical, who use cannabis both medicinally and as a spiritual aid. As Josiah, another Christian user, put it, 'I've been a Christian all my life, but due to traumatic family events, and possibly being autistic, I've struggled with debilitating anxiety and depression since childhood, and have struggled with a sense of being hated by God.' He continues, 'the last few years I've started smoking marijuana and I honestly feel like it's ...improved my relationship with God. It melts any fear or anger towards God I might feel, as I feel nothing but complete unconditional love. No judgement, no rage. Just a child who is loved by his Abba Father. It's also helped me read and understand the Bible from a more open-minded perspective.'[621] Again, a number of years ago, around 2002, I contacted a pioneering young activist who had founded the now defunct Christians for Cannabis. Her rationale for the organization was simple. Regardless of the discourses of profanation within mainstream Christianity, increasing numbers of believers were using cannabis and someone needed to defend their rights and offer sensible advice. Socially, culturally, and legally, the situation back then was significantly different from what it is now. Hence, I was surprised to learn that there were between 4,500 and 5,500 people a month visiting the Christians for Cannabis site and 358 subscribers to her newsletter. As she pointed out to me, 'it was actually Christians that had been telling me for years that there was much more to the issue than what I realised.' Moreover, while some readers might assume that such users must have been theologically progressive, this, in fact, was not the case. Some may have been, but, as she states of her own beliefs concerning cannabis, while they 'may be viewed as radical, I am a very conservative person. I came from a family of believers, with my grandfather and great grandmother having been ordained ministers ... I believe what God says, trust his Word and his promises.' As with many religious cannabis consumers, this young activist insisted that cannabis use was a natural, divinely ordained approach to spirituality.[622]

Beyond mainstream Christianity, however, there are a growing number of small cannabis-based religious organizations. While most are not explicitly Christian, we will see that a few are and, indeed, most do reference the Bible. These organizations include the Assembly of the Church of the Universe, the Farm, the Hawai'i Cannabis THC Ministry, the Church of Cognizance, Temple 420, Temple 420 of the Heartland, the Jah Healing Kemetic Temple of the Divine,[623] Igreja Niubingui Etíope Coptic de Sião do Brasil (which draws inspiration directly from Rastafari), and the First Church of Cannabis. There are also cannabis gurus, such as Swami Chaitanya, a Jnani yogi and follower of Swami Chidananda Giri, who emerged out of the hippie subculture of 1960s San Francisco, travelled for a number of years, lived in India, and eventually, with his partner Nikki Lastreto, established Swami Select, a successful cannabis business in Northern California's Mendocino County.[624] Since the 1990s, he has become increasingly well-known as a cannabis connoisseur, tournament judge, activist, and speaker. There is little need to discuss every cannabis church and guru, since, while there are obviously differences between them, as far as this book is concerned, the thrust of their ministry is largely the same, namely to promote the use of cannabis as a sacrament and as a source of healing and wellbeing.

The 1960s was a key moment in the history of the sacralization of cannabis. While the underground press 'actively championed marijuana's legalization',[625] many at the time believed that this was a far bigger issue that simply protecting the right of adults to get intoxicated in the way they chose. This was a matter of religious freedom. Psychoactive substances paved the way to authentic spirituality. 'If you are serious about your religion,' insisted Leary, 'if you really wish to commit yourself to the spiritual quest, you must learn how to use psychochemicals. Drugs are the religion of the twenty-first century.'[626] Again, Theodore Roszak reported in 1972 that 'the recent, eager unearthing of the psychedelic tradition signifies a revolution in consciousness. It revives the longing for sacramental experience.'[627] As Robert Cottrell has commented,

> Young people presumed that they could transform society and achieve spiritual bliss in a manner only the sanctified few had ever accomplished ... They were sure that their path toward illumination was eased or ensured altogether by lifestyle changes they effected, by discarding of the competitive and rational ways that had brought so much misery to so many, and by the ingesting of pharmacological substances that seemingly promised instant enlightenment.[628]

It was out of this countercultural milieu that the first drug religions emerged, one of the earliest of which was the Church of the Tree of Life, which promoted the sacramental use of a number of psychoactives, including cannabis: 'the most fundamental belief of the Church of the Tree of Life is that every human being has the right to do with himself whatever he pleases as long as his actions do not interfere with the rights of any other being. We believe that a person has the right ... to alter his consciousness with any psychoactive agent he wishes to use.'[629]

Perhaps the most well-known 'grass church'[630] to be founded during this period of countercultural revolution was the Farm, which was established in 1971 in Summertown, Tennessee, by former US Marine and tutor in English at San Francisco State College, Stephen Gaskin. After reading Huxley's *Doors of Perception* and experimenting with psychedelics,[631] he began to take on the role of a 'spiritual teacher.'[632] In particular, in 1967, in San Francisco, he organized weekly sessions, during which a number of eclectic spiritual, esoteric, and social ideas were explored. These became known as the 'Monday Night Class.'[633] Although these weekly sessions began as relatively small gatherings of like-minded hippies, the Monday Night Class quickly became 'the largest regularly occurring public meeting in the Bay area, attracting between 1,000 and 1,500 people each week.'[634] Eventually, it came to the attention of religious leaders who were intrigued by the appeal of Gaskin's ideas in an increasingly secular society, some of whom encouraged him to take his message around the country. 'A bunch of preachers met in San Francisco, and I was the only hippie who got to talk to them, and they liked me and, later, set me up with hometown churches. We got to meet people all over the country that way.'[635] Along with around 200 of his followers, 'the Caravan' began with 23 buses and ended up with more than 60 buses and numerous other vehicles travelling from state to state, stopping at colleges and churches to share Gaskin's hippie spirituality.[636] This naturally led to the formation of a sense of community. Gradually, the idea of a rural collective began to take shape and, after returning to California, they started to look for land. 'Going to the land is the old hippie dream, you know, but not practical in California. The land cost too much. We wanted to last. We wanted to not be a flash in the pan.'[637] Hence, while they'd managed to scrape together enough money for fifty acres in California, they decided to search in Tennessee where land was cheaper. Eventually, they purchased around 1,750 acres. The thought and care that went into the project was evident from that fact that it is still active today. Moreover, the Farm has become an important centre for environmental research and sustainable living. 'Gaskin's hippies learned the ancient virtues of hard work, good hygiene, and crop rotation. Deep in the Tennessee woods, they formed a spiritual commune... which has morphed... into a high-tech eco–think tank.'[638]

Gaskin identified his religion as 'hippy',[639] by which he appears to have meant that it began as a seeker spirituality with a wide range of influences, including Romanticism, Easternization, popular occultism, Christianity, and, of course, the use of psychoactives: 'I do various different kinds of things – I chant some and I do hatha yoga, and a few things like that, and also do a little grass and a little peyote... and I find out as I go along...'[640] As Robert Wuthnow has discussed, 'the 1960s had a dramatic impact on American spirituality. Research indicates that many people were influenced by the turmoil of these years to adopt a freewheeling and eclectic style of spirituality.'[641] Gaskin is a prime example of this. Indeed, Gaskin candidly admitted that 'we were not going to San Francisco and converting to religions; we were ransacking religions for goodies.'[642] What emerged was an eco-spirituality, informed by drug-induced experiences, and with a strong sense of social responsibility.[643] Although LSD was important for Gaskin, particularly in San Francisco, cannabis became the preferred sacrament at the Farm: 'It's like the Rastafarians say, you really don't need acid, because *dynamite reefer make you trip*'[644] – or, at least, it will get you high enough to induce a profound spiritual experience. 'I realized that I'd had an ego death and rebirth on one toke of hash.'[645]

Perhaps the key thing to note here is that, although Gaskin functioned as an authoritative charismatic teacher, actually the type of religion encouraged on the Farm was experiential. The emphasis was placed on the authority of individual 'peak experiences',[646] which, Gaskin believed, could be induced or amplified by cannabis. That said, it should be noted that research done in the San Francisco Bay Area at the time indicated that this type of spirituality was not purely self-oriented. It wasn't just a case of hippies getting high and withdrawing from society. Rather peak experiences were 'a reflective style of life.'[647] As demonstrated by members of the Farm, the cannabis experience encouraged users to be 'less concerned about status and possessions and more concerned with helping others.'[648]

As to Gaskin's particular understanding of the plant, this can be understood in terms of animism,[649] in that cannabis was understood to work with users as a teacher. As we have seen, this is a common understanding within cannabis religions. 'Grass is an ally,' in that 'it naturally engenders spirituality in the people who do it.'[650] It was this experience of learning to trust cannabis on a personal level, rather than as part of an external doctrinal tradition, that shaped his belief and practice. At the Farm there were a number of what might be called 'soft orthodoxies' about work, diet, family, and relationships that were encouraged, but, in the final analysis, spirituality was an individual's journey with cannabis. Members of the Farm could depend 'on marijuana for insight, for ceremonial purposes, and to enhance lovemaking'.[651] Indeed, as we have seen in the discussion of Rastafari, not only was cannabis understood to be able to generate peak experiences, but it also had the important effect of creating 'church', of binding individuals together into a spiritual community. Moreover, as many users will recognize, the process is circular, in that intoxication not only strengthens relationships, but the relationships formed enhance the individual's own cannabis experience, which in turn strengthens the sense of community, and so on. 'With cannabis you can have one joint, and two people, and you can get higher than if one smokes it. And if you share it with six people, you get still higher than if one person smoked it himself. There's a real gentle ritual, in that it gets passed from hand to hand with a gesture of "I'm passing something precious, and we're sharing communion with it."'[652] In a similar way to the collective understanding of individual Christians as 'the body of Christ' (1 Cor. 12.12–14), so Gaskin understood cannabis 'to integrate a bunch of heads into a head.'[653] A form of mystical communion takes place. 'We felt it was a church meeting *every time* good friends and good people got together and really got high and loved each other and went into being telepathic and high with one another.'[654]

The emphasis on telepathy was important for Gaskin, in that it was, in effect, central to his ecclesiology. 'After I was turned towards Spirit, the first thing I found out that blew my mind was that telepathy was real. That was the first thing, because I went into mind communication with people.'[655] 'It was if a light had been turned on. We were all completely telepathic in our head.'[656] As to how he understood telepathy, it can perhaps be understood as deep intimacy with another person. 'Now here's the thing about telepathy: telepathy is people's electrical fields being able to sense each other. See, everyone has an electrical field surrounding him, because part of your equipment's electrical, and anything electrical has a field around it. We call that field an aura.'[657] While we might want to question the cogency of this thesis, which was very common within the New Age milieu, the point is simply that, for Gaskin, this understanding was central to conflict resolution and the maintenance of good relationships within the community. Again, cannabis helped with the development of telepathy. Hence, he says, when relationships breakdown, in order to restore telepathic harmony, 'we go off and do the thing that we do to get cool: medicate, smoke cannabis, go for a walk in the woods, and get our peace back. That way we take anger out of the system, and no one has to suffer from it again.'[658] Likewise, the Sunday morning service was a 'good, stoned place' at which telepathic harmony was encouraged.[659]

Finally, it's worth noting that, while the Farm could have made money from selling homegrown cannabis, because the plant was set apart as special/sacred within the community, Gaskin argued that it should not be debased by commerce. Moreover, in using it as a sacrament, the user 'absorbed some of the karma of those who produced and distributed it.'[660] Dealers are interested only in financial gain and, as such, those who buy their cannabis from them have no idea what karma they are exposing themselves to. Hence, initially, it was grown within the community, by the community, for the community. This came to an end when, in 1973, the Farm was raided, their cannabis was seized, and Gaskin and three other members were arrested. Although an attempt was made to defend its sacramental use, it failed, and they were sent to prison for a year. Moreover, as a result of police surveillance, no more cannabis could be grown on the Farm. This meant a relaxing of the rules so that it could be donated (or bartered) by sympathetic outsiders.[661]

The Farm was not, however, the only 'grass church' to emerge during this period. The Church of the Universe was founded in Puslinch, Ontario, in 1969 by Walter Tucker and, for many years, was co-led by Michael Baldasaro. Up until 1986, when members were forcibly removed by the police, they occupied land that included a flooded former quarry, which Tucker had rented and renamed Clearwater Abbey. Here members were able to cultivate cannabis and embrace naturism, citing Adam's and Eve's prelapsarian nudity in the Garden of Eden. Their theological claim was that believers should stand before God naked and unashamed. 'The idea of taking your clothes off is to show that you are not guilty before God,' stated Tucker. 'You are willing to stand before God exactly as he created you, without shame.' Moreover, 'nudity has two aspects. One, the health aspect of being in God's creation with the golden sun shining down upon you. The other is that when you see yourself nude, along with other human beings, you understand that you are one of God's creatures.'[662] That said, since moving the Church headquarters to Hamilton, Ontario, the emphasis on nudity has declined. What has *not* declined, however, has been the focus on nature, which informs the Church's commitment to cannabis.

Until 17 October 2018, when cannabis was legalized for both recreational and medicinal purposes in Canada, the Church campaigned tirelessly for a change in the law. Indeed, Baldasaro was a classic case of a 'perennial candidate', that is a candidate for political office who is rarely, if ever successful. 'For decades the pot-smoking bushy-bearded Church of the Universe minister was the undisputed king of Hamilton's political fringe, a forerunner in a field which in recent years has become much more crowded ... Baldasaro's presence and off-beat commentary provided a welcome touch of comic relief that never failed to entertain voters at town halls and candidates' debates.'[663] He ran for mayor eight times, 'not to mention appearing on who knows how many provincial, federal, and council seat ballots.'[664] He ran as an independent candidate, as well as a candidate for both the Libertarian Party of Canada and also the Marijuana Party. While his campaigns touched on a number of issues, they were, of course, always primarily about the promotion of cannabis. The journalist Andrew Dreschel recalled the following in his 2016 obituary for Baldasaro, who had died on 9 June 2016, at the age of 67:

> In his earlier years, he nearly always managed to loop whatever topic was being discussed back to criticisms of Canada's restrictive drug laws. My favourite personal memories of Baldasaro tend to revolve around his advocacy for the legalization of pot, which the Church of the Universe uses as a sacrament ... I fondly recall his brotherly offers of a joint if I ever found myself in need of some religion. I also cheerfully remember the time *Spectator* editorial cartoonist Graeme MacKay called on Baldasaro at his church in a professional capacity and returned to the office with a tray of brownies ... Along the same lines, Baldasaro once brought a tray of hemp chocolate chip cookies to a meeting of the [*Spectator's*] editorial board with some of the fringe mayoral candidates ... In recent years, others have tried to play a similar outsider role on the political scene, but so far nobody has come close to matching Baldasaro's combination of good humour and human warmth. He really was a unique Hamilton character. We're going to miss him. The king is dead. There is no successor. And the city's political texture is dulled by his passing.[665]

Interestingly, while the Church recognized the need for political change in order that society might benefit from God's provision of cannabis, there was also a sense in which, for theological reasons, they didn't accept the law. God's provision of it trumped any human legislation outlawing it. As Tucker once commented when asked about the fact that his chosen sacrament was illegal, 'You seem to assume that I'm asking for someone's permission to live my life. I got that permission from God a long time ago. And no one can take that away. Only God.' Hence, he continues, 'I don't believe it's illegal.'[666]

As to the Church's use of cannabis, firstly, it declares that all parts of the plant should be utilised and, secondly, it should to be part of everyday life. Indeed, this is what it means to live a holy life, a life set apart for God. 'It's a matter of doing it every day,' declared Tucker. 'It's a matter of wearing the cloth. It's a matter of eating the seed. It's a matter of ingesting the Holy Weed into my chest, into my body, and allowing that spirit which is the plant spirit to combine with my spirit in worship of our Creator.'[667] This broadly animistic teaching is, of course, not dissimilar to the understandings of Harrison and Gaskin. The spirit of cannabis works with the individual to increase wellbeing and induce contemplation. 'When I want to calm my world, the immediate habitation of my soul, marijuana has a calming influence. And when I want to direct my thoughts internally, it has the ability to allow me to direct my thoughts where I want to without interference from negative forces.'[668]

Although the teaching of both Tucker and Baldasaro was similar to that of Gaskin, in that it was eclectic and focused on personal ecstatic experience, it was more explicitly informed by Judeo-Christian theism. Its core doctrines can be summed up as follows: 'The Church of the Universe is open to all creatures who believe God is God and obey the golden rules: 1. Don't hurt yourself. 2. Don't hurt anyone else.' It continues: 'The only prerequisite to becoming a Member of the Church of the Universe is that one must profess a belief in God's Spirit in you.'[669] More specifically, its theology of cannabis is constructed around a few key biblical verses, particularly those that mention 'the tree of life' (Gen. 1.29; Rev. 22.2, 14), which are believed to be direct references to cannabis. 'The Sacred Herb, God's Tree of Life, Marijuana ... is considered kosher, which is to say that [it] is a Holy Sacrament in the Church and as such it is imperative that ... [it] be grown by our own Herbalists/Farmers and distributed by our own Church Clergy.'[670]

There are similarities between the Church of the Universe and the more recently established Church of Cognizance. Having said that, while the latter appears to be informed by Christian culture, actually, it proudly claims to be 'predominantly Neo-Zoroastrian in nature.'[671] Founded in 1991 in Pima, Arizona, by Danuel and Mary Quaintance, its existence was formally announced on 12 August 1994, when the couple released a 'Declaration of Religious Sentiment' announcing the establishment of an 'Ethno-Socio-Religious Institute.'[672] Although Mary, who died on 8 March 2013, had been an atheist, significantly Danuel had been a member of the United Methodist Church and was, he claims, initially inspired to think of cannabis as a 'sacred herb' after reading the Bible. However, regardless of any formative biblical influence, the Church of Cognizance principally recognizes the scriptural authority of the *Avesta* – the ancient religious texts of Zoroastrianism, which had, initially, been communicated orally among Zoroastrian priests for more than a thousand years before being committed to writing and standardized between the third and seventh centuries CE.

Of particular importance for the Church is a sacramental understanding of cannabis based on references to '*haoma*' in the *Avesta*. 'There is a "mystery" surrounding an element of central focus throughout the scripture of the Zoroastrian religion. The "mystery" concerns the "true identity" of that central element of the "*Haoma* Offering", which is given in *Yasna* 11, just prior to the Zoroastrian Creed, given in the *Avesta* at *Yasna* 12.'[673] Unfortunately, argues Quaintance, the problem with contemporary Zoroastrianism is that is has 'given up adherence to this vital element of the *Haoma* Offering, or they substitute "Para" elements in place of the original. The problem is the "*parahaoma*" offers none of the benefits ascribed to the "original" *Haoma*.'[674] His point is that, although *haoma* is one of the ingredients of the *parahaoma* – a consecrated liquid prepared during the main act of worship – Zoroastrians tend to identify it as a variant of the non-psychoactive *ephedra*. This is a problem for Quaintance and, indeed, for a number of other cannabis apologists, not least Chris Bennett.[675] Again, the basic argument is that '*haoma*' is etymologically related to the word '*soma*', both of which are identified with cannabis – a theory that is now largely discredited.[676] However, again, we need not speculate about the cogency of this argument. The point is simply to note how ambiguous terms in ancient texts have been used by cannabis religionists and apologists to support the plant's sacralization.

Interestingly, it is rather surprising to discover that one of the key texts that members are encouraged to download from the website of the Church of Cognizance is a nineteenth-century pamphlet on Zoroastrianism by Henry Olcott, the co-founder and President of the Theosophical Society. However, in this pamphlet, Olcott he explicitly states that 'the Soma of the Aryans... was... not maddening like the Indian hemp, but exhilarating, illuminating, the begetter of divine visions.'[677] In other words, Olcott, while accepting that *haoma* had psychoactive properties, nevertheless, explicitly states that it should not be identified with cannabis. This is not addressed by the Church.

Again, it's worth noting here that there is an animist emphasis on the 'spirit residing within the plant'.[678] Indeed, like Harrison who identified the spirit in cannabis as the goddess Ma Ku, Quaintance is clear that 'the energy and spirit that is in marijuana is God. You consume the plant and you consume God. You are sacrificing your body to the deity.'[679] Again, without wanting to make too much of the similarities, some of this language is reminiscent of Christian understandings of the eucharist. 'Now as they were eating, Jesus took bread, and blessed, and broke it, and gave it to the disciples and said, "Take, eat; this is my body"' (Mt 26.26–28). (We will see below that this eucharistic understanding of cannabis is explicitly articulated by another cannabis church, Temple 420.) Again, members of the Church 'honor marijuana as the teacher, the provider, the protector.'[680] However, perhaps unsurprisingly, there are also similarities with the conception of *soma* in the *Ṛgveda*, in that *haoma*/cannabis is also revered as both a psychoactive and a deity – or, at least, the plant is very closely identified with the delity: '*haoma* is the name of the plant in which the deity named Haoma resides...'[681] In short, there is a confluence of theological ideas informing the Church's understanding of cannabis.

The influence of the Bible is more explicit in the theologies of two other cannabis churches, Temple 420 of the Heartland and the Assembly of Renown Plantation. Both were founded by Chapin Walton and are based in Kansas City. Eschewing the animistic understanding of cannabis, Walton makes it clear that he does not worship cannabis, but rather simply understands it to be a gift from the Creator.[682] Temple 420 of the Heartland also encourages an explicitly Bible-based theism. Indeed, there's a strong Jewish Christian emphasis to his teaching. Frequent references are made to Judaism, the preferred name for Jesus is 'Yeshua', and, as a mark of respect, 'God' is spelled 'G-d' – a custom popular within contemporary American Judaism. 'Inspired by a vision from G-d, Brother Walton started openly ministering about the provisions and truths of the Almighty Living G-d of the Bible. In 2003 he became ordained, in 2006 he joined the Judeo-Christian Ministry of Temple 420.'[683] Moreover, unlike a number of other cannabis churches, there is a pronounced emphasis on Bible teaching and evangelism. Indeed, some of their statements are strikingly similar to conservative Christian evangelistic literature. 'Have you been seeking more in life? Looking for salvation in yourself? You have the opportunity... to become a child of the Almighty Living God. God is graceful and opens this opportunity for all. We are all sinners. Accept Yeshua's sacrifice for you.'[684]

Also Jewish Christian in orientation, Temple 420, which is based in Los Angeles, is most closely associated with the veteran cannabis campaigner Craig X Rubin, an actor who played the proprietor of a medical cannabis dispensary in the series *Weeds* (2005–2012). Following the decision of the Supreme Court to grant an exemption to the Brazilian Spiritist organization, União do Vegetal, regarding the sacramental use of the powerful hallucinogen DMT (dimethyltryptamine), in 2006 Rubin founded Temple 420. Although he was brought up as a Jew with a grandfather who was a Rabbi, Rubin converted to Christianity. Interestingly, he claims that his conversion was the direct result of cannabis: 'pot made me from being just a Jew to a Jew for Jesus.'[685] That said, the process was probably a little more complex than this statement suggests, in that his conversion is clearly the result of his close relationship with the largely Christian Havasupai Native American tribe, which began when his mother took him to the reservation as a child. Rubin eventually built his own sweat lodge and began reading the Bible. The result was dramatic.

> I accepted Jesus as the messiah. I saw that He had fulfilled the prophecies of the Old Testament and having faith in Him gave me the peace in my life that I had been missing even though I was leading a 'spiritual' life. I still sweat with the Indians and enjoy taking peyote with them on occasion, although since putting my faith in Jesus my thinking became more Christ centred . . . It was then that some of my Christian friends who I had been chatting with online challenged me to spread the Word.

Rubin is now explicit about his commitment to the Christian conception of God and holds weekly Bible study sessions. 'We taught the Old Testament every Saturday at 4:20pm and on Sundays we taught the New Testament at the same stoner time.' (As discussed below, '420' is significant in cannabis culture.) Having said that, while his Bible teaching isn't limited to the spiritual understanding of cannabis, there are, nevertheless, a number of interpretations that some scholars might consider to be rather idiosyncratic. Of course, generally speaking, idiosyncrasy is not unusual for preachers who strive to make their sermons culturally relevant, but, for Rubin, the bias is towards cannabis. For example, he interprets Exodus 1:1–5 as follows: 'whenever the cannabis plant is burned it is putting the person who burns the cannabis on the mount with Moses who receives the Law. The Bible says, "the Lord dwells in the burning bush" and at Temple 420 we take that to heart.' Again, 'we feel that cannabis is the plant mentioned in the Book of Revelation that will be for "the healing of all nations," so we act on that belief by burning cannabis as a sacrament, just as when Jesus said, "Take this bread as my body and this wine as my blood."'[686]

Moreover, as we have seen, such organizations frequently challenge the common perception of users as lazy, disengaged dropouts. Certainly, there is little evidence to support the view that cannabis consumption necessarily leads to political quietism. Indeed, many years ago, Wuthnow found this in his early work on the counterculture – thereby challenging theories about mysticism posited by Max Weber and Ernst Troeltsch.[687] In everyday life, the cannabis user, like the mystic, doesn't simply recline and disengage from society. Some might do this of course, just as some teetotallers might, but it is not necessarily the case. Indeed, often, stoners and mystics seek change. Many are activists. As Rubin says of the work of Temple 420, 'we work with homeless kids to help them get jobs, we got one young porn star off the streets and into a women's shelter, and we even worked with pimps and prostitutes trying to help give them better lives ... Our Hollywood ministry is reaching many lost souls in a town that needs people who care. I think that the Father and Son would both be proud of what we are doing in His name.'[688]

420

As indicated above, '420' (pronounced 'four-twenty') is significant because, as many users will be aware, it refers both to the internationally observed day of cannabis culture, April 20 (4/20), and also to a time in the day set apart for toking. Indeed, although ostensibly secular, 20 April is celebrated as an international cannabis holy day. People take time off work, worship, meet up with friends, launch new products, promote new strains, attend cannabis industry conventions, and so on. It's become an enormously significant cultural phenomenon – so much so that it has earned an entry in the *Oxford English Dictionary*: 'Marijuana; the action of smoking marijuana. Frequently *attributive*. Often used with reference to the time 4:20 or the date April 20th (abbreviated 4/20 in the United States), considered as occasions for smoking or celebrating the smoking of marijuana.'

The reference to '420' originated in 1971 with the 'Waldos' – Steve Capper, Dave Reddix, Jeffrey Noel, Larry Schwartz, and Mark Gravich – a group of friends from San Rafael, Marin County, California, who used to meet up to chat, smoke, and have fun. One day, a friend of theirs gave them a map of the Point Reyes Peninsula drawn by Gary Newman.[689] They were told that it identified the spot where he had grown some cannabis. However, as a Coast Guard, he was becoming increasingly concerned that it might be discovered, which would lead to him getting fired. So, the friends arranged to drive to the area to look for it. They agreed to meet on the campus of San Rafael High School at 4.20pm next to a statue of Louis Pasteur (by the Italian American sculptor Beniamino Bufano). For several weeks they met up and searched for the crop, but without success. Nevertheless, over time, '420' became their secret code for cannabis: 'We did discover that we could talk about getting high in front of our parents, without them knowing, by using the phrase 420.'[690] However, of particular significance for the dissemination of the term was the fact that an older brother of Dave Reddix, one of the Waldos, was friendly with Phil Lesh, who played bass for The Grateful Dead. This eventually led to an invitation to roadie with bands associated with The Grateful Dead, which, in turn, led to the use of the term backstage by other roadies and musicians, such as David Crosby. Throughout this period, during which cannabis was demonized and illegal, 420 quickly became an important underground term, part of a secret language, just as we have seen terms like 'muggles' became part of the argot used by jazz musicians in the 1920s. However, it would be another twenty years before 420 would emerge from the countercultural underground in the US to gain widespread international recognition.

In 1990, a flyer promoting 420 began to circulate at Grateful Dead concerts in California. Although, by this time, few people were aware of its significance, a copy of the flyer made its way into the hands of Steve Bloom, a journalist working for *High Times*. During the 'last week of 1990', he tells us,

I went to several Grateful Dead shows at the Oakland Coliseum. I was walking in the parking lot and someone handed me a half-page flier. It had this message that people should smoke together at 4:20 and on 4/20. I brought it back to *High Times* in New York. We passed it around the office and everyone got a kick out of it. I was news editor at the time, so I transcribed the flyer and published it in the May 1991 issue. My little write up in *High Times* was the first time '420' got any national publicity.[691]

Having said that, the 1991 article included erroneous information regarding the origin of the term. It neglected to mention the Waldos and claimed that 420 began as a police code for 'marijuana smoking in progress.' This was eventually corrected in a 1998 *High Times* article, after Steve Capper contacted the editor, Steven Hager, in order to arrange a meeting with him to provide evidence regarding the true origin of the term.[692]

Although the flyer was not produced by the Waldos and included misleading information, it was significant for the popularization of 420. Apart from getting '420' into *High Times*, it led directly to the establishment of 4/20 as a 'day of celebration, the real time to get high, the grandmaster of all holidays'. Indeed, it encouraged users to 'get the day off work or school. We are going to meet at 4:20 on 4/20 for 420-ing in Marin County at the Bolinas Ridge sunset spot on Mt. Tamalpais.'[693] Hence, although explicitly focussed on consuming cannabis, 420 was, from the outset, always about friendship, sharing, and peace. As with cannabis-based religions, the emphasis was on the creation of a community. 'There is something fantastic about getting ripped at 4:20, when you know your brothers and sisters all over the country and even the planet are lighting up and toking up right along with you.'[694]

It Is unsurprising, therefore, that a cannabis-based new religion would reference 420. Indeed, all the organizations we have discussed so far could simply be referred to as '420 religions'.

Concluding comments

As a manifestation of the 'subjective turn' in the modern world, cannabis-based spiritualities can be understood as 'spiritualities of life'.[695] In other words, there is a conspicuous focus on 'the intrinsic spirituality of the person or the integral spirituality of the natural order as a whole.'[696] This type of spirituality tends to be epistemologically individualistic, focusing on the authority and significance of the experiencing self, rather than obedience to some external or transcendent source of authority. Although this may be combined with more traditional ideas about God – 'theistic spiritualities of life'[697] – and include a felt need for scriptural legitimation, the bias is always towards the experiencing self. This, of course, is to be expected. Psychoactive substances are all about inner experience: 'spirituality isn't about *what* we do, but *how* we do what we do. Whether we fast from food and pray for three days or roll a fatty [spliff] before our yoga class, the quality of our spiritual experiences is determined by the consciousness we bring to our actions.' And, in the final analysis, while it may not be for everyone, cannabis 'helps you to feel more connected to a loving higher purpose and takes you beyond limited ways of reacting to the world...'[698]

Moreover, related to this focus on inner experience, typically, there is also a focus on healing and wellbeing. Indeed, in accordance with much of what has been discussed in this chapter, Dussault has insisted that *'there's no such thing as "recreational" use.* Considering the imbalanced, incredibly stressful world we live in, all cannabis use is "medicinal."'[699] Cannabis use is therapeutic simply because it eases the passage through life. Furthermore, as well as helping 'to relax and balance the mind', it is also able to 'help even the most cynical sceptics find sacred reprieve from the onslaught of modernity.'[700] This is particularly the case, Dussault argues, if it is incorporated into a spiritual discipline such as yoga: 'yoga and cannabis produce altered states of consciousness on their own ... [but] work even more powerfully when combined ... With yoga and cannabis, the subtle, yet remarkable experiences of fully occupying the body and engaging a relaxed mind become more apparent. We feel *creative, magical, inspired, turned-on, present, satisfied*.'[701] In the final analysis, as discussed above, because the bias is toward the authority of inner experience, there is a loose relationship to tradition. The past is important, but it is viewed through a very particular lens, shaped primarily by personal experience. As such, we have seen that history and tradition tends to become repositories from which to plunder ideas. Sacred texts, archaeological evidence, and religious doctrines all tend to be reinterpreted and employed selectively.

Having noted the focus on inner experience, it's also important to remember that cannabis is a social drug and, as such, community is important. Joints are shared, bongs are passed round, the communal chalice is lifted, edibles are served, and everyone gathers together to celebrate 420. It's a drug that brings people together in an atmosphere of love and peace. Indeed, often this is encouraged through ritual. For example, Swami Chaitanya notes that he is 'part of an amorphous group who gather from time to time to specifically use cannabis as a sacrament with a creed and a defined ceremonial sequence, during which a gigantic cannabis cone joint is passed around the circle.' He continues: 'everyone brings a bit of flower to contribute to the communal joint. We pass it always to the right, with the right hand, and with the left hand covering the heart we look the recipient in the eye and say: "Cannamaste!" That person receives the cone with the right hand and repeats: "Cannamaste" covering their heart with their left hand and meeting your eyes.'[702]

Interestingly, recent research has shown that there is 'a direct association between non-medical cannabis use and positive psychological outcomes in otherwise healthy young adults.' In other words, cannabis tends to increase 'prosociality' – 'the intentional act of advancing the wellbeing of other people', including 'displays of empathy, providing assistance to others, and engaging in community service...'[703] This, moreover, seems to be supported by the emphasis placed on social activism by some cannabis-based spiritualities. As we have seen, key figures such as Gaskin, Rubin, Baldasaro, and Swami Chaitanya have all encouraged social responsibility and political activism. Again, as we have seen, this is an important point that directly challenges the popular perception of users as stupefied stoners. Indeed, Swami Chaitanya is clear that cannabis has been directly involved in the development of his activism: 'She has taught me political action and community organizing.'[704] Of course, there are times when cannabis users, like wine drinkers, relax with their chosen drug and get into a state in which it would be unwise to do very much at all, let alone get involved in social activism. But most users aren't stoned continuously and many have a keen sense of social responsibility.

Having said that, I suspect that, typically, social activism is less a direct result of the cannabis experience and more a consequence of other influences. As we have seen, users are typically motivated by a range of discourses from New Left ideology and countercultural politics to the Bible and Zoroastrian ethics. In other words, it usually takes more than simply getting high to become engaged in activism. Activists may, of course, gain inspiration when they are high, but there needs to be a larger ethical framework within which to interpret the ideas that emerge during intoxication. Nevertheless, it does seem clear that cannabis need not inhibit social activism and may, indeed, be a contributory factor to successful cultures of resistance and socially responsible behaviour.

We have also seen that, although many users will not subscribe to a particular form of cannabis spirituality, they nevertheless appreciate the insights gained during intoxication. Their lives are changed. For example, we have seen that, influenced by Baudelaire's *Artificial Paradises*, Walter Benjamin experimented with hashish in order to expand his consciousness and to explore its utility as an aesthetic, philosophical, and political technology of transcendence.[705] He was – in some respects, like Crowley before him – interested in its potential to dissolve the subject-object relationship, to loosen the constraining chains of reason, to manipulate time and space, to merge waking and sleeping states, to manifest the surreal, to make irregular connections between ideas, to punctuate experience with unexpected sensations, and, overall, to enable momentary thoughts and everyday objects to become sources of 'profane illumination'. As with the Romantics, he sought to explore the power of the imagination, which could be used to enhance one's experience of the world. Ordinary reality becomes non-ordinary reality; the familiar becomes unfamiliar; everyday spaces become 'heterotopias'.

This last point is worth unpacking a little because it is helpful for our understanding of the sacralization of cannabis. Following Foucault, the 'other spaces' generated during intoxication can be thought of as existing alongside, but distinct from hegemonic society and culture. Foucault identified two forms of space, 'utopias' and 'heterotopias'. The former are essentially unreal spaces that tend to present idealized forms of society: 'They present society itself in a perfected form, or else society turned upside down, but in any case these utopias are fundamentally unreal spaces.'[706] Heterotopias, on the other hand, are both 'real spaces' and 'counter-sites', in that they 'remain absolutely different from all the sites that they reflect and speak about'.[707] One might, for example, create a zen garden in the centre of London, similar to those found in Kyoto, which bears little relation to the life beyond the space it occupies. The two spaces are juxtaposed and remain intimately involved in the same world, but are fundamentally separated from each other. As such, the Zen garden can function as an idealized critique of wider society, as well as an escape from the frenetic hustle and bustle of everyday life. For Benjamin and for those spiritual users discussed in this chapter, cannabis is able to create inner utopias and heterotopias. Such profane illumination can, in turn, as Benjamin opined, have political potential. The cannabis experience might transport the user to a temporary heterotopia or, indeed, it might generate a utopian vision of what society could be, either of which is able to stimulate social activism.

For some writers, such as Ludlow, the heterotopias visited during the cannabis experience are objectively real. While this is not typical of the cannabis high, being a more common experience during psychedelic states, nevertheless, colourful descriptions of hashish heterotopias are often cited in religious and apologetic literature. Indeed, for Ludlow, these became part of his legitimation strategy. That is to say, as Huxley famously argued regarding the use of psychedelics,[708] psychoactive substances are able to induce genuine mystical experiences.

Concerning this last point, as James Lewis has noted regarding new religions, 'an important ideological resource for emergent movements, particularly in hostile social environments, is legitimacy. New religions actively seek legitimacy.'[709] Typically, they 'attempt to justify a new idea or a new social order by attributing to it the authority of tradition, but it is usually only through a radical reinterpretation of the past that they are able to portray themselves as the true embodiment of that "tradition."' He continues, 'one of the reasons why this particular legitimation strategy should have so much attraction is tied up with the prestige given to origins in almost all societies.'[710] This is, again, certainly the case when it comes to the religious and medicinal use of cannabis. Confirmation bias, selective use of the available evidence, neo-romantic constructions of the past, and a radical reinterpretation of history are all employed to legitimize and sacralize the use of cannabis. Having said that, while the notion of a 'legitimation strategy' might suggest the cynical manipulation of information, often this isn't the case. Confirmation bias easily and naturally informs the selection and interpretation of information. In a culture in which cannabis has been demonized for many years, constructing a sacred history of its importance as a sacrament used to induce religious experiences is important. Hence, we have seen that there has been an effort to legitimize cannabis using key sources of sacred authority, particularly scriptural authority – the Bible, the *Avesta*, the *Ṛgveda*, and so on. Again, more broadly, contemporary culture, which has witnessed an increased sacralization of nature and suspicion about the influence of multinational corporations, has had a formative impact on strategies of legitimation. Cannabis, we have seen, is framed as a plant-based alternative to the expensive and toxic chemicals produced by 'big pharma'. Having said that, we have seen that legitimation strategies do not necessarily entail fabrication. For example, as discussed in the previous chapter, the medical use of cannabis has included important healthcare research, which, in turn, has been enormously important for its legitimation in late-modern societies.

Notes

Introduction

1. Walter Benjamin, 'Hashish in Marseilles'. In Walter Benjamin, *On Hashish*. Edited by Howard Eiland (Cambridge: Harvard University Press, 2006), 118–119.
2. See Anonymous, 'The Effects of Marijuana on Consciousness'. In Charles Tart (ed.), *Altered States of Consciousness* (New York: Anchor Books, 1972), 343–364; Valerie Curran and Celia Morgan, 'Desired and Undesired Effects of Cannabis on the Human Mind and Psychological Well-being'. In Roger Pertwee (ed.), *Handbook of Cannabis* (Oxford: Oxford University Press, 2014), 647–660.
3. Benjamin, *On Hashish*, 145.
4. Ernst Bloch, *The Principle of Hope*, Vol. 1. Trans. by Neville Plaice, Stephen Plaice, and Paul Knight (Cambridge: MIT Press, 1986), 88–91.
5. Ibid., 89. On Bloch's understanding the 'daydream', see Michael Löwy and Robert Sayre, *Romanticism Against the Tide of Modernity*. Trans. by Catherine Porter (Durham: Duke University Press, 2001), 169–187.
6. 'Everything I said on the subject was directed polemically against the theosophists, whose experience and ignorance I find highly repugnant . . . First, genuine aura appears in all things, not just certain kinds of things, as people imagine.' Walter Benjamin, 'Hashish, Beginning of March 1930.' In Walter Benjamin, *On Hashish*. Edited by Howard Eiland (Cambridge: Harvard University Press, 2006), 58.
7. Walter Benjamin, 'A Small History of Photography.' In Walter Benjamin, *On Photography*. Trans. by Esther Leslie (London: Reaktion Books, 2015), 59–108.
8. Walter Benjamin, *The Work of Art in the Age of Its Technical Reproducibility, and Other Writings on Media*. Edited by Michael Jennings, Brigid Doherty, and Thomas Levin (Cambridge: Harvard University Press, 2008), 14.
9. Walter Benjamin, quoted in Rolf Goebel, 'Introduction: Benjamin's Actuality'. In Rolf Goebel (ed.), *A Companion to the Works of Walter Benjamin* Rochester: Camden House, 2009), 10–11.
10. Emil Brunner discusses the idea in *The Divine-human Encounter*. Trans Amandus Loos (Philadelphia: Westminster Press, 1943).
11. Quoted in Howard Eiland, 'Translator's Foreword', in Benjamin, *On Hashish*, vii.
12. Aldous Huxley, *The Doors of Perception; Heaven and Hell* (London: Flamingo, 1994); see also Christopher Partridge, *High Culture: Drugs, Mysticism, and the Pursuit of Transcendence in the Modern World* (New York: Oxford University Press, 2018).
13. Walter Benjamin, 'Surrealism: The Last Snapshot of the European Intelligentsia'. In *One-Way Street and Other Writings* (London: New Left Books, 1979), 227.
14. Eiland, 'Translator's Foreword', ix.
15. Ibid.
16. Walter Benjamin, *Reflections: Essays, Aphorisms, Autobiographical Writings*. Trans Edmund Jephcott (New York: Harcourt Brace Jovanovich, 1978), 177–192; Benjamin, *On Hashish*, 132–134.

17 Christina Halperin, 'Profane Illuminations: Classic Maya Molded Figurines in Comparative Context', *Res: Anthropology and Aesthetics* 71–72 (2019), 25–26.
18 Mircea Eliade, *The Sacred and the Profane: The Nature of Religion*. Trans. by Willard Trask (New York: Harcourt Brace Jovanovich, 1957); Robert C. Zaehner, *Mysticism, Sacred and Profane: An Inquiry Into Some Varieties of Praeternatural Experience* (London: Oxford University Press, 1961).
19 Eliade, *Sacred and Profane*, 11.
20 Ibid., 11.
21 Michel Foucault, *The Will to Knowledge: the History of Sexuality, Vol. 1*. Trans. by Robert Hurley (London: Penguin, 1990), 93.
22 Émile Durkheim, *The Rules of Sociological Method*. Trans. by Sarah Solovay and John Mueller (New York: The Free Press, 1938), 14.
23 Ibid., 3.
24 Ibid., 13.
25 Ibid.*d*, 10.
26 Zygmunt Bauman, 'Durkheim's Society Revisited'. In Jeffrey C. Alexander and Philip Smith (eds), *The Cambridge Companion to Durkheim* (Cambridge: Cambridge University Press, 2005), 363.
27 See particularly, Jeffrey Alexander, *The Meanings of Social Life: A Cultural Sociology* (New York: Oxford University Press, 2003); *The Civil Sphere* (New York: Oxford University Press, 2006).
28 Gordon Lynch, *The Sacred in the Modern World: A Cultural Sociological Approach* (Oxford: Oxford University Press, 2012), 5.
29 Linn Normand, *Demonization in International Politics* (New York: Palgrave Macmillan, 2016), 2.
30 For a good analysis of the 'politics of horror' in conservative religious cultures, see Jason Bivins, *Religion of Fear* (New York: Oxford University Press, 2008).
31 See Thomas De Witt, *The Weed that Bewitches* (New York: National Temperance Society and Publication House, 1885).
32 *Devil's Harvest*, IMDb: https://www.imdb.com/title/tt0157533/ (accessed 28 August,2020).
33 Alexander, *Meanings of Social Life*, 200.
34 Alexander, *Civil Sphere*, 62.
35 Supreme Court of the United States, 'Lee Brooker v. State of Alabama': https://eji.org/files/lee-brooker-us-cert-petition.pdf (accessed 3 January 2020).
36 See Jeffrey Alexander's discussion of the historical contingency of sacred forms in his analysis of shifting perceptions of the holocaust: *Meanings of Social Life*, 27–84.
37 See John Parascandola, 'The Drug Habit: the Association of the Word "Drug" with Abuse in American History'. In Roy Porter and Mikulas Teich (eds), *Drugs and Narcotics in History* (Cambridge: Cambridge University Press, 1995), 156–167.
38 Richard Rudgley, *The Alchemy of Culture: Intoxicants in Society* (London: British Museum Press, 1993); Paul Devereux, *The Long Trip: A Prehistory of Psychedelia* (Harmondsworth: Arkana, 1997).
39 See Guillermo Garat's discussion of the process and the challenges and opportunities it presented: 'Uruguay: A Way to Regulate the Cannabis Market'. In Beatriz Labate, Clancy Cavnar, and Thiago Rodrigues (eds), *Drug Policies and the Politics of Drugs in the Americas* (London: Springer, 2016), 209–226.
40 Bernie Sanders, 'Legalizing Marijuana', *BernieSanders.com*: https://berniesanders.com/issues/legalizing-marijuana (accessed 20 March 2020).

41 Howard Parker, Fiona Measham, and Judith Aldridge, *Drugs Futures: Changing Patterns of Drug Use Amongst English Youth* (London: Institute for the Study of Drug Dependence, 1995). See also, Shane Blackman, *Chilling Out: The Cultural Politics of Substance Consumption, Youth and Drug Policy* (Maidenhead: Open University Press, 2004), 127–147; Shane Blackman, '"See Emily Play": Youth Culture, Recreational Drug Use and Normalization', in Mark Simpson, Tracy Shildrick, and Robert MacDonald (eds), *Drugs in Britain: Supply, Consumption and Control* (London: Palgrave Macmillan, 2007), 39–59; Amy Pennay and Fiona Measham, 'The Normalisation Thesis – 20 Years Later', *Drugs: Education, Prevention, and Policy* 23.3 (2016), 187–189; Michael Shiner and Tim Newburn, 'Definitely, Maybe Not? The Normalisation of Recreational Drug Use Amongst Young People', *Sociology* 31.3 (1997), 511–529.
42 Shaun Ryder, in Anthony Bozza and Shawn Dahl (eds), *Rolling Stone Raves* (New York: Rolling Stone Press, 1999), 245–246.
43 See, for example, Jan van Amsterdam, David Nutt, Lawrence Phillips, and Wim van den Brink, 'European Rating of Drug Harms', *Journal of Psychopharmacology* 29.6 (2015), 655–660; Jan van Amsterdam and Wim van den Brink, 'Ranking of Drugs: A More Balanced Risk-assessment', *The Lancet* 376.9752 (2010), 1524–1525; Steve Fox, Paul Armentano, and Mason Tvert, *Marijuana is Safer: So Why Are We Driving People to Drink?* (White River Junction: Chelsea Green Publishing Company, 2009).
44 On 'specialness' in religion, see Ann Taves, *Religious Experience Reconsidered: A Building Block Approach to the Study of Religion and Other Special Things* (Princeton: Princeton University Press, 2009), 28–55.
45 For a popular guide to cannabis related films, see Shirley Halperin and Steve Bloom, *Reefer Movie Madness: The Ultimate Stoner Film Guide* (New York: Abrams Image, 2010). See also John Markert, *Hooked in Film: Substance Abuse on the Big Screen* (Lanham: Scarecrow Press, 2013), 33–86.
46 Kate Mossman, 'The Secret of *The Wicker Man*', *The New Statesman* (23–29 June 2023), 52.
47 See Sarah Thornton, *Club Cultures: Music, Media and Subcultural Capital* (Cambridge: Polity Press, 1995), which develops Pierre Bourdieu's ideas about 'cultural capital' to understand the cultural knowledge and commodities acquired by members of a subculture. Subcultural capital raises a person's status within a group and assists in differentiating members of that group from members of other groups. It may be the music listened to, the clothes worn, the argot employed, or, indeed, the drugs used.
48 Laura Garius and Amal Ari, *Regulating Right, Repairing Wrongs: Exploring Equity and Social Justice Initiatives within UK Cannabis Reform* (London: Release, 2022), 3.
49 Maddy Mussen and Emily Sheed, '16,000 Students Took Our Drugs Survey. Find Out How and What They're Taking This Term', *The Tab* (2020): https://thetab.com/uk/2020/12/22/16000-students-took-our-drugs-survey-find-out-how-and-what-theyre-taking-this-term-187354 (accessed 5 August 2023); Garius and Ari, *Regulating Right*, 3.
50 On 'cannabis clubs', see Mafalda Pardal (ed.), *The Cannabis Social Club* (London: Routledge, 2022).
51 Sarah Sinclair, 'Inside a UK Cannabis Club: Changing Lives, Tackling Stigma, Building Community', *Cannabis Health* (23 June 2023): https://cannabishealthnews.co.uk/2023/06/23/inside-a-uk-cannabis-club-saving-lives-tackling-stigma-building-community/ (accessed 5 August 2023).
52 Michael Fisher, quoted in ibid.
53 Ibid.

54 Damien Gayle, 'Durham Police Stop Targeting Pot Smokers and Small-scale Growers', *The Guardian* (22 July 2015): https://www.theguardian.com/society/2015/jul/22/durham-police-stop-targeting-pot-smokers-and-small-scale-growers (accessed 5 August, 2023).
55 Matta Busby, 'Prisons Should Trial Free Cannabis, Says UK's Former Chief Drug Adviser', *The Guardian* (27 February 2021): https://www.theguardian.com/society/2021/feb/27/prisons-should-trial-free-cannabis-says-former-top-drug-adviser (accessed 5 August, 2023).
56 R.D. Laing, 'Letter, 1 June, 1964'. In George Andrews and Simon Vinkenoog (eds), *The Book of Grass: An Anthology of Indian Hemp* (Harmondsworth: Penguin, 1972), 236.
57 David Nutt, *Cannabis (Seeing Through the Smoke): The New Science of Cannabis and Your Health* (London: Yellow Kite, 2021), 39.
58 Ibid., 22.
59 See, ibid., 38–46.
60 See, for example, Dawn MacKeen, 'What Are the Benefits of CBD?' *New York Times* (16 October 2019): https://www.nytimes.com/2019/10/16/style/self-care/cbd-oil-benefits.html (accessed 6 July 2023); Amber Smith, 'How to Help a Dog with Separation Anxiety', *Discover Magazine* (18 June 2023): https://www.discovermagazine.com/lifestyle/how-to-help-a-dog-with-separation-anxiety-full-guide-and-best-products (accessed 6 July 2023).
61 Megan Brenan, '14% of Americans Say They Use CBD Products', *Gallup News* (7 August 2019): https://news.gallup.com/poll/263147/americans-say-cbd-products.aspx#:~:text=WASHINGTON%2C%20D.C.%20%2D%2D%20One%20in,this%20hemp%20form%20of%20cannabis (accessed 23 May 2023).
62 Alena Hall, '64% Of US Adults Think CBD Is Safer Than Alcohol, Despite Legality Concerns', *Forbes Health* (21 April, 2022): https://www.forbes.com/health/body/2022-cbd-survey/ (accessed 23 May 2023).
63 Diana Gonimah, 'Everyday: Cannabis for Daily Consumption', *Eaze* (18 November 2020): https://www.eaze.com/article/everyday-cannabis-for-daily-consumption (accessed 6 June 2023).
64 'Five-a-day' is a national campaign developed in a number of countries to encourage the daily consumption of at least five portions of fruit and vegetables.
65 Fintan Smith and Lukas Paleckis, 'Decriminalising Cannabis in London: What do Londoners Think the Impact Would Be?' *YouGov* (7 December 2022): https://yougov.co.uk/topics/health/articles-reports/2022/09/07/decriminalising-cannabis-london-what-do-londoners- (accessed 23 May 2023).
66 Garius and Ari, *Regulating Right*, 3.
67 United Nations Office on Drugs and Crime, *World Drug Report 2022* (Vienna: United Nations Office on Drugs and Crime, 2022), 13.
68 Ibid., 16.
69 European Monitoring Centre for Drugs and Drug Addiction, *European Drug Report: Trends and Developments* (Luxembourg: Publications Office of the European Union, 2022), 8.
70 Ibid., 11.
71 Jeffrey Jones, 'Nearly Half of U.S. Adults Have Tried Marijuana', *Gallup News* (17 August 2021): https://news.gallup.com/poll/353645/nearly-half-adults-tried-marijuana.aspx (accessed 23 May 2023).
72 Amy Pennay and Fiona Measham, 'The Normalisation Thesis – 20 Years Later', *Drugs: Education, Prevention, and Policy* 23.3 (2016), 187.

73 Megan Brenan, 'Support for Legal Marijuana Inches Up to New High of 68%', *Gallup News* (9 November 2020): https://news.gallup.com/poll/323582/support-legal-marijuana-inches-new-high.aspx (accessed 20 August 2021). See also, NORC, 'Should Marijuana Be Made Legal? Key Trends', *NORC* (Chicago: University of Chicago, 2020): https://gssdataexplorer.norc.org/trends?category=Civil%20Liberties&measure=grass (accessed 23 May 2023).

74 Stephanie Kramer, 'Religious Americans are Less Likely to Endorse Legal Marijuana for Recreational Use', *Pew Research Center* (26 May 2021): https://www.pewresearch.org/short-reads/2021/05/26/religious-americans-are-less-likely-to-endorse-legal-marijuana-for-recreational-use/ (accessed 24 May 2023).

75 Brenan, 'Support for Legal Marijuana'.

76 Kramer, 'Religious Americans are Less Likely'.

77 See Christina Johns, 'The War on Drugs: Why the Administration Continues to Pursue a Policy of Criminalization and Enforcement', *Social Justice* 18.4 (1991), 147–165.

78 See Jonathan Merritt, 'The Christian Case for Marijuana', *New York Times* (20 June 2019): https://www.nytimes.com/2019/06/20/opinion/legalization-medical-marijuana-christianity.html (accessed 24 May 2023).

79 Kramer, 'Religious Americans are Less Likely'.

80 See, for example, Diana Kruzman, 'With "Christian Cannabis," a Pastor is Promoting the Spiritual Side of Marijuana', *Religion News Service* (29 March 2022): https://religionnews.com/2022/03/29/with-christian-cannabis-a-pastor-is-promoting-the-spiritual-side-of-marijuana/ (accessed 17 August 2022); Alyson Martin, 'Holy Rollers: These Devout Christians Are Using The Bible To Argue That Pot Is God's "Perfect Medicine"', *BuzzFeed News* (15 May 2017): https://www.buzzfeednews.com/article/alysonmartin/cannabis-reform-and-religion-in-the-south (accessed 7 July 2023).

81 See Timmen Cermak, *Marijuana on my Mind: The Science and Mystique of Cannabis* (Cambridge: Cambridge University Press, 2022), xv.

1 Cannabis

1 See, for example, Weston La Barre, *Culture in Context* (Durham NC: Duke University Press, 1980), 93–107; Guangpeng Ren, Xu Zhang, Ying Li, Kate Ridout, Martha Serrano-Serrano, Yongzhi Yang, Ai Liu, Gudasalamani Ravikanth, Muhammad Ali Nawaz, Abdul Samad Mumtaz, Nicolas Salamin, and Luca Fumagalli, 'Large-scale Whole-genome Resequencing Unravels the Domestication History of *Cannabis sativa*', *Science Advances* 7.29 (16 July 2021), 1–12; Meng Ren, Zihua Tang, Xinhua Wu, Robert Spengler, Hongen Jiang, Yimin Yang, and Nicole Boivin, 'The Origins of Cannabis Smoking: Chemical Residue Evidence from the First Millennium BCE in the Pamirs', *Science Advances* 5.6 (12 June 2019): https://www.science.org/doi/10.1126/sciadv.aaw1391 (accessed 20 October 2021).

2 See, for example, Robert Clarke and Mark Merlin, *Cannabis: Evolution and Ethnobotany* (Berkeley: California University Press, 2013); Mitch Earleywine (ed.), *Pot Politics: Marijuana and the Costs of Prohibition* (Oxford: Oxford University Press, 2007); Mark Ferrara, *Sacred Bliss: A Spiritual History of Cannabis* (Lanham: Rowman & Littlefield, 2016); Dale Jacquette (ed.), *Cannabis: Philosophy for Everyone: What Were We Just Talking About?* (Chichester: Wiley-Blackwell, 2010); Roger Pertwee (ed.), *Handbook of Cannabis* (Oxford: Oxford University Press, 2014); Gary Potter,

Weed, Need, and Greed: A Study of Domestic Cannabis Cultivation (London: Free Association Books, 2010); Lucas Richert and James Mills (eds), *Cannabis: Global Histories* (Cambridge: MIT Press, 2021); Vera Rubin (ed.), *Cannabis and Culture* (The Hague: Mouton Publishers, 1975); Barney Warf, 'High Points: A Historical Geography of Cannabis', *Geographical Review* 104 (2014), 414–438.

3 Brian Preston, *Pot Planet: Adventures in Global Marijuana Culture* (London: Atlantic Books, 2002).
4 'Cannabinaceae' is Rendle's spelling; 'Cannabaceae' is the contemporary spelling.
5 Alfred Barton Rendle, *The Classification of Flowering Plants*, Vol. 2 (Cambridge: Cambridge University Press, 1925), 56.
6 Clarke and Merlin, *Cannabis*, 312.
7 See, for example, Keith Villa, *Brewing with Cannabis: Using THC and CBD in Beer* (Boulder: Brewer's Publications, 2021), 21–32.
8 See Ernest Small, 'Evolution and Classification of *Cannabis sativa* (Marijuana, Hemp) in Relation to Human Utilization', *The Botanical Review* 81.3 (2015), 189–294.
9 Ernest Small and Arthur Cronquist, 'A Practical and Natural Taxonomy for *Cannabis*', *Taxon* 25.4 (1976), 405.
10 Karl Hillig, 'Genetic evidence for speciation in *Cannabis*(Cannabaceae)', *Genetic Resources and Crop Evolution* 52 (2005), 178.
11 For a good explanation of the key taxonomical issues, see Antonino Pollio, 'The Name of Cannabis: A Short Guide for Nonbotanists', *Cannabis and Cannabinoid Research* 1.1 (2016): https://www.ncbi.nlm.nih.gov/pmc/articles/PMC5531363/pdf/can.2016.0027.pdf (accessed 17 October 2021). See also, Lyle Craker and Zoë Gardner, 'The Botany of Cannabis'. In Julie Holland (ed.), *The Pot Book: A Complete Guide to Cannabis. Its Role in Medicine, Politics, Science, and Culture* (Rochester: Park Street Press, 2010), 35–43; Clarke and Merlin, *Cannabis*, 312–320; see also, John McPartland and Geoffrey Guy, 'Models of *Cannabis* Taxonomy, Cultural Bias, and Conflicts between Scientific and Vernacular Names', *The Botanical Review* 83 (2017), 327–381.
12 See Ernest Small, 'American Law and the Species Problem in Cannabis: Science and Semantics', *United Nations Bulletin on Narcotics* 28.3 (1975): https://www.unodc.org/unodc/en/data-and-analysis/bulletin/bulletin_1975-01-01_3_page002.html (accessed 23 April 2022).
13 See Holenarasipur Yoganarasimham Mohan Ram and Rina Sett, 'Induction of Fertile Male Flowers in Genetically Female *Cannabis sativa* Plants by Silver Nitrate and Silver Thiosulphate Anionic Complex', *Theoretical Applied Genetics* 62.4 (1982), 369–375.
14 Craker and Gardner, 'Botany of Cannabis', 38.
15 Ibid., 40.
16 Thomas Wood, Newton Spivey, and Thomas Easterfield, 'XL – Charas. The Resin of Indian Hemp', *Journal of the Chemical Society, Transactions* 69 (1896), 539–546; see also, Thomas Wood, Newton Spivey, and Thomas Easterfield, 'III – Cannabinol. Part 1', *Journal of the Chemical Society, Transactions* 75 (1899), 20–36.
17 Roger Adams, Madison Hunt, and J. H. Clark, 'Structure of Cannabidiol, a Product Isolated from the Marihuana Extract of Minnesota Wild Hemp. I', *Journal of the American Chemical Society* 62 (1940), 196–200.
18 See Ethan Russo, 'Taming THC: Potential Cannabis Synergy and Phytocannabinoid-terpenoid Entourage Effects', *British Journal of Pharmacology* 163.7 (2012), 1344.
19 See Roger Pertwee, 'Cannabinoid Pharmacology: The First 66 Years', *British Journal of Pharmacology* 147, Supplement 1 (2006), 163–171.

20 Raphael Mechoulam and Lumír Hanuš, 'Anandamide and More'. In Julie Holland (ed.), *The Pot Book: A Complete Guide to Cannabis. Its Role in Medicine, Politics, Science, and Culture* (Rochester: Park Street Press, 2010), 64.
21 Ibid., 64–65.
22 Ernest Small, 'Evolution and Classification of *Cannabis sativa* (Marijuana, Hemp) in Relation to Human Utilization', *The Botanical Review* 81 (2015), 190.
23 Clarke and Merlin, *Cannabis*, 49.
24 Ibid.
25 Desmond Slade, Zlatko Mehmedic, Suman Chandra, and Mahmoud ElSohly, 'Is Cannabis Becoming More Potent'. In David Castle, Robin Murray, and Deepak D'Souza (eds), *Marijuana and Madness*, second edition (Cambridge: Cambridge University Press, 2019), 51.
26 See Kat Petrilli, Lindsey Hines, Sally Adams, Celia Morgan, Valerie Curran, and Tom Freeman, 'High Potency Cannabis Use, Mental Health Symptoms and Cannabis Dependence: Triangulating the Evidence', *Addictive Behaviours* 144 (2023), 1–7: 'There was no association between high potency cannabis preference or THC concentration in cannabis and psychosis-like symptoms'.
27 Oaksterdam University: https://oaksterdamuniversity.com (accessed 9 Novemeber 2021).
28 Shimon Ben-Shabat, Ester Fride, Tzviel Sheskin, Tsippy Tamiri, Man-Hee Rhee, and Zvi Vogel, 'An Entourage Effect: Inactive Endogenous Fatty Acid Glycerol Esters Enhance 2-arachidonoyl-glycerol Cannabinoid Activity', *European Journal of Pharmacology* 353 (1998), 23–31.
29 See, for example, Ethan Russo, 'The Case for the Entourage Effect and Conventional Breeding of Clinical Cannabis: No "Strain," No Gain', *Frontiers in Plant Science* (9 January 2019): https://www.frontiersin.org/articles/10.3389/fpls.2018.01969/full (accessed 20 October 2021); Sari Goldstein Ferber, Dvora Namdar, Danielle Hen-Shoval, Gilad Eger, Hinanit Koltai, Gal Shoval, Liat Shbiro, and Aron Weller, 'The "Entourage Effect": Terpenes Coupled with Cannabinoids for the Treatment of Mood Disorders and Anxiety Disorders', *Current Neuropharmacology* 18 (2020), 87–96.
30 For popular discussions of numerous strains, see S.T. Oner (yes, it's a pseudonym), *Cannabis Sativa*, 3 vols (San Francisco: Green Candy Press, 2012, 2013, 2014); *Cannabis Indica*, 3 vols (San Francisco: Green Candy Press, 2011, 2012, 2014).
31 See, 'DJ Short Seeds': https://www.djgenetics.com (accessed: 20 October 2021).
32 Nick Jones, *Spliffs: A Celebration of Cannabis Culture* (London: Chrysalis Impact, 2003), 66.
33 Ibid., 75.
34 Ibid., 73.
35 Clarke and Merlin, *Cannabis*, 49.
36 See Cailun Tanney, Rachel Backer, Anja Geitmann, and Donald Smith, 'Cannabis Glandular Trichomes: A Cellular Metabolite Factory', *Frontiers in Plant Science* 12 (20 September 2021): https://www.frontiersin.org/articles/10.3389/fpls.2021.721986/full (accessed 24 April 2022).
37 Clarke and Merlin, *Cannabis*, 51.
38 Jones, *Spliffs*, 64.
39 Chris Duvall, *Cannabis* (London: Reaktion Books, 2015), 48.
40 Ibid., 139.
41 Joseph Berke and Calvin Hernton, *The Cannabis Experience: An Interpretative Study of the Effects of Marijuana and Hashish* (London: Quartet Books, 1977), 13.

42 Michael Schofield, *The Strange Case of Pot* (Harmondsworth: Penguin, 1971).
43 See Jonathon Green, *Days in the Life: Voices from the English Underground, 1961–1971* (London: Pimlico, 1998), 48, 52.
44 Danilo Marino, 'Hashish and Food: Arabic and European Medieval Dreams of Edible Paradises'. In Kirill Dmitriev, Julia Hauser, and Bilal Orfali (eds), *Insatiable Appetite: Food as Cultural Signifier in the Middle East and Beyond* (Leiden: Brill, 2019), 191.
45 Carsten Niebuhr, *Travels Through Arabia and Other Countries in the East*, 2 vols. Trans. by Robert Heron (Edinburgh: R. Morison & Son, 1792), 225.
46 Green, *Days in the Life*, 55.
47 Potter, *Weed, Need, and Greed*, 44.
48 See also Mel Thomas, 'The Glory Days of Haze: How I Came to Love Sativa'. In S.T. Oner, *Cannabis Sativa*, Vol. 2 (San Francisco: Green Candy Press, 2013), xiii.
49 Howard Marks, *Mr Nice* (London: Vintage, 1998), 64.
50 On the one hand, botanically, the word 'bud' refers to the compact growth on a plant that eventually develops into leaves, a flower, or a shoot. On the other hand, in cannabis culture, while the word 'bud' is used of the flower before harvesting, it is now frequently used of the harvested, dried, cured and consumable product. Hence, a user might refer to 'smoking some bud'.
51 See Julia Schultz, *The Influence of Spanish on the English Language Since 1801: A Lexical Investigation* (Newcastle: Cambridge Scholars Publishing, 2018), 206, 271.
52 Green, *Days in the Life*, 10, 27, 48, 52, 55.
53 See Marek Kohn, *Dope Girls: The Birth of the British Drug Underground* (London: Lawrence & Wishart, 1992).
54 Gilbert Shelton, *The Fabulous Furry Freak Brothers Omnibus* (London: Knockabout Comics, 2008), 27, 485.
55 Victor Maymudes and Jacob Maymudes, *Another Side of Bob Dylan: A Personal History on the Road and Off the Tracks* (New York: St. Martin's Press, 2014), 103–104; see also, Rob Chapman, *Psychedelia and Other Colours* (London: Faber & Faber, 2015), 268–270.
56 Green, *Days in the Life*, 10.
57 Milton 'Mezz' Mezzrow and Bernard Wolfe, *Really the Blues* (London: Secker & Warburg, 1957), 215.
58 See James H. Mills, *Cannabis Britannica: Empire, Trade, and Prohibition, 1800–1928* (Oxford: Oxford University Press, 2003), 51–66; Duvall, *Cannabis*, 46–49.
59 Alan Piper, 'The Mysterious Origins of the Word "Marihuana,"' *Sino-Platonic Papers* 153 (2005), 1–17.
60 Weston La Barre, *Culture in Context* (Durham NC: Duke University Press, 1980), 94.
61 Piper, 'Mysterious Origins', 5.
62 Chris Duvall, *The African Roots of Marijuana* (Durham: Duke University Press, 2019), 139.
63 Ibid., 140–141.
64 Ibid., 131.
65 Brian du Toit, 'Man and Cannabis in Africa: A Study of Diffusion', *African Economic History* 1 (1976), 17–35; 'Dagga: The History and Ethnographic Setting of *Cannabis Sativa* in Southern Africa'. In Vera Rubin (ed.), *Cannabis and Culture* (The Hague: Mouton Publishers, 1975), 81–116; see also Brian du Toit, *Cannabis in Africa. A Survey of Its Distribution in Africa, and a Study of Cannabis Use and Users in Multi-ethnic South Africa* (Rotterdam: A.A. Balkema, 1980); Nikolaas van der Merwe, 'Cannabis

Smoking in 13th-14th Century Ethiopia: Chemical Evidence'. In Vera Rubin (ed.), *Cannabis and Culture* (The Hague: Mouton Publishers, 1975), 77–80.
66 Duvall, *African Roots*, 229.
67 See, for example, Lester Grinspoon and James B. Bakalar, *Marihuana: The Forbidden Medicine* (New Haven: Yale University Press, 1993), 2.
68 See Mills, *Cannabis Britannica*, x–xi.
69 See du Toit, 'Man and Cannabis in Africa', 17–18.
70 Duvall, *African Roots*, 56.
71 Merwe, 'Cannabis Smoking', 77–80.
72 See Chris Duvall, *Cannabis* (London: Reaktion Books, 2015), 47.
73 See Vera Rubin and Lambros Comitas, *Ganja in Jamaica: The Effects of Marijuana Use* (New York: Anchor Books, 1976).
74 Kenneth Bilby, 'The Holy Herb: Notes on the Background of Cannabis in Jamaica'. In Rex Nettleford and Veronica Salter (eds), *Rastafari* (Mona: University of the West Indies Press, 1985), 83–86.
75 The 'Indian indenture system' was a system of legal servitude, by which more than a million Indians were taken to European colonies to replace African slaves, following the abolition of the slave trade in the early nineteenth century. See Lomarsh Roopnarine, *The Indian Caribbean: Migration and Identity in the Diaspora* (Jackson: University Press of Mississippi, 2018), 20–38; Verene Shepherd, *Transients to Settlers: the Experience of Indians in Jamaica, 1845-1950* (Leeds: Peepal Tree Press, 1994).
76 Shepherd, *Transients to Settlers*, 125; see also Rubin and Comitas, *Ganja in Jamaica*, 1.
77 Gurbakhsh Singh Chopra, 'Man and Marijuana', *International Journal of the Addictions* 4.2 (1969), 227.
78 Mills, *Cannabis Britannica*, 33.
79 Arthur Broughton, 'Hortus Eastensis'. In Bryan Edwards, *The History, Civil and Commercial, of the British West Indies*, Vol. 1 (London: John Stockdale, 1794), 493.
80 Ibid., 475.
81 Bilby, 'Holy Herb', 84.
82 Rubin and Comitas, *Ganja in Jamaica*, 16.
83 Ibid.
84 Ibid., 16–17.
85 On the Indian Hemp Drugs Commission, see Mills, *Cannabis Britannica*, 105–123.
86 Rubin and Comitas, *Ganja in Jamaica*, 16.
87 Ibid., 18–19.
88 See Jahlani Niaah, 'Ganja Terrorism and the Healing of the Nation'. In Beatriz Labate, Clancy Cavnar, and Thiago Rodrigues (eds), *Drug Policies and the Politics of Drugs in the Americas* (Cham: Springer International Publishing, 2016), 227–244.
89 Rubin and Comitas, *Ganja in Jamaica*, 21.
90 Excerpt from the *Daily Chronicle*, quoted in ibid., 22.
91 Niaah, 'Ganja Terrorism', 229–230.
92 Duvall, *African Roots*, 90.
93 Meng Ren, Zihua Tang, Xinhua Wu, Robert Spengler, Hongen Jiang, Yimin Yang, and Nicole Boivin, 'The Origins of Cannabis Smoking: Chemical Residue Evidence from the First Millennium BCE in the Pamirs', *Science Advances* 5.6 (12 June 2019): https://www.science.org/doi/10.1126/sciadv.aaw1391 (accessed 20 October 2021).
94 Clarke and Merlin, *Cannabis*, 1, 5, 6.

95 See, for example, Mei Wang, Yan-Hong Wang, Bharathi Avula, Mohamed M. Radwan, Amira S. Wanas, John van Antwerp, Jon Parcher, Mahmoud ElSohly, and Ikhlas A. Khan, 'Decarboxylation Study of Acidic Cannabinoids: A Novel Approach Using Ultra-High-Performance Supercritical Fluid Chromatography/Photodiode Array-Mass Spectrometry', *Cannabis and Cannabinoid Research* 1.1 (2016), 262.
96 See David Guba Jr, '"A Sovereign Remedy": Grimault & Co's Asthma Cigarette Empire' (18 February 2020): https://pointshistory.com/2020/02/18/a-sovereign-remedy-grimault-cos-asthma-cigarette-empire/ (accessed 23 December 2021): 'Already in 1840 the Conseil de Salubrité in Paris, the country's public health administration first created under Napoleon in 1802, took notice of the proliferation of medicinal cigarettes in the French pharmaceutical market. "It has been brought to our attention of the considerable number of pharmacists in Paris who are making cigarettes with stramonium, belladonna, digitalis, and jusquiame: some made them with the leaves of these same plants after their infusion in a solution of opium!" Believing these ingredients dangerous, the Conseil set about investigating medicinal cigarettes, discovering that "almost all the pharmacists of the capital sell such cigarettes. And use of these cigarettes leads to dizziness, nausea, intense headache, a sort of drunkenness, and finally a comatose state wish can be followed by more or less severe nervous symptoms." Despite these seemingly serious side effects, the Conseil concluded that "we must leave to the pharmacists, and to them alone, the right to prepare medicinal cigars, always on the condition of delivering them only after the prescription of a person skilled in the art, and in the typical form of other medications."'
97 See ibid.; see also Duvall, *Cannabis*, 135–137.
98 See ibid.
99 Mezzrow and Wolfe, *Really the Blues*, 214.
100 Ibid., 215.
101 Anonymous, 'Herbert Breakenridge the "Axe" Murderer is Sentenced to Death', *Kingston Daily Gleaner* (17 May 1929), 21.
102 Weedmaps.com, 'How to Roll a Blunt': https://weedmaps.com/learn/products-and-how-to-consume/how-to-roll-a-blunt (accessed 2 January 2022).
103 Ibid.
104 David Foster, 'How Blunts Came to Define Hip-Hop's Golden Age in New York City', *Elite Daily* (19 April 2016): https://www.elitedaily.com/life/blunts-hip-hop-golden-age-nyc/1464522 (accessed 13 December 2021).
105 Ibid. Redman's 'How to Roll a Blunt' was released on his debut album *Whut? Thee Album* (Rush Associated labels, 1992).
106 Ibid.
107 See Mezzrow and Wolfe, *Really the Blues*, 214.
108 Meyer Berger, 'Tea for a Viper', *The New Yorker* (12 March 1938), 36–37.
109 Richard Pollay and Timothy Dewhirst, 'The Dark Side of Marketing Seemingly "Light" Cigarettes: Successful Images and Failed Fact', *Tobacco Control* 11 – Supplement I (2002), i20.
110 Tobacco Control Research Group, 'Cigarette Filters', *Tobacco Tactics* (13 December 2021): https://tobaccotactics.org/wiki/cigarette-filters/ (accessed 3 August 2022).
111 Howard Becker, *Becoming a Marihuana User* (Chicago: Chicago University Press, 2015).
112 Ibid., 15.
113 Nicholas Lezard, *Bitter Experience Has Taught Me* (London: Faber and Faber, 2013), 118.

114 See Swami Chaitanya, 'Smoking a Joint Is a Journey', *Cannabis Now* (24 September 2023): https://cannabisnow.com/smoking-a-joint-is-a-journey/ (accessed 30 September 2023).
115 Tim Pilcher, *Spliffs 2: Further Adventures in Cannabis Culture* (London: Collins & Brown, 2004), 68.
116 Jones, *Spliffs*, 8.
117 Ibid.
118 See the comments by users in Berke and Hernton, *Cannabis Experience*.
119 Patrick Matthews, *Cannabis Culture* (London: Bloomsbury, 2003), 2.
120 Swami Chaitanya, 'A Sacramental High': https://swamiselect.com/a-sacramental-high/ (accessed 15 September 2023).
121 Preston, *Pot Planet*, 31–32.
122 See Noah Rubin, *How We Roll: The Art and Culture of Joints, Blunts, and Spliffs* (San Francisco: Chronicle Books, 2022).
123 See, for example, Norman Mailer, *The Armies of the Night: History as a Novel/The Novel as History* (New York: New American Library, 1968), 5. Again, in his song 'The Joker', Steve Miller refers to being 'a midnight toker' (Steve Miller Band, *The Joker*, 1973).
124 Quoted in Berke and Hernton, *Cannabis Experience*), 149.
125 Preston, *Pot Planet*, 32.
126 Quoted in Berke and Hernton, *Cannabis Experience*, 226.
127 See Peter Webster, 'Marijuana and Music: A Speculative Exploration', *Journal of Cannabis Therapeutics* 1.2 (2001), 93–105.
128 Quoted in Berke and Hernton, *Cannabis Experience*, 227.
129 Duvall, *African Roots*, 58–59.
130 Ibid., 59.
131 Ibid., 229.
132 Lewis Carroll, *Alice's Adventures in Wonderland* (London: The Folio Society, 1961), 36–37.
133 See Henry Yule and Arthur Coke Burnell, *A Glossary of Anglo-Indian Words*, second edition (London: Routledge, 1985), 195.
134 Preston, *Pot Planet*, 32.
135 See David Nutt, *Cannabis (Seeing Through the Smoke): The New Science of Cannabis and Your Health* (London: Yellow Kite, 2021), 203–214; Mark Wilding, 'The Story of Spice, the Street Drug That's Not Going Away', *Vice* (4 May 2017): https://www.vice.com/en/article/z4je55/the-story-of-spice-the-street-drug-thats-not-going-away (accessed 16 August 2022).
136 See, for example, Jamie Tahsin, 'If You Buy Weed Vapes in the UK, Beware – But Not for the Reason You Think', *Vice* (10 December 2019): https://www.vice.com/en/article/xweejk/cannabis-vapes-pens-buy-uk-spice (accessed 16 August 2022).
137 David Musto (ed.), *Drugs in America: A Documentary History* (New York: New York University Press, 2002), 460.
138 Danté Jordan, 'What are Moon Rocks and How Do You Smoke Them?' *Leafly* (9 May 2022): https://www.leafly.com/learn/consume/smoke/moon-rocks (accessed 18 July 2023).
139 See Robyn Griggs Lawrence, *Pot in Pans: A History of Eating Cannabis* (Lanham: Rowman & Littlefield, 2019).
140 See Danilo Marino, 'Hashish and Food: Arabic and European Medieval Dreams of Edible Paradises'. In Kirill Dmitriev, Julia Hauser, and Bilal Orfali (eds), *Insatiable*

Appetite: Food as Cultural Signifier in the Middle East and Beyond (Leiden: Brill, 2019), 194.
141 A Gunjah Wallah Company advertisement for 'Hasheesh Candy' printed in *Chicago Tribune* (14 April 1864), 3.
142 For a discussion of the book (but, not the hashish recipe) and an introduction to Toklas, see Sarah Garland, '"A Cookbook to be Read: What About It?", Gertrude Stein, Alice Toklas and the Language of the Kitchen', *Comparative American Studies* 7.1 (2009), 34–56; Rafia Zafar, 'Elegy and Remembrance in the Cookbooks of Alice B. Toklas and Edna Lewis', *MELUS: Multi-Ethnic Literature of the United States* 38 (2013), 32–51.
143 See John Geiger, *Nothing is True, Everything is Permitted. The Life of Brion Gysin* (New York: Disinformation Company, 2005), 105–107.
144 Alice B. Toklas, *Murder in the Kitchen* (London: Penguin, 2011), 80. Originally published as *The Alice B. Toklas Cookbook* (London: Michael Joseph, 1954).
145 Lawrence, *Pot in Pans*, 5.
146 See, for example, Elise McDonough, 'The History of Weed Brownies', *High Times* (20 September 2016): https://hightimes.com/edibles/everything-you-need-to-know-about-the-history-of-pot-brownies/ (accessed 21 April 2022).
147 Toklas, *Murder in the Kitchen*, 80.
148 Stephanie Hua and Coreen Carroll, *Edibles: Small Bites for the Modern Cannabis Kitchen* (San Francisco: Chronicle Books, 2018); Tracey Medeiros, *The Art of Cooking with Cannabis* (New York: Skyhorse Publishing, 2021); Laurie Wolf, *Cooking with Cannabis: Delicious Recipes for Edibles and Everyday Favorites* (Beverly: Quarry Books, 2016); Jamie Evans, 'A Beginner's Guide to Cooking with Cannabis': https://www.theherbsomm.com/single-post/a-beginners-guide-to-cooking-with-cannabis (accessed 18 April 2022). See also websites such as Kitchen Toke: https://kitchentoke.com (accessed 20 April 2022)
149 'Oral administration of THC results in its metabolism to 11-hydroxy-THC, which possesses up to 10 times greater potency.' Jahan Marcu, 'An Overview of Major and Minor Phytocannabinoids'. In Victor Preedy (ed.), *Neuropathology of Drug Addictions and Substance Misuse*, Vol. 1 (London: Academic Press, 2016), 674.
150 See William Notcutt and Emily Clarke, 'Cannabinoids in Clinical Practice: A UK Perspective.' In Roger Pertwee (ed.), *Handbook of Cannabis* (Oxford: Oxford University Press, 2014), 417.
151 See Margie Steer, 'Edible Marijuana: What We Need to Know', *The Conversation* (1 March 2017): https://theconversation.com/edible-marijuana-what-we-need-to-know-70898 (accessed 23 April 2022).
152 See, for example, Keith Villa, *Brewing with Cannabis: Using THC and CBD in Beer* (Boulder: Brewer's Publications, 2021), 21–32.
153 Lyden Henderson, quoted in Joe Baker, 'Flying High: What Will the Future of Cannabis-infused Drinks Look Like?' *Drinks Insight Network* (14 March 2019): https://www.drinks-insight-network.com/features/cannabis-infused-drinks/ (accessed 18 April 2022).
154 Pierre Bourdieu, *Distinction: A Social Critique of the Judgement of Taste*. Trans. by Richard Nice (Cambridge: Harvard University Press, 1984).
155 See Sarah Thornton, *Club Cultures: Music, Media and Subcultural Capital* (Cambridge: Polity, 1995), 11.
156 Bourdieu, *Distinction*, 475–479.
157 Thornton, *Club Cultures*, 105.

158 Nikki Lastreto and Swami Chaitanya, 'Our Story', *Swami Select*: https://swamiselect.com/our-story/ (accessed 17 August 2022).
159 See Potter's helpful discussion in *Weed, Need, and Greed*, 133–162.
160 Lastreto and Chaitanya, 'Our Story'.
161 Potter, *Weed, Need, and Greed*, 163.
162 See David Castle, Robin Murray, and Deepak D'Souza (eds), *Marijuana and Madness*, second edition (Cambridge: Cambridge University Press, 2019).
163 Nutt, *Cannabis*, 170.
164 Ibid., 180.
165 Adolph Steeze, 'On the Chaschisch of the Arabs (*Cannabis Sativa* or Hemp)', *Pharmaceutical Journal and Transactions* 5 (1846), 83.
166 Nutt, *Cannabis*, 76–77.
167 See Timmen Cermak, *Marijuana on my Mind: The Science and Mystique of Cannabis* (Cambridge: Cambridge University Press, 2022), 147–153, 233–236; see also the more recent analysis of the evidence in Kat Petrilli, Lindsey Hines, Sally Adams, Celia Morgan, Valerie Curran, and Tom Freeman, 'High Potency Cannabis Use, Mental Health Symptoms and Cannabis Dependence: Triangulating the Evidence', *Addictive Behaviours* 144 (2023), 1–7.
168 Erving Goffman, *Stigma: Notes on the Management of Spoiled Identity* (Harmondsworth: Penguin, 1968).

2 Profane Cannabis

1 See Harry Hubbell Kane, *Drugs That Enslave: The Opium, Morphine, Chloral and Hashisch Habits* (Philadelphia: Presley Blakiston, 1881), 206–218. See also James H. Mills, *Cannabis Britannica: Empire, Trade, and Prohibition, 1800-1928* (Oxford: Oxford University Press, 2003), 69–123.
2 See Michel Foucault, *The Will to Knowledge: the History of Sexuality, Vol. 1*. Trans. by Robert Hurley (London: Penguin, 1990).
3 Edward Mason, quoted in Madison Derbyshire, 'Higher Power: Church of England Backs Medicinal Cannabis', *Financial Times* (9 June 2019): https://www.ft.com/content/297f3234-88fa-11e9-97ea-05ac2431f453 (accessed 2 January 2020).
4 Kaya Burgess, 'Church of England Blesses Medicinal Use of Marijuana', *The Times* (10 June 2019): https://www.thetimes.co.uk/article/church-of-england-blesses-medicinal-use-of-marijuana-9pfnfkr2r# (accessed 2 January 2020).
5 Madison Derbyshire, 'Higher Power: Church of England Backs Medicinal Cannabis', *Financial Times* (9 June 2019): https://www.ft.com/content/297f3234-88fa-11e9-97ea-05ac2431f453 (accessed 2 January 2020).
6 See Joseph Gregorio, 'Physicians, Medical Marijuana, and the Law', *American Medical Association Journal of Ethics* 16. 9 (2014), 732–738.
7 For some background to this decision, see James Mills, *Cannabis Nation: Control and Consumption in Britain, 1928-2008* (Oxford: Oxford University Press, 2013), 204–215.
8 David Nutt, *Cannabis (Seeing Through the Smoke): The New Science of Cannabis and Your Health* (London: Yellow Kite, 2021), 31.
9 See EURAD, *Cannabis: Issues for Policy Makers* (Brussels, EURAD, 2012).
10 David Nutt, *Estimating Drug Harms: A Risky Business* (London: Centre for Crime and Justice Studies, 2009), 12.

11 Nutt, *Cannabis*, 35.
12 Anna Lewcock, 'Chemists Quit UK Drugs Council', *Chemistry World* (26 November 2009): https://www.chemistryworld.com/news/chemists-quit-uk-drugs-council/3000905.article (accessed 29 December 2021).
13 House of Commons, Home Affairs Committee, *Drugs: Breaking the Cycle, Ninth Report of Session 2012-13*, Vol. 1 (London: The Stationary Office, 2012), 100.
14 Les King, quoted in Lewcock, 'Chemists Quit UK Drugs Council'.
15 Lewcock, 'Chemists Quit UK Drugs Council'.
16 John Beddington, quoted in Steve Connor, 'Scientific Adviser Backs Sacked Drug "Tsar"', *Independent* (3 November 2009), https://www.independent.co.uk/news/science/scientific-adviser-backs-sacked-drug-tsar-1814041.html Accessed: 12 April 2020.
17 House of Commons, *Drugs*, 99.
18 Mark Fisher, *K-Punk: The Collected and Unpublished Writings of Mark Fisher (2004-2016)* (London: Repeater, 2018), 705.
19 Karl Marx, *Critique of Hegel's 'Philosophy or Right'*. Trans. by Annette Jolin and Joseph O'Malley (Cambridge: Cambridge University Press, 1977), 131.
20 Martine Skumlien, Claire Mokrysz, Tom P. Freeman, Vincent Valton, Matthew B. Wall, Michael Bloomfield, Rachel Lees, Anna Borissova, Kat Petrilli, Manuela Giugliano, Denisa Clisu, Christelle Langley, Barbara Sahakian, Valerie Curran, and Will Lawn, 'Anhedonia, Apathy, Pleasure, and Effort-Based Decision-Making in Adult and Adolescent Cannabis Users and Controls', *International Journal of Neuropsychopharmacology* 26.1 (2023), 10.
21 Kim Arlington, 'NSW Government's Stoner Sloth Anti-marijuana Campaign Cost Taxpayers $350,000', *Sydney Morning Herald* (19 February 2016): https://www.smh.com.au/national/nsw/nsw-governments-stoner-sloth-antimarijuana-campaign-cost-taxpayers-350000-20160218-gmxd8p.html (accessed 25 June 2023).
22 Ernst Bloch, *The Principle of Hope*, Vol. 1. Trans. by Neville Plaice, Stephen Plaice, and Paul Knight (Cambridge: MIT Press, 1986), 89.
23 Brocardus, quoted in Bernard Lewis, *Assassins: A Radical Sect of Islam* (New York: Basic Books, 2003), 1.
24 Farhad Daftary, *The Assassin Legends: Myths of the Isma'ilis* (London: I.B. Tauris, 1994), 2.
25 See Gérard Chaliand and Arnaud Blin, 'Zealots and Assassins'. In Gérard Chaliand and Arnaud Blin (eds), *The History of Terrorism: From Antiquity to ISIS* (Berkeley: University of California Press, 2016), 65–73.
26 Farhad Daftary, 'Ḥasan Ṣabbāḥ'. In Ehsan Yarshater (ed.), *Encyclopaedia Iranica*, Vol. 12, (New York: Encyclopaedia Iranica Foundation, 2004), 34.
27 John Hutnyk, *Pantomine Terror: Music and Politics* (Winchester: Zero Books, 2014), 1.
28 Bernard Lewis, *Assassins: A Radical Sect of Islam* (New York: Basic Books, 2003), 2.
29 Quoted in Lewis, *Assassins*, 2.
30 See Emanuel Mickel's helpful discussion in *The Artificial Paradises in French Literature: The Influence of Opium and Hashish on the Literature of French Romanticism and* Les Fluers Du Mal (Chapel Hill: University of North Carolina Press, 1969), 54–56.
31 Quoted in Lewis, *Assassins*, 3.
32 Lewis, *Assassins*, 3.
33 Quoted in ibid.

34 See Patrick Williams, 'The Assassination of Conrad of Montferrat: Another Suspect?' *Traditio* 26 (1970), 381–389; see also Farhad Daftary, *The Isma'ilis: Their History and Doctrines* (Cambridge: Cambridge University Press, 1990), 402.
35 Lewis, *Assassins*, 4.
36 Arnold of Lübeck, quoted in ibid., 4–5.
37 Daftary, *Ismailis*, 33.
38 See Mickel, *Artificial Paradises*, 57.
39 On hashish use in Egypt, see Gabriel Nahas, 'Hashish and Drug Abuse in Egypt During the 19th and 20th Centuries', *Bulletin of the New York Academy of Medicine* 61 (1985), 428–444.
40 David Guba Jr, *Taming Cannabis: Drugs and Empire in Nineteenth-Century France* (Montreal: McGill-Queen's University Press, 2020), 20–21.
41 Ibid., 40.
42 Edward Said, *Orientalism* (London: Penguin, 2003), 18.
43 See Daftary, *Assassin Legends*; David Guba Jr, 'Antoine Isaac Silvestre de Sacy and the Myth of the Hachichins: Orientalizing Hashish in Nineteenth-century France', *The Social History of Alcohol and Drugs* 30 (2016), 50–74.
44 Lewis, *Assassins*, 11.
45 Jacques-Joseph Moreau, *Hashish and Mental Illness*. Trans. Gordon J. Barnett (New York: Raven Press, 1973), 6.
46 Daftary, *Assassin Legends*, 91.
47 Edward William Lane, *An Account of the Manners and Customs of the Modern Egyptians*, Vol. 2 (London: Charles Knight & Co., 1837), 147.
48 Lewis, *Assassins*, 11–12.
49 Franz Rosenthal, *The Herb: Hashish versus Medieval Muslim Society*. In Franz Rosenthal, *Man Versus Society in Medieval Islam*, ed. by Dimitri Gutas (Leiden: Brill, 2014), 135; see also 152.
50 Ibid., 135. See also Rosenthal's discussion of al-Badrī's (1443–1489) treatment of the subject (148).
51 Daftary, *Assassin Legends*, 91–92. See also George Lane, 'The Mongols and the Advent of Hashish in Western Asia'. In Howard Marks (ed.), *The Howard Marks' Book of Dope Stories* (London: Vintage Books, 2001), 69–72.
52 Ibid.
53 Rosenthal, *The Herb*, 274.
54 On the subjective effects of cannabis, see Mitch Earleywine, 'Cannabis: Attending to Subjective Effects to Improve Drug Safety'. In Mitch Earleywine (ed.), *Mind-Altering Drugs: The Science of Subjective Experience* (Oxford: Oxford University Press, 2005), 240–257.
55 See Joseph von Hammer-Purgstall, *The History of the Assassins*. Trans Oswald Charles Wood (London: Smith and Elder, 1835), 137.
56 Ibid., 232–233.
57 Ibid., 233–234.
58 Ibid., 234–235 (emphasis added).
59 Henry Draper Steel, *Portable Instructions for Purchasing the Drugs and Spices of Asia and the East Indies* (London: D. Steel, 1779), 14. See also John Henry Grose, *A Voyage to the East Indies with Observations on Various Parts There* (London: Hooper & Morley, 1757).
60 Mordecai Cooke, *The Seven Sisters of Sleep* (London: James Blackwood, 1860), 247.
61 Ibid., 232.

62 Ibid., 247.
63 Ibid., 249.
64 Ibid., 247.
65 Ibid., 247–248.
66 Ibid., 241.
67 Ibid.
68 Mills, *Cannabis Britannica*, 69.
69 Michael Foucault, *History of Madness*. Trans by Jonathon Murphy and Jean Khalfa (London: Routledge, 2009), 208–250.
70 See Foucault, *History of Madness*, 147.
71 See Mills, *Cannabis Britannica*, 69.
72 Anonymous, 'Hasheesh and its Smokers and Eaters', *Scientific American* 14.7 (23 October 1858), 49.
73 Ibid.
74 Guba Jr, *Taming Cannabis*, 174.
75 Stanley Cohen, *Folk Devils and Moral Panics*, third edition (London: Routledge, 2002), 7.
76 See particularly Bill Thompson and Andy Williams, *The Myth of Moral Panics: Sex, Snuff, and Satan* (New York: Routledge, 2014).
77 Anonymous, 'Maniac Kills Patrolman', *El Paso Times* (2 January 1913). Reproduced in Trish Long, '1915: El Paso Becomes First City in United States to Outlaw Marijuana', *El Paso Times* (16 November 2019): https://eu.elpasotimes.com/story/news/2019/11/14/el-paso-history-pot-possession-first-city-outlaw-weed-tbt/2579079001/ (accessed 20 December 2019).
78 Howard Becker, *Outsiders: Studies in the Sociology of Deviance* (New York: The Free Press, 1963), 138.
79 Ibid., 146–163.
80 Anonymous, 'Maniac Kills Patrolman'.
81 Quoted in Long, '1915'.
82 Quoted in ibid.
83 Hugh Cummings, *Preliminary Report on Indian Hemp and Peyote* (1929), quoted in Richard Bonnie and Charles Whitebread II, *The Marijuana Conviction: A History of Marijuana Prohibition in the United States* (New York: The Lindesmith Center, 1999), 128.
84 Emily F. Murphy, *The Black Candle* (Toronto: Thomas Allen, 1922), 5.
85 Ibid., 336.
86 Ibid., 335.
87 Ibid., 332–333.
88 Ibid., 333.
89 Anonymous, 'Ban on Hashish Blocked Despite Ravages of Drug', *Chicago Daily Tribune* (3 June 1927), 20. See also, National Commission on Marihuana and Drug Abuse, *Appendix – Marihuana: A Signal of Misunderstanding. The Technical Papers of the First Report of the National Commission on Marihuana and Drug Abuse*, Vol. 1 (Washington: Government Printing Office, 1972), 485.
90 Anonymous, 'Mexican Family Go Insane. Five Said to Have Been Stricken by Eating Marihuana', *The New York Times* (6 July 1927), 10.
91 Anonymous, 'Marihuana Makes Fiends of Boys in 30 Days: Hashish Goads Users to Blood Lust', *San Francisco Examiner* (31 January 1923), 11.

92 Winifred Black, *Dope: The Story of the Living Dead* (New York: Star Company, 1928).
93 Ibid., 43.
94 Cohen, *Folk Devils and Moral Panics*, 49.
95 Anonymous, 'Marihuana Makes Fiends of Boys in 30 Days', 11.
96 David Musto, *The American Disease: Origins of Narcotic Control* (New York: Oxford University Press, 1987), 218.
97 *Notch Number One*. Director Ben Wilson (Arrow Film Corporation, 1924).
98 Anonymous, 'Marijuana Industry is Thriving in City. Children are Addicts', *New Orleans Tribune* (18 October 1926), 1.
99 US Treasury Department, *Traffic in Opium and Other Dangerous Drugs for the Year Ended December 31, 1931* (Washington: Government Printing Office, 1932), 51.
100 Anonymous, 'Marihuana Menaces Youth', *Scientific American* 154.3 (March, 1936), 151. See Trevor Hughes (ed.), *Reefer Madness* (Liscard: Zephyr, 1996).
101 Albert E. Fossier, 'The Marihuana Menace', *New Orleans Medical and Surgical Journal* 84.4 (1931), 247.
102 Ibid.
103 Becker, *Outsiders*, 147–148.
104 For a thoughtful overview of his life and career, see John C. McWilliams, *The Protectors: Harry J. Anslinger and the Federal Bureau of Narcotics, 1930–1962* (Newark: University of Delaware Press, 1990).
105 Harry Anslinger and Will Oursler, *The Murderers: The Story of the Narcotic Gangs* (New York: Farrar, Straus and Cudahy, 1961), 8.
106 Quoted in Bonnie and Whitebread II, *Marijuana Conviction*, 75.
107 Mark Thornton, *The Economics of Prohibition* (Salt Lake City: The University of Utah Press, 1991), 4.
108 As is well known, Coca-Cola contained cocaine until 1903, as did numerous other products, such as hay fever remedies. 'Opiates and cocaine became popular – if unrecognized – items in the everyday life of Americans'. Musto, *American Disease*, 3.
109 David Musto was Professor of the History of Medicine at Yale School of Medicine and, from 1973, a presidential adviser on drug policy.
110 Musto, *American Disease*, 3.
111 Harry Anslinger, quoted in Bonnie and Whitebread II, *Marijuana Conviction*, 149.
112 Quoted in Bonnie and Whitebread II, *Marijuana Conviction*, 81.
113 Bonnie and Whitebread II, *Marijuana Conviction*, 83.
114 Ibid., 90.
115 Anslinger, quoted in ibid., 92.
116 H. Wayne Morgan, *Drugs in America: A Social History, 1800-1980* (Syracuse: Syracuse University Press, 1981), 119.
117 McWilliams, *Protectors*, 112–113.
118 See Musto, *American Disease*, 192.
119 Quoted in Bonnie and Whitebread II, *Marijuana Conviction*, 108.
120 See Susan Speaker, '"The Struggle of Mankind against Its Deadliest Foe": Themes of Counter-Subversion in Anti-Narcotic Campaigns, 1920-1940', *Journal of Social History* 34.3 (2001), 591–610.
121 Becker, *Outsiders*, 142.
122 Ibid., 136.
123 Ibid.

124 Reinhold Niebuhr, quoted in Robert Moats Miller, 'The Protestant Churches and Lynching, 1919-1939', *The Journal of Negro History* 42 (1957), 118.
125 Jon Michael Spencer, *Blues and Evil* (Knoxville: University of Tennessee Press, 1993), 94.
126 Peetie Whaeatstraw, 'Mister Livingood/ The Good Lawd's Children' (Decca, 1941).
127 Richmond P. Hobson, 'Richmond P. Hobson Argues for Prohibition'. In Kathel Austin Kerr (ed.), *The Politics of Moral Behavior: Prohibition and Drug Abuse* (Reading: Addison-Wesley, 1973), 101.
128 Richard J. Bonnie and Charles H. Whitebread II, 'The Forbidden Fruit and the Tree of Knowledge: An Inquiry into the Legal History of American Marijuana Prohibition', *Virginia Law Review* 56.6 (1971), 1165–1166.
129 David Musto, 'The 1937 Marihuana Tax Act', *Archives of General Psychiatry* 26.2 (1972), 101–108.
130 While the Marihuana Tax Act of 1937 was not the first anti-cannabis law in the US (Pure Food and Drug Act, 1906; Harrison Act, 1914), it was the first national marijuana prohibition law. Managed by Anslinger following a nationwide moral crusade, it allowed states to enforce their own laws and to tax the cultivation and distribution of cannabis. While Anslinger was initially reluctant to get involved due to fears about the constitutionality of federal legislation, he was persuaded by the introduction of legislation to increase taxes on the use of hemp and, thereby, secure federal control of the plant. Hence, it did not criminalize the possession of cannabis *per se*, but rather it subjected it to a number of regulations. While it passed easily, it was opposed by the American Medical Association, which was concerned that taxes were now due from physicians who prescribed it and pharmacists who sold it. Similarly, farmers were opposed to the new requirement to acquire tax stamps for the production of hemp. In 1969, Timothy Leary, who had been arrested for possession, challenged the Act on the grounds that it required self-incrimination, which violated the Fifth Amendment. The court agreed. It was, therefore, declared unconstitutional and replaced by the Controlled Substances Act. See Alexandra Chasin, *Assassin of Youth: A Kaleidoscopic History of Harry J. Anslinger's War on Drugs* (Chicago: University of Chicago Press, 2016), 203–208
131 Musto, *American Disease*, 216–223.
132 See Bonnie and Whitebread II, *Marijuana Conviction*, 181.
133 Paul Garon, *Blues and the Poetic Spirit* (San Francisco: City Lights, 1996), 100. See also Christopher Partridge, *High Culture: Drugs, Mysticism, and the Pursuit of Transcendence in the Modern World* (New York: Oxford University Press, 2018).
134 Bonnie and Whitebread II, *Marijuana Conviction*, 181.
135 See Larry Sloman, *Reefer Madness: A History of Marijuana* (New York: St. Martin's Griffin, 1998), 126–151.
136 Johann Hari, 'The Hunting of Billie Holiday: How Lady Day was in the Middle of a Federal Bureau of Narcotics Fight for Survival', *Politico Magazine* (17 January 2015): https://www.politico.com/magazine/story/2015/01/drug-war-the-hunting-of-billie-holiday-114298 (accessed: 6 January 2020).
137 Anslinger, quoted in Sloman, *Reefer Madness*, 138.
138 Anslinger, quoted in ibid., 135.
139 Harry Anslinger and Courtney Cooper, 'Marijuana: Assassin of Youth.' In James A. Inciardi and Karen McElrath (eds), *The American Drug Scene: An Anthology*, fifth edition (New York: Oxford University Press, 2008), 111–112.

140 US Treasury Department, *Traffic in Opium and Other Dangerous Drugs for the Year Ended December 31, 1941* (Washington: Government Printing Office, 1942), 13.
141 Bonnie and Whitebread II, *Marijuana Conviction*, 185.
142 Anslinger, quoted in ibid., 185.
143 Joseph Bell, quoted in Sloman, *Reefer Madness*, 135.
144 Mike Levin, quoted in US Treasury Department', *Traffic in Opium*, 32.
145 Quoted in Sloman, *Reefer Madness*, 137.
146 Mike Levin, quoted in US Treasury Department, *Traffic in Opium*, 32.
147 A 1937 report, quoted in Chasin, *Assassin of Youth*, 188.
148 N.R. de Mexico, *Marijuana Girl* (New York: Universal Publishing and Distribution, 1951).
149 Anslinger and Cooper, 'Marijuana: Assassin of Youth', 108–113.
150 See ibid.
151 Anonymous, 'Dream Slayer Talks in Cell', *Tampa Daily Times* (18 October 1933), 1.
152 William D. Bush and Jack DeWitt, 'Marihuana Maniac', *Inside Detective* (July 1938), 44.
153 See John McWilliams, 'Through the Past Darkly: The Politics and Policies of America's Drug War', *Journal of Policy History* 3.4 (1991), 5–41.
154 His comments regarding Homer are, of course, ill-informed, in that, in *The Odyssey*, he refers only to the intoxicating and enchanting fruit offered by the Lotus-Eaters, not to cannabis. See Homer, *The Odyssey*. Trans. by Richard Lattimore (New York: Harper Perennial Modern Classics, 2007), 140.
155 Harry J. Anslinger, 'Marihuana Tax Act (1937): Statement of H. J. Anslinger, Commissioner of Narcotics, Bureau of Narcotics, Department of the Treasury': http://www.druglibrary.org/schaffer/hemp/taxact/taxact.htm (accessed 29 March 2016).
156 Jerry Mandel, 'Hashish, Assassins, and the Love of God', *Issues in Criminology* 2.2 (1966), 150.
157 G.R. McCormack, quoted in Mandel, 'Hashish, Assassins, and the Love of God', 150.
158 For a good, concise discussion of the issues relating to the identification of "Molekh" in the Hebrew Bible, see John Day, *Molech: A God of Human Sacrifice in the Old Testament* (Cambridge: Cambridge University Press, 1989).
159 Robert James Devine, *The Moloch of Marihuana* (Findlay, Ohio: Fundamental Truth Publishers, n.d.), 25.
160 *Kerry Drake Detective Cases* #10 (September 1948). Reprinted in Craig Yoe (ed.), *Reefer Madness Comics* (Milwaukee: Dark Horse Books, 2018), 63.
161 Craig Yoe, 'Satan's Lettuce', in Craig Yoe (ed.), *Reefer Madness Comics* (Milwaukee: Dark Horse Books, 2018), 25.
162 Yoe, 'Satan's Lettuce', 27.
163 From the film poster for *Marihuana: Weed With Its Roots in Hell*. See ibid., 15.
164 Anonymous, 'Terror! Just a Cigarette, You'd Think, but it was Made from a Sinister Weed and an Innocent Girl Falls Victim to This', *The Daily Mirror* (25 July 1939), 12.
165 Ibid.
166 Ibid.
167 See Roland Littlewood, 'Community-initiated Research: A Study of Psychiatrists' Conceptualizations of "Cannabis psychosis"', *Psychiatric Bulletin* 12.11 (1987), 486–488; Philip Carney and Maurice Lipsedge, 'Psychosis After Cannabis Abuse', *British Medical Journal* 288 (1984), 1381.
168 Dermot McGovern and Rosemarie Cope, 'First Psychiatric Admission Rates of First and Second Generation Afro-Caribbeans', *Social Psychiatry* 22 (1987), 139–149.

169 Ibid., 147–148.
170 Andrew Scull, *Madness in Civilization* (London: Thames & Hudson, 2016), 202.
171 Jamie Banks, 'Cannabis, Race, and Mental Illness in Britain, 1980–1993', *Historical Transactions* (4 July 2021): https://blog.royalhistsoc.org/2021/07/04/cannabis-race-and-mental-illness-in-britain-1980-1993/ (accessed 27 June 2022).
172 Chris Ranger, 'Race, Culture and "Cannabis Psychosis": The Role of Social Factors in the Construction of a Disease Category', *Journal of Ethnic and Migration Studies*, 15 (1989), 357.
173 Ibid., 362.
174 Ibid.
175 Glyn Lewis, Caroline Croft-Jeffreys, and Anthony David, 'Are British Psychiatrists Racist?' *British Journal of Psychiatry* 157.3 (1990) 410–415.
176 Clifford Broman, Harold Neighbors, Jorge Delva, Myriam Torres, and James Jackson, 'Prevalence of Substance Use Disorders Among African Americans and Caribbean Blacks in the National Survey of American Life', *American Journal of Public Health* 98.6 (2008), 1107.
177 For a recent philosophical challenge to both religious and non-religious arguments against recreational drug use, see Rob Lovering, *A Moral Defense of Recreational Drug Use* (New York: Palgrave Macmillan, 2015).
178 Catholic Answers, 'Is It Wrong to Alter Your Mind for Fun?' *Catholic Answers Magazine* (17 February 2022): https://www.catholic.com/magazine/print-edition/is-it-wrong-to-alter-your-mind-for-fun (accessed 2 October 2023).
179 John Piper, 'Christians and Marijuana', *Desiring God* (25 April 2013): https://www.desiringgod.org/interviews/christians-and-marijuana (accessed 11 July 2023).
180 Ibid.
181 For a good accessible introduction to the science and related issues, see David Nutt, *Cannabis (Seeing Through the Smoke): The New Science of Cannabis and Your Health* (London: Yellow Kite, 2021).
182 Catholic Answers, 'Is It Wrong to Alter Your Mind for Fun?'
183 See, for example, Jan van Amsterdam, David Nutt, Lawrence Phillips, and Wim van den Brink, 'European Rating of Drug Harms', *Journal of Psychopharmacology* 29.6 (2015), 655–660; Jan van Amsterdam and Wim van den Brink, 'Ranking of Drugs: A More Balanced Risk-assessment', *The Lancet* 376.9752 (2010), 1524–1525; Steve Fox, Paul Armentano, and Mason Tvert, *Marijuana is Safer: So Why Are We Driving People to Drink?* (White River Junction: Chelsea Green Publishing Company, 2009).
184 Leslie Iversen, *The Science of Marijuana*, second edition (Oxford: Oxford University Press, 2008), 98–99.
185 See Mary Douglas, *Purity and Danger: An Analysis of the Concept of Pollution and Taboo* (London: Routledge, 2002).
186 Todd Miles, *Cannabis and the Christian: What the Bible Says about Marijuana* (Nashville: B&H Publishing, 2021), 13.
187 Kevin Vanhoozer, 'Should Followers of Christ Use Recreational Marijuana?' *The Gospel Coalition* (16 January 2020): https://www.thegospelcoalition.org/article/followers-christ-use-recreational-marijuana/ (accessed 11 July 2023).
188 John Paul II, quoted in Catholic Answers, 'Is It Wrong to Alter Your Mind for Fun?'
189 Catholic Answers, 'Is It Wrong to Alter Your Mind for Fun?'
190 Ibid.
191 Ibid.
192 Gisela Kreglinger, *The Spirituality of Wine* (Grand Rapids: Eerdmans, 2016), 4.

193 Vanhoozer, 'Should Followers of Christ Use Recreational Marijuana?'
194 Miles, *Cannabis and the Christian*, 20.
195 Kreglinger, *Spirituality of Wine*, 98.
196 Ibid., 99.
197 Vanhoozer, 'Should Followers of Christ Use Recreational Marijuana?'
198 David Wilkerson, *The Cross and the Switchblade* (New York: Bernard Geis Associates, 1963).
199 Nicky Cruz, *Run Baby Run* (Gainsville: Bridge-Logos Publishers, 1968), 248–249.
200 Ibid., 266.
201 Miles, *Cannabis and the Christian*, 3.
202 Michel Foucault, *The Will to Knowledge: The History of Sexuality*, Vol. 1. Trans. by Robert Hurley (London: Penguin, 1990), 140–144.
203 Michel Foucault, *Society Must be Defended*. Trans. by David Macey (London: Penguin, 2003), 61.
204 See Michael Schaller, 'The Federal prohibition of Marihuana', *Journal of Social History* 4.1 (1970), 61–74.
205 Mark Thornton, *The Economics of Prohibition* (Salt Lake City: The University of Utah Press, 1991), 65.
206 This point was made by Robert Walton in *Marihuana: America's New Drug Problem* (Philadelphia: J.B. Lippincott, 1938). Although clearly informed by popular culture – which was shaped by Anslinger's rhetoric – Walton argued that cannabis can introduce users to 'more dangerous' drugs and, moreover, that it can lead to juvenile delinquency and extreme violence. Nevertheless, he admitted that there is a lack of scientific understanding about its effects.
207 Herbert Wollner, quoted in Bonnie and Whitebread II, *Marijuana Conviction*, 187.
208 Cohen, *Folk Devils and Moral Panics*, xiii.
209 Becker, *Outsiders*, 9.
210 Stephen Hilgartner and Charles Bosk, 'The Rise and Fall of Social Problems: the Public Arenas Model', *American Journal of Sociology* 94.1 (1988), 53.
211 Becker, *Outsiders*.
212 Joel Best, *Threatened Children: Rhetoric and Concern about Child-Victims* (Chicago: Chicago University Press, 1990), 40.
213 Ibid.
214 Ibid., 42.
215 Ibid.
216 See Yoe, *Reefer Madness Comics*.
217 See Lina Britto's interesting study of Columbian 'marijuana boom' in the 1970s, which was financed by North American suppliers capitalizing on the countercultural demand for the drug: *Marijuana Boom: The Rise and Fall of Colombia's First Drug Paradise* (Berkeley: University of California Press, 2020).

3 Medicinal Cannabis

1 Alex Halperin, *The Cannabis Dictionary* (London: Mitchell Beazley, 2020), 159. As we will see later in the chapter, because Reynolds was a 'Physician-in-Ordinary to Her Majesty's Household' there has been much speculation about Queen Victoria's cannabis usage.

2   See, for example, some of the discussions collected in Tod Mikuriya (ed.), *Cannabis: Collected Clinical Papers. Vol. 1, Marijuana: Medical Papers, 1839-1972* (Nevada City: Symposium Publishing, 2007).
3   Dee Dussault, *Ganja Yoga: A Practical Guide to Conscious Relaxation, Soothing Pain Relief, and Enlightened Self-discovery* (London: Hay House, 2017), 3.
4   Christian Rätsch, *Marijuana Medicine*. Trans. by John Baker (Rochester: Healing Arts Press, 2001), 178.
5   See Leslie Iversen, *The Science of Marijuana*, second edition (Oxford: Oxford University Press, 2008), 115–156; David Nutt, *Cannabis (Seeing Through the Smoke): The New Science of Cannabis and Your Health* (London: Yellow Kite, 2021); Roger Pertwee (ed.), *Handbook of Cannabis* (Oxford: Oxford University Press, 2014).
6   Sarah Sinclair, 'Hemp for Elephants: Inside the Zoo Giving Anxious Animals CBD', *Cannabis Health* (5 January 2021): https://cannabishealthnews.co.uk/2021/01/05/hemp-for-elephants-inside-the-zoo-giving-anxious-animals-cbd/ (accessed 27 September 2021).
7   Moran Hausman-Kedem, Shay Menascu, and Uri Kramer, 'Efficacy of CBD-enriched Medical Cannabis for Treatment of Refractory Epilepsy in Children and Adolescents – An Observational, Longitudinal Study', *Brain and Development* 40 (2018), 550.
8   Ibid.
9   See, for example, Andrew Sewell, Mohini Ranganathan, and Deepak Cyril D'Souza, 'Cannabinoids and Psychosis', *International Review of Psychiatry* 21.2 (2009), 152–162.
10 Dee Dussault, 'Benefits of Practicing Ganja Yoga': https://www.ganjayoga.online (accessed 9 April 2021).
11 Jack Herer, *The Emperor Wears No Clothes*, 14th edition (Woodland Hills: Herer Media & Publishing, 1998), 271.
12 Tammi Sweet, *The Wholistic Healing Guide to Cannabis* (North Adams: Storey Publishing, 2020), 9.
13 On romanticizing of the premodern, see Christopher Partridge, *The Re-Enchantment of the West: Alternative Spiritualities, Sacralization, Popular Culture and Occulture*, Vol. 1 (London: T. & T. Clark International, 2004), 77–78.
14 See Partridge, *Re-Enchantment of the West*, Vol. 2, 4–41.
15 Ashley Koshie, 'Going Green', *Treating Yourself: The Alternative Medicine Journal* 27 (2011), 17.
16 See Theodore Roszak, *The Making of a Counter Culture: Reflections on the Technocratic Society and Its Youthful Opposition* (London: Faber & Faber, 1970).
17 See Wendy Chapkis and Richard Webb, *Dying to Get High: Marijuana as Medicine* (New York: New York University Press, 2008), 148–149.
18 Emma Ockerman, 'The More Drugmakers Wowed Doctors with Gifts and Lunches, the More People Died of Drug Overdoses, Study Shows', *Vice News* (18 January 2019): https://www.vice.com/en/article/59xm4a/the-more-drugmakers-wowed-doctors-with-gifts-and-lunches-the-more-people-died-of-drug-overdoses-study-shows (accessed 18 April 2021). On conspiracies relating to 'big pharma', see, Robert Blaskiewicz, 'The Big Pharma Conspiracy Theory', *Medical Writing* 22.4 (2013), 259–261.
19 For a general introduction to the subject, see, Robert Blaskiewicz, 'The Big Pharma Conspiracy Theory', *Medical Writing* 22.4 (2013), 259–261.
20 Mark Miller, '10 Reasons Pot Is Better Than Prescription Drugs', *High Times* (23 August 2017): https://hightimes.com/news/10-reasons-pot-is-better-than-prescription-drugs/ (accessed 23 April, 2021).

21 Harry Resin, 'A History of Medical Cannabis', *Treating Yourself: The Alternative Medicine Journal*: https://treatingyourself.com/a-history-of-medical-cannabis/ (accessed 12 April 2021).
22 Marijuana Doctors, 'Cannabis and Cancer: Your Essential Guide to a Holistic Approach': https://www.marijuanadoctors.com/blog/cannabis-resources-for-cancer/ (accessed 12 April 2021).
23 Sven Hosford and Paloma Lehfeldt, 'The History of Medical Cannabis from Ancient Times to 1937 to Today', *Dispense Magazine Podcast* (2 November 2019): https://dispensemagazine.com/the-history-of-medical-cannabis-from-ancient-times-to-1937-to-today-an-interview-with-vireo-health-dr-paloma-lehfeldt/ (accessed 12 April 2021).
24 Richard Greer, quoted in Sven Hosford, 'Medical Cannabis: The Next Wave of Holistic Medicine', *Dispense Magazine* (1 March 2019): https://dispensemagazine.com/medical-cannabis-the-next-wave-of-holistic-medicine/#comments (accessed 12 April 2021).
25 Thomas Albright and Charles Perry, 'The Last Twelve Hours of the Whole Earth', *Rolling Stone* 86 (8 July 1971), 1.
26 See Caroline Maniaque-Benton and Meredith Gaglio, *Whole Earth Field Guide* (Cambridge: MIT Press, 2016).
27 See Roszak, *Making of a Counter Culture*; Theodore Roszak, *Where the Wasteland Ends: Politics and Transcendence in Postindustrial Society* (New York: Doubleday, 1972); Theodore Roszak, *Unfinished Animal: The Aquarian Frontier and the Evolution of Consciousness* (London: Faber & Faber, 1975); Charles Reich, *The Greening of America* (Harmondsworth: Penguin, 1971).
28 Roszak, *Making of a Counter Culture*, 258–259.
29 Christopher Partridge, 'A Beautiful Politics: Theodore Roszak's Romantic Radicalism and the Counterculture', *Journal for the Study of Radicalism* 12.2 (2018), 1–34.
30 Theodore Roszak, Tim Eiloart, Glyn Davies, Chris Cilchrist, and Dorothy Emmet, 'Is the Counter-culture Landscaping the Wasteland?' *Theoria to Theory* 12 (1979), 266.
31 Chellis Glendinning, *When Technology Wounds: The Human Consequences of Progress* (New York: William Morrow and Company, 1990), 15–16.
32 Charles Taylor, *The Ethics of Authenticity* (Cambridge: Harvard University Press, 1991), 26.
33 Robert Wuthnow, *After Heaven: Spiritualty in America Since the 1950s* (Berkeley: University of California Press, 1998), 160.
34 Wade Clark Roof, *The Spiritual Marketplace: Baby Boomers and the Remaking of American Religion* (Princeton: Princeton University Press, 1999), 106.
35 Ibid., 107. For a helpful overview of the main streams of contemporary spiritual healing in North America, see Meredith McGuire, *Ritual Healing in Suburban America* (London: Rutgers University Press, 1988).
36 See Mark Merlin, *Man and Marijuana: Some Aspects of Their Ancient Relationship* (Madison: Fairleigh Dickinson University Press, 1972).
37 Warren Dawson, 'Studies in the Egyptian Medical Texts III', *Journal of Egyptian Archaeology* 20.1 (1934), 44–45.
38 Ethan Russo, 'History of Cannabis and Its Preparations in Saga, Science, and Sobriquet', *Chemistry and Biodiversity* 4 (2007), 1622.
39 John Nunn, *Ancient Egyptian Medicine* (London: University of Oklahoma Press, 1996), 156.

40 Paula Veiga, 'To Prevent, Treat and Cure Love in Ancient Egypt. Aspects of Sexual Medicine and Practice in Ancient Egypt', *Proceedings of the Second International Congress for Young Egyptologists, Lisbon, November 2009*, 461: https://www.academia.edu/21822059/To_Prevent_Treat_and_Cure_Love_in_Ancient_Egypt_Aspects_of_Sexual_Medicine_and_Practice_in_Ancient_Egypt (accessed 27 March 2021).
41 Christian Rätsch, *Marijuana Medicine*. Trans. by John Baker (Rochester: Healing Arts Press, 2001), 86–87.
42 W. Benson Harer Jr, 'The Marijuana Myth in Ancient Egypt', *Journal of the American Research Center in Egypt* 51 (2015), 356–357; see also Gonzalo Sanchez and W. Benson Harer Jr, 'Toxicology in Ancient Egypt.' In Philip Wexler (ed.), *Toxicology in Antiquity*, second edition (London: Academic Press, 2019), 73–82.
43 Russo, 'History of Cannabis', 1625.
44 Ibid.
45 E.g. O.M.E. Abdel-Salam, A.F. Galal, S.A. ElShebiney, and A.E.D.M. Gaafar, 'International Aspects of Cannabis Use and Misuse: Egypt.' In Victor Preedy (ed.), *Handbook of Cannabis and Related Pathologies: Biology, Pharmacology, Diagnosis, and Treatment* (London: Academic Press, 2017), 111; Simon Wills, 'Cannabis Use and Abuse by Man: An Historical Perspective.' In David Brown (ed.), *Cannabis: The Genus Cannabis* (Amsterdam: Harwood Academic Publishers, 1998), 3.
46 Sergei Rudenko, *Frozen Tombs of Siberia: The Pazyryk Burials of Iron Age Horsemen*. Trans. by M.W. Tompson (Berkeley: University of California Press, 1970), 62.
47 See Robert Clarke and Mark Merlin, *Cannabis: Evolution and Ethnobotany* (Berkeley: California University Press, 2013), 13–28.
48 Chris Duvall, *Cannabis* (London: Reaktion Books, 2015), 30.
49 Mark Merlin, 'Archaeological Evidence for the Tradition of Psychoactive Plant Use in the Old World', *Economic Botany* 57.3 (2003), 312; see also Hui-Lin Li, 'The Origin and Use of Cannabis in Eastern Asia: Their Linguistic-Cultural Implications.' In Vera Rubin (ed.), *Cannabis and Culture* (The Hague: Mouton Publishers, 1975), 52.
50 Hong-En Jiang, Xiao Li, You-Xing Zhao, David K. Ferguson, Francis Hueber, Subir Bera, Yu-Fei Wang, Liang-Cheng Zhao, Chang-Jiang Liu, and Cheng-Sen Li, 'A New Insight into *Cannabis sativa* (Cannabaceae) Utilization from 2500-year-old Yanghai Tombs, Xinjiang, China', *Journal of Ethnopharmacology* 108 (2006), 420.
51 See Kocku Von Stuckrad, 'Constructions, Normativities, Identities: Recent Studies on Shamanism and Neo-shamanism', *Religious Studies Review* 31 (2005), 123–128; Dawne Sanson, 'New/Old Spiritualities in the West: Neo-Shamans and Neo Shamanism'. In James Lewis and Murphy Pizza (eds), *Handbook of Contemporary Paganism* (Leiden: Brill, 2009), 433–462.
52 See Ake Hulkrantz, *Shamanic Healing and Ritual Drama: Health and Medicine in Native North American Religious Traditions* (New York: Crossroad, 1992).
53 Mircea Eliade, *Shamanism: Archaic Techniques of Ecstasy*. Trans. by Willard Trask (London: Routledge & Kegan Paul, 1964), 390, 394–395, 399–403.
54 Jiang et al., 'A New Insight Into *Cannabis sativa* (Cannabaceae) Utilization from 2500-year-old Yanghai Tombs, Xinjiang, China', 420–421.
55 See Hui-Lin Li, 'The Origin and Use of Cannabis in Eastern Asia: Their Linguistic-Cultural Implications.' In Vera Rubin (ed.), *Cannabis and Culture* (The Hague: Mouton Publishers, 1975), 51.

56 Arthur Waley (trans. and ed.), *The Book of Songs* (London: George Allen & Unwin, 1937), 67, 166.
57 Joseph Brand and Zhongzhen Zhao, 'Cannabis in Chinese Medicine: Are Some Traditional Indications Referenced in Ancient Literature Related to Cannabinoids?' *Frontiers in Pharmacology* (10 March 2017): https://www.frontiersin.org/articles/10.3389/fphar.2017.00108/full (accessed 13 March 2021).
58 Li, 'The Origin and Use of Cannabis in Eastern Asia', 54.
59 Ibid., 51.
60 Ibid.
61 Brand and Zhao, 'Cannabis in Chinese Medicine'.
62 See Bi-Sheng Peng, 'From Religious Manual to Herbal Pharmacopoeia: A Textual Study of the Formation and Transformation of Shennong's Classic of *Materia Medica*', *Traditional Medicine Research* 5.5 (2020), 368–376.
63 JulieAnn Nugent-Head, 'The First Materia Medica: The Shen Nong Ben Cao Jing', *Journal of Chinese Medicine* 104 (2014), 24.
64 Ibid.
65 Ibid.
66 Ibid., 24–28.
67 See Chang Hsien-Che, 'The *Pen-ts' ao Pei-yao*: A Modern Interpretation of its Terminology and Contents.' In Paul U. Unschuld (ed) *Approaches to Traditional Chinese Medical Literature* (Dordrecht: Springer, 1989), 41.
68 See, for example, Nigel Wiseman and Feng Ye, *A Practical Dictionary of Chinese Medicine*, second edition (Brookline: Paradigm Publications, 1998), 399.
69 Brand and Zhao, 'Cannabis in Chinese Medicine'.
70 Ibid.
71 William Emboden, *Narcotic Plants* (London: Studio Vista, 1979), 53.
72 Wiseman and Ye, *A Practical Dictionary of Chinese Medicine*, 295.
73 Alexander Christison, 'On the Natural History, Action, and Uses of Indian Hemp', *Monthly Journal of Medical Science* 4.19 (1851): 26. See also Alexander Christison, 'On Cannabis indica, Indian Hemp', *The Annals and Magazine of Natural History, including Zoology, Botany, and Geology* 6 (1841), 483–493.
74 Solomon Snyder, *Uses of Marijuana* (New York: Oxford University Press, 1971), 19.
75 Rätsch, *Marijuana Medicine*, 22; William Emboden, 'Ritual Use of *Cannabis Sativa* L.: A Historical-Ethnographic Survey.' In Peter Furst (ed.), *Food of the Gods: The Ritual Use of Hallucinogens* London: George Allen & Unwin, 1972), 217.
76 Emboden, 'Ritual Use of *Cannabis Sativa* L.', 217.
77 See Ethan Russo, 'Cannabis in India: Ancient Lore and Modern Medicine'. In Raphael Mechoulam (ed.), *Cannabinoids as Therapeutics* (Basel: Birkhäuser Verlag, 2005), 1–22; Merlin, 'Archaeological Evidence', 295–323.
78 George Grierson, 'The Hemp Plant in Sanskrit and Hindi Literature', *The Indian Antiquary* 23 (1892), 260.
79 Duvall, *Cannabis*, 39.
80 Ibid.
81 Ralph Griffith (trans and ed.), *Hymns of the Atharva-Veda*, Vol. 2, second edition (Benares: E.J. Lazarus & Co., 1916), 74.
82 See Duvall, *Cannabis*, 47.
83 Griffith, *Hymns of the Atharva-Veda*, Vol. 1, 46. It's not entirely clear what *viṣkanda* means here. It typically means 'dispersing', or 'going away'.

84 Clarke and Merlin, *Cannabis*, 243.
85 Harold Kalant, 'Medicinal Use of Cannabis: History and Current Status', *Pain Research and Management* 6.2 (2001), 81; see also Ethan Russo, 'The Role of Cannabis and Cannabinoids in Pain Management.' In Richard Weiner (ed.), *Pain Management: A Practical Guide for Clinicians*, sixth edition (Boca Raton: CRC Press, 2002), 357–375; Dominik Wujastyk, *The Roots of Ayurveda: Selections from* Sankskrit *Medical Writings*, second edition (New Dehli: Penguin, 2001), 187, 304.
86 Vaidya Bhagwan Dash, *Materia Medica of Ayurveda: Based on Madanapala's Nighantu* (New Dehli: Health Harmony, 1991), 123.
87 Shri Dwarakanath, 'Use of Opium and Cannabis in the Traditional Systems of Medicine in India', United Nations Office on Drugs and Crime (1965): https://www.researchgate.net/publication/332736343_An_Indian_Perspective_on_Cannabis_for_Treatment_of_Pain (accessed 8 April 2021).
88 Kalant, 'Medicinal Use of Cannabis', 81; see also Russo, 'Role of Cannabis and Cannabinoids in Pain Management', 357–375.
89 Swagata Dilip Tavhare, Rabinarayan Acharya, Govind Reddy, and Kartar Singh Dhiman, 'Management of Chronic Pain with *Jalaprakshalana* (water-wash) *Shodhita* (processed) *Bhanga* (*Cannabis sativa* L.) in Cancer Patients with Deprived Quality of Life: An Open-label Single Arm Clinical Trial', *International Quarterly Journal of Research in Ayurveda* 40.1 (2019), 41.
90 Duvall, *Cannabis*, 43, 45.
91 R. Campbell Thompson, *A Dictionary of Assyrian Botany* (London: British Academy, 1949), 220.
92 *The Zend-Avesta. Part 1: The Venidad*, second edition. Trans. by James Darmesteter (Oxford: Oxford University Press, 1895), 179.
93 Joe Zlas, Harley Stark, Jon Seligman, Rina Levy, Ella Werker, Aviva Breuer, and Raphael Mechoulam, 'Early Medical Use of Cannabis', *Nature* 363 (1993), 215.
94 Ibid.
95 See A. Merzouki, F. Ed-derfoufi, and J. Molero Mesa, 'Hemp (*Cannabis sativa* L.) and Abortion', *Journal of Ethnopharmacology* 73 (2000), 501–503.
96 See, for example, Martin Lee's comments on Jamaican midwifery in *Smoke Signals: A Social History of Marijuana – Medical, Recreational, and Scientific* (New York: Scribner, 2012), 146.
97 E.g. Robert Burton, *The Anatomy of Melancholy* (London: B. Blake, 1621); William Lewis, *The New English Dispensatory* (London: J. Nourse, 1753); and William Lewis, *The Edinburgh New Dispensatory* (Worcester: Isaiah Thomas, 1794).
98 Thomas Short, *Medicina Britannica: or, a Treatise on Such Physical Plants as are Generally to be found in the Fields or Gardens in Great Britain* (London: R. Manby & H. Shute Cox, 1746), 137–138. See also Ethan Russo, 'Cannabis Treatments in Obstetrics and Gynaecology: A Historical Review', *Journal of Cannabis Therapeutics* 2.3-4 (2002), 5–35
99 See Noga Arikha, *Passions and Tempers: A History of the Humours* (New York: Ecco, 2007).
100 Burton, *Anatomy of Melancholy*, 251.
101 Nicholas Culpeper, *Culpeper's Complete Herbal, and English Physician Wherein Several Hundred Herbs, with a Display of their Medicinal and Occult Properties* (Manchester: J. Gleave & Son, 1826), 70–71.
102 Short, *Medicina Britannica*, 138.
103 Culpeper, *Culpeper's Complete Herbal*, 70–71.

104 *Papers Regarding the Cultivation of Hemp in India* (Agra: Secundra Orphan Press, 1855), Appendix iii.
105 Malachy Postlethwayt, *Universal Dictionary of Trade and Commerce*, Vol.1, third edition (London: H. Woodfall et al., 1766), 996–997.
106 Robert Wissett, *A Treatise on Hemp* (London: J. Harding, 1808), iii.
107 Mills, *Cannabis Britannica*, 47.
108 John Henry Grose, *A Voyage to the East Indies with Observations on Various Parts There* (London: Hooper & Morley, 1757).
109 Robert Wissett, *On the Cultivation and Preparation of Hemp* (London: Cox & Son, 1804), 18.
110 *Papers Regarding the Cultivation of Hemp in India*, Appendix iii (emphasis added).
111 Mills, *Cannabis Britannica*, 25.
112 See Juan Cole, *Napoleon's Egypt: Invading the Middle East* (New York: Palgrave Macmillan, 2008); Paul Strathern, *Napoleon in Egypt* (London: Vintage, 2008).
113 See Caroline Tully, 'Egyptosophy in the British Museum'. In Christine Ferguson and Andrew Radford (eds), *The Occult Imagination in Britain, 1875–1947* (Abingdon: Routledge, 2018), 131–145; see also Erik Hornung, *The Secret Lore of Egypt: Its Impact on the West*. Trans. by David Lorton (Ithaca: Cornell University Press, 2001).
114 See Mary M. Wood, 'Dominique-Jean Larrey, Chief Surgeon of the French Army with Napoleon in Egypt: Notes and Observations on Larrey's Medical Memoirs Based on the Egyptian Campaign', *Canadian Bulletin of Medical History* 25 (2008), 515–535.
115 Quoted in Paul Strathern, *Napoleon in Egypt* (London: Vintage, 2008), 37.
116 See Charles John Fedorak, 'The French Capitulation in Egypt and the Preliminary Anglo-French Treaty of Peace in October 1801: A Note', *The International History Review* 15 (1993), 525–534.
117 Menou, quoted in Guba Jr, *Taming Cannabis: Drugs and Empire in Nineteenth-Century France* (Montreal: McGill-Queen's University Press, 2020), 78–79.
118 Menou, quoted in ibid., 80.
119 Ibid., 14.
120 William Bynum, *Science and Practice of Medicine in the Nineteenth Century* (Cambridge: Cambridge University Press, 1994); Michael Worboys, 'Practice and the Science of Medicine in the Nineteenth Century', *ISIS* 102 (2011), 109–115
121 Michael Worboys, *Spreading Germs: Disease Theories and Medical Practice in Britain, 1865–1900* (Cambridge: Cambridge University Press, 2000).
122 See, for example, Bernhard Fronmüller, *Klinische Studien über die Schlafmachende Wirkung der Narkotischen Arzneimittel* (Erlangen: Verlag von Ferdinand Enke, 1869), 45–69.
123 Antoine Isaac Sylvestre de Sacy, 'Des preparations enivrantes faites avec le chanvre, mémoire li à l'Institut', *C.-T. ou Bulletin des societies méd. pub au nom de la Soc. méd. d'Emulation de Paris*, 4 (1809), 201–206.
124 Mills, *Cannabis Britannica*, 25.
125 William O'Shaughnessy, *On the Preparation of the Indian Hemp, or Gunjah, (Cannabis Indica). Their Effects of the Animal System in Health, and their Utility in the Treatment of Tetanus and other Convulsive Disorders* (Calcutta: Bishop's College Press, 1839).
126 William B.O'Shaughnessy, 'On the Preparation of the Indian Hemp, or Gunjah (*Cannabis Indica*); Their Effects of the Animal System in Health, and their Utility in the Treatment of Tetanus and other Convulsive Diseases'. In *Transactions of the*

Medical and Physical Society of Bengal, 1838-1840 (Calcutta: Medical and Physical Society of Bengal, 1840), 421–461; 'Cannabis.' In William O'Shaughnessy (ed.), *The Bengal Dispensatory. Chiefly Compiled from the Works of Roxburgh, Wallich, Ainslie, Wight, Arnot, Royle, Pereira, Lindley, Richard, and Feé, including the Results of Numerous Special Experiments* (Calcutta: W. Thacker and Co., 1842), 580–604; William O'Shaughnessy, 'On the Preparation of the Indian Hemp, or Gunjah (*Cannabis Indica*); their Effects of the Animal System in Health, and their Utility in the Treatment of Tetanus and other Convulsive Diseases', *Provincial Medical Journal and Retrospect of the Medical Sciences*, 123 (4 February 1843), 363–369.

127 Michael Aldrich, 'The Remarkable W.B. O'Shaughnessy', *O'Shaughnessy's: The Journal of Cannabis in Clinical Practice* (Spring 2006), 26; Lee, *Smoke Signals*, 23; Neil MacGillivrey, 'Sir William Brooke O'Shaughnessy (1808-1889), MD, FRS, LRCS Ed: Chemical Pathologist, Pharmacologist and Pioneer in Electric Telegraphy', *Journal of Medical Biography* 25 (2017), 186.

128 Bradley Borougerdi, 'The Cult of O'Shaughnessy', *Points* (24 July 2014): https://pointshistory.com/2014/07/24/the-cult-of-oshaughnessy/ (accessed 21 August 2021).

129 Stephanie Pain, 'High Times: The Victorian Doctor who Promoted Medical Marijuana', *New Scientist* (2 May 2018): https://www.newscientist.com/article/mg23831760-400-high-times-the-victorian-doctor-who-promoted-medical-marijuana/#ixzz70gz2UGww (accessed 15 July 2021).

130 John Moon, 'Sir William Brooke O'Shaughnessy – The Foundations of Fluid Therapy and the Indian Telegraph Service', *The New England Journal of Medicine* 276.5 (1967), 283.

131 Ibid.

132 See Mel Gorman, 'Sir William O'Shaughnessy, Lord Dalhousie, and the Establishment of the Telegraph System in India', *Technology and Culture: The International Quarterly of the Society for the History of Technology* 12 (1971), 581–601; J.A. Bridge, 'Sir William Brooke O'Shaughnessy, M.D., F.R.S., F.R.C.S., F.S.A.: A Biographical Appreciation by an Electrical Engineer', *Notes and Records: The Royal Society Journal of the History of Science* 52 (1998), 103–120.

133 O'Shaughnessy, *On the Preparation of the Indian Hemp*, 1.

134 Ibid., 11 (emphasis added).

135 O'Shaughnessy, 'On the Preparation of the Indian Hemp, or Gunjah, 363.

136 Ibid.

137 William O'Shaughnessy (ed.), *The Bengal Pharmacopœia, and General Conspectus of Medicinal Plants: Arranged According to the Natural and Therapeutical Systems* (Calcutta: Bishop's College Press, 1844), 291.

138 O'Shaughnessy, *On the Preparation of the Indian Hemp, or Gunjah*, (Cannabis Indica). *Their Effects of the Animal System in Health, and their Utility in the Treatment*, 36–37.

139 Anonymous, 'New Remedy for Tetanus and Other Convulsive Disorders, by W.B. O'Shaughnessy, MD, Calcutta', *The Lancet* 34 (1840), 539.

140 Ibid., 541.

141 O'Shaughnessy, *Bengal Dispensatory*.

142 O'Shaughnessy, 'On the Preparation of the Indian Hemp, or Gunjah', 363.

143 Ibid.

144 Ibid.

145 Ibid.

146 E.P. Whineray, 'A Pharmaceutical Study of Cannabis Sativa (Being a Collation of Facts as Known at the Present Date)', *The Equinox* 1.1 (1909), 233.
147 In the first issue of his journal, *The Equinox*, Crowley included an essay by another London pharmacist, E.P. Whineray (who he admired and whose shop on Stafford Street he frequently visited), in which he reveals that 'the important constituent is a resin. The active principle is stated to be a red oil, Cannabinol, which is liable to become oxidized and inert.' Ibid.
148 John Russell Reynolds, 'Therapeutic Uses and Toxic Effects of Cannabis Indica', *The Lancet* 135 (1890), 637.
149 Ibid., 637–638.
150 See, for example, Aldrich, 'Remarkable W.B. O'Shaughnessy'; Guy Coxall, Trev Coleman, and Steve Harrison, 'Cannabis and the Law: No Evidence, No Crime? A "Seed our Future Campaign" Report, October 2020': https://www.seedourfuture.co.uk/wp-content/uploads/sites/11/2020/10/Cannabis-and-the-Law-No-Evidence-No-Crime-MASTER-v1.3.pdf (accessed 28 September 2021), 5; Marc-Antoine Croq, 'History of Cannabis and the Endocannabinoid System', *Dialogues in Clinical Neuroscience* 22 (2020), 223-228; John Geluardi, *Cannabiz: The Explosive Rise of the Medical Marijuana Industry* (Abingdon: Routledge, 2016), 21; Iversen, *Science of Marijuana*, 120; Lee, *Smoke Signals*, 26; Philip Leveque, 'Premenstrual Syndrome, Medical Marijuana, and Queen Victoria', *Salem-News.com*: http://www.salem-news.com/articles/october162009/pms_mj_pl.php (accessed 21 July 2021); Russo, 'Cannabis Treatments in Obstetrics and Gynecology', 17.
151 Philip Leveque, 'Premenstrual Syndrome, Medical Marijuana, and Queen Victoria', *Salem-News.com*: http://www.salem-news.com/articles/october162009/pms_mj_pl.php (accessed 21 July 2021).
152 Russo, 'Cannabis Treatments in Obestrics and Gynecology', 17.
153 Anonymous, 'Dr Raphael Mechoulam and His Revolutionary Research', *Health Europa Quarterly* 10 (2019), 28.
154 House of Lords, Science and Technology Committee, *Cannabis: The Scientific and Medical Evidence*, Ninth Report (London, 1998): https://publications.parliament.uk/pa/ld199798/ldselect/ldsctech/151/15103.htm (accessed 22 July 2021). See also Virginia Berridge, 'Queen Victoria's Cannabis Use: Or, How History Does and Does Not Get Used in Drug Policy Making', *Addiction Research and Theory* 11.4 (2003), 213–215.
155 Amelia Gentleman, 'Ever Tried Cannabis? Prince Asks MS Sufferer', *The Guardian* (24 December 1998): https://www.theguardian.com/uk/1998/dec/24/monarchy.ameliagentleman (accessed 22 July 2021).
156 See Berridge's discussion: 'Queen Victoria's Cannabis Use: Or, How History Does and Does Not Get Used in Drug Policy Making', 214.
157 House of Lords, Science and Technology Committee, *Cannabis*. See also Berridge, 'Queen Victoria's Cannabis Use', 213–215.
158 See Alexander M. Cooke, 'Queen Victoria's Medical Household', *Medical History* 26 (1982), 307–320.
159 See also Chris Duvall's discussion of this 'knowledge laundering' about Queen Victoria's use of cannabis: *The African Roots of Marijuana* (Durham: Duke University Press, 2019), 222–228.
160 See a copy of this advertisement in Chris Bennett, 'The Incredible, Delectable, Miracle of 19th Century Medicine: Hasheesh Candy!' *Cannabis Culture* (7 February

2013): http://www.cannabisculture.com/content/2013/02/07/incredible-delectable-miracle-19th-century-medicine-hasheesh-candy (accessed 22 July 2021).
161 Bennett, 'Incredible, Delectable, Miracle'.
162 Stephen Snelders, Charles Kaplan, and Toine Pieters, 'On Cannabis, Chloral Hydrate, and Career Cycles of Psychotropic Drugs in Medicine', *Bulletin of the History of Medicine* 80.1 (2006), 107–114.
163 Aldrich, 'Remarkable W.B. O'Shaughnessy', 26; Lee, *Smoke Signals*, 23; Neil MacGillivrey, 'Sir William Brooke O'Shaughnessy (1808-1889), MD, FRS, LRCS Ed: Chemical Pathologist, Pharmacologist and Pioneer in Electric Telegraphy', *Journal of Medical Biography* 25 (2017), 186.
164 See David Guba Jr, 'Antoine Isaac Silvestre de Sacy and the Myth of the Hachichins: Orientalizing Hashish in Nineteenth-century France', *The Social History of Alcohol and Drugs* 30 (2016), 50–74.
165 Théophile Gautier, 'The Club of Assassins.' In Charles Baudelaire and Théophile Gautier, *Hashish, Wine, Opium*. Trans. by Maurice Strang (London: Calder and Boyars, 1972), 36.
166 David Guba Jr, 'France Forgets Own Golden Age of Medical Marijuana', *The Conversation* (24 September 2019): https://theconversation.com/france-forgets-own-golden-age-of-medical-marijuana-122584 (accessed 23 July 2021).
167 See Louis Rémy Aubert-Roche, *Rapport sur le choléra dans l'isthme de Suez Du 1er juin 1808 au 1er Juin 1869* (Paris : Chaix, 1869).
168 'Bey' is a Turkic honorific, which, despite his failure to convert to Islam, was bestowed on him by Muhammad Ali.
169 LaVerne Kuhnke, *Lives at Risk: Public Health in Nineteenth-Century Egypt* (Berkeley: University of California Press, 1990).
170 See, for example, Antoine-Barthélémy Clot, *Derniers mots sur la non-contagion de la peste* (Paris: Victor Masson & Fils, 1866).
171 Guba Jr, *Taming Cannabis*, 124.
172 Louis-Rémy Aubert-Roche, *De la peste ou typhus d'Orient: Documens et observations recueillis pendant les années 1834 à 1838, en Egypte, en Arabie, sur la Mer Rouge, en Abyssinie à Smyrne et à Constantinople* (Paris: Just Rouvier, 1840).
173 Guba Jr, *Taming Cannabis*, 124.
174 Aubert-Roche, *De la peste*, 271.
175 Ibid., 215.
176 Antoine Clot, 'Quelques réflexions sur les éffets du Haschich', *L'Abeille Médicale* 1 (January 1848), 93–94.
177 Alexandre Willemin, quoted in Guba Jr, *Taming Cannabis*, 107.
178 Guba Jr, *Taming Cannabis*, 108.
179 Ibid., 109.
180 Ibid., 125.
181 Aubert-Roche, *De la peste*, 212.
182 Ibid., 211.
183 Guba Jr, *Taming Cannabis*, 108.
184 Aubert-Roche, *De la peste*, 216; see also 212–213.
185 See his 'observations': ibid., 220–249.
186 Ibid., 216–217.
187 See, Guba Jr, 'Antoine Isaac Silvestre de Sacy', 50–74.
188 Antoine Ritti, *Éloge de J. Moreau (de Tours)* (Paris: Octave Doin Editeur, 1887); Jean-Pierre Luauté (ed.), *Les Moreau de Tours* (Paris: Glyphe, 2018); Eric Carlson,

'Cannabis indica in Nineteenth-Century Psychiatry', American Journal of Psychiatry 131 (1974), 1004–1007; Mike Jay, 'The Green Jam of "Dr X": Science and Literature at the Cub des Hashischins.' In Eugene Brennan and Russell Williams (eds), Literature and Intoxication: Writing, Politics, and the Experience of Excess (London: Palgrave Macmillan, 2015), 52–65.
189 Jacques-Joseph Moreau, Du Hachisch et de l'Aliénation mentale. Études psychologiques (Paris: De Fortin, Masson et Cie, 1845). Significant though it is in the history of psychiatry, it was only translated into English in 1973: Hashish and Mental Illness. Trans. Gordon J. Barnett (New York: Raven Press, 1973). As Jose Revuelta and Jose Villagrán have noted, this work him fame, not only 'for the timeliness of its appearance, but also – and mainly – for the originality of the ideas it contained.' Jose I. Pérez Revuelta and Jose M. Villagrán Moreno, 'Moreau de Tours: Organicism and Subjectivity. Part 1: Life and Work', History of Psychiatry 32 (2021), 167.
190 Moreau, Hashish and Mental Illness.
191 Ibid., 1.
192 Ibid., 17. See also Tony James, Dream, Creativity, and Madness in Nineteenth-Century France (Oxford: Oxford University Press, 1995), 99.
193 Datura Stramonium, he concluded, was able to 'exercise a beneficial effect on cases where delusions were primary . . .' Jacques-Joseph Moreau, 'On the Treatment of Hallucinations by Datura Stramonium', Provincial Medical and Surgical Journal 3.7 (1841), 127. See also Mémoire sur le traitement des hallucinations par le Datura Stramonium (Paris: J. Rouvier et E. Le Bouvier, 1841); 'Mémoire sur le traitement des hallucinations par le Datura stramonium', Gazette Médicale de Paris 9 (1841): 641–647, 673–680; Alexandre Brière de Boismont, Hallucinations or the Rational History of Apparitions, Visions, Dreams, Ecstasy, Magnetism, and Somnambulism (Philadelphia: Lindsay and Blakiston, 1853), 343–345.
194 'In France, the terms "fou" and "folie" (mad, madness) date back to the "Chanson de Roland" around 1080, while the more modern concept of "mental alienation" developed in the fourteenth century, leading to the identification of specialist physicians as "alienists" at the beginning of the nineteenth century. In France, the term "psychiatre" (psychiatrist) was accepted by the Académie in 1802, but its use became widespread only one century later, while the term "aliéniste" was becoming obsolete.' Julien Bogousslavsky and Thierry Moulin, 'From Alienism to the Birth of Modern Psychiatry: A Neurological Story?' European Neurology 62 (2009), 257–258.
195 Hélène Peters, 'Hashish and Mental Illness: The Experience and Observations of Moreau.' In Gabriel G. Nahas and Colette Latour (eds), Cannabis: Physiopathology, Epidemiology, Detection (Boca Raton: CRC Press, 1993), 343.
196 Bo Holmstedt, 'Introduction to Moreau de Tours'. In Jacques-Joseph Moreau, Hashish and Mental Illness. Trans. Gordon J. Barnett (New York: Raven Press, 1973), xix.
197 Alphonse Karr, Le Livre De Bord: Souvenirs, Portraits, Notes Au Crayon (Paris: Calmann-Lévy, 1880), 205–207.
198 See Takenori Yogo, 'Littérature et médecine à l'hôtel Pimodan', L'Année Baudelaire 13/14 (2009/2010), 158–159.
199 For comments on whether the date of his birth see Jose I. Pérez Revuelta and Jose M. Villagrán Moreno, 'Moreau de Tours: Organicism and Subjectivity. Part 1: Life and Work', History of Psychiatry 32 (2021), 170, n.2.
200 Jacques-Joseph Moreau, De la influence de physique relativement au désordre des facultés intellectuelles et en particulier dans cette varietés du délire désignée par M.

Esquirol sous le nom de monomania. Thèse pour le doctorat en médecine. No. 127 (Paris: Didot Le Jeune, 1830).
201 Moreau, *Du Hachisch.*
202 Philippe Pinel, *A Treatise on Insanity.* Trans. by D.D. Davis (Sheffield: Cadell and Davies, 1806), 108.
203 Ibid., 10.
204 Michel Foucault, *History of Madness.* Trans. by Jonathon Murphy and Jean Khalfa. (London: Routledge, 2006), 44–77.
205 Ibid., 463–511.
206 Rafael Huertas, 'Between Doctrine and Clinical Practice: Nosography and Semiology in the Work of Jean-Etienne-Dominique Esquirol (1772–1840)', *History of Psychiatry*, 19.2 (1939), 123.
207 M.K. Amdur and E. Messinger, 'Jean-Etienne-Dominique Esquirol: His Work and Importance for Modern Psychiatry', *American Journal of Psychiatry* 96.1 (1939), 129. See Jean Etienne Dominique Esquirol, *Mental Maladies: A Treatise on Insanity.* Trans. by E.K. Hunt (Philadelphia: Lee and Blanchard, 1845).
208 Esquirol, *Mental Maladies*, 93–110.
209 Ibid., 93.
210 Ibid., 81.
211 Ibid.
212 Holmstedt, 'Introduction', xiii–xiv.
213 See Rafael Huertas, 'Between Doctrine and Clinical Practice: Nosography and Semiology in the Work of Jean-Etienne-Dominique Esquirol (1772–1840)', *History of Psychiatry* 19.2 (1939), 124.
214 At the beginning of his study of hallucinations, he makes the following clear to readers: 'We admit the authenticity of the recitals both of the Old and the New Testament; we believe in the intervention of the Divinity to establish a religion, the founder of which proclaimed his mission by the destruction of the worship of false gods, by the abolition of slavery, and the creation of family ties.' Alexandre Brière de Boismont, *Hallucinations or the Rational History of Apparitions, Visions, Dreams, Ecstasy, Magnetism, and Somnambulism* (Philadelphia: Lindsay and Blakiston, 1853), 22.
215 This should be distinguished from the religion of Spiritualism, in that they were spiritualists, because they were alienists who focused on the 'spirit', the psyche, or the 'rational soul' of their patients.
216 Guba Jr, *Taming Cannabis*, 16.
217 Ibid., 156.
218 Foucault, *History of Madness*, 137.
219 Ibid.
220 See Alexandre Brière de Boismont, 'De l'influence de la civilisation sur le développement de la folie', *Annales d'hygiène publique et de médecine légale* 21.2 (1839), 241–295.
221 See Enric Novella and Rafael Huertas, 'Alexandre Brierre de Boismont and the Origins of the Spanish Psychiatric Profession', *History of Psychiatry* 22.4 (2011), 390.
222 Alexandre Brière de Boismont, *Des hallucinations ou histoire raisonnée des apparitions, des visions, des songes, de l'extase, du magnétisme et du somnambulisme* (Paris: Germer Baillière, 1845).
223 Brière de Boismont, *Hallucinations*, 27.
224 Ibid., viii.
225 Ibid., viii.

226 Ibid., viii–ix.
227 Brière de Boismont, 'De l'influence de la civilisation', 241–295.
228 Novella and Huertas, 'Alexandre Brierre de Boismont', 390.
229 Ibid.
230 See Brière de Boismont, *Hallucinations*, 333–334; ibid., 249–250.
231 Ibid., 342–343.
232 Guba Jr, *Taming Cannabis*, 158.
233 Brière de Boismont, *Hallucinations*, 342.
234 Ibid., 343.
235 Ibid.
236 Ibid.
237 Ibid., 343–345.
238 Guba Jr, *Taming Cannabis*, 157.
239 See Katrin Solhdju, 'Alienating Travels and Traveling into Alienation: Moreau de Tours's Experimental Attempts to Articulate the Body of Madness', *Dingdingdong* (25 December 2012), 16: http://dingdingdong.org/wp-content/uploads/alienatingtravels.pdf (accessed March 24, 2016).
240 Jacques-Joseph Moreau, *Recherches sur les aliénés en Orient* (Paris: Imprimerie de Bourgogne et Martinet, 1843).
241 Moreau, *Hashish and Mental Illness*, 1.
242 See Foucault, *History of Madness*, 336–337.
243 Jacques-Joseph Moreau, 'Lettres médicales sur la colonie des aliénés de Gheel', *La Revue Indépendante* 4(1842): 678–704.
244 See Moreau, *Recherches*.
245 Ibid., 29; Moreau, *Hashish and Mental Illness*, 2: 'Anyone who has visited the Orient knows how widely used hashish is, especially among the Arabs, who have developed no less pressing need for it than the Turks and Chinese for opium or the Europeans for alcoholic beverages.'
246 Bo Holmstedt, 'Introduction to Moreau de Tours'. In Moreau, *Hashish and Mental Illness*, xiv.
247 Moreau, *Hashish and Mental Illness*, 7–8 (emphasis added).
248 Ibid., 4.
249 He is referring to a deep well used to supply drinking water at the hospital where he was an attending psychiatrist.
250 Moreau, *Hashish and Mental Illness*, 8.
251 Holmstedt, 'Introduction to Moreau de Tours', xv.
252 Moreau, *Hashish and Mental Illness*, 27.
253 Ibid., 15.
254 Ibid., 19.
255 Ibid., 15.
256 Ibid., 16.
257 Ibid., 187; *Du Hachisch et de l'Aliénation mentale. Études psychologiques* (Paris: De Fortin, Masson et Cie, 1845), 357.
258 Ibid., 15.
259 Ibid., 1.
260 Ibid., 15–16
261 Ibid., 18.
262 Moreau, *Du Hachisch et de l'Aliénation mentale*, 36.
263 Moreau, *Hashish and Mental Illness*, 18.

264 Ibid., 18.
265 Ibid., 13.
266 Ibid., 16
267 Ibid., 91.
268 Ibid., 91.
269 Ibid., 94.
270 Brière de Boismont, *Hallucinations*, 339.
271 Amariah Brigham, 'Du Hachisch et de l'Aliénation mentale, par J. Moreau (de Tours) medicine de l'hospice, de Bicetre, etc.' *American Journal of Insanity* 2 (1845–1846), 276.
272 Ibid., 280.
273 It's worth noting that Foucault considered Moreau an important figure, both in the history of drugs and in the history of psychiatry. See Michel Foucault, *Psychiatric Power: Lectures at the Collège de France, 1973–1974*. Trans. by Graham Burchell (Basingstoke: Palgrave Macmillan, 2006), 278–293.
274 Considered by some to be a forerunner of the Nobel Prize, the Montyon Prize is awarded by the French Academy of Sciences and the Académie Française. For a helpful discussion of the significance of prizes in nineteenth-century France, see Maurice Crosland, 'From Prizes to Grants in the Support of Scientific Research in France in the Nineteenth Century: The Montyon Legacy', *Minerva* 17.3 (1979), 355–380.
275 Jacques-Joseph Moreau, 'De l'emploi du hachisch dans le cholera-morbus', *L'Union Médicale* 2 (1848), 491–492; 'Necessité pour l'autorité d'intervenir dans la question de l'hydrophobie – Proposition d'essai d'un nouveau moyen contre cette maladie', *L'Union Médicale* 6 (1852), 337; Edmond DeCourtive, *Haschisch. Étude Historique, Chimique et Physiologique* (Paris: Imprimirie d'Edouard Bautruche, 1848), 422–424.
276 Having said that, even in the twentieth century his work was mentioned by those with an interest in psychiatry and hashish, such as Pascal Brotteaux: *Hachich: Herbe de Folie et de Rêve* (Paris: Vega, 1934), 80ff.
277 Guba Jr, *Taming Cannabis*, 133.
278 Edmond DeCourtive, *Haschish: Étude historique, chimique et physiologique* (Paris: Imprimerie d'Éduard Bautruche, 1848).
279 For extracts of the thesis translated into English, see Ronald Siegel and Ada Hirschman, 'Edmond DeCourtive and the First Thesis on Hashish: A Historical Note and Translation', *Journal of Psychoactive Drugs* 23.1 (1991), 85–86.
280 Edmond DeCourtive, *Haschish: Étude historique, chimique et physiologique* (Paris: Imprimerie d'Éduard Bautruche, 1848), 18.
281 Guba Jr, *Taming Cannabis*, 136.
282 DeCourtive, *Haschish*, 13.
283 Guba Jr, *Taming Cannabis*, 136.
284 DeCourtive, quoted in ibid., 137.
285 Guba Jr, *Taming Cannabis*, 139.
286 Antoine Lieutaud, 'Du haschisch un canvre indien', *Bulletin trimestriel de la Société des Sciences, Belles-lettres et Arts du département du Var, séant à Toulon* (Toulon: L. Laurent, 1850), 17.
287 Guba Jr, *Taming Cannabis*, 139–140.
288 DeCourtive, quoted in ibid., 137.
289 See Iversen, *Science of Marijuana*, 122.
290 See Snelders, Kaplan, and Pieters, 'On Cannabis', 103.

291 George Beard, quoted in Eric Carlson, 'Cannabis indica in Nineteenth-Century Psychiatry', American Journal of Psychiatry 131 (1974), 1004.
292 See Giovanni Appendino, 'The Early History of Cannabinoid Research', Rendiconti Lincei. Scienze Fisiche e Naturali 31 (2020), 919–929.
293 See Roger Adams, 'Marihuana – Harvey Lecture, February 19, 1942', Bulletin of the New York Academy of Medicine (1942), 705–730.
294 Roger Pertwee, 'Cannabinoid Pharmacology: The First 66 Years', British Journal of Pharmacology 147, Supplement 1 (2006), 163; Raphael Mechoulam, 'Marihuana Chemistry', Science 168 (1970), 1159–1163.
295 Thomas Smith and Henry Smith, 'Process for Preparing Cannabine, or Hemp Resin', Pharmaceutical Journal and Transactions 6 (1846–1847), 171–173.
296 Ibid., 172–173.
297 Thomas Smith and Henry Smith, 'Préparation de la cannabine, principe actif du haschich', Bulletin générale thérapeutique médicale et chirurgicale 33 (1846), 135–136.
298 DeCourtive, Haschish, 24–25.
299 It's worth noting Dorvault's connection with the pharmaceutical firm, Grimault & Co., mentioned in the first chapter in relation to the manufacture of Cigarettes Indiennes. François Grimault was an apprentice working under Dorvault. Along with the investor Francisque-Jean-Baptiste Rigaud, in 1853 he established Grimault & Co. following the acquisition of majority shares in Dorvault's practice. While the relationship with Dorvault was acrimonious for several years, Grimault & Co. rapidly became an internationally recognized pharmaceutical brand, selling numerous medicines, including asthma cigarettes laced with cannabis.
300 Guba Jr, Taming Cannabis, 121.
301 The judgment of the Académie Nationale de Médicine, quoted in Guba Jr, Taming Cannabis, 134.
302 Joseph-Bernard Gastinel, quoted in Guba Jr, Taming Cannabis, 141.
303 Guba Jr, Taming Cannabis, 123 (emphasis added).
304 For a good discussion of the impact of cholera on French society, see Catherine Kudlick, Cholera in Post-Revolutionary Paris: A Cultural History (Berkeley: University of California Press, 1996). That said, as with other plague historians, Kudlick provides no significant analysis of the use of hashish.
305 Joseph-Bernard Gastinel, quoted in Guba Jr, Taming Cannabis, 142.
306 Alexandre Willemin, quoted in Guba Jr, Taming Cannabis, 142.
307 Anonymous, 'Abstract of the Proceedings of the Académie de Médicine, Paris: Cholera', Provincial Medical and Surgical Journal 13.14 (1849), 389.
308 Guba Jr, Taming Cannabis, 143.
309 See Kudlick, Cholera, 14–15.
310 Lieutaud, 'Du haschisch un canvre indien', 34.
311 François Dorvault, quoted in Guba Jr, Taming Cannabis, 145.
312 Brière de Boismont, Hallucinations, 342–343.
313 Brière de Boismont, quoted in Guba Jr, Taming Cannabis, 152.
314 See Brière de Boismont, Hallucinations, 333–334.
315 Ibid., 334. See also, Guba Jr, Taming Cannabis, 171–174.
316 Ibid., 338.
317 Mark Stewart, quoted in James Mills, 'Cannabis in the Commons: Colonial Networks, Missionary Politics and the origins of the Indian Hemp Drugs Commission 1893-4', Journal of Colonialism and Colonial History 6.1 (2005): https://muse.jhu.edu/article/181815 (accessed: 24 September 2021).

318 Louis Lewin, *Phantastica: Narcotic and Stimulating Drugs. Their Use and Abuse*. Trans. by P.H.A. Wirth (Rochester: Park Street Press, 1998), 100.
319 Snelders, Kaplan, and Pieters, 'On Cannabis', 104.
320 Iversen, *Science of Marijuana*, 121.
321 See, for example, Bernhard Fronmüller, *Klinische Studien über die Schlafmachende Wirkung der Narkotischen Arzneimittel* (Erlangen: Verlag von Ferdinand Enke, 1869), 45–69.
322 William Osler, *The Principles and Practice of Medicine: Designed for the Use of Practitioners and Students of Medicine* (Edinburgh: Young J. Pentland, 1892), 959; see also 847, 962.
323 For a brief discussion of these developments, see Simona Pisanti and Maurizio Bifulco, 'Modern History of Medical Cannabis: From Widespread Use to Prohibitionism and Back', *Trends in Pharmacological Sciences* 38.3 (2017), 195–198; Mary Bridgeman and Daniel Abazia, 'Medicinal Cannabis: History, Pharmacology, And Implications for the Acute Care Setting', *Pharmacy and Therapeutics* 42.3 (2017), 180–188.
324 'Seed Our Future Campaign': https://www.seedourfuture.co.uk (accessed 28 September 2021).
325 Jan van Amsterdam and Wimvan den Brink, 'Ranking of Drugs: A More Balanced Risk-assessment', *The Lancet* 376.9752 (2010), 1524–1525.
326 See Richard DeGrandpre, *The Cult of Pharmacology: How America Became the World's Most Troubled Drug Culture* (Durham: Duke University Press, 2006).
327 David Nutt, Leslie King, William Sualsbury, and Colin Blakemore, 'Development of a Rational Scale to Assess the Harm of Drugs of Potential Misuse', *The Lancet* 369 (2007), 1047–1053. For a popular discussion of this general issue, see Steve Fox, Paul Armentano, and Mason Tvert, *Marijuana is Safer: So Why Are We Driving People to Drink?* (White River Junction: Chelsea Green Publishing Company, 2009).
328 Anthony Storr, quoted in Soma, 'The Law Against Marijuana is Immoral in Principle and Unworkable in Practice', *The Times* (24 July 1967), 5.
329 Lester Grinspoon, *Marihuana Reconsidered* (Cambridge: Harvard University Press, 1971), 27.
330 Ibid., 4.
331 Ibid., 4–5.
332 Yuval Zolotov, 'Meet the Experts: Interview with Prof. Roger Pertwee', Fundación CANNA: Scientific Research and Cannabis Testing: https://www.fundacion-canna.es/en/meet-experts-interview-prof-roger-pertwee (accessed 30 September 2021).
333 Anonymous, 'Jive Girls Victims of Drug Racket', *The People* (19 November 1950), 5.
334 Duncan Webb, 'Dope: A Warning to Young People', *The People* (18 February 1951), 4.
335 Henry Bryan Spear, 'The British Experience', *John Marshall Journal of Practice and Procedure* 67 (1975), 85–86.
336 See Advisory Committee on Drug Dependence, *Cannabis* (London: Her Majesty's Stationary Office, 1968), 22–27.
337 R.D. Laing, 'Letter, 1 June, 1964.' In George Andrews and Simon Vinkenoog (eds), *The Book of Grass: An Anthology of Indian Hemp* (Harmondsworth: Penguin, 1972), 235.
338 Albert Rosenfeld, 'Marijuana: Millions of Turned-on Users', *LIFE* 63.1 (7 July 1967), 17.
339 Soma, 'The Law Against Marijuana is Immoral in Principle and Unworkable in Practice', 5.

340 Stephen Abrams, 'Soma, the Wootton Report and cannabis law reform in Britain during the 1960s and 1970s.' In Sharon Rödner Sznitman, Börje Olsson, and Robin Room (eds), *A Cannabis Reader: Global Issues and Local Experiences* (Lisbon: European Monitoring Centre for Drugs and Drug Addiction, 2008), 46.
341 Abrams, 'Soma, the Wootton Report and cannabis law reform in Britain during the 1960s and 1970s,' 44.
342 Anonymous, 'This Dangerous Man Must be Stopped', *News of the World* (7 July 1968), 1.
343 The Wootton Report was submitted to Parliament on 1 November 1968, and published in January 1969.
344 Advisory Committee on Drug Dependence, *Cannabis*, 1.
345 Ibid.
346 Ibid., 52. See also, Michael Schofield, *The Strange Case of Pot* (Harmondsworth: Penguin, 1971), 75–99.
347 *Hansard*, House of Commons, 'Cannabis: Wootton Report', vol. 776, column 959, (27 January 1969): https://hansard.parliament.uk/commons/1969-01-27/debates/1d97edb2-a083-4c62-8416-b0820669cc5a/Cannabis(WoottonReport) (accessed 2 October 2021).
348 Quintin Hogg, quoted in Abrams, 'Soma, the Wootton Report and cannabis law reform in Britain during the 1960s and 1970s,' 47.
349 Advisory Committee on Drug Dependence, *Cannabis*, 1.
350 Ibid., 32.
351 Ibid., 33.
352 Lee, *Smoke Signals*, 2–3.
353 See Lynn Zimmer and John Morgan, *Marijuana Myths, Marijuana Facts: A Review of the Scientific Evidence* (New York: Lindesmith Center, 1997).
354 Lester Grinspoon, 'A Cannabis Odyssey.' In Rick Cusick (ed.), *Cannabis – Philosophy for Everyone: What Were We Just Talking About?* (Chichester: Wiley-Blackwell, 2010), 22.
355 Grinspoon, 'A Cannabis Odyssey', 22–23.
356 See Amanda Reiman, *Medical Cannabis Facilities: Inside Cannabis Care* (Saarbrücken: VDM Verlag Dr. Müller, 2007), 4–8.
357 See Lee, *Smoke Signals*, 233.
358 See Olivia Waxman, 'Bill Clinton Said He "Didn't Inhale" 25 Years Ago', *Time* (29 March 2017): https://time.com/4711887/bill-clinton-didnt-inhale-marijuana-anniversary/ (accessed 8 October 2021).
359 Lee, *Smoke Signals*, 235.
360 Grinspoon, 'A Cannabis Odyssey', 23. Lester Grinspoon and James Bakalar, *Marihuana, the Forbidden Medicine* (New Haven: Yale University Press, 1993).
361 Julie Holland, 'Cannabinoids and Psychiatry.' In Julie Holland (ed.), *The Pot Book: A Complete Guide to Cannabis. Its Role in Medicine, Politics, Science, and Culture* (Rochester: Park Street Press, 2010), 282. See also: Kirsty Oswald, 'Cognitive Cannabis: the Emerging Evidence for Treating Mental Health Problems', *The Pharmaceutical Journal* (31 October 2019): https://pharmaceutical-journal.com/article/feature/cognitive-cannabis-the-emerging-evidence-for-treating-mental-health-problems (accessed: 7 April 2021).
362 See Tom Freeman, Chandni Hindocha, Sebastian Green, and Michael Bloomfield, 'Medicinal Use of Cannabis Based Products and Cannabinoids', *British Medical Journal* 365:l1141 (4 April 2019), 5: https://www.bmj.com/content/bmj/365/bmj.l1141.full.pdf (accessed 31 October 2021).

363 Mary Douglas, *Purity and Danger: An Analysis of the Concept of Pollution and Taboo* (London: Routledge, 2002), 9.
364 Hannah Deacon, 'Why I Campaign for Children Like my Son Alfie Dingley to be Able to Get Medical Cannabis', *British Medical Journal* (2019): https://www.bmj.com/content/365/bmj.l1921 (accessed 7 October 2021).
365 End Our Pain: https://endourpain.org (accessed 7 October 2021).
366 Mary Lou Smart, 'Cannabis and Chemo: How a patient Uses medical Marijuana to Cope with Breast Cancer', *Treating Yourself: The Alternative Medicine Journal* 27 (2011), 45.
367 American Cancer Society, 'Marijuana and Cancer', 2–3: https://www.cancer.org/content/dam/CRC/PDF/Public/8247.00.pdf (accessed 6 January 2020).
368 Guillermo Velasco, Cristina Sánchez, and Manuel Guzmán, 'Towards the Use of Cannabinoids as Antitumour Agents', *Nature Reviews: Cancer* 12.6 (2012), 436–444.
369 Anna Hodgekiss, 'Grandfather, 63, Claims he Cured Cancer with "Breaking Bad" Style Homemade Cannabis Oil', *Mail Online* (21 July 2014): https://www.dailymail.co.uk/health/article-2699875/I-cured-cancer-CANNABIS-OIL.html (accessed 29 September 2021).
370 Donald Abrams and Manuel Guzmán, 'Can Cannabis Cure Cancer?' *Journal of the American Medical Association: Oncology* (16 January 2020): https://realmofcaring.org/wp-content/uploads/2020/11/Can-Cannabis-Cure-Cancer.pdf (accessed 29 September 2021); American Cancer Society, 'Marijuana and Cancer', 2-3: https://www.cancer.org/content/dam/CRC/PDF/Public/8247.00.pdf (accessed: 6 January 2020).
371 Carl Roberts, Gerry Jager, Paul Christiansen, and Tim Kirkham, 'Exploring the Munchies: An Online Survey of Users' Experiences of Cannabis Effects on Appetite and the Development of a Cannabinoid Eating Experience Questionnaire', *Journal of Psychopharmacology (Oxford)* 33.9 (2019), 1149–1159; Patricia K. Riggs, Florin Vaida, Steven S. Rossi, Linda S. Sorkin, Ben Gouaux, Igor Grant, and Ronald J. Ellis, 'A Pilot Study of the Effects of Cannabis on Appetite Hormones in HIV-infected Adult Men', *Brain Research* 1431 (2012), 46–52.
372 See Shannon Nugent and Devan Kansagara, 'Cannabis for Chronic Pain: We Simply Don't Know', *Pain Medicine* 21.6 (2020), 1091–1092.
373 American Cancer Society, 'Marijuana and Cancer', 2–3.
374 Ibid.
375 Ibid.
376 Sarah Sinclair, 'I Just Medicate to Hoover', *Cannabis Health* 4 (2020), 62–63.
377 See Gary Potter, *Weed, Need, and Greed: A Study of Domestic Cannabis Cultivation* (London: Free Association Books, 2010), 72–73.
378 Paul Marinko, 'How Pensioner's Cooking Went to Pot', *The Guardian* (26 January 2005): https://www.theguardian.com/uk/2005/jan/26/drugsandalcohol (accessed 6 October 2021).
377 See for example, Tim Pilcher, *Spliffs 3: The Last Word in Cannabis Culture?* (London: Collins & Brown, 2005), 56–57.
380 Anonymous, 'Woman, 68, Avoids Jail for Growing Cannabis', *The Guardian* (7 March 2007): (accessed 6 October 2021).
381 Diane Riley and Eugene Oscapella, 'The Terry Parker Case: Marijuana for Epilepsy – and Soon for HIV/AIDS?' *Canadian HIV-AIDS Policy and Law Newsletter* 3–4 (Winter, 1997–1998), 20–23.
382 Government of Canada, 'Cannabis Legalization and Regulation': https://www.justice.gc.ca/eng/cj-jp/cannabis/ (accessed 5 October 2021).

383 Such reports, of which there is a steady flow, typically highlight sensational statements, such as: 'It felt like Edward Scissorhands was trying to grab my intestines and pull them out'. Laura Strickler and Steve Patterson, 'High Potency Weed Linked to Psychotic Episodes, Mysterious Vomiting Illness in Young Users', *NBC News* (11 July 2021): https://www.nbcnews.com/health/health-news/high-potency-weed-linked-psychotic-episodes-mysterious-vomiting-illness-young-n1273463?cid=sm_npd_nn_tw_ma (accessed 19 August 2021).

384 Mary Bridgeman and Daniel Abazia, 'Medicinal Cannabis: History, Pharmacology, and Implications for the Acute Care Setting', *Pharmacy and Therapeutics* 42.3 (2017), 187.

385 See, for example, Michael Lynch, 'Themes and Tones of Cannabis News Reports and Legalization Outcomes', *Media, Culture, and Society* 43.3 (2021), 570–581.

386 Liam O'Dowd, '52% of Britons Support the Legalisation of Cannabis in the UK', *Leafie* (6 April 2021): https://www.leafie.co.uk/news/52-percent-britons-support-legalisation-cannabis/ (accessed 6 October 2021).

387 Ted Van Green, 'Americans Overwhelmingly Say Marijuana Should be Legal for Recreational or Medical Use', Pew Research Center (22 November 2022): https://www.pewresearch.org/short-reads/2022/11/22/americans-overwhelmingly-say-marijuana-should-be-legal-for-medical-or-recreational-use/#:~:text=An%20overwhelming%20share%20of%20U.S.,medical%20use%20only%20(30%25). (accessed 2 February 2024).

388 The influence here has been Michel Foucault's *The Archaeology of Knowledge*. Trans. by Alan Sheridan (London: Tavistock Publications, 1972).

389 Gabriel Nahas, 'Hashish in Islam 9th to 18th Century', *Bulletin of the New York Academy of Medicine* 58.9 (1982), 830.

390 While there are a number of important recent books in the area, four of the most valuable are: David Castle, Robin Murray, and Deepak D'Souza (eds), *Marijuana and Madness*, second edition (Cambridge: Cambridge University Press, 2019); Roger Pertwee (ed.), *Handbook of Cannabis* (Oxford: Oxford University Press, 2014); David Nutt, *Cannabis (Seeing Through the Smoke): The New Science of Cannabis and Your Health* (London: Yellow Kite, 2021); Iversen, *Science of Marijuana*. While the first two books are of a more specialist academic nature, the latter two, written by leading British pharmacologists, are more accessible.

391 See, for example, Asia Mayfield, 'CBD for Children', *CBD Health and Wellness* (17 December 2018): https://cbdhealthandwellness.net/2018/12/17/cbd-for-children/ (accessed 20 August 2021).

392 Gordon Lynch, *The Sacred in the Modern World: A Cultural Sociological Approach* (Oxford: Oxford University Press, 2012), 28.

393 Ruby Grewal and Tony George, 'Cannabis-Induced Psychosis: A Review', *Psychiatric Times* 34.7 (2017): https://www.psychiatrictimes.com/view/cannabis-induced-psychosis-review (accessed 25 September 2021); Andrew Sewell, Mohini Ranganathan, and Deepak Cyril D'Souza, 'Cannabinoids and Psychosis', *International Review of Psychiatry* 21.2 (2009), 152–162; National Institute on Drug Abuse, *Marijuana Research Report* (13 April 2021): https://www.drugabuse.gov/download/1380/marijuana-research-report.pdf?v=d9e67cbd412ae5f340206c1a0d9c2bfd (accessed 25 September 2021).

394 Chris Smyth, 'Skunk Blamed for London Psychosis Epidemic', *The Times* (20 March 2019): https://www.thetimes.co.uk/article/skunk-blamed-for-london-psychosis-epidemic-kd2kdtz05 (accessed 12 October 2021); Stephen Adams, 'Scans Show

Drug's Impact on Brain, a Top Doctor Warns of a Psychosis, Paranoid Delusions and a Superskunk Schizophrenia Timebomb', *Mail Online* (24 March 2018): https://www.dailymail.co.uk/health/article-5539941/Top-doctor-warns-psychosis-paranoid-delusions-superskunk-schizophrenia-timebomb.html (accessed 12 October 2021); Hannah Devlin, 'Smoking Skunk Cannabis Triples Risk of Serious Psychotic Episodes', *The Guardian* (16 February 2015): https://www.theguardian.com/society/2015/feb/16/skunk-cannabis-triples-risk-psychotic-episodes-study (accessed 26 September 2021).
395 Essentia Pura, 'The Entourage Effect Explained': https://www.essentiapura.com/the-entourage-effect-explained/ (accessed 20 October 2021).
396 Rachna Patel, *The CBD Oil Solution: Treat Chronic Pain, Anxiety, Insomnia, and More – Without the High* (Indianapolis: DK Publishing, 2019), 11.
397 Ibid., 13.
398 'About the CBD Oil Solution': https://www.dk.com/uk/book/9780241405635-the-cbd-oil-solution/ (accessed 26 September 2021).
399 See Geluardi, *Cannabiz*, 91–172.
400 Jeffrey Jones, 'Nearly Half of US Adults Have Tried Marijuana', *Gallup News* (17 August 2021): https://news.gallup.com/poll/353645/nearly-half-adults-tried-marijuana.aspx (accessed 20 August 2021).
401 Megan Brenan, 'Support for Legal Marijuana Inches Up to New High of 68%', *Gallup News* (9 November 2020): https://news.gallup.com/poll/323582/support-legal-marijuana-inches-new-high.aspx (accessed 20 August 2021).
402 See, for example, Asia Mayfield, 'CBD for Children', *CBD Health and Wellness* (17 December 2018): https://cbdhealthandwellness.net/2018/12/17/cbd-for-children/ (accessed 20 August 2021).
403 Chapkis and Webb, *Dying to Get High*, 13.
404 Rachel Shteir, 'Julie Falco Goes West: Illinois Poster Girl for Legalizing Medicinal Cannabis Leaves Town.' In Jonathon Santlofer (ed.), *The Marijuana Chroinicles* (New York: Akashic Books, 2013), 216.
405 Stephen Young, 'Should This Woman Be Arrested?' *Chicago Reader* (10 February 2005): https://chicagoreader.com/news-politics/should-this-woman-be-arrested/ (accessed 14 October 2021).

4 Sacred Cannabis

1 Christopher Partridge, *High Culture: Drugs, Mysticism, and the Pursuit of Transcendence in the Modern World* (New York: Oxford University Press, 2018), 9–29.
2 Allen Ginsberg, 'The Great Marijuana Hoax: First Manifesto to End the Bringdown', *The Atlantic* (November 1966), 104.
3 Ram Dass, Joan Halifax, Robert Aitken, and Richard Baker, 'The Roundtable', *Tricycle: The Buddhist Review* 6.1 (1996), 108.
4 Walter Benjamin, *On Hashish*. Edited by Howard Eiland (Cambridge: Harvard University Press, 2006), 132–134. See also: Walter Benjamin, *Reflections*. Edited by Peter Demetz. Trans. by Edmund Jephcott (New York: Harcourt, Brace, Jovanovich, 1978), 179; Margaret Cohen, *Profane Illumination: Walter Benjamin and the Paris of Surrealist Revolution* (Berkeley: University of California Press, 1993)
5 Quoted in Howard Eiland, 'Translator's Foreword', in Benjamin, *On Hashish*, vii.

6 Dale Jacquette (ed.), *Cannabis: Philosophy for Everyone: What Were We Just Talking About?* (Chichester: Wiley-Blackwell, 2010).
7 Dale Jacquette, 'Philosophers Stoned', *The Philosopher's Magazine* (20 July 2016): https://www.philosophersmag.com/essays/137-philosophers-stoned (accessed 6 June 2023).
8 Ibid.
9 Mark Fisher, *K-Punk: The Collected and Unpublished Writings of Mark Fisher (2004-2016)* (London: Repeater, 2018), 705.
10 Dave Boothroyd, *Culture on Drugs: Narco-cultural Studies of High Modernity* (Manchester: Manchester University Press, 2006), 118.
11 Benjamin, *On Hashish*, 21.
12 Amanda Moser, Sharon Ballard, Jake Jensen, and Paige Averett, 'The Influence of Cannabis on Sexual Functioning and Satisfaction', *Journal of Cannabis Research* 5.2 (2023), 1–11. See also: Andrew Sun and Michael Eisenberg, 'Association Between Marijuana Use and Sexual Frequency in the United States: A Population-Based Study', *The Journal of Sexual Medicine* 14.11 (2017), 1342–1347; Becky Lynn, Julia López, Collin Miller, Judy Thompson, and Cristian Campian, 'The Relationship Between Marijuana Use Prior to Sex and Sexual Function in Women', *Sexual Medicine* 7.2 (2019), 192–197; Giuseppi Scimeca, Claudia Chisari, Maria Muscatello, Clemente Cedro, Gianluca Pandolfo, Rocco Zoccali, and Antonio Bruno, 'Cannabis and Sexual Behavior.' In Victor (ed.), *Handbook of Cannabis and Related Pathologies* (Cambridge: Academic Press, 2017), 180–187; Joseph Berke and Calvin Hernton, *The Cannabis Experience: An Interpretative Study of the Effects of Marijuana and Hashish* (London: Quartet Books, 1977), 133–148.
13 Earlier versions of some parts of this chapter were originally published in Partridge, *High Culture* and Partridge, 'Aleister Crowley on Drugs', *International Journal for the Study of New Religions* 7.2 (2016), 125–151.
14 Arthur Rimbaud, 'Morning of Drunkenness'. In *Collected Poems*. Trans. by Martin Sorrell (Oxford: Oxford University Press, 2001), 273. See also Robert Zaehner's discussion of Rimbaud's experiences of transcendence in Robert C. Zaehner, *Mysticism, Sacred and Profane: An Inquiry Into Some Varieties of Praeternatural Experience* (London: Oxford University Press, 1961), 61–83.
15 For a good English translation, see Théophile Gautier, 'The Club of Assassins.' In Charles Baudelaire and Théophile Gautier, *Hashish, Wine, Opium*. Trans. by Maurice Strang (London: Calder & Boyars, 1972), 31–56.
16 Gautier mentions Moreau in his earlier essay, 'Hashish.' In Baudelaire and Gautier, *Hashish, Wine, Opium*, 58.
17 Gautier, 'The Club of Assassins', 33–36.
18 Ibid., 40.
19 Ibid., 47. On Gautier's understanding of the Orient, see Elizabeth Dahab, 'Théophile Gautier and the Orient', *CLCWeb: Comparative Literature and Culture* 1.4 (1999), 1–7: http://docs.lib.purdue.edu/cgi/viewcontent.cgi?article=1054&context=clcweb (accessed 15 April 2016).
20 Gautier, 'The Club of Assassins', 47.
21 See Emanuel Mickel, *The Artificial Paradises in French Literature: The Influence of Opium and Hashish on the Literature of French Romanticism and* Les Fluers Du Mal (Chapel Hill: University of North Carolina Press, 1969).
22 Théophile Gautier, *Charles Baudelaire: His Life*. Trans. by Guy Thorne (Norderstedt: Vero Verlag, 2014), 77. See Charles Baudelaire, *Artificial Paradises*. Trans. by Stacy Diamond (New York: Citadel Press, 1996), 33.

23 Catherine Osborn, 'Artificial Paradises: Baudelaire and the Psychedelic Experience', *The American Scholar* 36:4 (Autumn, 1967), 660.
24 See Partridge, *High Culture*, 38–59.
25 See Frank Hilton, *Baudelaire in Chains: Portrait of the Artist as Drug Addict* (London: Peter Owen, 2004).
26 Baudelaire, *Artificial Paradises*, 74.
27 Baudelaire, 'Wine and Hashish', 90.
28 Ibid., 79.
29 Baudelaire, *Artificial Paradises*, 74.
30 Ibid., 85.
31 Ibid.
32 Ibid., 86.
33 Ibid., 88.
34 Ibid., 87.
35 Baudelaire, 'Wine and Hashish', 85–86.
36 Baudelaire, *Artificial Paradises*, 20.
37 Ibid., 70–71.
38 For a good overview of the relationship between drugs and music, see Jörg Fachner, 'Music and Drug-Induced Altered States of Consciousness'. In David Aldridge and Jörg Fachner (eds), *Music and Altered States: Consciousness, Transcendence, Therapy and Addictions* (London: Jessica Kingsley Publishers, 2006), 82–96. See also Berke and Hernton, *Cannabis Experience*, 157–164.
39 Baudelaire, 'Wine and Hashish', 86.
40 Baudelaire, *Artificial Paradises*, 73.
41 Baudelaire, 'Wine and Hashish', 87.
42 Ibid., 86–87.
43 Ibid., 86.
44 Baudelaire, *Artificial Paradises*, 32.
45 Gustave Flaubert, *The Letters of Gustave Flaubert: 1857-1880*. Edited and trans. by Francis Steegmuller (Cambridge: Harvard University Press, 1982), 20–21.
46 See Baudelaire's letter to Flaubert in Flaubert, *Letters*, 22–23. Gustave Flaubert, *The Temptation of Saint Anthony*. Trans. by Lafcadio Hearn (New York: Modern Library, 2001).
47 Michel Foucault, 'Introduction'. Trans. by Donald Bouchard and Sherry Simon. In Flaubert, *Temptation*, xxxvii.
48 Gustave Flaubert, *The Temptation of St. Anthony*. Trans. by Lafcadio Hearn (New York: The Modern Library, 2001), 190.
49 Ernst Bloch, *The Principle of Hope*, Vol. 1. Trans. by Neville Plaice, Stephen Plaice, and Paul Knight (Cambridge: MIT Press, 1986), 89.
50 Marcus Boon, *The Road of Excess: A History of Writing on Drugs* (Cambridge: Harvard University Press, 2002), 144. See also Trevor Hughes (ed.), *Hassan I Sabbah* (Liscard: Zephyr, 1995).
51 Hawkwind, 'Hassan I Sahba', *Quark, Strangeness and Charm* (Charisma, 1977). See also Hughes, *Hassan I Sabbah*; Trevor Hughes (ed.), *Reefer Madness* (Liscard: Zephyr, 1996).
52 See Robert Mack, 'Cultivating the Garden: Antoine Galland's *Arabian Nights* in the Traditions of English Literature'. In Saree Makdisi and Felicity Nussbaum (eds), *Arabian Nights in Historical Context: Between East and West* (Oxford: Oxford University Press, 2008), 51–82.
53 Sadie Plant, *Writing on Drugs* (New York: Farrar, Straus and Giroux, 1999), 48.

54 Harry Hubbell Kane, 'A Hashish-House in New York: The Curious Adventures of an Individual Who Indulged in a Few Pipefuls of the Narcotic Hemp', *Harper's New Monthly Magazine* 67 (November 1883), 946.
55 Anonymous, 'Mr Burroughs in Morocco', *Chemist and Druggist* (16 April 1892), 569.
56 Ibid.
57 Plant, *Writing on Drugs*, 48.
58 Alexandre Dumas, 'Sinbad the Sailor: Italy.' In *The Count of Monte Cristo* (Ware: Wordsworth Editions, 1997), Chapter 31. It's also worth noting Théophile Gautier's own contribution to the *Arabian Nights*, 'La mille et deuxième nuit': 'The Thousand and Second Night.' In Théophile Gautier, *The Works of Théophile Gautier*, Vol. 22. Trans. by F.C. de Sumichrast (New York: George D. Sproul, 1908), 227–270.
59 John Greenleaf Whittier, 'The Haschish'. In *The Complete Poetical Works of John Greenleaf Whittier* (Boston: James R. Osgood & Company, 1876), 201–202.
60 Ibid., 202.
61 Hawkwind, 'Hassan I Sahba.'
62 Bayard Taylor, 'The Vision of Hasheesh', *Putnam's Monthly Magazine of American Literature, Science and Art* 3.16 (April 1854), 402–408. See also Bayard Taylor, *A Journey to Central Africa; or, Life and Landscapes from Egypt to the Negro Kingdoms of the White Nile* (New York: G.P. Putnam, 1854), 518–519; Bayard Taylor, *The Lands of the Saracen; or, Pictures of Palestine, Asia Minor, Sicily, and Spain* (New York: G.P. Putnam, 1859), 133–148.
63 Taylor, 'The Vision of Hasheesh', 404.
64 Ibid.
65 Ibid., 404–405.
66 He considered himself a Pythagorian largely because he believed the philosopher to be an early user of hashish in his teaching. See Fitz Hugh Ludlow, *The Hasheesh Eater: Being Passages from the Life of a Pythagorean* (New York: Harper & Brothers, 1857), 176–187.
67 Ludlow, *Hasheesh Eater*, 18–19.
68 Boon, *Road of Excess*, 152.
69 See Donald Dulchinos, *Pioneer of Inner Space: The Life of Fitz Hugh Ludlow, Hasheesh Eater* (Brooklyn: Autonomedia, 1998), 71–72, 299.
70 William Blair, 'An Opium Eater in America', *The Knickerbocker; or, New York Monthly Magazine* (July, 1842), 47–57.
71 Ludlow, *Hasheesh Eater*, 17.
72 Ibid., 230.
73 Fitz Hugh Ludlow, 'The Apocalypse of Hasheesh', *Putnam's Monthly Magazine* 8.48 (December 1856), 233–239; reprinted in Ludlow, *Hasheesh Eater*, 280–289.
74 Ludlow, *Hasheesh Eater*. Cannabis was first recommended as a cure for lockjaw by O'Shaughnessy.
75 See, for example, Terence McKenna, *The Archaic Revival* (New York: Harper Collins, 1991), 3; Terence McKenna, *The Food of the Gods* (London: Rider, 1992), 163–165.
76 Dulchinos, *Pioneer*, 11. See also Fitz Hugh Ludlow, *The Annotated Hasheesh Eater*. Edited by David M. Gross (Self-published/CreateSpace, 2007), xvii.
77 Terence McKenna and Katherine Harrison McKenna, *Victorian Tales of Cannabis: An Audially Illuminated Manuscript from Sound Photosynthesis* (Mill Valley: Sound Photosynthesis, 2000). The tapes also include accounts of cannabis consumption by Bayard Taylor, Louisa May Alcott, and Richard Burton.
78 Ludlow, *Hasheesh Eater*, v.

79 Ibid., vi.
80 Ibid., vii.
81 Ibid., xiii.
82 Later, Ludlow would become familiar with opium addiction as a result of visits to an asylum to visit those who had succumbed to it. Indeed, in 1867, he produced the first article in a major American publication to address the issue: 'What Shall They Do to be Saved?' *Harper's New Monthly Magazine* (August 1867), 377–387.
83 Ludlow, *Hasheesh Eater*, ix.
84 Ibid., 123, 158.
85 Ibid., ix.
86 Ibid., x.
87 Plant, *Writing on Drugs*, 49.
88 Dulchinos, *Pioneer*, 58.
89 Ludlow, *Hasheesh Eater*, 106–107 (emphasis added).
90 Ibid., 108.
91 Ibid., 108.
92 Ibid., x.
93 Robert Irwin, *The Arabian Nights: A Companion* (London: Tauris Parke Paperbacks, 2005), 154.
94 *Thousand Nights and One Night*, Vol. 1, second edition. Trans. by Powys Mathers (London: Routledge, 1986), 567.
95 Bernard Reardon, *Religion in the Age of Romanticism* (Cambridge: Cambridge University Press, 1985), 3.
96 See, for example, Ludlow, *Hasheesh Eater*, 85. See also the discussion of hashish-induced near-death experience in Ronald Siegel and Ada Hirschman, 'Hashish Near-Death Experiences', *Anabiosis: Journal of Near-Death Studies* 4.1 (1984), 69–86.
97 Ludlow, *Hasheesh Eater*, 101.
98 See Leonard Jenkin, 'The Golden Wrong: A Life of Fitz Hugh Ludlow, with an Examination of His Writings' (doctoral dissertation, Columbia University, 1972).
99 Ludlow, *Hasheesh Eater*, 305.
100 Laurens Perseus Hickok, *Rational Psychology; or, The Subjective Idea and the Objective Law of All Intelligence* (New York: Iveson, Phinney & Co., 1861 [1849]). See also John Bare, 'Laurens Perseus Hickok: Philosopher, Theologian, and Psychologist.' In Gregory A. Kimble and Michael Wertheimer (eds), *Portraits of Pioneers in Psychology*, Vol. 3 (Washington: American Psychological Association, 1998), 1–15; John Bascom, 'Laurens Perseus Hickok', *The American Journal of Psychology* 19.3 (1908), 359–373.
101 See, for example, Bare, 'Laurens Perseus Hickok', 1–15; Bascom, 'Laurens Perseus Hickok', 359–373.
102 It is not mentioned at all by George Trumbull Ladd in *Elements of Physiological Psychology* (New York: Charles Scribner's Sons, 1887), Edwin Diller Starbuck in *The Psychology of Religion* (London: Walter Scott, 1899), or even William James in *Principles of Psychology* (New York: Henry Holt & Co., 1890) and *The Varieties of Religious Experience: A Study in Human Nature* (London: Longmans, Green and Co., 1902).
103 Hickok, *Rational Psychology*, 14.
104 See, for example, ibid., 48–49.
105 Ibid., 49.
106 Ibid., 2.
107 Ludlow, *Hasheesh Eater*, 301.

108 Ibid., 301–302. See Tommi Kakko, 'Hallucinatory Terror: the World of the Hashish Eater'. In Dale Jacquette (ed.), *Cannabis – Philosophy for Everyone: What Were We Just Talking About?* (Chichester: Wiley-Blackwell, 2010), 103–113.
109 Ludlow is almost certainly drawing on Kant's use of the concept in the *Critique of Pure Reason*. That is to say, although he was a member of a Bohemian group to which Emerson also belonged, he is not here referring *directly* to American Transcendentalism. Although Dulchinos makes much of the influence of Emerson (e.g. *Pioneer*, 78), in fact, he makes no reference to Emerson in either *The Hasheesh Eater* or 'The Apocalypse of Hasheesh'. Following Hickok, he is much more interested in Kant and subsequent Idealist thought.
110 Ludlow, *Hasheesh Eater*, 114.
111 Ibid., 305–306.
112 Ibid., 55, 100, 146, 162, 172, 204, 242.
113 Ibid., 148–149.
114 Ibid., 148.
115 Ibid.
116 Ibid., 149.
117 Ibid., 21, 148, 336–338.
118 Ibid., 341.
119 Frank Carpenter, quoted in Dulchinos, *Pioneer*, 280.
120 Dulchinos, *Pioneer*, 54.
121 There is, for example, some evidence that he was influenced by the ideas of Emmanuel Swedenborg, although it has to be said, that he makes no direct reference to his thought. See ibid., 77–78, 88.
122 Ludlow, *Hasheesh Eater*, 150.
123 Ibid., 152.
124 Ibid., 159.
125 Ibid., 144–145.
126 Ibid., 145–146.
127 Bernard McGinn (ed.), *Essential Writings of Christian Mysticism* (New York: Random House, 2006), 365–366.
128 Ludlow, *Hasheesh Eater*, 86.
129 McGinn, *Essential Writings*, xvi.
130 'Like Eblis, I refused to worship earth when I had seen heaven, and once more dared to assume his pride.' Ludlow, *Hasheesh Eater*, 214.
131 See, for example, Jeffrey Burton Russell, *Satan: The Early Christian Tradition* (Ithaca: Cornell University Press, 1981), 130–133.
132 Ludlow, *Hasheesh Eater*, 96.
133 Ibid., 74.
134 Ibid., 220.
135 Ibid., 96–97. These experiences of identification with Christ were initially discussed in Ludlow's earlier article, 'Apocalypse of Hasheesh', 629–630.
136 See Norman Zinberg, *Drug, Set, and Setting: The Basis for Controlled Intoxicant Use* (New Haven: Yale University Press, 1984).
137 Ludlow, 'Apocalypse of Hasheesh', 630.
138 Ludlow, *Hasheesh Eater*, 152.
139 Ibid., 75.
140 Ibid., 74.
141 Ibid., 74–75.

142 Ibid., 75.
143 Ibid., 64.
144 Ibid., 31.
145 Ibid., 64.
146 Ibid., 75.
147 Ludlow, 'Apocalypse of Hasheesh', 630.
148 For a useful philosophical analysis of this idea in Christian thought, see Charles Taliaferro, 'Human Nature, Personal Identity, and Eschatology.' In Jerry L. Walls (ed.), *The Oxford Handbook of Eschatology* (New York: Oxford University Press, 2008), 536–542. See also Stephen Patterson's discussion in *The Gospel of Thomas and Christian Origins: Essays on the Fifth Gospel* (Leiden: Brill, 2013), 61–92.
149 Ludlow, *Hasheesh Eater*, 164–165.
150 Ibid., 75.
151 See Wouter Hanegraaff, 'The First Psychonaut? Louis-Alphonse Cahagnet's Experiments with Narcotics', *International Journal for the Study of New Religions* 7.2 (2016), 105–123; Partridge, *High Culture*, 126–135.
152 Frank Podmore, *Modern Spiritualism: A History and a Criticism*, Vol. 1 (London: Methuen & Co., 1902), 82.
153 Ibid. See also Ronald Siegel and Ada E. Hirschman, 'Hashish Near-Death Experiences', *Anabiosis: Journal of Near-Death Studies* 4.1 (1984), 69–86.
154 Podmore, *Modern Spiritualism*, Vol. 1, 84.
155 John Patrick Deveney, *Paschal Beverly Randolph: A Nineteenth-Century American Spiritualist, Rosicrucian and Sex Magician* (Albany: State University of New York Press, 1997), 52.
156 Randolph betrays the influence of *The Celestial Telegraph* in his comments about, for example, the ability to contact living persons at distance by means of 'the telegraph of the soul.' Paschal Beverly Randolph, *Seership! The Magnetic Mirror: A Practical Guide for Those Who Aspire to Clairvoyance-Absolute: Original, and Selected from Various English and Asiatic Adepts* (Boston: Randolph & Co., 1870), 83.
157 See Deveney, *Paschal Beverly Randolph*, 4.
158 For example, see Marlene Tromp's discussion of Orientalism and gender in Spiritualism during this period: *Altered States: Sex, Nation, Drugs, and Self-Transformation in Victorian Spiritualism* (Albany: State University of New York Press, 2006), 77–96. See also Christopher Partridge, 'Lost Horizon: H.P. Blavatsky's Theosophical Orientalism'. In Mikael Rothstein and Olav Hammer (eds), *Handbook of the Theosophical Current* (Leiden: Brill, 2013), 309–333; Nicholas Goodrick-Clarke, 'The Theosophical Society, Orientalism, and the "Mystic East": Western Esotericism and Eastern Religion in Theosophy', *Theosophical History* 13.3 (2007), 3–28.
159 Throughout the latter part of the nineteenth century, popular texts such as Emma Hardinge Britten's *On the Road* commend Cahagnet's *Celestial Telegraph* to their readers. It is, she says, 'strongly recommended to the student, not only for the value of its facts and the soundness of its philosophy, but because it affords an excellent example of Spiritualism manifested through mesmerism, and presents the wonderful results obtained through clairvoyance and somnambulism.' Emma Hardinge Britten, *On the Road or The Spiritual Investigator: A Complete Compendium of the Science, Religion, Ethics, and Various Methods of Investigating Spiritualism* (Melbourne: George Robertson, 1878), 54. There is also evidence to suggest that it was being discussed in popular occult publications. See, for example, Fred Hockley, 'Remarks Upon the Rev. George Sandby's Review of Alphonse Cahagnet's *Arcanes de la Vie*

Future Devoilés, &c.', *The Zoist* 29 (April 1850), 54–64. Indeed, the article is followed by several pages of further discussion by other correspondents.
160   Louis-Alphonse Cahagnet, *Sanctuaire du Spiritualisme* (Paris: Germer Baillière, 1850).
161   Louis-Alphonse Cahagnet, 'Hashish Visions', *Spiritual Telegraph and Fireside Preacher* 8.36 (31 December 1859), 424–425.
162   Paschal Beverly Randolph, 'What Effects can Intoxicating Agents Have on the Soul of Man?' *Banner of Light* 8.7 (10 November 1860), 5.
163   Anonymous, 'Mr Wilkie Collins and "Precipitations,"' *Supplement to The Theosophist* 10 (October 1888), xxx (emphasis added).
164   J.A. Anderson, 'Alcohol', *The Pacific Theosophist* 5.4 (November 1894), 49.
165   Adolph d'Assier, *Posthumous Humanity: A Study of Phantoms*. Trans. by Henry S. Olcott (London: George Redway, 1887), 223. From the few comments Frank Podmore makes regarding drugs, it is clear that he too is not persuaded of their value as technologies of transcendence – see, for example, *Modern Spiritualism*, 330, 360.
166   Paschal Beverly Randolph, 'What is Life? What is Animal Life?' *Banner of Light* 8.13 (22 December 1860), 8.
167   Jules Hinde, 'Hashish', *Light: Journal of Psychical, Occult, and Mystical Research* 8.645 (20 May 1893), 233.
168   See Alan Gauld, *A History of Hypnotism* (Cambridge: Cambridge University Press, 1992).
169   See Adam Crabtree, *From Mesmer to Freud: Magnetic Sleep and the Roots of Psychological Healing* (New Haven: Yale University Press, 1993).
170   Adam Crabtree, 'Animal Magnetism and Mesmerism.' In Christopher Partridge (ed.), *The Occult World* (London: Routledge, 2015), 188.
171   Ibid., 188.
172   Ibid., 189.
173   Ibid.
174   Ibid.
175   Ibid.
176   William Gregory, *Letters to a Candid Inquirer, on Animal Magnetism* (Philadelphia: Blanchard & Lea, 1851), 138.
177   See, for example, Cahagnet's account of inducing Madame Pichard on August 31, 1848, in *Sanctuaire du Spiritualisme*, 165–176. As Antoine Faivre notes: 'Ainsi, le 31 août 1848 il fit absorber du haschich à une de ses patientes, Mme Pichard, qui se mit alors à tenir des discours visionnaires à caractère cosmique, eux aussi.' Faivre, '"Éloquence magique", ou descriptions des mondes de l'au-delà explorés par le magnétisme animal: au carrefour de la *Naturphilosophie* romantique et de la théosophie chrétienne (première moitié du XIXe siècle)', *Aries*, 8.2 (2008), 195. It is a little odd, therefore, that Susanna Crockford questions Faivre on this point, claiming that she is yet to find a reference to this. While Faivre may have inadvertently suggested that the account appears in *Arcanes de la Vie Future Devoilés* (*The Celestial Telegraph*), it is clear that he had *Sanctuaire du Spiritualisme* in mind: 'From Spiritualist Magnetism to Spiritism: The Development of Spiritualism in France, 1840-1870.' In Christopher Moreman (ed.), *The Spiritualist Movement: Speaking with the Dead in America and Around the World* (Santa Barbara: Praeger, 2013), 140.
178   Cahagnet, *Celestial Telegraph*, 68.
179   Ibid.

180 Éliphas Lévi, *The History of Magic*, second edition. Trans. by Arthur E. Waite (London: William Rider & Son, 1922), 106; see also 139, 436, 472.
181 Cahagnet, *Celestial Telegraph*, 3.
182 Ibid., 100.
183 Paschal Beverly Randolph, *Seership! The Magnetic Mirror: A Practical Guide for Those Who Aspire to Clairvoyance-Absolute: Original, and Selected from Various English and Asiatic Adepts* (Boston: Randolph & Co., 1870), 29–30.
184 Louis-Alphonse Cahagnet, *Magnetic Magic: A Digest of the Practical Parts of the Masterpieces of L.A. Cahagnet*. Edited and trans. by Robert Fryar (privately printed, 1898), 24.
185 Ibid., 17.
186 Ibid.
187 It should be noted, that his use of hashish seems measured. There is, in other words, little to support Ronald Siegel's unreferenced claim that, he used 'dosages of hashish ten times greater' than Gautier used. *Intoxication: The Universal Drive for Mind-Altering Substances* (Rochester: Park Street Press, 2005), 165.
188 Cahagnet, *Sanctuaire du Spiritualisme*, 4–8. Cahagnet, *Sanctuary of Spiritualism*, 3–6.
189 Cahagnet, *Sanctuary of Spiritualism*, 4–6, 14.
190 Ibid., 4.
191 Ibid., 57.
192 Ibid., 67.
193 Ibid., 64.
194 Ibid., 64.
195 Ibid., 64, 222.
196 Ibid., 29.
197 Ibid., 174–177; *Sanctuaire du Spiritualisme* (Paris: Germer Baillière, 1850), 283–287.
198 Ibid., 184; cf. 177
199 Ibid., 113.
200 Ibid., 4.
201 Cahagnet, 'Hashish Visions', 425; Cahagnet, *Sanctuary of Spiritualism*, 75.
202 Cahagnet, 'Hashish Visions', 425; Cahagnet, *Sanctuary of Spiritualism*, 75.
203 Cahagnet, *Sanctuary of Spiritualism*, 76.
204 Cahagnet, 'Hashish Visions', 425; Cahagnet, *Sanctuary of Spiritualism*, 76.
205 Cahagnet, 'Hashish Visions', 425.
206 Louis-Alphonse Cahagnet (ed.), *Abrégé des Merveilles du ciel et de l'enfer d'Emmanuel Swedenborg avec annotations et observations* (Paris: Germer-Baillière, 1854).
207 See Lynn Rosellen Wilkinson, *The Dream of an Absolute Language: Emanuel Swedenborg and French Literary Culture* (Albany: State University of New York Press, 1996), 109.
208 Cahagnet, *Sanctuary of Spiritualism*, 145.
209 See Partridge, *High Culture*, 9–29.
210 Cahagnet, 'Hashish Visions', 425.
211 Cahagnet, *Sanctuary of Spiritualism*, 67.
212 See Alan Gauld, *Mediumship and Survival: A Century of Investigations* (London: Heinemann, 1982), 220–224.
213 Cahagnet, *Sanctuary of Spiritualism*, 4, 77.
214 Ibid., 4.
215 Ibid., 67.
216 Cahagnet, *Sanctuaire du Spiritualisme*, 129.

217 Cahagnet, *Sanctuary of Spiritualism*, 66.
218 Randolph, 'What is Life?', 8.
219 Paschal Beverly Randolph, *Guide to Clairvoyance* (Boston: Rockwell & Rollins, 1867), 35.
220 Randolph, 'What is Life?', 8.
221 Hugh Urban, 'Paschal Beverly Randolph.' In Partridge, *Occult World*, 231.
222 Paschal Beverly Randolph, *P.B. Randolph, the 'Learned Pundit', and 'Man with Two Souls', His Curious Life, Works and Career* (Boston: Randolph Publishing Co., 1872).
223 He isn't mentioned at all in Emma Hardinge Britten's *Modern American Spiritualism: A Twenty Years' Record of the Communion Between Earth and the World of Spirits* (New York: self-published, 1870); and he is only mentioned in passing in Podmore's *Modern Spiritualism*, Vol. 2. The current scholarly interest in his work is largely the result of Deveney's study, *Paschal Beverly Randolph*.
224 See, for example, *The Two Worlds* 3.114 (17 January 1890), i.
225 Podmore, *Modern Spiritualism*, Vol. 2 (London: Methuen & Co., 1902), 23, 26, 31.
226 Ibid., 23, 26, 31.
227 For a discussion of Davy and nitrous oxide, see Partridge, *High Culture*, 61–67.
228 Lana Finley, 'Paschal Beverly Randolph in the African American Community'. In Stephen C. Finley, Margarita Simon Guillory, and Hugh R. Page, Jr. (eds), *Esotericism in African American Religious Experience* (Leiden: Brill, 2015), 37, 45.
229 Deveney, *Paschal Beverly Randolph*, 204.
230 See ibid., 237–240.
231 Max Nordau, *Degeneration* (New York: D. Appleton & Co., 1895 [1892]), 285–286.
232 Randolph, *Guide to Clairvoyance*, 48.
233 Paschal Beverly Randolph, 'Rosicrucian Papers No.5' *Religio-Philosophical Journal* 5.20 (6 February 1869), 3.
234 Randolph, *Seership!*, 30.
235 Randolph, 'What is Life?, 8.
236 Randolph, 'What Effects', 5.
237 Paschal Beverly Randolph, 'Hashish!' *Banner of Light* 8.4 (20 October 1860), 7.
238 Emma Hardinge Britten, quoted in Deveney, *Paschal Beverly Randolph*, 394. See also Podmore, *Modern Spiritualism*, Vol. 2, 23, 26, 31.
239 See Deveney, *Paschal Beverly Randolph*, 211–228.
240 Paschal Beverly Randolph, *Eulis! The History of Love* (Toledo: Randolph Publishing Co., 1874), 48.
241 Ibid.
242 Partridge, 'Lost Horizon', 309–333; Partridge, 'Orientalism and the Occult.' In Christopher Partridge (ed.), *The Occult World* (London: Routledge, 2015), 611–625. See also Goodrick-Clarke, 'Theosophical Society, Orientalism, and the "Mystic East"', 3–28.
243 Edward Said, *Orientalism* (London: Penguin, 2003), 177.
244 Ludlow, *Hasheesh Eater*, x.
245 Nordau, *Degeneration*, 218.
246 Randolph, *Guide to Clairvoyance*, 3.
247 Ibid.
248 Randolph, *Eulis!* 48.
249 Randolph, *Guide to Clairvoyance*, 17–18.
250 Randolph, 'What Effects', 5.

251 Randolph, *Guide to Clairvoyance*, 35–36.
252 Randolph, *Seership!* 29–30.
253 Randolph, *Guide to Clairvoyance*, 41.
254 Randolph, *P.B. Randolph, the 'Learned Pundit,' and 'Man with Two Souls,'* 9. He was particularly close to the Scottish medium Daniel Dunglas Home, whose best man he was and who had 'become the latest thing in Parisian society.' Arthur F. Davidson, *Alexandre Dumas (père): His Life and Works* (Westminster: Archibald Constable & Co., 1902), 319. See also Mme. (Julie) Home, *D.D. Home, His Life and Mission*. Edited by Arthur Conan Doyle (London: Kegan Paul, Trench, Trubner & Co., 1921), 61–64, 222.
255 Ludlow, *Hasheesh Eater*, 31, 37, 64, 92, 96, 102, 107, 111, 123, 227, 261; Robert Chambers, 'The Hashish', *Chamber's Edinburgh Journal* 9.256 (25 November 1848), 341. Reprinted in *Littell's Living Age* 20.246 (3 February 1849), 217.
256 See Gautier, 'Club of Assassins', 41–46; cf. Jacques-Joseph Moreau, *Hashish and Mental Illness*. Trans. Gordon J. Barnett (New York: Raven Press, 1973), 7, 11, 77.
257 Gautier, 'Club of Assassins', 34.
258 Baudelaire, *Artificial Paradises*, 36.
259 Randolph, 'What Effects', 5.
260 Ibid.
261 Ibid.
262 Ibid.
263 Randolph, *Guide to Clairvoyance*, 35.
264 Ibid., 47.
265 Randolph, *Eulis!* 48.
266 Paschal Beverly Randolph, *Dealings with the Dead; The Human Soul, Its Migrations and Its Transmigrations* (Utica: M.J. Randolph, 1862). This book notes that he was preparing a publication entitled *Hashish: Its Uses and Abuses*. There is, however, no known extant manuscript or, indeed, indication of whether it was eventually published.
267 On Platonic thought in early esotericism, see Dylan M. Burns, 'Ancient Esoteric Traditions: Mystery, Revelation, Gnosis.' In Partridge, *Occult World*, 17–33.
268 Deveney, *Paschal Beverly Randolph*, 103.
269 Randolph, *Dealings with the Dead*, 49.
270 Ibid., 25, 50; cf. 186.
271 Ibid., 25, 26.
272 He traces the journey of his monad through plant life, fish, and mammals, to 'Chimpanzee, Gorrilla ... Troglodyte ... Bosjesman, Hottentot, Negro, Malay, Kanaka, Digger, Indian, Tartar, Chinese, Hindoos, Persians, Arabian, Greek, Turk, German, Baul, Briton, American! There's the list, in general terms.' Ibid., 47–48.
273 Ibid., 48.
274 Ibid., 45.
275 Ibid., 21 (emphasis added).
276 Ibid., 54.
277 Cahagnet, 'Hashish Visions', 425.
278 Randolph, 'What is Life?' 8.
279 Ibid.
280 Ibid.
281 Ibid.
282 Helena Blavatsky, *Collected Writings*, Vol. 4. Edited by Boris de Zirkoff (Wheaton: Theosophical Publishing House, 1950), 351–352.

283 Hannah Wolff, 'Madame Blavatsky', *Two Worlds* 4.213 (11 December 1891), 671.
284 Albert Rawson, 'Mme. Blavatsky: A Theosophical Occult Apology', *Frank Leslie's Popular Monthly* (February 1892), 202. He even illustrates his article with a sketch of her with cigarette in hand (201).
285 Wolff, 'Madame Blavatsky', 672. Hannah Wolff, notes H.W. Burr, was 'the widow of the late John B. Wolff, President of the First Spiritual Society of Washington D.C.', who 'became acquainted with Blavatsky sometime before the publication of "Isis Unveiled."' *Madame Blavatsky* (s.l., s.n., 1893), 1–2.
286 See Randolph, *Guide to Clairvoyance*, 35–36.
287 Rawson, 'Mme. Blavatsky', 202.
288 Helena Blavatsky, quoted in ibid.
289 On Orientalism in early Theosophy, see Christopher Partridge, 'Adventures in "Wisdom-land": Orientalist Discourse in Early Theosophy'. In T. Rudbøg and E.R. Sand (eds), *Imagining the East: The Early Theosophical Society* (New York: Oxford University Press, 2020), 13–32.
290 Helena P. Blavatsky, *Isis Unveiled: A Master-Key to the Mysteries of Ancient and Modern Science and Theology*, Vol. 2 (Cambridge: Cambridge University Press, 2012 [1877]), 589.
291 Ibid., 589–590.
292 Ibid., 499.
293 Ibid., 378.
294 Ibid., 498.
295 Ibid., 45.
296 Ibid., 499.
297 Ibid., 498–499.
298 Ibid., Vol. 1, 523.
299 Helena P. Blavatsky, *The Secret Doctrine: The Synthesis of Science, Religion, and Philosophy*, Vol. 2 (Cambridge: Cambridge University Press, 2011 [1888]), 499.
300 Ibid., 124. For more on the Eleusinian Mysteries, see Christopher Partridge, 'Psychedelica Sub Rosa: The Eleusinian Mysteries and the Psychedelic Imagination'. In Hugh Urban and Paul C. Johnson (ed.), *Handbook of Religion and Secrecy* (Abingdon: Routledge, 2022), 57–70.
301 Helena Blavatsky, *Collected Writings*, Vol. 7. Edited by Boris de Zirkoff (Wheaton: Theosophical Publishing House, 1956), 58. See also Helena Blavatsky, *Secret Instructions to Probators of an Esoteric Occult School* (Pomeroy: Health Research, 1969), 99; *Secret Doctrine*, Vol. 3, 566.
302 Helena Blavatsky's editorial footnotes to extracts from Louis-Alphonse Cahagnet, *Cosmogonie et Anthropologies*: 'Cosmogony and Anthropology: Or, Deity, Earth and Man Studied by Analogy', *The Theosophist* 2.6 (March 1881), 133. See also Helena Blavatsky, 'Another Distinguished Fellow', *The Theosophist* 2.5 (February 1881), 104.
303 See Cahagnet's letter thanking the General Council of the Theosophical Society: Louis-Alphonse Cahagnet, 'M. Cahagnet's Letter', *The Theosophist* 2.5 (February 1881), 105. The letter indicates that he had included a copy of his work *Cosmogonie et Anthropologies*, extracts from which Blavatsky printed in the next issue of *The Theosophist*, along with her critical footnotes (see above).
304 Blavatsky, *Collected Writings*, Vol. 7, 58.
305 Ibid., 58.
306 'Theosophy teaches that we should be very careful not to alter our consciousness by artificial means, so many Theosophists shun the use of drugs, including alcohol and

tobacco, except under a doctor's orders.' Theosophical Society in America, 'Cults, the Occult, and Theosophy': https://www.theosophical.org/online-resources/leaflets/1793 (accessed 7 June 2016). See also Pablo Sender, 'Drugs and Spirituality: An Occult Perspective.' *Quest* 103.1 (Winter 2015), 16–19.

307 Maria Moritz, 'Looking for Spirituality in India: A German Theosophist's Experiments with *Ganga*, 1894-1896.' In Harald Fischer-Tiné and Jana Tschurenev (eds), *A History of Alcohol and Drugs in Modern South Asia: Intoxicating Affairs* (Abingdon: Routledge, 2015), 128.

308 See Annie Besant, *The Influence of Alcohol* (Adyar: Theosophical Publishing House 1892); Moritz, 'Looking for Spirituality in India', 128–129.

309 Charles Leadbeater, *The Chakras: A Monograph* (Adyar: Theosophical Publishing House, 2009).

310 Ibid.

311 Michael Saler, 'Introduction.' In Michael Saler (ed.), *The Fin-de-Siècle World* (London: Routledge, 2015), 3.

312 Alex Owen, *The Place of Enchantment: British Occultism and the Culture of the Modern* (Chicago: University of Chicago Press, 2004), 151.

313 See Joscelyn Godwin, Christian Chanel, & John Patrick Deveney, *The Hermetic Brotherhood of Luxor: Initiatic and Historical Documents of an Order of Practical Occultism* (York Beach: Samuel Weiser, 1995), 44.

314 Ibid., 74.

315 William Alexander Ayton, quoted in ibid., 75, 77.

316 See Robert A. Gilbert, 'The Hermetic Order of the Golden Dawn.' In Partridge, *Occult World*, 237–246; Robert A. Gilbert, *Revelations of the Golden Dawn: The Rise and Fall of a Magical Order* (London: Quantum, 1997).

317 Robert A. Gilbert, 'The Hermetic Order of the Golden Dawn.' In Partridge, *Occult World*, 237.

318 Owen, *Place of Enchantment*, 51–52.

319 Arthur Edward Waite, quoted in ibid., 52.

320 See Robert Fitzroy Foster, *W.B. Yeats: A Life. I: The Apprentice Mage* (Oxford: Oxford University Press, 1998), 108; Virginia Berridge, 'The Origins of the English Drug "Scene," 1890-1930', *Medical History* 32.1 (1988), 55.

321 Arthur Symons, quoted in Norman Alford, *The Rhymers' Club: Poets of the Tragic Generation* (Houndmills: Macmillan, 1994), 80.

322 Arthur Symons, quoted in ibid.

323 Margaret Mills Harper, 'Yeats and the Occult.' In Marjorie Howes and John Kelly (eds), *The Cambridge Companion to W.B. Yeats* (Cambridge: Cambridge University Press, 2006), 146. See also Denis Donoghue, *Irish Essays* (Cambridge: Cambridge University Press, 2011), 98–112; Mary Catherine Flannery, *Yeats and Magic: The Earlier Works* (Gerard's Cross: Colin Smythe, 1977); William Gorski, *Yeats and Alchemy* (Albany: State University of New York Press 1996); George Mills Harper, *Yeats's Golden Dawn: The Influence of the Hermetic Order of the Golden Dawn on the Life and Art of W. B. Yeats* (London: Macmillan, 1974); George Mills Harper (ed.), *Yeats and the Occult* (Toronto: Macmillan, 1975); George Mills Harper, *The Making of Yeats's 'A Vision': A Study of the Automatic Script*, 2 vols. (London: Macmillan, 1987); Heather Martin, *W.B. Yeats: Metaphysician as Dramatist* (Waterloo: Wilfred Laurier University Press, 1986); Virginia Moore, *The Unicorn: William Butler Yeats' Search for Reality* (New York: Macmillan, 1954).

324 W.B. Yeats, *The Collected Works of W.B. Yeats, Vol. 8. A Vision: The Original 1925 Version*. Edited by Catherine E. Paul and Margaret Mills Harper (New York: Scribner, 2008), liv–lv.
325 W.B. Yeats, quoted in Lawrence Sutin, *Do What Thou Wilt: A Life of Aleister Crowley* (New York: St. Martin's Griffin, 2000), 60.
326 Donoghue, *Irish Essays*, 104. It should be noted that, according to James Webb, Yeats had been introduced to Sinnett's work by Edward Dowden in Dublin. *The Flight From Reason* (London: Macdonald, 1971), 209.
327 See Harper, *Yeats's Golden Dawn*.
328 Harper, 'Yeats and the Occult', 144.
329 W.B. Yeats, *The Collected Works of W.B. Yeats, Vol. 5. Later Essays*. Edited by William H. O'Donnell (New York: Scribner, 1994), 186.
330 For a good overview of what we know of his thought in this area, see Kathleen Raine, *Yeats the Initiate: Essays on Certain Themes in the Work of W.B. Yeats* (Mountrath: Dolmen Press, 1986). Having said that, while Raine acknowledges his use 'drugs' (252), too little is made of this aspect of his occult practice.
331 It should also be noted that, particularly during periods when he was struggling emotionally, he was not above using drugs recreationally as a form of self-medication. See, for example, Foster, *W.B. Yeats*, 182–183.
332 See Foster, *W.B. Yeats*, 109.
333 W.B. Yeats, *Discoveries; A Volume of Essays* (Dundrum: Dun Emer Press, 1907), 24–25; cf. W.B. Yeats, *The Collected Works of W.B. Yeats, Vol. 3. Autobiographies*. Edited by William H. O'Donnell and Douglas N. Archibald (New York: Scribner, 1999), 264. Louis Claude de Saint-Martin was a French esoteric thinker influenced by Jakob Böhme, whose writings he translated into French. A student of Matinès de Pasqually and a central figure in the emergence of Martinism. See, Christian Giudice, 'Martinism in Eighteenth-Century France'. In Partridge, *Occult World*, 182–187.
334 Yeats, *Discoveries*, 25.
335 Ibid., 26.
336 Ibid., 27.
337 Flannery, *Yeats and Magic*, 99–100.
338 Ibid., 100–101.
339 Donoghue, *Irish Essays*, 105.
340 Anna MacBride White and A. Norman Jeffares (eds), *The Gonne-Yeats Letters, 1893-1938* (New York: W.W. Norton & Co., 1994), 70; see also Warwick Gould, '"The Music of Heaven": Dorothea Hunter'. In Deidre Toomey (ed.), *Yeats and Women: Yeats Annual, No. 9* (Houndmilss: Macmillan, 1992), 156.
341 White and Jeffares, *Gonne-Yeats Letters*, 71.
342 Foster, *W.B. Yeats*, 196.
343 Maude Gonne, *The Autobiography of Maud Gonne: A Servant of the Queen* (Chicago: University of Chicago Press, 1995), 204.
344 Ibid.
345 For more on Crowley's drug use, see Partridge, 'Aleister Crowley on Drugs'.
346 See Richard Kaczynski, *Perdurabo: The Life of Aleister Crowley* (Berkeley: North Atlantic Books, 2010), 394.
347 W.B. Yeats, quoted in Kaczynski, *Perdurabo*, 66, 73.
348 While Crowley's parents belonged to the Plymouth Brethren sect, his father Edward, who was an itinerant preacher, came from a wealthy Quaker family, who had made their fortune in the brewing industry.

349 Joris-Karl Huysmans, *Against Nature*. Trans. by Robert Baldick (Harmondsworth: Penguin, 1959).
350 Between 1909 and 1914 Crowley's journal *The Equinox* published a wide range of material, from poetry and short stories to discussions of yoga and the occult. The title reflects the fact that it was published twice a year on the vernal and autumnal equinoxes. Overall, there were ten issues.
351 E.P. Whineray, 'A Pharmaceutical Study of Cannabis Sativa (Being a Collation of Facts as Known at the Present Date)', *The Equinox* 1.1 (1909), 233–255; Aleister Crowley, 'The Psychology of Hashish', *The Equinox* 1.2 (1909), 31–89; Charles Baudelaire, 'The Poem of Hashish', *The Equinox* 1.3 (1910), 39–64; Fitz Hugh Ludlow, 'The Hasheesh Eater', *The Equinox* 1.4 (1910), 135–146. 'The Herb Dangerous' is available in Israel Regardie and Aleister Crowley, *Roll Away the Stone and The Herb Dangerous* (North Hollywood: Newcastle Publishing, 1994).
352 Abraham Maslow, *Religions, Values, and Peak Experiences* (Columbus: Ohio State University Press, 1964), 183.
353 Crowley, 'Psychology of Hashish', 115.
354 Martin Booth, *A Magick Life: A Biography of Aleister Crowley* (London: Hodder & Stoughton, 2000), 102.
355 This was the motto for Crowley's short-lived journal, *The Equinox*, 'the official organ' of the A∴A∴ – the occult order he established following his departure from the Hermetic Order of the Golden Dawn.
356 Aleister Crowley (published under the pseudonym 'A New York Specialist'). 'The Great Drug Delusion', *The English Review* (June 1922), 573.
357 Aleister Crowley, *The Book of the Law* (York Beach: Red Wheel/Weiser, 1976 [1938]), 9.
358 Aleister Crowley, *Magick: Liber ABA*, Book 4 (York Beach: Samuel Weiser, 2000 [1913]), 126.
359 See Crowley, *Book of the Law*, 10.
360 Ibid., 19.
361 Israel Regardie was Crowley's secretary from 1928 to 1932. He was also an influential occultist and an important figure in the popularization of the Golden Dawn. See Gerald Suster, *Crowley's Apprentice: The Life and Ideas of Israel Regardie* (London: Rider, 1989).
362 Israel Regardie, 'Roll Away the Stone'. In Regardie and Crowley, *Roll Away the Stone*, 23.
363 Israel Regardie, *The Eye in the Triangle: An Interpretation of Aleister Crowley* (Las Vegas: New Falcon Publications, 2014 [1970]), 117–118.
364 John F.C. Fuller, *The Star in the West: A Critical Essay Upon the Works of Aleister Crowley* (London: Walter Scott Publishing Co., 1907), 305.
365 Regardie, 'Roll Away the Stone', 24 (original emphasis). See also Crowley, 'Psychology of Hashish', 119.
366 See Partridge, 'Aleister Crowley on Drugs', 125–151.
367 Crowley, 'Psychology of Hashish', 119.
368 Regardie, 'Roll Away the Stone', 24 (emphasis added).
369 See Sutin, *Do What Thou Wilt*, 65.
370 Crowley, quoted in ibid.
371 Allan Bennett, quoted in Regardie, *Eye in the Triangle*, 117.
372 Regardie, *Eye in the Triangle*, 117.
373 Crowley, 'Psychology of Hashish', 121.

374 Ibid., 98; cf. John Symonds, *The Magic of Aleister Crowley* (London: Frederick Muller, 1958), 106–107.
375 Ibid.
376 Aleister Crowley, quoted in Richard Kaczynski, *The Weiser Concise Guide to Aleister Crowley* (San Francisco: Weiser, 2009), 64.
377 See, Sutin, *Do What Thou Wilt*, 35, 51.
378 Crowley, 'Psychology of Hashish', 95.
379 Ibid., 96.
380 Ibid., 98.
381 Ibid., 98–99.
382 Regardie, 'Roll Away the Stone', 20.
383 Ibid.
384 Ibid., 26–27.
385 Aleister Crowley, *The Book of Thoth* (York Beach: Weiser, 1974 [1944]), 124, 127.
386 Crowley, 'Psychology of Hashish', 95.
387 Ibid., 100. Fuller notes that the phrase originates in the Chaldean Oracles: 'the girders of the soul which give her breathing are easy to be loosed.' Fuller, *Star in the West*, 305, n.3.
388 Fuller, *Star in the West*, 305.
389 Crowley, 'Psychology of Hashish', 99.
390 Ibid., 95.
391 Crowley, *Magick: Liber ABA*, 501.
392 Crowley, *Book of Thoth*, 124.
393 'Lytton calls him Adonai in "Zanoni," and I often use this name in the note-books.' Aleister Crowley, 'The Temple of Solomon the King (Book 1)', *The Equinox* 1.1 (1909), 159; cf. Edward Bulwer Lytton, *Zanoni*, Vol. 1 (Edinburgh: William Blackwood & Sons, 1861), 130.
394 Lytton, *Zanoni*, Vol.1, 139; see also *Zanoni*, Vol.2 (Philadelphia: J.B. Lippincott, 1862), 46–61, 81, 99–111.
395 Lytton, *Zanoni*, Vol.1, 139; see also *Zanoni*, Vol.2, 31, 101.
396 See Lytton, *Zanoni*, Vol.1, 139; see also *Zanoni*, Vol.2, 102–104.
397 Lytton, *Zanoni*, Vol.1, 130.
398 Marco Pasi, 'The Varieties of Magical Experience: Aleister Crowley's Views on Occult Practice.' In Henrik Bogdan and Martin Starr (eds), *Aleister Crowley and Western Esotericism* (New York: Oxford University Press, 2012), 73.
399 Ibid., 73.
400 Crowley, 'Psychology of Hashish', 133.
401 Ibid., 141–142.
402 Ibid., 142.
403 Throughout his discussion, his estimation of Crowley is almost entirely lacking in critical distance and, indeed, approaches hagiography. For example, not only does he claim that his 'fine classical and scientific education at Cambridge' (omitting to mention that he failed to complete his studies) and 'his mountaineering exploits' equipped him to 'tackle the problem of psychedelic drugs' (how, he does not say), but he goes on to insist that 'Crowley was an experimental mystic of the highest magnitude. He had practiced yoga and magical techniques assiduously for many years until he had achieved a thoroughgoing mastery over both Eastern and Western methods. All of these rare skills were eventually brought to bear on his experimentation with a variety of drugs.' Moreover, Crowley's writings, he claims, 'bear witness to, and provide massive

evidence of, his objective and scientific attitude to the whole process.' This is actually very far from being the case. See Regardie, 'Roll Away the Stone', 42–43.
404 Suster, *Crowley's Apprentice*, 142.
405 Ibid., 143.
406 Ibid.
407 Ibid., 142.
408 See Regardie, 'Roll Away the Stone', 39.
409 Ibid., 40.
410 Ibid., 25.
411 Kenneth Grant, quoted in Suster, *Crowley's Apprentice*, 141.
412 See Regardie, 'Roll Away the Stone', 38–39.
413 Ibid., 41.
414 See Suster, *Crowley's Apprentice*, 140–144.
415 Ibid., 143–144.
416 See, for example, Tromp, *Altered States*, 153–155; Alex Owen, *The Darkened Room: Women, Power and Spiritualism in Late Victorian England* (Philadelphia: University of Pennsylvania Press, 1990), 64–65.
417 John Jones, *Spiritualism the Work of Demons* (Liverpool: Edward Howell, 1871), 6. See also the various responses to Jones's claims: Thomas Brevior, *Reply to the Rev. John Jones, on Spiritualism as 'The Work of Demons'* (Holborn: Thomas Scott, 1872); Florian Desprez, 'Reply to the Attack on Spiritualism by the Archbishop of Toulouse', *The Spiritualist* (11 June 1875), 284–285; Anonymous, *Spiritualism versus Satanism* (London: J. Burns, 1871).
418 Tromp, *Altered States*, 151.
419 See Marlene Tromp's useful discussion of gender, stress and alcoholism in late nineteenth-century Spiritualism. Ibid., 151–179.
420 Owen, *Darkened Room*, 65–66.
421 See Tromp, *Altered States*, 160–179.
422 Owen, *Darkened Room*, 65.
423 James Burns, quoted in ibid., 65.
424 Alfred Smedley, quoted in Marlene Tromp, 'Eating, Feeding and Flesh: Food in Victorian Spiritualism.' In Tatiana Kontou and Sarah Willbrun (eds), *The Ashgate Research Companion to Nineteenth-Century Spiritualism and the Occult* (Abingdon: Routledge, 2016), 298.
425 We might think here of Mary Douglas's famous structuralist analysis of dirt, contagion, and taboo in *Purity and Danger: An Analysis of Concepts of Pollution and Taboo* (London: Routledge, 2002).
426 Tromp, 'Eating, Feeding and Flesh', 298.
427 Emma Hardinge Britten (ed.), *Art Magic, or, Mundane, Sub-Mundane, and Super-Mundane Spiritualism* (New York: self-published, 1876), 170–171.
428 Ibid., 128–129.
429 Ibid., 162.
430 Emma Hardinge Britten (ed.), *Ghost Land; Or Researches Into the Mysteries of Occult Spiritism* (Boston: self-published, 1876), 34, 379.
431 Aleister Crowley, 'Cocaine', *The International* 11.10 (1917), 293.
432 Ibid.
433 Sutin, *Do What Thou Wilt*, 277.
434 Aleister Crowley, *Moonchild* (York Beach: Samuel Weiser, 1970 [1929]), 252.

435 Aleister Crowley, 'Liber XVIII: The Fountain of Hyacinth' (1921): http://hermetic.com/crowley/libers/lib93.html (accessed 4 July 2016).
436 Symonds, *Magic of Aleister Crowley*, 51.
437 The account is reproduced in Helen Norton Stevens, *Memorial Biography of Adele M. Fielde: Humanitarian* (New York: Fielde Memorial Committee, 1918), 51–53.
438 See Leonard Warren, *Adele Marion Fielde: Feminist, Social Activist, Scientist* (London: Routledge, 2002), 135–145.
439 Adele M. Fielde, 'An Experience in Hasheesh-Smoking', *The Therapeutic Gazette* 4 (1888), 449.
440 Ibid., 451.
441 Anonymous, 'The Psychic Effects of Hasheesh', *The Two Worlds* 3.114 (17 January 1890), 112. There are several basic errors in this article: as well as masculinizing her, the title of the original publication is cited as *Popular Science Monthly*, rather than *The Therapeutic Gazette*.
442 Anonymous, 'The Psychic Effects of Hasheesh', 112.
443 Fielde, 'Experience in Hasheesh-Smoking', 449.
444 Ibid., 449–450.
445 Ibid., 450.
446 Ibid.
447 Ibid.
448 In China, she had helped and worked with women who had suffered at the hands of husbands who were alcoholics or drug addicts. See Warren, *Adele Marion Fielde*, 89.
449 Partridge, *High Culture*, 26–27.
450 Gonne, *Autobiography*, 204
451 Max Weber, *The Protestant Ethic and the Spirit of Capitalism*. Trans. by Stephen Kalberg (Oxford: Blackwell, 2002).
452 Baudelaire, *Artificial Paradises*, 73.
453 Symonds, *Magic of Aleister Crowley*, 119.
454 Ennis Edmonds, *Rastafari: From Outcasts to Culture Bearers* (New York: Oxford University Press, 2003), 34.
455 Ibid.
456 See Patrick Taylor, 'Rastafari, the Other, and Exodus Politics: EATUP', *Journal of Religious Thought* 17 (1991), 102–103.
457 Dick Hebdige, *Subculture: The Meaning of Style* (London: Methuen,1979), 32–34. See also Yasus Afari, *Eye Pen: Philosophical Reasoning and Poetry* (Kingston: House of Honour Publishing and Senya-Cum, 2008), 76.
458 Hollis Lynch, *Edward Wilmott Blyden: Pan Negro Patriot 1832-1912* (Oxford: Oxford University Press, 1967).
459 See Christopher Partridge, 'Schism in Babylon: Colonialism, Afro-Christianity and Rastafari.' In James Lewis and Sarah Lewis (eds), *Sacred Schisms: How Religions Divide* (Cambridge: Cambridge University Press, 2009), 306–331.
460 Edward Blydon, quoted in Lynch, *Edward Wilmott Blyden*, 121.
461 Leonard Barrett, *The Rastafarians* (Boston: Beacon Press, 1997), 76.
462 Marcus Garvey, 'The British West Indies in the Mirror of Civilization: History Making by Colonial Negroes'. In Marcus Garvey, *Marcus Garvey and the Universal Negro Improvement Association Papers: Volume 1, 1826-August 1919*. Edited by Robert Hill (Berkeley: University of California Press, 1983), 27–32.

463 Peter Clarke, *Black Paradise: The Rastafarian Movement*, Black Political Studies No.5 (San Bernardino: Borgo Press, 1994), 37.
464 Marcus Garvey, *The Philosophy and Opinions of Marcus Garvey*. Edited by A. J. Garvey (Dover: Majority Press, 1986), 34.
465 Ibid., 61.
466 Barrett, *Rastafarians*, 81.
467 Clarke, *Black Paradise*, 36.
468 Barrett, *Rastafarians*, 128.
469 See, James H. Mills, *Cannabis Britannica: Empire, Trade, and Prohibition, 1800-1928* (Oxford: Oxford University Press, 2003), 51–66; Vera Rubin and Lambros Comitas, *Ganja in Jamaica: The Effects of Marijuana Use* (New York: Anchor Books, 1976), 37–38.
470 Lambros Comitas, 'The Social Nexus of *Ganja* in Jamaica'. In Vera Rubin (ed.), *Cannabis and Culture* (The Hague: Mouton Publishers, 1975), 120.
471 Barrett, *Rastafarians*, 129.
472 Ibid.
473 Marcus Garvey, quoted in Rupert Lewis, 'Marcus Garvey and the Early Rastafarians: Continuity and Discontinuity'. In Nathaniel Murrell, William Spencer, and Adrian McFarlane (eds), *Chanting Down Babylon: The Rastafari Reader* (Philadelphia: Temple University Press, 1998), 153.
474 Lewis, 'Marcus Garvey and the Early Rastafarians', 153.
475 Yasua Afari, *Overstanding Rastafari* (Knockpatrick: Senya-Cum, 2007), 90.
476 Ibid.
477 Peter Tosh, 'Legalize It'. *Legalize It* (Virgin, 1976).
478 Carole Yawney, 'Dread Wasteland: Rastafarian Ritual in West Kingston, Jamaica.' In Ross Crumrine (ed.), *Ritual, Symbolism and Ceremonialism in the Americas: Studies in Symbolic Anthropology* (Greenley: Museum of Anthropology, University of Northern Colorado, 1978), 169.
479 Rubin and Comitas, *Ganja in Jamaica*, 58.
480 See Kenneth Bilby, 'The Holy Herb: Notes on the Background of Cannabis in Jamaica.' In Rex (ed.), *Caribbean Quarterly Monograph: Rastafari* (Kingston: University of the West Indies, 1985), 86–89.
481 Yawney, 'Dread Wasteland', 169.
482 See Barrett, *Rastafarians*, 127–128.
483 Afari, *Eye Pen*, 76.
484 See Kelleyana Junique, *Rastafari? Rastafari For You: Rastafarianism Explained* (London: Athena Press, 2004), 16, 47.
485 See Jack Johnson-Hill, *I-Sight: The World of Rastafari: An Interpretive Sociological Account of Rastafarian Ethics* (Lanham: The Scarecrow Press, 1995), 143–199.
486 Velma Pollard, 'The Social History of Dread Talk', *Caribbean Quarterly* 28.2 (1982), 17.
487 Joseph Owens, 'The I-Words.' In Stephen Davis and Peter Simon (eds), *Reggae International* (London: Thames & Hudson, 1983) 62.
488 Johnson-Hill, *I-Sight*, 22.
489 Ibid., 22–23.
490 Afari, *Overstanding Rastafari*, 89.
491 Ennis Edmonds, 'The Structure and Ethos of Rastafari.' In Murrell, Spencer, and McFarlane, *Chanting Down Babylon*, 355.
492 While 'overstanding' is, for Rastas, a more positive term than '*under*standing', it also identifies a deeper and more significant comprehension of an issue.

493 Rubin and Comitas, *Ganja in Jamaica*, 58.
494 Afari, *Overstanding Rastafari*, 94.
495 Barry Chevannes, *Rastafari: Roots and Ideology* (Syracuse: Syracuse University Press, 1994), 199.
496 Afari, *Overstanding Rastafari*, 90.
497 Ibid.
498 Ibid., 90–91.
499 Ibid., 93.
500 Hunter S. Thompson, in Douglas Brinkley, 'Hunter S. Thompson: The Art of Journalism I', *The Paris Review* 42.156 (2000), 57–58.
501 Will Self, 'Introduction.' In *Revelation: The Canon Pocket Bible* (Edinburgh: Canongate Books, 1998), vii–xiv.
502 See Robert Clarke and Mark Merlin, *Cannabis: Evolution and Ethnobotany* (Berkeley: California University Press, 2013); Chris Duvall, *The African Roots of Marijuana* (Durham: Duke University Press, 2019). Also, although rather dated now, it is worth reading the various studies published in Rubin, *Cannabis and Culture*; David Guba, *Taming Cannabis: Drugs and Empire in Nineteenth-Century France* (Montreal: McGill-Queen's University Press, 2020); James Mills, *Cannabis Nation: Control and Consumption in Britain, 1928-2008* (Oxford: Oxford University Press, 2013).
503 Andrew Sherratt, quoted in Alexander Bauer, 'Life is Too Short for Faint-Heartedness: The Archaeology of Andrew Sherratt', *Journal of World Prehistory* 24 (2011), 99.
504 Andrew Sherratt, 'Sacred and Profane Substances: The Ritual Use of Narcotics in Later Neolithic Europe.' In Paul Garwood, David Jennings, Robin Skeates, and Judith Toms (eds), *Sacred and Profane: Proceedings of a Conference on Archaeology, Ritual and Religion* (Oxford: Oxford University Committee for Archaeology, 1991), 50–64; Andrew Sherratt, 'Alcohol and Its Alternatives: Symbol and Substance in Pre-industrial Cultures.' In Jordan Goodman, Paul Lovejoy, and Andrew Sherratt (eds), *Consuming Habits: Global and Historical Perspectives on How Cultures Define Drugs*, second edition (Abingdon: Routledge, 2007), 11–45.
505 Sherratt, 'Alcohol and Its Alternatives', 15. See also the discussion of Sherratt's work in Clarke and Merlin, *Cannabis*, 80–82, 106–107, 212–215.
506 Philip Farber, *High Magick: A Guide to Cannabis in Ritual and Mysticism* (Woodbury: Llewelllyn, 2020), 33 (emphasis added).
507 Steven Hager, 'Foreword.' In Chris Bennett, *Cannabis and the Soma Solution* (Walterville: TrineDay, 2010), 12.
508 Chris Bennett, 'Early/Ancient History.' In Julie Holland (ed.), *The Pot Book: A Complete Guide to Cannabis. Its Role in Medicine, Politics, Science, and Culture* (Rochester: Park Street Press, 2010), 17.
509 Ibid., 26.
510 Carol Sherman and Andrew Smith, *High Lights: An Illustrated History of Cannabis* (Berkeley: Ten Speed Press, 1999), 14.
511 See Daniel Sude and Sylvia Knobloch-Westerwick, 'Selective Exposure and Attention to Attitude-Consistent and Aptitude-Discrepant Information.' In Jesper Strömbäck, Åsa Wikforss, Kathrin Glüer, Torun Lindholm, and Henrik Oscarsson (eds), *Knowledge Resistance in High-Choice Information Environments* (Abingdon: Routledge, 2022), 88–105.
512 Christopher Partridge, *The Re-Enchantment of the West: Alternative Spiritualities, Sacralization, Popular Culture and Occulture*, Vol. 1 (London: T. & T. Clark International, 2004), 77–78.

513 Charles Taylor, *Modern Social Imaginaries* (Durham: Duke University Press, 2004), 23.
514 See Christopher Partridge, *The Re-Enchantment of the West: Alternative Spiritualities, Sacralization, Popular Culture and Occulture*, vols 1 and 2 (London: T. & T. Clark International, 2004, 2005).
515 See Matthew Ingram's engaging study, *Retreat: How the Counterculture Invented Wellness* (London: Repeater Books, 2020).
516 Paul Devereux, *The Long Trip: A Prehistory of Psychedelia* (Harmondsworth: Arkana, 1997), 28.
517 Ronald Hutton, *Shamans: Siberian Spirituality and the Western Imagination* (London: Hambledon Continuum, 2007), vii.
518 Graham Harvey, 'Animism Rather than Shamanism: New Approaches to What Shamans Do (for Other Animists).' In Bettina Schmidt and Lucy Huskinson (eds), *Spirit Possession and Trance: New Interdisciplinary Perspectives* (London: Continuum, 2010), 23–24. See also Robert Wallis, *Shamans/Neo-Shamans: Contested Ecstasies, Alternative Archaeologies, and Contemporary Pagans* (London: Routledge, 2003).
519 Hutton, *Shamans*, vii.
520 Ibid., viii.
521 Christian Rätsch, *Marijuana Medicine*. Trans. by John Baker (Rochester: Healing Arts Press, 2001), 15; see also William Emboden, 'Ritual Use of *Cannabis Sativa* L.: A Historical-Ethnographic Survey.' In Peter Furst (ed.), *Food of the Gods: The Ritual Use of Hallucinogens* (London: George Allen & Unwin, 1972), 223–224.
522 See, for example, Rätsch, *Marijuana Medicine*, 58; Chris Bennett, Lynn Osburn, and Judy Osburn, *Green Gold and the Tree of Life: Marijuana in Magic and Religion* (Frazier Park: Access Unlimited, 1995), 65–66.
523 Andrei Znamenski, *The Beauty of the Primitive: Shamanism and the Western Imagination* (New York: Oxford University Press, 2007), viii. See also, Partridge, *High Culture*, 19–23; David Wilson, *Redefining Shamanisms: Spiritualist Mediums and Other Traditional Shamans as Apprenticeships Outcomes* (London: Bloomsbury, 2014).
524 Mircea Eliade, *Shamanism: Archaic Techniques of Ecstasy*. Trans. by Willard Trask (New York: Bollingen Foundation, 1964), 390, 394, 399.
525 Ibid., 401.
526 Ibid.
527 Ibid., 400–401.
528 Richard Evans Schultes, 'Man and Marihuana', *Natural History* (August 1973), 62.
529 See, for example: Chris Bennett, *Liber 420: Cannabis, Magickal Herbs and the Occult* (Walterville: TrineDay, 2018), 11; Bennett, Osburn and Osburn, *Green Gold*, 3–4; Jeff Brown, *Marijuana and the Bible*, second edition (Clermont: Createspace, 2012), 2; Nick Brownlee, *Cannabis* (London: Sanctuary, 2002), 41; Robyn Lawrence, *Pot in Pans: A History of Eating Cannabis* (Lanham: Rowman & Littlefield, 2019), 15–16; Kayla Morgan, *Legalizing Marijuana* (Edina: ABDO Publishing Company, 2011); 22; Tim Pilcher, *Spliffs 3: The Last Word in Cannabis Culture?* (London: Collins & Brown, 2005), 35.
530 Gerardus van der Leeuw, *Religion in Essence and Manifestation*. Trans. by J.E. Turner (Princeton: Princeton University Press, 1964), 23.
531 Meng Ren, Zihua Tang, Xinhua Wu, Robert Spengler, Hongen Jiang, Yimin Yang, and Nicole Boivin, 'The Origins of Cannabis Smoking: Chemical Residue Evidence from the First Millennium BCE in the Pamirs', *Science Advances* 5.6 (12 June 2019): https://www.science.org/doi/10.1126/sciadv.aaw1391 (accessed 20 October 2021).

532 Ibid.
533 Clarke and Merlin, *Cannabis*, 57.
534 Bennett, 'Early/Ancient History', 26.
535 Roger Christie, 'The Hawaii Cannabis THC Ministry.' In Stephen Gray (ed.), *Cannabis and Spirituality: An Explorer's Guide to an Ancient Plant Spirit Ally* (Rochester: Park Street Press, 2017), 217.
536 John Oman, *The Natural and the Supernatural* (Cambridge: Cambridge University Press, 1931), 372.
537 See, for example, Pascal Boyer, *Explaining Religion: The Evolutionary Origins of Religious Thought* (New York: Basic Books, 2001); Robin Dunbar, *How Religion Evolved: And Why it Endures* (London: Pelican Books, 2022). For a helpful overview of the core theories in the study of religion, see James Thrower, *Religion: The Classical Theories* (Edinburgh: Edinburgh University Press).
538 Oman, *Natural and Supernatural*, 372
539 See, for example, Alan Sumler, *Cannabis in the Ancient Greek and Roman World* (Lanham: Lexington Books, 2018); Ren et al., 'The Origins of Cannabis Smoking.'
540 Bennett, Osburn, and Osburn, *Green Gold*, 4.
541 Guangpeng Ren, Xu Zhang, Ying Li, Kate Ridout, Martha Serrano-Serrano, Yongzhi Yang, Ai Liu, Gudasalamani Ravikanth, Muhammad Ali Nawaz, Abdul Samad Mumtaz, Nicolas Salamin, and Luca Fumagalli, 'Large-scale Whole-genome Resequencing Unravels the Domestication History of *Cannabis sativa*', *Science Advances* 7.29 (16 July 2021), 1.
542 Chris Duvall, *Cannabis* (London: Reaktion Books, 2015), 32.
543 Emboden, 'Ritual Use of *Cannabis Sativa* L.', 224–225.
544 Ainslie Embree, *The Hindu Tradition* (New York: Vintage, 1972), 21.
545 Aldous Huxley, *Brave New World* (London: Vintage, 2007 [1932]), 46, 47.
546 See R. Gordon Wasson, *Soma: Divine Mushroom of Immortality* (New York: Harcourt Brace, 1968).
547 Gordon Wasson, 'Persephone's Quest.' In Gordon Wasson, Stella Kramrisch, Jonathan Ott, and Carl Ruck, *Persephone's Quest: Entheogens and the Origins of Religion* (New Haven: Yale University Press, 1986), 32.
548 See also David Flattery and Martin Schwartz, *Haoma and Harmaline: The Botanical Identity of the Indo-Iranian Sacred Hallucinogen 'Soma' and its Legacy in Religion, Language, and Middle Eastern Folklore*, Near Eastern Studies 21 (Berkeley: University of California Press, 1989).
549 See Partridge, *High Culture*, 298–302.
550 John Brough, 'Soma and *Amanita muscaria*', *Bulletin of the School of Oriental and African Studies* 34 (1971), 331–362.
551 Ibid., 333.
552 Bennett, *Cannabis and the Soma Solution*.
553 Chris Bennett, 'Venerable Traditions: A Brief History of the Ritual and Religious Use of Cannabis.' In Gray, *Cannabis and Spirituality*, 52–57; Jeff Brown, *Marijuana and the Bible*, second edition (Clermont: Createspace, 2012); Jeff Brown, 'Ritual and Religious Use of Ganja in Jamaica.' In Gray, *Cannabis and Spirituality*, 144–151; Philip Farber, *High Magick: A Guide to Cannabis in Ritual and Mysticism* (Woodbury: Llewelllyn, 2020), 39–40, 131; George Andrews and Simon Vinkenoog (eds), *The Book of Grass: An Anthology of Indian Hemp* (Harmondsworth: Penguin, 1972), 39.

554 See, for example, Christie, 'Hawaii Cannabis THC Ministry', 209; Robyn Lawrence, *Pot in Pans: A History of Eating Cannabis* (Lanham: Rowman & Littlefield, 2019), 48. Sandra Hinchcliffe, *Your Cannabis Experience: A Beginner's Guide to Buying, Growing, Cooking and Healing with Cannabis* (New York Skyhorse Publishing, 2023), 4. See also Laurie Cozad's comments in *God on High: Religion, Cannabis, and the Quest for Legitimacy* (Lanham: Lexington Books, 2018), 3, 8, 47, 59.

555 Alyson Martin, 'Holy Rollers: These Devout Christians Are Using The Bible To Argue That Pot Is God's "Perfect Medicine"', *BuzzFeed News* (15 May 2017): https://www.buzzfeednews.com/article/alysonmartin/cannabis-reform-and-religion-in-the-south (accessed 7 July 2023).

556 See Gerhard Von Rad, *Genesis: A Commentary*. Trans. by John Marks (Philadelphia: Westminster Press, 1961), 61; Martin Kessler and Karel Duerloo, *A Commentary on Genesis: The Book of Beginnings* (Mahwah: Paulist Press, 2004), 33–34.

557 See Joseph Blenkinsopp, *Ezekiel* (Louisville: John Knox Press, 1990), 160–161.

558 Harold Moldenke and Alma Moldenke, *Plants of the Bible* (New York: Ronald Press Company, 1952), 131.

559 Craig Gross, 'Convictions', *Christian Cannabis*: https://christiancannabis.com/convictions/ (accessed 10 July 2023). See also Jonathon Merritt, 'The Christian Case for Marijuana', *New York Times* (20 June 2019): https://www.nytimes.com/2019/06/20/opinion/legalization-medical-marijuana-christianity.html (accessed 24 May 2023).

560 Sula Benet, 'Early Diffusion and Folk Uses of Hemp'. In Vera Rubin (ed.), *Cannabis and Culture* (The Hague: Mouton Publishers, 1975), 40–41.

561 Lytton John Musselman, *A Dictionary of Bible Plants* (Cambridge: Cambridge University Press, 2012), 32; see also 121–122.

562 Ibid., 32.

563 Michael Zohary, *Plants of the Bible* (Cambridge: Cambridge University Press, 1982), 134.

564 Ibid.

565 Musselman, *Dictionary of Bible Plants*, 121–122.

566 Zohary, *Plants of the Bible*, 196.

567 See, for example, James Strong, *Exhaustive Concordance of the Bible* (New York: Abingdon Press, 1890), 24, 104; Francis Brown, Samuel Driver, and Charles Briggs, *A Hebrew and English Lexicon of the Old Testament* (Oxford: Oxford University Press, 1906), 141, 889.

568 Dioscorides, quoted in Theodore Brunner, 'Marijuana in Ancient Greece and Rome: The Literary Evidence', *Bulletin of the History of Medicine* 47.4 (1973), 349.

569 Edward Dodge, 'How Moses and the Israelites Used Cannabis', *Merry Jane* (15 November 2016): https://merryjane.com/news/bible-moses-israelites-cannabis (accessed 6 September 2023).

570 Farber, *High Magick*, 5.

571 Will Johnson, *Cannabis in Spiritual Practice: The Ecstasy of Shiva, the Calm of the Buddha* (Rochester: Inner Traditions, 2018), 44.

572 Bennett, Osburn, and Osburn, *Green Gold*, 36.

573 Ibid., 101.

574 Christian Rätsch, *Encyclopedia of Psychoactive Plants: Ethnopharmacology and its Applications*. Trans. by John Baker (Rochester: Park Street Press, 1998), 146.

575 See Chris Bennett, 'Marijuana and the Goddess', *Zen Zion Coptic Orthodox Church* (1 September 1998): https://zzco.org/chris_bennett/goddess.html (accessed 23 July

2023); Chris Bennett, 'The Magical and Ceremonial Use of Cannabis in the Ancient World.' In Harold Ellens (ed.), *Seeking the Sacred with Psychoactive Substances: Chemical Paths to Spirituality and to God*. Vol.1 (Santa Barbara: ABC-CLIO, 2014), 23–56; Chris Bennett, 'The Mother Plant of the Goddess – Cannabis', *Cannabis Culture* (31 May 2019): https://www.cannabisculture.com/content/2019/05/31/the-mother-plant-of-the-goddess-cannabis/ (accessed 24 July 2023); Bennett, Osburn, and Osburn, *Green Gold*, 36, 51, 109–112, 274; Jamie Della, 'Cannabis: A Herbal Ally', *Jamie Della: Blogs* (7 April 2022): https://jamiedella.com/blog/cannabis-an-herbal-ally (accessed 12 July 2023); Dee Dussault, *Ganja Yoga: A Practical Guide to Conscious Relaxation, Soothing Pain Relief, and Enlightened Self-discovery* (London: Hay House, 2017), 44–46; Patrick Lynch, 'How Marijuana Thrived in Certain Cultures: Ancient Egypt', *Way of Leaf* (3 March 2020): https://wayofleaf.com/blog/how-cannabis-became-part-of-thriving-culture-ancient-egypt (accessed 23 July 2023); Christian Rätsch, *Marijuana Medicine*. Trans. by John Baker (Rochester: Healing Arts Press, 2001), 85–87, 100–103; Riley Winters, 'Magu: The Hemp Goddess Who Healed Ancient Asia', *Ancient Origins* (31 August 2017): https://www.ancient-origins.net/myths-legends-asia/magu-hemp-goddess-who-healed-ancient-asia-008709 (accessed 16 July 2023).

576 Daniel Overmyer, *Local Religion in North China in the Twentieth Century* (Leiden: Brill, 2009), 135.
577 Joseph Needham, *Science and Civilization in China*, Vol.5, Part 2 (Cambridge: Cambridge University Press, 1974), 152.
578 Kathleen Harrison, 'Who Is She? The Personification of Cannabis in Cultural and Individual Experience.' In Gray, *Cannabis and Spirituality*, 23–24; see also Della, 'Cannabis: A Herbal Ally.'
579 Della, 'Cannabis: A Herbal Ally.'
580 See, for example, Mark Ferrara, *Sacred Bliss: A Spiritual History of Cannabis* (Lanham: Rowman & Littlefield, 2016), 110–112.
581 See Barry Cunliffe, *The Scythians: Nomad Warriors of the Steppe* (Oxford: Oxford University Press, 2019).
582 Herodotus, *The Histories*. Trans. by Robin Waterfield (Oxford: Oxford University Press, 1998), 259–260; see also Barry Cunliffe, *The Scythians: Nomad Warriors of the Steppe* (Oxford: Oxford University Press, 2019), 46, 194, 293.
583 Sergei Rudenko, *Frozen Tombs of Siberia: The Pazyryk Burials of Iron Age Horsemen*. Trans. by M.W. Tompson (Berkeley: University of California Press, 1970).
584 See David Asheri, Alan Lloyd, and Aldo Corcella, *A Commentary on Herodotus Books I–IV* (Oxford: Oxford University Press, 2007), 213, 635.
585 See Marie-Françoise Guédon, 'Sacred Smokes in Circumboreal Countries: An Ethnobotanical Exploration', *The Northern Review* 22 (2000), 29–42; Marcello Pennacchio, Lara Jefferson, and Kayri Havens, *Uses and Abuses of Plant-Derived Smoke: Its Ethnobotany as Hallucinogen, Perfume, Incense, and Medicine* (Oxford: Oxford University Press, 2010).
586 See Max Nelson, *The Barbarian's Beverage: The History of Beer in Ancient Europe* (Abingdon: Routledge, 2005), 38–44.
587 Alan Sumler, *Cannabis in the Ancient Greek and Roman World* (Lanham: Lexington Books, 2018), 15.
588 Yi Yang, Melissa Lewis, Angelica Bello, Ewa Wasilewski, Hance Clarke, and Lakshmi P. Kotra, '*Cannabis sativa* (Hemp) Seeds, Δ^9-Tetrahydrocannabinol, and Potential Overdose', *Cannabis and Cannabinoid Research* 2.1 (2017), 274.

589 Sumler, *Cannabis*, 5.
590 Ibid., 64.
591 Galen, quoted in Brunner, 'Marijuana in Ancient Greece and Rome', 350.
592 It's also worth noting that Theophrastus (*c.* 371–*c.* 287) not only differentiates between monocotyledons and dicotyledons, but also has a 'definite idea . . . of the relation of flower to fruit'. Indeed, as Arthur Pease discusses, numerous botanical distinctions can be 'found in the *Historia Plantarum*, the ninth book of which . . . is our earliest extant herbal.' For example, 'in the *De Causis Plantarum* he discusses kinds of reproduction by seeds and cuttings; he believes that most so-called "spontaneous generation" is explicable by small and inconspicuous seeds . . .' Arthur Pease, 'A Sketch of The Development of Ancient Botany', *Phoenix* 6.2 (1952), 46–47.
593 Dioscorides, quoted in Brunner, 'Marijuana in Ancient Greece and Rome', 349.
594 Leslie Iversen, 'How Cannabis Works in the Brain.' In David Caastle, Robin Murray, and Deepak D'Souza (eds), *Marijuana and Madness*, second edition (Cambridge: Cambridge University Press, 2012), 9.
595 Mitch Earleywine, 'Cannabis: Attending to Subjective Effects to Improve Drug Safety'. In Mitch Earleywine (ed.), *Mind-Altering Drugs: The Science of Subjective Experience* (Oxford: Oxford University Press, 2005), 246.
596 Renate Rolle, *The World of the Scythians*. Trans. by F.G. Walls (Berkeley: University of California Press, 1989), 93.
597 See, for example, Sumler, *Cannabis*; Michael Rinella, *Pharmakon: Plato, Drug Culture, and Identity in Ancient Athens* (Lanham: Lexington Books, 2012).
598 See James Butrica, 'The Medical Use of Cannabis Among the Greeks and Romans', *Journal of Cannabis Therapeutics* 2 (2002), 51–70.
599 Brunner, 'Marijuana in Ancient Greece and Rome', 345.
600 Ibid., 354.
601 Ibid., 349.
602 Dioscorides, quoted in ibid., 349.
603 Ibid., 354.
604 Ibid., 350.
605 Ibid., 354.
606 Ibid.
607 Ibid., 355.
608 Stephen Gray, 'The Basics: Practical Guidance for Working with Cannabis as a Spiritual Ally'. In Gray, *Cannabis and Spirituality*, 67–88.
609 Stephen Gray, 'Working with the Spirits: An Interview with Cannabis Shaman Hamilton Souther.' In Gray, *Cannabis and Spirituality*, 130, 131.
610 Swami Chaitanya, 'A Sacramental High': https://swamiselect.com/a-sacramental-high/ (accessed 15 September 2023).
611 Doug Rushkoff, 'Cannabis: Stealth Goddess.' In Julie Holland (ed.), *The Pot Book: A Complete Guide to Cannabis. Its Role in Medicine, Politics, Science, and Culture* (Rochester: Park Street Press, 2010), 371.
612 Harrison, 'Who Is She?' 32.
613 Ibid., 25–27.
614 Dussault, *Ganja Yoga*, 130.
615 Douglas Osto, *Altered States: Buddhism and Psychedelic Spirituality in America* (New York: Columbia University Press, 2016), 142.
616 Quoted in ibid., 142–143.
617 Quoted in ibid.

618 Quoted in ibid.
619 Quoted in ibid.
620 Craig Gross, 'Why?' *Christian Cannabis*: https://christiancannabis.com/why/ (accessed 10 July 2023). See also Jonathon Merritt, 'The Christian Case for Marijuana', *New York Times* (20 June 2019): https://www.nytimes.com/2019/06/20/opinion/legalization-medical-marijuana-christianity.html (accessed 24 May 2023).
621 'Josiah', on *Christian Cannabis*: https://christiancannabis.com/josiah/ (accessed 5 November 2023).
622 Personal correspondence: see Partridge, *Re-Enchantment of the West*, Vol. 2, 125–126.
623 The Jah Healing Kemetic Temple of the Divine, based in Big Bear City, was closed by San Bernardino County because of claims that it was illegally functioning as a cannabis dispensary. See Joe Nelson, 'Shuttered Big Bear Cannabis Church Loses Court Appeal to Reopen, Vows to Continue Fight', *San Bernardino Sun* (20 October 2022): https://www.sbsun.com/2022/10/14/shuttered-big-bear-cannabis-church-loses-court-appeal-to-reopen-vows-to-continue-fight/#:~:text=Jah%20Healing%20Kemetic%20Temple%20of%20the%20Divine%20Church%2C%20which%20considers,June%202020%20decision%20ordering%20a (accessed 5 November 2023).
624 Swami Chaitanya, 'Swami Chaitanya's Journey to Becoming Swami': https://swamiselect.com/swami-chaitanyas-journey/ (accessed 15 September 2023).
625 John McMillian, *Smoking Typewriters: The Sixties Underground Press and the Rise of Alternative Media in America* (New York: Oxford University Press, 2011), 128.
626 Timothy Leary, *The Politics of Ecstasy* (London: Paladin, 1970 [1968]), 38.
627 Theodore Roszak, *Sources* (New York: Harper Colophon Books, 1972), 40.
628 Robert C. Cottrell, *Sex, Drugs, and Rock 'n' Roll: the Rise of America's 1960s Counterculture* (Lanham: Rowman & Littlefield, 2015), ix.
629 John Mann (ed.), *The First Book of Sacraments of the Church of the Tree of Life* (San Francisco: Tree of Life Press, 1972), 4.
630 Michael Traugot, 'The Farm.' In William Zellner and Marc Petrowsky (eds), *Sects, Cults, and Spiritual Communities: A Sociological Analysis* (Westport: Praeger, 1998), 48.
631 See Gabriel Patrick Morley, 'Tripping with Stephen Gaskin: An Exploration of an Adult Hippie Educator', doctoral dissertation, University of Southern Mississippi, 2012, 106–107.
632 'I've been a spiritual teacher for about five years now. The way it worked out is that I was just talking to folks, folks asking me about Spirit, and maybe about tripping, and in time I found that I was doing the job of the parish priest ... Upon researching that question, I found out that spiritual teachers are where you find them, and if that's what I seemed to be doing ... I should do it. I know about kundalini yoga and chakras, and energy and telepathy and astral projection and mind-reading and all that kind of stuff.' Steven Gaskin, *The Caravan* (New York: Random House/The Foundation, 1972), 152–153.
633 See Stephen Gaskin, *Monday Night Class* (San Francisco: Book Publishing Company, 2005).
634 Traugot, 'The Farm', 42.
635 Stephen Gaskin, in Arthur Versluis and Morgan Shipley, 'Stephen Gaskin Interview', *Journal for the Study of Radicalism* 4.1 (2010), 147.
636 See Gaskin, *Caravan*.
637 Stephen Gaskin, in Versluis and Shipley, 'Stephen Gaskin Interview', 149.
638 Jim Windolf, 'Sex, Drugs, and Soybeans', *Vanity Fair* (5 April 2007): https://www.vanityfair.com/news/2007/05/thefarm200705 (accessed 17 August 2023).

639 Morley, 'Tripping with Stephen Gaskin, ii.
640 Gaskin, *Monday Night Class*, 118.
641 Robert Wuthnow, *After Heaven: Spirituality in America Since the 1950s* (Berkeley: University of California Press, 1998), 53; see also Robert Wuthnow, *Experimentation in American Religion* (Berkeley: University of California Press, 1978).
642 Versluis and Shipley, 'Stephen Gaskin Interview', 142.
643 Stephen Gaskin, *This Season's People: A Book of Spiritual Teachings* (Summertown: Book Publishing Company, 1976), 165. See Wuthnow, *Experimentation*, 157–160.
644 Stephen Gaskin, *Amazing Dope Tales and Haight Street Flashbacks* (Summertown: Book Publishing Company, 1980), 15.
645 Ibid., 13.
646 Maslow, *Religion, Values, and Peak Experiences*.
647 Wuthnow, *Experimentation*, 112.
648 Ibid., 114.
649 Animism is a notoriously slippery term. For a good introduction to the subject, see Graham Harvey (ed.), *The Handbook of Contemporary Animism* (London: Routledge, 2014).
650 Stephen Gaskin, *Cannabis Spirituality* (Los Angeles: High Times Press, 1996), 74.
651 Traugot, 'The Farm', 48.
652 Gaskin, *Cannabis Spirituality*, 40.
653 Gaskin, *Caravan*, 103.
654 Gaskin, *Amazing Dope Tales*, 62 (original emphasis).
655 Gaskin, *Caravan*, 7.
656 Gaskin, *Amazing Dope Tales*, 45.
657 Gaskin, *Caravan*, 15.
658 Gaskin, *Cannabis Spirituality*, 30–31.
659 Stephen Gaskin, *Volume One: Sunday Morning Services on The Farm* (Summertown: Book Publishing Company, 1977), 21.
660 Traugot, 'The Farm', 48.
661 See Laurie Cozad, *God on High: Religion, Cannabis, and the Quest for Legitimacy* (Lanham: Lexington Books, 2018), 21–22.
662 Walter Tucker, quoted in Dan Leohndorf, 'The Beliefs of the Church of the Universe', *Cannabis Culture* (1 June 1997): https://www.cannabisculture.com/content/1997/06/01/1227/ (accessed 18 August 2023).
663 Andrew Dreschel, 'Baldasaro Was King of the Political Fringe', *The Hamilton Spectator* (9 June 2016): https://www.thespec.com/opinion/columnists/dreschel-baldasaro-was-king-of-the-political-fringe/article_721d4a11-f5c2-523d-ae50-5e5b14391ea4.html (accessed 19 August 2023).
664 Ibid.
665 Ibid.
666 Walter Tucker, quoted in Leohndorf, 'Beliefs of the Church of the Universe',.
667 Walter Tucker, quoted in ibid.
668 Walter Tucker, quoted in ibid.
669 Church of the Universe, 'About This Group': https://www.facebook.com/groups/Church.ot.Universe/about (accessed 18 August 2023).
670 Church of the Universe, 'Sacraments and Terminologies': https://iamm-sab.tripod.com/id11.html (accessed 19 August 2023).
671 Church of Cognizance, 'Church of Cognizance': http://haoma.org/wiki/tiki-index.php?page=Church+Of+Cognizance (accessed 20 August 2023).

672 Ibid.
673 Ibid.
674 Ibid.
675 Bennett, *Cannabis and the Soma Solution*; Bennett, 'Magical and Ceremonial', 39–51.
676 For a useful overview of the evidence and the debates, see Dieter Taillieu, 'Haoma: Botany'. In Ehsan Yarshater (ed.), *Encyclopædia Iranica*, Vol. 11 (New York: Encyclopædia Iranica Foundation, 2012), https://www.iranicaonline.org/articles/haoma-i (accessed 6 November 2023).
677 Henry Olcott, *The Spirit of the Zoroastrian Religion* (Bombay: 'published by public subscription', 1882), 27.
678 Danuel Quaintance, 'In Loving Memory of Mary Helen Quaintance': http://haoma.org (accessed 20 August 2023).
679 Danuel Quaintance, quoted in Stephanie Innes, 'With Its 2 Founder Serving Time, Church of Pot is Devastated', *Arizona Daily Star* (9 September 2009).
680 Danuel Quaintance, quoted in ibid.
681 Danuel Quaintance, quoted in Cozad, *God on High*, 36.
682 Temple 420, 'Salvation is For You Too!': https://www.temple420kansascity.org/salvation (accessed 21 August 2023). Click on the section entitled 'Popular Questions'.
683 Temple 420, 'About Us': https://www.temple420kansascity.org (accessed 21 August 2023).
684 Temple 420, 'Salvation is For You Too!'
685 Craig X Rubin, quoted in David Critchell, 'Showtime's Mr. Bong', *GQ* (11 July 2006): https://www.gq.com/story/craig-x-rubin-weeds-mary-louise-parker (accessed 21 August 2023).
686 Craig X Rubin, 'Reverend of Temple 420 Plans to Use Religious Defense', *Cannabis Culture* (16 December 2006): https://www.cannabisculture.com/content/2006/12/16/4877/ (accessed 21 August 2023).
687 Wuthnow, *Experimentation*, 78–114.
688 Rubin, 'Reverend of Temple 420'.
689 Elissa Einhorn, 'Meet the Waldos: the True Story of the Marin Stoners Who Coined "420"', *The Jewish News of North California* (19 April 2018): https://jweekly.com/2018/04/19/meet-waldos-true-story-marin-stoners-coined-420/ (accessed 6 September 2023).
690 The Waldos, quoted in Steven Hager, '420 or Fight', *High Times* (December 1998), 12.
691 Chris Goldstein, 'The Original Flier That Sparked the 420 Phenomenon', *Freedom Leaf* (15 April 2016): https://www.freedomleaf.com/420-flyer/ (accessed 6 September 2023).
692 Hager, '420 or Fight', 12.
693 Goldstein, 'Original Flier'.
694 Ibid.
695 Partridge, *Re-Enchantment of the West*, Vol. 2, 6–22.
696 Linda Woodhead and Paul Heelas, 'Spiritualities of Life: Introduction'. In Linda Woodhead and Paul Heelas (eds), *Religion in Modern Times: An Interpretative Anthology* (Oxford: Blackwell, 2000), 110.
697 See Paul Heelas, 'The Spiritual Revolution: From "Religion" to "Spirituality"'. In Linda Woodhead, Paul Fletcher, Hiroko Kawanami, and David Smith (eds), *Religions in the Modern World*, first edition (London: Routledge, 2002), 366–369.
698 Dussault, *Ganja Yoga*, 56.

699 Ibid., 2 (original emphasis).
700 Ibid., 26–27.
701 Ibid., 83 (original emphasis).
702 Chaitanya, 'Sacramental High.'
703 Jacob Miguel Vigil, Sarah S. Stith, and Tiphanie Chanel, 'Cannabis Consumption and Prosociality', *Scientific Reports* 12: 8352 (2022): https://www.nature.com/articles/s41598-022-12202-8 (accessed 7 September 2023).
704 Chaitanya, 'Sacramental High'.
705 Benjamin, *On Hashish*.
706 Michel Foucault, 'Of Other Spaces', *Diacritics* 16 (1986), 24.
707 Ibid.
708 Aldous Huxley, *The Doors of Perception; Heaven and Hell* (London: Flamingo, 1994).
709 James Lewis, *Legitimating New Religions* (New Brunswick: Rutgers University Press, 2003), 11.
710 Ibid., 143.

Bibliography

Abdel-Salam, O.M.E., A.F. Galal, S.A. ElShebiney, and A.E.D.M. Gaafar, 'International Aspects of Cannabis Use and Misuse: Egypt'. In Victor Preedy (ed.), *Handbook of Cannabis and Related Pathologies: Biology, Pharmacology, Diagnosis, and Treatment* (London: Academic Press, 2017), 110–121.
Abel, Ernest, *Marijuana: The First Twelve Thousand Years* (New York: Springer, 1980).
Abrams, Donald and Manuel Guzmán, 'Can Cannabis Cure Cancer?' *Journal of the American Medical Association: Oncology* (16 January 2020): https://realmofcaring.org/wp-content/uploads/2020/11/Can-Cannabis-Cure-Cancer.pdf (accessed 29 September 2021).
Abrams, Stephen, 'Soma, the Wootton Report and cannabis law reform in Britain during the 1960s and 1970s'. In Sharon Rödner Sznitman, Börje Olsson, and Robin Room (eds), *A Cannabis Reader: Global Issues and Local Experiences* (Lisbon: European Monitoring Centre for Drugs and Drug Addiction, 2008), 39–49.
Adams, Roger, 'Marihuana—Harvey Lecture, February 19, 1942', *Bulletin of the New York Academy of Medicine* (1942), 705–730.
Adams, Roger, Madison Hunt, and J. H. Clark, 'Structure of Cannabidiol, a Product Isolated from the Marihuana Extract of Minnesota Wild Hemp. I', *Journal of the American Chemical Society* 62 (1940), 196–200.
Adams, Stephen, 'Scans Show Drug's Impact on Brain, a Top Doctor Warns of a Psychosis, Paranoid Delusions and a Superskunk Schizophrenia Timebomb', *Mail Online* (24 March 2018): https://www.dailymail.co.uk/health/article-5539941/Top-doctor-warns-psychosis-paranoid-delusions-superskunk-schizophrenia-timebomb.html (accessed 12 October 2021).
Advisory Committee on Drug Dependence, *Cannabis* (London: Her Majesty's Stationary Office, 1968).
Afari, Yasus, *Eye Pen: Philosophical Reasoning and Poetry* (Kingston: House of Honour Publishing and Senya-Cum, 2008).
Afari, Yasus, *Overstanding Rastafari* (Knockpatrick: Senya-Cum, 2007).
Aggrawal, Anil, *APC Forensic Medicine and Toxicology for Homeopathy* (New Dehli: Avichal Publishing Company, 2014).
Albright, Thomas and Charles Perry, 'The Last Twelve Hours of the Whole Earth', *Rolling Stone* 86 (8 July 1971), 1, 6.
Aldrich, Michael, 'The Remarkable W.B. O'Shaughnessy', *O'Shaughnessy's: The Journal of Cannabis in Clinical Practice* (Spring 2006), 26–27.
Alexander, Jeffrey, *The Civil Sphere* (New York: Oxford University Press, 2006).
Alexander, Jeffrey, *The Meanings of Social Life: A Cultural Sociology* (New York: Oxford University Press, 2003).
Alford, Norman, *The Rhymers' Club: Poets of the Tragic Generation* (Houndmills: Macmillan, 1994).
Amdur, M.K. and E. Messinger, 'Jean-Etienne-Dominique Esquirol: His Work and Importance for Modern Psychiatry', *American Journal of Psychiatry* 96.1 (1939), 129–135.

American Cancer Society, 'Marijuana and Cancer': https://www.cancer.org/content/dam/CRC/PDF/Public/8247.00.pdf (accessed 6 January 2020)
Amsterdam, Jan van and Wim van den Brink, 'Ranking of Drugs: A More Balanced Risk-assessment', *The Lancet* 376.9752 (2010), 1524–1525.
Amsterdam, Jan van, David Nutt, Lawrence Phillips, and Wim van den Brink, 'European Rating of Drug Harms', *Journal of Psychopharmacology* 29.6 (2015), 655–660.
Anderson, J.A., 'Alcohol', *The Pacific Theosophist* 5.4 (November 1894), 49.
Andrews, George and Simon Vinkenoog (eds), *The Book of Grass: An Anthology of Indian Hemp* (Harmondsworth: Penguin, 1972).
Anonymous, 'Abstract of the Proceedings of the Académie de Médicine, Paris: Cholera', *Provincial Medical and Surgical Journal* 13.14 (1849), 389.
Anonymous, 'Ban on Hashish Blocked Despite Ravages of Drug', *Chicago Daily Tribune* (3 June 1927), 20.
Anonymous, 'Dr Raphael Mechoulam and His Revolutionary Research', *Health Europa Quarterly* 10 (2019), 28–31.
Anonymous, 'Dream Slayer Talks in Cell', *Tampa Daily Times* (18 October 1933), 1.
Anonymous, 'Hasheesh and its Smokers and Eaters', *Scientific American* 14.7 (23 October 1858), 49.
Anonymous, 'Herbert Breakenridge the "Axe" Murderer is Sentenced to Death', *Kingston Daily Gleaner* (17 May 1929), 21.
Anonymous, 'History of Cannabis', BBC, *Panorama*: http://news.bbc.co.uk/1/hi/programmes/panorama/1632726.stm (accessed 21 July 2021)
Anonymous, 'Jive Girls Victims of Drug Racket', *The People* (19 November 1950), 5.
Anonymous, 'Marihuana Makes Fiends of Boys in 30 Days: Hashish Goads Users to Blood Lust', *San Francisco Examiner* (January 31, 1923), 11.
Anonymous, 'Marihuana Menaces Youth', *Scientific American* 154.3 (March 1936), 151.
Anonymous, 'Marijuana Industry is Thriving in City. Children are Addicts', *New Orleans Tribune* (18 October 1926), 1.
Anonymous, 'Mexican Family Go Insane. Five Said to Have Been Stricken by Eating Marihuana', *The New York Times* (6 July 1927), 10.
Anonymous, 'Mr Burroughs in Morocco', *Chemist and Druggist* (16 April 1892), 569.
Anonymous, 'Mr Wilkie Collins and "Precipitations"', *Supplement to The Theosophist* 10 (October 1888), xxx.
Anonymous, 'New Remedy for Tetanus and Other Convulsive Disorders, by W.B. O'Shaughnessy, MD, Calcutta', *The Lancet* 34 (1840), 539–541.
Anonymous, 'Terror! Just a Cigarette, You'd Think, but it was Made from a Sinister Weed and an Innocent Girl Falls Victim to This', *The Daily Mirror* (25 July 1939), 12.
Anonymous, 'The Effects of Marijuana on Consciousness'. In Charles Tart (ed.), *Altered States of Consciousness* (New York: Anchor Books, 1972), 343–364.
Anonymous, 'The Psychic Effects of Hasheesh', *The Two Worlds* 3.114 (January 17, 1890), 112.
Anonymous, 'This Dangerous Man Must be Stopped', *News of the World* (7 July 1968), 1.
Anonymous, 'Woman, 68, Avoids Jail for Growing Cannabis', *The Guardian* (7 March 2007).
Anonymous, *Spiritualism versus Satanism* (London: J. Burns, 1871).
Anslinger, Harry J., 'Marihuana Tax Act (1937): Statement of H. J. Anslinger, Commissioner of Narcotics, Bureau of Narcotics, Department of the Treasury': http://www.druglibrary.org/schaffer/hemp/taxact/taxact.htm (accessed 29 March 2016).
Anslinger, Harry J. and Courtney Cooper, 'Marijuana: Assassin of Youth', *American Magazine* 124 no.1 (July 1937), 18–19, 150–153. Reprinted in James A. Inciardi and

Karen McElrath (eds), *The American Drug Scene: An Anthology*, fifth edition (New York: Oxford University Press, 2008), 108–113.
Anslinger, Harry J. and Will Oursler, *The Murderers: The Story of the Narcotic Gangs* (New York: Farrar, Straus, and Cudahy, 1961).
Anslinger, Harry J., *The Traffic in Narcotics* (New York: Funk and Wagnalls, 1953).
Appendino, Giovanni, 'The Early History of Cannabinoid Research', *Rendiconti Lincei. Scienze Fisiche e Naturali* 31 (2020), 919–929.
Arikha, Noga, *Passions and Tempers: A History of the Humours* (New York: Ecco, 2007).
Arlington, Kim, 'NSW Government's Stoner Sloth Anti-marijuana Campaign Cost Taxpayers $350,000', *Sydney Morning Herald* (19 February 2016): https://www.smh.com.au/national/nsw/nsw-governments-stoner-sloth-antimarijuana-campaign-cost-taxpayers-350000-20160218-gmxd8p.html (accessed 25 June 2023).
Armstrong, William and John Parascandola, 'The American Concern Over Marihuana in the 1930s', *Pharmacy in History* 14.1 (1972), 25–35.
Arveiller, Jacques, 'Hachich, romantisme et voyage initiatique', *L'Information psychiatrique* 66.5 (1990), 493–504.
Arveiller, Jacques, 'Le Cannabis en France au xixe siècle: une histoire médicale', *L'Évolution Psychiatrique* 78.3 (2013), 451–484.
Asheri, David, Alan Lloyd, and Aldo Corcella, *A Commentary on Herodotus Books I-IV* (Oxford: Oxford University Press, 2007).
Aubert-Roche, Louis Rémy, *De la peste, ou, typhus d'Orient, documents et observations recueillies pendant les années 1834 à 1838, en Egypte, en Arabie, sur la Mer-Rouge, en Abyssinie, a Smyrne et à Constantinople, suivis d'un essai sur le Hachisch et son emploi dans le traitement de la peste* (Paris: Rouvier, 1843).
Aubert-Roche, Louis Rémy, *Rapport sur le choléra dans l'isthme de Suez Du 1er juin 1808 au 1er Juin 1869* (Paris: Chaix, 1869).
Aubert-Roche, Louis-Rémy, *De la peste ou typhus d'Orient: Documens et observations recueillis pendant les années 1834 à 1838, en Egypte, en Arabie, sur la Mer Rouge, en Abyssinie à Smyrne et à Constantinople* (Paris: Just Rouvier, 1840).
Baker, Joe, 'Flying High: What Will the Future of Cannabis-infused Drinks Look Like?' *Drinks Insight Network* (14 March 2019): https://www.drinks-insight-network.com/features/cannabis-infused-drinks/ (accessed 18 April 2022).
Ball, Benjamin, 'Hallucinations de la vue et de l'ouïe. Intermittence. Traitement par le haschisch. Guérison', *Gazette des hôpitaux civils et militaires* 29.90 (1856), 359–360.
Banks, Jamie, 'Cannabis, Race, and Mental Illness in Britain, 1980–1993', *Historical Transactions* (4 July 2021): https://blog.royalhistsoc.org/2021/07/04/cannabis-race-and-mental-illness-in-britain-1980-1993/ (accessed 27 June 2022).
Barberet, John, '"Un mets nouveau": Hashish and hashish Narratives in Nineteenth-Century Paris'. In Henry Freeman (ed.), *Beginnings in French Literature* (Amsterdam: Rodopi, 2002), 79–90.
Bare, John, 'Laurens Perseus Hickok: Philosopher, Theologian, and Psychologist'. In Gregory Kimble and Michael Wertheimer (eds), *Portraits of Pioneers in Psychology*, Vol. 3 (Washington: American Psychological Association, 1998).
Barrett, Leonard, *The Rastafarians* (Boston: Beacon Press, 1997).
Bascom, John, 'Laurens Perseus Hickok', *The American Journal of Psychology* 19.3 (1908), 359–373.
Bates, Albert, 'The Farm'. In Timothy Miller (ed.), *Spiritual and Visionary Communities: Out to Save the World* (Abingdon: Routledge, 2016), 212–138.

Baudelaire, Charles, 'Wine and Hashish: Compared as Means for the Multiplication of Personality'. In Charles Baudelaire and Théophile Gautier, *Hashish, Wine, Opium*. Trans. by Maurice Strang (London: Calder and Boyars, 1972), 65–92.

Baudelaire, Charles, *Artificial Paradises*. Trans. by Stacy Diamond (New York: Citadel Press, 1996).

Bauer, Alexander, 'Life is Too Short for Faint-Heartedness: The Archaeology of Andrew Sherratt', *Journal of World Prehistory* 24 (2011), 99–105.

Bauman, Zygmunt, 'Durkheim's Society Revisited'. In Jeffrey C. Alexander and Philip Smith (eds), *The Cambridge Companion to Durkheim* (Cambridge: Cambridge University Press, 2005), 360–382.

Becker, Howard, *Becoming a Marihuana User* (Chicago: Chicago University Press, 2015).

Becker, Howard, *Outsiders: Studies in the Sociology of Deviance* (New York: The Free Press, 1963).

Bello, Joan, 'The Physical, Psychological, and Spiritual Benefits of Marijuana'. In Thomas Lyttle (ed.), *Psychedelics Reimagined* (New York: Autonomedia, 1999), 41–64.

Ben-Shabat, Shimon, Ester Fride, Tzviel Sheskin, Tsippy Tamiri, Man-Hee Rhee, and Zvi Vogel, 'An Entourage Effect: Inactive Endogenous Fatty Acid Glycerol Esters Enhance 2-arachidonoyl-glycerol Cannabinoid Activity', *European Journal of Pharmacology* 353 (1998), 23–31.

Benet, Sula, 'Early Diffusion and Folk Uses of Hemp'. In Vera Rubin (ed.), *Cannabis and Culture* (The Hague: Mouton Publishers, 1975), 39–49.

Benjamin, Walter, *On Hashish*. Edited by Howard Eiland (Cambridge: Harvard University Press, 2006).

Benjamin, Walter, *One-Way Street and Other Writings* (London: New Left Books, 1979).

Benjamin, Walter, *Reflections: Essays, Aphorisms, Autobiographical Writings*. Trans. by Edmund Jephcott (New York: Harcourt Brace Jovanovich, 1978).

Benjamin, Walter, *Reflections*. Edited by Peter Demetz. Trans. by Edmund Jephcott (New York: Harcourt, Brace, Jovanovich, 1978).

Benjamin, Walter, *The Work of Art in the Age of Its technical Reproducibility, and Other Writings on Media*. Edited by Michael Jennings, Brigid Doherty, and Thomas Levin (Cambridge: Harvard University Press, 2008).

Benjamin, Walter, 'A Small History of Photography'. In Walter Benjamin, *On Photography*. Trans. by Esther Leslie (London: Reaktion Books, 2015), 59–108.

Bennett, Bradley, 'Doctrine of Signatures: An Explanation of Medicinal Plant Discovery or Dissemination of Knowledge?' *Economic Botany* 61 (2007), 246–255.

Bennett, Chris, 'Early/Ancient History'. In Julie Holland (ed.), *The Pot Book: A Complete Guide to Cannabis. Its Role in Medicine, Politics, Science, and Culture* (Rochester: Park Street Press, 2010), 17–26.

Bennett, Chris, 'Marijuana and the Goddess', *Zen Zion Coptic Orthodox Church* (1 September 1998): https://zzco.org/chris_bennett/goddess.html (accessed 23 July 2023).

Bennett, Chris, 'The Incredible, Delectable, Miracle of 19th Century Medicine: Hasheesh Candy!' *Cannabis Culture* (7 February 2013): http://www.cannabisculture.com/content/2013/02/07/incredible-delectable-miracle-19th-century-medicine-hasheesh-candy (accessed 22 July 2021).

Bennett, Chris, 'The Magical and Ceremonial Use of Cannabis in the Ancient World'. In Harold Ellens (ed.), *Seeking the Sacred with Psychoactive Substances: Chemical Paths to Spirituality and to God*. Vol. 1 (Santa Barbara: ABC-CLIO, 2014), 23–56.

Bennett, Chris, 'The Mother Plant of the Goddess—Cannabis', *Cannabis Culture* (31 May 2019): https://www.cannabisculture.com/content/2019/05/31/the-mother-plant-of-the-goddess-cannabis/ (accessed 24 July 2023);

Bennett, Chris, 'Venerable Traditions: A Brief History of the Ritual and Religious Use of Cannabis'. In Stephen Gray (ed.), *Cannabis and Spirituality: An Explorer's Guide to an Ancient Plant Spirit Ally* (Rochester: Park Street Press, 2017), 38–58.

Bennett, Chris, 'Was Jesus a Stoner?', *High Times* (1 February 2003), 68–71.

Bennett, Chris, *Cannabis and the Soma Solution* (Walterville: TrineDay, 2010).

Bennett, Chris, *Cannabis: Lost Sacrament of the Ancient World* (Walterville: TrineDay, 2023).

Bennett, Chris, *Liber 420: Cannabis, Magickal Herbs and the Occult* (Walterville: TrineDay, 2018).

Bennett, Chris, Lynn Osburn, and Judy Osburn, *Green Gold and the Tree of Life: Marijuana in Magic and Religion* (Frazier Park: Access Unlimited, 1995).

Berger, Meyer, 'Tea for a Viper', *The New Yorker* (12 March 1938), 36–37.

Berke, Joseph and Calvin Hernton, *The Cannabis Experience: An Interpretative Study of the Effects of Marijuana and Hashish* (London: Quartet Books, 1977).

Bern, Paul, *Cannabis Legalization and the Bible: Compatible or Not?* (Atlanta: Progressive Christian Ministries of Greater Atlanta, 2016).

Berridge, Virginia, 'Queen Victoria's Cannabis Use: Or, How History Does and Does Not Get Used in Drug Policy Making', *Addiction Research and Theory* 11.4 (2003), 213–215.

Berridge, Virginia, 'The Origins of the English Drug "Scene," 1890-1930', *Medical History* 32.1 (1988), 51–64.

Berthault, Edouard, *Du Haschisch, son Histoire, ses Effets Physiologiques et Thérapeutiques*. Thèse pour le Doctorat en Médecine, Faculté de Médecine de Paris, No 258 (Paris: Imprimerie de Rignoux, 1854).

Berthier, Pierre, 'Essais sur les propriétés hypnotiques du hachisch dans les maladies mentales', *Journal de Médicine Mentale* 8 (1868), 432–436.

Besant, Annie, *The Influence of Alcohol* (Adyar: Theosophical Publishing House 1892).

Best, Joel, *Threatened Children: Rhetoric and Concern about Child-Victims* (Chicago: Chicago University Press, 1990).

Bey, Hakim and Abel Zug (eds), *Orgies of the Hemp Eaters: Five Hundred Years of Cannabis Cuisine, Slang, Ritual, Literature* (New York: Autonomedia, 2004).

Bibra, Ernst Freiherr von, *Pant Intoxicants*. Trans. by Hedwig Schleiffer (Rochester: Healing Arts Press, 1995).

Bienenstock, David, 'Psychiatrist Lester Grinspoon Smoked Pot with Carl Sagan—A Lot', *Vice* (29 October 2013): https://www.vice.com/en/article/9ak93p/psychiatrist-lester-grinspoon-smoked-weed-with-carl-sagana-lot#:~:text=I%20do%20not%20consider%20myself,surroundings%2C%20both%20animate%20and%20inanimate (accessed 7 September 2023).

Bienenstock, David, 'The Anointed One: Did Jesus Perform His Miracles with Cannabis Oil?' *Vice* (12 December 2013): https://www.vice.com/en/article/bn5z7v/did-jesus-perform-his-miracles-with-cannabis-oil (accessed 03 August 2023).

Bilby, Kenneth, 'The Holy Herb: Notes on the Background of Cannabis in Jamaica'. In Rex Nettleford (ed.), *Caribbean Quarterly Monograph: Rastafari* (Kingston: University of the West Indies, 1985), 82–95.

Bivins, Jason, *Religion of Fear* (New York: Oxford University Press, 2008).

Black, Winifred, *Dope: The Story of the Living Dead* (New York: Star Company, 1928).

Blackman, Shane, '"See Emily Play": Youth Culture, Recreational Drug Use and Normalization', in Mark Simpson, Tracy Shildrick, and Robert MacDonald (eds),

Drugs in Britain: Supply, Consumption and Control (London: Palgrave Macmillan, 2007), 39–59.

Blackman, Shane, *Chilling Out: The Cultural Politics of Substance Consumption, Youth and Drug Policy* (Maidenhead: Open University Press, 2004).

Blair, William, 'An Opium Eater in America', *The Knickerbocker; or, New York Monthly Magazine* (July 1842), 47–57.

Blaskiewicz, Robert, 'The Big Pharma Conspiracy Theory', *Medical Writing* 22.4 (2013), 259–261.

Blavatsky, Helena P., 'Another Distinguished Fellow', *The Theosophist* 2.5 (February 1881), 104.

Blavatsky, Helena P., *Collected Writings*, 15 vols. Edited by Boris de Zirkoff (Wheaton: Theosophical Publishing House, 1950).

Blavatsky, Helena P., *Isis Unveiled: A Master-Key to the Mysteries of Ancient and Modern Science and Theology*, 2 vols (Cambridge: Cambridge University Press, 2012).

Blavatsky, Helena P., *Secret Instructions to Probators of an Esoteric Occult School* (Pomeroy: Health Research, 1969).

Blavatsky, Helena P., *The Secret Doctrine: The Synthesis of Science, Religion, and Philosophy*, 3 vols (Cambridge: Cambridge University Press, 2011).

Blenkinsopp, Joseph, *Ezekiel* (Louisville: John Knox Press, 1990).

Bloch, Ernst, 'Protocol of the Same Experiment'. Trans. by Howard Eiland. In Walter Benjamin, *On Hashish*. Edited by Howard Eiland (Cambridge: Harvard University Press, 2006), 30–32.

Bloch, Ernst, *The Principle of Hope*, Vol. 1. Trans. by Neville Plaice, Stephen Plaice, and Paul Knight (Cambridge: MIT Press, 1986).

Bogousslavsky, Julien and Thierry Moulin, 'From Alienism to the Birth of Modern Psychiatry: A Neurological Story?' *European Neurology* 62 (2009), 257–263.

Bonnie, Richard J. and Charles H. Whitebread II, 'The Forbidden Fruit and the Tree of Knowledge: An Inquiry into the Legal History of American Marijuana Prohibition', *Virginia Law Review* 56.6 (1971), 971–1169.

Bonnie, Richard and Charles Whitebread II, *The Marijuana Conviction: A History of Marijuana Prohibition in the United States* (New York: The Lindesmith Center, 1999).

Boon, Marcus, *The Road of Excess: A History of Writing on Drugs* (Cambridge: Harvard University Press, 2002).

Booth, Martin, *A Magick Life: A Biography of Aleister Crowley* (London: Hodder & Stoughton, 2000).

Boothroyd, Dave, *Culture on Drugs: Narco-cultural Studies of High Modernity* (Manchester: Manchester University Press, 2006).

Borougerdi, Bradley, 'The Cult of O'Shaughnessy', *Points* (24 July 2014): https://pointshistory.com/2014/07/24/the-cult-of-oshaughnessy/ (accessed 21 August 2021).

Borougerdi, Bradley, *Commodifying Cannabis: A Cultural History of a Complex Plant in the Atlantic World* (Lanham: Lexington Books, 2018).

Bourdieu, Pierre, *Distinction: A Social Critique of the Judgement of Taste*. Trans. by Richard Nice (Cambridge: Harvard University Press, 1984).

Bowes, Amelia, 'Cannabis in Conservative Christian Communities', *Natural Care* (6 September 2018): https://naturalcaregroup.com/cannabis-in-conservative-christian-communities/ (accessed 10 July 2023).

Boyer, Pascal, *Explaining Religion: The Evolutionary Origins of Religious Thought* (New York: Basic Books, 2001).

Bozza, Anthony and Shawn Dahl (eds), *Rolling Stone Raves* (New York: Rolling Stone Press, 1999).
Brand, Joseph and Zhongzhen Zhao, 'Cannabis in Chinese Medicine: Are Some Traditional Indications Referenced in Ancient Literature Related to Cannabinoids?' *Frontiers in Pharmacology* (10 March 2017): https://www.frontiersin.org/articles/10.3389/fphar.2017.00108/full (accessed 13 March 2021).
Brenan, Megan, '14% of Americans Say They Use CBD Products', *Gallup News* (7 August 2019): https://news.gallup.com/poll/263147/americans-say-cbd-products.aspx#:~:text=WASHINGTON%2C%20D.C.%20%2D%2D%20One%20in,this%20hemp%20form%20of%20cannabis (accessed 23 May 2023).
Brenan, Megan, 'Support for Legal Marijuana Inches Up to New High of 68%', *Gallup News* (9 November 2020): https://news.gallup.com/poll/323582/support-legal-marijuana-inches-new-high.aspx (accessed 20 August 2021).
Brent, James, 'Communication Using the Heart and Cannabis', *Society of Cannabis Clinicians* (28 May 2021): https://www.cannabisclinicians.org/2021/05/28/communication-using-the-heart-and-cannabis/ (accessed 16 July 2023).
Brevior, Thomas, *Reply to the Rev. John Jones, on Spiritualism as 'The Work of Demons'* (Holborn: Thomas Scott, 1872).
Bridge, J.A., 'Sir William Brooke O'Shaughnessy, M.D., F.R.S., F.R.C.S., F.S.A.: A Biographical Appreciation by an Electrical Engineer', *Notes and Records: The Royal Society Journal of the History of Science* 52 (1998), 103–120.
Bridgeman, Mary and Daniel Abazia, 'Medicinal Cannabis: History, Pharmacology, And Implications for the Acute Care Setting', *Pharmacy and Therapeutics* 42.3 (2017), 180–188.
Brière de Boismont, Alexandre, 'De l'influence de la civilisation sur le développement de la folie', *Annales d'hygiène publique et de médecine légale* 21.2 (1839), 241–295.
Brière de Boismont, Alexandre, *Des hallucinations ou histoire raisonnée des apparitions, des visions, des songes, de l'extase, du magnétisme et du somnambulisme* (Paris, Germer Baillière, 1845).
Brière de Boismont, Alexandre, *Hallucinations or the Rational History of Apparitions, Visions, Dreams, Ecstasy, Magnetism, and Somnambulism* (Philadelphia: Lindsay and Blakiston, 1853).
Brigham, Amariah, 'Du Hachisch et de l'Aliénation mentale, par J. Moreau (de Tours) medicine de l'hospice, de Bicetre, etc'. *American Journal of Insanity* 2 (1845–1846), 275–281.
Brinkley, Douglas, 'Hunter S. Thompson: The Art of Journalism I', *The Paris Review* 42.156 (2000), 42–75.
Britten, Emma Hardinge (ed.), *Ghost Land; Or Researches Into the Mysteries of Occult Spiritism* (Boston: self-published, 1876).
Britten, Emma Hardinge, *Art Magic, or, Mundane, Sub-Mundane, and Super-Mundane Spiritualism* (New York: self-published, 1876).
Britten, Emma Hardinge, *Modern American Spiritualism: A Twenty Years' Record of the Communion Between Earth and the World of Spirits* (New York: self-published, 1870).
Britten, Emma Hardinge, *On the Road or The Spiritual Investigator: A Complete Compendium of the Science, Religion, Ethics, and Various Methods of Investigating Spiritualism* (Melbourne: George Robertson, 1878).
Britto, Lena, *Marijuana Boom: The Rise and Fall of Colombia's First Drug Paradise* (Berkeley: University of California Press, 2020).
Broman, Clifford, Harold Neighbors, Jorge Delva, Myriam Torres, and James Jackson, 'Prevalence of Substance Use Disorders Among African Americans and Caribbean

Blacks in the National Survey of American Life', *American Journal of Public Health* 98.6 (2008), 1107–1114.

Brotteaux, Pascal, 'The Ancient Greeks'. In George Andrews and Simon Vinkenoog (eds), *The Book of Grass: An Anthology of Indian Hemp* (Harmondsworth: Penguin, 1972), 27–28.

Brotteaux, Pascal, *Hachich: Herbe de Folie et de Rêve* (Paris: Vega, 1934).

Brough, John, 'Soma and *Amanita muscaria*', *Bulletin of the School of Oriental and African Studies* 34 (1971), 331–362.

Broughton, Arthur, 'Hortus Eastensis'. In Bryan Edwards, *The History, Civil and Commercial, of the British West Indies*, Vol. 1 (London: John Stockdale, 1794), 473–494.

Brown, David (ed.), *Cannabis: The Genus Cannabis* (Amsterdam: Harwood Academic Publishers, 1998).

Brown, Francis, Samuel Driver, and Charles Briggs, *A Hebrew and English Lexicon of the Old Testament* (Oxford: Oxford University Press, 1906).

Brown, Jeff, 'Ritual and Religious Use of Ganja in Jamaica'. In Stephen Gray (ed.), *Cannabis and Spirituality: An Explorer's Guide to an Ancient Plant Spirit Ally* (Rochester: Park Street Press, 2017), 144–151.

Brown, Jeff, *Marijuana and the Bible*, second edition (Clermont: Createspace, 2012).

Brownlee, Nick, *Cannabis* (London: Sanctuary, 2002).

Brunner, Emil, *The Divine-human Encounter*. Trans Amandus Loos (Philadelphia: Westminster Press, 1943).

Brunner, Theodore, 'Marijuana in Ancient Greece and Rome: The Literary Evidence', *Bulletin of the History of Medicine* 47.4 (1973), 344–355

Burgess, Kaya, 'Church of England Blesses Medicinal Use of Marijuana', *The Times* (10 June 2019): https://www.thetimes.co.uk/article/church-of-england-blesses-medicinal-use-of-marijuana-9pfnfkr2r# (accessed 2 January 2020).

Burns, Dylan, 'Ancient Esoteric Traditions: Mystery, Revelation, Gnosis'. In Christopher Partridge (ed.), *The Occult World* (London: Routledge, 2015), 17–33.

Burton, Robert, *Anatomy of Melancholy*, ed. by Holbrook Jackson (New York: New York Review of Books, 2001); *The Anatomy of Melancholy* (London: B. Blake, 1621).

Busby, Matta, 'Prisons Should Trial Free Cannabis, Says UK's Former Chief Drug Adviser', *The Guardian* (27 February 2021): https://www.theguardian.com/society/2021/feb/27/prisons-should-trial-free-cannabis-says-former-top-drug-adviser (accessed 5 August 2023).

Bush, William D. and Jack DeWitt, 'Marihuana Maniac', *Inside Detective* (July 1938).

Butrica, James, 'The Medical Use of Cannabis Among the Greeks and Romans', *Journal of Cannabis Therapeutics* 2 (2002), 51–70.

Bynum, William, *Science and Practice of Medicine in the Nineteenth Century* (Cambridge: Cambridge University Press, 1994)

Cahagnet, Louis-Alphonse (ed.), *Abrégé des Merveilles du ciel et de l'enfer d'Emmanuel Swedenborg avec annotations et observations* (Paris: Germer-Baillière, 1848).

Cahagnet, Louis-Alphonse, *Sanctuaire du Spiritualisme* (Paris: Germer Baillière, 1850).

Cahagnet, Louis-Alphonse, *The Celestial Telegraph; or Secrets of the Life to Come, Revealed Through Magnetism*, 2 vols. (New York: J.S. Redfield, 1851).

Cahagnet, Louis-Alphonse, *The Sanctuary of Spiritualism; A Study of Human Soul, and of Its Relations with The Universe, Through Somnambulism and Ecstasy*. Trans. M. Flinders Pearson (London: George Peirce, 1851).

Cahagnet, Louis-Alphonse, 'Hashish Visions', *Spiritual Telegraph and Fireside Preacher* 8.36 (31 December 1859), 424–425.
Cahagnet, Louis-Alphonse, 'M. Cahagnet's Letter', *The Theosophist* 2.5 (February 1881), 105.
Cahagnet, Louis-Alphonse, 'Cosmogony and Anthropology: Or, Deity, Earth and Man Studied by Analogy', *The Theosophist* 2.6 (March 1881), 133–134.
Cahagnet, Louis-Alphonse, *Magnetic Magic: A Digest of the Practical Parts of the Masterpieces of L.A. Cahagnet*. Edited and trans. by Robert Fryar (privately published, 1898).
Campbell, James, 'Note on the Religion of Hemp', *Indian Hemp Drugs Commission*, Vol. 3: Appendices. Miscellaneous (Simla: Government Central Printing Office, 1894), 250–252.
Carlson, Eric, '*Cannabis indica* in Nineteenth-Century Psychiatry' *American Journal of Psychiatry* 131 (1974), 1004–1007.
Carney, Philip and Maurice Lipsedge, 'Psychosis After Cannabis Abuse', *British Medical Journal* 288 (1984), 1381.
Caroll, Lewis, *Alice's Adventures in Wonderland* (London: The Folio Society, 1961).
Castle, David, Robin Murray, and Deepak D'Souza (eds), *Marijuana and Madness*, second edition (Cambridge: Cambridge University Press, 2019).
Catholic Answers, 'Is It Wrong to Alter Your Mind for Fun?' *Catholic Answers Magazine* (17 February 2022): https://www.catholic.com/magazine/print-edition/is-it-wrong-to-alter-your-mind-for-fun (accessed 2 October 2023).
Cermak, Timmen, *Marijuana on my Mind: The Science and Mystique of Cannabis* (Cambridge: Cambridge University Press, 2022).
Chaitanya, Swami, 'A Sacramental High': https://swamiselect.com/a-sacramental-high/ (accessed 15 September 2023).
Chaitanya, Swami, 'Swami Chaitanya's Journey to Becoming Swami': https://swamiselect.com/swami-chaitanyas-journey/ (accessed 15 September 2023).
Chaitanya, Swami, 'Smoking a Joint Is a Journey', *Cannabis Now* (24 September 2023): https://cannabisnow.com/smoking-a-joint-is-a-journey/ (accessed 30 September 2023).
Chaliand, Gérard and Arnaud Blin, 'Zealots and Assassins'. In Gérard Chaliand and Arnaud Blin (eds), *The History of Terrorism: From Antiquity to ISIS* (Berkeley: University of California Press, 2016), 65–73.
Chambers, Robert, 'The Hashish', *Chamber's Edinburgh Journal* 9.256 (25 November 1848), 341–344.
Chapkis, Wendy and Richard Webb, *Dying to Get High: Marijuana as Medicine* (New York: New York University Press, 2008).
Chapman, Rob, *Psychedelia and Other Colours* (London: Faber & Faber, 2015).
Chasin, Alexandra, *Assassin of Youth: A Kaleidoscopic History of Harry J. Anslinger's War on Drugs* (Chicago: University of Chicago Press, 2016).
Chein, Isidor, Donald L. Gerard, Robert S. Lee, and Eva Rosenfeld, *The Road to H: Narcotics, Delinquency and Social Policy* (New York: Basic Books, 1964).
Chevannes, Barry, *Rastafari: Roots and Ideology* (Syracuse: Syracuse University Press, 1994).
Chopra, Gurbakhsh Singh, 'Man and Marijuana', *International Journal of the Addictions* 4.2 (1969), 215–247.
Christie, Roger, 'The Hawaii Cannabis THC Ministry'. In Stephen Gray (ed.), *Cannabis and Spirituality: An Explorer's Guide to an Ancient Plant Spirit Ally* (Rochester: Park Street Press, 2017), 207–214.

Christison, Alexander, 'On *Cannabis* indica, *Indian Hemp*', *The Annals and Magazine of Natural History, including Zoology, Botany, and Geology* 6 (1841), 483–493.
Christison, Alexander, 'On the Natural History, Action, and Uses of Indian Hemp', *Monthly Journal of Medical Science* 4.19 (1851): 26–45.
Church of Cognizance, 'Church of Cognizance': http://haoma.org/wiki/tiki-index.php?page=Church+Of+Cognizance (accessed 20 August 2023).
Church of the Universe, 'About This Group': https://www.facebook.com/groups/Church.ot.Universe/about (accessed 18 August 2023).
Church of the Universe, 'Sacraments and Terminologies': https://iamm-sab.tripod.com/id11.html (accessed 19 August 2023).
Cirone, Victor, 'Cannabis: Medicine or Poison?' *Everything Herbal* (23 January 2022): https://everythingherbal.ca/cannabis-medicine-or-poison/ (accessed 10 July 2023).
Clarke, Peter, *Black Paradise: The Rastafarian Movement*, Black Political Studies No.5 (San Bernardino: Borgo Press, 1994).
Clarke, Robert and Mark Merlin, *Cannabis: Evolution and Ethnobotany* (Berkeley: California University Press, 2013).
Clot, Antoine-Barthélémy, 'Quelques réflexions sur les éffets du Haschich', *L'Abeille Médicale* 1 (January 1848), 93–94.
Clot, Antoine-Barthélémy, *Derniers mots sur la non-contagion de la peste* (Paris: Victor Masson & Fils, 1866).
Cohen, Margaret, *Profane Illumination: Walter Benjamin and the Paris of Surrealist Revolution* (Berkeley: University of California Press, 1993).
Cohen, Stanley and Laurie Taylor, *Escape Attempts: The Theory and Practice of Resistance to Everyday Life* (London: Allen Lane, 1976).
Cohen, Stanley, *Folk Devils and Moral Panics*, third edition (London: Routledge, 2002).
Cole, Juan, *Napoleon's Egypt: Invading the Middle East* (New York: Palgrave Macmillan, 2008).
Coles, William, *Adam in Eden or Nature's Paradise* (London: J Streater, 1657).
Comitas, Lambros, 'Cannabis and Work in Jamaica: A Refutation of the Amotivational Syndrome', *Annals of the New York Academy of Sciences* 282.1 (1976), 24–32.
Comitas, Lambros, 'The Social Nexus of *Ganja* in Jamaica'. In Vera Rubin (ed.), *Cannabis and Culture* (The Hague: Mouton Publishers, 1975), 119–132.
Connor, Steve, 'Scientific Adviser Backs Sacked Drug "Tsar"', *Independent* (3 November 2009), https://www.independent.co.uk/news/science/scientific-adviser-backs-sacked-drug-tsar-1814041.html Accessed: 12 April 2020.
Cooke, Alexander M., 'Queen Victoria's Medical Household', *Medical History* 26 (1982), 307–320
Cooke, Mordecai, *The Seven Sisters of Sleep* (London: James Blackwood, 1860).
Coxall, Guy, Trev Coleman, and Steve Harrison, 'Cannabis and the Law: No Evidence, No Crime? A "Seed our Future Campaign" Report, October 2020': https://www.seedourfuture.co.uk/wp-content/uploads/sites/11/2020/10/Cannabis-and-the-Law-No-Evidence-No-Crime-MASTER-v1.3.pdf (accessed 28 September 2021).
Cozad, Laurie, *God on High: Religion, Cannabis, and the Quest for Legitimacy* (Lanham: Lexington Books, 2018).
Crabtree, Adam, 'Animal Magnetism and Mesmerism'. In Christopher Partridge (ed.), *The Occult World* (London: Routledge, 2015), 188–194.
Crabtree, Adam, *From Mesmer to Freud: Magnetic Sleep and the Roots of Psychological Healing* (New Haven: Yale University Press, 1993).

Craker, Lyle and Zoë Gardner, 'The Botany of Cannabis'. In Julie Holland (ed.), *The Pot Book: A Complete Guide to Cannabis. Its Role in Medicine, Politics, Science, and Culture* (Rochester: Park Street Press, 2010), 35-43.
Critchell, David, 'Showtime's Mr. Bong', *GQ* (11 July 2006): https://www.gq.com/story/craig-x-rubin-weeds-mary-louise-parker (accessed 21 August 2023).
Crockford, Susanna, 'From Spiritualist Magnetism to Spiritism: The Development of Spiritualism in France, 1840-1870'. In Christopher Moreman (ed.), *The Spiritualist Movement: Speaking with the Dead in America and Around the World* (Santa Barbara: Praeger, 2013), 129-144.
Croq, Marc-Antoine, 'History of Cannabis and the Endocannabinoid System', *Dialogues in Clinical Neuroscience* 22 (2020), 223-228.
Crosland, Maurice, 'From Prizes to Grants in the Support of Scientific Research in France in the Nineteenth Century: The Montyon Legacy', *Minerva* 17.3 (1979), 355-380.
Crowley, Aleister (writing under the pseudonym 'A New York Specialist'), 'The Great Drug Delusion', *The English Review* (June 1922), 571-576.
Crowley, Aleister, 'Cocaine', *The International* (October 1917), 291-294.
Crowley, Aleister, 'Liber XVIII: The Fountain of Hyacinth' (1921): http://hermetic.com/crowley/libers/lib93.html (accessed July 4, 2016).
Crowley, Aleister, 'The Psychology of Hashish', *The Equinox* 1.2 (1909), 31-89.
Crowley, Aleister, 'The Temple of Solomon the King (Book 1)', *The Equinox* 1.1 (1909), 141-230.
Crowley, Aleister, 'The Temple of Solomon the King (Book 4)', *The Equinox* 1.4 (1910), 43-118.
Crowley, Aleister, *Book of the Law* (York Beach: Red Wheel/Weiser, 1976).
Crowley, Aleister, *Magick: Liber ABA, Book 4* (York Beach: Samuel Weiser, 2000).
Crowley, Aleister, *Moonchild* (York Beach: Samuel Weiser, 1970).
Crowley, Aleister, *The Book of the Law* (York Beach: Red Wheel/Weiser, 1976).
Crowley, Aleister, *The Book of Thoth* (York Beach: Weiser, 1974).
Cruz, Nicky, *Run Baby Run* (Gainsville: Bridge-Logos Publishers, 1968).
Culpeper, Nicholas, *Culpeper's Complete Herbal, and English Physician Wherein Several Hundred Herbs, with a Display of their Medicinal and Occult Properties* (Manchester: J. Gleave & Son, 1826).
Cunliffe, Barry, *The Scythians: Nomad Warriors of the Steppe* (Oxford: Oxford University Press, 2019).
Curran, Valerie and Celia Morgan, 'Desired and Undesired Effects of Cannabis on the Human Mind and Psychological Well-being'. In Roger Pertwee (ed.), *Handbook of Cannabis* (Oxford: Oxford University Press, 2014), 647-660.
d'Assier, Adolph, *Posthumous Humanity: A Study of Phantoms*. Trans. by Henry S. Olcott (London: George Redway, 1887).
Daftary, Farhad, 'Ḥasan Ṣabbāḥ'. In Ehsan Yarshater (ed.), *Encyclopaedia Iranica*, Vol. 12, (New York: Encyclopaedia Iranica Foundation, 2004), 34-37.
Daftary, Farhad, *Ismailis in Medieval Muslim Societies* (London: I.B. Tauris, 2005).
Daftary, Farhad, *The Assassin Legends: Myths of the Isma'ilis* (London: I.B. Tauris, 1994).
Daftary, Farhad, *The Isma'ilis: Their History and Doctrines* (Cambridge: Cambridge University Press, 1990).
Dahab, Elizabeth, 'Théophile Gautier and the Orient', *CLCWeb: Comparative Literature and Culture* 1.4 (1999), 1-7: http://docs.lib.purdue.edu/cgi/viewcontent.cgi?article=1054andcontext=clcweb (accessed 15 April 2016).

Dash, Vaidya Bhagwan, *Materia Medica of Ayurveda: Based on Madanapala's Nighantu* (New Dehli: Health Harmony, 1991).
Davidson, Arthur, *Alexandre Dumas (père): His Life and Works* (Westminster: Archibald Constable & Co., 1902).
Davidson, Katey, 'Why Do We Need Endorphins?' *Healthline* (30 November 2021): https://www.healthline.com/health/endorphins (accessed 31 August 2022).
Davis, Stephen, *Bob Marley: Conquering Lion of Reggae* (London: Plexus, 1994).
Dawson, Warren, 'Studies in the Egyptian Medical Texts III', *Journal of Egyptian Archaeology* 20 (1934), 41–46.
Day, John, *Molech: A God of Human Sacrifice in the Old Testament* (Cambridge: Cambridge University Press, 1989).
De Quincey, Thomas, *Confessions of an English Opium-Eater and Other Writings* (Oxford: Oxford University Press, 2013).
De Witt, Thomas, *The Weed that Bewitches* (New York: National Temperance Society and Publication House, 1885).
Deacon, Hannah, 'Why I Campaign for Children Like my Son Alfie Dingley to be Able to Get Medical Cannabis', *British Medical Journal* (2019): https://www.bmj.com/content/365/bmj.l1921 (accessed 7 October 2021).
Dean, Mitchell and Daniel Zamora, *The Last Man Takes LSD: Foucault and the End of Revolution* (London: Verso, 2021).
DeCourtive, Edmond, *Haschish: Étude historique, chimique et physiologique* (Paris: Imprimerie d'Éduard Bautruche, 1848).
DeGrandpre, Richard, *The Cult of Pharmacology: How America Became the World's Most Troubled Drug Culture* (Durham: Duke University Press, 2006).
Della, Jamie, 'Cannabis: A Herbal Ally', *Jamie Della: Blogs* (7 April 2022): https://jamiedella.com/blog/cannabis-an-herbal-ally (accessed 12 July 2023).
Derbyshire, Madison, 'Higher Power: Church of England Backs Medicinal Cannabis', *Financial Times* (9 June 2019): https://www.ft.com/content/297f3234-88fa-11e9-97ea-05ac2431f453 (accessed 2 January 2020).
Desprez, Florian, 'Reply to the Attack on Spiritualism by the Archbishop of Toulouse', *The Spiritualist* (11 June 1875), 284–285.
Deveney, John Patrick, *Paschal Beverly Randolph: A Nineteenth-Century American Spiritualist, Rosicrucian and Sex Magician* (Albany: State University of New York Press, 1997).
Devereux, Paul, *The Long Trip: A Prehistory of Psychedelia* (Harmondsworth: Arkana, 1997).
Devine, Robert James, *The Assassin of Youth: Marihuana* (Findlay, Ohio: Fundamental Truth Publishers, 1937).
Devine, Robert James, *The Moloch of Marihuana* (Findlay, Ohio: Fundamental Truth Publishers, n.d.).
Devlin, Hannah, 'Smoking Skunk Cannabis Triples Risk of Serious Psychotic Episodes', *The Guardian* (16 February 2015): https://www.theguardian.com/society/2015/feb/16/skunk-cannabis-triples-risk-psychotic-episodes-study (accessed 26 September 2021).
Dodge, Edward, 'How Moses and the Israelites Used Cannabis', *Merry Jane* (15 November 2016): https://merryjane.com/news/bible-moses-israelites-cannabis (accessed 6 September 2023).
Doniger O'Flaherty, Wendy, 'The Post-Vedic History of the Soma Plant'. In R. Gordon Wasson (ed.), *Soma: Divine Mushroom of Immortality* (New York: Harcourt Brace, 1968), 95–147

Donoghue, Denis, *Irish Essays* (Cambridge: Cambridge University Press, 2011).
Douglas, Mary, *Purity and Danger: An Analysis of the Concept of Pollution and Taboo* (London: Routledge, 2002).
Dowbiggin, Ian, *Inheriting Madness: Professionalization and Psychiatric Knowledge in Nineteenth-Century France* (Berkeley: California University Press, 1991).
Dreschel, Andrew, 'Baldasaro Was King of the Political Fringe', *The Hamilton Spectator* (9 June 2016): https://www.thespec.com/opinion/columnists/dreschel-baldasaro-was-king-of-the-political-fringe/article_721d4a11-f5c2-523d-ae50-5e5b14391ea4.html (accessed 19 August 2023).
du Toit, Brian, 'Dagga: The History and Ethnographic Setting of *Cannabis Sativa* in Southern Africa'. In Vera Rubin (ed.), *Cannabis and Culture* (The Hague: Mouton Publishers, 1975), 81–116.
du Toit, Brian, 'Man and Cannabis in Africa: A Study of Diffusion', *African Economic History* 1 (1976), 17–35.
du Toit, Brian, *Cannabis in Africa. A Survey of Its Distribution in Africa, and a Study of Cannabis Use and Users in Multi-ethnic South Africa* (Rotterdam: A.A. Balkema, 1980).
Dufton, Emily, *Grass Roots: The Rise and Fall and Rise of Marijuana in America* New York: Basic Books, 2017).
Dulchinos, Donald, *Pioneer of Inner Space: The Life of Fitz Hugh Ludlow, Hasheesh Eater* (Brooklyn: Autonomedia, 1998).
Dumas, Alexandre, *The Count of Monte Cristo* (Ware: Wordsworth Editions, 1997).
Dunbar, Robin, *How Religion Evolved: And Why it Endures* (Dublin: Pelican Books, 2022).
Durkheim, Émile, *The Elementary Forms of Religious Life*. Trans. by Carol Cosman (Oxford: Oxford University Press, 2001).
Durkheim, Émile, *The Rules of Sociological Method*. Trans. by Sarah Solovay and John Mueller (New York: The Free Press, 1938).
Dussault, Dee, 'Benefits of Practicing Ganja Yoga': https://www.ganjayoga.online (accessed 9 April 2021).
Dussault, Dee, *Ganja Yoga: A Practical Guide to Conscious Relaxation, Soothing Pain Relief, and Enlightened Self-discovery* (London: Hay House, 2017).
Duvall, Chris, *Cannabis* (London: Reaktion Books, 2015).
Duvall, Chris, *The African Roots of Marijuana* (Durham: Duke University Press, 2019).
Dwarakanath, Shri, 'Use of Opium and Cannabis in the Traditional Systems of Medicine in India', United Nations Office on Drugs and Crime (1965): https://www.researchgate.net/publication/332736343_An_Indian_Perspective_on_Cannabis_for_Treatment_of_Pain (accessed 8 April 2021).
Earleywine, Mitch (ed.), *Mind-Altering Drugs: The Science of Subjective Experience* (Oxford: Oxford University Press, 2005).
Earleywine, Mitch (ed.), *Pot Politics: Marijuana and the Costs of Prohibition* (Oxford: Oxford University Press, 2007).
Earleywine, Mitch, 'Cannabis: Attending to Subjective Effects to Improve Drug Safety'. In Mitch Earleywine (ed.), *Mind-Altering Drugs: The Science of Subjective Experience* (Oxford: Oxford University Press, 2005), 240–257.
Earleywine, Mitch, *Understanding Marijuana: A New Look at the Scientific Evidence* (Oxford: Oxford University Press, 2002).
Edmonds, Ennis, 'The Structure and Ethos of Rastafari'. In Nathaniel Murrell, William Spencer, and Adrian McFarlane (eds), *Chanting Down Babylon: The Rastafari Reader* (Philadelphia: Temple University Press, 1998), 349–360.

Edmonds, Ennis, *Rastafari: From Outcasts to Culture Bearers* (New York: Oxford University Press, 2003).

Eiland, Howard, 'Translator's Foreword'. In Walter Benjamin, *On Hashish*. Edited by Howard Eiland (Cambridge: Harvard University Press, 2006), vii–xii.

Einhorn, Elissa, 'Meet the Waldos: the True Story of the Marin Stoners Who Coined "420"', *The Jewish News of North California* (19 April 2018): https://jweekly.com/2018/04/19/meet-waldos-true-story-marin-stoners-coined-420/ (accessed 6 September 2023).

Elenbaas, Ashley Litecky, 'Reviving the Doctrine of Signatures: How to Start Seeing Signatures in the Natural World', *The Alchemist's Kitchen* (31 July 2015): https://wisdom.thealchemistskitchen.com/reviving-the-doctrine-of-signatures-how-to-start-seeing-the-signatures-in-the-natural-world/ (accessed 15 July 2023).

Eliade, Mircea, *Shamanism: Archaic Techniques of Ecstasy*. Trans. by Willard Trask (London: Routledge & Kegan Paul, 1964).

Eliade, Mircea, *The Sacred and the Profane: The Nature of Religion*. Trans. by Willard Trask (New York: Harcourt Brace Jovanovich, 1957).

Elliott, Iris, *Poverty and Mental Health: A Review to Inform the Joseph Rowntree Foundation's Anti-Poverty Strategy* (London: Mental Health Foundation, 2016).

Emboden, William, 'Cannabis—A Polytypic Genus', *Economic Botany* 28.3 (1974), 304–310.

Emboden, William, 'Ritual Use of *Cannabis Sativa* L.: A Historical-Ethnographic Survey'. In Peter Furst (ed.), *Food of the Gods: The Ritual Use of Hallucinogens* London: George Allen & Unwin, 1972), 214–236.

Emboden, William, *Narcotic Plants* (London: Studio Vista, 1979).

Embree, Ainslie, *The Hindu Tradition* (New York: Vintage, 1972).

Esquirol, Jean Etienne Dominique, *Mental Maladies: A Treatise on Insanity*. Trans. by E.K. Hunt (Philadelphia: Lee and Blanchard, 1845).

Etorre, Elizabeth M., 'The Society for the Study of Addiction: Temperance, Treatment or Tolerance? (1930–1961)', *Drug and Alcohol Dependence* 16.1 (1985), 51–60.

EURAD, *Cannabis: Issues for Policy Makers* (Brussels: EURAD, 2012).

European Monitoring Centre for Drugs and Drug Addiction, *European Drug Report: Trends and Developments* (Luxembourg: Publications Office of the European Union, 2022).

Evans-Pritchard, Edward E., *Witchcraft, Oracles, and magic Among the Azande* (Oxford: Oxford University Press, 1937).

Evans, Jamie, 'A Beginner's Guide to Cooking with Cannabis': https://www.theherbsomm.com/single-post/a-beginners-guide-to-cooking-with-cannabis (accessed 18 April 2022).

Fachner, Jörg, 'Music and Drug-Induced Altered States of Consciousness'. In David Aldridge and Jörg Fachner (eds.), *Music and Altered States: Consciousness, Transcendence, Therapy and Addictions* (London: Jessica Kingsley Publishers, 2006), 82–96.

Faivre, Antoine, '"Éloquence magique", ou descriptions des mondes de l'au-delà explorés par le magnétisme animal: au carrefour de la *Naturphilosophie* romantique et de la théosophie chrétienne (première moitié du XIXe siècle)', *Aries*, 8.2 (2008), 191–228.

Farber, Philip, *High Magick: A Guide to Cannabis in Ritual and Mysticism* (Woodbury: Llewelllyn, 2020).

Fedorak, Charles John, 'The French Capitulation in Egypt and the Preliminary Anglo-French Treaty of Peace in October 1801: A Note', *The International History Review* 15 (1993), 525–534.

Ferber, Sari Goldstein, Dvora Namdar, Danielle Hen-Shoval, Gilad Eger, Hinanit Koltai, Gal Shoval, Liat Shbiro, and Aron Weller, 'The "Entourage Effect": Terpenes Coupled with Cannabinoids for the Treatment of Mood Disorders and Anxiety Disorders', *Current Neuropharmacology* 18 (2020), 87–96.

Ferrara, Mark, *Sacred Bliss: A Spiritual History of Cannabis* (Lanham: Rowman & Littlefield, 2016).

Fielde, Adele M., 'An Experience in Hasheesh-Smoking', *The Therapeutic Gazette* 4 (1888), 449–451.

Fisher, Mark, *K-Punk: The Collected and Unpublished Writings of Mark Fisher (2004-2016)* (London: Repeater, 2018).

Flannery, Mary Catherine, *Yeats and Magic: The Earlier Works* (Gerard's Cross: Colin Smythe, 1977).

Flattery, David and Martin Schwartz, *Haoma and Harmaline: The Botanical Identity of the Indo-Iranian Sacred Hallucinogen 'Soma' and its Legacy in Religion, Language, and Middle Eastern Folklore*, Near Eastern Studies 21 (Berkeley: University of California Press, 1989).

Flaubert, Gustave, *The Letters of Gustave Flaubert: 1857-1880*. Ed. and trans. by Francis Steegmuller (Cambridge: Harvard University Press, 1982).

Flaubert, Gustave, *The Temptation of Saint Anthony*. Trans. by Lafcadio Hearn (New York: Modern Library, 2001).

Fossier, Albert E., 'The Marihuana Menace', *New Orleans Medical and Surgical Journal* 84.4 (1931), 247–252.

Foster, David, 'How Blunts Came to Define Hip-Hop's Golden Age in New York City', *Elite Daily* (19 April 2016): https://www.elitedaily.com/life/blunts-hip-hop-golden-age-nyc/1464522 (accessed 13 December 2021).

Foster, Robert Fitzroy, *W.B. Yeats: A Life. I: The Apprentice Mage* (Oxford: Oxford University Press, 1998).

Foucault, Michel, *Psychiatric Power: Lectures at the Collège de France, 1973–1974*. Trans. by Graham Burchell (Basingstoke: Palgrave Macmillan, 2006).

Foucault, Michel, 'Introduction'. Trans. by Donald Bouchard and Sherry Simon. In Gustave Flaubert, *The Temptation of Saint Anthony*. Trans. by Lafcadio Hearn (New York: Modern Library, 2001), xiii–xliv.

Foucault, Michel, 'Technologies of the Self'. In Luther Martin, Huck Gutman, and Patrick Hutton (eds), *Technologies of the Self: A Seminar with Michel Foucault* (Amherst: University of Massachusetts Press, 1988), 16–49.

Foucault, Michel, *History of Madness*. Trans by Jonathon Murphy and Jean Khalfa (London: Routledge, 2006).

Foucault, Michel, *Society Must be Defended*. Trans. by David Macey (London: Penguin, 2003).

Foucault, Michel, *The Archaeology of Knowledge*. Trans. by Alan Sheridan (London: Tavistock Publications, 1972).

Foucault, Michel, *The Will to Knowledge: The History of Sexuality, Vol. 1*. Trans. by Robert Hurley (London: Penguin, 1990).

Fox, Steve, Paul Armentano, and Mason Tvert, *Marijuana is Safer: So Why Are We Driving People to Drink?* (White River Junction: Chelsea Green Publishing Company, 2009).

Freeman, Daniel, Graham Dunn, Robin Murray, Nicole Evans, Rachel Lister, Angus Antley, and Paul Morrison, 'How Cannabis Causes Paranoia: Using the Intravenous Administration of Δ9-tetrahydrocannabinol (THC) to Identify Key Cognitive Mechanisms Leading to Paranoia', *Schizophrenia Bulletin* 41.2 (2015), 391–399.

Freeman, Tom, Chandni Hindocha, Sebastian Green, and Michael Bloomfield, 'Medicinal Use of Cannabis Based Products and Cannabinoids', *British Medical Journal* 365:l1141 (4 April 2019), 1–7: https://www.bmj.com/content/bmj/365/bmj.l1141.full.pdf (accessed 31 October 2021).

Fronmüller, Bernhard, *Klinische Studien über die Schlafmachende Wirkung der Narkotischen Arzneimittel* (Erlangen: Verlag von Ferdinand Enke, 1869).

Fuller, John F.C., *The Star in the West: A Critical Essay Upon the Works of Aleister Crowley* (London: Walter Scott Publishing Co., 1907).

Garat, Guillermo, 'Uruguay: A Way to Regulate the Cannabis Market'. In Beatriz Labate, Clancy Cavnar, and Thiago Rodrigues (eds), *Drug Policies and the Politics of Drugs in the Americas* (London: Springer, 2016), 209–226.

Garius, Laura and Amal Ari, *Regulating Right, Repairing Wrongs: Exploring Equity and Social Justice Initiatives within UK Cannabis Reform* (London: Release, 2022).

Garland, Sarah, '"A Cookbook to be Read: What About It?", Gertrude Stein, Alice Toklas and the Language of the Kitchen', *Comparative American Studies* 7.1 (2009), 34–56.

Garon, Paul, *Blues and the Poetic Spirit* (San Francisco: City Lights, 1996).

Garvey, Marcus, *Marcus Garvey and the Universal Negro Improvement Association Papers: Volume 1, 1826–August 1919*. Ed. by Robert Hill (Berkeley: University of California Press, 1983).

Garvey, Marcus, *The Philosophy and Opinions of Marcus Garvey*. Ed. by Amy J. Garvey (Dover: Majority Press, 1986).

Gaskin, Stephen, *Amazing Dope Tales and Haight Street Flashbacks* (Summertown: Book Publishing Company, 1980).

Gaskin, Stephen, *Cannabis Spirituality* (Los Angeles: High Times Press, 1996).

Gaskin, Stephen, *Monday Night Class* (San Francisco: Book Publishing Company, 2005).

Gaskin, Stephen, *This Season's People: A Book of Spiritual Teachings* (Summertown: Book Publishing Company, 1976).

Gaskin, Stephen, *Volume One: Sunday Morning Services on The Farm* (Summertown: Book Publishing Company, 1977).

Gauld, Alan, *A History of Hypnotism* (Cambridge: Cambridge University Press, 1992).

Gauld, Alan, *Mediumship and Survival: A Century of Investigations* (London: Heinemann, 1982).

Gautier, Théophile, 'Hashish'. In Charles Baudelaire and Théophile Gautier, *Hashish, Wine, Opium*. Trans. by Maurice Strang (London: Calder and Boyars, 1972), 57–62.

Gautier, Théophile, 'The Club of Assassins'. In Charles Baudelaire and Théophile Gautier, *Hashish, Wine, Opium*. Trans. by Maurice Strang (London: Calder and Boyars, 1972), 31–56.

Gautier, Théophile, 'The Thousand and Second Night'. In Théophile Gautier, *The Works of Théophile Gautier*, Vol. 22. Trans. by F.C. de Sumichrast (New York: George D. Sproul, 1908), 227–270.

Gautier, Théophile, *Charles Baudelaire: His Life*. Trans. by Guy Thorne (Norderstedt: Vero Verlag, 2014).

Gayle, Damien, 'Durham Police Stop Targeting Pot Smokers and Small-scale Growers', *The Guardian* (22 July 2015): https://www.theguardian.com/society/2015/jul/22/durham-police-stop-targeting-pot-smokers-and-small-scale-growers (accessed 5 August 2023).

Geiger, John, *Nothing is True, Everything is Permitted. The Life of Brion Gysin* (New York: Disinformation Company, 2005).

Geluardi, John, *Cannabiz: The Explosive Rise of the Medical Marijuana Industry* (Abingdon: Routledge, 2016).

Gentleman, Amelia, 'Ever Tried Cannabis? Prince Asks MS Sufferer', *The Guardian* (24 December 1998): https://www.theguardian.com/uk/1998/dec/24/monarchy.ameliagentleman (accessed 22 July 2021).

Gilbert, Robert, 'The Hermetic Order of the Golden Dawn'. In Christopher Partridge (ed.), *The Occult World* (London: Routledge, 2015), 237–246.

Gilbert, Robert, *Revelations of the Golden Dawn: The Rise and Fall of a Magical Order* (London: Quantum, 1997).

Ginsberg, Allen, 'The Great Marijuana Hoax: First Manifesto to End the Bringdown', *The Atlantic* (November 1966), 104, 107–112.

Giudice, Christian, 'Martinism in Eighteenth-Century France'. In Christopher Partridge (ed.), *The Occult World* (London: Routledge, 2015), 182–187.

Glendinning, Chellis, *When Technology Wounds: The Human Consequences of Progress* (New York: William Morrow and Company, 1990).

Godwin, Joscelyn, Christian Chanel, and John Patrick Deveney, *The Hermetic Brotherhood of Luxor: Initiatic and Historical Documents of an Order of Practical Occultism* (York Beach: Samuel Weiser, 1995).

Goebel, Rolf, 'Introduction: Benjamin's Actuality'. In Rolf Goebel (ed.), *A Companion to the Works of Walter Benjamin* (Rochester: Camden House, 2009), 1–22.

Goffman, Erving, *Stigma: Notes on the Management of Spoiled Identity* (Harmondsworth: Penguin, 1968).

Goldstein, Chris, 'The Original Flier That Sparked the 420 Phenomenon', *Freedom Leaf* (15 April 2016): https://www.freedomleaf.com/420-flyer/ (accessed 6 September 2023).

Gonimah, Diana, 'Everyday: Cannabis for Daily Consumption', *Eaze* (18 November 2020): https://www.eaze.com/article/everyday-cannabis-for-daily-consumption (accessed, 6 June 2023).

Gonne, Maude, *The Autobiography of Maud Gonne: A Servant of the Queen* (Chicago: University of Chicago Press, 1995).

Goodrick-Clarke, Nicholas, 'The Theosophical Society, Orientalism, and the "Mystic East": Western Esotericism and Eastern Religion in Theosophy', *Theosophical History* 13.3 (2007), 3–28.

Gorman, Mel, 'Sir William O'Shaughnessy, Lord Dalhousie, and the Establishment of the Telegraph System in India', *Technology and Culture: The International Quarterly of the Society for the History of Technology* 12 (1971), 581–601.

Gorski, William, *Yeats and Alchemy* (Albany: State University of New York Press 1996).

Gould, Warwick, '"The Music of Heaven": Dorothea Hunter'. In Deidre Toomey (ed.), *Yeats and Women: Yeats Annual, No. 9* (Houndmills: Macmillan, 1992), 132–188.

Grady, Dennis P., 'From *Reefer Madness* to *Freddy's Dead*: The Portrayal of Marijuana in Motion Pictures'. In Paul Loukides and Linda Fuller (eds), *Beyond the Stars, Vol. 3: The Material World in American Popular Film* (Bowling Green: Bowling Green University Popular Press, 1993), 51–62.

Gray, Stephen (ed.), *Cannabis and Spirituality: An Explorer's Guide to an Ancient Plant Spirit Ally* (Rochester: Park Street Press, 2017).

Gray, Stephen, 'The Basics: Practical Guidance for Working with Cannabis as a Spiritual Ally'. In Stephen Gray (ed.), *Cannabis and Spirituality: An Explorer's Guide to an Ancient Plant Spirit Ally* (Rochester: Park Street Press, 2017), 67–88.

Gray, Stephen, 'Working with the Spirits: An Interview with Cannabis Shaman Hamilton Souther'. In Stephen Gray (ed.), *Cannabis and Spirituality: An Explorer's Guide to an Ancient Plant Spirit Ally* (Rochester: Park Street Press, 2017), 129–137.

Gregorio, Joseph, 'Physicians, Medical Marijuana, and the Law', *American Medical Association Journal of Ethics* 16. 9 (2014), 732–738.

Gregory, William, *Letters to a Candid Inquirer, on Animal Magnetism* (Philadelphia: Blanchard & Lea, 1851).

Grewal, Ruby and Tony George, 'Cannabis-Induced Psychosis: A Review', *Psychiatric Times* 34.7 (2017): https://www.psychiatrictimes.com/view/cannabis-induced-psychosis-review (accessed 25 September 2021).

Grierson, George Abraham, 'The Hemp Plant in Sanskrit and Hindi Literature', *The Indian Antiquary* 23 (1892), 260–262.

Griffith, Ralph (trans and ed.), *Hymns of the Atharva-Veda*, 2 vols, second edition (Benares: E.J. Lazarus & Co., 1916).

Grinspoon, Lester, 'A Cannabis Odyssey'. In Rick Cusick (ed.), *Cannabis—Philosophy for Everyone: What Were We Just Talking About?* (Chichester: Wiley-Blackwell, 2010), 22–34.

Grinspoon, Lester, 'Medical Marihuana in a Time of Prohibition'. In James Inciardi and Karen McElrath (eds), *The American Drug Scene: An Anthology* (New York: Oxford University Press, 2008), 114–123.

Grinspoon, Lester and James Bakalar, *Marihuana, the Forbidden Medicine* New Haven: Yale University Press, 1993).

Grinspoon, Lester, *Marihuana Reconsidered* (Cambridge: Harvard University Press, 1971).

Grose, John Henry, *A Voyage to the East Indies with Observations on Various Parts There* (London: Hooper & Morley, 1757).

Gross, Craig, 'Why?' *Christian Cannabis*: https://christiancannabis.com/why/ (accessed 10 July 2023).

Gross, Craig, 'Convictions', *Christian Cannabis*: https://christiancannabis.com/convictions/ (accessed 10 July 2023).

Guba, David, '"A Sovereign Remedy": Grimault & Co's Asthma Cigarette Empire' (18 February 2020): https://pointshistory.com/2020/02/18/a-sovereign-remedy-grimault-cos-asthma-cigarette-empire/ (accessed 23 December 2021).

Guba, David, 'Antoine Isaac Silvestre de Sacy and the Myth of the Hachichins: Orientalizing Hashish in Nineteenth-century France', *The Social History of Alcohol and Drugs* 30 (2016), 50–74.

Guba, David, 'France Forgets Own Golden Age of Medical Marijuana', *The Conversation* (24 September 2019): https://theconversation.com/france-forgets-own-golden-age-of-medical-marijuana-122584 (accessed 23 July 2021).

Guba, David, 'Taming the Orient: France and the First Global Movement to Medicalize Cannabis, ca. 1800–1850'. In Lucas Richert and James Mills (eds), *Cannabis: Global Histories* (Cambridge: MIT Press, 2021), 3–28.

Guba, David, *Taming Cannabis: Drugs and Empire in Nineteenth-Century France* (Montreal: McGill-Queen's University Press, 2020).

Guédon, Marie-Françoise, 'Sacred Smokes in Circumboreal Countries: An Ethnobotanical Exploration', *The Northern Review* 22 (2000), 29–42.

Hager, Steven, '420 or Fight', *High Times* (December 1998), 12.

Hager, Steven, 'Foreword'. In Chris Bennett, *Cannabis and the Soma Solution* (Walterville: TrineDay, 2010), 11–12.

Hall, Alena, '64% Of US Adults Think CBD Is Safer Than Alcohol, Despite Legality Concerns', *Forbes Health* (21 April 2022): https://www.forbes.com/health/body/2022-cbd-survey/ (accessed 23 May 2023).

Hall, Katelyn, Andrew Monte, Tae Chang, Jacob Fox, Cody Brevik, Daniel Vigil, Mike Van Dyke, and Katherine James, 'Mental Health-related Emergency Department Visits Associated With Cannabis in Colorado', *Academic Emergency Medicine* 25.5 (2018), 526–537.

Halperin, Alex, *The Cannabis Dictionary* (London: Mitchell Beazley, 2020).

Halperin, Christina, 'Profane Illuminations: Classic Maya Molded Figurines in Comparative Context', *Res: Anthropology and Aesthetics* 71–72 (2019), 25–39.

Halperin, Shirley and Steve Bloom, *Reefer Movie Madness: The Ultimate Stoner Film Guide* (New York: Abrams Image, 2010).

Hammer-Purgstall, Joseph von, *The History of the Assassins: Derived from Oriental Sources*. Trans. by Oswald Charles Wood (London: Smith and Elder, 1935).

Hanegraaff, Wouter, 'The First Psychonaut? Louis-Alphonse Cahagnet's Experiments with Narcotics', *International Journal for the Study of New Religions* 7.2 (2016), 105–123.

Hansard, House of Commons, 'Cannabis: Wootton Report', vol. 776 (27 January 1969): https://hansard.parliament.uk/commons/1969-01-27/debates/1d97edb2-a083-4c62-8416-b0820669cc5a/Cannabis(WoottonReport) (accessed 2 October 2021).

Harer Jr., W. Benson, 'The Marijuana Myth in Ancient Egypt', *Journal of the American Research Center in Egypt* 51 (2015), 356–357.

Hari, Johann, 'The Hunting of Billie Holiday: How Lady Day was in the Middle of a Federal Bureau of Narcotics Fight for Survival', *Politico Magazine* (17 January 2015): https://www.politico.com/magazine/story/2015/01/drug-war-the-hunting-of-billie-holiday-114298 (accessed 6 January 2020).

Harper, George Mills (ed.), *Yeats and the Occult* (Toronto: Macmillan, 1975)

Harper, George Mills, *The Making of Yeats's 'A Vision': A Study of the Automatic Script*, 2 vols. (London: Macmillan, 1987).

Harper, George Mills, *Yeats's Golden Dawn: The Influence of the Hermetic Order of the Golden Dawn on the Life and Art of W. B. Yeats* (London: Macmillan, 1974).

Harper, Margaret Mills, 'Yeats and the Occult'. In Marjorie Howes and John Kelly (eds), *The Cambridge Companion to W.B. Yeats* (Cambridge: Cambridge University Press, 2006), 144–166.

Harrison, Kathleen, 'Who Is She? The Personification of Cannabis in Cultural and Individual Experience'. In Stephen Gray (ed.), *Cannabis and Spirituality: An Explorer's Guide to an Ancient Plant Spirit Ally* (Rochester: Park Street Press, 2017), 18–37.

Harvey, Graham (ed.), *The Handbook of Contemporary Animism* (London: Routledge, 2014).

Harvey, Graham, 'Animism Rather than Shamanism: New Approaches to What Shamans Do (for Other Animists)'. In Bettina Schmidt and Lucy Huskinson (eds), *Spirit Possession and Trance: New Interdisciplinary Perspectives* (London: Continuum, 2010), 16–34.

Hausman-Kedem, Moran, Shay Menascu, and Uri Kramer, 'Efficacy of CBD-enriched Medical Cannabis for Treatment of Refractory Epilepsy in Children and Adolescents— An Observational, Longitudinal Study', *Brain and Development* 40 (2018), 544–551.

Hebdige, Dick, *Subculture: The Meaning of Style* (London: Methuen, 1979).

Heelas, Paul, 'The Spiritual Revolution: From "Religion" to "Spirituality"'. In Linda Woodhead, Paul Fletcher, Hiroko Kawanami, and David Smith (eds), *Religions in the Modern World*, first edition (London: Routledge, 2002), 357–378.

Herer, Jack, *The Emperor Wears No Clothes*, 14th edition (Woodland Hills: Herer Media & Publishing, 1998).

Herodotus, *The Histories*. Trans. by Robin Waterfield (Oxford: Oxford University Press, 1998).

Hickok, Laurens Perseus, *Rational Psychology; or, The Subjective Idea and the Objective Law of All Intelligence* (New York: Iveson, Phinney & Co., 1861 [1849]).
Hilgartner, Stephen and Charles Bosk, 'The Rise and Fall of Social Problems: the Public Arenas Model', *American Journal of Sociology* 94.1 (1988), 53–78.
Hillig, Karl, 'Genetic evidence for speciation in *Cannabis*(Cannabaceae)', *Genetic Resources and Crop Evolution* 52 (2005), 161–180.
Hillman, David C.A., *The Chemical Muse: Drug Use and the Roots of Western Civilization* (New York: Thomas Dunne, 2008).
Hilton, Frank, *Baudelaire in Chains: Portrait of the Artist as Drug Addict* (London: Peter Owen, 2004).
Hinchcliffe, Sandra, *Your Cannabis Experience: A Beginner's Guide to Buying, Growing, Cooking and Healing with Cannabis* (New York: Skyhorse Publishing, 2023).
Hinde, Jules, 'Hashish', *Light: Journal of Psychical, Occult, and Mystical Research* 8.645 (May 20, 1893), 233.
Hobson, Richmond P., 'Richmond P. Hobson Argues for Prohibition'. In Kathel Austin Kerr (ed.), *The Politics of Moral Behavior: Prohibition and Drug Abuse* (Reading: Addison-Wesley, 1973), 97–102.
Hockley, Fred, 'Remarks Upon the Rev. George Sandby's Review of M. Alphonse Cahagnet's *Arcanes de la Vie Future Devoilés, & c*', *The Zoist* 29 (April 1850), 54–64.
Hodgekiss, Anna, 'Grandfather, 63, Claims he Cured Cancer with "Breaking Bad" Style Homemade Cannabis Oil', *Mail Online* (21 July 2014): https://www.dailymail.co.uk/health/article-2699875/I-cured-cancer-CANNABIS-OIL.html (accessed 29 September 2021).
Holland, Julie, 'Cannabinoids and Psychiatry'. In Julie Holland (ed.), *The Pot Book: A Complete Guide to Cannabis. Its Role in Medicine, Politics, Science, and Culture* (Rochester: Park Street Press, 2010), 282–294.
Holland, Julie (ed.), *The Pot Book: A Complete Guide to Cannabis. Its Role in Medicine, Politics, Science, and Culture* (Rochester: Park Street Press, 2010).
Holmstedt, Bo, 'Introduction to Moreau de Tours'. In Jacques-Joseph Moreau, *Hashish and Mental Illness*. Trans. Gordon J. Barnett (New York: Raven Press, 1973), ix–xxii.
Home, Julie, *D.D. Home, His Life and Mission*. Edited by Arthur Conan Doyle (London: Kegan Paul, Trench, Trubner & Co., 1921).
Homer, *The Odyssey*. Trans. by Richard Lattimore (New York: Harper Perennial Modern Classics, 2007).
Hornung, Erik, *The Secret Lore of Egypt: Its Impact on the West*. Trans. by David Lorton (Ithaca: Cornell University Press, 2001).
Hosford, Sven, 'Medical Cannabis: The Next Wave of Holistic Medicine', *Dispense Magazine* (1 March 2019): https://dispensemagazine.com/medical-cannabis-the-next-wave-of-holistic-medicine/#comments (accessed 12 April 2021).
Hosford, Sven and Paloma Lehfeldt, 'The History of Medical Cannabis from Ancient Times to 1937 to Today', *Dispense Magazine Podcast* (2 November 2019): https://dispensemagazine.com/the-history-of-medical-cannabis-from-ancient-times-to-1937-to-today-an-interview-with-vireo-health-dr-paloma-lehfeldt/ (accessed 12 April 2021).
House of Commons, Home Affairs Committee, *Drugs: Breaking the Cycle, Ninth Report of Session 2012–13*, Vol. 1 (London: The Stationary Office, 2012).
House of Lords, Science and Technology Committee, *Cannabis: The Scientific and Medical Evidence*, Ninth Report (London, 1998): https://publications.parliament.uk/pa/ld199798/ldselect/ldsctech/151/15103.htm (accessed 22 July 2021).

Hsien-Che, Chang, 'The *Pen-ts' ao Pei-yao*: A Modern Interpretation of its Terminology and Contents'. In Paul Unschuld (ed.), *Approaches to Traditional Chinese Medical Literature* (Dordrecht: Springer, 1989), 41–51.
Hua, Stephanie and Coreen Carroll, *Edibles: Small Bites for the Modern Cannabis Kitchen* (San Francisco: Chronicle Books, 2018).
Huertas, Rafael, 'Between Doctrine and Clinical Practice: Nosography and Semiology in the Work of Jean-Etienne-Dominique Esquirol (1772–1840)', *History of Psychiatry*, 19.2 (1939), 123–140.
Hughes, Jennifer Scheper, 'Contemporary Popular Catholicism in Latin America'. In Virginia Garrard-Burnett, Paul Freston, and Stephen Dove (eds), *The Cambridge History of Religions in Latin America* (Cambridge: Cambridge University Press, 2016), 480–490.
Hughes, Trevor (ed.), *Hassan I Sabbah* (Liscard: Zephyr, 1995).
Hughes, Trevor (ed.), *Reefer Madness* (Liscard: Zephyr, 1996).
Hulkrantz, Ake, *Shamanic Healing and Ritual Drama: Health and Medicine in Native North American Religious Traditions* (New York: Crossroad, 1992).
Hutnyk, John, *Pantomine Terror: Music and Politics* (Winchester: Zero Books, 2014).
Hutton, Ronald, *Shamans: Siberian Spirituality and the Western Imagination* (London: Hambledon Continuum, 2007).
Huxley, Aldous, *Brave New World* (London: Vintage, 2007).
Huxley, Aldous, *The Doors of Perception; Heaven and Hell* (London: Flamingo, 1994).
Huysmans, Joris-Karl, *Against Nature*. Trans. by Robert Baldick (Harmondsworth: Penguin, 1959).
Indian Hemp Drugs Commission, *Report of Indian Hemp Drugs Commission, 1893–1894*, 8 vols. (Simla: Government Central Printing Office, 1894).
Ingram, Matthew, *Retreat: How the Counterculture Invented Wellness* (London: Repeater Books, 2020).
Innes, Stephanie, 'With Its 2 Founder Serving Time, Church of Pot is Devastated', *Arizona Daily Star* (9 September 2009).
Irwin, Robert, *The Arabian Nights: A Companion* (London: Tauris Parke Paperbacks, 2005).
Iversen, Leslie, 'How Cannabis Works in the Brain'. In David Castle, Robin Murray, and Deepak D'Souza (eds), *Marijuana and Madness*, second edition (Cambridge: Cambridge University Press, 2012), 1–16.
Iversen, Leslie, *The Science of Marijuana*, second edition (Oxford: Oxford University Press, 2008).
Jacquette, Dale (ed.), *Cannabis: Philosophy for Everyone: What Were We Just Talking About?* (Chichester: Wiley-Blackwell, 2010).
Jacquette, Dale, 'Philosophers Stoned', *The Philosopher's Magazine* (20 July 2016): https://www.philosophersmag.com/essays/137-philosophers-stoned (accessed 6 June 2023).
James, Tony, *Dream, Creativity, and Madness in Nineteenth-Century France* (Oxford: Oxford University Press, 1995).
James, William, *Principles of Psychology* (New York: Henry Holt & Co., 1890).
James, William, *The Varieties of Religious Experience: A Study in Human Nature* (London: Longmans, Green and Co., 1902).
Jay, Mike, 'The Green Jam of "Dr X": Science and Literature at the Cub des Hashischins'. In Eugene Brennan and Russell Williams (eds), *Literature and Intoxication: Writing, Politics, and the Experience of Excess* (London: Palgrave Macmillan, 2015), 52–65.
Jenkin, Leonard, 'The Golden Wrong: A Life of Fitz Hugh Ludlow, with an Examination of His Writings' (doctoral dissertation, Columbia University, 1972).

Jiang, Hong-En, Xiao Li, You-Xing Zhao, David K. Ferguson, Francis Hueber, Subir Bera, Yu-Fei Wang, Liang-Cheng Zhao, Chang-Jiang Liu, and Cheng-Sen Li, 'A New Insight Into *Cannabis sativa* (Cannabaceae) Utilization from 2500-year-old Yanghai Tombs, Xinjiang, China', *Journal of Ethnopharmacology* 108 (2006), 414–422.

Johns, Christina, 'The War on Drugs: Why the Administration Continues to Pursue a Policy of Criminalization and Enforcement', *Social Justice* 18.4 (1991), 147–165.

Johnson-Hill, Jack, *I-Sight: The World of Rastafari: An Interpretive Sociological Account of Rastafarian Ethics* (Lanham: The Scarecrow Press, 1995).

Johnson, Donald, *Indian Hemp: A Social Menace* (London: Christopher Johnson, 1952).

Johnson, Will, *Cannabis in Spiritual Practice: the Ecstasy of Shiva, the Calm of the Buddha* (Rochester: Inner Traditions, 2018).

Jones, Jeffrey, 'Nearly Half of US Adults Have Tried Marijuana', *Gallup News* (17 August 2021): https://news.gallup.com/poll/353645/nearly-half-adults-tried-marijuana.aspx (accessed 20 August 2021).

Jones, John, *Spiritualism the Work of Demons* (Liverpool: Edward Howell, 1871).

Jones, Nick, *Spliffs: A Celebration of Cannabis Culture* (London: Chrysalis Impact, 2003).

Jordan, Danté, 'What are Moon Rocks and How Do You Smoke Them?' *Leafly* (9 May 2022): https://www.leafly.com/learn/consume/smoke/moon-rocks (accessed 18 July 2023).

Kaczynski, Richard, *Perdurabo: The Life of Aleister Crowley* (Berkeley: North Atlantic Books, 2010).

Kaczynski, Richard, *The Weiser Concise Guide to Aleister Crowley* (San Francisco: Weiser, 2009).

Kakko, Tommi, 'Hallucinatory Terror: the World of the Hashish Eater'. In Dale Jacquette (ed.), *Cannabis—Philosophy for Everyone: What Were We Just Talking About?* (Chichester: Wiley-Blackwell, 2010), 103–113.

Kalant, Harold, 'Medicinal Use of Cannabis: History and Current Status', *Pain Research and Management* 6.2 (2001), 80–91.

Kane, Harry Hubbell, 'A Hashish-House in New York: The Curious Adventures of an Individual Who Indulged in a Few Pipefuls of the Narcotic Hemp', *Harper's New Monthly Magazine* 67 (November 1883), 944–949.

Kane, Harry Hubbell, *Drugs That Enslave: The Opium, Morphine, Chloral and Hashisch Habits* (Philadelphia: Presley Blakiston, 1881).

Kane, Harry Hubbell, *Opium-Smoking in America and China: A Study of its Prevalence, and Effects, Immediate and Remote, on the Individual and the Nation* (New York: G.P. Putnam's and Sons, 1882).

Karr, Alphonse, *Le Livre De Bord: Souvenirs, Portraits, Notes Au Crayon* (Paris: Calmann-Lévy, 1880).

Kerr, Kathel Austin (ed.), *The Politics of Moral Behavior: Prohibition and Drug Abuse* (Reading: Addison-Wesley, 1973).

Kessler, Martin and Karel Duerloo, *A Commentary on Genesis: The Book of Beginnings* (Mahwah: Paulist Press, 2004).

Kirsch, Adam, 'The Philosopher Stoned: What Drugs Taught Walter Benjamin', *The New Yorker* (13 August 2006): https://www.newyorker.com/magazine/2006/08/21/the-philosopher-stoned#:~:text=Under%20the%20influence%20of%20hashish,the%20trance%20that%20fathered%20it. (accessed 6 June 2023).

Kohn, Marek, *Dope Girls: The Birth of the British Drug Underground* (London: Lawrence & Wishart, 1992).

Koshie, Ashley, 'Going Green', *Treating Yourself: The Alternative Medicine Journal* 27 (2011), 16–17.

Kramer, Joan, 'Medical Marijuana for Cancer', *CA: Cancer Journal for Clinicians* 65.2 (2015), 109–122.
Kramer, Stephanie, 'Religious Americans are Less Likely to Endorse Legal Marijuana for Recreational Use', *Pew Research Center* (26 May 2021): https://www.pewresearch.org/short-reads/2021/05/26/religious-americans-are-less-likely-to-endorse-legal-marijuana-for-recreational-use/ (accessed 24 May 2023).
Kreglinger, Gisela, *The Spirituality of Wine* (Grand Rapids: Eerdmans, 2016).
Kruzman, Diana, 'With "Christian Cannabis," a Pastor is Promoting the Spiritual Side of Marijuana', *Religion News Service* (29 March 2022): https://religionnews.com/2022/03/29/with-christian-cannabis-a-pastor-is-promoting-the-spiritual-side-of-marijuana/ (accessed 17 August 2022).
Kudlick, Catherine, *Cholera in Post-Revolutionary Paris: A Cultural History* (Berkeley: University of California Press, 1996).
Kuhnke, LaVerne, *Lives at Risk: Public Health in Nineteenth-Century Egypt* (Berkeley: University of California Press, 1990).
La Barre, Weston, *Culture in Context* (Durham NC: Duke University Press, 1980).
La Rue, George Michael, 'Treating Black Deaths in Egypt: Clot-Bey, African Slaves, and the Plague Epidemic of 1834–1835'. In Anna Winterbottom and Facil Tesfaye (eds), *Histories of Medicine and Healing in the Indian Ocean World: The Modern Period* (New York: Palgrave Macmillan, 2016), 27–59.
Ladd, George Trumbull, *Elements of Physiological Psychology* (New York: Charles Scribner's Sons, 1887).
Laing, R.D., 'Letter, 1 June, 1964'. In George Andrews and Simon Vinkenoog (eds), *The Book of Grass: An Anthology of Indian Hemp* (Harmondsworth: Penguin, 1972), 235–236.
Lamont, Michèle, *Money, Morals, and Manners: The Culture of the French and American Upper-Middle Class* (Chicago: Chicago University Press, 1992).
Lane, Edward William, *An Account of the Manners and Customs of the Modern Egyptians*, Vol. 2 (London: Charles Knight & Co., 1837).
Lastreto, Nikki and Swami Chaitanya, 'Our Story', *Swami Select*: https://swamiselect.com/our-story/ (accessed 17 August 2022).
Lawrence, Robyn Griggs, *Pot in Pans: A History of Eating Cannabis* (Lanham: Rowman & Littlefield, 2019).
Leadbeater, Charles, *The Chakras: A Monograph* (Adyar: Theosophical Publishing House, 2009).
Leary, Timothy, *The Politics of Ecstasy* (London: Paladin, 1970).
Ledermann, François, 'Pharmacie, médicaments et psychiatrie vers 1850: le cas de Jacques-Joseph Moreau de Tours', *Revue d'Histoire de la Pharmacie* 35.276 (1988), 67–76.
Lee, Martin, *Smoke Signals: A Social History of Marijuana—Medical, Recreational, and Scientific* (New York: Scribner, 2012).
Leohndorf, Dan, 'The Beliefs of the Church of the Universe', *Cannabis Culture* (1 June 1997): https://www.cannabisculture.com/content/1997/06/01/1227/ (accessed 18 August 2023).
Leveque, Philip, 'Premenstrual Syndrome, Medical Marijuana, and Queen Victoria', *Salem-News.com* (16 October 2009): http://www.salem-news.com/articles/october162009/pms_mj_pl.php (accessed 21 July 2021).
Lévi, Éliphas, *The History of Magic*, second edition. Trans. by Arthur E. Waite (London: William Rider & Son, 1922).
Lewcock, Anna, 'Chemists Quit UK Drugs Council', *Chemistry World* (26 November 2009): https://www.chemistryworld.com/news/chemists-quit-uk-drugs-council/3000905.article (accessed 29 December 2021).

Lewin, Louis, *Phantastica: Narcotic and Stimulating Drugs. Their Use and Abuse*. Trans. by P.H.A. Wirth (Rochester: Park Street Press, 1998).
Lewis, Bernard, *Assassins: A Radical Sect of Islam* (New York: Basic Books, 2003).
Lewis, Glyn, Caroline Croft-Jeffreys, and Anthony David, 'Are British Psychiatrists Racist?' *British Journal of Psychiatry* 157.3 (1990) 410–415.
Lewis, James, *Legitimating New Religions* (New Brunswick: Rutgers University Press, 2003).
Lewis, Rupert, 'Marcus Garvey and the Early Rastafarians: Continuity and Discontinuity'. In Nathaniel Murrell, William Spencer, and Adrian McFarlane (eds), *Chanting Down Babylon: The Rastafari Reader* (Philadelphia: Temple University Press, 1998), 145–158.
Lewis, William, *The Edinburgh New Dispensatory* (Worcester: Isaiah Thomas, 1794)
Lewis, William, *The New English Dispensatory* (London: J. Nourse, 1753).
Lezard, Nicholas, *Bitter Experience Has Taught Me* (London: Faber and Faber, 2013).
Li, Hui-Lin, 'The Origin and Use of Cannabis in Eastern Asia: Their Linguistic-Cultural Implications'. In Vera Rubin (ed.), *Cannabis and Culture* (The Hague: Mouton Publishers, 1975), 51–62.
Libreria Editrice Vaticana, *The Catechism of the Catholic Church*, second edition (Huntington: Our Sunday Visitor, 1997).
Lieutaud, Antoine, 'Du haschisch un canvre indien', *Bulletin trimestriel de la Société des Sciences, Belles-lettres et Arts du département du Var, séant à Toulon* (Toulon: L. Laurent, 1850), 17–36.
Linsey, Mark and David Lester, *Suicide by Cop: Committing Suicide by Provoking Police to Shoot You* (New York: Baywood Publishing, 2004).
Littlewood, Roland, 'Community-initiated Research: A Study of Psychiatrists' Conceptualizations of "Cannabis psychosis"', *Psychiatric Bulletin* 12.11 (1987), 486–488.
Littlewood, Roland and Maurice Lipsedge, *Aliens and Alienists: Ethnic Minorities and Psychiatry*, third edition (London: Routledge, 1997).
Long, Trish, '1915: El Paso Becomes First City in United States to Outlaw Marijuana', *El Paso Times* (16 November 2019): https://eu.elpasotimes.com/story/news/2019/11/14/el-paso-history-pot-possession-first-city-outlaw-weed-tbt/2579079001/ (accessed 20 December 2019).
Löwy Michael and Robert Sayre, *Romanticism Against the Tide of Modernity*. Trans. by Catherine Porter (Durham: Duke University Press, 2001).
Luauté, Jean-Pierre (ed.), *Les Moreau de Tours* (Paris: Glyphe, 2018).
Lovering, Rob, *A Moral Defense of Recreational Drug Use* (New York: Palgrave Macmillan, 2015).
Ludlow, Fitz Hugh, 'The Apocalypse of Hasheesh', *Putnam's Monthly Magazine* 8.48 (December 1856), 233–239; reprinted in Fitz Hugh Ludlow, *The Hashish Eater: Being Passages from the Life of a Pythagorean* (New York: Theophania Publishing, 2011), 280–289.
Ludlow, Fitz Hugh, 'The Hasheesh Eater', *The Equinox* 1.4 (1910), 135–146.
Ludlow, Fitz Hugh, 'What Shall They Do to be Saved?' *Harper's New Monthly Magazine* (August 1867), 377–387; reprinted in Horace B. Day (ed.), *The Opium Habit, with Suggestions as to the Remedy* (New York: Harper and Brothers, 1868), 250–284.
Ludlow, Fitz Hugh, *The Annotated Hasheesh Eater*. Edited by David M. Gross (Self-published/CreateSpace, 2007).
Ludlow, Fitz Hugh, *The Hasheesh Eater: Being Passages from the Life of a Pythagorean* (New York: Harper and Brothers, 1857; reprinted New York: Theophania Publishing, 2011).

Lynch, Gordon, *The Sacred in the Modern World: A Cultural Sociological Approach* (Oxford: Oxford University Press, 2012).
Lynch, Hollis, *Edward Wilmott Blyden: Pan Negro Patriot 1832–1912* (Oxford: Oxford University Press, 1967).
Lynch, Michael, 'Themes and Tones of Cannabis News Reports and Legalization Outcomes', *Media, Culture, and Society* 43.3 (2021), 570–581.
Lynch, Patrick, 'How Marijuana Thrived in Certain Cultures: Ancient Egypt', *Way of Leaf* (3 March 2020): https://wayofleaf.com/blog/how-cannabis-became-part-of-thriving-culture-ancient-egypt (accessed 23 July 2023).
Lynn, Becky, Julia López, Collin Miller, Judy Thompson, and Cristian Campian, 'The Relationship Between Marijuana Use Prior to Sex and Sexual Function in Women', *Sexual Medicine* 7.2 (2019), 192–197.
Lytton, Edward Bulwer, *Zanoni*, 2 vols. (Edinburgh: William Blackwood & Sons, 1861, 1862).
MacGillivrey, Neil, 'Sir William Brooke O'Shaughnessy (1808–1889), MD, FRS, LRCS Ed: Chemical Pathologist, Pharmacologist and Pioneer in Electric Telegraphy', *Journal of Medical Biography* 25 (2017), 186–196.
Mack, Robert, 'Cultivating the Garden: Antoine Galland's *Arabian Nights* in the Traditions of English Literature'. In Saree Makdisi and Felicity Nussbaum (eds), *Arabian Nights in Historical Context: Between East and West* (Oxford: Oxford University Press, 2008), 51–82.
MacKeen, Dawn, 'What Are the Benefits of CBD?' *New York Times* (16 October 2019): https://www.nytimes.com/2019/10/16/style/self-care/cbd-oil-benefits.html (accessed 6 July 2023).
Maher, John T., *Cannabis Sativa: A Lecture* (Washington: Department of Justice, Drug Enforcement Administration, National Training Institute, 1976).
Mailer, Norman, *The Armies of the Night: History as a Novel/The Novel as History* (New York: New American Library, 1968).
Majercik, Ruth, *The Chaldean Oracles: Text, Translation, and Commentary* (Leiden: Brill, 1989).
Mandel, Jerry, 'Hashish, Assassins, and the Love of God', *Issues in Criminology* 2.2 (1966), 149–156.
Maniaque-Benton, Caroline and Meredith Gaglio, *Whole Earth Field Guide* (Cambridge: MIT Press, 2016).
Mann, John (ed.), *The First Book of Sacraments of the Church of the Tree of Life* (San Francisco: Tree of Life Press, 1972).
Marcu, Jahan, 'An Overview of Major and Minor Phytocannabinoids'. In Victor Preedy (ed.), *Neuropathology of Drug Addictions and Substance Misuse*, Vol. 1 (London: Academic Press, 2016), 672–701.
Marijuana Doctors, 'Cannabis and Cancer: Your Essential Guide to a Holistic Approach': https://www.marijuanadoctors.com/blog/cannabis-resources-for-cancer/ (accessed 12 April 2021).
Marincolo, Sebastian, *High: Insights on Marijuana* (). Indianapolis: Dog Ear Publishing, 2010).
Marincolo, Sebastian, *What Hashish Did to Walter Benjamin: Mind-Altering Essays on Cannabis* (Stuttgart: Khargala Press, 2015).
Marinko, Paul, 'How Pensioner's Cooking Went to Pot', *The Guardian* (26 January 2005): https://www.theguardian.com/uk/2005/jan/26/drugsandalcohol (accessed 6 October 2021).

Marino, Danilo, 'Hashish and Food: Arabic and European Medieval Dreams of Edible Paradises'. In Kirill Dmitriev, Julia Hauser, and Bilal Orfali (eds), *Insatiable Appetite: Food as Cultural Signifier in the Middle East and Beyond* (Leiden: Brill, 2019), 190–213.

Markert, John, *Hooked in Film: Substance Abuse on the Big Screen* (Lanham: Scarecrow Press, 2013).

Marks, Amber, *Becoming Mr Nice: the Howard Marks Archive* (Harpenden: No Exit Press, 2021).

Marks, Howard (ed.), *The Howard Marks' Book of Dope Stories* (London: Vintage, 2001).

Marks, Howard, *Mr Nice* (London: Vintage, 1998).

Martin, Alyson, 'Holy Rollers: These Devout Christians Are Using The Bible To Argue That Pot Is God's "Perfect Medicine"', *BuzzFeed News* (15 May 2017): https://www.buzzfeednews.com/article/alysonmartin/cannabis-reform-and-religion-in-the-south (accessed 7 July 2023).

Martin, Heather, *W.B. Yeats: Metaphysician as Dramatist* (Waterloo: Wilfred Laurier University Press, 1986).

Marx, Karl, *Critique of Hegel's 'Philosophy or Right'*. Trans. by Annette Jolin and Joseph O'Malley (Cambridge: Cambridge University Press, 1977).

Maslow, Abraham, *Religion, Values, and Peak Experiences* (Columbus: Ohio State University Press, 1964).

Matthews, Patrick, *Cannabis Culture* (London: Bloomsbury, 2003).

Mayfield, Asia, 'CBD for Children', *CBD Health and Wellness* (17 December 2018): https://cbdhealthandwellness.net/2018/12/17/cbd-for-children/ (accessed 20 August 2021).

Maymudes, Victor and Jacob Maymudes, *Another Side of Bob Dylan: A Personal History on the Road and Off the Tracks* (New York: St. Martin's Press, 2014).

McCrackin, Carmen, 'New research Exposes 15 Most Dangerous Drugs', *Addiction Center* (18 August 2019) https://www.addictioncenter.com/news/2019/08/15-most-dangerous-drugs/ (accessed 16 September 2023).

McDonough, Elise, 'The History of Weed Brownies', *High Times* (20 September 2016): https://hightimes.com/edibles/everything-you-need-to-know-about-the-history-of-pot-brownies/ (accessed 21 April 2022).

McGinn, Bernard (ed.), *Essential Writings of Christian Mysticism* (New York: Random House, 2006).

McGovern, Dermot and Rosemarie Cope, 'First Psychiatric Admission Rates of First and Second Generation Afro-Caribbeans', *Social Psychiatry* 22 (1987), 139–149.

McGuire, Meredith, *Ritual Healing in Suburban America* (London: Rutgers University Press, 1988)

McKenna, Terence, *The Archaic Revival* (New York: Harper Collins, 1991).

McKenna, Terence, *The Food of the Gods: A Radical History of Plants, Drugs, and Human Evolution* (London: Rider, 1992).

McKenna, Terence and Katherine Harrison McKenna, *Victorian Tales of Cannabis: An Audially Illuminated Manuscript from Sound Photosynthesis* (Mill Valley: Sound Photosynthesis, 2000).

McMillian, John, *Smoking Typewriters: The Sixties Underground Press and the Rise of Alternative Media in America* (New York: Oxford University Press, 2011).

McPartland, John and Geoffrey Guy, 'Models of *Cannabis* Taxonomy, Cultural Bias, and Conflicts between Scientific and Vernacular Names', *The Botanical Review* 83 (2017), 327–381.

McWilliams, John C., *The Protectors: Harry J. Anslinger and the Federal Bureau of Narcotics, 1930–1962* (Newark: University of Delaware Press, 1990).

McWilliams, John, 'Through the Past Darkly: The Politics and Policies of America's Drug War', *Journal of Policy History* 3.4 (1991), 5–41.
Mechoulam, Raphael (ed.), *Cannabinoids as Therapeutics* (Basel: Birkhäuser Verlag, 2005).
Mechoulam, Raphael, 'Marihuana Chemistry', *Science* 168 (1970), 1159–1163.
Mechoulam, Raphael and Lumír Hanuš, 'Anandamide and More'. In Julie Holland (ed.), *The Pot Book: A Complete Guide to Cannabis. Its Role in Medicine, Politics, Science, and Culture* (Rochester: Park Street Press, 2010), 63–72.
Medeiros, Tracey, *The Art of Cooking with Cannabis* (New York: Skyhorse Publishing, 2021).
Memedovich, Ally, Laura Dowsett, Eldon Spackman, Tom Noseworthy and Fiona Clement, 'The Adverse Health Effects and Harms Related to Marijuana Use: An Overview Review', *Canadian Medical Association Journal Open* 6 (2018), E339–E346.
Merlin, Mark, 'Archaeological Evidence for the Tradition of Psychoactive Plant Use in the Old World', *Economic Botany* 57.3 (2003), 295–323.
Merlin, Mark, *Man and Marijuana: Some Aspects of Their Ancient Relationship* (Madison: Fairleigh Dickinson University Press, 1972).
Merritt, Jonathan, 'The Christian Case for Marijuana', *New York Times* (20 June 2019): https://www.nytimes.com/2019/06/20/opinion/legalization-medical-marijuana-christianity.html (accessed 24 May 2023).
Merwe, Nikolaas van der, 'Cannabis Smoking in 13th–14th Century Ethiopia: Chemical Evidence'. In Vera Rubin (ed.), *Cannabis and Culture* (The Hague: Mouton Publishers, 1975), 77–80.
Merzouki, A., F. Ed-derfoufi, and J. Molero Mesa, 'Hemp (*Cannabis sativa* L.) and Abortion', *Journal of Ethnopharmacology* 73 (2000), 501–503.
Mexico, N.R. de, *Marijuana Girl* (New York: Universal Publishing and Distribution, 1951).
Mezzrow, Milton 'Mezz' and Bernard Wolfe, *Really the Blues* (London: Secker & Warburg, 1957).
Mickel, Emanuel, *The Artificial Paradises in French Literature: The Influence of Opium and Hashish on the Literature of French Romanticism* and Les Fluers Du Mal (Chapel Hill: University of North Carolina Press, 1969).
Mikuriya, Tod (ed.), *Cannabis: Collected Clinical Papers. Vol. 1, Marijuana: Medical Papers, 1839–1972* (Nevada City: Symposium Publishing, 2007).
Miles, Todd, *Cannabis and the Christian: What the Bible Says about Marijuana* (Nashville: B&H Publishing, 2021).
Millar, Aaron, 'Holy Smoke! The Church of Cannabis', *The Observer* (13 August 2017): https://www.theguardian.com/global/2017/aug/13/church-of-cannabis-denver-colorado (accessed 25 August 2022).
Miller, Robert Moats, 'The Protestant Churches and Lynching, 1919–1939', *The Journal of Negro History* 42 (1957), 118–131.
Mills, James, 'Cannabis in the Commons: Colonial Networks, Missionary Politics and the origins of the Indian Hemp Drugs Commission 1893–4', *Journal of Colonialism and Colonial History* 6.1 (2005): https://muse.jhu.edu/article/181815 (accessed 24 September 2021).
Mills, James, *Cannabis Britannica: Empire, Trade, and Prohibition, 1800–1928* (Oxford: Oxford University Press, 2003).
Mills, James, *Cannabis Nation: Control and Consumption in Britain, 1928–2008* (Oxford: Oxford University Press, 2013).
Mohan Ram, Holenarasipur Yoganarasimham, and Rina Sett, 'Induction of Fertile Male Flowers in Genetically Female *Cannabis sativa* Plants by Silver Nitrate and Silver Thiosulphate Anionic Complex', *Theoretical Applied Genetics*. 62.4 (1982), 369–375.

Moldenke, Harold and Alma Moldenke, *Plants of the Bible* (New York: Ronald Press Company, 1952).
Monte, Andrew, Richard Zane, and Kennon Heard, 'The Implications of Marijuana Legalization in Colorado', *Journal of the American Medical Association* 313 (2015), 241–242.
Moon, John, 'Sir William Brooke O'Shaughnessy—The Foundations of Fluid Therapy and the Indian Telegraph Service', *The New England Journal of Medicine* 276.5 (1967), 283–274.
Moore, Virginia, *The Unicorn: William Butler Yeats' Search for Reality* (New York: Macmillan, 1954).
Moreau, Jacques-Joseph, 'De l'emploi du hachisch dans le choléra-morbus', *L'Union Médicale* 2 (1848), 491–492.
Moreau, Jacques-Joseph, 'De l'identité de l'état de rêve et de la folie', *Annales médico psychologiques* 1 (1855): 361–408.
Moreau, Jacques-Joseph, 'Lettres médicales sur la colonie des aliénés de Gheel', *La Revue Indépendante* 4 (1842): 678–704.
Moreau, Jacques-Joseph, 'Necessité pour l'autorité d'intervenir dans la question de l'hydrophobie—Proposition d'essai d'un nouveau moyen contre cette maladie', *L'Union Médicale* 6 (1852), 337.
Moreau, Jacques-Joseph, 'On the Treatment of Hallucinations by *Datura Stramonium*', *Provincial Medical and Surgical Journal* 3.7 (1841), 126–127.
Moreau, Jacques-Joseph, *De la influence de physique relativement au désordre des facultés intellectuelles et en particulier dans cette varietés du délire désignée par M. Esquirol sous le nom de monomania.* Thèse pour le doctorat en médecine. No. 127 (Paris: Didot Le Jeune, 1830).
Moreau, Jacques-Joseph, *Du Hachisch et de l'Aliénation mentale. Études psychologiques* (Paris: De Fortin, Masson et Cie, 1845).
Moreau, Jacques-Joseph, *Hashish and Mental Illness*. Trans. Gordon J. Barnett (New York: Raven Press, 1973).
Moreau, Jacques-Joseph, *Mémoire sur le traitement des hallucinations par le Datura Stramonium* (Paris: J. Rouvier et E. Le Bouvier, 1841); also published as: 'Mémoire sur le traitement des hallucinations par le Datura stramonium', *Gazette Médicale de Paris* 9 (1841), 641–647, 673–680.
Moreau, Jacques-Joseph, *Recherches sur les aliénés en Orient* (Paris: Imprimerie de Bourgogne et Martinet, 1843); also published as: 'Recherches sur les aliénés en Orient', *Annales Médico Psychologiques* 1 (1843), 103–132.
Morgan, Kayla, *Legalizing Marijuana* (Edina: ABDO Publishing Company, 2011).
Morgan, Wayne, *Drugs in America: A Social History, 1800–1980* (Syracuse: Syracuse University Press, 1981).
Moritz, Maria, 'Looking for Spirituality in India: A German Theosophist's Experiments with *Ganga*, 1894–1896'. In Harald Fischer-Tiné and Jana Tschurenev (eds), *A History of Alcohol and Drugs in Modern South Asia: Intoxicating Affairs* (Abingdon: Routledge, 2015), 117–135.
Morley, Gabriel Patrick, 'Tripping with Stephen Gaskin: An Exploration of an Adult Hippie Educator' (doctoral dissertation, University of Southern Mississippi, 2012).
Moser, Amanda, Sharon Ballard, Jake Jensen, and Paige Averett, 'The Influence of Cannabis on Sexual Functioning and Satisfaction', *Journal of Cannabis Research* 5.2 (2023), 1–11.
Mossman, Kate, 'The Secret of *The Wicker Man*', *The New Statesman* (23–29 June 2023), 52–53.

Mukherjee, Braja Lal, 'The Soma Plant', *The Journal of the Royal Asiatic Society of Great Britain and Ireland* (1921), 241–244.
Mukherjee, Braja Lal, *The Soma Plant* (Calcutta: Weekly Notes Printing Press, 1922).
Mulgrew, Ian, *Bud Inc. Inside Canada's Marijuana Industry* (Toronto: Random House Canada, 2005).
Müller-Ebeling, Claudia, Christian Rätsch, and Wolf-Dieter Storl, *Witchcraft Medicine: Healing Arts, Shamanic Practices, and Forbidden Plants* (Rochester: Inner Traditions, 1998).
Murphy, Emily F., *The Black Candle* (Toronto: Thomas Allen, 1922).
Musselman, Lytton John, *A Dictionary of Bible Plants* (Cambridge: Cambridge University Press, 2012).
Mussen, Maddy and Emily Sheed, '16,000 Students Took Our Drugs Survey. Find Out How and What They're Taking This Term', *The Tab* (22 December 2020): https://thetab.com/uk/2020/12/22/16000-students-took-our-drugs-survey-find-out-how-and-what-theyre-taking-this-term-187354 (accessed 5 August 2023).
Musto, David (ed.), *Drugs in America: A Documentary History* (New York: New York University Press, 2002).
Musto, David, 'The 1937 Marihuana Tax Act', *Archives of General Psychiatry* 26.2 (1972), 101–108.
Musto, David, *The American Disease: Origins of Narcotic Control* (New York: Oxford University Press, 1987).
Nahas, Gabriel, 'Hashish and Drug Abuse in Egypt During the 19th and 20th Centuries', *Bulletin of the New York Academy of Medicine* 61 (1985), 428–444.
Nahas, Gabriel, 'Hashish in Islam 9th to 18th Century', *Bulletin of the New York Academy of Medicine* 58.9 (1982), 814–831.
National Commission on Marihuana and Drug Abuse, *Appendix – Marihuana: A Signal of Misunderstanding. The Technical Papers of the First Report of the National Commission on Marihuana and Drug Abuse*, Vol. 1 (Washington: Government Printing Office, 1972).
National Institute on Drug Abuse, *Marijuana Research Report* (13 April 2021): https://www.drugabuse.gov/download/1380/marijuana-research-report.pdf?v=d9e67cbd412ae5f340206c1a0d9c2bfd (accessed 25 September 2021).
Needham, Joseph, *Science and Civilization in China*, Vol. 5, Part 2 (Cambridge: Cambridge University Press, 1974).
Nelson, Joe, 'Shuttered Big Bear Cannabis Church Loses Court Appeal to Reopen, Vows to Continue Fight', *San Bernardino Sun* (20 October 2022): https://www.sbsun.com/2022/10/14/shuttered-big-bear-cannabis-church-loses-court-appeal-to-reopen-vows-to-continue-fight/#:~:text=Jah%20Healing%20Kemetic%20Temple%20of%20the%20Divine%20Church%2C%20which%20considers,June%202020%20decision%20ordering%20a (accessed 5 November 2023).
Nelson, Max, *The Barbarian's Beverage: The History of Beer in Ancient Europe* (Abingdon: Routledge, 2005).
Niaah, Jahlani, 'Ganja Terrorism and the Healing of the Nation'. In Beatriz Labate, Clancy Cavnar, and Thiago Rodrigues (eds), *Drug Policies and the Politics of Drugs in the Americas* (Cham: Springer International Publishing, 2016), 227–244
Niebuhr, Carsten, *Travels Through Arabia and Other Countries in the East*, 2 vols. Trans. by Robert Heron (Edinburgh: R. Morison & Son, 1792).
NORC, 'Should Marijuana Be Made Legal? Key Trends', *NORC* (Chicago: University of Chicago, 2020): https://gssdataexplorer.norc.org/trends?category=Civil%20Liberties&measure=grass (accessed 23 May 2023).

Nordau, Max, *Degeneration* (New York: D. Appleton & Co., 1895).
Normand, Linn, *Demonization in International Politics* (New York: Palgrave Macmillan, 2016).
Notcutt, William and Emily Clarke, 'Cannabinoids in Clinical Practice: A UK Perspective'. In Roger Pertwee (ed.), *Handbook of Cannabis* (Oxford: Oxford University Press, 2014), 415–432.
Novak, William, *High Culture: Marijuana in the Lives of Americans* (New York: Alfred A. Knopf, 1980).
Novella, Enric and Rafael Huertas, 'Alexandre Brierre de Boismont and the Origins of the Spanish Psychiatric Profession', *History of Psychiatry* 22.4 (2011), 387–402.
Nugent-Head, JulieAnn, 'The First Materia Medica: The Shen Nong Ben Cao Jing', *Journal of Chinese Medicine* 104 (2014), 24–28.
Nugent, Shannon and Devan Kansagara, 'Cannabis for Chronic Pain: We Simply Don't Know', *Pain Medicine* 21.6 (2020), 1091–1092.
Nunn, John, *Ancient Egyptian Medicine* (London: University of Oklahoma Press, 1996).
Nutt, David, *Cannabis (Seeing Through the Smoke): The New Science of Cannabis and Your Health* (London: Yellow Kite, 2021).
Nutt, David, *Estimating Drug Harms: A Risky Business* (London: Centre for Crime and Justice Studies, 2009).
Nutt, David, Leslie King, William Sualsbury, and Colin Blakemore, 'Development of a Rational Scale to Assess the Harm of Drugs of Potential Misuse', *The Lancet* 369 (2007), 1047–1053.
O'Dowd, Liam, '52% of Britons Support the Legalisation of Cannabis in the UK', *Leafie* (6 April 2021): https://www.leafie.co.uk/news/52-percent-britons-support-legalisation-cannabis/ (accessed 6 October 2021).
O'Shaughnessy, William B. (ed.), *The Bengal Dispensatory and Pharmacopœia* (Calcutta: Bishop's College Press, 1841).
O'Shaughnessy, William B. (ed.), *The Bengal Dispensatory. Chiefly Compiled from the Works of Roxburgh, Wallich, Ainslie, Wight, Arnot, Royle, Pereira, Lindley, Richard, and Feé, including the Results of Numerous Special Experiments* (Calcutta: W. Thacker and Co., 1842).
O'Shaughnessy, William B. (ed.), *The Bengal Pharmacopœia, and General Conspectus of Medicinal Plants: Arranged According to the Natural and Therapeutical Systems* (Calcutta: Bishop's College Press, 1844).
O'Shaughnessy, William B., 'Cannabis'. In William O'Shaughnessy (ed.), *The Bengal Dispensatory. Chiefly Compiled from the Works of Roxburgh, Wallich, Ainslie, Wight, Arnot, Royle, Pereira, Lindley, Richard, and Feé, including the Results of Numerous Special Experiments* (Calcutta: W. Thacker and Co., 1842), 580–604.
O'Shaughnessy, William B., 'On the Preparation of the Indian Hemp, or Gunjah (*Cannabis Indica*); their Effects of the Animal System in Health, and their Utility in the Treatment of Tetanus and other Convulsive Diseases', *Transactions of the Medical and Physical Society of Bengal*, 1838–1840 (Calcutta: Medical and Physical Society of Bengal, 1840), 421–461; also available in Tod Mikuriya (ed.), *Cannabis: Collected Clinical Papers. Vol. 1, Marijuana: Medical Papers, 1839–1972* (Nevada City: Symposium Publishing, 2007), 3–30.
O'Shaughnessy, William B., 'On the Preparation of the Indian Hemp, or Gunjah (*Cannabis Indica*); their Effects of the Animal System in Health, and their Utility in the Treatment of Tetanus and other Convulsive Diseases', *Provincial Medical Journal and Retrospect of the Medical Sciences* 123 (4 February 1843), 343–347, 363–369.
O'Shaughnessy, William B., *On the Preparation of the Indian Hemp, or Gunjah, (Cannabis Indica). Their Effects of the Animal System in Health, and their Utility in the*

Treatment of Tetanus and other Convulsive Disorders (Calcutta: Bishop's College Press, 1839).
Ockerman, Emma, 'The More Drugmakers Wowed Doctors with Gifts and Lunches, the More People Died of Drug Overdoses, Study Shows', *Vice News* (18 January 2019): https://www.vice.com/en/article/59xm4a/the-more-drugmakers-wowed-doctors-with-gifts-and-lunches-the-more-people-died-of-drug-overdoses-study-shows (accessed 18 April 2021).
Olcott, Henry, *The Spirit of the Zoroastrian Religion* (Bombay: 'published by public subscription', 1882).
Oman, John, *The Natural and the Supernatural* (Cambridge: Cambridge University Press, 1931).
Oner, S.T., *Cannabis Indica*, 3 vols (San Francisco: Green Candy Press, 2011, 2012, 2014).
Oner, S.T., *Cannabis Sativa*, 3 vols (San Francisco: Green Candy Press, 2012, 2013, 2014).
Osborn, Catherine, 'Artificial Paradises: Baudelaire and the Psychedelic Experience', *The American Scholar* 36:4 (Autumn 1967), 660–668.
Osler, William, *The Principles and Practice of Medicine: Designed for the Use of Practitioners and Students of Medicine* (Edinburgh: Young J. Pentland, 1892).
Osto, Douglas, *Altered States: Buddhism and Psychedelic Spirituality in America* (New York: Columbia University Press, 2016).
Oswald, Kirsty, 'Cognitive Cannabis: the Emerging Evidence for Treating Mental Health Problems', *The Pharmaceutical Journal* 33 (31 October 2019): https://pharmaceutical-journal.com/article/feature/cognitive-cannabis-the-emerging-evidence-for-treating-mental-health-problems (accessed: 16 March 2021).
Otto, Rudolf, *The Idea of the Holy*. Trans. by John Harvey (Oxford: Oxford University Press, 1958).
Overmyer, Daniel, *Local Religion in North China in the Twentieth Century* (Leiden: Brill, 2009).
Owen, Alex, *The Darkened Room: Women, Power and Spiritualism in Late Victorian England* (Philadelphia: University of Pennsylvania Press, 1990).
Owen, Alex, *The Place of Enchantment: British Occultism and the Culture of the Modern* (Chicago: University of Chicago Press, 2004).
Owens, Joseph, 'The I-Words'. In Stephen Davis and Peter Simon (eds), *Reggae International* (London: Thames & Hudson, 1983) 62.
Pain, Stephanie, 'High Times: The Victorian Doctor who Promoted Medical Marijuana', *New Scientist* (2 May 2018): https://www.newscientist.com/article/mg23831760-400-high-times-the-victorian-doctor-who-promoted-medical-marijuana/#ixzz70gz2UGww (accessed 15 July 2021).
Papers Regarding the Cultivation of Hemp in India (Agra: Secundra Orphan Press, 1855).
Parascandola, John, 'The Drug Habit: the Association of the Word "Drug" with Abuse in American History'. In Roy Porter and Mikulas Teich (eds), *Drugs and Narcotics in History* (Cambridge: Cambridge University Press, 1995), 156–167.
Pardal, Mafalda (ed.), *The Cannabis Social Club* (London: Routledge, 2022).
Parker, Howard, Fiona Measham, and Judith Aldridge, *Drugs Futures: Changing Patterns of Drug Use Amongst English Youth* (London: Institute for the Study of Drug Dependence, 1995).
Parker, Scott, 'Introduction'. In Scott Parker (ed.), *Conversations with Ken Kesey* (Jackson: University Press of Mississippi, 2014), 7–9.

Partridge, Christopher, 'Schism in Babylon: Colonialism, Afro-Christianity and Rastafari'. In James Lewis and Sarah Lewis (eds), *Sacred Schisms: How Religions Divide* (Cambridge: Cambridge University Press, 2009): 306–331

Partridge, Christopher, 'A Beautiful Politics: Theodore Roszak's Romantic Radicalism and the Counterculture', *Journal for the Study of Radicalism* 12.2 (2018), 1–34.

Partridge, Christopher, 'Adventures in "Wisdom-land": Orientalist Discourse in Early Theosophy'. In T. Rudbøg and E.R. Sand (eds), *Imagining the East: The Early Theosophical Society* (New York: Oxford University Press, 2020), 13–32.

Partridge, Christopher, 'Aleister Crowley on Drugs', *International Journal for the Study of New Religions* 7.2 (2016), 125–151.

Partridge, Christopher, 'Lost Horizon: H.P. Blavatsky's Theosophical Orientalism'. In Mikael Rothstein and Olav Hammer (eds), *Handbook of the Theosophical Current* (Leiden: Brill, 2013), 309–333.

Partridge, Christopher, 'Orientalism and the Occult'. In Christopher Partridge (ed.), *The Occult World* (London: Routledge, 2015), 611–625.

Partridge, Christopher, 'Psychedelica Sub Rosa: The Eleusinian Mysteries and the Psychedelic Imagination'. In Hugh Urban and Paul C. Johnson (ed.), *Handbook of Religion and Secrecy* (Abingdon: Routledge, 2022), 57–70.

Partridge, Christopher, *Dub in Babylon: Understanding the Evolution and Significance of Dub Reggae in Jamaica and Britain from King Tubby to Post-punk* (London: Equinox, 2010).

Partridge, Christopher, *High Culture: Drugs, Mysticism, and the Pursuit of Transcendence in the Modern World* (New York: Oxford University Press, 2018).

Partridge, Christopher, *The Lyre of Orpheus: Popular Music, the Sacred, and the Profane* (Oxford: Oxford University Press, 2014).

Partridge, Christopher, *The Re-Enchantment of the West: Alternative Spiritualities, Sacralization, Popular Culture and Occulture*, 2 vols (London: T. & T. Clark International, 2004, 2005).

Pasi, Marco, 'The Varieties of Magical Experience: Aleister Crowley's Views on Occult Practice'. In Henrik Bogdan and Martin Starr (eds), *Aleister Crowley and Western Esotericism* (New York: Oxford University Press, 2012), 53–87.

Patel, Rachna, *The CBD Oil Solution: Treat Chronic Pain, Anxiety, Insomnia, and More—Without the High* (Indianapolis: DK Publishing, 2019).

Patterson, Stephen, *The Gospel of Thomas and Christian Origins: Essays on the Fifth Gospel* (Leiden: Brill, 2013).

Pease, Arthur, 'A Sketch of The Development of Ancient Botany', *Phoenix* 6.2 (1952), 44–51.

Peng, Bi-Sheng, 'From Religious Manual to Herbal Pharmacopoeia: A Textual Study of the Formation and Transformation of Shennong's Classic of *Materia Medica*', *Traditional Medicine Research* 5.5 (2020), 368–376.

Pennacchio, Marcello, Lara Jefferson, and Kayri Havens, *Uses and Abuses of Plant-Derived Smoke: Its Ethnobotany as Hallucinogen, Perfume, Incense, and Medicine* (Oxford: Oxford University Press, 2010).

Pennay, Amy and Fiona Measham, 'The Normalisation Thesis—20 Years Later', *Drugs: Education, Prevention, and Policy* 23.3 (2016), 187–189.

Pertwee, Roger (ed.), *Handbook of Cannabis* (Oxford: Oxford University Press, 2014).

Pertwee, Roger, 'Cannabinoid Pharmacology: The First 66 Years', *British Journal of Pharmacology* 147, Supplement 1 (2006), 163–171.

Peters, Hélène, 'Hashish and Mental Illness: The Experience and Observations of Moreau'. In Gabriel G. Nahas and Colette Latour (eds), *Cannabis: Physiopathology, Epidemiology, Detection* (Boca Raton: CRC Press, 1993), 343–357.

Petrilli, Kat, Lindsey Hines, Sally Adams, Celia Morgan, Valerie Curran, and Tom Freeman, 'High Potency Cannabis Use, Mental Health Symptoms and Cannabis Dependence: Triangulating the Evidence', *Addictive Behaviours* 144 (2023), 1–7.
Pilcher, Tim, *Spliffs 2: Further Adventures in Cannabis Culture* (London: Collins & Brown, 2004).
Pilcher, Tim, *Spliffs 3: The Last Word in Cannabis Culture?* (London: Collins & Brown, 2005).
Pinel, Philippe, *A Treatise on Insanity*. Trans. by D.D. Davis (Sheffield: Cadell and Davies, 1806).
Piper, Alan, 'The Mysterious Origins of the Word "Marihuana,"' *Sino-Platonic Papers* 153 (2005), 1–17.
Piper, John, 'Christians and Marijuana', *Desiring God* (25 April 2013): https://www.desiringgod.org/interviews/christians-and-marijuana (accessed: 11 July 2023).
Pisanti, Simona and Maurizio Bifulco, 'Modern History of Medical Cannabis: From Widespread Use to Prohibitionism and Back', *Trends in Pharmacological Sciences* 38.3 (2017), 195–198.
Plant, Sadie, *Writing on Drugs* (New York: Farrar, Straus and Giroux, 1999).
Pocock, Lewis Greville, *Reality and Allegory in the Odyssey* (Amsterdam: A. M. Hakkert, 1959).
Podmore, Frank, *Modern Spiritualism: A History and a Criticism*, 2 vols. (London: Methuen & Co., 1902).
Pollard, Velma, 'The Social History of Dread Talk', *Caribbean Quarterly* 28.2 (1982), 17–40.
Pollay, Richard and Timothy Dewhirst, 'The Dark Side of Marketing Seemingly "Light" Cigarettes: Successful Images and Failed Fact', *Tobacco Control* 11—Supplement I (2002), i18–i31.
Pollio, Antonino, 'The Name of Cannabis: A Short Guide for Nonbotanists', *Cannabis and Cannabinoid Research* 1.1 (2016): https://www.ncbi.nlm.nih.gov/pmc/articles/PMC5531363/pdf/can.2016.0027.pdf (accessed 17 October 2021).
Postlethwayt, Malachy, *Universal Dictionary of Trade and Commerce*, Vol.1, third edition (London : H. Woodfall et. al., 1766).
Potter, Gary, *Weed, Need, and Greed: A Study of Domestic Cannabis Cultivation* (London: Free Association Books, 2010).
Preedy, Victor (ed.), *Handbook of Cannabis and Related Pathologies: Biology, Pharmacology, Diagnosis, and Treatment* (London: Academic Press, 2017).
Preston, Brian, *Pot Planet: Adventures in Global Marijuana Culture* (London: Atlantic Books, 2002)
Preston, Martin, 'Top 10 Most Dangerous Drugs', *Delamere* (3 February 2022): https://delamere.com/blog/top-10-most-dangerous-drugs (accessed 16 September 2023).
Prioreschi, Plinio and Donald Babin, 'Ancient Use of Cannabis', *Nature* 364. 6439 (1993): 680.
Quaintance, Danuel, 'In Loving Memory of Mary Helen Quaintance': http://haoma.org (accessed 20 August 2023).
Raine, Kathleen, *Yeats the Initiate: Essays on Certain Themes in the Work of W.B. Yeats* (Mountrath: Dolmen Press, 1986).
Raja, Satyen, 'Consciousness Transformation and the Ancient Wisdom of the Sadhus of India'. In Stephen Gray (ed.), *Cannabis and Spirituality: An Explorer's Guide to an Ancient Plant Spirit Ally* (Rochester: Park Street Press, 2017), 152–161.
Ram Dass, Joan Halifax, Robert Aitken, and Richard Baker, 'The Roundtable', *Tricycle: The Buddhist Review* 6.1 (1996), 101–109.

Randolph, Paschal Beverly, 'Hashish!' *Banner of Light* 8.4 (October 20, 1860), 7.
Randolph, Paschal Beverly, 'Rosicrucian Papers No.5', *Religio-Philosophical Journal* 5.20 (6 February 1869), 3.
Randolph, Paschal Beverly, 'What Effects Can Intoxicating Agents Have on the Soul of Man?' *Banner of Light* 8.7 (10 November 1860), 5.
Randolph, Paschal Beverly, 'What is Life? What is Animal Life?' *Banner of Light* 8.13 (22 December 1860), 8.
Randolph, Paschal Beverly, *Dealings With the Dead; The Human Soul, Its Migrations and Its Transmigrations* (Utica: M.J. Randolph, 1862).
Randolph, Paschal Beverly, *Eulis! The History of Love* (Toledo: Randolph Publishing Co., 1874).
Randolph, Paschal Beverly, *Guide to Clairvoyance* (Boston: Rockwell and Rollins, 1867).
Randolph, Paschal Beverly, *P.B. Randolph, the 'Learned Pundit', and 'Man with Two Souls', His Curious Life, Works and Career* (Boston: Randolph Publishing Co., 1872).
Randolph, Paschal Beverly, *Seership! The Magnetic Mirror: A Practical Guide for Those Who Aspire to Clairvoyance-Absolute: Original, and Selected from Various English and Asiatic Adepts* (Boston: Randolph & Co., 1870).
Ranger, Chris, 'Race, Culture and "Cannabis Psychosis": The Role of Social Factors in the Construction of a Disease Category', *Journal of Ethnic and Migration Studies* 15.3 (1989), 357–369.
Rätsch, Christian, *Encyclopedia of Psychoactive Plants: Ethnopharmacology and its Applications*. Trans. by John Baker (Rochester: Park Street Press, 1998).
Rätsch, Christian, *Marijuana Medicine*. Trans. by John Baker (Rochester: Healing Arts Press, 2001).
Rawson, Albert, 'Mme. Blavatsky: A Theosophical Occult Apology', *Frank Leslie's Popular Monthly* (February 1892), 199–208.
Reardon, Bernard, *Religion in the Age of Romanticism* (Cambridge: Cambridge University Press, 1985).
Regardie, Israel, 'Introduction'. In Christopher Hyatt, *Undoing Yourself With Energized Meditation and Other Devices*, ninth edition (Tempe: New Falcon Publications, 2002), xxi–xxii.
Regardie, Israel, 'Roll Away the Stone'. In Israel Regardie and Aleister Crowley, *Roll Away the Stone and The Herb Dangerous* (North Hollywood: Newcastle Publishing, 1994), 1–65.
Regardie, Israel and Aleister Crowley, *Roll Away the Stone: An Introduction to Aleister Crowley's Essays on the Psychology of Hashish, with the Complete Text of Aleister Crowley's 'The Herb Dangerous'* (North Hollywood: Newcastle Publishing, 1994).
Regardie, Israel, *The Eye in the Triangle: An Interpretation of Aleister Crowley* (Las Vegas: New Falcon Publications, 2014).
Reich, Charles, *The Greening of America* (Harmondsworth: Penguin, 1971).
Reiman, Amanda, *Medical Cannabis Facilities: Inside Cannabis Care* (Saarbrücken: VDM Verlag Dr. Müller, 2007).
Reinoso Niche, Jorgelina, 'Santa Rosa and Singing from the Heart of the Bädi', *Anthropology of Consciousness* 33 (2022), 229–254.
Ren, Guangpeng, Xu Zhang, Ying Li, Kate Ridout, Martha Serrano-Serrano, Yongzhi Yang, Ai Liu, Gudasalamani Ravikanth, Muhammad Ali Nawaz, Abdul Samad Mumtaz, Nicolas Salamin, and Luca Fumagalli, 'Large-scale Whole-genome Resequencing Unravels the Domestication History of *Cannabis sativa*', *Science Advances* 7.29 (16 July 2021), 1–12.

Ren, Meng, Zihua Tang, Xinhua Wu, Robert Spengler, Hongen Jiang, Yimin Yang, and Nicole Boivin, 'The Origins of Cannabis Smoking: Chemical Residue Evidence from the First Millennium BCE in the Pamirs', *Science Advances* 5.6 (12 June 2019): https://www.science.org/doi/10.1126/sciadv.aaw1391 (accessed 20 October 2021).

Rendle, Alfred Barton, *The Classification of Flowering Plants*, Vol. 2 (Cambridge: Cambridge University Press, 1925).

Resin, Harry, 'A History of Medical Cannabis', *Treating Yourself: The Alternative Medicine Journal*: https://treatingyourself.com/a-history-of-medical-cannabis/ (accessed 12 April 2021).

Revuelta, Jose I. Pérez, and Jose M. Villagrán Moreno, 'Moreau de Tours: Organicism and Subjectivity. Part 1: Life and Work', *History of Psychiatry* 32 (2021), 162–175.

Revuelta, Jose I. Pérez, and Jose M. Villagrán Moreno, 'Moreau de Tours: Organicism and Subjectivity. Part 2: Moreau as Psychopathologist', *History of Psychiatry* 32 (2021), 255–269.

Reynolds, John Russell, 'On the Therapeutic Uses and Toxic Effects of *Cannabis Indica*', *The Lancet* 135 (1890), 637–638. Also available in Tod Mikuriya (ed.), *Cannabis: Collected Clinical Papers. Vol. 1, Marijuana: Medical Papers, 1839-1972* (Nevada City: Symposium Publishing, 2007), 145–149.

Richert, Lucas and James Mills (eds), *Cannabis: Global Histories* (Cambridge: MIT Press, 2021).

Riggs, Patricia, Florin Vaida, Steven S. Rossi, Linda S. Sorkin, Ben Gouaux, Igor Grant, and Ronald J. Ellis, 'A Pilot Study of the Effects of Cannabis on Appetite Hormones in HIV-infected Adult Men', *Brain Research* 1431 (2012), 46–52.

Riley, Diane and Eugene Oscapella, 'The Terry Parker Case: Marijuana for Epilepsy—and Soon for HIV/AIDS?' *Canadian HIV-AIDS Policy and Law Newsletter* 3-4 (Winter 1997-1998), 20–23.

Rimbaud, Arthur, *Collected Poems*. Trans. by Martin Sorrell (Oxford: Oxford University Press, 2001).

Rinella, Michael, *Pharmakon: Plato, Drug Culture, and Identity in Ancient Athens* (Lanham: Lexington Books, 2012).

Ritti, Antoine, *Éloge de J. Moreau (de Tours)* (Paris: Octave Doin Editeur, 1887).

Roberts, Carl, Gerry Jager, Paul Christiansen, and Tim Kirkham, 'Exploring the Munchies: An Online Survey of Users' Experiences of Cannabis Effects on Appetite and the Development of a Cannabinoid Eating Experience Questionnaire', *Journal of Psychopharmacology (Oxford)* 33.9 (2019), 1149–1159.

Rogers, Athlyi, *The Holy Piby* (Kingston: Headstart; Chicago: Research Associates School Times Publication, 2000).

Rolle, Renate, *The World of the Scythians*. Trans. by F.G. Walls (Berkeley: University of California Press, 1989).

Roof, Wade Clark, *The Spiritual Marketplace: Baby Boomers and the Remaking of American Religion* (Princeton: Princeton University Press, 1999)

Roopnarine, Lomarsh, *The Indian Caribbean: Migration and Identity in the Diaspora* (Jackson: University Press of Mississippi, 2018).

Rosenfeld, Albert, 'Marijuana: Millions of Turned-on Users', *LIFE* 63.1 (7 July 1967), 16–23.

Rosenthal, Franz, *The Herb: Hashish versus Medieval Muslim Society*. In Franz Rosenthal, *Man Versus Society in Medieval Islam*, ed. by Dimitri Gutas (Leiden: Brill, 2014), 131–334.

Ross, Samir, Hala ElSohly, ElSayeda ElKashoury, and Mahmoud ElSohly, 'Fatty Acids of Cannabis Seeds', *Phytochemical Analysis* 7.6 (1996), 279–283.

Roszak, Theodore, *Sources* (New York: Harper Colophon Books, 1972).

Roszak, Theodore, *The Making of a Counter Culture: Reflections on the Technocratic Society and Its Youthful Opposition* (London: Faber & Faber, 1970).
Roszak, Theodore, Tim Eiloart, Glyn Davies, Chris Cilchrist, and Dorothy Emmet, 'Is the Counter-culture Landscaping the Wasteland?' *Theoria to Theory* 12 (1979), 255–268.
Roszak, Theodore, *Unfinished Animal: The Aquarian Frontier and the Evolution of Consciousness* (London: Faber & Faber, 1975).
Roszak, Theodore, *Where the Wasteland Ends: Politics and Transcendence in Postindustrial Society* (New York: Doubleday, 1972).
Rubin, Craig X, 'Reverend of Temple 420 Plans to Use Religious Defense', *Cannabis Culture* (16 December 2006): https://www.cannabisculture.com/content/2006/12/16/4877/ (accessed 21 August 2023).
Rubin, Noah, *How We Roll: The Art and Culture of Joints, Blunts, and Spliffs* (San Francisco: Chronicle Books, 2022).
Rubin, Vera (ed.), *Cannabis and Culture* (The Hague: Mouton Publishers, 1975).
Rubin, Vera and Lambros Comitas, *Ganja in Jamaica: The Effects of Marijuana Use* (New York: Anchor Books, 1976).
Rudenko, Sergei, *Frozen Tombs of Siberia: The Pazyryk Burials of Iron Age Horsemen*. Trans. by M.W. Tompson (Berkeley: University of California Press, 1970).
Rudgley, Richard, *The Alchemy of Culture: Intoxicants in Society* (London: British Museum Press, 1993).
Rushkoff, Doug, 'Cannabis: Stealth Goddess'. In Julie Holland (ed.), *The Pot Book: A Complete Guide to Cannabis. Its Role in Medicine, Politics, Science, and Culture* (Rochester: Park Street Press, 2010), 366–372.
Russell, Jeffrey Burton, *Satan: The Early Christian Tradition* (Ithaca: Cornell University Press, 1981).
Russo, Ethan, 'Cannabis in India: Ancient Lore and Modern Medicine'. In Raphael Mechoulam (ed.), *Cannabinoids as Therapeutics* (Basel: Birkhäuser Verlag, 2005), 1–22.
Russo, Ethan, 'Cannabis Treatments in Obstetrics and Gynaecology: A Historical Review'. In Ethan Russo, Melanie Creagan Dreher, and Mary Lynn Mathre (eds), *Women and Cannabis: Medicine, Science, and Sociology* (New York: Haworth Integrative Healing Press, 2002), 5–36.
Russo, Ethan, 'Cannabis Treatments in Obstetrics and Gynaecology: A Historical Review', *Journal of Cannabis Therapeutics* 2.3-4 (2002), 5–35.
Russo, Ethan, 'Cognoscenti of Cannabis I: Jacques-Joseph Moreau (1804–1884)', *Journal of Cannabis Therapeutics* 1.1 (2001), 85–88.
Russo, Ethan, 'History of Cannabis and Its Preparations in Saga, Science, and Sobriquet', *Chemistry and Biodiversity* 4 (2007), 1614–1648.
Russo, Ethan, 'Taming THC: Potential Cannabis Synergy and Phytocannabinoid-terpenoid Entourage Effects', *British Journal of Pharmacology* 163.7 (2012), 1344–1364.
Russo, Ethan, 'The Case for the Entourage Effect and Conventional Breeding of Clinical Cannabis: No "Strain," No Gain', *Frontiers in Plant Science* (9 January 2019): https://www.frontiersin.org/articles/10.3389/fpls.2018.01969/full (accessed 20 October 2021).
Russo, Ethan, 'The Role of Cannabis and Cannabinoids in Pain Management'. In Richard Weiner (ed.), *Pain Management: A Practical Guide for Clinicians*, sixth edition (Boca Raton: CRC Press, 2002), 357–375.
Russo, Ethan and Geoffrey Guy, 'A Tale of Two Cannabinoids: The Therapeutic Rationale for Combining Tetrahydrocannabinol and Cannabidiol', *Medical Hypotheses* 66.2 (2006), 234–246.

Russo, Ethan, Melanie Creagan Dreher, and Mary Lynn Mathre (eds), *Women and Cannabis: Medicine, Science, and Sociology* (New York: Haworth Integrative Healing Press, 2002).
Sabina, María, *Selections*. Edited by Jerome Rothenberg (Berkeley: University of California Press, 2003).
Sacy, Antoine Isaac Sylvestre de, 'Des preparations enivrantes faites avec le chanvre, mémoire li à l'Institut', *C.-T. ou Bulletin des societies méd. pub au nom de la Soc. méd. d'Emulation de Paris*, 4 (1809), 201–206.
Said, Edward, *Orientalism* (London: Penguin, 2003).
Saler, Michael, 'Introduction'. In Michael Saler (ed.), *The Fin-de-Siècle World* (London: Routledge, 2015), 1–8.
Sanchez, Gonzalo and W. Benson Harer Jr., 'Toxicology in Ancient Egypt'. In Philip Wexler (ed.), *Toxicology in Antiquity*, second edition (London: Academic Press, 2019), 73–82.
Sanders, Bernie, 'Legalizing Marijuana', *BernieSanders.com*: https://berniesanders.com/issues/legalizing-marijuana (accessed 20 March 2020).
Sandstrom, Alan and Pamela Effrein Sandstrom, *Pilgrimage to Broken Mountain: Nahua Sacred Journeys in Mexico's Huasteca Veracruzana* (Denver: University of Colorado Press, 2023).
Sanson, Dawne, 'New/Old Spiritualities in the West: Neo-Shamans and Neo Shamanism'. In James Lewis and Murphy Pizza (eds), *Handbook of Contemporary Paganism* (Leiden: Brill, 2009), 433–462.
Santlofer, Jonathon (ed.) *The Marijuana Chroinicles* (New York: Akashic Books, 2013).
Schaller, Michael, 'The Federal prohibition of Marihuana', *Journal of Social History* 4.1 (1970), 61–74.
Schofield, Michael, *The Strange Case of Pot* (Harmondsworth: Penguin, 1971).
Schultes, Richard Evans, 'Man and Marihuana', *Natural History* (August 1973), 59–63, 80, 82.
Schultes, Richard Evans, Albert Hofmann, and Christian Rätsch, *Plants Of The Gods. Their Sacred Healing And Hallucinogenic Powers* (Rochester: Healing Arts Press, 1992)
Schultes, Richard Evans, William Klein, Timothy Plowman, and Tom Lockwood, 'Cannabis: An Example of Taxonomic Neglect'. In Vera Rubin (ed.), *Cannabis and Culture* (The Hague: Mouton Publishers, 1975), 21–38.
Schultz, Julia, *The Influence of Spanish on the English Language Since 1801: A Lexical Investigation* (Newcastle: Cambridge Scholars Publishing, 2018).
Scimeca, Giuseppi, Claudia Chisari, Maria Muscatello, Clemente Cedro, Gianluca Pandolfo, Rocco Zoccali, and Antonio Bruno, 'Cannabis and Sexual Behavior'. In Victor Preedy (ed.), *Handbook of Cannabis and Related Pathologies* (Cambridge: Academic Press, 2017), 180–187.
Scull, Andrew, *Madness in Civilization* (London: Thames & Hudson, 2016).
Seibert, Shawn, Pankaj Kumar, Patrick Gomez, Christina Gomez, Laura Miller, and Matt Logsdon, 'Cannabis in Cancer Patients to Improve Quality of Life and Cancer Related Symptoms', *Journal of Clinical Oncology* 36.15 (2018): https://ascopubs-org.ezproxy.lancs.ac.uk/doi/abs/10.1200/JCO.2018.36.15_suppl.e18812 (accessed 18 August 2021).
Self, Will, 'Introduction'. In *Revelation: The Canon Pocket Bible* (Edinburgh: Canongate Books, 1998), vii–xiv.
Sender, Pablo, 'Drugs and Spirituality: An Occult Perspective'. *Quest* 103.1 (Winter 2015), 16–19.
Sewell, Andrew, Mohini Ranganathan, and Deepak Cyril D'Souza, 'Cannabinoids and Psychosis', *International Review of Psychiatry* 21.2 (2009), 152–162.

Shelton, Gilbert, *The Fabulous Furry Freak Brothers Omnibus* (London: Knockabout Comics, 2008).
Shepherd, Verene, *Transients to Settlers: the Experience of Indians in Jamaica, 1845–1950* (Leeds: Peepal Tree Press, 1994).
Sherman, Carol and Andrew Smith, *High Lights: An Illustrated History of Cannabis* (Berkeley: Ten Speed Press, 1999).
Sherratt, Andrew, 'Alcohol and Its Alternatives: Symbol and Substance in Pre-industrial Cultures'. In Jordan Goodman, Paul Lovejoy, and Andrew Sherratt (eds), *Consuming Habits: Global and Historical Perspectives on How Cultures Define Drugs*, second edition (Abingdon: Routledge, 2007), 11–45.
Sherratt, Andrew, 'Sacred and Profane Substances: The Ritual Use of Narcotics in Later Neolithic Europe'. In Paul Garwood, David Jennings, Robin Skeates, and Judith Toms (eds), *Sacred and Profane: Proceedings of a Conference on Archaeology, Ritual and Religion* (Oxford: Oxford University Committee for Archaeology, 1991), 50–64.
Shiner, Michael and Tim Newburn, 'Definitely, Maybe Not? The Normalisation of Recreational Drug Use Amongst Young People', *Sociology* 31.3 (1997), 511–529.
Short, Thomas, *Medicina Britannica: or, a Treatise on Such Physical Plants as are Generally to be found in the Fields or Gardens in Great Britain* (London: R. Manby & H. Shute Cox, 1746).
Shteir, Rachel, 'Julie Falco Goes West: Illinois Poster Girl for Legalizing Medicinal Cannabis Leaves Town'. In Jonathon Santlofer (ed.), *The Marijuana Chroinicles* (New York: Akashic Books, 2013), 214–222.
Siegel, Ronald and Ada Hirschman, 'Edmond DeCourtive and the First Thesis on Hashish: A Historical Note and Translation', *Journal of Psychoactive Drugs* 23.1 (1991), 85–86.
Siegel, Ronald, *Intoxication: Life in Pursuit of Artificial Paradise* (London: Simon & Schuster, 1989).
Sinclair, Sarah, 'Hemp for Elephants: Inside the Zoo Giving Anxious Animals CBD', *Cannabis Health* (5 January 2021): https://cannabishealthnews.co.uk/2021/01/05/hemp-for-elephants-inside-the-zoo-giving-anxious-animals-cbd/ (accessed 27 September 2021).
Sinclair, Sarah, 'I Just Medicate to Hoover', *Cannabis Health* 4 (2020), 62–63.
Sinclair, Sarah, 'Inside a UK Cannabis Club: Changing Lives, Tackling Stigma, Building Community', *Cannabis Health* (23 June 2023): https://cannabishealthnews.co.uk/2023/06/23/inside-a-uk-cannabis-club-saving-lives-tackling-stigma-building-community/ (accessed 5 August 2023).
Skumlien, Martine, Claire Mokrysz, Tom P Freeman, Vincent Valton, Matthew B Wall, Michael Bloomfield, Rachel Lees, Anna Borissova, Kat Petrilli, Manuela Giugliano, Denisa Clisu, Christelle Langley, Barbara Sahakian, Valerie Curran, and Will Lawn, 'Anhedonia, Apathy, Pleasure, and Effort-Based Decision-Making in Adult and Adolescent Cannabis Users and Controls', *International Journal of Neuropsychopharmacology* 26.1 (2023), 9–19.
Slade, Desmond, Zlatko Mehmedic, Suman Chandra, and Mahmoud ElSohly, 'Is Cannabis Becoming More Potent'. In David Castle, Robin Murray, and Deepak D'Souza (eds), *Marijuana and Madness*, second edition (Cambridge: Cambridge University Press, 2019), 35–54.
Sloman, Larry, *Reefer Madness: A History of Marijuana* (New York: St. Martin's Griffin, 1998).
Small, Ernest, 'American Law and the Species Problem in Cannabis: Science and Semantics', *United Nations Bulletin on Narcotics* 28.3 (1975): https://www.unodc.org/

unodc/en/data-and-analysis/bulletin/bulletin_1975-01-01_3_page002.html (accessed 23 April 2022).

Small, Ernest, 'Evolution and Classification of *Cannabis sativa* (Marijuana, Hemp) in Relation to Human Utilization', *The Botanical Review* 81 (2015), 189–294.

Small, Ernest and Arthur Cronquist, 'A Practical and Natural Taxonomy for *Cannabis*', *Taxon* 25.4 (1976), 405–435.

Smart, Mary Lou, 'Cannabis and Chemo: How a patient Uses medical Marijuana to Cope with Breast Cancer', *Treating Yourself: The Alternative Medicine Journal* 27 (2011), 42–45.

Smith, Amber, 'How to Help a Dog with Separation Anxiety', *Discover Magazine* (18 June 2023): https://www.discovermagazine.com/lifestyle/how-to-help-a-dog-with-separation-anxiety-full-guide-and-best-products (accessed 06 July 2023).

Smith, Fintan and Lukas Paleckis, 'Decriminalising Cannabis in London: What do Londoners Think the Impact Would Be?' *YouGov* (7 December 2022): https://yougov.co.uk/topics/health/articles-reports/2022/09/07/decriminalising-cannabis-london-what-do-londoners- (accessed 23 May 2023).

Smith, Thomas and Henry Smith, 'Préparation de la cannabine, principe actif du haschich', *Bulletin générale thérapeutique médicale et chirurgicale* 33 (1846), 135–136.

Smith, Thomas and Henry Smith, 'Process for Preparing Cannabine, or Hemp Resin', *Pharmaceutical Journal and Transactions* 6 (1846–1847), 171–173.

Smyth, Chris, 'Skunk Blamed for London Psychosis Epidemic', *The Times* (20 March 2019): https://www.thetimes.co.uk/article/skunk-blamed-for-london-psychosis-epidemic-kd2kdtz05 (accessed 12 October 2021).

Snelders, Stephen, Charles Kaplan, and Toine Pieters, 'On Cannabis, Chloral Hydrate, and Career Cycles of Psychotropic Drugs in Medicine', *Bulletin of the History of Medicine* 80.1 (2006), 95–114.

Snyder, Solomon H., *Uses of Marijuana* (New York: Oxford University Press, 1971).

Société Orientale de France, *Société Orientale de France fondée à Paris en 1841 reconnue et autorisée par décision des ministres de l'intérieur et de l'instruction publique* (Paris: J. Rouvier, 1843).

Sohn, Emily, 'Weighing the Dangers of Cannabis', *Nature: Outlook* (28 August 2019): https://www.nature.com/articles/d41586-019-02530-7 (accessed 22 June 2021).

Solhdju, Katrin, 'Alienating Travels and Traveling into Alienation: Moreau de Tours's Experimental Attempts to Articulate the Body of Madness', *Dingdingdong* (25 December 2012), 16: http://dingdingdong.org/wp-content/uploads/alienatingtravels.pdf (accessed March 24, 2016).

Solomon, David (ed.), *The Marijuana Papers* (New York: Signet Books, 1968).

Soma, 'The Law Against Marijuana is Immoral in Principle and Unworkable in Practice', *The Times* (24 July 1967), 5.

South, Nigel (ed.), *Drugs: Culture, Controls, and Everyday Life* (London: Sage, 1999).

Speaker, Susan, '"The Struggle of Mankind against Its Deadliest Foe": Themes of Counter-Subversion in Anti-Narcotic Campaigns, 1920-1940', *Journal of Social History* 34.3 (2001), 591–610.

Spear, Henry Bryan, 'The British Experience', *John Marshall Journal of Practice and Procedure* 67 (1975), 67–98.

Spencer, Jon Michael, *Blues and Evil* (Knoxville: University of Tennessee Press, 1993).

Spencer, William, 'The First Chant: Leonard Howell's *The Promised Key*'. In Nathaniel Murrell, William Spencer, and Adrian McFarlane (eds), *Chanting Down Babylon: The Rastafari Reader* (Philadelphia: Temple University Press, 1998), 361–389.

Starbuck, Edwin Diller, *The Psychology of Religion* (London: Walter Scott, 1899).

Steel, Henry Draper, *Portable Instructions for Purchasing the Drugs and Spices of Asia and the East Indies* (London: D. Steel, 1779), 14.
Steer, Margie, 'Edible Marijuana: What We Need to Know', *The Conversation* (1 March 2017): https://theconversation.com/edible-marijuana-what-we-need-to-know-70898 (accessed 23 April 2022).
Steeze, Adolph, 'On the Chaschisch of the Arabs (*Cannabis Sativa* or Hemp)', *Pharmaceutical Journal and Transactions* 5 (1846), 83.
Stelzer, Emily, 'Euphrasy, Rue, Polysemy, and Repairing the Ruins'. In Thomas Festa and Kevin Donovan (eds), *Scholarly Milton* (Clemson: Clemson University Press, 2019), 185–208.
Stevens, Helen Norton, *Memorial Biography of Adele M. Fielde: Humanitarian* (New York: Fielde Memorial Committee, 1918).
Strathern, Paul, *Napoleon in Egypt* (London: Vintage, 2008).
Strickler, Laura and Steve Patterson, 'High Potency Weed Linked to Psychotic Episodes, Mysterious Vomiting Illness in Young Users', *NBC News* (11 July 2021): https://www.nbcnews.com/health/health-news/high-potency-weed-linked-psychotic-episodes-mysterious-vomiting-illness-young-n1273463?cid=sm_npd_nn_tw_ma (accessed 19 August 2021).
Strong, James, *Exhaustive Concordance of the Bible* (New York: Abingdon Press, 1890).
Sude, Daniel and Sylvia Knobloch-Westerwick, 'Selective Exposure and Attention to Attitude-Consistent and Aptitude-Discrepant Information'. In Jesper Strömbäck, Åsa Wikforss, Kathrin Glüer, Torun Lindholm, and Henrik Oscarsson (eds), *Knowledge Resistance in High-Choice Information Environments* (Abingdon: Routledge, 2022), 88–105.
Sumler, Alan, *Cannabis in the Ancient Greek and Roman World* (Lanham: Lexington Books, 2018).
Sun, Andrew and Michael Eisenberg, 'Association Between Marijuana Use and Sexual Frequency in the United States: A Population-Based Study', *Journal of Sexual Medicine* 14.11 (2017), 1342–1347.
Supreme Court of the United States, 'Lee Brooker v. State of Alabama': https://eji.org/files/lee-brooker-us-cert-petition.pdf (accessed 3 January 2020).
Suster, Gerald, *Crowley's Apprentice: The Life and Ideas of Israel Regardie* (London: Rider, 1989).
Sutin, Lawrence, *Do What Thou Wilt: A Life of Aleister Crowley* (New York: St. Martin's Griffin, 2000).
Sweet, Tammi, *The Wholistic Healing Guide to Cannabis* (North Adams: Storey Publishing, 2020).
Symonds, John, *The Magic of Aleister Crowley* (London: Frederick Muller, 1958).
Sznitman, Sharon Rödner, Börje Olsson, and Robin Room (eds), *A Cannabis Reader: Global Issues and Local Experiences* (Lisbon: European Monitoring Centre for Drugs and Drug Addiction, 2008).
Tahsin, Jamie, 'If You Buy Weed Vapes in the UK, Beware—But Not for the Reason You Think', *Vice* (10 December 2019): https://www.vice.com/en/article/xweejk/cannabis-vapes-pens-buy-uk-spice (accessed 16 August 2022).
Taillieu, Dieter, 'Haoma: Botany'. In Ehsan Yarshater (ed.), *Encyclopædia Iranica*, Vol. 11 (New York: Encyclopædia Iranica Foundation, 2012), https://www.iranicaonline.org/articles/haoma-i (accessed 6 November 2023).
Taliaferro, Charles, 'Human Nature, Personal Identity, and Eschatology'. In Jerry Walls (ed.), *The Oxford Handbook of Eschatology* (New York: Oxford University Press, 2008), 534–547.

Tanney, Cailun, Rachel Backer, Anja Geitmann, and Donald Smith, 'Cannabis Glandular Trichomes: A Cellular Metabolite Factory', *Frontiers in Plant Science* 12 (20 September 2021): https://www.frontiersin.org/articles/10.3389/fpls.2021.721986/full (accessed 24 April 2022).

Taves, Ann, *Religious Experience Reconsidered: A Building Block Approach to the Study of Religion and Other Special Things* (Princeton: Princeton University Press, 2009).

Tavhare, Swagata Dilip, Rabinarayan Acharya, Govind Reddy, and Kartar Singh Dhiman, 'Management of Chronic Pain with *Jalaprakshalana* (water-wash) *Shodhita* (processed) *Bhanga* (*Cannabis sativa* L.) in Cancer Patients with Deprived Quality of Life: An Open-label Single Arm Clinical Trial', *International Quarterly Journal of Research in Ayurveda* 40.1 (2019), 34–43

Taylor, Bayard, 'The Vision of Hasheesh', *Putnam's Monthly Magazine of American Literature, Science and Art* 3.16 (April 1854), 402–408.

Taylor, Bayard, *A Journey to Central Africa; or, Life and Landscapes from Egypt to the Negro Kingdoms of the White Nile* (New York: G.P. Putnam, 1854).

Taylor, Bayard, *The Lands of the Saracen; or, Pictures of Palestine, Asia Minor, Sicily, and Spain* (New York: G.P. Putnam, 1859).

Taylor, Charles, *Modern Social Imaginaries* (Durham: Duke University Press, 2004).

Taylor, Charles, *The Ethics of Authenticity* (Cambridge: Harvard University Press, 1991).

Taylor, Patrick, 'Rastafari, the Other, and Exodus Politics: EATUP', *Journal of Religious Thought* 17 (1991), 95–107.

Temple 420, 'About Us': https://www.temple420kansascity.org (accessed 21 August 2023).

Temple 420, 'Salvation is For You Too!': https://www.temple420kansascity.org/salvation (accessed 21 August 2023).

Theosophical Society in America, 'Cults, the Occult, and Theosophy': https://www.theosophical.org/online-resources/leaflets/1793 (accessed 7 June 2016).

Thomas, Mel, 'The Glory Days of Haze: How I Came to Love Sativa'. In S.T. Oner, *Cannabis Sativa*, Vol. 2 (San Francisco: Green Candy Press, 2013), xiii–xviii.

Thompson, Bill and Andy Williams, *The Myth of Moral Panics: Sex, Snuff, and Satan* (New York: Routledge, 2014).

Thompson, R. Campbell, *A Dictionary of Assyrian Botany* (London: British Academy, 1949).

Thornton, Mark, *The Economics of Prohibition* (Salt Lake City: The University of Utah Press, 1991).

Thornton, Sarah, *Club Cultures: Music, Media and Subcultural Capital* (Cambridge: Polity Press, 1995).

Thousand Nights and One Night, Vol. 1, second edition. Trans. by Powys Mathers (London: Routledge, 1986).

Thrower, James, *Religion: The Classical Theories* (Edinburgh: Edinburgh University Press).

Tobacco Control Research Group, 'Cigarette Filters', *Tobacco Tactics* (13 December 2021): https://tobaccotactics.org/wiki/cigarette-filters/ (accessed 3 August 2022).

Toklas, Alice B., *Murder in the Kitchen* (London: Penguin, 2011).

Traugot, Michael, 'The Farm'. In William Zellner and Marc Petrowsky (eds), *Sects, Cults, and Spiritual Communities: A Sociological Analysis* (Westport: Praeger, 1998), 41–62.

Tromp, Marlene, 'Eating, Feeding and Flesh: Food in Victorian Spiritualism'. In Tatiana Kontou and Sarah Willbrun (eds), *The Ashgate Research Companion to Nineteenth-Century Spiritualism and the Occult* (Abingdon: Routledge, 2016), 285–310.

Tromp, Marlene, *Altered States: Sex, Nation, Drugs, and Self-Transformation in Victorian Spiritualism* (Albany: State University of New York Press, 2006).

Tully, Caroline, 'Egyptosophy in the British Museum'. In Christine Ferguson and Andrew Radford (eds), *The Occult Imagination in Britain, 1875–1947* (Abingdon: Routledge, 2018), 131–145.

United Nations Office on Drugs and Crime, *World Drug Report 2022* (Vienna: United Nations Office on Drugs and Crime, 2022).

Urban, Hugh, 'Paschal Beverly Randolph'. In Christopher Partridge (ed.), *The Occult World* (London: Routledge, 2015), 231–233.

US Treasury Department, *Traffic in Opium and Other Dangerous Drugs for the Year Ended December 31, 1941* (Washington: Government Printing Office, 1942).

US Treasury Department, *Traffic in Opium and Other Dangerous Drugs for the Year Ended December 31, 1931* (Washington: Government Printing Office, 1932).

van der Leeuw, Gerardus, *Religion in Essence and Manifestation*. Trans. by J.E. Turner (Princeton: Princeton University Press, 1964).

Van Green, Ted, 'Americans Overwhelmingly Aay Marijuana Should be Legal for Recreational or Medical Use', Pew Research Center (16 April 2021): https://www.pewresearch.org/fact-tank/2021/04/16/americans-overwhelmingly-say-marijuana-should-be-legal-for-recreational-or-medical-use/ (accessed 7 October 2021).

Van Green, Ted, 'Americans Overwhelmingly Say Marijuana Should be Legal for Medical or Recreational Use', Pew Research Center (22 November 2022): https://www.pewresearch.org/short-reads/2022/11/22/americans-overwhelmingly-say-marijuana-should-be-legal-for-medical-or-recreational-use/#:~:text=An%20overwhelming%20share%20of%20U.S.,medical%20use%20only%20(30%25) (accessed 2 February 2024).

Vanhoozer, Kevin, 'Should Followers of Christ Use Recreational Marijuana?' *The Gospel Coalition* (16 January 2020): https://www.thegospelcoalition.org/article/followers-christ-use-recreational-marijuana/ (accessed 11 July 2023).

Veiga, Paula, 'To Prevent, Treat and Cure Love in Ancient Egypt. Aspects of Sexual Medicine and Practice in Ancient Egypt', *Proceedings of the Second International Congress for Young Egyptologists, Lisbon, November 2009*, 453–465: https://www.academia.edu/21822059/To_Prevent_Treat_and_Cure_Love_in_Ancient_Egypt_Aspects_of_Sexual_Medicine_and_Practice_in_Ancient_Egypt (accessed 27 March 2021).

Velasco, Guillermo, Cristina Sánchez, and Manuel Guzmán, 'Towards the Use of Cannabinoids as Antitumour Agents', *Nature Reviews: Cancer* 12.6 (2012), 436–444.

Versluis, Arthur and Morgan Shipley, 'Stephen Gaskin Interview', *Journal for the Study of Radicalism* 4.1 (2010), 141–158.

Vigdor, Neil, 'The Other CBD: Christian Book Distributors Changes Name After Cannabis Confusion', *New York Times* (13 July 2019): https://www.nytimes.com/2019/07/13/us/christian-book-cbd-cannabidiol.html (accessed 16 September 2023).

Vigil, Jacob Miguel, Sarah S. Stith, and Tiphanie Chanel, 'Cannabis Consumption and Prosociality', *Scientific Reports* 12: 8352 (2022): https://www.nature.com/articles/s41598-022-12202-8 (accessed 7 September 2023).

Villa, Keith, *Brewing with Cannabis: Using THC and CBD in Beer* (Boulder: Brewer's Publications, 2021).

Von Rad, Gerhard, *Genesis: A Commentary*. Trans. by John Marks (Philadelphia: Westminster Press, 1961).

Von Stuckrad, Kocku, 'Constructions, Normativities, Identities: Recent Studies on Shamanism and Neo-shamanism', *Religious Studies Review* 31 (2005), 123–128.

Wade, Simeon, *Foucault in California* (Berkeley: Heyday, 2019).

Wadell, Paul, *Happiness and the Christian Moral Life*, second edition (Lanham: Sheed & Ward, 2012).

Waley, Arthur (trans. and ed.), *The Book of Songs* (London: George Allen & Unwin, 1937).
Walton, Robert P., *Marihuana: America's New Drug Problem* (Philadelphia: J.B. Lippincott, 1938).
Walusinski, Olivier, 'Benjamin Ball (1834–1893), premier titulaire de la chaire des maladiesmentales', *Annales Médico-Psychologiques* 179.1 (2021), 107–112.
Wang, Mei, Yan-Hong Wang, Bharathi Avula, Mohamed M. Radwan, Amira S. Wanas, John van Antwerp, Jon Parcher, Mahmoud ElSohly, and Ikhlas A. Khan, 'Decarboxylation Study of Acidic Cannabinoids: A Novel Approach Using Ultra-High-Performance Supercritical Fluid Chromatography/Photodiode Array-Mass Spectrometry', *Cannabis and Cannabinoid Research* 1.1 (2016), 262–271.
Warf, Barney, 'High Points: A Historical Geography of Cannabis', *Geographical Review* 104 (2014), 414–438.
Warren, Leonard, *Adele Marion Fielde: Feminist, Social Activist, Scientist* (London: Routledge, 2002).
Wasson, R. Gordon, 'Persephone's Quest'. In R. Gordon Wasson, Stella Kramrisch, Jonathon Ott, and Carl Ruck, *Persephone's Quest: Entheogens and the Origins of Religion* (New Haven: Yale University Press, 1986), 17–81.
Wasson, R. Gordon, 'Seeking the Magic Mushroom', *Life* (13 May 1957), 100–107, 109–110, 112–113, 117–118, 120.
Wasson, R. Gordon, 'The Hallucinogenic Fungi of Mexico: An Inquiry into the Origins of the Religious Idea Among Primitive Peoples', *The Psychedelic Review* 1.1 (1963), 27–42.
Wasson, R. Gordon, *Soma: Divine Mushroom of Immortality* (New York: Harcourt Brace, 1968).
Wasson, Valentina and Gordon Wasson, *Mushrooms, Russia, and History*, Vol. 2 (New York: Pantheon Books, 1957).
Waxman, Olivia, 'Bill Clinton Said He "Didn't Inhale" 25 Years Ago', *Time* (29 March 2017): https://time.com/4711887/bill-clinton-didnt-inhale-marijuana-anniversary/ (accessed 8 October 2021).
Webb, Duncan, 'Dope: A Warning to Young People', *The People* (18 February 1951), 4.
Weber, Max, *The Protestant Ethic and the Spirit of Capitalism*. Trans. by Stephen Kalberg (Oxford: Blackwell, 2002).
Webster, Peter, 'Marijuana and Music: A Speculative Exploration', *Journal of Cannabis Therapeutics* 1.2 (2001), 93–105.
Weedmaps.com, 'How to Roll a Blunt': https://weedmaps.com/learn/products-and-how-to-consume/how-to-roll-a-blunt (accessed 2 January 2022).
Whineray, E.P., 'A Pharmaceutical Study of Cannabis Sativa (Being a Collation of Facts as Known at the Present Date)', *The Equinox* 1.1 (1909), 233–255; reproduced in Israel Regardie, *Roll Away the Stone: An Introduction to Aleister Crowley's Essays on the Psychology of Hashish, with the Complete Text of Aleister Crowley's 'The Herb Dangerous'* (North Hollywood: Newcastle Publishing, 1994), 69–92.
White, Anna MacBride and A. Norman Jeffares (eds), *The Gonne-Yeats Letters, 1893–1938* (New York: W.W. Norton & Co., 1994).
Whittier, John Greenleaf, *The Complete Poetical Works of John Greenleaf Whittier* (Boston: James R. Osgood & Company, 1876).
Wilding, Mark, 'The Story of Spice, the Street Drug That's Not Going Away', *Vice* (4 May 2017): https://www.vice.com/en/article/z4je55/the-story-of-spice-the-street-drug-thats-not-going-away (accessed 16 August 2022).
Wilkerson, David, *The Cross and the Switchblade* (New York: Bernard Geis Associates, 1963).

Wilkinson Lynn, Rosellen, *The Dream of an Absolute Language: Emanuel Swedenborg and French Literary Culture* (Albany: State University of New York Press, 1996).
Williams-Garcia, Roberto, 'The Ritual Use of Cannabis in Mexico'. In Vera Rubin (ed.), *Cannabis and Culture* (The Hague: Mouton Publishers, 1975), 133–145.
Williams, Patrick, 'The Assassination of Conrad of Montferrat: Another Suspect?' *Traditio* 26 (1970), 381–389.
Willoughby, Jessica, Stacey Hust, Leticia Couto, Jiayu Li, Soojung Kang, Christina Nickerson, Ron Price, and Sandy Tlachi-Munoz, 'The Impact of Sexual Scripts in Brand-generated Cannabis Social Media Posts on Sex-related Cannabis Expectancies: Does Body Appreciation Moderate Effects?' *Drug and Alcohol Review* (17 February 2023), 1–10.
Wills, Simon, 'Cannabis Use and Abuse by Man: An Historical Perspective'. In David Brown (ed.), *Cannabis: The Genus Cannabis* (Amsterdam: Harwood Academic Publishers, 1998), 1–27.
Wilson, David, *Redefining Shamanisms: Spiritualist Mediums and Other Traditional Shamans as Apprenticeships Outcomes* (London: Bloomsbury, 2014).
Windolf, Jim, 'Sex, Drugs, and Soybeans', *Vanity Fair* (5 April 2007): https://www.vanityfair.com/news/2007/05/thefarm200705 (accessed 17 August 2023)
Winters, Riley, 'Magu: The Hemp Goddess Who Healed Ancient Asia', *Ancient Origins* (31 August 2017): https://www.ancient-origins.net/myths-legends-asia/magu-hemp-goddess-who-healed-ancient-asia-008709 (accessed 16 July 2023).
Wiseman, Nigel and Feng Ye, *A Practical Dictionary of Chinese Medicine*, second edition. (Brookline: Paradigm Publications, 1998).
Wissett, Robert, *A Treatise on Hemp* (London: J. Harding, 1808).
Wissett, Robert, *On the Cultivation and Preparation of Hemp* (London: Cox & Son, 1804).
Wolf, Laurie, *Cooking with Cannabis: Delicious Recipes for Edibles and Everyday Favorites* (Beverly: Quarry Books, 2016).
Wolff, Hannah M., 'Madame Blavatsky', *Two Worlds* 4.213 (11 December 1891), 671–672.
Wood, Mary, M., 'Dominique-Jean Larrey, Chief Surgeon of the French Army with Napoleon in Egypt: Notes and Observations on Larrey's Medical Memoirs Based on the Egyptian Campaign', *Canadian Bulletin of Medical History* 25 (2008), 515–535.
Wood, Matthew, *The Magical Staff: The Vitalist Tradition in Western Medicine* (Berkeley: North Atlantic Books, 1992).
Wood, Thomas, Newton Spivey, and Thomas Easterfield, 'III—Cannabinol. Part 1', *Journal of the Chemical Society, Transactions* 75 (1899), 20–36.
Wood, Thomas, Newton Spivey and Thomas Easterfield, 'XL—Charas. The Resin of Indian Hemp', *Journal of the Chemical Society, Transactions* 69 (1896), 539–546.
Woodhead, Linda and Paul Heelas (eds), *Religion in Modern Times: An Interpretative Anthology* (Oxford: Blackwell, 2000).
Worboys, Michael, 'Practice and the Science of Medicine in the Nineteenth Century', *ISIS* 102 (2011), 109–115.
Worboys, Michael, *Spreading Germs: Disease Theories and Medical Practice in Britain, 1865–1900* (Cambridge: Cambridge University Press, 2000).
Wujastyk, Dominik, *The Roots of Ayurveda: Selections from Sanskrit Medical Writings*, second edition (New Dehli: Penguin, 2001).
Wuthnow, Robert, *After Heaven: Spiritualty in America Since the 1950s* (Berkeley: University of California Press, 1998).
Wuthnow, Robert, *Experimentation in American Religion* (Berkeley: University of California Press, 1978).

Yang, Yi, Melissa Lewis, Angelica Bello, Ewa Wasilewski, Hance Clarke, and Lakshmi P. Kotra, 'Cannabis sativa (Hemp) Seeds, $Δ^9$-Tetrahydrocannabinol, and Potential Overdose', *Cannabis and Cannabinoid Research* 2.1 (2017), 274–281

Yawney, Carole, 'Dread Wasteland: Rastafarian Ritual in West Kingston, Jamaica'. In Ross Crumrine (ed.), *Ritual, Symbolism and Ceremonialism in the Americas: Studies in Symbolic Anthropology* (Greenley: Museum of Anthropology, University of Northern Colorado, 1978), 154–174.

Yeats, W.B., *Discoveries; A Volume of Essays* (Dundrum: Dun Emer Press, 1907).

Yeats, W.B., *The Collected Works of W.B. Yeats, Vol. 3. Autobiographies*. Edited by William H. O'Donnell and Douglas N. Archibald (New York: Scribner, 1999).

Yeats, W.B., *The Collected Works of W.B. Yeats, Vol. 5. Later Essays*. Edited by William H. O'Donnell (New York: Scribner, 1994).

Yeats, W.B., *The Collected Works of W.B. Yeats, Vol. 8. A Vision: The Original 1925 Version*. Edited by Catherine E. Paul and Margaret Mills Harper (New York: Scribner, 2008).

Yoe, Craig (ed.), *Reefer Madness Comics* (Milwaukee: Dark Horse Books, 2018).

Yoe, Craig, 'Satan's Lettuce', in Craig Yoe (ed.), *Reefer Madness Comics* (Milwaukee: Dark Horse Books, 2018), 11–31.

Yogo, Takenori, 'Littérature et médecine à l'hôtel Pimodan', *L'Année Baudelaire* 13/14 (2009/2010), 157–180.

Young, Stephen, 'Should This Woman Be Arrested?' *Chicago Reader* (10 February 2005): https://chicagoreader.com/news-politics/should-this-woman-be-arrested/ (accessed 14 October 2021).

Yule, Henry and Arthur Coke Burnell, *A Glossary of Anglo-Indian Words*, second edition (London: Routledge, 1985).

Zaehner, Robert C., *Mysticism, Sacred and Profane: An Inquiry Into Some Varieties of Praeternatural Experience* (London: Oxford University Press, 1961).

Zafar, Rafia, 'Elegy and Remembrance in the Cookbooks of Alice B. Toklas and Edna Lewis', *MELUS: Multi-Ethnic Literature of the United States* 38 (2013), 32–51.

Zend-Avesta, Part 1: The Venidad, second edition. Trans. by James Darmesteter (Oxford: Oxford University Press, 1895).

Zimmer, Lynn and John Morgan, *Marijuana Myths, Marijuana Facts: A Review of the Scientific Evidence* (New York: Lindesmith Center, 1997).

Zinberg, Norman, *Drug, Set, and Setting: The Basis for Controlled Intoxicant Use* (New Haven: Yale University Press, 1984).

Zlas, Joe, Harley Stark, Jon Seligman, Rina Levy, Ella Werker, Aviva Breuer, and Raphael Mechoulam, 'Early Medical Use of Cannabis', *Nature* 363 (1993), 215.

Znamenski, Andrei, *The Beauty of the Primitive: Shamanism and the Western Imagination* (New York: Oxford University Press, 2007).

Zohary, Michael, *Plants of the Bible* (Cambridge: Cambridge University Press, 1982).

Zolotov, Yuval, 'Meet the Experts: Interview with Prof. Roger Pertwee', Fundación CANNA: Scientific Research and Cannabis Testing: https://www.fundacion-canna.es/en/meet-experts-interview-prof-roger-pertwee (accessed 30 September 2021).

Discography

Bad Brains, *Reefer Madness* (Leafy Records, 1992).
Big Bud, *Infinity + Infinity* (Good Looking Records, 1999)
Diamond D, *Stunts, Blunts and Hip Hop* (Chemistry Records, 1992).

The Fall, *Backdrop* (Cog Sinister, 2001).
Hawkwind, *Astounding Sounds, Amazing Music* (Charisma, 1976).
Hawkwind, *Quark, Strangeness and Charm* (Charisma, 1977).
Jah Power Band vs. Sly and the Revolutionaries, *Sensi Dub*, Vol. 7/1 (Original Music, n.d.).
Peetie Whaeatstraw, 'Mister Livingood/ The Good Lawd's Children' (Decca, 1941).
Peter Tosh, *Legalize It* (Virgin Records, 1976).
Redman, *Whut? Thee Album* (Rush Associated Labels, 1992).
Steve Miller Band, *The Joker* (Capitol Records, 1973).
UB40, *Signing Off* (Graduate Records, 1980).
Vagina Dentata Organ, *Music For The Hashishins: In Memoriam Of Hasan Sabbah* (WSNS, 1983).
Various artists, *Reefer Madness* (Stash Records, 1979).
Various artists, *Reefer Madness: A Collection Of Vintage Drug Songs, 1927–1945* (Buzzola, 2004).

Filmography

Films

The Big Lebowski. Directors: Joel Coen and Ethan Coen (Working Title Films, 1998).
Green is Gold. Director: Ryon Baxter (Transition Pictures, 2016).
I Love You, Alice B. Toklas. Director: Hy Averback (Warner Brothers, 1968).
Notch Number One. Director: Ben Wilson (Arrow Film Corporation, 1924).
Pineapple Express. Director: David Gordon Green (Columbia Pictures, 2007)
Reefer Madness. Director: Louis J. Gasnier (G&H Productions, 1936).
Saving Grace. Director: Nigel Cole (20th Century Fox, 2000)
Ted. Director Seth MacFarlane (Universal Pictures, 2012).
Up in Smoke. Director: Lou Adler (Paramount Pictures, 1978).

TV series

Brassic. Creators: Daniel Brocklehurst and Joe Gilgun (Calamity Films, 2019–),
High Maintenance. Creators: Ben Sinclair and Katja Blitchfeld (Janky Clown Productions, 2012–2020)
Ideal. Creator: Graham Duff (Baby Cow Productions, 2005–2011),
Weeds. Creator: Jenji Kohan (Tilted Productions; Lionsgate Television; Showtime Networks, 2005–2012),

Index

Abazia, Daniel, 134, 260, 263
Abdel-Salam, O.M.E., 248
Abramelin Operation, 184
Abrams, Donald, 262
Abrams, Stephen, 261
Acharya, Rabinarayan, 250
ad-Din Sinān, Rashid, 50
Adams, Roger, 15, 120, 230, 259
Adams, Sally, 231, 237
Adams, Steven, 127, 264
addiction, 9–10, 40, 51–52, 57, 59–61, 63, 64–65, 68, 69, 70, 72, 73, 76, 78, 84, 113, 125, 127, 128, 171, 179, 181, 185, 186, 187, 188
Additional Records of Famous Physicians, 91–92
Adversa, 130
Advisory Council on the Misuse of Drugs, 44
Afari, Yasus, 281
AIDS, 129–130
Aitken, Robert, 265
Albright, Thomas, 86, 247
alcohol, 5, 7, 8, 9, 10, 17, 18, 20, 21, 38, 40, 41, 46, 62, 65, 66, 69, 75, 76–79, 82, 92, 93, 99, 102, 120, 121, 125, 128, 129, 142, 150, 162, 165, 168, 174, 186, 187, 196, 202, 207, 218, 222
Aldrich, Michael, 252, 253
Aldridge, Judith, 227
Alexander, Jeffrey, 5–6, 226
Alford, Norman, 276
Ali, Muhammad, 106, 254
Allison, William, 100
ally, cannabis spiritual, 209, 213
Alzheimer's disease, 83
AMCD, *see* Advisory Council on the Misuse of Drugs
Amdur, M.K., 256
Amsterdam, 18
Amsterdam, Jan van, 227, 244, 260

Anderson, J.A., 271
Anderson, Larry, 6
Andrews, George, 286
Andriola, Alfred, 72
animal magnetism, 159–160
animism, 213
Anslinger, Harry J., 61–73, 80–81, 242, 243, 245
Anthony, Saint, 145
Antwerp, John van, 234
anxiety, 10, 41, 75, 81, 83, 84, 94, 113, 130, 132, 210, 228
Appendino, Giovanni, 259
Arabian Nights, 51, 145, 146, 147, 148, 149, 150, 167, 169, 182
Ari, Amal, 227
Arikha, Noga, 250
Arlington, Kim, 238
Armentano, Paul, 227, 244
Armstrong, Louis (music), 67–68
Arnold of Lübeck, 49–50
Aronowitz, Al, 21
arthritis, 83
Asheri, David, 287
Ashurbanipal, 94
Assassins, 47–60, 71, 101, 105, 107, 123, 141, 145, 146, 168
Assembly of Renown Plantation, 217
Atharvaveda, 23, 93
Aubert-Roche, Louis Rémy, 106–108, 119, 141, 254
Augoeides invocations, 183–184
aura, 22, 174, 225
Averett, Paige, 265
Avesta, 94, 203, 216, 223
Avula, Bharathi, 234
Ayton, William Alexander, 175, 276
Ayurveda, 93

Backer, Rachel, 231
Bakalar, James, 130, 233, 261

Baker, Joe, 236
Baker, Richard, 265
Baldasaro, Michael, 214–216, 221
Ballard, Sharon, 265
Balzac, Honoré de, 36, 141
Bangertus, Henricus, 50
Banks, Jamie, 74, 244
Bantu, 22
Barbarossa, Frederick, 49
Bare, John, 268
Barrett, Leonard, 191, 193, 282
Bascom, John, 268
Batilly, Denis Labey de, 50
Baudelaire, Charles, 36, 141–146, 148, 151, 162, 165, 168, 179, 184, 190, 222, 254, 266, 274, 278, 281
Bauer, Alexander, 283
Bauman, Zygmunt, 5, 226
Beard, George, 119, 258
Beardsley, Aubrey, 148
Beatles, The (music), 21, 127
beatniks, 8
Beats, the, 7, 22, 148
Becker, Howard, 30–31, 61, 65, 66, 72, 80, 234, 240, 241, 245
Beddington, John, 46
Bello, Angelica, 288
Ben-Shabat, Shimon, 18, 231
Bencao Gangmu, 90–91
Benet, Sula, 204–205, 286
Benjamin, Walter, 1–3, 139, 140, 222, 225, 265
Bennett, Allan, 176, 181, 184, 279
Bennett, Chris, 197, 201–203, 216, 253, 254, 283, 284, 285, 286, 287, 291
Berger, Meyer, 29, 234
Berke, Joseph, 20–21, 231, 235, 266
Berner, 17
Berridge, Edmund William, 174
Berridge, Virginia, 253, 276
Besant, Annie, 174, 276
Best, Joel, 80, 245
bhāṅg, 23–26, 35, 37, 92–94, 97, 169, 203, 205
Bifulco, Maurizio, 260
Big Bud (music), 29
The Big Lebowski (film), 8, 47
Bilby, Kenneth, 24, 233, 282
biopolitics, 79

biopower, 43
Bivins, Jason, 226
Black, Winifred, 58, 241
Blackman, Shane, 227
Blackwood, Algernon, 148
Blair, William, 147, 267
Blakemore, Colin, 260
Bland, Lorna, 133
Blaskiewicz, Robert, 246
Blavatsky, Helena P., 171–174, 176, 184, 275, 276
Blenkinsopp, Joseph, 286
Blin, Arnaud, 238
Bloch, Ernst, 2, 145, 225, 238
Bloom, Steve, 219–220, 227
Bloomfield, Michael, 238, 262
blues, 22, 28, 66–69, 81, 82
blunts, 28–30, 33, 34, 39
Blyden, Edward Wilmott, 191
Bogousslavsky, Julien, 255
Boivin, Nicole, 229, 233, 285
Bonaparte, Napoleon, 50, 55, 98, 99
bong, 27, 31, 34, 35, 221
Bonnie, Richard J., 63, 66, 240, 241, 242, 243, 245
Book of Odes, 90
Boon, Marcus, 145, 147, 267
Booth, Martin, 179, 278
Boothroyd, Dave, 140, 265
Borougerdi, Bradley, 252
Bosk, Charles, 80, 245
Bourdieu, Pierre, 39, 227, 236
Boyer, Pascal, 285
Bozza, Anthony, 227
Bragg, Robert Campbell, *see* Mexico, N.R. de
Brand, Joseph, 90, 249
Brassic (TV series), 8
Breakenridge, Herbert, 234
Brenan, Megan, 228, 229, 264
Bretonnau, Pierre-Fidèle, 109
Breuer, Aviva, 250
Brevior, Thomas, 280
Bridge, J.A., 252
Bridgeman, Mary, 134, 260, 263
Brière de Boismont, Alexandre, 108, 111–112, 116, 119, 123, 255, 256, 257, 258, 259
Brigham, Amariah, 117
Brink, Wim van den, 227, 244, 260

Brinkley, Douglas, 283
Britten, Emma Hardinge, 187–188, 271, 273, 281
Britto, Lena, 245
Broman, Clifford, 244
Brooker, Lee Carroll, 6
Brotteaux, Pascal, 258
Brough, John, 203, 286
Broughton, Arthur, 24, 233
Brown, Gordon, 44–45
Brown, Jeff, 284–285, 286
Brown, John Collis, 103
Brown, Ricardo Emmanuel, *see* Korupt
Brownlee, Nick, 285
Brunner, Emil, 2, 225
Brunner, Theodore, 208, 286, 288
Bruno, Antonio, 265
Bucke, R.M., 185
Buddhism, 176, 181, 209
Burgess, Kaya, 237
Burnell, Arthur Coke, 235
Burns, Dylan, 274
Burns, James, 186, 280
Burroughs, Silas, 146
Burroughs, William, 142
Burton, Richard, 182, 268
Burton, Robert, 95–96, 250
Busby, Matta, 228
Bush, William D., 243
Butrica, James, 288
Buzurg-Ummid, Kiyā, 48
Buzurg-Ummid, Muhammad, 48
Bynum, William, 251

Cahagnet, Louis-Alphonse, 158–179, 187, 270, 271, 272, 273, 275, 276
Caldwell, Billy, 44, 131
Callaghan, James, 128
Calloway, Cab (music), 67
Calvert, Robert (music), 145–146
Campian, Cristian, 265
Canada, 7, 14, 28, 57, 68, 131, 134, 214, 215
cancer, 83, 835, 94, 117, 131, 132, 133
cannabidiol, *see* CBD
cannabine, 120, 122
Cannabis Act (2018), 134
cannabis compassion clubs, 133
Cannabis Cup, 18

Cannabis indica, 14, 15, 18, 19, 26, 50, 93, 103, 107, 108, 118, 124
cannabis resin, *see* hashish
Cannabis ruderalis, 14–15
Cannabis sativa, 13–15, 17–19, 24, 26, 37, 50, 51, 88, 89, 93, 94, 118, 119, 179
cannabutter, 37
Capper, Steve, 219, 220
Carlson, Eric, 254, 258
Carney, Philip, 243
Carpenter, Frank, 153, 269
Carroll, Coreen, 236
Carroll, Lewis, 34, 235
Castle, David, 237, 263
CBD, 8, 10, 15, 37, 83, 120, 132, 133, 136, 137, 210
Cedro, Clemente, 265
Cermak, Timmen, 229, 237
Cesamet, 130
Chaitanya, Swami, 31, 39–40, 211, 221, 235, 237, 289, 292
chakras, 174
Chaliand, Gérard, 238
chalice, 195–196, 221
Chambers, Robert, 274
Chandra, Suman, 231
Chanel, Christian, 276
Chanel, Tiphanie, 292
Chapkis, Wendy, 138, 246, 264
Chapman, Rob, 232
charas, 23, 26
Charles, Prince, 104
Chasin, Alexandra, 242, 243
Cheech and Chong, 35, 207
chemotherapy, 130, 132
Chevannes, Barry, 283
chillum, 20, 25, 27, 33, 34, 195
China, 26, 88–92, 164, 188, 202, 205, 248, 281
Chisari, Claudia, 265
cholera, 100–101, 107, 117, 122, 123
Chopra, Gurbakhsh Singh, 24, 233
Christianity, 5, 7, 12, 43, 48, 49, 54, 56, 58, 66, 71, 72, 75–79, 81–83, 88, 105, 111, 119, 145, 148, 153, 154, 155, 156, 167, 186, 188, 189, 193–196, 202, 203, 210–213, 216–218
Christiansen, Paul, 262
Christie, Roger, 201, 285, 286

Christison, Alexander, 92, 249
Church of Cognizance, 211, 216–217
Church of England, 44, 105
Church of the Tree of Life, 211
Church of the Universe, 211, 214–216
cigarette filters, 29–30
Clarke, Emily, 236
Clarke, Hance, 288
Clarke, Peter, 282
Clarke, Robert, 13–14, 16, 17, 19, 26, 93, 229, 230, 231, 233, 248, 250, 283, 285
Clearwater Abbey, 214
Clemente, Cedro, 265
Clinton, Bill, 130
Clot Bey, *see* Clot, Antoine-Barthélémy
Clot, Antoine-Barthélémy, 106, 254
Club des Hachichins, 36, 37, 109, 141, 146, 147, 158, 166, 168, 174
Club Eleven, 126
Club of Assassins, *see Club des Hachichins*
cocaine, 62, 64, 72, 126, 181, 185, 187, 188, 241
Cohen, Margaret, 265
Cohen, Stanley, 56, 80, 240, 241, 245
cold method, 38
Cole, Juan, 251
Coleman, Trev, 253
Coleridge, Samuel Taylor, 145, 148
Collins, Wilkie, 159
colonialism, 23, 25, 74, 121, 136, 190, 194
Comitas, Lambros, 24–25, 192, 194, 195, 233, 282, 283
Confucius, 164
Connor, Steve, 238
Conrad of Montferrat, 49
Cooke, Alexander M., 253
Cooke, Mordecai, 54, 240
Cookies Farm, 17
Cooper, Courtney Ryley, 70, 242, 243
Cope, Rosemarie, 73, 74, 243
Corcella, Aldo, 287
Corson, Kate, 165
Cotton Club, 68
counterculture, 1, 8, 10, 20, 22, 29, 30, 31, 32, 35, 37, 69, 82, 85, 87, 130, 133, 137, 138, 148, 185, 198, 199, 210, 211, 212, 218, 219, 222, 245
Courtive, Edmond de, 117–122, 258, 259
Coxall, Guy, 253

Cozad, Laurie, 286, 290, 291
Crabtree, Adam, 160, 271
Craker, Lyle, 230
Crick, Francis, 127
Critchell, David, 291
Crockford, Susanna, 272
Croft-Jeffreys, Caroline, 244
Croq, Marc-Antoine, 253
Crosby, David (music), 219
Crosland, Maurice, 258
Crowley, Aleister, 148, 176, 179–187, 190, 222, 253, 278, 279, 280, 281
Crusades, 48–51, 55, 56, 57
Cruz, Nicky, 78–79, 245
Culpeper, Nicholas, 96, 250
cultural capital, 39
Cummings, Hugh, 57
Cunliffe, Barry, 287
Curran, Valerie, 225, 231, 237, 238
Curry, J.N., 72

d'Assier, Adolph, 159, 271
d'Espérance, Elizabeth, 187
D'Souza, Deepak, 231, 237, 246, 264, 288
Daftary, Farhad, 48, 50, 51, 238, 239
dagga, 25
Dahab, Elizabeth, 266
Dahl, Shawn, 227
Dangerous Drugs Act (1920), 181
Dangerous Drugs Act (1928), 126
Daniel, Price, 64–65
Daoism, 205
Dash, Vaidya Bhagwan, 250
datura, 27, 92, 108, 120
Daumier, Honoré, 141
David, Anthony, 244
Davidson, Arthur, 274
Davy, Humphry, 165, 273
dawamesc, 36, 37, 108, 114, 117, 119, 121, 130, 138, 167–169, 171
Dawson, Warren, 88–89, 247
Day, John, 243
De Quincey, Thomas, 142, 148, 150, 151, 152, 153
De Witt, Thomas, 226
Deacon, Hannah, 262
decarboxylation, 27, 37
Decker, Lydia, 203
DeCourtive, Edmond, 117–122, 258, 259

DeGrandpre, Richard, 260
Delacroix, Eugène, 141
Della, Jamie, 205, 287
Delva, Jorge, 244
demon/demonic, 48, 50, 58, 72, 81, 136, 155
demonization, 4, 5, 6, 7, 8, 17, 21, 25, 43–82, 84, 85, 101, 112, 118, 119–124, 127, 132, 133, 134, 135, 136, 137, 197, 219, 223
depression, 36, 41, 83, 94, 130, 132, 195, 210
Derbyshire, Madison, 237
Desert Fathers, 145
Desprez, Florian, 280
Detroit Federation of Musicians, 69
Deveney, John Patrick, 158, 270, 273, 274, 276
Devereux, Paul, 226, 284
Devine, Robert James, 71, 243
Devlin, Hannah, 264
Dewhirst, Timothy, 234
DeWitt, Jack, 243
Dharmapala, Angarika, 174
Dhiman, Kartar Singh, 250
Diamond D (music), 29
Dimbleby, David, 127
Dingley, Alfie, 44, 131
Dioscorides, Pedanius, 205, 207–208
Divine Farmer's Classic of Materia Medica, see *Shennong Bencaojing*
DMT (dimethyltryptamine), 218
Dodge, Edward, 287
Donoghue, Denis, 176, 178
Donovan (music), 126
Dorvault, François, 121, 122, 259
Douglas, Mary, 131, 262, 280
dowam meskh, *see dawamesc*
dowameskh, *see dawamesc*
Dowson, Ernest, 176
dread talk, 194
dreams, 2, 47, 50, 67, 70, 116–118, 139, 141, 143, 145, 148, 149, 157, 162, 168, 172, 173, 178, 190, 207, 225
Dreschel, Andrew, 215, 290
dronabinol, 130
drum 'n' bass, 29
du Toit, Brian, 23, 232, 233
Dublin Hermetic Society, 176

Duerloo, Karel, 286
Dulchinos, Donald, 148, 153, 267, 268, 269
Dumas, Alexandre, 36, 141, 146, 150, 165, 168, 267
Dunbar, Robin, 285
Dunkley, Archibald, 192
Durkheim, Émile, 4, 5, 6, 43, 227
Dussault, Dee, 83, 84, 209, 221, 246, 287, 289, 292
Duvall, Chris, 19, 22, 23, 26, 33, 92, 94, 202, 231, 232, 233, 234, 235, 248, 250, 253, 285
Dwarakanath, Shri, 93, 250
Dylan, Bob (music), 21
Dymphna, 113

Earleywine, Mitch, 207, 229, 239, 288
East India Company, 25, 96, 101, 147, 192
East, Hinton, 24
Easterfield, Thomas, 230
Ebers Papyrus, 88–89, 94
Eckhart, Meister, 155
ecstasy, 3, 27, 36, 50, 52, 65, 66, 67, 142, 156, 161, 173, 169, 177, 179, 180, 187, 189, 199–201, 216, 248
Ed-derfoufi, F., 250
edibles, 27, 30, 35–38, 114, 221
Edmonds, Ennis, 191, 281, 283
Egyptosophy, 98
Einhorn, Elissa, 291
Eisenberg, Michael, 265
El-Halebi, Suliman, 98
Eleusinian Mysteries, 173, 275
Eliade, Mircea, 3, 6, 199–200, 226, 248, 284
elixir of life, 83, 164, 167, 172, 173, 182, 183
elixir vitae, see elixir of life
Elizabeth I, Queen, 96
Ellis, Havelock, 176, 178
Ellis, Ronald J., 262
ElShebiney, S.A., 248
ElSohly, Mahmoud, 231, 234
Emboden, William, 14, 92, 202, 249, 284, 285
Embree, Ainslie, 285
Emerald Cup, 18
Emerald Triangle, 39–40
End Our Pain, 132
endocannabinoids, 126
entourage effect, 18

Epidyolex, 130, 138
epilepsy, 44, 83, 130, 131, 132, 134
Ernst, Rudolf, 33
Esquirol, Jean Etienne Dominique, 108–113, 116, 256
Ethiopia, 24, 33, 190–192
Ethiopian Orthodox Tewahedo Church, 194
Ethiopian Salvation Society, 192
Ethiopianism, 190–192
EURAD, *see* Europe Against Drugs
Europe Against Drugs, 45
Evans, Jamie, 236

Fabulous Furry Freak Brothers, 21
Fachner, Jörg, 266
Faivre, Antoine, 271, 272
Falco, Julie, 138
Falconet, Étienne Maurice, 50
Fall, The (music), 46
Farber, Philip, 197, 283, 286, 287
Farm, The, 211, 212–214
FBN, *see* Federal Bureau of Narcotics
Federal Bureau of Narcotics, 61–70, 72, 80–82
Fedorak, Charles John, 251
Ferrara, Mark, 229, 287
Fichte, Johan Gottlieb, 152
Fielde, Adele Marion, 188–189, 281
Finger, Henry, 58
Finley, Lana, 165, 273
First Church of Cannabis, 211
First International Opium Conference, 58
Fisher, Mark, 46–47, 140, 265
Fisher, Michael, 9, 227
Fitzgerald, Ella (music), 67
Flannery, Mary Catherine, 177, 277
Flattery, David, 285
Flaubert, Gustave, 144, 145, 147, 266
flavonoids, 18, 83
fly agaric mushroom, 200, 202, 203
Foley, Edward, 68
Fossier, Albert E., 59, 241
Foster, David, 29, 234
Foster, Robert Fitzroy, 276, 277, 278
Foucault, Michel, 4, 55, 79, 109, 110, 111, 145, 222, 226, 237, 240, 245, 256, 257, 258, 263, 266, 292
420, 219–220, 221

Fox sisters, 173
Fox, Kate, 186
Fox, Steve, 227, 244, 260
Freeman, Tom, 231, 237, 238, 262
Freemasonry, 175
Freya, 205, 208
Fronmüller, Bernhard, 124, 251, 260
Fuchs, Leonhart, 95
Fuller, John F.C., 183, 279

Gaafar, A.E.D.M., 249
Gaglio, Meredith, 247
Galal, A.F., 248
Galen, 95, 207, 208
Galland, Antoine, 145
ganga, see *ganja*
ganja, 22–26, 28, 74, 93, 97, 123, 130, 171, 172, 192–195
ganja yoga, 209
Gaoni, Yehiel, 120
Garat, Guillermo, 226
Garden of Eden, 214
Gardner, Zoë, 230
Garius, Laura, 227, 228
Garland, Sarah, 236
Garon, Paul, 67, 242
Garvey, Marcus, 191–194, 282
Gaskin, Stephen, 212–216, 221, 290
Gastinel Affair, 121
Gastinel, Joseph-Bernard, 107, 121–123
gateway drug, 9, 64, 72
Gauld, Alan, 271, 273
Gautier, Théophile, 36, 105, 141, 142, 147, 165, 167, 168, 173, 254, 265, 266, 267, 272, 274
Gayle, Damien, 228
Geiger, John, 236
Geitmann, Anja, 231
Geluardi, John, 253, 264
Gentleman, Amelia, 104, 253
George, Tony, 263
Germany, 7, 28, 61, 124
Gilbert, Robert, 175, 276
Ginsberg, Allen, 22, 139, 148, 264
Giudice, Christian, 277
Glendinning, Chellis, 87, 247
gnosis, 173
Godwin, Joscelyn, 276
Goebel, Rolf, 225

Goffman, Erving, 41, 237
Golden Dawn, *see* Hermetic Order of the Golden Dawn
Goldstein, Chris, 292
Gonimah, Diana, 228
Gonne, Maude, 176, 178, 181, 189, 278.
Goodrick-Clarke, Nicholas, 270
Gorman, Mel, 252
Gorski, William, 277
Gouaux, Ben, 262
Gould, Warwick, 277
Grandsagne, Stéphane Ajasson de, 108–109
Grant, Igor, 262
Grant, Kenneth, 185, 280
Grateful Dead, The (music), 219–220
Graves, Robert, 202
Gravich, Mark, 219
Gray, Stephen, 288
Great Depression, 59, 63
green dragon method, *see* hot method
Green is Gold (film), 8
Green Thumb Industries, 17
green-out, *see* white-out
Green, Jonathon, 21, 232
Green, Sebastian, 262
Greene, Graham, 127
greening, *see* white-out
Greer, Richard, 86, 247
Gregorio, Joseph, 237
Gregory, William, 161, 271
Grewal, Ruby, 263
Grierson, George Abraham, 92, 249
Griffith, Ralph, 249
grinder, 31–32
Grinspoon, Lester, 125, 129, 130, 233, 260, 261
Grose, John Henry, 53, 97, 239, 251
grounding, 195
Guba Jr, David, 50, 55, 99, 105, 106, 107, 111, 118, 119, 121, 122, 234, 239, 240, 251, 254, 256, 257, 258, 259, 283
Guédon, Marie-Françoise, 288
Gunjah Wallah Company, 36, 236
Guy, Geoffrey, 230
Guzmán, Manuel, 262
gynaecology, 94
Gysin, Brion, 36

Hager, Steven, 18, 197, 220, 283, 291
Haile Selassie I, 192, 194–195
Halifax, Joan, 265
Halperin, Alex, 245
Halperin, Christina, 3, 226
Halperin, Shirley, 227
Hamfats, Harlam (music), 67
Hammer-Purgstall, Joseph von, 52, 54, 239
Hanegraaff, Wouter, 270
Hanuš, Lumír, 231
Haoma Offering, 216
haoma, 203, 216–217
Harer Jr, William Benson, 88, 248
Hari, Johann, 67, 242
Harney, Malachi, 65
Harris, Evan, 46
Harrison McKenna, Katherine, 148, 268
Harrison Narcotics Act (1914), 62
Harrison, Kathleen, 205, 209, 215, 217, 287, 289
Harrison, Steve, 253
Harrowing of Hell, 154
Harvey, Graham, 199, 284, 290
Hasan II, 48–49
Ḥasan Ṣabbāḥ, *see* Ḥasan-e Ṣabbāḥ
Ḥasan ʿAlā Zikrihi's Salām, *see* Hasan II
Ḥasan-e Ṣabbāḥ, 47–53, 60, 145
hash brownie, 36, 37, 75, 77, 78, 215
hashish, 1–2, 16, 19, 20, 21, 22, 26, 35, 36, 43, 50–53, 55–60, 71, 89, 99, 100, 105–124, 135, 136, 141–154, 156–159, 161–189, 222, 236
ḥashīshīyyīn, *see* Assassins
Hausman-Kedem, Moran, 246
Havens, Kayri, 288
Hawai'i Cannabis THC Ministry, 211
Hawkwind (music), 145, 267
Hearst, William Randolph, 58
Hebdige, Dick, 191, 281
Heelas, Paul, 292
Hegel, G.W.F., 152, 170
Heim, Roger, 202
Hemmingway, Ernest, 36
hemp, 8, 13, 19–20, 22, 24–27, 38, 50, 51, 54, 57, 59, 60, 71, 83, 88, 89–98, 100, 102, 103, 107, 119, 120, 136, 146, 147, 159, 161–162, 168, 169, 177, 197, 199, 200, 202, 204, 205, 208, 215, 217
Herer, Jack, 84, 246

Hermetic Brotherhood of Luxor, 174
Hermetic Order of the Golden Dawn, 174–176, 179, 181, 184
Hernton, Calvin, 20, 21, 231, 235, 265, 266
Herodotus, 205–208
heroin, 61, 64, 65, 72, 126, 129, 179, 181, 185, 187, 188
Hesychius of Alexandria, 208
Hibbert, Joseph, 192
Hickok, Laurens Perseus, 151–153, 268, 269
High Maintenance (TV series), 8
High on the Range (film), see *Notch Number One*
High Style Brewing Company, 38
Hilgartner, Stephen, 80, 245
Hillig, Karl, 14, 230
Hilton, Frank, 266
Hinchcliffe, Sandra, 286
Hinde, Jules, 271
Hindocha, Chandni, 262
Hinds, Robert, 192
Hines, Lindsey, 231, 237
hip-hop, 29
hippies, 8, 21, 37, 39, 40, 142, 148, 185, 211, 212, 213
Hirschman, Ada, 258, 268, 270
HIV, 132
Hobson, Richmond Pearson, 65, 66, 242
Hockley, Fred, 271
Hockney, David, 127
Hodgekiss, Anna, 262
Hofmann, Albert, 203
Hogg, Quintin, 128
Hogg, Ron, 9
Holland, Julie, 130, 261
Holmstedt, Bo, 110, 113, 114, 255, 256, 257
Homer, 71, 243
Hornung, Erik, 251
Hosford, Sven, 247
hot knives, 27
hot method, 38
hotboxing, 35, 207
Howard, Rosetta (music), 67
Howell, Leonard, 192–193
Hsien-Che, Chang, 249
Hua Tuo, 92
Hua, Stephanie, 236
Hübbe-Schleiden, Wilhelm, 173

Huertas, Rafael, 110, 256, 257
Hughes, Trevor, 241, 267
Hugo, Victor, 36, 141
Hulkrantz, Ake, 248
Hume, David, 151, 152
humoral theory, 94, 100
Hutnyk, John, 48, 238
Hutton, Ronald, 199, 284
Huxley, Aldous, 2, 3, 185, 202, 212, 223, 225, 285, 292
Huxley, Francis, 127
Huysmans, Joris-Karl, 179, 278
hypnotism, 159–160, 189

I Love You, Alice B. Toklas (film), 36, 37
Ideal (TV series), 8
Idealism, 145, 151, 152, 153, 189
Igreja Niubingui Etíope Coptic de Sião do Brasil, 211
Indian Hemp Drugs Commission, 25, 233
Ingram, Matthew, 284
Innes, Stephanie, 291
International Narcotic Education Association, 65
International Opium Convention (1912), 26, 58
Irish, William, 69
Irwin, Robert, 150, 268
Isis, 205, 208
Islam, 20, 35, 47–53, 99, 101, 112, 123, 148
Isma῾ili, 47–53, 60
Iversen, Leslie, 124, 244, 246, 253, 258, 263, 288

Jackson, James, 244
Jacquette, Dale, 139, 229, 265, 269
Jager, Gerry, 262
Jagger, Mick (music), 126
Jah Healing Kemetic Temple of the Divine, 211, 289
Jah Power Band (music), 194
Jamaica, 18, 22, 24–28, 190–194
James, Tony, 255
James, William, 180, 185, 269
Javid, Sajid, 43, 46, 81, 131
Jay, Mike, 255
jazz, 22, 28, 29, 66–69, 70, 80, 81, 82, 126, 219

Jeffares, A. Norman, 277, 278
Jefferson, Lara, 288
Jenkin, Leonard, 268
Jenks, Kenneth, 129
Jensen, Jake, 265
Jesus, 78, 79, 195, 217, 218
Jiang, Hongen, 229, 233, 285
Johns, Christina, 229
Johnson-Hill, Jack, 194, 282, 283
Johnson, Alan, 44–46, 81
Johnson, Charles, 176
Johnson, Will, 287
joint, 28–33, 78, 81, 210, 213, 215, 221
Jones, Jeffrey, 228, 264
Jones, John, 280
Jones, Nick, 30–31, 235
Jordan, Danté, 235
Judaism, 104, 139, 184, 217, 218

Kaczynski, Richard, 278, 279
Kakko, Tommi, 269
Kalant, Harold, 93, 250
Kali, 205, 208
Kane, Harry Hubbell, 146, 237, 267
kaneh, 204
Kansagara, Devan, 262
Kant, Immanuel, 151, 152, 153, 269
Kaplan, Charles, 123, 254, 258, 260
Kardashian, Kim, 10
Karr, Alphonse, 108, 141, 255
keef, *see* kief
Kelly, Rose, 182
Kerouac, Jack, 22, 148
Kessler, Martin, 286
Khan, Ikhlas A., 234
kief, 32, 35, 142, 144
King, Les, 45, 238, 260
Kirkham, Tim, 262
Kléber, Jean-Baptiste, 98–99
Knobloch-Westerwick, Sylvia, 284
Kohn, Marek, 232
Korsakoff syndrome, 76
Korupt (music), 35
Koshie, Ashley, 84, 246
Kotra, Lakshmi P., 288
Kramer, Stephanie, 229
Kramer, Uri, 246
Kreglinger, Gisela, 77, 244, 245
Kruzman, Diana, 229

Kudlick, Catherine, 259
Kuhnke, LaVerne, 254

l-Bayṭār, Ibn, 20
La Barre, Weston, 22, 203, 229, 232
Ladd, George Trumbull, 269
Laing, R.D., 10, 20, 127, 228, 260
landrace cannabis, 19, 202
Lane, Edward William, 51, 239
Larrey, Dominique-Jean, 251
Lastreto, Nikki, 39–40, 211, 237
laudanum, 38, 103
Lawrence, Robyn Griggs, 37, 235, 236, 285, 286
Leadbeater, Charles Webster, 174, 276
Leary, Timothy, 148, 184, 185, 211, 242, 289
Lee, Martin, 129, 250, 252, 253, 254, 261
Lees, Rachel, 238
Leeuw, Gerardus van der, 200, 285
Leite, George Thurston, *see* Scott, Thurston
Leohndorf, Dan, 290, 291
Lesh, Phil (music), 219
Leuret, François, 113
Leveque, Philip, 103, 253
Lévi-Strauss, Claude, 203
Lévi, Éliphas, 161, 184, 272
Levin, Mike, 69, 243
Levy, Rina, 250
Lewcock, Anna, 238
Lewin, Louis, 123, 260
Lewis, Bernard, 48, 51, 238, 239
Lewis, Glyn, 244
Lewis, James, 223, 292
Lewis, Melissa, 288
Lewis, Rupert, 282
Lewis, William, 250
Lezard, Nicholas, 30, 234
Li, Hui-Lin, 91, 248, 249
Licata, Victor, 70, 71, 73
Lieutaud, Antoine, 119, 258, 259
Lipsedge, Maurice, 243
Littlewood, Roland, 243
Lloyd, Alan, 287
Locke, John, 151
Loja, Franco, 18
Long, Trish, 240

López, Julia, 265
Lovecraft, Howard Phillips, 148
Lovering, Rob, 244
Löwy, Michael, 225
LSD, 41, 127, 128, 185, 212
Luauté, Jean-Pierre, 254
Ludlow, Fitz Hugh, 147–158, 165, 167, 168, 169, 174, 179, 182, 183, 184, 189, 200, 223, 267, 268, 270, 274, 278
Lynch, Gordon, 5, 136, 226
Lynch, Hollis, 282
Lynch, Michael, 263
Lynch, Patrick, 287
Lynn, Becky, 265
Lytton, Edward Bulwer, 183–184, 279

Ma Ku, 205, 208, 217
MacGillivrey, Neil, 252, 254
Mack, Robert, 267
MacKeen, Dawn, 228
mafen, 91–92
magick, 180, 183
Maginot, Adèle, 160–161, 163
magnetic fluid, 160
magnetic sleep, 160, 161
magnetism, 159–162, 169, 186, 187
Magu, *see* Ma Ku
Mailer, Norman, 235
Mair, Victor, 22
majoon, see *majoun*
majoun, 35–37 103
Mandel, Jerry, 71, 243
Maniaque-Benton, Caroline, 247
Mann, John, 289
Marcu, Jahan, 236
Marihuana Tax Act (1937), 79
Marinko, Paul, 262
Marino, Danilo, 35, 130, 232, 235
Marinol, 130
Markert, John, 227
Marks, Howard, 21, 232
Martin, Alyson, 229, 286
Martin, Heather, 277
Martinism, 177
Martinov, Ivan, 13
Marx, Karl, 46, 238
Maslow, Abraham, 179, 185, 278, 290
Mason, Edward, 44, 237
materia medica, 88, 90, 91, 93, 197

Mathers, Samuel Liddell MacGregor, 175, 176, 184
Matthews, Patrick, 31, 235
Mayfield, Asia, 263, 264
Maymudes, Jacob, 232
Maymudes, Victor, 232
McCartney, Paul (music), 127
McDonough, Elise, 236
McGinn, Bernard, 154, 155, 269
McGovern, Dermot, 73–74, 243
McGuire, Meredith, 247
McKenna, Terence, 148, 268
McMillian, John, 289
McPartland, John, 230
McWilliams, John C., 241, 243
Measham, Fiona, 227, 228
Mechoulam, Raphael, 15–16, 18, 103, 120, 231, 249, 250, 253, 259, 294
Medeiros, Tracey, 236
medical marijuana cooperatives, 133
medicinal cannabis, 6–8, 11–12, 13, 15, 16, 17, 19, 26, 27, 28, 40, 44, 55, 60, 62–65, 71, 74–75, 81, 83–138, 140–141, 160–161, 207–208, 210, 214, 217, 221, 223
Mehmedic, Zlatko, 231
melancholy, 95, 112
Menascu, Shay, 246
Menou, Jacques-François de, 98, 99
Merlin, Mark, 13–14, 16, 17, 19, 26, 89, 93, 229, 230, 231, 233, 247, 248, 249, 250, 283, 285
Merritt, Jonathan, 229, 286, 289
Merwe, Nikolaas van der, 24, 232, 233
Merzouki, A., 250
Mesa, J. Molero, 250
mescalin, 178, 190
Mesmer, Franz Anton, 159–160
mesmerism, 123, 158–174, 175, 271
Messinger, E., 256
Mexican Revolution (1910), 56
Mexico, N.R. de, 69–70
Mezzrow, Milton 'Mezz', 22, 28, 232, 234
Mickel, Emanuel, 238, 239, 266
Mikuriya, Tod, 246
Milam Jr, Gilbert Antony, *see* Berner
Miles, Todd, 76–79, 244, 245
Miller, Collin, 265
Miller, Jonathon, 127

Miller, Mark, 85, 246
Miller, Robert Moats, 242
Mills Harper, George, 176, 277
Mills Harper, Margaret, 176, 276, 277
Mills, James, 55, 97, 98, 100, 230, 232, 233, 237, 240, 251, 259, 282, 283
Ming Yi Bie Lu, see *Additional Records of Famous Physicians*
Misuse of Drugs Act (1971), 9, 45, 128
Moldenke, Alma, 286
Moldenke, Harold, 286
Molech, *see* Moloch
Moloch, 72, 243
moon rocks, 35
Moon, John, 252
Moore, Virginia, 277
Moreau, Jacques-Joseph, 36, 108–120, 141, 162, 168, 174, 189, 239, 255, 256, 257, 258, 265, 274
Moreno, Jose M. Villagrán, 255
Morgan, Celia, 225, 231, 237
Morgan, John, 261
Morgan, Kayla, 285
Morgan, Wayne, 64, 241
Moritz, Maria, 276
Morley, Gabriel Patrick, 289, 290
morphine, 61, 181, 188
Moser, Amanda, 265
Moses, 191, 204, 205, 218
Mossman, Kate, 227
Moulin, Thierry, 255
multiple sclerosis, 83, 104, 130, 138
munchies, 54, 132
mundane, 3, 7–10, 43, 96, 135, 139, 140, 170
Murphy, Emily, 57, 240
Murray, Robin, 231, 237, 288
Muscatello, Maria, 265
music, 1, 8, 9, 22, 29, 31, 33, 39, 40, 66–69, 60, 80, 90, 114, 126, 127, 140, 144, 145, 150, 155, 187, 189, 191, 219
Musselman, Lytton John, 204, 286
Mussen, Maddy, 227
Musto, David, 62, 66, 235, 241, 242
mysticism, 1, 2, 3, 35, 84, 111, 139, 141–147, 149, 153, 154, 155, 160, 163, 64, 165, 167, 172, 175, 179, 180, 181, 182, 183, 185, 189, 190, 196, 197, 199, 200, 210, 213, 218, 223

nabilone, 130
nabiximols, 130
Nahas, Gabriel, 135, 239, 255, 263
Napoleon, *see* Bonaparte, Napoleon
Needham, Joseph, 203, 205, 287
Neighbors, Harold, 244
Nelson, Horatio, 98
Nelson, Joe, 289
Nelson, Max, 288
Neoplatonism, 162, 169, 170, 178, 183
Nerval, Gérard de, 36, 141
Nettleford, Rex, 233
New Age, 214
Newburn, Tim, 227
Niaah, Jahlani, 233
Niebuhr, Carsten, 20, 232
Niebuhr, Reinhold, 66, 242
nitrous oxide, 173, 180, 273
Noel, Jeffrey, 219
Nordau, Max, 167
normalisation,
Normand, Linn, 226
Notch Number One (film), 58
Notcutt, William, 236
Novella, Enric, 256, 257
Nowell-Smith, Patrick, 127
Nugent-Head, JulieAnn, 91, 249
Nugent, Shannon, 262
Nunn, John, 88, 247
Nutt, David, 10, 40, 45, 46, 81, 150, 157, 169, 227, 235, 237, 238, 244, 246, 260, 263

O'Dowd, Liam, 263
O'Shaughnessy, William Brooke, 100–108, 120, 253, 254, 268
Oaksterdam University, 17
obstetrics, 94
Ockerman, Emma, 246
Olcott, Henry S., 159, 217, 291
Old Man of the Mountain, *see* Ḥasan-e Ṣabbāḥ
Olsson, Börje, 261
Oman, John, 201–202, 285
Oner, S.T., 231, 232
opium, 26, 38, 46, 52, 55, 56, 58, 62, 72, 93, 101, 102, 103, 105, 118, 120, 142, 143, 144, 147, 148, 162, 172, 173, 181, 187, 197, 234

Order of the Stella Matutina, 176
Oribasius, 208
orientalism, 33, 47–55, 57, 74, 98, 101, 105, 107, 111, 112, 118–120, 122, 124, 135, 141, 142, 145, 146, 148, 150, 166, 168, 172, 182
Osborn, Catherine, 142, 266
Osburn, Judy, 202, 284, 285, 287
Osburn, Lynn, 202, 284, 285, 287
Oscapella, Eugene, 263
Osiris, 205, 208
Osler, William, 124, 260
Osto, Douglas, 289
Oswald, Kirsty, 261
Oursler, Will, 241
Overmyer, Daniel, 287
Owen, Alex, 174, 175, 186, 276, 280
Owens, Joseph, 194, 283

Pain, Stephanie, 252
Paleckis, Lukas, 228
Pan-Africanism, 191
Pandolfo, Gianluca, 265
parahaoma, 216
Paramount Dance Hall, 126
paranoia, 46, 120
Parascandola, John, 226
Parcher, Jon, 234
Pardal, Mafalda, 227
Parker, Howard, 227
Parker, Terrance, 134
Parkinson's disease, 83
Partridge, Christopher, 225, 242, 246, 247, 264, 265, 266, 270, 273, 275, 278, 279, 281, 282, 284, 285, 289, 292
Pasi, Marco, 184, 279
Patel, Rachna, 137, 264
Patterson, Stephen, 279
Patterson, Steve, 263
Pease, Arthur, 288
Pennacchio, Marcello, 288
Pennay, Amy, 227, 228
Perry, Charles, 86, 247
Pertwee, Roger, 125, 128, 229, 230, 236, 246, 259, 260, 263
Peters, Hélène, 255
Petrilli, Kat, 231, 237, 238
Petrillo, James, 68
peyote, 177, 183, 212, 218

Phillips, Lawrence, 227, 244
Pieters, Toine, 123, 254, 258, 260
Pilcher, Tim, 30, 235, 263, 285
Pineapple Express (film), 8
Pinel, Philippe, 109, 110, 256
Pinnacle plantation, 192
Piper, Alan, 22
Piper, John, 75
Pisanti, Simona, 260
Plant, Sadie, 146, 267, 268
Pliny the Elder, 208
Podmore, Frank, 158, 270, 2721, 273
Pollard, Velma, 194, 283
Pollay, Richard, 234
Pollexfen, George, 176
Pollio, Antonino, 230
Polo, Marco, 48, 52, 118, 145
Postlethwayt, Malachy, 96, 251
Potet, Jules du, 158
Potter, Gary, 20–21, 40, 229, 232, 237, 262
Pravaz, Charles, 124
Preston, Brian, 13, 32–33, 34, 230, 235
profane illumination, 2–3, 139–140, 222
Prohibition (1920–1933), 62, 81
psychedelics, 41, 185, 212, 223
psychiatry, 10, 20, 36, 55, 70, 73–74, 108–119, 125, 127, 130, 134, 162
psychosis, 17, 41, 73–74, 76, 116, 136, 196, 231
Pure Food and Drug Act (1914), 62
Puységur, Marquis de, 160
Pythagoras, 164

Quaintance, Danuel, 216–217, 291
Quaintance, Mary Helen, 216
Qur'an, 48

racism, 22, 25, 53–61, 66, 73–74, 126
Radwan, Mohamed M., 234
Raine, Kathleen, 277
Ram Dass, 139, 265
Ram, Holenarasipur Yoganarasimham Mohan, 230
Randolph, Paschal Beverly, 158–159, 161–175, 179, 187, 271, 272, 273, 274, 275
Ranganathan, Mohini, 246, 264
Ranger, Chris, 74, 244

Rastafari, 22, 24, 74, 190–196, 203, 211, 212, 213
Rätsch, Christian, 83, 88, 92, 246, 248, 249, 284, 287
Rawson, Albert, 172, 275
Raynor, Johnson, 185
Reardon, Bernard, 151, 268
reasoning session, 195
Reddix, Dave, 219
Reddy, Govind, 250
Redman (music), 29
Reefer Madness (film), 60
reefer madness, 49–50, 68, 71, 72, 73, 82, 138
Regardie, Israel, 180–181, 182, 184, 185, 278, 279, 280
reggae, 22, 190, 191
Reich, Charles, 86, 247
Reiman, Amanda, 261
Ren, Meng, 229, 233
Rendle, Alfred Barton, 13, 230
resin, cannabis, *see* hashish
Resin, Harry, 247
Revuelta, Jose I. Pérez, 255
Reynolds, John Russell, 103, 104, 245, 253
Ṛgveda, 172, 202, 203, 217, 223
Richard I, 49
Richards, Keith (music), 126
Richert, Lucas, 230
Rig Veda, see *Ṛgveda*
Riggs, Patricia, 262
Riley, Diane, 263
Rimbaud, Arthur, 141, 265
Rinella, Michael, 288
Ritti, Antoine, 254
ritual, 25, 26, 30, 31, 90, 138, 172, 175, 178, 183, 184, 195, 196, 197, 200–203, 205, 206, 207, 209, 213, 221, 247
roach, 29–30, 32, 34
Roberts, Carl, 262
Robinson, J. Russell (music), 67
Rolle, Renate, 288
Roman Catholicism, 2, 75, 76, 144
Romanticism, 142, 149, 212, 225, 238, 266
Roof, Wade Clark, 87, 247
Room, Robin, 261
Roopnarine, Lomarsh, 233
Rosenfeld, Albert, 260
Rosenthal, Franz, 51, 239

Rosicrucianism, 175, 183
Rossi, Steven S., 262
Roszak, Theodore, 86, 211, 246, 247, 289
Rubin, Craig X, 217–218, 221
Rubin, Noah, 235
Rubin, Vera, 24–25, 194, 195, 230, 232, 282, 283
Rudenko, Sergei, 89. 206, 248, 287
Rudgley, Richard, 226
Rudolph, Paul (music), 145
Rushkoff, Douglas, 209, 289
Russell, George, 176
Russell, Jeffrey Burton, 269
Russo, Ethan, 88, 89, 103, 230, 231, 247, 248, 249, 250, 253
Ryder, Shaun (music), 8

sacrament, 31, 47, 190, 193, 195, 197, 203, 205, 211, 212, 214, 215, 216, 218, 221, 223
Sacy, Antoine Isaac Silvestre de, 48, 51, 100, 105, 107, 108, 118, 123, 251
Said, Edward, 167, 239
Saladin, 49
Saler, Michael, 276
Sánchez, Cristina, 262
Sanchez, Gonzalo, 248
Sanders, Bernie, 7, 226
Sanson, Dawne, 248
Santlofer, Jonathon, 264
Saracens, 49, 101
Sartre, Jean-Paul, 148
Satanism, 179
Sativex, *see* nabiximols
Saving Grace (film), 8
Sayre, Robert, 225
Schelling, Friedrich W. J., 152
schizophrenia, 84, 136
Schofield, Michael, 20, 232, 261
Scholem, Gershom, 139
Schultes, Richard Evans, 14, 200, 284
Schultz, Julia, 232
Schwartz, Larry, 219
Schwartz, Martin, 285
Scimeca, Giuseppi, 265
Scott, Jody, *see* Scott, Thurston
Scott, Thurston, 69–70
Scull, Andrew, 74, 244
Scythians, 89, 204–208

Self, Will, 196, 283
Seligman, Jon, 250
Sellers, Peter, 37
Sender, Pablo, 276
set and setting, 31, 207
Sett, Rina, 230
Sewell, Andrew, 246, 264
shamanism, 84, 90, 199, 200, 203, 208, 209
Sheed, Emily, 227
Shelton, Gilbert, 21, 232
shemshemet, 88–89
Shennong Bencaojing, 91
Shennong, 91
Shepherd, Verene, 233
Sherman, Carol, 197, 284
Sherratt, Andrew, 196, 197, 283
Shijing, see *Book of Odes*
Shiner, Michael, 227
Shipley, Morgan, 280
Shiva, 205, 208
Short, Daniel John,18
Short, Thomas, 95, 96, 250
Shteir, Rachel, 264
Shuster, Joe, 72
Siberia, 89, 199, 203, 206
Siegel, Jerry, 72
Siegel, Ronald, 258, 270, 272
Sinclair, Sarah, 227, 246
Sinnett, Alfred Percy, 176, 277
skunk, 17, 18, 45, 136, 200
Slade, Desmond,
slavery, 23, 24, 58, 62, 69, 146, 152, 164, 188, 190, 194, 233, 256
Sleep of Sialam, 175
Sloman, Larry, 242, 243
Sly and the Revolutionaries (music), 194
Small, Ernest, 14, 16, 230, 231
Smart, Mary Lou, 262
Smedley, Alfred, 186, 280
Smith, Amber, 228
Smith, Andrew, 197, 284
Smith, Donald, 231
Smith, Edward Sutton, 172
Smith, Fintan, 228
Smith, Henry, 120, 259
Smith, Mark E. (music), 46
Smith, Thomas, 120, 259
Smyth, Chris, 264
Snelders, Stephen, 123, 254, 258, 260

Snyder, Solomon, 92, 249
social imaginary, 198–199, 208
Societas Rosicruciana in Anglia, 175
Society of Psychical Research, 176, 188
Solhdju, Katrin, 257
Solomon, David, 185
Solomon, King, 192, 194
Soma Research Association, 127–128
soma, 93, 172–173, 175, 187, 202, 203, 208, 216, 217
somnambulism, 111, 158, 160, 187
Sorkin, Linda S., 262
space cakes, 37
Speaker, Susan, 241
Spear, Henry Bryan, 126, 260
Spencer, Jon Michael, 66, 242
Spencer, William, 282, 283
Spengler, Robert, 229, 233, 285
spice (drug), 34
Spiritism, 167
Spiritualism, 111, 158–171, 173–174, 187–190
Spivey, Newton, 230
spliff, 28–30, 32, 33, 195, 220
Squire, Peter, 103
Starbuck, Edwin Diller, 269
Stark, Harley, 250
stash box, 32
Steel, Henry Draper, 53, 239
Steer, Margie, 236
Steeze, Adolph, 41, 237
Stein, Gertrude, 36
Steve Miller Band (music), 235
Stevens, Helen Norton, 281
Stewart, Mark, 123
stigmatization, 5, 9, 46, 138, 144, 190
Stith, Sarah S., 292
Storr, Anthony, 125, 127
Strathern, Paul, 251
Strickler, Laura, 263
Strong, James, 286
Sualsbury, William, 260
subcultural capital, 8, 21, 22, 29, 30, 32, 38, 40, 82
Sude, Daniel, 284
Sumler, Alan, 207, 285, 288
Sun, Andrew, 265
Suster, Gerald, 185, 278, 280
Sutin, Lawrence, 277, 279, 291

Swedenborg, Emanuel, 158, 161, 163, 164, 177, 269
Sweet, Tammi, 246
Symonds, John Addington, 176, 188, 190, 279, 281
Symons, Arthur, 176, 177, 276
Syndros, 130
Sznitman, Sharon Rödner, 261, 293

Tabram, Pat, 133
Tahsin, Jamie, 235
Taillieu, Dieter, 291
Taliaferro, Charles, 270
Tang, Zihua, 229, 233, 285
Tanney, Cailun, 231
Taves, Ann, 227
Tavhare, Swagata Dilip, 250
Taylor-Young, Leigh, 37
Taylor, Bayard, 147–148, 150, 165, 166, 172, 267, 268
Taylor, Charles, 87, 198, 247, 284
Taylor, Joyce, 70
Taylor, Patrick, 281
Teach your Children (film), see *Reefer Madness*
Ted (film), 8
Teesside Cannabis Club and Exhale Harm Reduction Centre, 9–10
telepathy, 213–214, 290
temperance, 62, 173, 186–190
Temple 420 of the Heartland, 211, 217
Temple 420, 211, 217–219
terpenes, 18, 31
THC (tetrahydrocannabinol), 15–19, 26, 27, 35, 37, 38, 45, 83, 84, 103, 114, 120, 132, 136, 137, 196, 200, 201, 206, 207, 208
THCA (tetrahydrocannabinolic acid), 27, 37
Thelemic philosophy, 180
Theosophical Society, 159, 173, 175, 176, 217
Thomas, Mel, 21, 232
Thompson, Bill, 240
Thompson, Hunter S., 196, 283
Thompson, Judy, 265
Thompson, Reginald Campbell, 94, 250
Thornton, Mark, 62, 79, 241, 245
Thornton, Sarah, 39, 227

Thoth, 205, 208
Thousand Nights and One Nights, see *Arabian Nights*
Thracians, 206
Thrower, James, 285
tincture, 38, 103, 104, 121, 122, 123, 124, 126, 128, 130, 138, 182
toke, 8, 33, 213, 235
Toklas, Alice B., 36, 37, 236
Torres, Myriam, 244
Tosh, Peter (music), 193, 282
Traugot, Michael, 289, 290
trichomes, 18, 19, 32, 206
Troeltsch, Ernst, 218
Tromp, Marlene, 186, 270, 280, 281
Trump, Donald, 35
Tucker, Walter, 214–216, 290, 291
Tuke, William, 109
Tully, Caroline, 251
Tvert, Mason, 227, 244, 260
Tynan, Kenneth, 127
Tyson, Mike, 17

underground press, 211
Underhill, Evelyn, 185
UNIA, *see* Universal Negro Improvement Association
União do Vegetal, 218
Uniform State Narcotic Drug Act (1934),
Universal Negro Improvement Association, 191
Up in Smoke (film), 35
Urban, Hugh, 273, 275
Uruguay, 7

Vagina Dentata Organ (music), 145
Vaida, Florin, 262
Van Green, Ted, 263
Vanhoozer, Kevin, 76–78, 244, 245
vaporizer, 27
Veiga, Paula, 88, 247
Velasco, Guillermo, 262
Versluis, Arthur, 290
Victoria, Queen, 101–104, 105
Vigil, Jacob Miguel, 292
Villa, Keith, 230, 236
Villagrán, Jose, 255
Vinkenoog, Simon, 286

Von Rad, Gerhard, 286
Von Stuckrad, Kocku, 248
Von Worms, Abraham, 184

Waldos, the, 219–220
Waley, Arthur, 248
Walker, Marion, 45
Walton, Chapin, 217
Walton, Robert P., 245
Wanas, Amira S., 234
Wang, Mei, 234
Wang, Yan-Hong, 234
Wang, Yu-Fei, 248
Warf, Barney, 230
Warren, Leonard, 281
Wasilewski, Ewa, 288
Wasson, R. Gordon, 202–203, 285
Waxman, Olivia, 261
Webb, Chick (music), 67
Webb, Duncan, 260
Webb, James, 277
Webb, Richard, 138, 246, 264
Weber, Max, 189–190, 218, 281
Webster, Peter, 235
Weeds (TV series), 8, 217
wellbeing, 8, 10, 27, 31, 40, 44, 83, 84, 85, 86, 87, 95, 105, 125, 131, 134, 136, 198, 205, 211, 215, 221
Wellcome, Henry, 146
Werker, Ella, 250
Wesley, John, 104–105
Westcott, William Wynn, 175
Wheatstraw, Peetie (music), 66
Whineray, E.P., 179, 253, 278
white-out, 41
White, Anna MacBride, 277
Whitebread II, Charles H., 63, 66, 240, 241, 243, 245
Whittier, John Greenleaf, 146
Whole Earth Catalog, 86
Wilding, Mark, 235
Wilkerson, David, 78, 245
Wilkinson Lynn, Rosellen, 272
Willemin, Alexandre, 106–107, 108, 122, 123, 254, 259
Williams, Andy, 240
Williams, Patrick, 239
Wills, Simon, 248

Wilson, David, 284
Windolf, Jim, 290
wine, 8, 17, 18, 76–79, 92, 142, 162, 196, 218, 222
Winters, Riley, 287
Wiseman, Nigel, 249
Wissett, Robert, 96, 97, 251
witchcraft, 50, 106
Wolf, Laurie, 236
Wolfe, Bernard, 232, 234
Wolff, Hannah, 171, 275
Wollner, Herbert, 79, 245
Wood, Alexander, 124
Wood, Mary, M., 251
Wood, Thomas, 230
Woodhead, Linda, 292
Woodman, William Robert, 175
Woodward, William, 64
Woolrich, Cornell, *see* Irish, William
Wootton Committee, 127–129
Wootton Report, 127–129
Wootton, Barbara, 127
Worboys, Michael, 251
World Conference on Narcotic Education (1926), 65
World Narcotic Defense Association, 65
Wu, Xinhua, 229, 233, 285
Wujastyk, Dominik, 250
Wuthnow, Robert, 87, 212, 218, 247, 290, 291

Yang, Yi, 288
Yang, Yimin, 229, 233, 285
Yang, Yongzhi, 229, 285
Yanghai Tombs, 90
Yawney, Carole, 282
Ye, Feng, 249
Yeats, William Butler, 176–179, 277
Yoe, Craig, 72, 243, 245
Yogo, Takenori, 255
Young, Stephen, 264
Yule, Henry, 235

Zaehner, Robert C., 3, 6, 226, 265
Zafar, Rafia, 236
Zend-Avesta, 94, 250
Zephaniah, Benjamin, 193
Zhao, Liang-Cheng, 248

Zhao, You-Xing, 248
Zhao, Zhongzhen, 90, 249
Zimmer, Lynn, 261
Zinberg, Norman, 270
Zlas, Joe, 250

Znamenski, Andrei, 199, 284
Zoccali, Rocco, 265
Zohary, Michael, 204, 286
Zolotov, Yuval, 260
Zoroastrianism, 94, 203, 216–217, 222